Map by Quenton Staff and Safari Press

MONTHS OF THE SUN

Months of the Sun

Forty years of elephant hunting in the Zambezi Valley

Ian Nyschens

Safari Press Inc.

Nyschens, Ian

Second edition

Safari Press Inc.

1997, Long Beach, California

ISBN 1-57157-106-X

Library of Congress Catalog Card Number 96-69077

10 9 8 7 6 5 4 3 2

Readers wishing to receive the Safari Press catalog, featuring many fine books on big-game hunting, wingshooting, and sporting firearms should write to Safari Press, Inc., P.O. Box 3095, Long Beach, CA 90803-0095, USA.. Tel: (714) 894-9080, or visit our Web site at www.safaripress.com.

Contents

Acknowledgments

I sincerely acknowledge and am grateful to Angela Dabbs for her feat of converting my original handwritten draft into typewritten format; Maureen Smit, who spent considerable time in further drafting; Phino Battigelli for his work on reproducing old photographs into book illustrations. Tim Barnes, 'The Man of the River'; Kyle Forrester; Alex Tait; Jane and Dave West; the Vlahakis and Hinzie families; Dubbles Draper; Cheryl Morck (née Nyschens); Clive Nyschens; Joan Nyschens (now Boyle); Barrie Ball; Bruce Austen; and John Posselt—all for encouragement and photographs to authenticate events. Brian Marsh, a fellow author who drove me on, resulting in the publication of this book. Some pictures were provided by the Ministry of Information and the National Archives of Zimbabwe. And finally, thanks to Elijah Garriremo for the computer documentation and Quenton Staff for drawing the original map.

Dedication

I dedicate the past events to my son, Clive, my daughter, Cheryl, and my ex-wife Joan; and in the wild sense to the incomparable trackers and my staunch hunting companions; and to the great beasts of Africa.

Author's Note

I hope the record of these past events will enlighten readers who may be interested and yet are less fortunate than those of us who, I now realize, were privileged to have lived through the portrayed events in an era now gone forever.

I am not an author as such and I found that to impart what happened was at times a desperate attempt at communication. Words are not always adequate to fully describe happenings, people, and especially the great wildernesses and rivers of Africa. It is one thing to live experiences and another to pen them, and because of this I have omitted many events, concentrating on those that may be of greatest interest.

Above all, it is my concern that readers may momentarily escape from the modern pressures of present-day life, if only as a diversion, while reading *The Months of the Sun*.

In the history of this book I have tried to take the reader not only into the world of the wilds but also into the wilderness of man's mind, as seen through the eyes of the ivory hunter.

G R Nyschens

Foreword

When I entered the room, I saw a man on his knees blowing the reluctant kindling in the fireplace. When he stood up, he extended his right hand, saying, "I can't stand to be in the cold out of the sun." I then realized I had met Ian Nyschens.

The place was Harare, Zimbabwe, and I had been invited to dinner at a friend's home. It was there I met Ian. His name is pronounced "nations," and he later told me it was of Danish origin. In the next three days we met several times discussing the details of his opus. Always he would either sit by the fire or in the garden in the sunshine. As soon as the warmth reached him he came alive, but the shade and cold made him withdraw and lose his sense of humor. I could easily see that he would be most in his element in the heat of the Zambezi Valley, preferably during the Months of the Sun as he likes to refer to the hot season.

I had been told by one of his friends, "He is a law unto himself, comes and goes when he likes. Even now after all these years he disappears for weeks into his beloved Zambezi Valley without a word as to when he will be back." I was to discover that indeed he is an anachronism, one of those rare eccentric characters of which there are, sadly, very few left in this world.

I normally do not write an introduction or foreword to the books we publish, feeling that there are nearly always people who know the author better than I do. However, I had read Ian's manuscript the year before, and his story had impressed me tremendously. In fact, I was so impressed that by the time I was a third through the manuscript I thought of Negely Farson, who had written the introduction to Walter Bell's *Karamojo Safari*. In it Farson said, ". . . try as you might, you will not find a story to equal the one you are about to read."

Well, I had found such a story, which I consider to be a tremendous statement. Walter Bell is generally recognized among old African hands to be the father of all elephant hunters. He was a tremendous shot whose physique and reflexes were superb. His marksmanship is legendary, and his deeds are discussed by young and old African hunters year in, year out, to this day. He was also a master storyteller.

Ian Nyschens' story in some ways surpasses Bell's. He shot just as many elephant (both men killed over 1,000), but Ian shot them under much more difficult circumstances. Ian stalked elephant in the thick *jess* bush of the Zambezi Valley while Bell shot in more open terrain. Ian shot elephant that were educated to man and his guns, hunting well into the 1950s. Walter Bell hunted unsophisticated herds at the turn of the century, many of which had never seen a white man, much less had heard the report of a firearm. This is by no means an attempt to belittle Bell's accomplishments in the least; I merely offer them as a comparison.

When I discuss Ian Nyschens' elephant days, I am not talking about a man who has shot his elephant during cropping operations that typically have large backup crews, semiautomatic weapons, and multiple marksmen shooting at cows, calves, and bulls alike. With today's necessity to crop excess elephant in numbers in certain areas, it is no wonder that some of the experts have taken many more elephant than any of the old-timers. But it's an entirely different enterprise from the way Nyschens and Bell hunted. Virtually every single one of Ian's elephant were individual bulls or the menacing "Zambezi Ladies," and they were mostly shot with a double rifle. There is no doubt that Ian's courage is tremendous. His attitude is quite matter of fact, however, as I discovered when he said, "We are all afraid when following a wounded elephant in impenetrable bush; it is just a matter of controlling your fears. Anybody who tells you otherwise is lying."

Ian does not need nor does he try to impress with blown-up stories. In fact he is a man who likes to converse but rarely talks about his own deeds. When he does make a statement, he comes straight to the point. I remember him telling me, "The only three good things coming out of Britain are double rifles, English women, and bloody good horses." He downplayed his own accomplishments, saying there were hunters who had shot at least as many elephant as he had, and some had much greater experience. You will find a few of these great hunters mentioned in this book.

Of course the hours we spent were much too short. I asked him about various incidents described in the manuscript. He told me about them and others he had not written about. I was mesmerized, absorbing every word like sand does to water in the desert. The time flew by. We were still talking on the last day of my visit to Harare when I was reminded that my plane would leave in a few hours. So good were the stories that it was hard to believe three days had flown by. Ian invited me on a canoe trip down the Zambezi when I returned. Given that the Zambezi is twenty-six hours by airplane from my home, I doubt that I will be able to come, but I shall try.

And so I lay here before you the words of a remarkable man. I will not say, as Negely Farson did, that the equal of this story does not exist, but I will say that it is unlikely, very unlikely. Living legends are few and far between.

Ludo J. Wurfbain, publisher
July 1, 1995
Harare, Zimbabwe

Prologue

Pretoria to Rhodesia - From the city to the African wilds

In 1947, while struggling through the usual bitter cold winter of South Africa's Transvaal highveld, I received a letter from an acquaintance. His name was Faanie Jooste, and he had previously gone north into the country then known as Southern Rhodesia. He described it as a better and warmer place, and invited me to join him. The cold of the Transvaal, especially at night, was such that I quickly made up my mind, and in a few days I had hitchhiked across the South African border into Rhodesia.

I located Faanie in the town of Bulawayo, where he had bought safari equipment. It was new and exciting to me: camping gear, snakebite outfit with the other medical supplies, and the bright shine of cartridges and feel of rifles. Faanie was a magnificent specimen, physically and mentally hardened. He needed a companion to go up the Zambezi River above the Victoria Falls. I, on the other hand, was by comparison a weakling. As a child I had suffered from rheumatic fever, which had left me with a faulty heart valve.

"Well," Faanie said, "what do you want to do, look for a job or pool in with me and go up the Zambezi River where there is still adventure and a warmer climate?"

With our gear and packs we hitchhiked to the Victoria Falls, easy in those days since few people would motor past a hitchhiker. We viewed the grandeur of the falls and walked around the rain forest, finishing at the Devil's Cataract. Here I examined the statue of explorer David Livingstone and tried to picture his travels through this country.

Faanie put me in the picture. "All you have to know is that Livingstone had a good constitution, the sympathy of the tribes, a medical degree so that he could keep disease at bay, and a special Bible because it was backed up by the London Mission Society in England. He was instrumental in eradicating the slave trade in Africa, in his day still plied by the Arabs."

"How the hell would you know that?" I asked.

"From my brother Martin at Pretoria University," he said. Then he gave me another one of his versions of history, referring to me as "Englander" from the German word. I am not English, only culturally so—but I certainly was to an Afrikaner like Faanie! "Listen, Englander," he said, "Livingstone was a Boer hater. My forefathers discovered these falls before Livingstone and probably the Portuguese and Arabs before the Afrikaners. But they did not come from England with that special Bible. So Livingstone discovered the Victoria Falls." Though Faanie had fought in World War II with the Allies, underneath it all he was still an Afrikaner nationalist, but intelligently so, as war and

travel had altered and widened his mind. "To hell with Livingstone," he said. "How do we get up the river?"

"Let's talk to the boat people," I suggested. So we bought some food and took our gear and walked the north bank above the falls, where there were some small agricultural holdings on the river. We came across a man trying to repair a pump in the water. "English, of course," Faanie said.

It was a diesel motor. Faanie was always bright and practical in his own strange ways and in a short time the engine was running and pumping water to the house. We were consequently invited in and treated well, and learned most of what was necessary of the area and the Zambezi River above Victoria Falls. We spent the night there, discussing the practical aspects of river travel and through our host we leased a small canoelike craft cheaply and had a go at the river. "Stick to the soft side-water," our host said, "and don't come back over the falls."

After a full two days' rowing, the top of my shoulders and back ached. We saw occasional crocodiles and hippopotami, and traveled wide expanses of water with occasional islands on which were palm and other trees, some growing with their root systems in the water. On the third day the river lost its great expanse, and having mastered the art of canoeing Faanie decided to cross the river to the south bank. We rowed hard in the main current and experienced the frightening power of the mighty Zambezi River. As a result we were forced far downstream but eventually landed on the south bank. Here we discovered the spoor of wild animals. Faanie recognized some of them, but I did not until I saw elephant spoor. Only an elephant could have such large feet. I examined its intricate patterns, trying to determine which way it had gone. We camped in pleasant shaded surroundings and at night listened to the noises of animals around us, all strange, new, and intriguing. From the moment I saw the elephant spoor, there was an awakening in me, and now it grew stronger. Sun, warm air, exercise, and incredible freedom were having their effects, as I slowly felt new strength coming into my system.

"Englander," Faanie said, "you are beginning to look better."

"We have no more tinned beef, so I am going to hunt a buck," I announced.

We were far up the river now, and the return of the canoe was overdue. There was no point in going farther. "Remember," Faanie said, "The English said there were rapids up ahead." At midday we camped in a suitable spot. Faanie went downstream and I up, both to try to shoot a buck. Unfamiliarity affected my judgment and confidence, but at least I felt the master of myself with a rifle in hand. I got occasional glimpses of antelope running off, but no chance of a shot. I had heard stories of lion, and apprehensively watched the ground for their spoor.

After a mile or so I crossed an open area and entered an adjoining forest. Suddenly I had to stop short. Close in front of me was a herd of elephant. I did not know what to do, so in fear stood stock-still, and then slowly tried to move behind a tree. I froze as a large elephant turned with raised head and outstretched ears to gaze in my direction. I could feel my heart pounding and although I had a faulty heart valve, I felt everything was working at

top pace. Never before had I been both fearful yet highly alert at the same time. When I realized how massive the elephant was, the gun in my hand felt like a piece of firewood. Others had shot elephant with .303 rifles like the one I carried, but seldom successfully from the front. This elephant was huge at close quarters, facing me menacingly and slowly coming on in stages. In desperation I felt I must take a shot at its face as I could not wait for it to close the gap between us. Then it suddenly stopped, gazed intently with ears flapping, shook its massive head from side to side and then ponderously turned around and rejoined the herd. Heart still pounding, I slowly retreated, trying to use the tree as a visual shield.

I had finished backing up, having gained some ground, and turned to walk away slowly when a gunshot sounded inland from the river. Suddenly the forest became a nightmare of elephant bodies trumpeting in high-pitched fear and fury. Instinctively, I recognized this uncontrollable danger and thought this was the last place on earth that I wanted to be at the moment. Consequently I took fright and ran across the open area, hoping that none of the elephants would pursue me. Halfway across, in fear and uncertainty, I turned slightly to see the rustling vegetation and elephant running inland through the forest. As they got into thicker vegetation, I heard them crashing off in the distance, with occasional high-pitched trumpeting sounds telling me that the welcome distance between us was widening.

After this experience I was shaken. I made my way to the riverbank where I sat in an opening, looking inland to where the elephant had stampeded. My heart started to slow down. I sprinkled my face and drank some water, then wondered what Faanie was doing so close to me because the last time I had seen him he was walking downstream. Curse the bastard anyway. Or perhaps it was somebody else, an African with a rifle. Not likely, I thought, and at this stage I was not going inland to find out!

I selected some shade and tried to relax and was doing just that when another shot rang out. By the sound, it was a .303 rifle. I thought perhaps Faanie was in trouble, so I fired an answering shot and after some time he emerged across the opening, quite content. He came up to me saying, “I shot a bushbuck, gutted him, and placed him off the ground in a tree, so you can help me carry him to the river,”

“Do you know,” I said, “that I was standing next to a herd of elephant when you fired?”

“What for?” he enquired.

“Because I walked into them.”

“What did they say?” he said.

Obviously he was in one of his humourous moods. I showed him the elephant spoor where they had stood and later stampeded.

“Can’t see your spoor,” he said. So I pointed it out to him.

“Must have been exciting.” And again he asked, “What did they say?” At that moment I felt like blowing his brains out.

“Never mind, Englander, never fear. You are far from dead,” he told me.

Stupid, insensitive bastard, I thought.

For the next few days we proceeded leisurely downriver and had the opportunity to absorb the environment in detail. There was the necessity to avoid hippo in our flimsy canoe, and we experienced the hideous sight and primeval dread of large crocodiles as they took refuge from our sudden appearance, swimming speedily to pass under the canoe. I was consoled by the fact that they did not know how to attack our craft. We at times saw wildfowl flying near or nesting on islands and heard the calls of many unknown birds. We sensed that wild animals, descendants of millions of years of untamed Africa, lurked somewhere on the banks and farther inland. The vegetation was to us all new, which added to our fascination. Our nights were spent around the campfires with animal noises unfamiliar to us in the background.

On our return, as we were about to land the canoe above the falls, Faanie quietly said, as if to himself, "A sample of this life has made me vow not to cross south of the Limpopo River unless I have to." In this short period I, too, had realized that we no longer had grand illusions about crowded civilization. Back in Bulawayo there were other ways of life. Many people worked all week, only to get drunk on weekends. It was the only escape for people who were bored and unadventurous, or possibly over-disciplined by the laws of society. In any case, my weak body could not take such abuse, so I realized civilization was not an option for me.

Bull Elephant:

Learning the Hard Way – 1947

After the Victoria Falls trip, Faanie was gripped by gold fever, which developed into an obsession. I accompanied him to mining sites on the Angwa River, about 130 miles northwest of the capital city of Salisbury. On arrival I realized gold had little appeal for me as there was nothing wild in the work, only the sweat of hard labour under primitive conditions, panning the river for the slightest traces of gold.

Faanie, however, was possessed of tremendous drive. Standing next to a noisy mining stamp mill, I detected in him the delight, anticipation, and ambition he felt for this yellow metal. He was content to struggle ahead under harsh conditions, always hoping to strike gold. But to me the earth was for vegetation and rocks, a defiance to man. It also seemed the real science was the detection of minerals—mostly unrewarding, given the time and effort spent, since the ancients had mined all known surface deposits for hundreds of years prior to our arrival in Africa. Consequently the search possessed no interest or excitement for me, and so Faanie and I parted.

Later, with two Greeks, Venturas and Galanakis, I went to Mozambique. Galanakis' father had a trading store in the town of Umtali on the eastern border of Rhodesia. He also had property at Gondola, a small village in Mozambique—then Portuguese East Africa. Within miles around the towns every Portuguese considered himself a *casadore* (hunter) and consequently fired at anything wild he saw. Game always represented profit in the form of food to consume or barter with the indigenous people. The Portuguese traded after a fashion in bananas, dried game meat, occasional illegal shotguns, or whatever was in demand—in fact, anything for a buck. The system was very much like Mozambique itself: everything for Portugal and nothing put back. Gondola was not much of a place, and I was glad when we left it to go to the Amatonga forest.

Here we met Jianaki, also a young Greek, sent by his father to supervise the felling of the forest trees. The logs were hauled to the Gondola railhead, part of the Rhodesia/Beira, Mozambique railway, and sent to Salisbury and Johannesburg for furniture manufacture. I had by now grown stronger, and because of this was disturbed by Jianaki's weak stoop and yellow complexion. It seemed to me that if he stayed in the forest he would die. I spoke to Venturas about it, and he said Jianaki's father kept him here, away from their distant fruit farm, because they had a concession here and there was money in the timber. We moved on, and we talked Jianaki into coming with us, which pleased me. That night we camped at the edge of the Amatonga forest.

We were planning to torch hunt, using dazzling lights to blind our antelope quarry. The primary danger was from our own rifles. Venturas at the time was ill, and, not wanting to hunt, I stayed in camp with him.

The forest at night had a hazy atmosphere, and I noticed that Venturas seemed mentally blank. Afterward I wondered if he was afraid of the dark and had taken drugs. Sometime during the night I woke to a subhuman shriek somewhere in the trees; there was a pause, and then three or four more shrieks. It was unnerving, to say the least. Feeling fearful, I raked and fed the fire and, rifle in hand, tried in vain to wake Venturas. He muttered something vaguely. In desperation I clouted him, but to no avail. With a companion so useless, it was the same as being alone.

Sitting against a large tree next to him, I listened and watched intently. At first I thought the screams might be human, but I reasoned they could not be because they seemed to come from high above the ground. In puzzlement and fear I tried to stay awake but must eventually have slumbered, for I woke to the distant drone of a motor vehicle approaching. It was the party returning, having shot reedbuck. I mentioned the fearful screeches of the night, but they were tired and took little notice of me. Now that they were here I hoped the creature would wail again, but it did not.

In the morning we moved off to some open game country and camped at a delightful running river called the Toa. It had a wide waterfall, and you could stand under it on a rock shelf, hidden from view. I enjoyed some time there and later took a rifle to stroll down the bank of the Toa. There was nothing of interest, other than old hyena and buffalo spoor, so after a long walk I returned to the campfire at dusk.

The reedbuck meat had been cut into biltong strips and the skins treated with salt. What a lot of bother it was to commercialize small antelope, unless they were wanted for one's own use. I have never liked meat camps and still don't, so in the morning when they all decided to hunt, I welcomed the opportunity, jokingly saying I was going to shoot a *kambaku* (a giant elephant). I had a 10.75mm rifle, supposedly suitable for big game, and an assortment of soft and solid bullets. We came across eland spoor and I changed the magazine to softnose, but later the eland got into that nonstop trot of theirs in which they can go all day, so we thought it best to abandon them to search elsewhere.

As we emerged from an open forest, and were crossing a narrow *vlei* (grassland), we heard the crack of branches and at the top of the *vlei* saw an elephant at the forest fringe feeding off leaves. Suddenly, without hesitation or warning, Galanakis grabbed the 10.75 rifle from me and fired at the elephant's head from about 150 yards. I saw dust fly from its skin, and then it spun around and came straight down the *vlei*, charging silently. Galanakis took fright and ran off with my rifle, leaving me standing there with the ammunition. The elephant was now coming straight at us.

Venturas had a light 7mm rifle loaded with softnose bullets and said, "Here, shoot it." I did not want to antagonize the elephant further, and hoped that it might not have seen us, but it had. I told Venturas, "Split up! That way the elephant can only get one of us."

Venturas, however, was in a total funk, and muttered something about the Madonna, so I pushed him one way and I went the other. At that instant Forey, a tribesman of our party, ran from the side where Galanakis had disappeared and called loudly to distract the elephant. His timely action saved us, for the beast paused, momentarily confused, which allowed us all to scatter. We did not see Galanakis until we reached camp. Later that night around the fire, I looked at these people and wondered about tribesmen like Forey, whom I considered superior and who yet was dependent on Europeans. I said nothing, but I was disturbed and disgusted by the actions of the Europeans. They argued amongst themselves into the night, eventually falling asleep. In the morning, pointing to Forey, I said that if it were not for him, one of us would be dead.

A photograph of Forey, whom I considered superior and yet was dependent on Europeans.

It dawned on me that the privileged in Mozambique were so steeped in their self-importance that they could not understand my reasoning. They must have felt much the same as the ancient pharaohs did, taking privilege as part of their heritage. There was no appreciation for the courage that had saved one of us, and so, disillusioned, I left them. There was nothing of interest at the so-called game area of

Shangara, so I returned to Rhodesia, crossing farther north via the Nyamapanda border post.

Here there was a large tsetse-fly-control campaign. Hunting was encouraged to rid the area of all wildlife, and this was probably the most backward policy in all Africa, certainly as far as game was concerned. While crossing a dry watercourse named the Nangogo, I saw the tail end of an elephant herd moving across it. I followed and got close to two bulls, firing single shots into each one's shoulder. I then watched them stampede off with the others. The bush was sparse, so I followed and, to my surprise, found the two bulls dead on their sides. I did not consider this hunting as all I did was follow a while and fire two shots in open country.

The ivory from these elephant gave me more money in this short time than I could have earned elsewhere in months. But the 10.75 rifle was of inferior quality and became unreliable. As I had heard other complaints about this particular make, I switched to a converted military .303 rifle, which I bought for £8 in, of all places, a furniture shop in Bulawayo. In those days there were many types of rifles on the market. Some of them were very good, but it was essentially a matter of what you could afford. The excellent ones were very expensive, as was the ammunition.

During World War II all guns had been handed in to the government for safekeeping, but after the war many of them, including many surplus military .303 rifles, were made available to the public. Licensing then was the opposite to the way it is done now. Then you merely purchased the rifle and the license was forwarded to you at a later date—sometimes never.

There were all sorts of influences on a would-be elephant hunter. There were the theorists who knew everything except in practice; the buck hunters who greatly exaggerated their exploits with dangerous game; the armchair hunters who had absorbed most of the written works of previous hunters and spoke with authority as if they had experienced it all; and the farmers who had hunting holidays mostly to make biltong for labor rations. Generally, dangerous big game was the target of hired indigenous hunters, often improperly armed and employed by traders to obtain meat, ivory, and horn. Another type was the backup hunter; they assisted each other by all firing at a single animal until it collapsed.

Finally, there were the real hunters, the few men living in the far-off wilds, seeming to want to isolate themselves from the rest of civilization. They were but a handful, but these people knew what was required to survive in isolation in a remote wilderness. They were professionals. They had an understandable intolerance toward others, most noticeable during the winter hunting seasons, when licensed once-a-year hunters from various surrounding countries would come to Mozambique and penetrate what the professionals considered their own preserves. They always tried to keep the details of their areas as secret as possible.

The professional's lifestyle required a different stamp of man, as I was to learn later. He had a code of honor that few city folk could live up to, and he had to develop exceptional mental, emotional, and physical stamina and nerve.

It was nothing for him to follow the spoor of wandering elephant bulls for many days with only the barest essentials of life: water, fire, food, and rifle. Other hunters would favour stalking resident herds with bulls, but even there, many failed and wounding incidents were high.

I had glanced through an old hunting book that depicted various vital shots of elephant. They were in diagram form, and I marked them in my memory for future use. Everything was clear now, at least in theory. So, with the foolhardiness of youth, inexperience, and with the object of hunting elephant, I arrived at the Urema area in Mozambique.

I went through the usual preliminaries: walking, searching, and making enquiries as to the whereabouts of elephant bulls. I was told that a lone bull was said to have chased some women away from a water hole. We found the new spoor of such a bull. Despite my inexperience, I was fresh and eager, armed with a .303 rifle with a ten-shot magazine and a *rota* (ash bag).

The tribesmen started tracking the elephant. About midday the bull descended into a large bowl-like depression filled with scrub forest, occasional large trees, and giant green, widespread, leafy ferns, some taller than a man. From its lush appearance, the depression obviously held water during the rainy season, and it became noticeable that the bull was taking his time, no doubt feeling secure in the tangled vegetation. The same could not be said of the tribesmen, for they, one after the other, seemed to flit away behind me as we progressed.

These people needed meat, and in order to obtain it, at least one of them was needed to spoor the bull while I watched the thick vegetation ahead. With the last tribesman in front of me, I could see from his face and manner that he was fearful of the dense vegetation.

It seemed as if no air stirred here, and the tracker, now tense and fearful, tried to pass by me to leave. I checked him, asking, "What is it? We haven't seen the elephant yet." He slowly drew off and silently disappeared down a bend of the elephant path. I wondered how the tribesmen could voluntarily move off without the protection of my rifle. Apparently, the farther they got from the elephant the better they felt.

Alone now, I stood on the elephant path, *rota* in hand, testing the wind. It was still, the ash falling straight to the earth. I stood in great silence broken only by the gentle twitter of some small birds. One in particular cocked its head to look down at me. The birds moved off, jumping from branch to branch. There was not even the movement of a leaf. I stood for some minutes listening to the great silence as there was no visual indication of animal presence.

I thought of the bull, knowing that he was probably close ahead of me, and said to myself, "So, this is your sanctuary, a great silent forest where you sleep during the heat of the day."

I continued to absorb the atmosphere of the place, but was reluctant to move forward and fearfully thought that I might spend hours standing and hoping that the bull would move off, which might give me the advantage of hearing him.

Because the trackers had abandoned me so suddenly, I knew the bull must be very close. I now wondered how I had voluntarily maneuvered myself into this predicament. I could have retreated but became more and more aware of the feeling of the rifle in my hands. It fitted well, and I told myself I was not an unarmed primitive. Courage came gradually as the need arose; eventually I shook the feeling of being alone and confidence took control of me. I slowly moved forward, tense and alert.

Some minutes passed, and I could afford only an occasional glance at the ground to confirm the bull's spoor. I felt a gradual change, an unsure feeling, and my instincts told me the bull was aware of me. Imagination, perhaps, but whatever it was, I took heed of these inner warnings of danger. When I reached a slight turn in the path, my instincts told me to proceed no farther. I reasoned that although the vegetation was thick it was mostly green, so I should be able to see the gray of an elephant's body easily enough.

Once more I tested with the *rota*—the wind was right. I slowly tucked the ash bag under my gun-belt and took the rifle's fore-end in my left hand. I thought and felt that man and beast were conscious of each other, and I stood in dead silence, listening to nothing but with a strong feeling of animal presence. I scanned the vegetation, then slowly, like a startling vision, the upper part of an elephant's head came into shape. It was staring at me, as stationary and silent as a large gray ghost.

I scanned the vegetation, then slowly, like a startling vision, the upper part of an elephant's head staring at me came into shape.

I felt flushes of blood pounding my temples and was conscious of my beating heart. Instinctively I raised the rifle and fired just as the bull lurched forward. The vegetation was dense, and I saw only the upper portion of his forehead. It was not a charge as such, but a quick, silent rush to get at me. The shot had no effect; the bull came on, and I turned to run, firing a hasty shot at his temple. I barely had time to throw myself aside as he passed close enough for me to see the detailed wrinkles on his skin. He crashed on for a short distance, and then suddenly a total silence descended, almost as if nothing had happened.

I was amazed at my escape and thought the bull must now be listening close by. I raised myself, mostly hidden by the green ferns, and detected a slight scraping sound on vegetation. The elephant was moving in a half-circle, his body too large to move silently in the dense scrub. It dawned on me that this was not an ordinary elephant but one that had been hunted before and was wise to the ways of man. In my inexperienced circumstances, it was a frightening thought.

The occasional scrape of his body gave me his direction; then total silence developed again. I could feel he was moving, but I could not hear exactly where. I had time now, so I took the *rota* and tested the wind. The ash fell slowly to the earth, indicating no air movement. I returned the ash bag and was just going to raise myself full length when I heard the bull moving on fallen leaves. That meant he was on an elephant path—the one close to me. His movement was slow, and I knew he was listening, trying to flush me out. He was clever, and in my fear he was beginning to unnerve me. Then his great pads came down the path.

My vision was limited to his lower legs as he paused, now and then changing weight from one front foot to another—no doubt listening as he did so. He kept coming. The nearer he came, the louder my heartbeat sounded. He passed me at a few yards and then stopped. Immediately I realized that he had an idea of my location. I saw the expansion of his front pads as he shifted his weight, no doubt turning his head from side to side, listening and scenting.

I knew he could not see me because of the green ferns, but if the wind changed in his favour I would be dead. He did not move from that particular spot, repeatedly transferring his weight to one or the other of his front legs, indicating that he was still listening and scenting. Although he could not see or smell me, he knew that I was close by.

I felt now that I had to gamble with my life. Having had enough of this one-sided game of fear, I would have to go into action before I lost my nerve. To hell with it, then. I slowly raised myself and saw an opening in the ferns to the side of the bull's head, slightly ahead of me. I fired at what I thought was the brain, but the shot had no effect, so I immediately fired again. The bull roared and turned on me. I took to the path and ran for my life. If he followed, I knew he would outrun and kill me, and even if I turned and faced him again I doubted that I could stop him. Whose side were the gods on now?

To my great relief I heard him crashing and turning to and fro near my last position. This gave me hope, and with the strength of desperation I kept running along the path. It twisted and turned; I knew I was losing my sense of direction and could be going deeper into the forest. But distance between us was all that mattered then. He trumpeted and roared with rage, no doubt incensed by my scent.

I ran farther and heard the welcome yodeling calls from the tribesmen in the distance. They were trying to distract the bull in the hope that it would become confused. Their timing was late, but it helped me get my sense of direction again. I switched to another elephant path leading out of the dense vegetation. I was feeling the effects of nervous strain and heart stress. My breath came in great gasps; I felt light-headed and had to slow down.

The tribesmen's yodelings gradually became fainter. After few more minutes a gentle incline indicated that I was leaving the depression. I paused halfway up, leaning on the rifle, feeling my heart strain again, and realized that it was not only the elephant that could kill me. Later I left the depression and entered more open country. I slumped down slowly against a tree.

By that time it was midday; I was worn out and thirsty, and I cursed the water carrier for deserting me.

In fact there was little chance of the tribesmen finding me. They had heard the elephant trumpeting after my last shot, so they knew he was not dead. There went their dreams of meat and mine of ivory, and I thought if I went on hunting in this way, ivory would cost me my life. Exhausted, I did not particularly care at that moment. A weak, relaxed feeling came over me, but my heart continued to pound and there was a frightening pain in the chest.

This physical strain and fear were having an effect, and I succumbed to it. Later I became conscious of sand on my face and fingers, and the forest took shape again. I felt weak and thirsty. The sun's angle indicated late afternoon, so I must have been unconscious for some time.

The village was about seven miles off, and with luck I would reach it at sundown. The need for water was so great that I pressed on, sometimes using the *rota* to test the wind. After covering perhaps two miles, I felt safe and fired a shot in the hope that some of the tribesmen would still be about. I rested again and moved on another mile or so, and then a hunch developed. I did not know quite what it was, but hastened to a slight ridge. After a while I saw a handful of tribesmen tracking me, so I called and showed myself.

They hastened their steps, and when they arrived I recognized my waterbag, which was handed to me. They had left some water in it. I detected a sheepishness—they were like ashamed little children. I told them of my experience. "Do you see, bwana, why we left you?" they said. It was only now that I learned this bull elephant had a bad reputation for killing people.

I asked them why they hadn't told me this before.

They replied, "Meat, bwana, meat—we thought you might get him." Then they posed a keen question: "Did I think he might die of the head shots?"

I doubted it and said, "Why don't you all go in there and find out?" They burst into laughter. It was the end of the hunt for us, and we reached the village just after sunset.

In the morning I woke to a sun well up and the cry of a naughty child being chastised. Most of the village was deserted; there were no signs of men cutting poles for *kias* (huts) or women collecting firewood and water. An old man came out of a hut and entered the shade of the council chamber roof, his wrinkled, lean body draped with a black loincloth tied around his waist. There followed the usual greeting and palaver. The older men of a tribe are usually more accurate and interesting to talk to. He said, "So, you escaped where others had failed?"

"I see the village is nearly deserted," I said. "Have they gone off to cut the elephant meat?" After looking at me for a while, he laughed. It appeared that my elephant was not always resident but moved over a large area and raided village crops during the growing seasons.

"Well," I said, "whatever he does I will not be here to see or hear him, so I give him to you." We both laughed.

The woman who had previously chastised her squalling child now approached and offered me a plate of cooked mealie-meal, boiled vegetables, and leaves. Not tasty, but because of her kindness and my appreciation I ate it, thankful that it was not a plate of large wood-worms or flying ants.

I stayed a few days, but did not want to hunt that particular elephant. Under different circumstances, with a more suitable weapon, I may have tried it. In any case, they reported that the bull no longer came to the water holes.

I thought of the unfortunate people who would have to chase him out of their lands in the coming crop season. In spite of my efforts, all I had experienced here was a nerve-wracking failure. Having courted death in wild country, you would have thought that the refuge of civilization would be appealing. This was not so, as thereafter I became ever more bored of living in an age of dull conformity. And so I moved on.

Time has no urgency in the wilds of Africa, yet it puts an inner, spiritual strength and confidence into a man. You are not subjected to the pressures of the rat race, and consequently you become calmer of nature, clearer of mind, and develop an insight into the relationship between man, beast, and environment. Here, having struggled against the threat to my life, I felt I had matured quickly, and I knew that I was a lot smarter than when I had first started.

Gold Fever:

The Folly of Youthful Ignorance—1947

My lines of thought and ways of life were changing. I began to realize that elephant hunting was expensive; it involved licenses, good equipment, the ability to range vast areas, knowing how to converse with the tribes, and how to avoid or cope with tropical diseases—but I was determined to shoot a living out of the bush. I wondered how Faanie was doing in the gold fields and decided to seek him out on the higher Angwa River, where I eventually found him. He looked strained and lean from having overworked himself and living on bare rations, and he was sunburnt from working on the open rocks, sand, and water along the Angwa River. He had a friendly relationship with the Hinzie family, who were the local mine owners.

They had advised and assisted Faanie in his ventures but to no avail; he had not struck paydirt. I stayed at Old Man Hinzie's for a while, a place of scattered rondavels. At night Hinzie studied the stars with a powerful mounted telescope, and I watched him with great interest. Before this I had been lost in the bush at night and had to wait for dawn before getting my bearings again. Now, in Old Man Hinzie I had an excellent teacher. There was too much to absorb, but he taught me how to read the stars for the practical purpose of not getting lost at night.

Hinzie was interesting, and I spent some pleasant times with him. He explained what Rhodesia had been like in the past and how it was changing. Most of the area, except for the high upper plateau of the eastern mountains, consisted of mile upon mile of forest with *vlei* (areas of grasslands) in between. Of particular interest was the Great Dyke. This hill range rises from the earth in a snakelike formation, crossing the country. In East Africa and to the north it becomes part of the Great Rift Valley and Lakes Regions, where it recedes below the earth's surface to reach the Red Sea.

In later years I was to hunt those areas, but that is another episode. Now my interest was in the trees of the Great Dyke in Rhodesia. Large herds of elephant from far and wide, perhaps seeking the minerals from the leaves, had previously browsed these trees. It interested me that elephant, feeding by instinct, would range from so far off to feed in the Dyke. In later years I noted elephant-feeding habits, which helped me locate their feeding grounds.

Our journey down the Angwa River using pack donkeys. Faanie is in the foreground with the cap.

The Rhodesian government was then implementing plans to resettle soldiers returning from World War II. The soldiers were being given grants of land with eventual title. Tobacco, the major and better-paying crop in Rhodesia, Old Man Hinzie stated, was the cause of the continuing deforestation. Timber was being used to fire the barns for curing the tobacco leaf. Like Faanie, these returning soldiers were of a good stamp. War and travel had enriched them, and those lagging behind soon matured with the challenge of their new enterprises.

At Hinzie's camp two thoughts had emerged. One was that I had hunted elephant unsuccessfully, and the second was that Faanie had pursued gold that had so far eluded him. On the strength of this, we decided to make a journey down the length of the Angwa River with the use of pack donkeys. From harebrained people come harebrained schemes. With the help of Hinzie's contacts we scoured the area and managed to locate and purchase eight donkeys. With advice from Hinzie, Faanie and I headed out.

Our journey was to take us along the banks of the Angwa River. It was my intention and hope to locate elephant in the mountainous area of the Zambezi escarpment, in what I thought was an unoccupied area. Faanie had dreams of finding gold in this comparatively unexplored region. After a few days we found ourselves in steep, hilly country, often losing sight of the river. The hills and gorges acted as barriers, and we would go for as much as a day before the necessity of water made us find the river again. It was both mentally and physically trying, especially with one donkey that we named "Rizillio." He had a mangled ear, much like a wrestler friend of ours who had a cauliflower ear and carried the same name.

From the top of a hill this damned animal would suddenly buck and pitch its pack, causing it to roll down the steep slopes. After days of this practice, I watched Faanie coming to the end of his tether. He would have to descend the slope to retrieve the pack and carry it up the hill again. The donkey would sometimes carry the pack, but it would also go through moods where it would chuck the pack six or seven times a day. I knew its day would come. It was just a matter of time out here battling in the raw before Faanie's impatience would give way to rage. Then came the day when I heard a shot and saw this donkey with some of its guts hanging out. I did not like it, so I said, "Shoot it in the head, stupid." He gazed at the donkey and said, "Let it suffer; I have been suffering for days myself."

I shot it in the brain and distributed the load amongst the others as best I could. Our travel was better now and toward dusk we sighted baboons, the only animals we had seen in the last five days. We were camped at a pleasant spot, so Faanie prospected the area for a few days. He had tools, dynamite, and fuses, and I often heard him blasting up and down the river—all to no avail; his only traces of gold were found while panning the river. No gold and no ivory, but we continued.

After many days we felt we were dropping in altitude and the heat was intensifying. There was occasional buck spoor, and I hoped in days to come that they would become numerous. My spirits rose at the thought of elephant and ivory. We camped in a small valley near the Angwa River, and that night I thought I heard something stealthy near the campfire, something that let out great drawn-out sighs. "Lion," I said. It could only be lion, and in this country they would be hungry.

I had been raised with horses and was familiar with the signs of equine panic, so I told Faanie to tie his three donkeys securely on his side of the campfire as I was doing on mine. Away from the firelight it was dark, and unbeknownst to us lion had crept up close. I had a favourite refined donkey called Neddy, and I kept her as close as possible. Some of the donkeys were noticeably restless, and as I raked the fire to generate more light there was a ferocious roar. The donkeys strained to break loose. Faanie's lot took off, and for a second I saw the side of a lion rushing past in the firelight. The donkeys had been panicked into other waiting lion. There followed a few muffled squeals from the donkeys, and then it was all over.

In a while we heard the lion fighting ferociously and dragging the carcasses farther off. I threw some lighted firebrands, trying to illuminate the scene, but they were too far away. We listened to them consuming our pack animals, and, sitting close around a large fire, we spent a frightening and uneasy night. In the morning there was almost nothing left of two donkeys. The third apparently had run off in a different direction.

I said to Faanie, "The cats have nerve at night, so let's see how much they have in daylight." Rifle in hand, I examined the lion spoor and started following it—against Faanie's advice. His parting words were, "I'll have your gear and maybe your rifle if the lion get you. Leave them, it will change nothing."

Answering to strong, revengeful hunting instincts, I took the lion spoor. I had learned how to spoor elephant reasonably well, but lion spoor is something else unless on soft ground. After a few hours of painstaking tracking, I found where they had lain down, but the spoor continued into stony country broken by gullies, so I had to abandon it.

I backtracked and eventually found the other donkey grazing unconcernedly on a slope, so I led it back to our camp. We left this place at midday, hoping that the lion had had enough meat and would leave us alone, but it was not to be.

Two days later it was evident that antelope numbers were increasing, and Faanie shot a young kudu bull for rations. As an additive it went down well, and we cut the remainder into strips for drying. It was now obvious that we were dropping in altitude and getting into game country, but that night we had another visit from lion, whether the same ones or not we did not know.

There were many uprooted dead trees about, probably from elephant activity during the past rains. Some of these we collected in a heap to make a large bonfire which gave off a certain penetrating light into the darkness. I noticed my small donkey listening and scenting, and her nervousness alarmed me. "Faanie, they are here again," I said. "Shoot at anything you see and make sure you shoot low."

The fear went from one animal to the next, but this time we had tied them securely to large trees within yards of the fire. There were no sounds beyond the perimeter of the firelight, but I sensed the cats watching us for an opportunity. The donkeys one and all turned to stare in different directions, indicating that the lion were changing their positions. The inaction became nerve-wracking, so I fired a shot in the darkness. Other than a short, loud grunt, there was no sign of movement.

Later we spotted a lion on the fringe of the firelight. Noiselessly and stealthily it approached our donkeys. We both fired, and the lion seemed to turn over in the air, leaving dust to linger in the firelight as it departed into the darkness.

I wondered if it would die. "Do they charge after having retreated?" I asked. But Faanie did not know. We now had a bright fire with many lion grunting nearby. "Fire at the sounds but high—I don't need a charging lion coming into the firelight," I said.

We fired into the darkness and listened to the grunts receding. The cats were still there at some distance, and for all we knew they might remain all night. So we decided to take turns staying awake and feeding the fire. Later

I said, "Faanie, for Christ's sake, if you feel sleepy wake me, don't leave it too late." And so we spent a fitful night, thankful when the dawn came. On first light we fanned out and found a large dead lioness about a hundred yards from the camp. It looked as if one of the bullets had taken her in the lungs as dried frothy blood was in evidence.

"My first lion," Faanie said.

In reply I answered, "Yes, it could be, but two donkeys later."

"Doubt that they are the same; the others were bolder," he said.

"All lion are bold at night, depending on how hungry they are," I answered.

In the daylight we proceeded. The country was changing. The trees were becoming larger, the bush was thickening, and the air was becoming hotter, all indications that we were descending in elevation. Upon reaching a crest, we saw it below us—the wide panorama of the great Zambezi Valley. The smoky gray-blue haze disappeared into the vast distance. What a sight this magnificent valley was, a lost world for man to explore. I flushed warm with excitement with expectations of things to come; it was a place for adventure and dreams. We spent a long time gazing and talking from this high elevation. The Angwa River dropped to the valley floor somewhere to our right, and on looking slightly back we saw distant smoke. Habitation, I wondered, in this vast wild area?

I scanned the opposite areas—no smoke. There could be people there, but because of the heat and evident bush it was also a sanctuary for game. Faanie was of the opinion that there was no habitation in the lower valley. We needed water. "To the valley then; we must find water at all costs," he said. I did not want to leave this spot, but Faanie reasoned: "You cannot stay here forever." Then there was a change of urgency in his voice: "There are tsetse flies on the donkeys!"

Hell, I thought. Old Man Hinzie had said there were no flies in the lower foothills away from the Angwa. Anger rose in me. Either the fly had changed its locality or the old man had never been here. "Get them out of the shade," I said.

We painstakingly caught the flies, using our hunting knives to trap their front legs, and squashed them. To those unfamiliar, a tsetse fly is a tough insect; sometimes, after you have swatted them, they fly off.

After the intriguing sight of the valley when I had been so relaxed, we were rapidly plunged into a dilemma, and we were frustrated. We had come so far through the hills, and now we were almost in the big-game world—plagued first by lion, now tsetse flies, and even the probable habitations of man. What a wasted effort of physical hardship it was. We had come all the way through the mountains, a bold, stupid effort caused by false information. Disturbed, I found it hard to think calmly. The sun increased in intensity, and the country became hot. We moved to higher ground and started thinking of our immediate needs. Number one, of course, was water.

Green fingers of trees below us indicated watercourses. I did not want to leave this site, so Faanie volunteered and disappeared down into the valley. The forest and bush swallowed him up as he vanished out of view.

Many thoughts and hours afterward Faanie returned saying the valley floor was very dry with no signs of water, not even from digging into the sand of the watercourses. But game spoor was plentiful. We now had no option but to head for the Angwa River.

The Angwa River, we learned, joins the Hunyani to become the Manyami. Without water, the heat would weaken the donkeys even though they got a daily handful of corn. "What difference does it make," I thought to myself, "They have been stung and will die anyway. To the river then and let us have water."

The Angwa was farther than anticipated. Traveling the escarpment foothills for a night with howling hyena about, we reached it the next day. There were flies on the donkeys from time to time, but now in the valley proper we no longer bothered to keep them off except for Neddy, whom I led close to me so I could swish her with branches occasionally. She was such a willing little creature, and with the likelihood of our donkeys dying of *nagana* (sleeping sickness), I doubled her ration of corn.

We found a pleasant spot on the Angwa and next day took stock. I left Faanie in the camp and walked down the Manyami riverbanks. There was quite a lot of game in this country, and I saw cow elephant spoor at places along the banks and going into thick bush inland. The country intrigued me, and I only returned as the sun was setting. Both of us having been alone for some time, we had each tried to come to the best conclusion to solve our dilemma. I was for continuing to cross the valley floor to reach the mighty Zambezi River. "Englander, you have got it bad," Faanie said.

"What bad?" I asked.

Faanie retorted, "Bull fever!"

"Bullshit," I answered. But he was right. Having come so far, though, I was only trying to find a way out of the dilemma.

"Englander, you are licked and don't know it—save your resources and let us return while the donkeys have strength."

He was correct: We had to turn back. So next morning, regretfully, we headed back onto the escarpment, haunted by the ignorance and folly of youth. From a height, I turned with Neddy on a rope to gaze once more at the alluring sight of the magnificent Zambezi Valley, a panorama of vast spaces. I spoke to Neddy: "You must be one of the only donkeys to have come here and when you show signs of weakness, I will mercifully shoot you in the brain. You are only a donkey and will expect and know nothing." I gently held her by her ear and gazed below me at the inhospitable, intriguing valley of thickets and forests. Land of both big and small game—beasts and birds of prey and sudden death to the unwary.

The heat haze seemed to say, "Follow me, and you will experience all." What is it about this valley that seems to calm and satisfy my soul? I had a long last look, then turned to follow Faanie.

"Feel lousy, Englander?" he asked.

"No," I said. "I feel like dancing!"

He retorted, "That's one of the signs."

"What signs?" I asked.

"The signs of the bush tap."

"What's that?" I queried.

"It's a madness you get when in the bush too long away from people. A tap-tap-tapping develops in your head and then you go mad. But first you have to feel like dancing." We both laughed, and I did not look back any more.

We had crossed to the opposite bank of the Angwa, hoping it would be easier, but the country became tougher, especially away from the winding river. On the second day I told Faanie, "We must recross and take the side previously traveled."

He felt the going might improve where we were, so I went along with him. But it got worse. It was the same story here: no game animals. Perhaps the hills were too steep for game to frequently go down to the waters. The donkeys were becoming sluggish, or was it my imagination? Neddy still walked briskly, perhaps because of the double rations. I suggested we increase the corn to the donkeys as they looked a bit lean. "It's all this hard work in the hills," Faanie said. "If we increase their rations there will not be enough to last."

It was the same story here: no game animals. Perhaps the hills were too steep for game to frequently go down to the waters.

"They will die anyhow," I said, "maybe before getting back, so let us feed them well while they are still alive."

"What about our gear?" he queried.

"Well, if we lose it what can we do? We should learn to travel light in our treks. Donkeys only encourage weight. No, we will lose it anyway," I said.

"And you?" Faanie asked.

"Well, I have made up my mind the donkeys will die, especially carrying weight, and I will settle for my rifle, water bags, and food."

We were at cross-purposes, and I lost patience, saying in the morning if I found a suitable place I would ford the Angwa River. Faanie did not take me seriously, but the instincts to survive surpassed even our friendship, especially now that our thoughts were different. Even if I was wrong, I had to use my own judgment. At midday I still could not find a suitable crossing because of the steep hills. In late afternoon I found a place and, taking Neddy plus one other donkey, forded the river. Faanie hesitated on the ridge above the river.

I signaled him to follow and continued up the opposite rise. My second donkey stumbled and fell, so I gave it time. Finally we topped the ridge. I

I had made up my mind the donkeys would die, so I would settle for my rifle, water bags, and food.

felt my decision and direction were right. After a mile or so I camped and prepared for the night. No Faanie. Perhaps he would stick to the other side. I listened to the gentle calls of owls and night jars. It was a bit eerie here alone, but there were no animal spoors, so I felt I could sleep safely. I had water, corn, and light gear on the second donkey. I gave the donkeys another drink.

In the morning I continued. I wondered how far the river was to my left, but my direction was generally good. In late afternoon the second donkey showed signs of distress. I turned at a right angle, hoping to reach the river, but the donkey was exhausted. So I carried water to it and then camped. As night fell I wondered how Faanie was faring. He was probably miles from me on the opposite bank. *Stupid bastard,* I thought, it would be better if he were here. I woke at dawn to see the second donkey down on its side. I encouraged it to rise, but it was unable to do so. I examined its bars and eye membranes; its color was anemic. I checked Neddy—she was fine—then examined the packs. I told myself to settle for the water bags and added these to Neddy's load. Discarding the rest, I moved on. About twenty yards away, I turned and shot the second donkey in the brain. Neddy ran on a bit, but the other donkey remained flat without moving. I caught Neddy, and we continued.

I wanted to be out of these hills and wished that I had never entered them. I moved through the usual gameless country, each hill almost the same as the last. At dusk I reached the Angwa River, again slept, and moved on. Another two days and Neddy was still perky and walking well. Every day I examined her eye membranes. I suspected that she didn't have *nagana,* but time would tell. She grazed alertly that night, tied close, and I felt safe and fell asleep. At dawn she was down. I examined her and encouraged her to rise. She came up easily. This donkey was healthy and in her own way strong.

Where was Faanie? I hoped he had crossed the river. Because my beast was strong, I thought I should recross and search for Faanie's spoor on the opposite bank. I did so and wasted a day as there was no sign. Perhaps I was ahead of him, so I spent the day close to the river, recrossed in the morning, and continued on my side of the river. *Where is that man,* I wondered? I had given him plenty of time. I slowed down and at midday unpacked in some shade. The country was less hilly now but still hard going. I dozed, waking to hear something other than Neddy, and saw Faanie walking toward me.

"Man, but you move!" he said.

"Good donkey," said I.

"How come she is not dead? Mine all are," he said.

"Leave them?" I queried.

"No, shot them of course," he said.

"Must have been far as I heard nothing," I said.

"These hills deflect sound, no doubt."

"What are you carrying?" I asked.

"Can't you see water and food?" he answered.

I found it amusing. "Same as me," I said. I stayed a while at Old Man Hinzie's and then moved on to leave Faanie with his dreams of gold.

Cow Elephant:

Encounters and Dangers—1948

After the almost disastrous elephant bull episode, I bought a Jeffrey .404 magazine rifle in Salisbury, which cost me seventy pounds sterling. Ammunition I got from Marcel Mitton, an elderly occasional hunter, supposedly the father of Tommy Mitton, who was resident in the Portuguese corridor of Mozambique where I eventually arrived. Tommy spoke Portuguese, English, and the local dialect, and he traded with and armed locals to hunt anything profitable. He kindly lent me two trackers and organized carriers for my use. We crossed the Zambezi River into the northwestern area toward Northern Rhodesia.

It was enticing new country, and as I progressed I found myself in a land unique, in an atmosphere charged with primitive men and wild beasts. Each day brought the intrigue of penetrating beautiful forests, grassy glades, bushlands, and uninviting swamps, with occasional hills and sometimes massive mountain ranges looming on the brilliant skyline at great distances. The sun shone from a clear sky to warm the earth on a place known as Mozambique. Here time stood still—as if waiting for me to discover the land's wild wonders and ways. It was entirely African, steeped in beauty and danger as only wild Africa can be.

My safari went from scattered village to village seeking the whereabouts of bull elephant. In one village an old tribesman who had been to Rhodesia told me that some of the bulls had been shot or driven from this area and that black hunters were shooting in the distant wilderness on a reward basis for their employers, who traded elsewhere. But the old man said, "There are many cow elephant resident here and very cheeky, raiding our crops in the growing seasons. We use muzzleloaders (*chigeedas*) and drums to try to chase them from our lands, but we know how cheeky they can get and sometimes we have to run for our lives and leave these elephant herds at the loss of our crops."

The old man told the trackers where the elephant herds might be watering, and in the morning we found and followed their spoor. They numbered some ninety to a hundred animals, and I hoped that there would be some fair-sized bulls amongst them. On the occasions when they fanned out, the spoor seemed to indicate no bulls, but I still hoped there might be.

I had had my share of elephant scares, and the fearful reputation of the cow elephant is generally well known. An ignorant, inexperienced person like myself could easily get killed even before realizing what it was about. Here, struggling and trying to hunt, I was forced to mature quickly. Because the forest was sparse, I decided to follow the elephant. The herd moved through scrub and forest, feeding occasionally with the wind constantly in our favour. From the fresh droppings, we saw that we might be able to overtake the herd toward midday. But as the heat increased, the elephant left the light forest to enter the cover of thicker bush and dense scrub. After miles of these trying conditions, the carriers disappeared.

I was down to two trackers, one carrying a water bottle and the front one a *rota*. The silent concentration on tracking and scanning ahead with such limited vision caused fatigue and strain on our nervous systems. I reasoned to myself that I was not qualified to tackle a cow herd, especially in such large numbers, but having come so far we continued. The trackers from time to time paused as we listened to the slight air currents rustling the leaves. There was none of the customary bird calls, and it was as if there was nothing to fear here except our imaginations. But the spoor was evident and very fresh. A little ahead we came across shining elephant dung, which caused the two trackers to become more alert and to slow their pace.

With the first tracker spooring and the other scanning the bush ahead, the fearful strain became evident. Soon the second tracker paused and said softly, "I fear cow elephant, and sometimes I think I see them where there are none."

I told them that we were all afraid, and the fear before the action was the greatest. They did not understand or did not want to. Then I heard a noise, like "kok-kok-kok" on branches.

"Elephant?" I inquired.

They did not confirm it, but I pondered, almost sure. We moved forward again, much slower, straining our senses, and then I smelled elephants.

I bird-called the trackers to a halt and shook the *rota* gently. The air direction was in our favour and had been all day. I was puzzled. Why can't the trackers smell the elephants? Did their smoking habits dull their sense of smell?

I handed the ash bag to the foremost tracker and took up a position behind him. Their instincts made them reluctant to follow, and they listened intently, hand-rolling their crude cigarettes and seeming to enjoy every inhalation they took. It had an effect because their fingers shook less, but I could see by their eyes that they were apprehensive. Perhaps their tobacco was laced with *m'bange* (hashish or the dagga drug).

Slowly and reluctantly they moved on again with me between them. The ground cover was good, and they tracked slowly ahead almost soundlessly. I felt a warmth toward them. These men knew the reputation of this particular cow herd, and yet they bravely sought them totally unarmed with only their senses and instincts to rely on. The elephant must be very close now, and, as we moved into a clearing only slightly less thick, the front tracker instantly froze. In front of us appeared a large herd of elephant, spread out. We had not been alert enough as some were too close. The foremost tracker, instead of remaining stationary, moved to get behind me and softly said, "*koo heenya*" (to sh-- in fear). In the tracker's mind this was a warning of things to come.

Two large cows had seen his movements, and they came forward with raised heads and ears outspread to threaten us. It was a frightening sight, and I tried to remain calm, but my blood was racing. The wind was still in our favour, but these two elephant cows slowly, in stages, came toward us menacingly. At the same time I sensed more than saw a stirring in the herd. We were much too close, and the elephant had us in full view. There were two cows so close together that I realized if they charged one might get me. Facing them, I heard the trackers running as they disappeared. The crackle of leaves under their flying feet seemed to trigger the nearest cow. With a dip of her back legs, she trumpeted loudly and charged.

In a flash I felt terror from that trumpet blast. My life hung in balance. I fired at her forehead and she dropped; whereupon I instantly reloaded and concentrated on the second cow, which was nearly upon me. She also dropped, and in seconds the whole herd went berserk and turned into a bunch of angry neurotics all seeking something to obliterate. I was only partly hidden behind the nearest dead cow.

They grouped in front of me beyond the dead cows, and there developed a wide movement toward me. Fearfully, I saw them gather momentum. Realizing I may have paused too long, I took the initiative and fired hastily. The elephant started collapsing as I continued a rapid fire, and they checked their actions slightly. One came very close, and then turned sideways, so I fired. She staggered but did not drop. I had figured out the frontal brain shots, but where was the brain position from the side? The elephants were many, too close to me, and running about in angry confusion, not quite knowing what they were looking for.

Out of dire necessity I had to take a few forward steps to try to find refuge up against the stomach and between the legs of the first dead cow. The herd saw this and reacted by moving closer and spreading around me, some near the dead cow's head and some near the back feet. An old cow with a sunken, hollow head took over the herd. Trumpeting loudly, she turned to lead the others around the dead shield cows and in so doing exposed her hollow head side-on. I fired, and instantly she collapsed. In that moment I knew I had also determined the side brain shot. The elephant, now in a half-circle, closed in on the dead cows in front of me. Their size and numbers were overwhelming. My life now depended on nerve and fast, accurate firepower. Although I felt it was hopeless, I had to fight to the last.

Fearing attacks, I kept firing fast frontal and side shots. At this quick rate of firing, the shells from the front of my belt and shoulder bandoliers were soon used up, and I started loading from the back. The process was slower, but the elephant numbers were less. Perhaps because of the rapid fire, they seemed confused. There was another anxiety now: How many shells were left? I kept on firing while the strong smell of Cordite permeated the air. The elephant noises finally receded, and the fearful trumpeting shrieks and roars came to an end. The remainder of the herd had stopped moving and stood at various angles in a half-circle of immobility, uttering low gurgling sounds and developing drooped physical attitudes.

My shoulder was bruised and extremely painful. As I topped up the rifle magazine again, they saw and heard me but thankfully there was no reaction. I wondered why. Perhaps they were leaderless or demoralized. I waited, still in fear, knowing that cows also attack as individuals, but they all remained stationary. Because of my fears, I dared not disturb them. I stood stock-still, my ammunition low. I wanted desperately to get out of there while the elephant were inactive, but I did not know how; to move might trigger some dreaded reaction.

Then, unexpectedly, I heard movements behind me in the bushes, and a nerve-shattering trumpet followed by the crashing of vegetation. *Not again,* I thought, *I'll never make it.* I had no option but to brace myself and hope to shoot those that came up behind me through the thick bush. It seemed my life was already fading.

These elephant suddenly broke into view close by but to the side of the clearing. They went past, and the others became alert and followed them. I heard their shrill trumpets of rage and fear as they crashed off, racing through the bush until the sound receded. I gazed at the passageway of flattened trees and bushes in their wake. Then there were no sounds other than distant shrill trumpeting. I listened as the sounds receded in the distance, knowing it was unlikely that the elephant would come back on their tracks.

Slowly a great silence developed in the clearing. Dead elephant were strewn everywhere, at all angles. Eventually I could no longer hear my heart beating. The great silence and the sight of dead elephant contrasted with the chaos I had just experienced. I gazed around silently and slowly as if not to disturb anything for a while, fear slowly subsiding within me. What a sight it was. All the elephant were on their sides. So this is killing, with all the ferocious and spectacular majesty of these great beasts having come to an end.

I was absorbed in the silence and the immensity of my surroundings. Just me and my lifesaving ally, the rifle. I experienced neither elation nor shame, but somehow regrets developed, which dampened my primitive hunting instincts. Then I experienced a feeling of extreme exhaustion. Weariness overcame me;

the effect, perhaps, of my overworked nervous system. I sensed the need to go to earth, so I sat down against a tree on the fringe of the clearing.

Thirsty, I thought of water. My fingers, like the trackers', trembled as I checked the number of shells left. In the great silence I felt the vastness of this forest bushland, and I theorized on the effect of a man with a gun penetrating and changing it. It made me think deeply, and I reached the conclusion that the day would come when man would destroy the wilds—changing the face of this earth, even the trees and bush, for such is the nature and needs of man. Man is the most constructive and yet decisively destructive creature on earth, and I am man.

My mind went back to my own kind in society, to the occasions when I had to suffer, and "suffer" is the word, the social niceties of others with their practiced charms. I had been subjected to misplaced opinions and overwhelmingly false sentiments. The sentimentalists unknowingly feed themselves on a diet of distorted fact. They are usually all meat eaters and have other people kill prime domestic stock for their tables, both for eating and to entertain others. They reproduce themselves with offspring and thus have to have more land, industry, commerce, and farms. Although they do not kill, their increasing masses are the main reason for the destruction of wild animals. Curiously enough, other than a few of our own ignoramuses, these people are not from Africa but mainly from overseas where they have almost wiped out their own wild animals; now they sentimentalize about ours. It is, I found, an ignorant conceit of false beliefs and hypocrisy.

Because of the notoriety of this cow herd, the news of its having been shot spread rapidly through the area. Strangely enough, I had heard of them in the local language only as the "cheeky ones." I did not know that they had a reputation for killing people at water holes and especially in cultivated areas when people tried to dislodge them. My original information was secondhand, without detail. Apparently these elephant had been well-led in three separate herds by old cow matriarchs that, when disturbed, brought the whole lot down en masse on any unfortunate persons hunting or protecting their crops. Had I known the full facts, I would not have hunted them. I now understood that when you face mortal danger you get to know yourself, particularly in such a different world.

Elephant with extended ears and heads raised in alarm are fearsome. Their attitudes prior to what could become attacks alarmed and frightened me. But I was soon to learn that silent charges with ears thrown back and trunks curled to the chest were the deadliest of all. Sound effects from trumpeting, roaring, and charging elephant were unnerving and demoralizing, but not as terrible as the charge itself. Eventually I became partly conditioned to it. But it remained frightening and always awe-inspiring: I came to realize I was not facing just wild elephant but the ferocity of an ancient Africa.

There are moments when men, through fear and strain, reach the limits of physical and mental stamina, when they surrender to what they consider inescapable death, a submission to their fate. But ever since I hunted the first elephant bull that chased me in the Mozambique forest depression, I

Elephant with extended ears and heads raised in alarm are fearsome.

determined never to cease fighting, even if the situation seemed futile. It was this philosophy that carried me through what, at times, seemed impossible odds.

In the case of the cow elephant herd, I had not only ignorantly attempted to hunt a large herd, I had by force of circumstances learned the hard way how to fight cow elephant in their midst. No doubt fate was on my side.

I later came to realize that, irrespective of the type of event, I could not afford to be dogmatic. No hard and fast rules applied. Indeed, for survival I had to be flexible and above all determined. The alternative was fear, dominating all. That fear had to be brought under effective control when confronted by these large beasts. No animal on earth can match the power of an infuriated elephant. To hunt elephant successfully, it was vital that I understand some of their senses and instincts.

I had learned much about elephant and often thought of them. When a hunter tangles with dangerous game, he must accept the fact that once the action is about to happen or starts, the circumstances—especially in large elephant herds—can and do go wrong. He has no control over numbers of animals close by, especially since he often finds himself surrounded in bush with limited visibility. It then becomes a matter of attack or defend and most times both. In such circumstances, when elephant do not panic and flee, they either group close to each other or communicate by sound signals.

Under these conditions it is not uncommon to have sections of cow herds and individuals coming at you from different angles, especially if drawn by scent and then, when they get closer, by sight. They are affected by each other and get into frenzies. Their neurotic trumpeting and roars of rage are unnerving, even to veteran hunters who have had the experience to steel themselves to such occasions. These are not the undisturbed elephant you see when motoring through a game reserve or national park. They are very impressive and admirable giants, absolutely spectacular in their determined attacks.

Once you've seen elephant under these conditions at close quarters, you have experienced the most impressive animal fury in Africa. It stays in the mind until it becomes part of you. In the moments of action, survival usually rides on your ability to hide effectively until the rapidity of your fire reduces their numbers. This lesson was one I was to learn well in the years to come.

It is not uncommon to have sections of cow herds and individuals coming at you from different angles.

Drums sending their message from village to village, eventually reaching Tommy Mitton.

Here in Zambezia that night and for a few more the drums sent their message from village to village to eventually reach Tommy Mitton, so he knew within two days of the fight that I had tangled with the cow-elephant herd. The meat of the dead elephant was given to the locals from all around on condition, through the chiefs, that the ivory would be delivered to Tommy Mitton, who would sell it for me. I pushed on toward the Northern Rhodesia border and managed to get nine bulls in twos and threes.

After the cow-herd attack, it seemed comparatively mild to hunt bulls in small numbers. Experience with elephant reactions, plus common sense coupled with the instincts to survive, were teaching me fast, and I was living both hard and dangerously. I had to adjust to a primitive way of life and had now, both professionally and emotionally, become an ivory hunter in order to survive in the wilderness.

Now, with the goal of returning, I moved east and after a week turned south to reach the Zambezi River. The journey gave me greater understanding of both the potential for game and the villages in the area. I could have continued north, but it was a vast hinterland, and I was not yet equipped for traveling these large spaces. However, I continued into this fascinating world of nature. There was an impressive mountain range to the west. On coming down its gentle lower slopes, with the mountains towering in the background, we traversed well-shaded forests and eventually saw before us a grass plain extending for some miles. At its fringes we made a camp. In late afternoon I heard a dull shot about a mile off, farther up the plain. Thinking I might get a gamebird for myself, I took an old-fashioned exposed hammer shotgun and strolled up to see who the hunter was.

At this time of year the place was well-stocked with buffalo, lion, and hyena, so I took care to walk the fringe of the forest with a view of the grasslands where I had heard the shot. In the distance I saw two tribesmen with a dead immature buffalo on its side. A little farther I came on the fresh spoor of a buffalo herd where they had run into the forest for cover. I stuck to the shade of the forest and on coming closer saw the men in some detail. The taller one had what looked like an old muzzleloader of Arab origin. Even at a distance I could tell by the shape of the stock. The other carried a light spear. I was pleased to see them, but the pleasure was not returned. As I approached, the spear man alerted the other, who immediately turned and fired at me. He had, when aiming, paused too long, and I dropped onto the ground, for the moment losing the shotgun.

I distinctly heard the heavy slow slug pass over me and then hit within the forest behind me. An uncontrollable rage rose in me. After my experiences of danger, it was infuriating to have someone try to take my life with a gun! I grabbed at the shotgun, getting it back to front with the stock forward. As I rose I saw the two men running off. It was urgent that the assassin be prevented from reloading, so I instantly gave chase. I was physically hard and fit. As I neared them they split, so I followed the armed one. I was almost on him when he spun around to use the muzzleloader as a club to defend himself. I came through it and brained him with the shotgun, the two exposed hammers penetrating his skull so that I had to kick the shotgun from the bottom to release the hammers from his head. In so doing, I came close to killing myself as one barrel went off to the side of my groin. It was nearly a double tragedy, but in my anger I did not want to think about it; I was now looking for the spear man, who had disappeared into the forest.

The impact had broken off the shotgun stock, and only then did I realize that I should have fired the gun instead of using it as a club. No doubt in those moments my primitive instincts had taken over. They say one is influenced by one's environment and in my case this was definitely so. I still had half a shotgun, so I followed the spear-man's tracks. It was plain that he kept running fast. I followed for a while, hoping that he would try to hide, in which case I would flush him out. But the man continued at such a high speed that I eventually had to abandon the chase. It took me a long time to calm down, and by that time it was late afternoon.

On reaching my camp, I rustled up the porters to load. I wanted to move a few miles in case others came back at night to attack us. I pushed the porters hard and they complained, not knowing what had happened. We camped past midnight and moved on early in the morning. We came across fresh bull spoor, but I had to leave it to move out of the area for what I considered our safety.

Another week passed, in which time I got five bull elephant. I was well loaded and felt satisfied when we reached the Zambezi. On its beautiful banks I camped for a while to allow the porters to collect meat they had left drying in a village. The incredible appetite all tribesmen have to consume large amounts of meat, fresh or otherwise, has to be seen to be believed.

Tommy Mitton had long since heard of the cow hunt and on my return expressed his disappointment at not being able to get the meat, saying that by now there would not even be stains on the ground. On the third day two *cipais* (police messengers) arrived with a letter saying that I had overshot my license and must report to the *chefe do poste* (the local commissioner).

Overshot, I thought, in an area where elephant, because of their crop-raiding activities, were considered by the authorities as vermin with no limit on their numbers! Tommy Mitton warned me that this was not Rhodesia; the authorities could stage anything to suit themselves. An unpaid fine would mean imprisonment, and a corrupt

Another week passed, in which time I got five bull elephant. I was well loaded and felt satisfied when we reached the Zambezi.

official could enrich himself on the confiscation of my equipment and ivory. The porters and trackers were apprehensive, not wanting to be involved. For a long time they had been in subservience to the absolute power of officialdom. It was a strange, isolated feeling to be so alone, as if everyone stood aside to await my downfall. What of the gunman, I thought? Why no official mention of him?

This was all in contrast to Rhodesia, where tribesmen aired grievances with their chiefs and then forwarded them to the officials. I always thought it bad policy anywhere in Africa to appoint officials who where not born to the culture of the country, especially on the lower levels where contact with the locals was necessary. I had two options: Break out and head for the Rhodesian escarpment or consider my own future here in Mozambique and see what the officials had to say. Should I break out, I would not be legally able to enter Mozambique again.

I decided on the latter course and some days later appeared before the *chefe do poste*. He was a Latin, all right, but of Africa, with shining black hair and sallow skin coloring. Although young, he had an expression of maturity in his eyes. The room was big and long, and behind a desk he paced slowly up and down while others took various positions. All my papers had been presented and the questions started through a half-caste interpreter.

"Are you the one who shot up the big elephant herd?" he asked.

"Yes," I replied.

"How many were you?" he asked.

"The carriers, the trackers, and myself," I said.

"No," he interjected, "how many were you when shooting?"

"I was alone," I said. "The trackers ran off at the last moment."

Then to my surprise the trackers were brought in, questioned briefly in Portuguese, and sent out. I did not understand them, but there was a silence and stares.

All the time at the back of my mind was the unmentioned episode of the muzzleloader gunman; I felt they would bring it out last as a final blow. Strangely enough, no charges were read out to me as the accused.

"*Estrangeiros*" (foreigners), the *chefe do poste* said, almost amused. "Here in Mozambique you are trouble. In the wild parts you are worse!" He carried on, obviously biased against anything that was not Portuguese.

I wondered if this was to become an abusive lecture, so unlike a court proceeding. I was on the point of asking permission to speak to enquire what the specific charges were, but I remembered Tommy Mitton's words of warning about Portuguese officialdom.

Through the interpreter, the *chefe do poste* continued, sometimes too fast, so I missed some of his statements. Then, he said, "You *estrangeiros*"—that word of contempt again—"you cause a lot of discomfort and embarrassment. You are always on the coast or hunting. It is better when you *caçadores* (hunters, pronounced *casadores*) are on the coast. From time to time you get killed. That is the end of the hunt, but only the beginning for us. Unless reliable people come forward to identify you and make burial arrangements, we have to freeze your stinking bodies and most of the time keep them until they are removed to their country of origin. You could easily have been such a nuisance."

Then he went on to a policy statement: "It is not always right here to completely remove dangerous game problems. If the people here (meaning the tribespeople) don't have to worry, their minds turn to other things. There is not enough relaxation and you *casadores* intensify it. You are fortunate that you hunt with our permission."

At that moment I realized I was not going to be prosecuted. The whole of this affair seemed to me an exercise of official power and personal expression. He certainly did not like foreigners, especially hunters, in his country.

I was partly confused and wondered what the hearing was really all about. Was there so much I had missed through the interpreter? Then, without the slightest indication, the proceedings came to an end. I waited for my papers, which the interpreter gave me, while the *chefe do poste* came closer and stared. I wondered what bombshell was about to explode as I had the would-be assassin in the back of my mind all the time.

"Men like you," he said, "belong on the northern frontier: more elephant, wilder, even man-eaters sometimes to keep you awake at night. I have a young relative there, also a *casadore*, by name Antonio Alves. You people always seem to find each other, so if you do, tell him the story of your cow elephant. It may help him to leave and go back to Lourenço Marques where his parents worry about him."

The hearing being finished, I told the *chefe do poste*, through the interpreter, that where I came from we have Portuguese friends, but we do not think of them as *estrangeiros*.

"I am born a son of Africa—can you say the same?" I asked.

His calm, indifferent attitude changed as he said: "Is that all you have to think of? You have been named '*Moomi*' by the trackers. We will know now wherever you are." I wondered what it was with this bastard. "*Moomi*" is a degrading name meaning wild dog. But I counted my blessings and left. Later I felt good about it all. The tyrants were not tyrants, and I still had free range in this vast wild land.

Kabora Bassa:

The Roaring Zambezi River—1948

I had planned to return to Rhodesia via the towns of Tete and Gondola, but before doing so, I explored the region of the Zambezi River known as Kebra Bassa (Kabora Bassa). The Portuguese told me its waters were absolutely impassable, and after a fearsome and futile attempt on the frightening, rough waters I quickly realized this was indeed so. I then approached the river gorges from the land, where I spent many days moving over broken, rugged, hellish country that was difficult to negotiate and lacked water. I was constantly thirsty within miles of where millions of gallons roared through many deep gorges.

I spent a few days moving farther downriver. From my vantage points at the tops of the rocky cliffs, I gazed on a turbulent, powerful, even fearfully rushing river mass. I was absolutely intrigued. It was hard getting to these vantage points because I had to negotiate huge black rocks that reflected the sun. It became so rugged that I began to doubt if a man could actually walk the lengths of the gorges, much less ride the waters.

The savage nature of this terrain alone was an obstacle to success. At one place I emerged to gaze on the mighty Zambezi River going through a narrows not more than thirty yards wide. The fast-flowing current driving the full stream was trying to escape up and downward. I guessed this surging mass could be about a quarter-mile deep.

I spent many hours gazing down on such sights. I had a Machikunda tribesman with me, and we shared the portage of food and necessities. At first awed and impressed, he later became fearful and expressed the desire to leave the area, saying that if we slept too close to the current the "gods of the river" could cause us to be lured into the surging waters at night, never to be seen or heard of again.

I spent many days moving over broken, rugged, hellish country that was difficult to negotiate and lacked water.

The might of the flowing mass also had its effect on me, and for the first time I began to understand the primitive workings of the pagan mind. At one stage, on returning to the river by a different route, I heard the distant roar about a quarter-mile away. We slowly approached over rough country and discovered a huge slab of rock the size of a few houses suspended in the current, the water rushing at it and raising it into the air in a mass, then crashing back again into its own waters further on.

Faanie was always a man at home on water and I thought of him and said to myself, *Well, Faanie, let me see you take a swim here!* I laughed at this thought.

The Machikunda had become frightened again, and, as it was so hellish trying to move through this country, we left the river. I was never to see these scenes again because all this is now under the waters of the Kabora Bassa dam. At that time, reaching these places was an expedition in itself, even when fit and traveling light. As we moved away from the river, it was heartening to see the landscape leveling out and familiar vegetation taking over again.

JAILBIRD:

CIVILIZATION BUSH STYLE—1948

I passed through Tete, a town on the Zambezi River, then headed south, inland, to Gondola. Here I had friends, and while I was there a message came through requesting that I assist a farmer who was being troubled by elephant raiding his banana plantations. It was an area that grew tropical fruit for export. There were several bull elephant raiding the plantations in late afternoons and at night. There were no resident elephant in this area, so these bulls must have come from far off.

It was an amusing sight but also a dangerous one to see the desperate farmer and many laborers advancing on the elephants, all banging drums and tins. Some were armed with a rifle and a shotgun, and collectively they were trying to stop the destruction of the plantation. They would get to a certain point and then the elephants, in the cover of the banana trees, would refuse to move. The farmer and his assistants then fired into the plantation, the elephant charged, and everybody panicked and ran for their lives.

"Stand firm! Stand firm!" I heard the farmer shout in Portuguese, but they sprinted like greyhounds and were away in a flash. It was just as well, for they might have wounded or enraged the elephants.

My hunting permits were for the valley corridor and north of the Zambezi, but the farmer assured me that his resident's permit covered this situation. Unknown to me, it did not. The agreement was that the ivory was mine and the meat was for the farmer's use. By the time I arrived at the scene, it was late afternoon, and amidst much chattering, ordering, and countermanding, the men were trying to regroup again. I warned them to be silent and stay clear. I checked the wind, then walked up to the edge of the plantation where I could hear the elephant feeding. From about 150 yards away I saw an elephant's head here and there and sometimes portions of elephant bodies. Because of the broad leaves of the banana trees, I would have to get close to the elephant. I listened for the positions of the individuals and came up to the back legs of a bull with another farther on facing me.

I had a rough idea of shot placement by now, so I fired at the farther bull, whose head was facing me. He collapsed, but the one with his back legs toward me spun around from eight paces, turning on me. I managed to get him just as he began the dip action of charging. He collapsed, but a third bull came rushing in anger, ears upraised. He offered a side-brain shot, and I took it. There followed a total silence, with all the other elephant positioned farther off on the plantation.

Then I heard the almost silent blurps of elephant communication. I waited for the others to show themselves or stampede off, but there was no movement—only total silence. I reasoned that if I were quiet enough I could move up closer to view the unseen elephant. Just as I thought of this line of action, all the noise of the drums, shrieking, and chanting started again about a hundred paces behind me. It was followed immediately by the trumpeting and roaring of live elephant bearing down on me. I managed to shoot two of them and another two hurried past me toward the beaters, who were assembled in the open.

Immediately I took advantage of this by coming up close behind them. They stopped at the fringe, and I heard the beaters running off in the distance. Tins and drums were silent now. One elephant, giving a deep roar of rage and frustration, turned slowly and walked toward me. He did not know of my presence, and as his head cleared the banana leaves I shot him. This caused the other one to go berserk. Breaking through to his companion, he spun around, seeking an enemy.

On sighting me close by, he became a picture of majestic fury, and as he changed his stance I shot him in the brain from the side. There was the danger of other elephant undetected in heavy cover, so I waited silently for some time. If there were others, they had probably moved off by now. As I stood listening intently, I realized this was possibly the shortest hunt I would ever have; I had walked only about two hundred paces. There were no more elephant indications. As I emerged, the beaters saw me and came rushing up, excitedly beating tins, drums, and yelling again.

It took some time before they were silent enough for me to tell them that elephant might remain deeper in the plantation. On realizing this, they dashed off again for safety, as noisy as hell. I could not help laughing. What a crazy bunch of noisy bastards they were! It was hard to associate their antics with their primitive brethren; no doubt the influence of commercialization had changed their lives. They certainly were collective, but only in noise.

The battle did not end with the killing of the elephant, however. Days later, when I tried to load the tusks, I was confronted by the farmer, his friends, and laborers. He made a claim to half the ivory. They faced me, armed with two guns and about fifty pangas. Believing himself to be in a position of power, the farmer caught me by the arm to emphasize my position relative to his. There was no comparison between the danger of hunting elephant and a Mozambican farmer. I was young, I was tough, and when I heard the farmer going back on his promise, I saw red. I pushed him aside. Then he called for physical backing in Portuguese. I lunged and thrust the point of my gun barrel onto his throat, and he went down gurgling and gasping for breath.

I had to fight the terrible rage I felt to finish him off, but at the same time I also had to watch his friends—one in particular, who was armed. That one knew I was aware of his gun and consequently he made no attempt to help the farmer. It was clear that I would have shot him had he pointed his gun at me. They all stared, undecided, and did nothing. I had made the stupid mistake of assaulting a Portuguese citizen. My own helpers and I managed to load the ivory under these threatening conditions and drove off. On thinking about it, I later motored through the night back to Tete to be far from the scene.

I had made previous arrangements with an old Swedish hunter to dispose of my ivory through him. So I went to one of his camping sites outside the town of Tete, on the Zambezi riverbanks. No one there, but a night later, about two in the morning, I thought a lion had pounced on me. I wakened with a start. It was the black Portuguese police. They pushed my face into the ground and got on me while they tied my hands behind my back. Just before sunup they started walking me back to Tete. At the town I was taken to the jail. During my incarceration they would let me out during the day with an armed guard to keep an eye on me. No doubt the purpose was that if I should try to escape the guard would shoot me, whereupon they could confiscate my property.

The charges, although I had not yet been informed of them, were for assault and hunting without a permit. Though I was not really behind bars, the waste of time and the uncertainty were frustrating. In the meantime, the ivory and all my goods were being held by the authorities pending the hearing. I whiled away some time in a local dingy wine shop while housewives shopped and children peeped to see the foreigner who was in the calaboose.

As I watched the pontoon ferry being hauled across the Zambezi, a truck came over on it with a Pretoria number plate. As the ferry was being tied to the shore, I recognized two friends, who called to me. We had been at school together; they, having heard that I had disappeared into the wilds, were pleased to see me again. They had just come back from Lake Nyasa on holiday. Full of enthusiasm and keen to hear of my adventures, they insisted on drinks and supper at the local hotel, which at that time was not a hotel as such but only a temporary refuge for travelers.

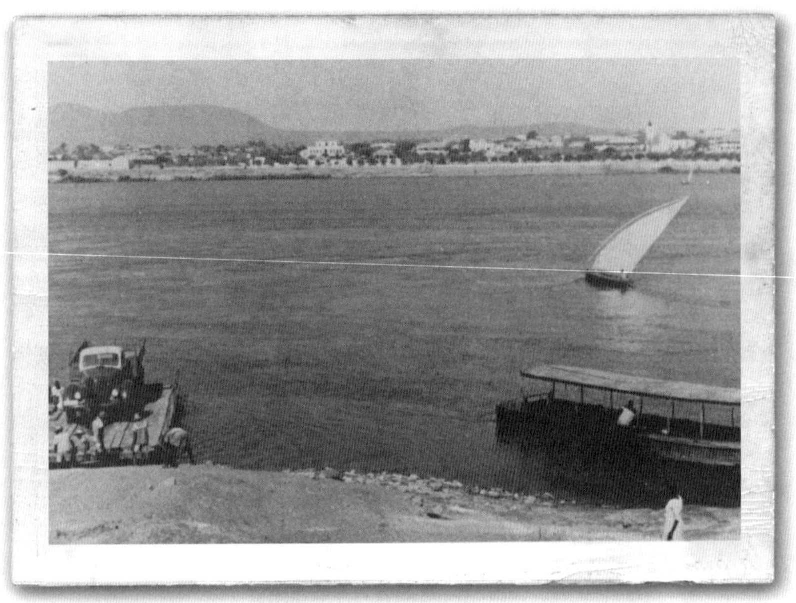

As I watched the pontoon ferry being hauled across the Zambezi, a truck came over on it with a Pretoria number plate.

Then my friends became conscious of my guard, armed with what we called a Portuguese Mauser rifle. It was recognizable by the straight bolt handle, not curved like other Mauser rifles.

"Is this bloke a friend of yours?" they asked. "What does he want?"

Their reaction was amusing, but I did not think so at the time. I had to tell them I was a jailbird. They stared unbelieving at first and then aghast; I could read it in their eyes. Me, a jailbird in a foreign jail! Being a jailbird did not bother me, but being in jail did. Having realized that we were in different worlds, they promised to see what could be done from their end, and they moved off to the hotel and I to the jail house. Laughingly, I thought it was not exactly a successful social event. My friends seemed pleased to see the last of me.

In the jail that night an incident occurred. I heard excited talking in Portuguese, and at the jail door there appeared a new prisoner, a large-boned man. He had been assaulted and his captors, four policemen, had also had their share, evidenced by bruises and blood here and there. The prisoner was handcuffed and vigorously pushed into my cell, not so much in brutality but as if to get rid of him. He was a giant in stature, and it was evident by the bumps I could see through his thinning hair that someone had made liberal use of a baton.

Slowly he took in his surroundings, but he was obviously still in a rage. He glanced at the other prisoners, a Portuguese and some mulattoes, all incarcerated for minor offenses from what I had gathered. Eventually he calmed down enough for me to be able to speak to him, but he remained agitated. After looking at the coloreds and the Portuguese, he muttered the words in Afrikaans "*Wit man.*" (white man), meaning me. Apparently he did not expect people of the so-called higher order to be in, as he put it, a "dago jail."

I was amused and reminded him that he, a white man, was also in the dago jail.

"Not for long," he said. "When I get to South Africa, I will kill the dago bastards there."

He spoke broken English in a strong Afrikaans accent, which made it more amusing.

It was enlightening to see a foreigner besides myself in trouble. I did not let on that I could understand his language as I was enjoying him, his expressions, and what I considered his murdering of the English language. He swore at me and the Portuguese in Afrikaans and then said something about his wife. The coloreds were the luckiest as he gave them no verbal abuse. He settled down and in the morning complained about this hot country, which he said had stupefied the dago brain. Then the story came out.

Apparently he had arrived at the hotel from Nyasaland, left his wife in the car, and gone inside to obtain accommodation. The bar and lounge were one, and while he was inside a drunken Portuguese came out. Muttering, probably something about foreigners (*estrangeiros*), he urinated on the back wheel of my new friend's car. The wife, sitting in the front, overreacted and got herself into a state. She screamed and went into histrionics, no doubt to draw her husband's attention from inside of the building.

Another Portuguese had come from the bar to see what the excitement was about, with the husband following close behind. Enraged and no doubt influenced by his wife, he first beat up the original Portuguese, and then his companions. He must have done a good job because the police arrived shortly thereafter. When the giant resisted arrest, he was baton-beaten and handcuffed. The whole affair had been humorous, but stupid and unnecessary.

Apparently this giant was very much influenced by his wife, and I said so. He glared. I told him the Portuguese had a different culture, but had he done this in South Africa the result would have been the same. His wife no doubt was living at the hotel, and perhaps this new surrounding may have helped to broaden her narrow mind. It was obvious they both suffered from the same mentality, but he more so under her influence.

In the morning his behavior was more normal so his handcuffs were removed. At midmorning I was taken to the court hearing of my own case. A Swede, a fellow hunter who spoke Portuguese fluently, came to defend me, and after much palaver I was found guilty and fined 8,000 escudos or the equivalent of £80, a lot of money in those days. My ivory was confiscated, this being a disturbing loss as its value was at least four times that of the fine, but my equipment was returned to me. The farmer involved was also fined the same amount for calling me to shoot the elephant when he knew that neither of us had the proper license. Having got my freedom again, I thought the best of this place was the road out of it. So, I moved on.

PORTUGUESE CORRIDOR:

ENCOUNTERS AND LEARNING THE WILD WAYS—1948

Having seen the Zambezi River at its most turbulent at the Kabora Bassa gorges, I now appreciated its calmer waters as I traversed the Portuguese Mozambique corridor close to the two Rhodesias by dugout. The north bank was occupied by scattered villages, but not so the south bank. There were, however, the occasional far-flung small villages and a few at water points inland.

In the process of trying to familiarize myself with this wild and savage environment I lived the same poor existence as the tribesmen, sharing the same hardships. In the emotional sense one could feel rich without wealth, but this new way of life taxed my constitution almost to its limits since, compared to the European way of life that I was used to, I now had to live in a state of near-malnutrition. Other than game meat, all other food was of a much lower standard. Primitive Africa was having its influence, and under these conditions I soon became wild, indeed at times more savage than the tribesmen, except I had the advantage of a rifle. I hunted in nothing other than sandals and a piece of cloth (*n'koo kota*—loincloth) around my waist and a spare one tucked under my gun belt in case of excessive sun exposure to head and shoulders. In these self-imposed conditions, I had escaped from the rat-race but was paying a price for my escape.

The valley was bushy and well-forested with numerous spoor of a variety of game; in particular there was buffalo, some of which I shot as good will for the people. In semi-open and trampled grasses, the buffalo were not dangerous targets to hunt if shoulder shots were used. However, I wounded one in the open through the interference of a local armed with a muzzleloader. It ran after its herd, which had entered the thickets. The wounded bull stayed at the back of the herd and then, perhaps feeling its wound, veered off to leave them and entered thick scrub.

The situation having changed, I tried to reason myself out of the new danger, asking myself why I was following a wounded buffalo for meat that I did not want for myself. But after clouting the local tracker for continually talking on the spoor, I dismissed them all and followed alone. It is strange and so different from other hunters how I almost from the beginning preferred to close in alone on a dangerous animal. Essentially it must have been that I did not want any other presence except the hunted. Going after a wounded animal alone sharpened my senses and concentration so that I felt certain of my ability to defend myself.

The heat had set in and the buffalo stopped from time to time, no doubt to get an advantage. Twice, judging by his spoor, he had stood in thick bush close to the elephant paths, waiting for me, but had then moved off again. I knew that at a suitable spot he would take an aggressive stand. The buffalo is reputed to be tough and courageous when wounded.

With the .404 rifle in hand—which I considered inadequate for such occasions—I slowly followed. I had a tense fright when unexpectedly some gamebirds flew up close to my feet, giving away my position and the advantage to my fearsome opponent. I listened to a slight crosswind through the leaves and checked it with the *rota*. Here uncertainty took over, so, patiently and very slowly, I advanced, for it was the kind of place for a wounded buffalo to make a stand. I moved a hundred paces or so, sweat running down into my eyes. Then my instincts told me he was there.

Other than the spoor and an incredible feeling of stillness in the vegetation, there was nothing to indicate the buffalo's presence. I stopped to scan the bush in a half-circle. Unknown to me, my eyes had passed over him where he waited off the path. Then I heard movement and the bush gave way to body sounds. Through the bush I saw the curved horns and the darkness of body as he rushed me. I took a chance by firing through the bush into what I thought was the 'V' of his chest. He broke out on the path very much alive, and I managed a quick second shot at the center of his chest. He staggered slightly but kept coming on—head extended, black nose horizontal, eyes intently fixed on me. I doubted I had time for a third shot and in desperation fired from my hip into his head. He seemed too close to dodge, and there was no more time. On receiving the last shot, he faltered, semi-stunned. Then he staggered down onto his chest, his hindquarters collapsed, and he bellowed a most disturbing drawn-out bawl.

In seconds life left him. Shaken, I felt grateful it was him instead of me. I was very impressed by his tenacity, unflinching courage, and determination. No wonder buffalo have the reputation for having killed more hunters than any other animal!

On hearing the shots, the tribesmen waited for some time and then sought me. I examined the two bullet holes in the chest. The line roughly showed heart shots. This had been my first charge; I did not want the next one to be my last. So I had to know the exact result of each shot, because the way he came on at me after the shots was frightening. Eventually the tribesmen crowded the scene. Some had their customary light choppers, and I watched as they hacked the buffalo and reached his heart. They brought it out only partly intact as it had been ripped by one bullet. I concluded that the other bullet had reached a lung. To survive I had to learn exactly how to stop dangerous game. I realized that in theory the buffalo should have been dead after the first of those shots, but he must have continued his movement with the blood in the artery still feeding the brain until the heart had totally collapsed. This was my theory, but I needed to confirm it. The lesson I learned from this encounter was to keep a wounded buffalo at a reasonable distance to allow the heart time to collapse.

In seconds life left him. Shaken, I felt grateful it was him instead of me.

On my instructions the tribesmen cut the head open and split the horns for examination. I viewed a small brain, about the size of a polo ball, well protected by the massive boss of the horns. It could be reached with a perfectly placed bullet, but I did not feel confident with that shot. The next best shot would be to try to stun the buffalo in the head if he faced me. Well, I thought, I would just have to see when the occasion arose. I knew for certain that I did not want to stand to a charge from these determined beasts at close quarters, at least not until I could devise a method of immediately immobilizing them.

Ranging through the area by boat, I enjoyed helping the people, standing by sometimes to shoot the occasional crocodile caught in the fishing nets. This reptile, unless hit in the brain, always got away into the deep waters; even wounded, it took only a few movements of the tail for it to disappear into the

Ranging through the area by dugout, I enjoyed helping people, standing by sometimes to shoot the occasional crocodile caught in the fishing nets.

depths. Crocodiles in these parts, as in most wild areas, seize women collecting water and children playing in the shallows, particularly in the heat of the Months of the Sun or *chireemo* in native dialect, the very hot period before the rains. There was a sense of fatalism about crocodile attacks among these tribes, much of it due to the chief's authority. At other places I had found large wooden stakes driven into the water's edge in half-circles to allow the women to collect water in safety. But the attitude here was that it could not happen to them.

When one considers the sheer terror of being seized, mauled, and drowned by one of these hideous, loathsome reptiles, it would be the first creature I would take precautions against. During this period I saw a crocodile seize and drown a long buffalo bull in the Zambezi River. It was unusual as I never saw it happen to a buffalo again. It was in late afternoon, and I watched from a high bank while game came down to drink in a shallow area with a strong deep current running close by.

A herd of buffalo, some fifty or sixty in number, crowded the shoreline, had their drink, and slowly moved away. At the tail end of the herd an old buffalo came to the water's edge, started drinking, then looked out over the expanse of water. It turned its head once to look at the slowly departing herd, and as it put its head down to drink again there was a sudden eruption of the waters and a large crocodile seized the buffalo by its muzzle. From my vantage point I could see the crocodile with its short, powerful legs reversing into the water, using its tail for leverage. Foolishly the buffalo, courageous even with its muzzle in the crocodile's mouth, tried to ram the crocodile with its head and also chop with its front feet. Then it found itself in deeper water. Once the buffalo lost its footing, the drama was over. I saw it turn and kick in desperation a few times, drowning, and then it disappeared.

There is a false sense of security in the wilds, particularly near the beautiful and mighty Zambezi River. Along the tranquil waters of Africa, merciless killings take place with sudden, violent explosion, and almost immediately afterward the scene reverts to its former beauty and tranquillity. I thought of how often we flitted across the shimmering African rivers while below us lay another deadly jungle. I was thankful that crocodiles did not have the intelligence or experience to tip us out of the dugouts into the water. It would have made these beautiful rivers a hideously frightening place to be.

Here in this unspoiled wilderness, wild animals wandered at will under the dictum of rains and dry seasons. By virtue of the necessities of forest survival these animals experienced superior fitness and well being. These fascinating forms of fauna in a timeless land made me realize for the first time that mankind's existence in evolution is but a "fleeting" instant—and yet a man's life span is *his* eternity. In this endlessly intriguing atmosphere of the bush forest, I developed a clear perspective on my new maverick lifestyle.

And so I ranged through a vast area to learn everything possible, both new and intriguing. There was a wide variety, though not a great abundance, of antelope—impala, waterbuck, zebra, bushbuck, kudu, eland—and I often came across them in the course of elephant hunting. I heard the lion roar into the early hours of morning; I heard the maniacal, frightening, disturbing, shrieking laughs of hyena close around the campfires.

The locals tried to encourage me to shoot antelope, but I have always considered antelope to be attractively marked, athletic creatures. They always seemed inoffensive and defenseless against firearms, and unless I was in desperate need of meat I left them alone. I had the time and opportunity to study game around water holes or at other convenient places, and I fell in love with their surroundings.

These scenes were at times disturbed by lion, with all the action, speed, and drama of escape and killing. To humans, lion are merciless killers, and I witnessed young lion attacking single animals and mauling them to death, and lionesses seizing the throat of their prey and slowly strangling the victim through the great pressure of their jaws.

I once saw wild dogs tackle an old lion. By instinct they seemed to know the lion was coming to his end. The dogs ran past and then turned to test him. The lion kept his back to thick bush, but the dogs closed in and suddenly one rushed in from the side, and ripped a portion of the lion. The lion cuffed the dog aside. Wild dogs, like all hunting creatures, sense weakness as a sign to attack. All fear vanished as the whole pack literally ripped the lion apart. It was all over quickly, except for the feasting and tearing of the carcass.

I wondered how often lion were attacked and how other lion in their old age had to die. In the wilderness, the driving forces are food, water, and the mating instinct. There is no refinement and certainly no mercy as we know it. Advantage is of the moment and must be taken immediately in order to survive or procreate. These principles of survival go from the largest to the smallest of creatures.

The elephant in his great bulk seems less subject to these mundane principles. Other than the mating instincts and the emotional disposition of cow herds, the elephant above all seeks a vast range in which to find food, peace, and solitude. His only enemies seemed to be man, lightning, and the loss of land. But no doubt he suffers parasites and diseases unknown, to us.

Here on the Zambezi I estimated that I could not be more than forty-odd miles distant from where Faanie and I had descended the escarpment and where our donkeys had been stung by tsetse flies. On that occasion, another forty miles or so would have brought us to the banks of the mighty river. In the higher branches of a large *musango* tree I tried to view the escarpment, but distance was blurred by the heat haze.

Elephant were much on my mind here in the corridor. I had managed to get seventeen tusks of medium-sized bulls from various small troops. I stashed them in an isolated place close to the south bank of the Zambezi.

Being so close to the two Rhodesian borders, I decided to continue upstream in a dugout, using a tribesman to assist me. We reached the Portuguese border post of Zumbo on the north side of the Zambezi. As a precaution we paddled upstream at night to pass it, then went on to the Luangwa River confluence to camp a few miles up on the north bank of the Zambezi in Northern Rhodesia. At this stage I was beginning to experience fatigue and depression and spent the whole day and night there; then we moved on again and in a few days were well into the narrowing, fast waters of the Mupata Gorge.

Notwithstanding the hardships and danger, this land had a romance about it. But my progress was slowed as I steadily became weak and listless through living too long on unsuitable native foods. There was nothing else to eat except the now-unappetizing sight of meat, and in the gorge the frighteningly powerful current daily sapped my strength. Under these conditions, I felt I could not last into the unknown ahead of me. We reluctantly turned the dugout into the main current to go back downriver, as I no longer had the strength to fight the currents.

Immediately we experienced the speed and power of the river in the confined space between the hills of the gorge. Since we no longer had to fight the powerful current, my morale rose and I was able to concentrate on negotiating the fast-flowing waters. It must be understood that all gorges below Kariba were bigger and faster than they are now after the building of the Kariba Dam. We crossed the Luangwa River junction, and here I stored away the idea of one day traversing the Luangwa overland to see what game might be there. We passed the border post at Zumbo after sunset and slept on a sandbar a few miles below.

Early next morning, using the river's strongest current, we stayed in the mainstream and at midday landed by some huts on the north bank. Here we had good luck and traded dried meat for fresh fish, which we cooked on a spit next to a fire. It was good food and a welcome change. Another day at the paddles and in late afternoon we arrived at a small village on the south bank about ten miles above my ivory cache.

We bargained, and I shot an old elephant cow in return for the use of an extra dugout. Within hours my hidden ivory was loaded, and, with both of us in single dugouts, we continued, moving fast downstream. Life was easier and we slept where it suited us: at night on sandbar islands and during the heat under shade on the banks.

Not being much of a meat eater, especially game, I began to experience a disturbing craving for vegetables, butter, and fruit. It was as if I had no guts in me, and I tried to substitute crude leaves and wild fruit, but I had let my system go too far. Further cravings and weaknesses developed with the added misery of dysentery, and thankful I was to reach food supplies, even of the tinned, artificial type, at my base at the Panyami River junction. There I paid my paddler, then motored overland to the town of Quelimane, where there were vegetables, tropical fruit in abundance, and sea foods. In addition I had the pleasures of the warm Indian Ocean, the reassurance of acquaintances, and the benefits of an organized community.

Under these conditions I improved tremendously, and on one occasion was able to visit the outpost of Vila Cabral, where I found John Taylor—"*Pondoro*" (the lion)—a hunter of great repute. His experience and knowledge, especially in rifles and calibers was exceptional, and he generously shared that knowledge with me. I could not have received a better education. In my life I had never listened so attentively as I did when I closed my eyes at the campfire and heard John Taylor's words of wisdom. He was at the time contemplating writing another book. I always remember John Taylor as the man who put me on the right track to survive in Africa. There were all sorts of experts extant at the time, and their explanations, I soon realized, were all show and theory without background to back it up. I was never gullible when it came to life-and-death matters, not even in the early days of youthful ignorance. I found the genuine article as I listened to John Taylor's words of experience and for the first time gained a clear picture of what before had been a blurred vision, like the distant unknown.

However, in later events involving various circumstances, I at times held some of his advice in dispute. I also take into account that John Taylor had a precise and measured outlook, particularly when amongst elephant herds. This I did not always have, and I tended to rely heavily on my instincts, which were stronger. Indeed, while hunting with Taylor, I proved my instincts were my first line of defense. He encouraged me in this, saying he had never seen a "sixth sense" so highly developed in a white man. The ability to sense unseen danger is innate. We use the phrase "sixth sense" to describe an extension of the other five. But I doubt if this is an accurate description; to me it is instinct—an instinctive feeling caused by physical threat. Perhaps intuition is a closer description.

In my experience instinct is a stimulus caused by the fear of death, and it is particularly strong when I am following on the spoor of dangerous wounded animals in dense vegetation. Logically, if you do not follow them, there are no such stimuli to sharpen your senses. On the other hand, the greater the tensions are under these conditions, the greater the stimuli become—especially if you are alone, and provided you have those instincts.

For some people it is traumatic to follow wounded animals, especially into thick brush. When forced to do so, they are reduced to such a state of inefficiency as to become useless. In such cases there is no intelligent instinctive stimulus, only an overwhelming, dominant fear. These people are a menace because they can easily cause the deaths of others. They possess the ability to hunt only when everything is in their favour. But I have on rare occasions seen men with concrete-jungle backgrounds—city men—who instinctively rose to the occasion of extreme danger, indeed impressively so. I conclude that such people have strong instincts to survive.

I think my sense of survival was brought about by fear and uncertainty. Circumstances and events had an influence. Ever since I was attacked by the herd of killer cow elephant with such fury and in such close quarters, I have developed strong instincts to know when I was in danger from concealed animals, especially elephant, lion, and buffalo—in that order. An inexplicable sense warns me of danger.

Of all the dangerous game, the leopard puzzles me most. These creatures can kill domestic dogs, unseen, unheard, and unknown to their victims. They even enter houses and successfully do the same. Does their presence not give off a feeling of impending death? Why is it that dogs, with their wonderful senses, do not sense the presence of a leopard until it is too late? On one occasion, when asleep in camp, I had instinctively awakened to feelings of danger, only to discover a lion stalking my bed under a mosquito net. On another occasion I woke with the feeling of danger. I knew it was elephant, and the fear had a stifling effect on my nostrils and lungs. I barely managed to slip out under the mosquito net as the bull attacked my bedding.

There are other instances that show me we have abilities other than the five senses. It is not just man that experiences such events; these extra senses are much more developed in animals, even domestic ones. But enough of this controversial subject for now; I will leave it for future happenings.

Taylor, in his book *Big Game and Big Game Rifles*, says, "Any rifle which shows a knockout value of not less than fifty (referring to his theory of quantitative knock out values) can be relied upon to knock an elephant down in any circumstance." Any circumstance? Even for an experienced hunter, in dense bush this is more than a small challenge. I personally have had terrifying experiences with elephant in bush so dense that I had to wait for the last moment to fire up through the underside of an elephant's jowls to try to reach the brain. Great risks had to be taken as there were no alternatives. At such angles there is no clear picture of brain positions, which makes a shot even more uncertain. In such cases there is little transmission of shock, as there is when using medium to heavy rifles on frontal head shots. By "medium" I mean rifles in the .375 to .425 class; I consider "heavy" to be from .450 upward.

These are my views for what they are worth. Other than shooting cows in large herds my successes were mostly with rifles in the .450 class, by which I mean .450 to .500. If I were of a heavier build, I would have constantly used a larger caliber than .450, but this was the rifle most suited to my weight. With acquired knowledge and skill, this caliber carried me through dangerous escapades. Indeed it was more than just a rifle to me, and it became an extension of my power.

I think most people can shoot elephant under ideal conditions, especially if they are knowledgeable and precise. Wounded animals are an entirely different matter; they move into dense sanctuaries, and if you find wounded elephant disturbing, try lion or leopard, especially leopard. After much experience I reached the conclusion that hunters seldom track up the last two, and what they did not know their instincts told them. It was as though the big cats were saying, "Follow me at the cost of your life."

I read somewhere that it is virtually impossible to knock an elephant down with a body shot other than in the spine. This is not so; a good right and left barrel to the hip ball-and-socket joints will suffice, and a shot at the large aorta area of the heart puts them down in seconds. A shot to the spine where it joins the back of the brain is also instantaneous. So is the large cord in the neck, and a high shoulder shot will cause a standing elephant to fall toward you, but most times it has to be finished with another shot.

Advice is all very well, but there is much controversy in the hunting world caused by people offering advice without the experience to support it. Some people enjoy these debates. I don't, because they remind me of my early days before I was put right by John Taylor. This is what I mean by Pondoro being precise and factual. It is not a matter of who is right but *what* is right, and the average man is not in a position to know. He has to depend on others, and sometimes they actually know less than he does. So much is written by people who had gleaned information from others here and there. It is then turned into a state of debate, like listening to petty politicians. Simply stick to the practical principles.

No animal deliberately charges sideways. On the frontal head shots, especially on big-boned bull elephant, a heavy bullet with plenty of weight to diameter and with the right velocity will penetrate through to lodge itself beyond the brain. The calculations of ballistic experts show that this penetration will reach through an elephant's body to lodge in the opposite shoulder, and so on. On the other hand, when bullet diameter is increased at the loss of weight, it lacks sufficient penetration. The 10.75mm cartridge is an example. Even an increased powder charge is not the answer, for there must be a balance between diameter, bullet weight, and velocity. Bullet shape is also important to keep a true course.

A good example is the .375 caliber. It has tremendous drive and true course, but its high velocity sometimes takes it through an animal, which is not what you want, because for a bullet to have proper effect on elephant it must not completely penetrate and pass through the target. A solid bullet, therefore, should have sufficient diameter, speed, and weight to penetrate—preferably just past the vital organs. This then has full effect.

An example of a wrong-shaped bullet is the sharp-nosed .303 British bullet that was designed for combat. It was at one time commonly used for hunting, especially on soft-skinned game, but on frontal shots on elephant it barely reaches the brain because it loses its course. From the side I have managed to shoot elephant in the brain with the .303. However, this is anything but a hunting rifle, and I only mention it as a bad example. In my early days I had a bull elephant chase the hell out of me when I was using a .303, which brings to mind another disturbing incident.

I once shot a large, aggressive cow elephant from the front, just as she turned on me. The shot was taken in haste as she was very close. She dropped but rose quickly and staggered a matter of yards before I deliberately aimed for the brain again. She reeled slightly back on her haunches but in seconds spun around to dash off. I was using a .450 double, and the thought flashed through my mind that someone may have tampered with my sights. In desperation, not wanting to follow her wounded, I shot her on the high, arched part of her massive spine. She was immobilized and rolled over. This was not hunting as I know it now, and even at that stage, I felt inadequate, like a clumsy, bungling executioner. In addition to causing the animal to suffer unnecessarily, I was firing off ammunition that, even back then, in Mozambique, cost one pound sterling a round. By now very much alarmed, I shot her close to the breast formation in her underside. This was a shot that I sometimes used to make sure of a fallen elephant, because the bullet lodges in the heart or lung.

The bulls in the herd by now had run off, and I returned to camp, disturbed by failure and absolutely confused. I examined the rifle, and it appeared fine. Nevertheless, I was worried that the affair had robbed me of some of my confidence. I slept badly that night, dreaming of some power bewitching my rifle.

It was possible that the shells had been underloaded or that the bullets had broken up. In the morning I dissected the elephant to find that it had a malformed brain cavity, the brain being much lower and flatter than normal. My bullets had passed well above the brain. I know this sounds incredible, but I was firing at what amounted to a brainless elephant, a frightening thought. It was the first and last time that occurred. I sometimes wonder if this has happened to other hunters, with elephant or other dangerous game.

On Taylor's advice, I visited Lake Nyasa and the sea coast up to the Tanganyika border, relaxing and enjoying a good climate and conditions. The Mozambique coast is particularly relaxing, beautiful, and interesting. With its lovely beaches and warm climate, it is an unspoiled wonderland, or at least it was back then. Having regained my health there, I started thinking of Faanie and the northern frontier. After a while I became restless, a sure sign of returning health. This being low country and the rains imminent, I left for Rhodesia. I thought that Faanie would be interested in exploring the northern territory with me. It embraced vast areas across the Zambezi River north to the Tanganyika border and east of Lake Nyasa. In the Portuguese language this area was referred to as the Tete Zambezia, Niassa, and Cabodelgado districts.

Hoping that Faanie would by now have either struck it rich or exhausted his spirit seeking gold, I looked for him at the gold diggings on the Angwa River in Rhodesia. I was disappointed to discover that he had left to establish himself with a drilling rig in Kenya. It amused me to think of him digging into the earth again. I could think of no one more suitable for the coming venture and even thought of following him, but, considering the distance and my chances of finding him, I abandoned it.

While in the town of Bulawayo, I bought a Rigby .450 No. 2, a short-barreled double rifle with 300 sealed rounds of ammunition. It was old and had been extensively used and was a model discontinued and out of date, but it was the best rifle I was ever to own. I doubt if other double rifles were in its class. It was a handy stopper. The big brass cases were 3½ inches long with low chamber pressures and when one considers how all heavy-caliber rifles pound one's shoulders, this rifle for comfort and effect was the best for me.

With the limit of 300 rounds—and little likelihood of obtaining more—I hoarded my ammo and used it sparingly, reserving it mostly for wounded dangerous game. I had acquired a good battery now, a .404 magazine rifle and a .450 double rifle. I left a contact address for Faanie with Old Man Hinzie on the Angwa River gold fields and prepared light equipment for myself.

I had learned the hard way to travel lightly, even at times being held at ransom by locals when I urgently required their knowledge of areas or physical assistance. So I limited my kit to a minimum of essentials. I figured to be light is to travel fast and, if need be, undetected.

TETE – ZAMBEZIA

ELEPHANTS AND MAN-EATERS—1949

On the Rhodesian plateau I experienced the slow change of the coming season. The first nip of cold morning air suggested the time was at hand for me to descend to the low country and cross the Zambezi River into northern Mozambique. On traveling down the escarpment, I had exciting and pleasant thoughts of the sheer freedom to range over the vast elephant areas, deep into the warmer country and richer air of the low-lying lands.

I was uncertain of the unknown, however. There would be hardships including demands on human stamina, terrifying threats of thirst, as well as physical contact with wild beasts that could maim or kill me. The prospect of tropical diseases was frightening. Then there would be the irritating, nerve-sapping hassle of having to tolerate and cooperate with the locals, who would scheme to exploit weaknesses and situations to their own benefits. Another anxiety was the uncertainty of acquiring unlimited elephant on a legal license. The character and whims of the all-powerful Portuguese officials and the spy systems of their secret police had to be taken into account. Last but not least, there were the dietary requirements of the white hunter in the black man's primitive wilderness. I had experienced some of it before with less equipment, living like a tribesman, but the past had also taught me that, living alone, if I became hurt or sick it could be the end of me. And so in this wilderness my thoughts turned to Faanie, he on a drilling rig burrowing into the earth somewhere in Kenya.

Having motored to the valley floor, I left my vehicle at a village and crossed the Zambezi River in dugouts, camping on the north bank and organizing carriers to move between distant villages. Bearing in mind that I would need assistance in hunting, I tried to judge the local individuals and their bows and arrows, choppers, and spears. They carried them for confidence and by tradition. The farther north I ranged, the more noticeable and numerous the elephant populations became, many in large herds of cows with the occasional bull, and sometimes mixed groups. As usual, they were raiding the hell out of native cultivated lands. These powerful beasts knew exactly how much pressure was needed to break open watermelons so they could feed on them.

With the tribe's primitive methods of attempting to keep elephant out of the cultivated lands, half the crop went to the cultivators and half to the elephant. The damage by trampling alone was high, and hundreds of melons of mixed variety were smashed open and half eaten. It was a free-for-all, a fight between anxious, noisy, angry men and mighty beasts. Drums, tins, arrows, and occasional muzzleloaders were used, all to no avail; the elephant were able to condition themselves to man's puny efforts and irritating noises. With the concern of angry, desperate people, they drove arrows and threw spears at raiding elephant, which sometimes smashed their huts in retaliation, scattering the people in fearful panic. In desperation the tribes fell back on their faith, much as we do on ours. They hung charms and magic potions around the cultivated lands. It was not their efforts that made me laugh but the thought that any animal would be influenced by such antics.

I pitied them in their misery as they seemed to know no other way of life. Here were the poorest of the poor, the wretched of this land—yet they somehow managed to keep body and soul together. They foraged in the forests and bushlands, eating woodworms, ants, mice, roots, wild fruits, reptiles, and the occasional animal that their primitive weapons could bring down. But without crops they could not maintain their food needs, hence their emaciation. This was not the ideal place for men of the soil, but they knew no other, and home is where the heart is.

It was unprofitable for me to shoot these large herds of mostly cow elephant. I listened to the locals lamenting their prospects of near starvation. It was the age-old battle between man and beast. The areas were sparsely inhabited, and even if the people went elsewhere to live, the elephant in their wanderings would always find the cultivated lands. At the time there were no restrictions as the land was vast and unwanted; villages were long distances apart.

In this primitive life, it appeared that if the balance of man and beast were to be maintained, some of both were destined to die. To somehow kill or drive the marauders off was a constant threat and challenge as it required ingenuity, skill, and courage. No doubt some children and adults must starve. In the poor living conditions of this land, where others had so little, I prized my essential possessions, and I was at least effective against elephant.

Some men were very brave in their desperation as they tried at great risk to stave off the vast numbers of elephant. Others had been killed trying to do so. In the midst of these elephant depredations, a man named Chakama, having already thrown one spear but still armed with another, shouted emotionally: "They will bring us to starvation, and we will have to abandon our villages. I kill them even if I die!" Just in time I caught him by the upper arm, restraining him as he attempted single-handedly to move forward and attack the elephant mass. I realized that if I did not stop him I would soon witness the elephant smashing him.

At another village the same elephant raiders were so bold, attacking in full daylight, that in pity for the tribesmen I shot seven old cow elephant. It was a large herd, and the remainder reluctantly moved off to take cover in an adjoining forest. They stood there in defiance, waiting for nightfall, when they would raid the lands again—that is, if the smell of their dead did not deter them.

I then witnessed the locals' antics as they vented their hatred on the dead elephant. Some rushed at the carcasses with spears, throwing them but only partly penetrating the thick hides. Some spears that were not thrown straight bent at the spearheads. Other people hacked off the animal's tails to stamp on them and throw them into the air. Still others speared the sexual organs. Their hatred was all-consuming.

Suddenly, large numbers of nearly naked women, wearing nothing other than animal skins or short skirts of beaten bark, arrived—God knows from where! They were armed with primitive large knives, pangas, choppers, and spears. They converged on the dead elephant and ripped open the guts, hacking and pulling the large intestines to the sides, talking, shouting, and excitedly calling to each other for encouragement and assistance. Each family feverishly hacked away, knowing that this opportunity might never occur again. One woman with a large bloody knife said, "I will take my crops from your guts."

What was at first humour now changed as the locals urgently hacked away, some taking more meat than others, thus causing arguments. The shape of the beasts changed when parts were cut and pulled away. Organs were put on display as signs of ownership on the mixture of soil and trampled maize stalks.

Amid this frenzy of butchery, the natives cooperated in raising large portions of elephant meat and then lowering them onto the heads of others, who, with that African sense of balance, shuffled off to their various destinations. A wild African is never so lively and industrious as when he is hacking at the carcasses of elephant. Within hours there were only bloodstains and dung heaps on the ground. Even the massive head bones were hacked into manageable proportions and carried away.

My safari camped a few miles upstream at a pool away from the village. I had not yet encountered bulls worth shooting, and this particular area was at times known for its ivory. Three days later and farther on, however, I struck the first large bulls, a troop of about a dozen in ideal conditions. With the exception of one bull that turned to attack, I shot seven without incident, and the remainder slipped off silently into the forest. The ivory was large, and we had to camp for days to remove it. To allow the full use of labour, I traversed the surroundings alone, finding it reasonably stocked with a variety of game.

In a heavy forest I discovered antelope spoor that I was not familiar with, probably a small duiker. Examining the water holes gave me a fair idea of the resident game populations. There was much evidence of elephant here in the rainy seasons, with deep spoor in hardened mud everywhere, as well as indications of numerous herds moving between the grassy glades and the beautiful semi-open, shaded forests. On dense slopes I found fresh spoor of leopard, where they had watched me and then moved off.

A honey guide bird took to me, persistently twittering and desperately trying to get me to follow it. Bees and I are not friends, and since I did not have the locals with me to extract the honey, I took no notice of the bird's frantic calls. It dived and darted, indicating the direction to follow. But it was not my direction, and as I moved away it perched, emitting weaker twitterings, no doubt wondering how this man-creature could be so stupid. Toward sundown I came across large elephant spoor a few miles from camp, possibly twelve or more animals, their toes dug into the sand, indicating haste of movement.

That night in the firelight I considered whether I should take the trackers and water carriers to live for some days on the elephant spoor, and try to overtake the elephant. I had a fifty-fifty chance of catching them. In the predawn I awoke to the roaring of lion close by. They put on a grand show of sound, making me think they were next to camp, but they were more than four hundred yards away.

The roars woke everyone, so fires were rekindled and reluctantly activity commenced. I figured that if we left now at predawn we could be on the bull elephant's tracks at sunrise. We picked up the spoor farther on from where I had previously seen it. The elephant stayed together and were easy to follow through the open forest, mile upon mile. Then they moved into thick green foliage, feeding extensively. Here they must have lingered the night, and before dawn they headed straight to arrive at a water hole. It was now after midday, and I figured we were at least six hours behind them. As we proceeded, the country thickened and there were signs of much elephant feeding. As there was no danger at this stage, I pressed the trackers and we kept a fast, continuous pace.

That night we camped and replenished the water bags at a pool where the elephant had also watered. I thought them to be about two hours ahead of us. Depending on how much they fed, they would have the advantage of the coming night. At first light we were back on the spoor again. The elephant walked along low ranges and fed heavily in adjoining valleys, but at predawn they left the valleys, and to my surprise we arrived at an abandoned village. I saw where they had grazed old maize stalks and must have moved out at dawn. Within a mile they entered heavy forest. It was not yet midday, and I felt we were only hours behind them. We replenished at a water hole, and I noticed that only one of the elephant had bothered to drink.

They were not restless but were moving over long distances between their feeding places. We, on the other hand, were becoming fatigued, living on rice, dried meat, and water and using all the hours of daylight for tracking without breaks. At sundown I examined fresh, warm dung droppings. The forest here was thick with scrub and the light faded fast. It was dangerous to pursue without enough vision, and so we spent the night on the elephant spoor again with carried water and rations. I noticed the trackers were becoming demoralized.

That night I stopped their talking around the firelight, and in a little while they fell asleep—that being my purpose. At dawn we again followed, arriving at a picturesque pool surrounded by large, spreading forest trees. Here the elephant had watered and mud-bathed, lingering some time. There was plenty of game, and as we approached, the animals moved away from us: impala, sable, kudu, and eland, along with fresh buffalo and lion spoor. Vultures circled close by, and we deviated slightly to come up silently on a pride of lion feeding on a buffalo. We witnessed their spectacular ferocity as they fought for feeding positions around the carcass. There was a selfish, primitive cruelty to the cubs, which in their hunger were desperately trying to get in position to feed—and were generally savagely driven off the buffalo and forced to stand hungry beyond the circle of feeding adults.

We hastened off after the elephant into well-treed, leafy bush country. I kicked open a dung dropping and it was cold inside. The elephant were zigzagging here and there—a sure sign that we would make up some time. I took the opportunity to show the trackers the economy of moving on central spoors to avoid meandering. Slowly the heat of the day increased, and we arrived at a beautifully shaded spot of dense forest. Here the elephant had rested some considerable time, it being a requirement of their digestive system to slumber for hours in the intense heat of midday after feeding heavily during the night. They had slept a long time; within half a mile I kicked open a dung dropping and tested the temperature with the back of my hand. It was warm, but the intense sun may have kept it so. The elephant were more relaxed after their rest, feeding and halting for short periods. Then, to my dismay, the spoors indicated a straight course of direction.

I began to have doubts of overtaking the animals as they could suddenly decide on a far destination. In urgency I pressed the already fatigued trackers because I felt we could not maintain the pace on the following, fourth, day. Then we came across more dung droppings, these new and shining. I tested one and it was hot; then I observed some newly chewed leaves and bark. The elephant were close now, and the trackers became cautious, slowing their pace. They wind-tested, and I took my position behind the forwardmost tracker. After a short while he began to falter, a sure sign of nerve strain, so I put the other tracker in his place and used the one behind me for sighting.

All signs were fresh, and I had the advantage of no dense bush scrub. In these inviting conditions we heard the elephant feeding on leaves. As we approached, their massive shapes were loosely clustered and they appeared unaware of us, their feeding noises unchanged. I double-checked my rifle magazine and cartridge belts, then watched the wind-testing of the foremost tracker and cautiously moved forward, waiting for an opportunity when the elephant would bunch closer.

The fatiguing past days seemed to have robbed the trackers of nerve, so I took the lead. We were directly behind the elephant, and as we moved forward, more came into view. Trees and branches precluded full views of them, but parts of bodies and glimpses of heavy ivory showed. For the most success I felt I must get right inside the herd as far as the wind would allow. I passed three of them partly hidden on my left, feeding, and heard others close in front but not visible. For our safety we got into a position to avoid stampede, then I started firing at the heads facing me. In moments four elephant were down. A fifth, a very large-headed bull, dropped on an accurately placed frontal shot but quickly rose.

(This caused disturbing thoughts. Perhaps the bullet deflected within the skull cavity or did not penetrate to the brain. Whatever, it was not a hunting failure on my part, and it proved—as I had previously suspected—that rifles below the .450 class were on the light side for elephant hunting.)

This elephant rose in seconds, undazed, and as it moved forward and turned, I drove a shot into its exposed shoulder. It ran off as if nothing had happened, trumpeting at a hundred yards or so just before it collapsed from the heart shot.

During that period all caution was thrown to the wind as I moved forward and shot others, including one just turning to rush me, which I shot in the brain from the side. The elephant I had passed on my left were now moving parallel to me, and we saw each other simultaneously. One turned on us and was impressive and frightening at close quarters. A tracker completely lost his nerve and sprinted to one side triggering the bull's aggression, and the elephant trumpeted immediately and chased the tracker. Seconds earlier when the same bull had turned on us, I had been about to shoot. When he suddenly changed

After days of tracking, we finally overtook the herd of elephants.

course, I had to focus my attention anew on this enraged elephant, which was trumpeting and about to reach the tracker, who was running for his life.

I heard the man wail, "*Mai-ee-we-manderegera*" (My mother you are leaving me to die) as his running form was hidden by the elephant's pursuing bulk. I had to try an extreme angle behind the beast's ear, in the neck at the brain. It was either a brain shot or suffer a dead tracker with the bother of official enquiries. In a second of concentration I fired, and to my surprise the bull collapsed. As I reloaded a single cartridge into the magazine, he got up on his feet again. In urgency I fired again, this time farther back. Now he collapsed totally with his back feet extending, and the body mass no longer moved. I came up to him and put my hand where I could feel his heart still beating, but with the brain destroyed, the heartbeats slowly receded into lifelessness.

I had in those last tense moments wasted time and opportunity to get other bulls, and I cursed the running tracker. Well, it was emergency over greed. The elephant that had received a body shot was found dead close by. I had seven bulls with large ivory and we were all alive. In an exhausted state we camped close by. We had enough water for drinking and cooking until morning and knew we could reach more at the nearest water hole. Within two days we were back at the camp.

Four days passed, and upon arrival at a village I examined the remains of cultivated lands for spoor in the semidarkness of a setting sun. The land had been heavily trampled, for the elephant had reverted to eating the remainder of the maize stalks. They did not return that night. In the morning, because I was short of good rations, I questioned the villagers on the whereabouts of buffalo. In reply there was much chatter, lies, and confusion. At last the head man arrived. He appeared coarse and slow-minded, a degenerate-looking specimen. Although he lived here he knew nothing. Some of the others were repeating the name Keto, the honey hunter. He was sent for, but he was some distance away, and so we had to wait for him.

Eventually Keto arrived, and I could see at a glance that he was different. We questioned him about buffalo, and he mentioned some water holes that these animals frequented. It was already late, usually a bad procedure in hunting, but the honey hunter was sure, and so we reached the first water hole, but the buffalo spoor was two days old. At the second watering place, in a depression with large trees close to the water's edge and surrounded by open forest in a most splendid setting, we found spoor of early morning, probably predawn.

Over many miles we experienced the usual change of vegetation, scrub, and high grasses, the latter trampled in places by a variety of game. We saw waterbuck moving away unalarmed and stopping at a few hundred yards to gaze back. On a fringe of forest we sighted a large herd of beautifully coloured impala, full of energy, snorting as they made athletic, curved leaps, the high-jumpers of the savannas.

We kept on the buffalo spoor, and on a slight rise the trackers paused. We would, I thought, be lucky to get the buffalo in this open country. Ahead we saw movement about two hundred yards away in some deep shade. A kudu bull rose to his feet, then cows came into shape. We stared at each other; then they became alert and suspicious. The bull emitted a penetrating bark as they all turned and dashed off in graceful, long strides, disappearing into the vegetation. I thought of the harmlessness of all antelope, except perhaps sable at close quarters. Even wounded, there is no real danger of attack unless the hunter closes in on them.

Large herds of *gondonga* (hartebeest) slowly ambled along, though they are probably the fastest buck in Africa. As we continued, the vegetation changed again to heavy, tall grasses and bush. This was a buffalo refuge, and when we found fresh dung we slowed in order to keep the element of surprise. Then there appeared indistinct black shapes, many lying down and others standing. Though we had no clear view of a single animal, some individuals began to stare in our direction, having seen our movements. Then the bush came to life with snorts and buffalo bodies as the herd rose, alarmed, and got direction from the leaders to surge toward us, even though not fully aware of our presence. Upon leaving camp that morning, I had loaded the .404 magazine rifle with three old, well-exposed, softnose bullets that I wanted to expend, thinking they might eventually become undependable. These cartridges would teach me how to stop oncoming buffalo in their tracks.

I had learned much of buffalo habits and reactions from other hunts, but in the face of such a surging mass I was not completely confident, so I used the heavier double-barreled rifle. The leading animals came into view with the mass pressing behind them at about forty yards. I fired for the chest of a large cow. She did not deviate but within seconds collapsed and amidst the noise of hooves and horns, bawled in her death throes. Hastily I fired the second barrel, a similar shot at a large bull. He dropped within a few yards, but I did not hear him bawling because of the noise. Amidst the dust and body noises, the animals started to turn to one side. I kept firing the .450 rifle, panicking a little as the herd by now should have veered well off.

Perhaps I had not killed the leaders, I thought. There was no time to ponder, so I grabbed the .404 rifle. To my surprise two oncoming buffalo fell instantly to frontal head shots with the softnose ammunition, and as they did so there was a directional change. To keep it going I fired point-blank at angled chests and turning shoulders. The buffalo swerved, and as Pondoro Taylor had advised me, I fired at the base of the spine behind the brain of one animal. It dropped instantly and was covered by dust as the sounds of many hooves and banging horns swept past us. The buffalo dashed away, finally stampeding out of earshot.

After such excitement we needed to recover our nerves and release tension. I thought of the buffalo that dropped instantly to the spine shot. There was no need to examine inner details of its neck; it was obvious that the spine was shattered immediately behind or where it joins the brain cavity. All very well, but animals don't charge sideways. So there must be a way to instantly drop buffalo from the front.

I needed knowledge vital to survival. Though I failed to realize it at the moment of firing, I had actually learned how to immobilize oncoming buffalo.

Pleased with my shooting of the .404 rifle, I wondered how it could have been more effective than the .450 double barrel, so I opened the two buffalo skulls. I was intrigued to discover that the softnose bullets had expanded between the horns and disintegrated on impact to spread some of the shrapnel into to the brain. On later occasions, I used such softnose shots on wounded buffalo in the thickets.

But I mostly carried solids and cut into them with a broken, old hacksaw blade to form a star on the bullet head. These loads had at least the same effect as the softnose bullets.

We reserved a dead buffalo for ourselves and covered them all with branches to baffle the encircling vultures, which often hover high in the sky beyond the vision of human eyes. We walked back through a stretch of gameless country—though we did see pheasant and guinea fowl—to arrive at the next settlement. Here too were the usual devastated croplands, and we spoke to the headman of the village as others crowded around.

I noted disturbing signs of pellagra in these people, a diet deficiency that affects the skin and the digestive and nervous systems. No doubt that would have happened to me had I not turned my dugout to take the downstream current at the Mupata Gorge on the Zambezi River. What were a white man's chances here without some sort of balanced diet? It occurred to me that an ivory hunter must have athletic stamina. Like all athletes, his food intake can mean success or failure. This was one of the many important things to be learned about this isolated way of life, beyond the danger, excitement, and rewards of ivory hunting.

We gave these hard-up villagers all but one of the buffalo and watched them dash off for their knives, spears, and choppers, then disappear in the direction we had just come from. In a short time the village was mostly deserted.

We continued a few miles and found a murky water hole, where we camped. I did not like the sight of it and issued orders for all our drinking water to be boiled. There was contentment here, and much eating of buffalo meat.

Early the next morning I heard lion roaring far off, usually an indication of game numbers. Just after dawn, as we proceeded, game became numerous and water holes showed the spoor of the hunting animals: lion, leopard, and the scavenging hyena. There was good game feed in this parklike country of savanna and woodlands with occasional depressions holding water from the past rainy season.

We came across signs of large herds of eland, sable, and some rhinoceros spoor, and eventually I sighted a rhino amongst some trees. I had heard they were crazy when disturbed and prone to blundering attacks, so I tested this theory. The animal was not fully grown, having short horns, and so I, well covered by a tree, called to it. At first it stood still, listening, but then became alarmed and agitated. It turned on a small tree, bashing it a few times, and then trotted off. I was to learn later from tales told around campfires at night that rhino were not always that amusing,

The light forests were shady and game-filled. It was the type of country where you wanted to linger forever. There were elephant including herd bulls, but considering the heavy ivory we already had, they were not worth hunting. One afternoon, after snaring wildfowl at a small water hole in the company of a tracker, we topped a slight rise to see lion lying close to a herd of well over a thousand buffalo. The buffalo, at least on the outer fringes, were aware of the killer cats.

On other occasions I had watched the stalking tactics of lion. First they would get the buffalo restless enough to move off; then suddenly they would flank them, sometimes landing on the buffalo's backs and shoulders to claw and dig deep into them or bend back their noses and necks. Invariably the buffalo would collapse to earth, where they would be seized and strangled by powerful jaws.

Lion did not always kill in this fashion, but it was their preferred method with the bovine species. It is fascinating to witness lion closing in on their quarry with their alert, catlike actions. And now, with the wind favourable and us concealed, I watched this scene of lion and buffalo, and tried to analyze the situation: Both hunters and hunted were aware of each other's presence and nothing was happening. Perhaps the situation would change at nightfall.

We arrived at our camp at sundown to see a stranger emerge from the forest and stand spear in hand some distance from the campfires. I beckoned him to advance. Africans, having so little, usually wanted something: meat, a service of some kind, or perhaps to give you the impossible task of trying to save a dying relative. The newcomer came forward slowly as if feeling his way into a new world, briefly speaking to my water carrier as he approached us. This was no beggar but a muscular and well-proportioned man in his prime.

I moved forward in a gesture of welcome and at close quarters looked into the face of a man very badly scarred by facial mutilations. There was no way of recognizing what he had once looked like. My first impression was that of someone evil to be feared, but I displayed no signs of disturbance. Unlike most wild Africans, his greeting was to the point, with no clapping of hands or gesticulation. Something in his physical balance and his voice gave me the feeling that under that mutilated facial exterior there was a lot of man. His looks took some getting used to. Because I could not completely understand his Lomwe language, I stared at the fire and conversed with him through the trackers. He had come from the Rio Ruvuma, a river on the Tanganyika border, and lived by hunting leopard to sell their skins, and trade their claws and teeth to the medicine men and chiefs.

If true, I found his words more than merely interesting because hunting the stealthy leopard requires the greatest of skills. I suspected that he must have an illegal hidden rifle or shotgun.

We all talked, ate, and relaxed in the atmosphere of the campfire, and in a pleasant way I questioned the newcomer on the country ahead and the Rio Ruvuma. He knew it well and informed us that it is a place of many large tuskers as the Zambezia and Nyasa crop areas lured bulls across the Ruvuma River into Mozambique to raid toward the end of the crop season, which was about now. Then the bulls would gradually return. I asked him what spoor he had seen.

"Plenty," he said. "Large herds and a lot of scattered big bulls."

Hearing this made me optimistic.

"Where will they be in the coming winter season?" I asked.

"Most of them go back into the lion man-eater country of Tanganyika," he said.

I got the picture.

"So where are you hunting now?" I asked.

"I am not hunting yet," he said. "I come to hunt with the 'wild dog' and can lead him to where the large bulls water. All this country I know better than others."

I was disillusioned at his disclosure of my identity as "wild dog"; it meant that no matter where I went I would be known. I had planned to flit alone on excursions across the border into Tanganyika. Well, as the saying goes, so much for the best-laid plans of mice and men. I did not know what decision to make with this faceless one and so let things take their course. We moved around the area for a few more days, getting to know each other. He was infinitely better than any tracker I had so far used. It was not only his fast tracking but his ability to anticipate the reactions of game, and I noticed that the men treated him with fearful yet friendly respect.

He mentioned that the time was fast approaching for most of the raiding bulls to return to Tanganyika, so we moved on from this wonderland under the guidance of the new tracker, Chirenge (meaning someone with powerful, muscular legs). We no longer moved in a straight northern direction but rather from water hole to water hole and sometimes along small streams. At this time in 1949, the great drought of East Africa was raging in the north, causing wild animals to attempt to migrate elsewhere for food and water.

On the fourth day we found fresh spoor of a large troop of elephant bulls. Chirenge's tracking speed was too fast for us—he tended to run on the spoor. We had gone miles through attractive savanna, but then in the heat of midday the elephant entered thick bush, green and well leafed. Here they fed extensively, giving us the opportunity to close the gap. Even in the thick bush Chirenge's pace was too fast and he too enthusiastic. I had to put another tracker in his place who was used to me and who approached the elephants slowly. Chirenge, who was carrying the double rifle with two bandoliers, suddenly pushed forward and indicated a movement, and the head, shoulders, and front feet of an elephant appeared. The bull had large ivory, and I was tempted to go for the side brain shot. Chirenge, next to me using the *rota*, whispered "straggler" and so it was that there were no others close by. We waited and the bull eventually turned slowly and ambled off in the direction of the others. I put Chirenge back on the spoor, cautioning him to proceed at a slow pace. His "slow" was quite fast, and then he paused, intently listening. He remained where he was, hand slightly raised for attention and silence.

Then we all heard a branch break and leaves rustling. Still Chirenge did not move and kept testing the wind with the *rota.* Not satisfied, he moved off at an angle to approach the herd from a different position. We quarter-circled them, and Chirenge boldly and expertly closed in, confidently following the elephant at a distance of about twenty yards. The rustling noises told me we were up against elephant, some feeding, others standing, fanning their ears. At Chirenge's side, I could see parts of elephant and protrusions of large ivory here and there.

Chirenge signaled with his eyes, and I saw, portions of large bulls with tusks, protruding from a bush, very close in front, facing us. I indicated to the others to stay close, and fired the .404 rifle. The bull dropped, and there was complete silence. It lasted only seconds before new movement revealed others. I took two more frontal shots and the bulls dropped instantly. Now what bull heads we could still see were raised, ears outspread in alarm. Elephant first experience alarm, then fear, and finally, out of fear, become quickly and unexpectedly enraged and attack. From experience and observation, I knew this to be their pattern. If a hunter is faced by more than three elephant alarmed in this manner, it could be his end if they charge simultaneously. Because of the thick bush, the animals are hunted at very close quarters; to have them charging in different directions greatly increases the hunter's risk.

I saw two bulls moving away from the troop to my right and shot them. Then, to my surprise, Chirenge, like a dog breaking its leash, and with great agility, suddenly moved his sinuous body forward to my left and went into action with my double-barreled rifle. From my vantage point, I could not see him, but I instinctively knew it was time for me to advance to the center of the troop, and immediately did so, taking shots to clear the way. Chirenge was close, but still out of sight, and I heard him firing again. It meant he knew how to load a double rifle, and I hoped to God he was killing and not just wounding them. The remaining bulls went through the bush ahead of me, and we heard them crashing off, the sounds receding in the distance.

The dead were not all in view, so I scouted around and was impressed by the large ivory—at a guess, the tusks weighed sixty to one hundred pounds a side. Along with the bulls I had shot previously, I had enough wealth to last me one year. Because there was enough for all, my intentions were to handsomely reward everyone. These were my thoughts as Chirenge came back and indicated by his fingers that eleven elephant were down. He became impatient, saying there was a water hole some miles off and that we must move if we were to get there before dark.

That night Chirenge and I discussed the day's hunt and the four elephant he had shot. I waited for an explanation but he volunteered none. However, he said it was the first time he had used a double rifle but knew that it worked like a shotgun. He said it was getting late in the season and that we should leave the carriers to the ivory extraction and take the two other trackers to travel light and hunt elephant ahead. It all made sense, but I explained that besides this ivory I had more hidden from whence I had come. Three days of hard work and it was removed. With our goods, the weight of the ivory was hard to carry, so we hid it.

At this stage, it was essential to keep the safari together, as desertion of any of its members could lead to the theft of hard-earned hidden ivory. This had to be avoided at all cost, and so I devised a plan of wealth-sharing. I had noticed that the farther trackers and helpers were from their homes the less enthusiastic they became, some even deserted unseen to go hundreds of miles back to their homes unrewarded. Deserters tend to steal anything of value—sometimes items essential to the safari.

We passed the lower slopes of the impressive Milange Mountains and many days later saw distant ranges ahead. This vast rugged area was known as the land of the Lomwe people, and our trackers referred to some of the ranges as Mabu and Maripee. Here we hunted elephant, but it was mostly high country and at times cold and damp, with frequent drizzling rains.

I much prefer low-lying warm country, so in discomfort we abandoned this place, turning east and north, eventually following the Lugenda River. Here two rivers came together, and to the northeast we could see the stream drop into a valley. Chirenge advised that the Rio Ruvuma should be about a week's walk from here. He was for lingering to scout the area of the Chiutezi River before proceeding north again, and it was not so much the rivers but his knowledge of the water holes that gave us the bull elephant we were seeking.

The massive forest and bushlands of northern Mozambique had a strange and enticing atmosphere, and as I penetrated them I became intrigued—partly by the beauty and movement of the many wild animals, especially the antelope, and always by the lure of dangerous game. In a few days we were in well-stocked antelope and buffalo country with water holes, savanna, grass, and bush. Lion, leopard, hyena, and wild dog were seen. It was another one of those inviting places to linger. The time had come for me to find out about Chirenge. So, while at a water hole snaring wildfowl, I questioned him. He told me he was a Tanganyikan but lived on the Mozambique side of the Ruvuma River. He owned a 9.3mm Mauser rifle but had not had ammunition for two years. I did not bother to ask the origin of the rifle, for no doubt it had been stolen or illegally traded for something. He had a brother, a chief, who was his mortal enemy, having caused him to be imprisoned in Dar es Salaam for illegal ivory dealing.

Chirenge killed leopard, mostly with poisoned arrows, in order to stay well established on the Mozambique side, where he gave the teeth and claws to *murios* (witch doctors) and *nangas* (medicine men), who in turn had the chiefs turn blind eyes to his activities. Apparently word of his poaching went no farther than the chiefs, whose authority silenced the people. Chirenge was skilled at trapping and spear-fishing and seldom went without meat, which he traded for other items.

Considering the poverty here, this enterprising man was in a very good position to survive. He stayed on the Ruvuma River as a precaution in case he had to cross either way. And he had three very large hidden tusks. I was later to see these and estimated them to be between 140 and 150 pounds each. Because of his previous ivory dealing and jail sentence, he was undecided as to how to capitalize on the ivory.

"'Wild dog'—where did you hear that?" I asked.

"On the Ruvuma," he replied. "They have heard of the big cow elephant shoot-up and know you are not from Mozambique but an *estrangeiro*."

"And on the strength of that you found me?"

Chirenge gave the teeth and claws of leopards to murios (witch doctors) like the one shown here, and nangas (medicine men) who in turn had the chiefs turn blind eyes to his activities.

"Yes, but it was not easy with us both coming from different directions."

I heard a fluttering of wings as a pheasant was caught in the snare. He dashed off to kill it, and on his return I was smiling. He was also amused, not knowing why—or maybe he thought it had something to do with the snared bird. I burst out laughing and said, "You people, you always want something—what is it you want?"

We were both amused, and he said, "Bwana, I need you to sell ivory."

For my part, I wondered if he could be trusted to collect my hidden ivory, as the sale of some of the tusks could finance me to Kenya, where I might make contact with Faanie. I would go up the coast to Mombasa and then inland. The next season we would be safer and more efficient, hunting in partnership. It was not good for a hunter to be alone in this wild, enticing, yet risky country. But the ivory trail had become a way of life, and so I penetrated farther northward.

I had heard of other hunters elsewhere in the wilds but did not think it was convenient to find them. No doubt I would meet some of them later in Nampula or other places. I missed my culture and the company of my own kind, and I felt old and isolated. In addition, continuous elephant hunting plays hell on the nervous system, and without a break now and then you become irritable, nervous, and short-tempered. This did not make for good relationships between myself and the trackers, who were experiencing the same symptoms, but to a lesser degree.

When overstrained from too much dangerous hunting, you imagine seeing elephant where there are none. It develops into a frightful anticipation of imaginary dangers and an inability to know the real from the unreal. I was feeling dangerously close to this condition and considered the merits of a hiatus from elephant hunting. I had heard of men who never recovered from this condition and eventually had to change their professions. They missed the wilds, but a persistent, lingering fear dominated their hearts and minds. However, if you survive this stage, and become more familiar with elephant, you come partly under their spell, ever conscious of their presence. But you never loose your fear of them, especially in dense vegetation.

Perhaps this is a good place to describe in detail what it was like to make a living hunting elephant—the challenge, difficulties, physical and mental demands, and the rewards as well. If your first encounter should involve a large herd of cow elephant in thick bush, I doubt if your nerves would last. So this is essentially a description of bull hunting. In the usual procedure you find the spoor of a troop of bulls just after sunrise. These elephant have lazed around all night drinking and feeding extensively without insects to worry them. They move off at predawn with great strides—equal to three of yours—and walk miles through forest and bushlands to one of their many places of rest and sanctuary. This is not a great exertion to them, but their normal manner of travel, and they do it voluntarily. They are gregarious, having contact with each other even in the dense bush. Occasionally they may linger to feed. They may walk thirty miles or more, but a typical day's travel is about twenty miles, even less in very dense bush. At midday they seek thick bush for shade and rest. This is not sleeping as we know it but a loitering, dozing laziness in proximity to each other. Some animals actually sleep lying down on the slopes of large antheaps. Lighter animals lie flat on the ground, but the majority stand sleeping on their feet.

You have followed them, carrying much-needed water, rifles, etc. You are clothed and thus usually very hot. Elephant ears have many blood vessels that act as radiators to cool their bodies. As the heat increases, they may feed continuously in a state of pleasure and linger here and there in shade. Eventually they move off. Under the blazing midmorning sun of the African low country, you feel the need for rest and water. Drink you must, but rest you can't.

The heat increases rapidly and insects become pests. Tsetse flies seek your blood and mopane flies make life miserable by flocking to the liquid of your eyes as you look down at tracks or peer ahead in case the elephant have stopped for a break. All the time the heat reflects off the ground, and then the bush thickens and you're forced to slow down and proceed with caution, to make sure of the spoor and the distance between you and your quarry. Sometimes the soles of your feet burn, having made too much contact with the earth. You sweat profusely, but it makes you feel good—provided you have water and salt to replace the body loss; otherwise, you fatigue quicker than usual and get into a desperate state of thirst.

Water is life, and without it you die in a state of madness. You feel your physical power and stamina diminishing. It is not so much food you require but relaxation and rest. But you cannot rest as time lost here could mean the loss of elephant. As you linger, they move in great strides ahead of you. Elephant usually take refuge in thick bush in the morning and plow through it for miles, sometimes on well-worn, narrow paths. You face these conditions at midday and will travel many more miles at the worst time of day, painstakingly tracking and anticipating. If the animals remain stationary for a long time, you could suddenly walk into them, and so you continue for hours, the heat and trying conditions sapping what little resources you have left. Eventually it is only stamina and willpower that keep you going—these and the prospect of ivory.

Your stomach is lean and hollow, and you feel that any overexertion will be your last. But the spoor freshens and you have to show new mental interest, so you drive yourself on, hoping to make contact while you still have some strength left. All signs are fresh, but the elephant keep moving ahead. You have no alternative but to follow doggedly. I used to imagine I was sitting on a horse with my burning feet dangling. It was a lovely picture. Eventually, warm dung droppings, chewed leaves, sounds, scent, or instinct tell you of your quarry's proximity. You now have to summon what reserves of nervous energy, courage, and skill you have left for the final, fearful contact. Your vision is limited because of the bush; animal sounds act as guides to your coming actions.

The wind, when not in your favour, will warn your quarry, which may bolt and waste the day's efforts. If the air is swirling in all directions, no amount of skill will help, other than rushing ahead at speed. It is important to know that wounded or determined, aggressive animals can and do use erratic wind currents to move, even in large semicircles, into position to suddenly come at you or patiently wait, aware of your approach.

Hunters believe wounded buffalo circle to wait in ambush. You may be spooring directly ahead when unexpectedly you hear the bush crashing as animals come at you from the side, having caught your scent in the wind swirls. With elephant, if the herd is well led, you may find yourself in a minor stampede. It is one of the reasons I prefer bush conditions: You are semi-hidden and some of the animals may pass you. Unless some form of team communication signals them to attack, they will continue crashing through the bush away from you.

A herd of elephant in coordinated attack is fearless and formidable, as each animal concentrates on the hunter. A white man is foreign and more easily identified in thick bush than the dark-skinned tribesmen, and the elephant will select him, especially if the tracker and water carrier remain stationary while the hunter moves into action. An elephant's concentration is keenly intense, and it is vital that you break up this intensity before an attack, even if it means making everyone move. I am talking of a herd of elephant in the open viewing you. In other words, if you give the animals more than one object to concentrate on, you become more difficult to pinpoint as the target of a concerted attack; your chances are better if their attentions are diverted by even temporary confusion. Even if you break up the menace of a concerted attack, you still have to deal with them as individuals. But if the wind is in your favour, the tracker can approach in the right direction.

There is a naive belief that elephant cannot see clearly. I personally have tested their sight from a dugout offshore. At 150 yards they are conscious of you. At eighty yards they can make positive identification, and at fifty yards they are subject to being disturbed, frightened, or angry. I am talking of elephant that have at some time been hunted. But here you are now, so close to them in thick bush, where they are mostly hidden, that you can smell them and feel their presence. Most times you hear the soft gurgling sounds of elephant communicating with each other; occasionally they make harsh, growling roars.

You are now voluntarily in the midst of the mightiest wild animals on earth, and at this range you cannot escape the intimidation that their presence brings. They are massive, sometimes twelve feet at the shoulders, the large ones weighing six tons and more—the record height is thirteen feet, two inches or 4.01 meters; estimated weight, twelve imperial tons—and they move through thick bush as easily as you walk through grass. There is no way of escaping the feeling that you are, by comparison, fearfully puny—because that is exactly what you are.

They are right next to you, sometimes a matter of a few paces, and you may have partial vision of some of their bodies. You are in a sea of dense vegetation trying to peer through gaps. Although you cannot see all of the animals, their standing positions relative to yours are vital because when the action starts, some elephant may come down on you. It is usually impossible to position them all.

If the ash from the *rota* sinks straight to earth, you are unseen and safe for the moment. You have dreads and doubts, and in these final moments you are totally alone, even if the trackers are near and giving you their own fear, of which you already have enough. Even if you are amongst a troop of bulls, not just one or two, you have to draw on inner reserves, which you may feel are dwindling. With your life in the balance, you have to force yourself to take the first shot. Whatever happens, your action will trigger multiple reactions. Now the moment of truth has arrived as you raise the rifle for the shot at the first bull. All shots, when possible, must be at the brain for instant results, to keep the target from rushing at you or disturbing others into action. If you have strong hunting instincts, it will help to dampen some of your fears. You fire the first shot, knowing all hell will break loose around you—knowing, too, that in seconds you will find yourself amidst a background of animal fear and fury.

You try to suppress your own fears and concentrate on shooting at heads facing you. Other hidden animals may already be moving in your direction. In the thick bush, it's a deadly game of nerve and skill of killing speed, coordination, and maneuver. The elephant are in a better position to see you as they crash through the heavy bush. And they have an amazing sense of communication that seems inexplicable to the human brain and probably includes sound effects inaudible to us.

Because of panic, fear, and anger, a herd of elephant is not fully functional. This is to your advantage; where the opportunity arises, you must shoot with speed and accuracy for the safety of everyone. The faster you drop them, the safer you begin to feel. There are many huge beasts crashing around unseen, and a few may try to flush you out and hunt you. You lose all contact with time, realizing only that this crisis is lasting too long for your nervous system. Then to your great relief and joy, you hear the elephant stampeding away from you,

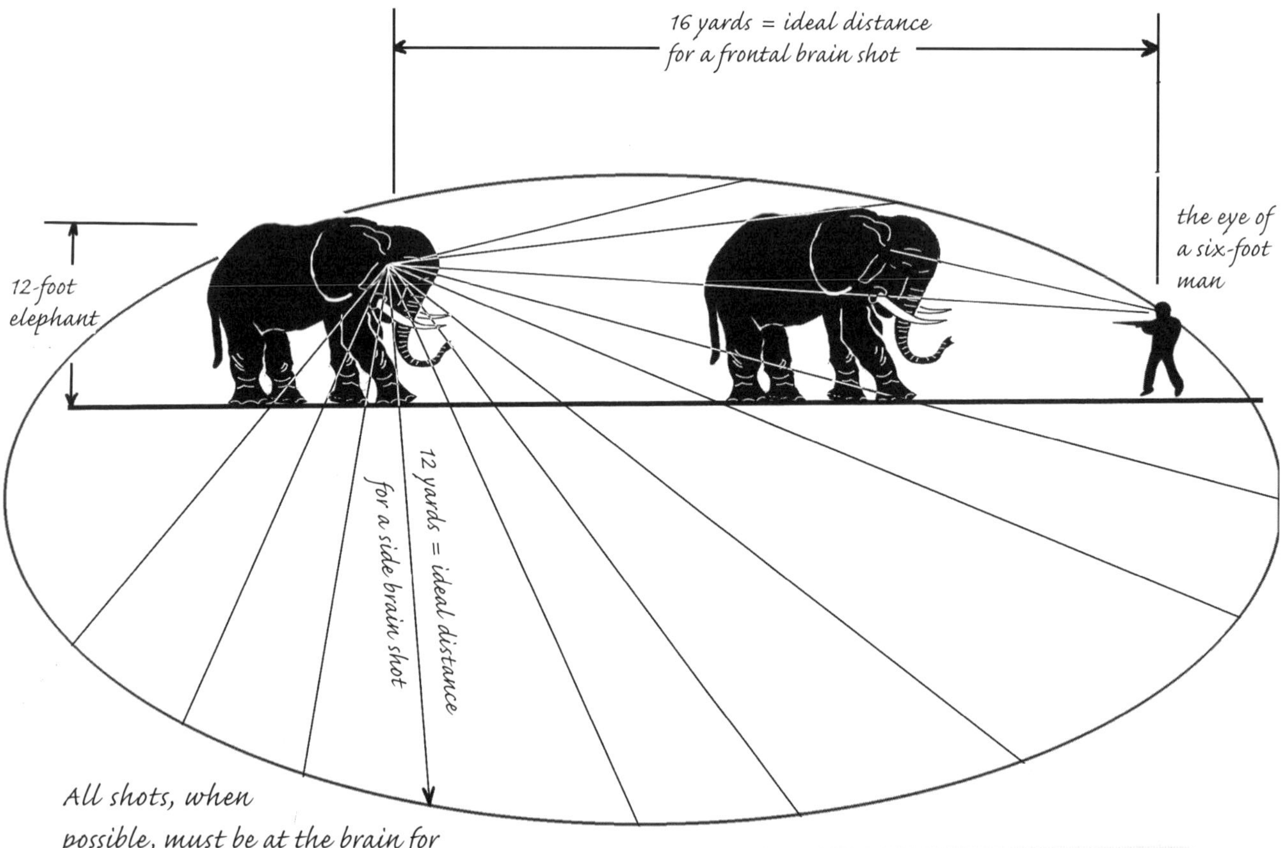

All shots, when possible, must be at the brain for instant results, to keep the target from rushing at you or disturbing others into action.

trumpeting and roaring. Your senses tell you there may be stragglers or wounded lurking, and so you remain alert as the great welcome silence envelopes you, amidst the dust and the mixed smells of elephant and Cordite. Your rifle has become a treasured lifesaver.

Your nervous system has been drained and you feel the need to go to earth, to sit or lie down to regain your equilibrium. Undamaged, you feel fully alive and have that great sense of well-being that can only be experienced in the wilderness. Your thirst is intense, and if you're lucky enough to have water you savour its cooling relief running down your throat. You have profited by taking ivory, and, for the moment, take your leisure in the wilds. But in the days to come you will hunt again and again, severely taxing your nervous system, at increasingly greater risk of the breakdown I spoke of earlier—seeing elephant where there are none.

Now let us return to the hunt at hand: In this part of Mozambique there was enough ivory for the hunter, but the grass on the other side always seems greener, and so, with illegal entry into Tanganyika in mind, we moved closer to the Ruvuma River. My intention was to hunt bulls there eventually, but I was already stretched out with caches of ivory to the south behind me. I moved ever northward in this intriguing land, an unusual place endowed with natural abundance, from puny mice to the mightiest elephant on earth, and the beauty of massive forests, bush lands, and occasional *vleis* of tall grasses. At this time of year there were abundant water pans and flowing rivers in a warm, comfortable, relaxing climate. I wanted to linger, but I had a destination—the Rio Ruvuma on the Mozambique/Tanganyika frontier, where even more impressive places might await across the river—and so I reluctantly moved from this wonderland.

I left the main camp and traveled light with Chirenge as a guide. With the aid of an acquaintance and the use of his dugout, we crossed the Ruvuma at midday and camped well into Tanganyika. The area was populated by people, but before the sun went down we came across large bull-elephant spoor. Chirenge took me well inland to watering places where I was excited to find so many signs of large elephant. I had seen enough for the time being and returned to Mozambique. Chirenge explained much to me, and I got to know which areas to avoid. This new Tanganyikan area, I thought, might well have even more game than Mozambique.

We had been gone about eight days and on our return heard of lion attacks on a village. Lion had apparently killed a woman coming from the water and that night had pulled a man, woman, and child from a hut. Man-eaters don't mean much until they are in your vicinity, and then they mean everything. Chirenge was of the opinion that they were transient lion as people here had not been attacked for many years, but I had difficulty with that theory since lion are usually territorial, and rarely hunt outside an established range.

It was here that Chirenge told me of being attacked by hyenas while sleeping. It was a hot night, and he slept outside the front doorway of his hut, waking to terrible pain on his face as he was dragged by a hyena close to the dying embers of the fire. Reaching for his face, he felt fur and realized his face was in the jaws of a hyena. He kicked out at it and in so doing most of the flesh of his face came away.

For seconds he saw hyena around him, and then they seized him again by his face. His wife, hearing the struggle, emerged with spear and chopper to assist. She must have been a woman of great courage because the hyena were in a pack and already had the taste of blood. She closed in on them and hacked at them with the chopper. Chirenge, who was being mauled again, managed to kick himself free a second time, and his brave wife put the spear in his hands. Together they defended with chopper and spear and managed to drive the hyena off.

I had seen hyena packs pull down game efficiently, and had heard of hyena seizing sleeping people and tearing out chunks of flesh. This attack on Chirenge was disturbing to me, and it made me think of the many nights I had spent sleeping alone next to a fire in so-called security.

With Chirenge's experience and the man-eaters on my mind, we recrossed the Ruvuma. Here we saw a large crocodile—probably sixteen feet or more with enormous girth. It saw us approaching at a distance, seemingly unconcerned. But as we got close, it slipped into the water. I doubt if anybody seized by such a river monster would be able to fight or get away.

Our main camp was on a small stream south of the Ruvuma River. Before reaching it, we were informed by a group of locals that one of our carriers had been seized a few nights before by lion. At first I doubted it, but Chirenge did not, and wondered who it was. At camp the other two trackers confirmed the news. The victim was Kasoko, whom I had named "Grumble" because, although willing enough, that was what he was always doing. With the exception of some spears and choppers, the trackers were unarmed. At the camp they had built a stockade of chopped trees and branches for defense. It was firm enough, but determined lion could jump over the top.

The story was that they were all sleeping around two fires, and in the morning Kasoko was missing. They thought nothing of it, supposing he had gone off to urinate or something. But when they saw drag marks and lion spoor, they became alarmed. Armed with spears, they followed and after a distance saw where lion had fought over the body.

Other than some bloodstained clothing, nothing was found. The lion had dragged Kasoko's remains beyond where our men were willing to go. I thought to myself that the skull must still be there. We discussed it. With or without evidence, this matter had to be reported to the *chefe do poste*. If man-eater activities continued, I would have to abandon my intended trip up the coast to Kenya, keep my staff intact, and retrace our way south.

We moved to the Ruvuma, living off hunted buffalo, fish, and native vegetables, relaxing on this pleasant river. A few days later we heard of other people having been killed by man-eaters, including one at a village that we knew about twenty miles south of us. That was the deciding factor: There would be no peace from the man-eaters now, so I decided—to the relief of all—to sell some ivory for expenses and to move south. We reequipped with essential supplies at Nampula, many miles south. From there we returned on the southern route to collect other ivory caches, eventually reaching the Zambezi River. Then on to Tete and Quelimane on the coast, a distance of many hundreds of miles. We were well off the beaten tracks and at times reached villages and heard the intonation of the drums informing us that the man-eaters' activities had seriously increased behind us.

To those unfamiliar with the activities of man-eating lion and, rarely, leopard, it is a terrifying experience, probably the worst one can have in wild Africa. The man-eaters stalk women in the croplands, at water holes, and

Night belongs to the man-eaters.

when collecting firewood. Children are also victims, and I know of two ivory hunters who were killed and eaten. It is pitiful to see the measly human remains of lion attacks. In the villages one can see and feel the terror creeping into people's souls as the sun begins setting, for the night belongs to the man-eaters.

The village inhabitants' only refuges are their huts and trees; strangely enough, they prefer the former and pass their nights between sleep and terror. Even the children are mostly silent out of fear. The fear is like a plague, making the people submissive and fearfully ineffective with their bows and arrows, spears, and choppers. Lion are extremely powerful, and a good blow from one of their paws can take a man's head off. I have stayed under the night shade of overhanging roofs of village huts waiting for man-eaters to appear and felt the people's fear, though our's was lessened because of our firearms and the stout company of the trackers. On those occasions we adopted the habit of sleeping during the day, something I could easily do, especially in the heat and after staying awake all night from sunset to sunrise. Lion are not always adept at killing humans and certainly do not do it with the same efficiency they display with game. If a person is seized by the neck or head, death is instant, but if not, it results from being dragged and mauled.

There is no way a man can physically fight a lion unless he is well armed, and I know of only one case of success. This was Harry Wolhunter, a game ranger employed by Kruger National Park. He managed to kill a lion with a knife to its heart as it dragged him. Certainly he had great courage and presence of mind, but had he missed the stab to the heart, he would have been mauled to death. It is not widely known that lion reach out with their forepaws to pull you into them and are particularly damaging when they use the dew claws on their inner front feet.

Unknown to me, all hunting activities had been suspended by the Portuguese authorities until such time as the man-eaters were accounted for. It meant that all hunters, in order to pursue their normal lives, had to turn their efforts to the destruction of the man-eaters. It also meant that any lion seen would be shot in the hope that they were man-eaters.

At this stage I was grateful to be far enough south away from the scene. The crop season was finished, and I had done well enough on elephant. Winter was coming up on the plateaus, and even when we reached the coast at Quelimane we could feel a slight change from the heat. It brought about perfect weather, and at night I enjoyed the company of people while sitting at the pavement cafes with good food and wine. The Mozambique coast is sheer pleasure, a relaxing place of decent and cheap facilities. Nothing, of course, lasts forever, but it was indeed good not having to rough it for a time.

Before returning to Salisbury, I amply rewarded my staff, especially Chirenge, who returned north again. He had actually planned to walk back alone to the Rio Ruvuma, but I overruled him and managed to get him a cheap berth on a tramp steamer to the northern port of Mocimboa da Praia.

From the Portuguese I heard of the great numbers of buffalo in the Marromeu district, residing on the flats and open plains—the *tunda* as they called it. I was later to learn that it is not just *tunda* but a variety of vegetation with swamps, *barrossa* palm forests with their wide leaves noisy in the winds, and places continually watered with permanent jungle growth. But the area was dominated by vast open plains with lush grasses. I arrived there to find a profusion of the usual variety of African wild animals on a coastal plain with rivers draining from the interiors into the lowlands. This lower section is part of the land of the Sena people.

In early Portuguese colonial history, men in suits of armour penetrated to the upper reaches of this country, but the tiny malaria mosquito became the master of their destinies. At the time, malaria was a mystery disease. The mosquitoes, plus intrigues and minor wars caused the Portuguese *conquistadores* to retreat to the coastline, where they used the local inhabitants to penetrate the interior lands for trading purposes. The lures were gold, ivory, and slaves—particularly gold, which was carried in the hollows of porcupine quills. No doubt the source of much of the gold was the land of Monomatapa, now part of Zimbabwe. Slaves carried the ivory to the coast.

I was so impressed with the game herds of the *tunda* that I stayed to explore it in some detail, traveling through swamp lands to the sea dunes where the *tunda* ends. Here I gazed out across the warm, inviting Indian Ocean, stretching to the horizon. But my greatest pleasure was to see the minor herds of buffalo on the beaches, particularly some old bulls standing in the sea waves. It was a sight beyond my imagination, and I sat for hours watching the buffalo on their beachfront. Nature totally undisturbed by man is indeed marvellous. Later, on the distant northern coastline, I was to see elephant on the beaches, suggesting that it was a part of their way of life from ancient times.

My next step was the Sena Sugar Estates, well inland in this fertile country, where sugar cane is grown for commercial purposes. Big herds of buffalo were hunted in comparative safety from trucks, to provide meat for the labour forces. For the sake of experience, I assisted them and found that the safety factor changed when wounded buffalo took cover within their own herds or broke off to seek sanctuary in dense vegetation, swamps, or, worse still, in the *barrossa* forests where winds make it a place of exaggerated noisy leaf movements. This factor gave the buffalo the element of surprise as the hunter had to approach in the confusion of forest sounds. It became a nerve-wracking follow-up as the buffalo, more familiar with such conditions, confidently waited for your approach.

The commercial meat hunter there was Gustav Guex, of Swiss origin with a slight accent, a wiry man highly experienced with buffalo—especially on the plains. To get used to the large herds, I hunted with him. This country was interlaced with channel swamps where crude wooden bridges had to be almost constantly repaired because of termite activities and annual floods.

At one stage I had an American hunter, Ralf Richard, with me. He was the right stamp of man and excellent as a hunter, but always point-blank refused to fire the first shot, saying he was fearful of what he might stir in the herds. "You ain't never seen nothing like it," he would say in his infectious twang, as we approached the massive buffalo herds on the open plains. By this time I had learned much about buffalo reactions on these plains, but on foot and up close to a mighty herd, I always had feelings of awe and uncertainty.

On a few of those occasions, buffalo previously wounded by someone else detached themselves from the herd to charge, and I had to stop them in their tracks before others followed. Here my experience firing softnose bullets to the upper nasal cavities was vital since it instantly immobilized them. What disturbed me at the time were the deliberate charges by buffalo that were not wounded and appeared not to be diseased.

On one particular occasion, viewing buffalo from a high elevation, I estimated that I was gazing on a moving mass of about 5,000 to 6,000 animals. The many miles of excellent grazing supported such large numbers. To come up to such a herd caused fear and at the same time fascination. This was ancient Africa. The buffalo's overwhelming numbers, contact noises, and bold, concentrated stares made you feel puny in their wild, enticing presence. You became conscious of large flocks of egrets and oxpecker birds hovering over or resting on their backs, but you didn't really bother to watch them as the intent, menacing bovine stares and the way they jostled each other to approach still closer held your attention. Their numbers alone made you doubt your abilities and stripped you of all pretensions. Any sign of retreat at such a stage could cause them to suddenly follow and then stampede over you.

Our one advantage was in the buffalo's reaction to gunfire—they tended to shy away from it. But if we had been caught in a stampede of such numbers, I doubt if any trace of us would have been found. I would have felt infinitely better with a trained and fast horse under me.

I left Marromeu to return to Salisbury, where I bought a partnership in a business. It proved unsound, and I pulled out, minus much money but with more experience. It was ivory money down the drain and was not the first time that I had entered the competition of the rat-race. Because of these adverse experiences and the lure of wildlife, I continued hunting elephant.

MUPATA GORGE:

THE STORM UNLEASHED — 1949

In Salisbury I received a letter from Faanie describing his activities in Kenya and in reply requested that he join me here in Rhodesia to go to Zambezia, across the Zambezi River in Mozambique. I waited for a reply that never came and consequently missed an opportunity to visit the Sabi-Wanezi River area in Mozambique on the Rhodesian border.

In Espungabera, a village in central Mozambique, I had met an old Portuguese hunter who befriended me and advised that there was a good elephant bull population in the area. But my lifestyle was now based more on the seasons than previously, and the Months of the Sun were upon me. So I decided to venture up the Mupata Gorge, to again travel the Zambezi River from Mozambique into Northern and Southern Rhodesia. After motoring down the escarpment, I reached the Zambezi at its junction with the Panyame in the Portuguese Corridor.

In mid-November I bought a carefully selected dugout canoe, and as I thought about a paddler companion, one voluntarily came forward. The man, named

Dakati, had come from Northern Rhodesia. He looked bright and seemed built well enough for the future task. He was armed with the customary spear and bow and arrows (known as *p'fumo-dati-m'seve*), an indication that he knew something about the bush. We went upstream on the Zambezi, paddling in the calmer waters near shore. The sun's extreme heat had a languishing effect on us. I would usually condition myself by not wearing a hat, but here the sun was so strong that we both had to tie loincloths to our heads for protection.

For days we battled against the current, sleeping on sandbar islands and going inland at times to check for bull-elephant spoor. I managed to shoot three close to the river without incident. The ivory was not impressive, about forty pounds a side. We hid it in a gully where it could not be dragged away by scavengers. There were watercourses with evaporating pools close to the main river, and I set snares there and caught wildfowl. My favorite was the red-necked francolin, the kind that screeches so loudly at dawn.

On a wide portion of the river I recognized features from my previous travels, and on the north bank I saw huts where I had traded meat for fish when I had suffered from diet deficiency. For old time's sake I was tempted to cross to that north shore, but later dismissed it as not worth the exertion in the excessive heat.

The dugout at times passed over them, and should any have emerged at the wrong moment, we would have been flung out into the river.

After many days of paddling and fighting the current, we passed the Portuguese post of Zumbo at night. The hippo must have been persecuted since I was last here because, upon hearing or sensing us, they dashed from the shore to escape into the water. Sometimes they rose too close to us, to disappear and reappear on the surface. The dugout at times passed over them, and should any have emerged at the wrong moment, we would have been flung out into the river.

Water is most enjoyable in hot country at the right time and place, but it is not man's natural environment, especially at night with panicking hippo bobbing up and down and crocodiles lurking beneath the surface. I found it unnerving and consequently regretted not having taken the north bank. By paddling as silently as possible through the hippo menace, we managed to put some distance between us and the Zumbo border post. The next day we passed the Luangwa River junction without incident, crossed to the northern bank, and entered the Mupata Gorge. We had to stay close to the shore in the slower current.

In the surging flow of the gorge, progress was slow, and it took days of hard physical exertion. Eventually we passed four minor dry gullies coming into the main gorge, two on each side but miles apart. I was tempted to explore them upward into foothills, but we kept on, hoping to do so on the return journey.

After many days fighting the current, we eventually emerged above the gorge and landed. As there were lots of tsetse flies, I selected an open, shaded spot and hid our dugout close by in a thick reedbed. After our battles against the current we rested, but on the second day I decided to walk downstream toward some nearby foothills to see what game was there. Dakati carried his short spear and a water bottle. It was incredibly hot, but game was plentiful and close to the river, sometimes in large herds running in front of us, away from the river into the bush for sanctuary. We came across fresh buffalo spoor with lion in their wake. It was obvious that the lion were hunting, so we followed the spoor for a while in the hope of seeing them.

It was unusual, I thought, for them to be hunting early in the morning heat. Then, to my surprise, the fresh spoor of a large troop of elephant bulls crossed the buffalo and lion tracks. The elephant were in a leisurely walk, heading toward the foothills. Naturally we abandoned the lion and buffalo spoor to follow the elephant.

Here on open ground tracking was easy, so we walked a few paces apart and followed at our leisure, testing the wind occasionally. The elephant entered a small area of *jess*—thick, sharp thickets where visibility is very limited—and Dakati kept losing the spoor. Repeatedly I pointed it out to him, but he became reluctant to follow. Something was wrong, and I felt he was purposely trying to irritate and confuse me. As the bush thickened, he stalled time and time again, making excuses about there being too many elephant too close. In anger and disgust I took the spoor and told him to watch the bush ahead of me, assuming he would do this properly. The *jess* thinned out and within a short while we emerged into a sparse, leafless forest. Then, to my surprise, I discovered that Dakati was no longer with me. I waited a long time, hoping that he would arrive, but to no avail. Alone, I had to take the spoor and try to sight the elephant ahead at the same time. They had entered the low foothills, feeding here and there. The big tracks were impressive, and this was the largest troop of bulls I had so far come across, probably about thirty elephant.

I looked back hoping that Dakati might be following, but there was no sign of him. On areas of higher ground I gazed on open patches of the valley floor below me. It was all new country and new circumstances. To hunt here alone in this unfamiliar wilderness with so many bulls in front of me was not appealing. It was not just the idea of closing in on them alone—that I actually preferred and was conditioned to—but spooring and watching at the same time was a strain. Now, having to do everything alone, I realized I had previously been spoiled by having had excellent trackers.

Here there was no loneliness as such but rather a feeling of being alone, and a sense of uneasiness. Occasionally, looking up from the spoor, I noticed a blue-purple mass on the skyline above the scrub. It was a tropical storm speeding toward me, and the heat was so intense that I looked forward to it. My reluctance to follow now diminished as I realized the oncoming storm could obliterate the elephant spoor. Despondency increased at the thought of losing the spoor of so many bulls, which by now had become paramount in my mind. The elephant were close, but so was the rain. The storm loomed up quickly and was awe-inspiring, with a powerful wind ahead of it bending the scrub to the snapping point. It seemed that I might yet be able to close in and get to the bulls. Lightning flashed and thunder reverberated. A small shower of rain fell, then a deluge, with dangerous flashes of lightning all around. I used my head cloth to wrap my clothing and protect the bullets. The lightning strikes on the ground were fearsome, and I sought sanctuary. I felt insignificant and wondered, amused, whether God was angry or just talking. In the distance below me lightning forked out and disappeared into the earth, with the vibration of thunder in its wake.

I had lost direction and turned to look for some sort of depression to shelter in. There in front of me, huddled together, was a massive troop of bull elephant. The storm by now was moving off. Instinctively I closed in, not knowing what to expect. From what I could see and sense, the elephant were confused. If I opened fire, they could turn on me and I would not be able to stop them. I had to make a decision to shoot or get away. I tried to balance my chances—what if I got killed or injured? Then a tremendous flash illuminated the scene, bringing me out of my dilemma.

I selected a large tusker facing me and fired, then fired at others in rapid succession. They dropped where they were; the others were perplexed. I continued a rate of fire so fast that my shoulder became sore. The elephant that were hit stayed down, and the others stood in the same positions. My first mistake occurred as I missed a side brain shot. The bull crashed but in seconds was up again. A change came over the troop now as I shot the wounded one. Some faced me in formidable attitudes with outstretched ears, but my fire was too rapid, and as they dropped I realized they were leaderless or confused by my rifle fire and the lightning. It was almost an automatic procedure as I mercilessly finished them off.

The storm abated, but the wind was strong now in the opposite direction. Suddenly I saw movement, and an elephant rose with another behind it. I fired and dropped them in the middle of the heap and waited for others, but there was no more movement. I stood almost thoughtless, conscious only of the sight in front of me and the now receding lightning storm. Behind me the sun became brighter, giving details to the fallen giants. Their skin showed their clear slate color wet with rain, bright tusks, and the bottoms of large washed feet that would never tread again.

Disturbed and trembling, I wondered if they had ever known gunfire. Wet and cool now, I listened to the storm recede in the distance, and the silence became great. *What the hell*, I thought, *one dead elephant is the same as many.*

But this was not so; sometimes hell is within yourself. The heaps of elephant bothered me deeply. As I put the rifle stock to the ground and clasped the barrel, it was hot enough to burn my fingers, but I was so perplexed as not to feel it fully. Ivory, I always wanted ivory—now what could I do with it? I was in rugged, strange country, and even if I found assistance, there were so many dead elephant that this fearful event would eventually leak out.

I felt deep regret for this deed, which I saw as a crime against the wilds of unspoiled Africa. I could not shake it and cursed myself for allowing it to become the hell that was developing within me. What a waste of magnificent bulls, too much even for hyena and vultures. Why did I not think of this before I started shooting?

With a conscious effort I partly pushed my feelings aside, in favour of concern about my own survival. In this wilderness I realized that I had only five cartridges left. How rich and yet poor do you feel? Those five bullets represented my survival.

I reasoned that eventually these dead elephant would disappear as if the debacle had never happened. No people where likely to come here except someone like myself, for the gorge country was uninhabited and desolate. Certainly no one would venture here in the rains. I gazed at the distant storm with occasional flashes still streaking the sky. In despondency I turned and found a place to look out from the low hills toward the river. Considerable time must have passed. I was miles from the river. Would I get lost now that I was alone? All the past strain was making me lose confidence.

There was an uncomfortable rise in humidity. I gazed at the sun's position, wondering if I would find the river before dark. I thought of man-eaters. How could there be man-eaters if there were no people? Feelings of uncertainty and fear gripped me, then suspicion and foreboding. What had happened to Dakati? Would my dugout still be in the reedbeds? If not, how would I find the sustenance other than meat to walk out of here? How much time did I have? What if the elephant carcasses were discovered by chance? The vultures would hover here for weeks. Why was I talking to myself? I was thinking less of the elephant and more of myself now as my predicament rose to the fore.

The sun indicated late afternoon, and all spoor and other ground signs had been obliterated by the rains. I strode out and started to become myself again. I came to a small rock formation where I found storm water. It tasted good, but my stomach was empty and I had a nagging discomfort. Perhaps a nervous reaction? Why not? Everything could be put down to nerves. Only five bullets left. I must remain alert and get a firm grip on myself. I had no thirst. It was warm country, and by night I should reach the Zambezi. I saw lower country below me. I wanted to stay on the higher ground, but had to descend to the lower, less open country because that is where I had come from. I walked on, trying not to think of elephant.

The sun was low and starting to silhouette the tree branches in the west. For the last mile new spoor was evident on the washed ground. I entered some scrub and could sense something ahead of me, something big. Suddenly the shrieking cries of oxpecker birds warned of my approach, indicating a rhino close-by. I circled the area and continued. I entered forest verging on scrub and got glimpses of waterbuck and many herds of impala running off. It was getting dark now, and feelings of loneliness and fear assailed me. Again I felt the cartridges in my belt, like gold on my fingers—but only five of them. The river was still some considerable distance off, and I did not want to walk into danger unexpectedly at night where animals were concentrated—with the probability of lion hunting there. So I found a suitable place to spend the night at the base of a large, climbable tree. It was warm, but without the comfort of a fire the night was a long and uninviting prospect.

I listened to the many insects and, later, lion far off roaring to each other. All these sounds I had experienced many times before but not while disturbed and alone. It made me accept that a man in the wilds without a place of refuge is vulnerable, especially at night without firelight and his own kind to assist him. Eventually I succumbed to sleep and woke early, anxious and restless for the light of day. I walked carefully in the predawn. As the sun began illuminating the earth I started hearing bird chirps and the noisy gamebirds, especially the red-necked francolin. Dawn was a slow explosion of light, with the trees and bushes gradually coming into detailed shape. There was little spoor at first, but then it became numerous and I knew I was nearing the river. Later I sighted a lot of game, especially impala and waterbuck and a few lion tracks.

The riverine vegetation appeared—large shady trees—and then the river itself. The banks were vertical, with places here and there where big game had broken the soil down to reach the water. Warily I selected the right spot and drank. It was not as good as the rainwater I'd had the previous day. I reasoned my camp was upstream and walked steadily through sparse bush and savanna. The game moved inland in front of me.

I sighted a large herd of buffalo with a herd of cow elephant in the background, and I moved around them. The terrain became open savanna with large *musango* and sausage trees. I heard the call of the fish eagles and always in the background my favourite sound, the haunting, lonely call of the spotted wood doves. Finally I saw in the distance the trees I had selected for a campsite.

I noted there was only an old campfire. It had been extinguished by rain. No human spoor—no Dakati. Apprehensive, I made for the bank and went down into the reedbed. Rifle at the ready, I pushed my way through the reeds and saw part of the dugout, the rest hidden. What a relief—without the boat I would have been stranded away from any human contact. Here, more so than in other places, the mother river was the artery of life. Without her all travel would be overland and the traveler would face the frightening madness that is thirst. These thoughts soon disappeared as I looked into the dugout—two paddles, a fishing spear, and a water bottle; everything else was gone.

I scrambled up the steep bank and searched for the sealed containers of ammunition I had left at the camp in a hollow at the base of a tree. They were also gone. There was no spoor, which meant that Dakati had stolen my essential possessions before the storm—ammunition, snake outfit, an extra pair of hunting sandals, a *kaross*, and other essential articles.

Searching in ever-widening circles, I found an abandoned pot, a stabbing knife, and my magnifying glass, used for making fires. Dakati's direction must have been west toward the distant mountains of Northern Rhodesia, not visible from here. There were no tracks.

I had two options. One was to try to follow in a general direction in the hope of finding his tracks outside the sphere of the storm. The other was to move from my position before nightfall in case Dakati returned to murder me for the rifle now that he had the hundred rounds of ammunition.

Since I could not be sure of following Dakati and he had the alternative of attacking me at night, I decided to take to the river and cross to the opposite bank. It took quite an exertion to drag the dugout from the reedbed, and only when I had it in the current did I feel better. I began the crossing immediately, knowing that by the time I reached the other bank the current would have taken me almost a mile downstream. I urgently needed to find small pools at which to snare gamebirds, as I had to eat before the sun set again. But I found no pools and spent my second night without food. Dakati had taken everything edible. I cursed the bastard but did not feel any better. I reasoned that I would have to use a cartridge to get meat to last me out of this.

After a hungry, restless night I awoke to a brilliant dawn as the mighty river and surrounding forests took shape and the wild birds came to life—a chorus of the creator that would slowly diminish as the heat rose. And this particular day seemed to have an aura of danger to come.

Later in the morning, while watching hundreds of impala and not knowing which one to shoot, I was attracted by a honey guide bird. I followed it to a bee entrance in a hollow tree and then returned and brought the dugout closer. I collected dried sticks and leaves and used the magnifying glass to start a fire and smoke the bees out. Hungry as I was, I did not scorn scavenging. I gave the bees a long time to vacate as they are one of my greatest fears, and then inserted my hand into the opening. I brought out a large dark-yellow comb of honey and some bees at the same time, so I ran off fast through heavy bush to dislodge them. It worked. But to my great surprise and dismay I heard a snort and at the same time felt a hard impact and was lifted violently into the air. I knew I had been pitched by a rhino and tried to cling to the rifle, but I hit the ground on one leg and my back. Beset by pain and fear, I groped for the rifle but found that I could not stand properly on one leg. I sat on my backside, then spun around, feeling fortunate so far for not having been attacked again. There was nothing in sight, only dust hanging in the bush. I listened intently to allay my fears. No sound. The pain in my back slowly receded, but my foot hurt excruciatingly. I exclaimed aloud as to why this should happen here while I was all alone. My hatred for Dakati was intense, but pain overruled it.

Slowly the pain receded some, but the throbbing persisted. When I moved, some pain returned as if warning me not to do so. Upon seeing my hard-won honeycomb, I reached for it and sat a while waiting for the pain to ease. My hunger was gnawing, and I ate the honeycomb, dust and all. At first I experienced a sickly feeling; then my stomach accepted it, and in a short while I felt energy in my system.

With the use of the rifle as a crutch, I managed to get to the river. I glanced down over the steep banks to see large crocodiles basking on narrow shelves of sand near deep currents. They saw me and slid slowly into the water. I found a break in the bank and cleaned my hands and had a drink next to the dugout. Like it or not, I had to expend a bullet to get food, so I dragged my leg to the floodplain. Impala bristled and jumped aside. Game at this time of year was still well concentrated. I hesitated, deciding which one to shoot. They were so athletic—stopping, staring, and jumping. I felt shaky, and if I fired when one jumped, I might miss and expend a precious bullet for nothing. They moved past me in a delightful pattern of colour and movement.

Then I saw a bushbuck standing in low scrub. He looked ancient and tough. Perhaps I would be doing him a favour by taking him, but he too moved off, my vision blurred by the dry sticks. In my condition it was essential to shoot close to the riverbank. At the edge of a swamp a herd of kudu emerged. A handsome bull with spiral horns was surrounded by hornless cows. I saw a half-grown one and fired. The heavy .450 bullet took it in the shoulder. It curled over on a front leg, slumped, and was dead in seconds. It was so unlike shooting elephant for ivory. I dislike buck hunting, and for a few seconds before it died I watched the movements of its nostrils as it gasped its last. Antelope have so many fascinating and admirable qualities in addition to their beauty. Beyond their speed of flight, they are defenseless.

I returned to the dugout to paddle it downstream closer to the kill. Crocodiles saw me and reluctantly disappeared into the water. One big one did not want to move. I shouted in fear and slowly it submerged and blended into the deep current. My isolation made me fearfully conscious of the dugout being nothing other than a hollowed-out tree trunk on which I had to share the river with crocodiles. *Loathsome creatures,* I thought, *why did God make them?*

I landed by the kudu and struggled up the bank. There had been a change here. No longer were any antelope close. The impala were six hundred yards away under trees. Perhaps a cat was lurking, most likely leopard. In any case, there was enough meat and good luck to it. I cut the neck off the kudu and removed the guts. On my backside I moved in stages; with the end of the dugout rope I dragged the carcass while the heat increased steadily. On my knees now, I managed to turn the young kudu into the dugout. With a paddle I pushed away from the bank and into the current, my immediate destination the mouth of the gorge. The water's surface had a distant curve, indicating a quickening of the current, and in a while I entered the gorge. There was dead vegetation on the hills and a constant hot breeze coming up the river. How pleasant it would be if it were not so hot, I thought. I searched for a green tree for shade, one not too close to the shoreline as crocodiles might emerge to get at my meat.

The miles melted fast as I moved down-current in the gorge. Eventually I saw a suitable landing place and made for it. It had a stony bank and semi-flat surface with a small shady tree.

I hadn't the strength to pull the carcass ashore, so I cut off the legs and then managed it. I sliced some meat and put it on small, sharpened sticks, roasting it at an angle to the fire. I'm not really a meat eater, but I was hungry.

The water's surface had a distant curve, indicating a quickening of the current, and in a while I entered the gorge.

It smelled good and I could hardly wait for it to roast. Some of it burned in the flames, but this part was especially tasty. I had a good feed and realized how the hungry primitives must feel after hacking into a dead elephant. I sharpened the stabbing knife on a coarse rock, skinned the kudu to use the hide as a cover, and cut the meat into small, long strips for drying. It was essential in the rainy season that meat be smoked dry. So I collected dead branches and some green leaves to properly smoke the meat. Other than my pain, I was all right. I had meat, water, the transport of a dugout, and a fast current to take me to my base at the Panyame River in Mozambique. Barring further mishap, I would reach my destination.

My mind was no longer on the heap of dead elephant, but I wondered about the possibility of collecting the ivory in the future. With twenty-seven dead, there was considerable money in the ivory lying up there. With effort and organization it could be recovered, but right now there were more important obstacles, such as continuous rain. Should rain come, the climate would remain warm but the kudu's meat would go bad, leaving me nothing to trade at the coming river villages. I had tinned supplies at the Panyame camp, but it was a considerable distance, especially for someone immobile.

I might yet have to use the four cartridges for protection. I spent two days at this site in the gorge, allowing my pain to subside, and moved off on the third day, pushing the dugout into the fast-flowing midriver current. The current was fast everywhere, but I preferred the middle because the hippo stayed close to the banks. I didn't know what they found to eat, beyond a bit of edible greenery near the banks. I heard the plopping of fish as they broke the water's surface. There was no evidence of crocodiles because of the rugged shoreline, but I knew they were there hunting fish in their jungles under the surface.

I experienced a wonderful feeling of freedom and mobility as I did not have to use my leg and the current did most of the work. I pulled up at a dry gully sloping down from the hills on my right. Small sand beds and soft ground showed the unmistakable spoor of large crocodiles and recent evidence of rhino and three large elephant bulls. Nothing I could do about it, so I pushed the dugout into the current again. The sun was powerful at midday, but the hot breeze up over the water seemed to help.

The sloping hills on either shore were covered in stunted trees that got water only in the rains, which ran off quickly while millions of gallons flowed nearby. Consequently the hills were stark, dry, and uninviting with rocks and boulders strewn about. Sometimes crocodiles appeared, their eyes and snout tips gliding across the water. I felt secure in knowing their habits, and only when they got too close to the dugout did I beat the paddle on the surface, making them slowly submerge.

At times I saw them gliding under the dugout. Experience had so far shown that they are, thank God, without the intellect to tip a dugout, and I hoped they would remain that way. However, I always had to scan the surface for hippo heads, for to be overturned by one of those beasts could be fatal. There were no sounds of life on the slopes except occasional bird noises, including the comforting calls of the spotted wood doves. I had heard these birds just about everywhere in the valleys, hills, and forests of the low country. We seemed to haunt the same places. And I always felt they were in contact with me, calling out, "Some birds lay one egg, I lay two, two, too-too-too-too-too," until the call receded and was taken up by others. It is a haunting, melancholy sound that always helped me to relax.

In late afternoon the brightness of the gorge changed to gloomy shade as the hills blocked out the direct sunlight. It was depressing—the demons of despair come to haunt me. To boost my morale I shouted defiance at the hills and listened to the last part of the echoes: "Where are you? What are you?" In Portuguese I answered, "I am *Casadore,* I am *casadore de elephantes*." I thought to myself, *Stop making conversations with yourself and watch the waters or you may be a hunter of nothing, or worse still, the hunted.* Sometimes I stopped to wash where I could find sand. It helped keep my pores clean in the excessive heat.

In the late afternoon I started looking for a safe place to camp. I knew the gloomy feeling and depression would again descend upon me. Bird noises were less, and only the occasional flop of a fish and the sound of the mighty Zambezi constantly flowing on its way broke the silence. The river made a slight turn, the hills narrowed, and the current quickened. There appeared to be disturbances across the gorge. An obstacle deep down partly blocked the river, causing the current to well up and flow faster. Disturbed at the sight, I fearfully paddled hard to rush through it. Then, far in the distance, I saw something—a slow, slight movement—*humans?* I sighted a dugout beached on its side, and joy swept over me. I paddled closer, still watchful of hippo. A man, woman, and child, perhaps Machikunda tribespeople. The current brought me down fast. I ran the dugout onto some sand and greeted the man in *korekore.* He responded, speaking the same.

What a pleasure it was to see him. The child stared, afraid; the woman stayed at a customary distance. The man looked at me and said, "You have been lost."

"Yes, lost in the head," I replied. We laughed.

"You travel alone?" he inquired.

"My paddler deserted me," I said.

"In this country? To go where?" he inquired.

"To the mountains west from the river above the gorge. That is why I am so pleased to see you," I said.

Studying me, he smiled, saying, "White man in a black man's wilderness." We both laughed simultaneously.

The child came closer and said "*In diane eewe*?" (Who is that?)

"*Murungu*" (European), the father replied.

I asked, "Have you fish?"

"Yes," he said, "from this morning."

I struggled from the dugout and had to use the rifle as a crutch. He stared at my swollen feet. Briefly I told him the story. He laughed loudly. "So the bees made you mad and you ran blind. Where is that rhino?"

"I don't know, he ran off." He seemed disappointed. "I have mountains of meat," I said.

"Where?" he asked.

I paused, becoming secretive. "Here in my head," I said.

He stared at me. "You have been alone too long and too far away," he replied. With his help we pulled my dugout up the slope and tied it. I told him that I had a gnawing pain in my stomach that only fish could take away. He spoke to the woman and she brought fish from their dugout. She opened, cooked, and smoked them. They did not look good but tasted better. It was getting dark now, and they kindled a fire well above the water line. I gave them plenty of meat strips, and they supplied *hupfu* and *matamba* (gravy with mealie-meal and pumpkin), which gave us a meal. Here in the gorge it tasted better than a sumptuous dinner. He wanted tobacco, but I did not smoke. Not many white men at that time and place did not smoke.

"Where are you from?" he asked. We had a large, glowing fire next to the cooking fire, and it lighted up the waters below us.

"From Northern Rhodesia," I lied. "Where there are many tsetse flies."

"You have been there, all right," he said.

I lied again and told him that I must return to Kanyemba downriver. He wanted to know where the bullets from my belt were, and I said they had been stolen by the paddler with my other equipment.

He said he would ask me no more. In conversation I learned that he was indeed a Machikunda. He had come on a three-day journey from below Zumbo to resettle far upstream in Chief Chiawa's country in Northern Rhodesia where his wife had been born. He wanted to know why the Portuguese plagued them with restrictions on weapons and licenses. "What is it with white men when they use police of our own people to plague us with game hunting and trapping?" he said. "We have needs and cannot live on corn alone. We must have meat, but the valley is fly-ridden, and we have no cattle like other tribes do."

I told him the rulers are men not used to hardships and who do not realize or care; they follow orders from others in Salisbury and Lourenço Marques.

The man's name was Kampari, and it was his ambition to work in the Johannesburg gold mines. He said he would come back rich and have many wives and children who would care for him when he was old. I did not want to disillusion him, for he might not even get to Johannesburg, so I left him with his ambitions but warned that when he got there, "You will dream of warm places, even this hot gorge."

That night we heard lion roaring in the hills above the gorge. I wondered how I would have felt, disabled and alone here without these good people. In the morning we checked the shoreline to see if game had come to drink. Nothing had except hippo and a lone rhino. But there was also old spoor of bull elephant. They would probably not return now that there was water in the hills. I felt gratitude toward this man. He had so willingly shared what he had that I gave him a third of my meat. I was tempted to shoot a hippo for him, but the thought of using another bullet put it from my mind.

We stayed another day, and I felt very welcome as a member of this primitive family. The child had lost its fear and the mother joined us around the campfire. It was mostly male conversation, but when he spoke to his wife in *Machikunda* I picked up words here and there. I watched the child's face in the firelight and wondered how many children would experience such places and the grateful company of a lone white man here in this wild gorge.

Kampari's wife had caught many small fish, which she smoked, and together with some maize meal she presented it to me. It would last most of my journey. Since I had enough, I gave them another large portion of kudu meat, retaining some to barter, should the need arise. Kampari often got fish, but not game. Game meat meant nothing to me as I could shoot it in bulk if required. We had appreciated each other, and I thought what a good hunting companion he would make if it were not for the fact that he was going to settle beyond my reach. When I see some of the human trash around, I wonder at the fate of such good people as these.

I had gleaned a lot of information from Kampari about the country above the gorge. There were two main chiefs far upriver. One was Dandawa. The other was Chiawa, who was more important and had a greater sphere of influence. That was all tsetse-fly country, meaning there were no cattle. There was also a chief by the name of Chundu at the eastern escarpment, where they kept a metal god called Chimombe. I was later to learn that some of the personalities that cast this land in legend were very real.

Kampari, with his family, and I parted in the early morning, he going slowly upstream and I going down much faster. At a distance I turned to see him poling his craft and his wife waved to me. She must have said something to Kampari as he waved too. I did the same, but had to concentrate ahead as the gorge got faster with some large whirlpools, which I paddled through at a pace. No doubt Kampari watched me for a while as he was in a position to do so, but I had to glide on and the current parted us quickly. We would never meet again.

Although he did not know it, his company for the past few days had helped to reestablish me mentally, when I most needed it. In these later days I often think of the good people I have known. I like the idea that they may also remember me.

I traveled far that day, wanting to emerge from the confinement of the gorge to experience the open waters again. I stopped only for bathing to get relief from the heat. I could see a buildup of rain and storms behind me in Kampari's direction. No doubt he knew how to cope with it. The discomfort of rain caused me little concern as I knew it would remain warm. If worse came to worse and I could not get relief, I would lever the dugout onto the shore, turn it upside down, and take refuge under it. That night at sunset I reached the Luangwa River confluence and continued in the dark, passing the Portuguese post of Zumbo.

A few miles on I landed on an island. Too weary to cook, I ate some fish and fell asleep. In the predawn I watched the riverbanks take shape. Bird noises drifted over to me with the flight of early morning ducks. There were no huts in sight, so I gathered driftwood for a fire and had a filling meal of maize and fish. I had pushed myself too hard the day before and could feel stiffness and pain in my neck and shoulders, but the swelling in my leg was going down.

Then it was off into the mainstream again. By midmorning the sun was so hot that I felt the danger of excessive sunburn and used my loincloths to cover myself. I had no trousers as such, only two pieces of loincloth—one for the waist and the other for my head and shoulders.

I had been gone quite some time and figured it must be past Christmas, possibly 31 December, my birthday. That afternoon I experienced a frightening storm and the Zambezi became so rough with rain, lightning, and wind that no craft could possibly travel it. The wind caused waves not imaginable on a river. Luckily I was close to the shore when it struck. There were some fallen trees, and I tied the dugout to them. I removed the essentials and took refuge atop the bank.

Here I watched the storm, spectacular and frightening, with the trees giving way to the winds. The river was at first choppy and then big waves came upstream against the current, lapping onto the islands and covering sandbars. This was a heavy tropical downpour, and flashes of lightning occasionally lit up the darkness. Nature in its fury is not to be underestimated, but the best I could do was take refuge in a gully. Here I had a passageway to look out on the river and saw lightning strikes on both banks and on the river itself. Tropical

That night at sunset I reached the Luangwa River confluence.

storms can be devastating. In the middle of such storms there seems to be an abatement and then it continues with wind in the opposite direction from which it started.

I traveled far that day, wanting to emerge from the confinement to experience the open waters again.

Eventually the storm's fury moved up the valley, but the Zambezi remained rough and unnavigable. As the sky cleared, what leaves were left glistened, the ground seemed washed clean and the river was a dull light brown with receding choppy waves.

The dugout was stuck completely under water. Everything was soaked except my rifle and ammunition and the paddles, which I had with me. It was of no great concern as I was close to the Panyami River junction, where I had other essential supplies. My pot was gone, and I had no option but to bail the water with my hands, a long and tedious task.

I managed to remove enough water so that I could drag the dugout, and with leverage, tip it. It was only a matter of miles to the Panyami, but the river was still rough and I waited for it to calm down. But it did not, and as I did not wish to spend a night there, I decided to go overland to the junction. I hid the paddles and walked downstream. My leg was sore but bearable. There was not a lot of game, but what I saw was lively and dashed off or crashed through the vegetation. All seemed to be nervous or excited. Eventually I struck a path leading in the right direction. I continued on it, eventually arriving at the village after dark.

The tribesmen sitting at their fires were surprised to see me emerge from the darkness. My supplies of tinned foods were there. They questioned me, and I told them only what they needed to know: My paddler had abandoned me, stealing my equipment. I had shot three elephant and would eventually collect the ivory. With a good description of the place, they could do it for me. I stayed a few days, collecting the dugout, and leaving it for their use at the village. We had clear weather with slowly receding humidity, a sign that the country was drying out again. But I knew it was only temporary as the main rains had not yet arrived.

I was anxious to get up to the escarpment and onto the plateau before more rains occurred, so I made the attempt while it was still clear. The rains held off in the valley and on the escarpment and although I could see storms on the plateau, I made it back to Salisbury and a totally different way of life.

I was no sooner there than Faanie arrived—a season late, the son of a bitch. He liked Kenya and had made money but said he thought the British had "stuffed it up." I was pleased to see him, and we relaxed, drinking a bottle of whisky at a restaurant. Quite keenly I told him of the twenty-seven bulls and the ivory. I remember his words: "Either you are drunk, or I don't hear right."

I had previously given it a lot of thought and with the object of getting him away from gold ventures and into the ivory scene, I made my proposition. "I will split the take with you," I said, "but we must take the gorge in the main rains, which are almost here, and whether the ivory is there or not, we hunt Zambezia and Niassa in the crop season and cross the Ruvuma River into Tanganyika." He did not give the straight answer I was hoping for and ordered more whisky. I had noticed since last seeing him that he had acquired a large capacity for liquor. He said, "You know, Englander, I can't see myself struggling like you up that gorge."

I thought that was his final decision, but then he said, "I have some money now." Then he asked, "Does it have to be a dugout?"

"Yes," I answered, "European-type boats are a giveaway."

He said, "Do you know, Englander, that I am a river boy?" And then, "Why can't we fit motors onto dugouts?"

I pictured this and thought about it. "Yes, the wood could be altered to suit motors." It meant we could carry more supplies. With these conditions agreed upon, we were ready to retrieve my ivory.

WADOMA:

BITTER REWARD—1950

It was a hazardous journey full of hardship, discomforts, and at times short tempers. The escarpment road was wet, but since we were going mostly down, not up, we managed to slither to its base. We had a four-wheel-drive vehicle, but the valley was so soaked by the rains that in many places we got stuck in huge puddles. In the mopane forest the wheels sank into the soil. We sometimes had to walk for miles to obtain extra manpower from the locals to extract the vehicle. It took a few days to cross the valley floor to our destination. Faanie said he had never worked so hard, not even while looking for gold on the Angwa. On the Zambezi River we got a few days of sunshine, and in a short while the heat started to dry out our surroundings.

Faanie had gone to considerable lengths to organize slings—light buck sails, ground sheets, outboard engines—to carry our ivory. He had acquired a small Geiger counter to prospect what we knew as Wadoma, the hills that formed the Mupata Gorge, sometimes referred to as the Kapsuku Range or Red Range. I got my original dugout back and purchased another large one, to which we fitted the motors. To travel against the current required that we carry a lot of fuel and load all our goods judiciously. As in all upriver travel, perishables are discarded as you progress, lightening the loads until only the essentials remain for the easy downstream travel.

For days we motored without mishap in miserable drizzle. The dugouts became unstable when speeded up too fast with engine power. So we had to adjust to an even pace for proper control. We made good progress against the current in deep side waters where there was less resistance, but sometimes the motors caught on hidden obstacles. As far as I was concerned, the dugout with the paddles—not considering the human energy spent—was still the way to go. But with the luxury of power propelling us upstream, I was content to be idle. We passed places easily where I had previously battled the current manually for hours on end. Faanie was proved right, and I had concede to the practicality and pleasure of power on the river.

We had spread the story around that we were to search for minerals in the hills of the gorge, and so as Faanie and I approached Zumbo, the Portuguese post, I insisted that we paddle the two canoes upstream so as to make a soundless passage. Even in the calmer side waters it was a strenuous undertaking for two men paddling loaded dugouts at night. As soon as I thought it safe, we motored a few miles and camped. The next morning we were in the gorge, and here we eased off. The Zambezi was rising; the water was nearer the old flood marks than when I had traveled it before. And it had coloured to a light brown, indicating that other rivers were already flowing into the Zambezi. I explained this to Faanie, showing him old high-water marks indicating the river would later become a raging torrent, depending on the severity of the rains and the time of year.

Because we did not know when the water in the gorge might rise, we spent the full day traveling up it. It pleased me to motor past places with comparative ease where I had struggled with paddles before. Everything now seemed different. The trees covering the hills were no longer stark but bright green; the birds were active, the piercing cries of fish eagles resounding; and reed growth had taken over in some sandy places.

The rains had altered the gorge. The river was more formidable, but we had horsepower and eventually reached the top of the gorge, emerging into the country of my experiences in the early rains. Here all vegetation was green, the Zambezi was wider and brown with flotsam here and there, and the place was alive with the noises of insect life. The crocodiles were no longer as visible as before, and vision was more limited because of the leaves and grass growth, the latter in places taller than ourselves. That late afternoon I barely had time to define the direction of our search and was not sure of our course.

In the morning, although we did not expect to see any humans, I took the precaution of hiding our gear and dugouts in a dense reedbed, and we camped at a distance from it in thick forest. Animal spoor was pronounced, showing clearly on soft, damp ground, but there was not much of it close to the river. The bush was completely changed, and the distant hills, now very clear because of the rains, were the only recognizable landmark. They helped me pick up the original gulch where I had ascended the range.

Without the heat and dry, harsh conditions of my earlier visit, travel was easy by comparison and in a short while we were in the hills. The topography guided me, and I soon realized the place of slaughter was somewhere hereabouts. Then Faanie saw bleached elephant skulls in the sunlight; some with ivory intact and others from which the ivory had fallen.

"You must have had a war here," he said.

"No," I answered. "Regretfully, it was more like an execution." I looked at the place and tried to picture the original scene but could not because of all the regrowth of bush and grass.

The bones were scattered all over. No doubt scavenging animals had cleared the meat away in a matter of weeks, and the rain and sun had done the rest. There was not even the vestige of a piece of skin. To my surprise, I found the spoor of hyena and porcupine, no doubt still having a go at the bones. We walked separately and counted the tusks: Fifty from twenty-seven elephant. This meant that some elephant had carried single tusks. I circled the place to see if any tusks had been dragged, but there were no signs. I looked out from where I had stood after shooting and could clearly see the mountains of both escarpments. The rains had cleared the air, making everything sharp and distinct; in this clear atmosphere one had the eyesight of a bird of prey. Gazing in the direction of the river, I turned as Faanie came up. "I fully understand what you were telling me now," he said.

For the next twelve days we slaved in heat, humidity, and rain to deliver the ivory the four miles to the river. This was the second time Faanie had said that he had never worked so hard, not even on the gold sites. But I reminded him that this was at least rewarding. "It will be more than ordinarily rewarding," he said, "though we will have to spread out the sales of the ivory."

We were getting less sunshine and more rains, and I noticed that the river had risen since our arrival. "We have to make haste to get through the gorge," I suggested.

After discarding goods no longer required, we embarked on the current, moving slowly. Our boat had the capacity to carry all the ivory, but as a precaution I reloaded some of it into the smaller craft. The waters of the gorge were not only higher but also a lot rougher, and we worried about losing the ivory after all the trouble and effort. The motors were a great success, keeping our speed ahead of that of the current. We almost made it through the gorge in half a day, but at the narrows the current was now turbulent, which caused us added anxiety and required careful maneuvering.

The next morning in heavy rains we emerged out of the gorge and traveled in the middle current of the wide river. No banks were visible. We cut the motors and drifted for a few miles to where I guessed Zumbo might be. I did not like traveling in heavy rain because of difficulty in seeing the schools of hippo. And glad I was when we pulled up on an island and erected the tarpaulins. It rained the whole afternoon and night but in the morning the skies cleared, so we pushed off again. Within the hour, though, a continuous drizzle blurred everything at a distance.

I was all for camping on a small island, but Faanie insisted on traveling, saying that we had so far remained safely unidentified. So we continued in discomfort to the Panyami River junction—always anxious about hippo and all the other dangers of traveling on a river with limited vision—where we landed close to a path leading to the Panyame village. We had to take greater precautions here, for fear of anyone seeing the large quantity of ivory.

I arrived at the village the next day at sunup, collected our truck, and drove along the path, flattening small trees here and there to arrive at our camp on the river. We immediately loaded the ivory and covered it with tarpaulins. Some ivory we left around the camp for curious eyes, and when someone arrived that day, I said it was from elephant that we had shot while prospecting. At the camp we had enough tinned foods and some luxuries under shelter. We could wait for a break in the weather to dry the valley floor enough so we could pass over it.

In the meantime the river had risen again and was now a chocolate mass, and I was glad we would no longer be on it. Next day we pulled the dugouts well out of the rising waters, leaving instructions for them to be moved to the village for safekeeping. In our isolated camp away from the village we waited for an opportunity to travel overland, and within two weeks we were on the plateau. Here we took a ten-day break to reequip and prepare for our next safari far to the north, where we planned to reach the Tanganyika border across the Ruvuma River.

Rio Ruvuma:

Elephant, Men, Man-Eaters, and Revenge—1951

We were better organized now, but because of the wetness we sometimes had to haul the truck, which was our mobile base. We had hired local people as carriers, but not so many, and used them to venture into otherwise inaccessible places. We came across villages not seen before, with the usual signs of crop-raiding by large herds of elephant. Occasionally we shot herd bulls or "visiting" animals, and I got the impression from tusk size that they were resident elephant and not from northern Mozambique or southern Tanganyika, where tusk size tended to be larger.

I imparted to Faanie what I had learned the hard way, providing him a shortcut to avoid the dangers of my youthful stupidity. We were not encountering large troops of bulls, so I stood back and watched Faanie while we closed in on smaller troops. A few times he miscalculated but, on realizing the animals' positions, quickly moved aside or went into action to protect himself. He was an absolute individualist and a natural at hunting dangerous game; he was athletic and instantaneously responded to frightening situations. But there was one bad sign: He lacked enough fear.

We came across an isolated large village where there was nothing to delight the eye; malaria and tropical diseases had sapped the physiques of these poor people with their weak, crying, scrawny children, derelict mud huts, filth, and squalor. Because of elephant depredations, these people were without food crops. I looked at their emaciated bodies and thought of Jack London's words, "The function of man is to live, not just exist." It seemed all they had left were starving bodies and souls. They obviously were strictly agriculturalists, not hunters. They could not cope with the elephant crop-raiders. It was a place of large herds of cow elephant with occasional bulls, all raiding lands until only the maize stalks were left.

Faanie and I thought that taking a few large elephant would at least change this for a while. We acquired a few mediocre trackers, sending them off in different directions to where the villagers said there were favourable feeding grounds. They returned that afternoon, one saying he had found a large elephant herd living in the scrub forest and drinking in the water depressions.

Faanie was a man who converted fear into excitement and was at times more than I could cope with. He was a difficult person to tone down. His lack of fear and his reckless actions worried me, and I did not want to land alone on the Rio Ruvuma, with him under the ground somewhere. I told him that because of his physical and mental abilities he was underestimating his quarry.

His usual reply was, "Don't worry, Englander, you are neurotic," or some similar exaggeration.

In the hopes of toning Faanie down, I asked him if he wanted to tackle a cow herd, and he agreed. The next morning we found them at midday, leisurely feeding. We heard them from about two hundred yards. The bush was thick but not tall, and it would probably give us an occasional view of their heads.

Here I said, "As far as rifle power is concerned, you are on your own. Take the *rota* and a tracker, and I will be behind him."

He moved ahead of the tracker, but when he was halfway to the herd, I had to check him saying, "This is not a small herd of bulls—you are moving in too fast."

"How do you know—there are none on your side?" he replied.

"Well, if there are, we will just have to shoot them."

I looked at him for a few seconds, wondering about the generations of stubborn genetics that must have gone into his brain. Because of the proximity of the elephant, we were in no position to discuss the matter. So in sheer frustration and annoyance I bowed to him, indicating the path the elephant had taken. He moved off, but again too quickly, paying no attention to the bush on his sides. Cow elephant have a bad effect on most trackers. I noticed that this one, Kari, was nervous and apprehensive, so I placed him behind me and took his position behind Faanie, looking ahead to sight the quarry.

As we approached, the elephant were mostly silent, except for the odd low, gushing roar. I saw the first patches of elephant skin through the vegetation and then we saw parts of others coming into view. Behind them there must have been many more. I turned my fingers to my right, indicating the presence of other elephant. There were no sounds but I felt they were there. Because we could smell elephant, there was no need any more for the *rota*, so I took it from Faanie to free his hands and tucked it under my gunbelt, indicating for him to search for heads facing him.

To my right there was a well-worn elephant path. I turned my head slightly to listen in that direction and immediately had to turn back as Faanie opened fire. A crash of vegetation told me a cow was down, another, and then total silence, followed by the slight blurbs of communication warning the herd. In the silence I indicated to Faanie that we should not move, since the elephant were trying to place us. In these moments there must be no human movement or sound. Then we heard two matriarch cows trumpet with rage, and I knew that they might swerve in our direction. A bush came to violent life as heavy bodies crashed through it. There was another trumpet signal, and as the animals moved off to our left we saw some of them. To my amazement, Faanie dashed off alongside them while the tracker panicked and fled down the elephant path.

Faanie was out of sight now but close, firing. The idiot was hunting like a fox terrier in thick bush. I had to back him up, fearing he could unknowingly turn elephant toward me. Over the trumpeting of elephant and crashing of bush, I heard what sounded like a human scream. I struggled through a particularly thick patch of bush and watched Faanie. He was spectacular. With his great physical coordination, he was running alongside the herd, shooting them in the brain at a few paces, sometimes having to force his way past thick bush. I admired the sheer recklessness of it. I knew I would never have such a hunting companion again, but unless I could convince him to take more reasonable action, he was surely going to be smashed and trampled or, worse still, impaled on a tusk.

A confidence caused by my presence seemed to stimulate him. How this could be so under these circumstances I did not know, as there was so much thick bush between us. Upon reaching him, I heard a crash of bush behind and turned, barely having time to shoot a cow coming down on me. The shot halted Faanie, and he faced me.

I was stupefied by his actions. Most of the advice I had imparted to him he had thrown to the winds. He was reckless to the point of endangering our lives unnecessarily. The pattern of elephant hunting I had devised for survival meant nothing to him; only his individualism mattered. Having gained his attention and suspecting the worst, I said to Faanie, "I think they got the tracker—I heard a scream."

We changed position to get the wind in our favour and came at a part of the herd from a different angle. The fury of the elephant herd is unnerving at close quarters; we saw flattened trees, smashed bush, infuriated elephant, and dust. If we closed in now, it would be a war to the finish as they would certainly attack us en masse. For the first time, I saw Faanie hesitate, but he was still game to go in. I had to stop him, saying, "Only a nerveless idiot would attempt it."

We moved out and away from there. The sight of elephant anger had its effect on Faanie, but not enough. He had shot seven cows, more than were required for the villagers, and was, in my opinion, lucky to be alive. It was not his hunting sense but his athletic abilities and speed of reactions that had aided him. If he continued in this fashion, he would, by the law of averages, die a young hunter. I asked him why he wasted my hard-won experience. He said he was carried away by the moment.

"Carried away by the moment? What carried you away?" I asked.

"The way the elephant drop and crash," he said.

I said: "Do you realize those elephant crashed the tracker as well? Man is the thinking animal. Do you think here in the wilds that excludes you? You are no good to anyone dead."

"Stuff you, Englander," he said.

We returned to our camp near the village, where they knew about the hunt from the other guide who had been left behind at the herd. Runners were sent to nearby villages and the drums rolled out their messages, the communication of the bush, the sounds alternating in intonations. Just about everybody disappeared in the direction of the dead elephant, and we hoped that their noisy numbers would disperse any remainder of the herd. We had informed them of the dead tracker. The people remained there that night, cutting and eating elephant meat to their heart's content.

When we arrived in the morning, smoking meat racks were everywhere and people from other villages worked furiously and argued amongst themselves. The presence of so many seemed to heighten their excitement. We moved off where the tracker had been and examined the ground closely. The only signs of him were his sandals, some cloth mixed with blood and sand, and some minor bones and part of his skull. The rest was trampled under the ground.

Faanie said, "I have seen men shot up, but there is usually more than this left of them."

"Yes, the work of many great, angry feet."

At the camp we sent a runner to the nearest chief, who in turn, after examining the spot with us, would by normal procedure notify the nearest authority, many miles away.

Faanie, to gain more experience, was to keep the camp supplied with meat as I had done the previous year by hunting buffalo. We moved farther north, and late one afternoon he came into camp saying he had shot two buffalo and seen evidence of fresh lion spoor around. With the object of hunting the lion, he wanted us to go there in the morning, hoping that the lion would be feasting on the buffalo.

On arrival we found that the lion had recently moved away from the carcasses after feeding. We were alone. Because the area was fairly open and Faanie was keen, I took the position of tracker, warning him to be sure not to wound. We were after a large pride with three-quarters-grown cubs. Occasionally we could see from the spoor where these cubs expended their energies playing with each other, but the adult animals kept on at a steady pace.

As usually happens, animals seeking sanctuary enter the densest bush available. I hoped to have quick contact as I did not fancy hours of painstaking, fearful tracking. Tracking lion calls for special abilities because their spoor, depending on the ground, is not always visible, and their camouflage is incredible. They are not normally prone to attack, but if you persist and they know they are being harassed, there is every chance an individual lion may turn to attack you.

In bush and grasses a wounded lion blends so well that it takes an exceptional hunter or tracker to detect it at close quarters before it is too late. Having this in mind, I again warned Faanie: If he wounded any, he would become the tracker even if I had to point the spoor out to him from time to time. In this thick bush around us, I felt uncertain of my abilities.

Faanie had learned the bird calls hunters use to signal each other. Calls of the birds common to the area do not disturb or alarm game. On hearing Faanie call, I stopped and gazed intently but saw nothing. We were standing together as Faanie slowly raised his rifle. There followed a blast and a growl as a lion leaped clear above the bush, then disappeared. We heard the grunts of others.

Until this moment I had seen nothing of them. Now I saw parts of lion ambling away. Then another quick shot and a lion hit the ground with its back legs in the air, falling over and in rage pawing at anything in contact. After another shot, it become motionless. We stood in silence, hoping that the others had all moved away. I was concerned with the lion he had first hit. Faanie went forward to the dead lion, then signaled. He had found the first lion dead as well. It had taken a bullet through the point of shoulder into its lower heart. The second one had two shots penetrating its lungs, evident by some frothing blood. I felt a lesser, slower man would have wounded a lion under these circumstances.

Faanie was for skinning and carrying the two lion, but the camp was far and the skins were awkward to carry, so we covered the carcasses with branches for the porters to collect later. With luck, hyena would not find them before the morning, and so it was. But Faanie was disappointed because the head porter had discarded the lion heads, contrary to his instructions, and by this time the hyena would have got at them.

Faanie was thoroughly annoyed with the porters; therefore, he placed the main culprit with the trackers on the spoor of elephant to let him experience fear. He then informed the porter that he who was responsible for losing the heads would be hunted by the spirit of the cats. This statement disturbed the porter and he deserted, but reappeared a day later saying he had slept at a village but lion had roared so close that he felt safer back with us. And so Faanie put him with the trackers on elephant spoor again. He wanted to get him amongst a cow herd to teach him the supreme lesson, but I thought it was not worth the risk and bother.

It so happened that lion roared near our camp that night. The next night the porter pulled the now-treated lion skins into the bush, believing that if he returned the lion, pursuing spirits would leave him. In the morning one of the trackers discovered the remains of the lion skins, scavenged by hyena. I knew there would be a murder, so I quickly got hold of this porter, paid him and gave him some rations, even agreed with him that he was now free of lion spirits, and sent him on his way. It caused Faanie to go into a silent rage. Well, so much for bush politics, and since the porter was getting farther and farther from us, I dismissed the matter from my mind.

We moved on, discovering other places and shooting elephant, but the ivory was not as impressive as I had obtained near the Rio Ruvuma the previous season. The rains were diminishing now, and the insect life was prolific. We saw many varieties of beautifully marked butterflies and experienced a temporary cessation of tsetse-fly activity. These butterflies tended to flock to the elephant spoor, concentrating at the remains of elephant urine. Hundreds of dung beetles were breaking up the large elephant droppings and rolling them into small balls to maneuver to their holes. They were sometimes so active that they interfered with our spooring; all we could at times see were damp marks where the dung had been rolled away by the beetles so they could lay their larvae in it. Other small beetles (known as Christmas beetles) were in the forests in thousands and gave off continuous shrieks that were both penetrating and maddening. Once I fired a shot and the whole forest became silent—but only for about eight seconds. Within a minute the forest was again taken over by their piercing screeching. They were so many that it sounded like one continuous noise.

Finally I left Faanie to his mood, and as a change, took some porters to where I thought there may be some isolated bulls. I ranged a large area over five days, getting two bulls from a water hole and seeing the spoor of many cows. As a diversion, I left these bulls intact, covered with branches, to attract lion rather than vultures. For two days in early morning, I checked the carcasses but had no luck. The day-and-a-half return trip took me through attractive country with many antelope, buffalo, and lion spoors.

We were a few hours from the camp when, in an open, shady forest, one of the porters drew attention to dark stain marks on a tree trunk indicating a beehive. Two of the porters were keen to remove the honey, but I walked on with the others, knowing that some of the honey would be saved for us. Some time after we arrived at the main camp, one porter came running up in a sweat. He informed us that his friend, on inserting his hand into the beehive, had been bitten by a snake. He waited in fear for a while and then panicked and ran in our direction. After a short distance he collapsed, and his friend overtook him, then continued on to reach us. I had just gotten back and was relaxing on a ground sheet spread on the grass, so Faanie volunteered and took a rifle and snakebite outfit and set off with the distressed porter.

They returned just after sunset, saying that the collapsed porter was swollen and dead, having been bitten on one hand. They had covered him with branches. I lay there thinking: one tracker dead by elephant, one porter nearly dead by Faanie, and one dead by snakebite. We were in for more drama with another chief having to be taken to the site, where the villagers would have to bury the latest victim.

We had breaks of dry weather and, with the scarcity of bull elephant, decided to hunt the numerous buffalo to make dry rations of biltong. The buffalo did not always run off. On one occasion a large herd stood its ground in open country with only a tree here and there. I was puzzled to see the leaders come forward as if to meet us, then stop, shake their heads, and paw and chop the ground. These leaders were magnificent bulls, and I got the impression that their only previous human contact was with men carrying spear or bow and arrow. Others jostled from the back of the herd in curiosity; there must have been at least a few hundred spread out in front of us and staring. It was awe-inspiring, and I realized we were getting glimpses into ancient Africa.

We were so fascinated we did not wish to molest them, but three large bull leaders came keenly forward in stages, the others following a short distance behind them. At forty yards we began to doubt our ability to stop them, except perhaps with fast firepower. The tension was rising, and with rifles ready Faanie and I raised a free arm and shouted. The bulls paused, their shiny black noses and great curved horns facing us. They were massively threatening but also undecided, so I coordinated with Faanie to take chest shots.

Then, to our relief, the bulls emitted snorts as signals and lumbered off at a canter, taking the others with them. There followed a few bellows from the mass of black-gray bodies and the clash of many horns as they moved away from us in a cloud of drifting dust. We watched the oxpecker birds in the dust as they alighted from the disturbed herd. The wind had switched, and there was no doubt the buffalo, besides viewing us, had also got our scent.

We were at this time visiting far-flung places to drive raiding bulls from cultivated lands and from new feeding grounds unknown from my last visit. Here we found the evidence of "pilot" bulls, animals that would leave the herds to go hundreds of miles in search of new feeding grounds and then return so that the herds could follow. If these bulls became disturbed or suspicious while scouting, the herds did not follow. I often thought that interrupting pilot bulls could be a practical way of keeping large cow herds from the human settlements and croplands. Because most of these bulls carried poor ivory, we left them.

Some of these areas were particularly lush and well shaded, and it was a pleasure to see the great variety of antelope and wildfowl at the watering pans, with lion and leopard spoor evident as well. We often heard them roaring and grunting at night.

Leopard would emit rasping grunts as they walked past our camps in the dark. We decided to take the spoor of a particularly big one, and for hours it played us out, leading us through hellish, broken country. A master hunter, it always heard us coming and moved ahead. But we persisted, and at midday it got into some low hills strewn with boulders and heavy vegetation. This meant that at all times it would be well ahead of and above us.

I had hunted leopard at other times but not under these circumstances. And I had learned that a cornered or charging leopard turns into a quick streak, and unless the cat is visible and the hunter prepared, it gets to the hunter before he can fire effectively—a deadly ambush. The leopard does not always manage to kill the hunter outright, but a mauling from this cat leaves the hunter in such a shredded mess that without medical treatment he succumbs in pain and delirium. I personally would prefer to hunt lion. This particular leopard kept its spots—we knew we were licked, and we abandoned the hunt.

News reached us that a district commissioner from the adjoining British territory of Nyasaland had crossed Lake Nyasa to help the locals on the Portuguese side who were experiencing the terrors of man-eating lion. I guessed he must be a hundred miles northwest of us, and since bulls here did not seem worthwhile, I said to Faanie that we should go there as a diversion. He had his own ideas and suggested other places to check for elephant. I had seen enough of minor bulls and cow elephant. I even saw the pattern of their skins in my sleep. We decided to separate for a while, Faanie moving north with the main base and I northwest.

The country at this time of year was so beautiful and intriguing that I always felt like moving through it. I told Faanie to send runners to kraals or blaze trees to advise me of his direction. I took four carriers plus a tracker and a guide.

On the third day we came across many rhino spoor in a thorn-scrub area. Then we saw fresh spoor of a lone, very big lion. Thinking of Faanie's lost lion head, I took the spoor. Thorn scrub was a favourite place for rhino, and I could see where they had eaten large areas of leaf. It improved the vision, and as the lion was so far undisturbed and somewhere close, we confidently followed. Suddenly, there was a crash in the thorn scrub, and I heard the snort of a disturbed rhino coming in our direction. There was a convenient thick patch near an elephant path, and we waited there. In seconds the rhino and two others lumbered past. Besides being a bloody nuisance, they gave us a fright. Lion that have been hunted are wise, and if this one was close enough he would have heard the crashing noise. I was hoping to keep him undisturbed and stationary, and this rhino business had lessened the chances.

We continued, and within minutes I got a glimpse of a large lion trotting across an opening. Hastily I fired, thinking that under the conditions I might not get another chance. I realized the moment the rifle kicked my shoulder that anxiety and stupidity had caused me to wound the lion. I heard it thrashing in the thorn scrub. There were a few throaty grunts, then total silence.

I cursed those rhino, but in actual fact I was the one who had made the amateur mistake of firing wildly and hoping for success. Besides nerve and skill, the successful hunting of dangerous game calls for absolute control and intelligence, regardless of disturbances and emotions. I knew all this and had practiced it so many times, but I failed to heed my own experience. Now I had wounded a lion, of all animals.

Most hunters allow a time period for wounded game to stiffen up, but right or wrong I was anxious to sort out my bugger-up, so I immediately followed. There was a small amount of blood and then none. The sun was high now and the heat took over, dulling the senses.

We continued spooring, and soon the tracker showed signs of losing confidence. We were in soft sand, ideal ground for spooring, but he kept losing it and I kept pointing it out to him. I asked him if he was afraid.

"No, of course not," he lied.

I said, "Why are you purposely losing the spoor to confuse me?"

He answered, "I see blood before my eyes."

It is an expression elephant trackers use to show that they have had enough eye strain and stress. Normally in such a case I would have switched to the other tracker, but he had gone off with Faanie. I knew the lion was close and aware of us, and at that moment I had murderous feelings about the tracker, but I had to reserve all my nervous energy, so I took the spoor myself, and I placed the tracker behind me with the water bag. The porters I had already left a few miles distant at a small watercourse.

Experience had taught me that hunting cats required careful movement and intense concentration. Now, with the added strain of tracking, I was being overtaxed. As we progressed, I became aware of the noisy tracker behind me. I warned him once, but it got worse. So, now, I had a wounded lion somewhere in front and a noisy tracker behind me. He apparently thought his safety lay in creating enough noise so that the lion would continuously move off in front of us. Through his antics, the tracker had made himself master of the hunt. We all have our breaking point and mine erupted.

I turned and thrust him in the throat with the rifle butt. He collapsed, gurgling and gasping for breath, and while he was in what I angrily considered a satisfactory condition, I took the water bag and started tracking the lion again. Within a short while I hid the water bag and continued on the spoor. The strain and fear were there but less so, for now I could feel the great silence of the bush around me: The only noises at midday would be insects, the occasional bird, myself, and perhaps my quarry in front of me. But though conditions had greatly improved, having to lower my eyes constantly to the spoor increased the danger of sudden attack.

At times I could smell lion scent lingering in the bush, and my senses told me to move cautiously. I stood in one spot, testing the wind and listening intently. It is thought that lion have a poor sense of smell, but that all depends on what they are smelling. On the ground in front of me were distinct and very large pug marks, at a guess over an hour old. I considered the possibility of it being a man-eater. I had shot the occasional man-eater before, but not alone during long-distance spooring.

The smell of lion was strong, so it had to be close in front of me. Reluctantly I proceeded, seldom looking down at spoor but following its general direction. I came into a thinning out of bush and a small clearing of lower scrub, then felt a switch of wind direction and the cat smell became fainter. My instincts, regardless of spoor and wind, told me the lion was close by. My approach had been painstakingly silent, but I realized I must be at least partly visible here on the fringe of the clearing.

In readiness I scanned across the twenty-yard opening and silently cursed the perfect way a lion can conceal itself. I reasoned that if it had seen me, it would have reacted in some way by now. If it was a man-eater, however, it might not react normally. Such reasoning only brought added fear and confusion.

Of one thing I was sure: The great cat was here with me now, and it had the advantage of being stationary to look and listen. I am always aware of the great silence and immensity of forests and bush. This awareness now became pronounced. It was like the setting of a stage. How could I have such unfocused thoughts? This could be life or death now or, worse still, a terrible mauling. Concentrate, I said to myself, as you do with the elephant, only more so. There was a sort of timelessness in the air that could come only with danger or great peace of mind. The latter I did not have.

A small, blue, bright-chested bird I had not noticed before cocked its head, looking down at an angle. Intently I gazed in that direction and at first saw nothing, only thick leaf cover. As my eyes were about to move on, I suddenly saw two ears flatten down on the very top of a lion's head.

There was a grunting snarl, and a great, fierce head came at me in an instant, low at first, but then leaping. My life was in the balance. The lion's size was exaggerated by its being well off the ground. It had barely got into its spring when my .450 bullet took it in the forehead. It collapsed, curled, and then quivered. I knew that my shot had hit above its brain, only stunning it, so I gave it a second shot.

No doubt the lion had watched, concealed in the leaves, waiting for me to enter the low scrub clearing. My looking at it must have triggered its charge. It had not waited long enough for me to come close enough to make absolutely sure of its attack.

I found a conveniently shaded spot and sat down against a tree. It took some time for my heart and pulse rate to become normal again. I sat a long time. There was no sign of the tracker. Eventually I covered the lion carcass with broken branches and returned on the spoor. I found the water bag and was grateful for it, then reached the spot where I'd had the drama with the tracker. The signs indicated that he had lain and struggled there for some time and then retreated. He must have heard the shots from the heavy rifle. So perhaps he was pleased to think that I might be dead. In the morning I sent him back with others to bring the lion skin and skull, and they found them intact.

Next day I arrived at a small village. The headman showed me where the district commissioner was camped. But he was off on the spoor of man-eaters that had seized a woman and child from some other village. I spoke with the headman about game, and he said I had come from a wild area, unlike this place. Here there were lots of small villages a few miles apart, and game, because of the illegal trade in muzzleloaders and trapping, had tended to move away. It was the old story: As human numbers increased, game populations decreased.

He described the living conditions of the area. Even if half of it were true, it was a terrifying place. There were large prides of very bold man-eaters, in twos and threes, as well as isolated single animals. Even allowing for exaggeration, I wondered how there could be so many lion. From what I knew of past events, there was usually something—a wound or an illness—that prevented man-eaters from catching game successfully. I asked the headman why the lion did not move to the wild area I had just come from. He said lion all have their own territories, like us. Game here was now scarce and humans had become the game. Because of the man-eater activities, some of the people had reaped their crops and left for Lake Nyasa.

I questioned him about crop-raiding elephant. He said they come during the crop season, the forerunners being mostly bulls, which the villagers try to shoot and wound—anything to keep them from the cultivated lands. If the forerunners are not discouraged, the elephant come in large numbers. This we had learned. It is not a real problem, he said, because the villagers all converge with many muzzleloading guns. The guns do not kill instantly but drive the elephant away. Though he did not know it, he was mostly talking about pilot bulls.

I questioned him also about the district commissioner. I was told that he had shot eleven man-eaters in a month. They call him Katasoro, meaning the man who shoots more than one animal with a single bullet.

I wanted to know more about the cats. "Do the lion walk far?" I asked.

Sometimes, he said, they walk all day if they know they are being followed, and then a few days later they appear to hunt people in the croplands, at water holes, or when they collect firewood.

He said, "We barricade ourselves in our huts at night and wait with spears and muzzleloaders, but there are many more huts than muzzleloaders." And the lion would brave the single shot of a muzzleloader to rip open the roof thatch of a hut.

My visit to the district commissioner, whom I thought was just out for some hunting excitement with the man-eaters, had taken me into a terror-stricken area. I asked why Katasoro camped in the village; the answer was that he wanted to be near the lion should they return. Apparently Katasoro slept wherever he expected lion movements.

I felt that Katasoro would be pleased to see me, and camped near him. It was late afternoon, so I instructed my carriers who wished to sleep to do so now, as we would have to take turns guarding at night, and God help a man if I found him sleeping later.

On request I went out with the villagers to collect firewood and water. They were relaxed, but as the night approached, fear took over and they retreated to their huts to barricade themselves in. The lion had so terrorized them that should a nearby hut be raided, the others stayed where they were, not assisting in any way. They were simply thankful that it was not they, even though their turn to face this frightful death could well come later. I had read of the Roman principle of divide and rule, but here the problem was a combination of fear and cowardice. Well, who was I to judge? Perhaps later I would be less critical. I had large fires for light and assigned guard duties, but Katasoro did not return.

In the morning I accompanied the women and a few men to the water holes, and there the recent spoor of lion was pointed out to me. I thought of following them, but because of the women and my inefficient tracker, I returned with the villagers for their safety. At the camp were four runners armed with muzzleloaders and spears who informed me that lion had killed three people at an adjoining village. At this point, I realized that I was being asked to help eliminate man-eaters, no easy task, but the difficulty was compounded by the fact that I had a human jackal for a tracker and no worthwhile hunting staff. I told the messengers these facts. They huddled together at a distance, gesturing to emphasize what they were saying. The sun was well up when they approached me again. They knew a man, they said, who could follow lion under all conditions but were not sure if he would assist in a dangerous venture.

"Well," I said, "if he has no stomach for it, why bother asking him?"

They replied that he was both skilled and courageous but was a solitary fellow who preferred to live alone in the forest.

"How far?" I asked.

A full day's walk, I was told, meaning twenty miles or so. He had two huts in trees far apart and was on the fringe of the game country. He had a family in this area but lived in isolation, seeing them from time to time. He sounded like a recluse hiding in the sticks, I thought.

"Well," I said, "it's two days' walk to get him here—that is, if he agrees."

I had met a few recluses, and all seemed to have something in common—a dislike for people. The notion seemed impractical, so I dismissed it.

That afternoon the white man Katasoro returned with his helpers. At a short distance he looked like one of those typical weak English specimens with legs like sticks with bone showing through the flesh, clothed in a helmet and ridiculous-looking short trousers that were actually rather long. But he was wiry and could probably walk all day long. He was a piece of biltong, as we used to say, with plenty of stamina. He reminded me of an undernourished cleric. His accent and mannerisms were typical of the English from India, always a source of amusement to me. But, despite these observations, I realized that he was also probably a tough, courageous, and skilled man.

He was a storehouse of information and had, on other occasions, hunted the Mozambique side of Lake Nyasa right up near Nampula. He had killed five man-eaters, and had the skins and heads to show for it. He warned me about sleeping without guards at night and even offered me the hospitality of his camp for safety. I accepted, moving my own gear over.

On listening to him, I realized that Katasoro's knowledge of man-eaters was astounding; in a week I learned what otherwise might have taken a lifetime. He was such an expert in his field that I wanted to hunt with him, and he agreed. Here, I felt, was a practical approach to learning, and it turned out that way. I mentioned the recluse, and Katasoro said he had used him and that he was probably the best tracker in the area and that he had lots of nerve. However, he had the shortcoming that he would suddenly disappear for days, even a week at a time—brilliant but undependable.

Katasoro said he had spent the last two days checking water holes and visiting villages, but found only old spoor and no killings. "That's how it goes," Katasoro said. "Then suddenly there will be a wave of terror. If you stay long enough, you will experience it."

On the third morning the same runners came up to the camp, informing us that man-eaters had killed and eaten a family at their village. I mentioned that

I had seen pug marks at the nearby water hole after the previous killing. Katasoro jumped into action, calling for his trackers, water carriers, and food.

It had happened again. There in front of us at the water hole was lion spoor about three hours old. Katasoro explained that man-eaters often watered well away from the scene of their kills, especially if there were no cubs in the group, and this was the case here, judging by the spoor. Katasoro's trackers were exceptionally good at their work and moved well, no doubt having spoored many times. By midday we were close on the lion, and we slowed down as the signs became fresh.

In soft sand Katasoro showed me pug marks indicating that one lion had a foot problem, not putting its full weight on the ground. My guess, he said, is that this lion had been damaged in the shoulder and has taught the others to be man-eaters. This one, then, would be the leader.

The tracks seemed to indicate about seven animals, but Katasoro said more likely there were nine or ten of them. He explained that the lion's digestive systems sometimes made them sleep long hours, but if disturbed they could keep moving all day.

Pointing, he said, "See how the ones at the rear want to come to a halt."

In a short while his trackers stopped and signaled with their eyes. Katasoro used lighted tobacco to determine wind direction. They were more cautious than I was on elephant spoor and occasionally stood to listen for long periods. At an eye signal, Katasoro followed the first tracker, and I took my position behind them. They moved so cautiously, slowly, and silently that I thought of Faanie: Under these circumstances he would have approached slowly and then rushed the lion.

I heard a purring call, and suddenly lion arose from the ground where they had been sleeping. The scrub cover was thick, and it all happened so quickly. Two fast shots, a few grunts, and all the lion disappeared ahead in the scrub.

After a bit of silence, we heard the moaning of a lion in distress and anger. I have respect for a wounded lion as well as an instinct to survive, so I repositioned myself behind the second tracker.

The pattern of follow-up changed now. Leadman was a tracker with a shotgun, then Katasoro, also armed, then the second tracker and me. I am not one to go crazy over weapons, but I must mention that Katasoro had an unusual gun, made in Germany or Austria, if memory serves me right. It had three barrels—the lower two were 9.3mm with rifling and the top one a heavy shotgun. It was a handy gun and at the time probably the best type of weapon for lion attacks. With that gun, a lion could reach you only if your nerve failed or you were caught off guard.

I felt better now because the wounded lion would in theory have to get past three people to reach me. As we passed one dead lion, the other one's moaning stopped. Katasoro took the lead, indicating for us to remain where we were. In a short while I heard a rustle of leaves, then two quick shots. The trackers instantly moved forward; they knew from hunting with Katasoro that the lion was dead. Katasoro explained to me how the lion had taken a paralyzing shot close along the rear spine as it had run off. Apparently he often used this shot.

Following wounded lion certainly affected Katasoro much less than it did me, and I thought, *Well, to each his own.*

As the lion were being skinned, he explained that the spread-out villages and sections of bush and forest were interspersed over an area of about sixty miles by twenty, making the man-eaters difficult to pinpoint, except sometimes at water holes and in the villages at night. The lion killed people at and after sunset. Then they usually, but not always, moved off to water, which would give them the advantage of about six hours before daylight.

Katasoro's best successes had been realized by sitting up amongst huts and, when called to fresh spoor by the tribesmen, moving between villages. He had a pattern of lion movements in his head and said the time had come when the pride would be raiding one of two villages about seven miles apart. He asked me to sit up in one of them under the darkness of the thatch overhangs of hut roofs. I agreed. He gave me his best tracker and some supplies. We lingered and slept during the day, waiting for nightfall.

Close to sunset I took my position under the thatch-roof overhang with the hut wall at my back. Katasoro's tracker was on the other side armed with a shotgun. Not really knowing him and because he was armed, I was afraid of misdirected gunfire. Fear had a place in everybody's minds: Before sundown the villagers barricaded themselves in their huts—a reflection of the disturbing atmosphere of terror among the tribespeople.

Moonlight cast shadows under the hut roofs and some sparse trees, but the open ground was brightly lit. At a few hundred yards there were some large trees, the rest having been cut down for fuel. In the distance were the remains of maize lands. I felt up to staying awake in the uncanny silence of what was normally a village of talkative people—but in which we now heard only an occasional cough or the whimper of a child.

Then, within the hour of sundown, I heard sighs from powerful lungs. To see the rifle's ivory front sight, I had merely to push the rifle out of the shade of the overhang roof and forward into the moonlight. Looking ahead, I saw lion at about fifty yards—all walking boldly and unconcernedly in my direction. In the excitement I was on the point of trying to contact the tracker on the opposite side of the hut when the lead lion effortlessly leaped onto a hut roof, forcing its way with paws and weight through the thatch. I heard wails and pitiful screams from inside. I fired as the other lion kept coming on. I put three down, one growling, struggling, and clawing, the two others motionless. As the wounded lion's struggles ceased, I was amazed to see the others standing around as if looking to see what had happened. So I kept firing at chests and shoulders. Eventually the few remaining lion trotted off in their peculiar gait, disappearing behind huts. Being man-eaters, I thought they might lie there in wait.

Unknown to me, the tracker had come around the hut, and as the last lion was about to leave he gave it the heavy load from the shotgun up its backside. It leaped up behind the others and disappeared. The fearful screams from the hut the first lion had entered had ceased during my firing, but we could still hear snarls and feeding inside. This lion had carried on unconcerned about the shooting, in total contrast to the previous daylight hunt where the lion had scattered. I knew from my urgent shooting that I had wounded one lion and the one with the heavy shot up its backside made two. The tracker and I approached the hut in the moonlight, and I was about to signal him to circle it when all feasting noises ceased. The lion might have winded us—even I could smell the Cordite from my expended shells.

The tracker moved forward to circle the hut, but I caught his arm, thinking lion might be lurking in the shade of other huts. Suddenly there was a deep, disturbing purr and the lion sprang up from inside the hut, breaking through the opening in the thatch and landing to one side of us. It had a large piece of human remains in its jaw. We both fired, and it slumped over and died. We waited a while to listen, and slowly both of us moved together from hut to hut through the village.

There were no more lion anywhere. We tried to entice the villagers to come out, but only a few emerged, armed with spears. They were fearful until they saw the dead cats. Then the village erupted with excited people. We had to warn and restrain them from spearing the dead lion and damaging the skins. In the midst of this enthusiastic chattering of relief, I had forgotten about the hut that was raided. The tracker reminded me, so we approached, but I did not care to see the sight I knew must be there, so I left the tracker to inspect it. We broke down the door, and he entered. After a few moments I heard him say, "*Waafa zehzeh*," meaning all were dead. I called to some village men, and they assisted by bringing out the bodies and placing them with the remains that the dead lion had carried.

There in the moonlight was an orderly array of dead, mauled humans—a man, woman, and four children—with the lion lying behind them, a ghastly but moving sight. I saw where the man-eater had eaten through the loincloth of the man, and into the stomach and buttocks of a child. The little evidence of biting indicated that the family was killed by heavy blows from the lion's paws, with many deep, ripping claw marks. It was not so much the sight but the thought that the people were so helpless against the terror of the lion. I tried to imagine the last few final thoughts of the terrified children.

I felt a rising and consuming hatred of man-eaters, and I fully understood why Katasoro sacrificed his efforts and risked his life to hunt them, as in my state I felt the same. In all honesty I now had fleeting regrets about how I penetrated elephant herds, killing them—admittedly sometimes to protect people and crops but more often for profit and way of life. It was no wonder that elephant attacked me. But then I told myself the situations were not comparable: *You are getting sensitive and soft—watch yourself, or you will land up on a tusk*, I chided myself.

Fires were rekindled in front of the village huts, with families standing around them. I had a large one built for ourselves and cautioned the people about the possibilities of the man-eaters lingering. They started to neglect their fires and finally barricaded themselves back into their huts again. Sitting around the fire, looking past the gleaming black skins of a few tribesmen at the dead lion and people, I thought about the overcivilized, self-righteous, and opinionated people who thought hunters were unfeeling, indifferent, and even mad. They should see such sights as this.

Where would I have been if it were not for the wild? Most probably in a factory or some equally unthinkable place, mentally conditioned to believe it was a good way of life . . . striving to pay off a house in thirty years by the credit system . . . raising children to do the same to their children—all for the sake of fostering commerce and building civilizations. In time the madness would reach even these wilds, and for what? So that in the end, rival civilizations can go to war with each other.

Life is for living, and the individual is but a blip in the overall pattern of organized civilizations. The hunter is only an instrument of minor destruction, in this instance in a vast wilderness with too many animals to count. The real destructive power is the need of man to procreate, increase his numbers, and take the land from the game. Nothing in the long run is more certain to eliminate wild animals from this earth than the increase in human population.

Picture Europe, America, and Asia as they once were, with vast numbers of wild animals. These civilizations are pushing their influences and ways into Africa with the same object. Humankind procreates and at the same time has the hypocritical audacity to lecture on game preservation. The whole process is a lie, a false promise. In time we will have only game parks, reserves, and zoos—and, in the long run, only museums. All this will occur unless man somehow controls his reproductive capacity.

Here I would like to quote a sentence from David Livingstone's journals. He was speaking of the Zambezi and Kafue River junctions of the Zambezi Valley, viewing it from the western escarpment. It was the year 1855:

"The plain below us at the left of the Kafue had more large game on it than anywhere else I had seen in Africa."

In 1953, ninety-eight years later, I personally covered this area with Faanie while visiting Chief Chiawa. We crossed the valley and spoke to many villagers. There were almost no living creatures left. More recently—1987—because of constant human settlement, even the forest trees are few and far between, having been used for fuel.

This environment of wild animals and vegetation has been removed *forever* from the greatest big-game area in Africa, as seen by David Livingstone. It could have existed that way for millions of years, but in 135 years man's increasing numbers have totally destroyed it.

I was brought back from these thoughts to the realities of my present situation. I thought Katasoro would be pleased by the dead man-eaters, but there was more to it than that. Tomorrow the tracker and I had two wounded lion to follow. I did not relish the idea. After arranging the tribesmen into guard duties, I fell asleep at the fireside. I heard them talking in low tones and mentally compared them to their noisy, shouting, half-civilized brothers in the towns. It is a fact that primitive black people do not have a rowdy culture and are polite and well-mannered.

Here in Mozambique criminal activities were few, and I had to live among the people to appreciate them and see some of the bad faults of my own society. Our sphere of influence is unrelenting and continuous. No doubt the primitive's descendants in future generations will lose all tribal values and become concrete-worshipping creatures like ourselves.

I woke at dawn. There was no screeching of wildfowl, distant trumpet of elephant, or roar of hunting lion—only a few small twittering birds and the distant call of doves. There was nothing really wild here except the wild terror of the man-eaters. I called for water and looked at the bodies of the dead people and lion, now fully illuminated by a rising sun. Many flies buzzed at the bodies, and I called for the headman.

"What are you going to do now?" I asked him, indicating the mauled corpses.

"Notify the *chefe do poste*," he said.

"I mean, those people there!" I said irritably.

"Bury them," he said.

"Well, do it now—can't you hear the flies are gathering?" I said.

I had them skin the lion for Katasoro. I was anxious to leave this place. At first, out of curiosity, the tracker and I circled the village to find where the lion had entered. Then we found where the remaining cats, including the two wounded ones, had left the village.

The tracker was highly skilled on lion spoor, and between us we tried to determine whether the lion with the faulty shoulder was among them. After painstakingly examining the spoor for a distance, the tracker was sure this lion was not one of them. So this was a different pride. I began to appreciate how Katasoro could determine the identity of lion and pattern their activities. We returned to the task at hand—tracking the wounded lion's spoors. We two knowing men, both well armed, took hard rations and water and moved on. But my heart was not fully in it. We saw that the two wounded lion had separated.

"This one dies first," the tracker said, indicating one set of tracks.

I thought he meant we would shoot this one first, but within a half-mile we saw a dead lion lying in a small clearing. It was the one I had wounded. We broke off and carried branches to protect the carcass from vultures, and then we returned to the other wounded lion's spoor. The heat of day had started, and the sun no longer slanted on the spoor to create shadows that make distinction easier.

I was impressed by this tracker. He had an attitude of confidence and ease about him, and the shotgun seemed to fit like a toy in his hands. In some respects he reminded me of Faanie. He had the ability to spoor quickly, but later his attitude changed to one of caution.

We came to deep shade and hid the water bag and rations. I took the opportunity to question him. He spoke the Chinyanja language and was from Nyasaland. I was amazed to learn that Katasoro, although from Nyasaland, was not a district commissioner at all. It was something that had started as a rumour on the Mozambique side of the lake, and because it had its advantages, it was left at that.

"And the other tracker?" I asked.

He answered, "We are all from Port Herald, the bwana also."

"And where did you learn to track like you do?" I asked.

In honesty he replied, "I was not always good until we learned how to get *nyama* (game meat) on the Portuguese side of the lake."

We both laughed. He meant he had been a poacher, and poachers are usually the best trackers. He told me amusing stories of poaching activities in dugouts on the lake.

"And the spooring of lion?" I asked.

"It came naturally," he said. "My eyes have always been sharp."

In comparison to my human jackal back at the camp, I fancied this man here as both tracker and companion, but I knew this was not possible because he was also a farmer: His primary role in life was cultivating crops at his village. In addition, he was important to Katasoro in ridding the area of man-eaters.

We again took up the lion spoor. My heart was in it now, and I felt it would have to be an unusual lion to get at us. The tracker explained that the heavy shotgun load was not fatal, but the lion would be in pain and angry because the pellets would have penetrated into his back and hind leg muscles. Because any movement would be painful, he would probably lie up somewhere close to make his stand.

This tracker had humour. Pointing the shotgun, he said laughing, "That 'somewhere' is the place where *machende pamusoro*."

African humour is hilarious, especially during a dangerous hunt. It is difficult to fully translate into English, but what he had meant was that where we would meet the lion was the place where our stomachs would contract from fear and cause our testicles to raise up and tighten like stones. The African mind seems to believe that as this is the most important part of his anatomy, it will be the last part to suffer should he be attacked. Often, when I noticed one of the party becoming fearful upon stalking dangerous game, I would laughingly accuse him of "*machende pamusoro*." It would always generate laughter and most times it relaxed whoever was the fearful one.

But now, on the lion spoor again, the humour waned. I felt this would be my last hunt here and hoped that nothing would happen to me because I wanted to get back to Faanie as arranged. It had been a good experience, and I had learned much in this short period. The lion spoor was many hours old, but the tracker was cautious. We heard something and paused, glimpsing a lone bushbuck racing off. A wildfowl flew from beneath our feet and caused my heart to flutter. The moment of "*machende pamusoro*" had not yet arrived—but by the tracker's movements I knew it was close.

The trees thinned out, and we entered dense scrub. This must be the place, I thought. I tested the wind with the *rota* and it was in our favour. The tracker indicated that the lion was here. As in all dangerous hunting, we call it the "moment of truth"—we would see what we were made of.

I felt the tracker and I were a good combination, but the bush was so dense—and we had a wounded lion in front of us. There was no alternative but to concentrate intently. All nerves and instincts were sharp and ready to trigger physical actions. The tracker paused, motionless, like a statue, so I had to do the same. A good ten minutes passed. He stood with the shotgun raised to his waist. We all have certain instincts, and in the wilds they become more pronounced. In some men they are uncanny.

The spoor was old, but the tracker indicated with his eyes that the lion was here with us. He did not move and urged no movement from me, not even the *rota.* I got a faint whiff of lion, but that did not always signify close presence; scent sometimes lingers where there is no wind in dense bush. In these moments of uncertainty and tense fear, I realized that this was no ordinary lion we had followed. He was used to the ways of man, but this was probably the first time he had felt pain and partial disablement. And above all, man had followed him into his refuge. There was the remote possibility of his being unaware of us. But I dismissed this as wishful thinking.

The tracker now was fixedly staring at a place, and the gun ever so slowly came up to his shoulder. He remained in this awkward position, so I got ready and concentrated on the spot, low thickets in full leaf cover about ten paces away. I felt something was going to happen, a charge or runoff. Time was working on my already strained nerves. The tracker and I were side by side now, a few feet apart, with me slightly behind.

The leaves parted in an instant, with no grunt or snarl of warning. A lion's head emerged, and its body came through the air at the tracker's waist. This lion's nerves were obviously more stretched than ours, and in midair it took the shotgun's blast full in the face. I saw bits of fluff blow from its head as it landed on the ground and disappeared, violently thrashing under the low scrub almost at the tracker's feet. We both fired into the movement of leaves. It thrashed and clawed an opening in the thickets and became partly visible, and we continued shooting until there was no more movement. Our many shots made the skin useless.

That hunt made me think of a persistent dream, almost a nightmare, I'd had of a lion clawing at my leg. This dream was often in the back of my mind as I followed lion under dangerous conditions.

We needed relaxation, so we abandoned the lion, uncovered, to the eventual arrival of vultures and hyena and walked out of the thickets to take our ease under some shade. Eventually we backtracked and ambled to the place where we had left our rations and water. Under deep shade here, it was home-away-from-home and with good company. All our fears had gone, and we appreciated the feeling of being alive. Those who do not face danger never experience this feeling because safety for them is always taken for granted.

In the afternoon we reached Katasoro's camp. He came out to greet us, jovial and pleased. He knew what had happened, except for our last hunt, and I told him of it.

"Quite a tracker," he said.

"A jewel in the palm of a poor man's hand," I replied.

"Well," he said, "don't get any ideas about him for your elephant hunting. He lives on the lake, you know, and besides, they get a share in the rewards."

"What rewards?" I asked.

"Well," he said, "the Portuguese are now paying rewards and administrative privileges to those who destroy the man-eaters. In addition, I sell the skin and skull of each man-eater with a story of its final days to the tourists, mostly Americans, in East Africa. They buy anything like that, you know!"

"You enterprising bastard," I said.

"Yes, I am," he replied, quite pleased with all the dead lion skins and skulls. "But you shall have your share."

He was like a little boy dividing sweets amongst his friends. What a funny little Englishman he was. I wondered what Faanie would have thought of him after always referring to me as an Englander.

"The knowledge and experience I have acquired from you is enough payment," I said. "I do not want any other."

He then said, "You must have a pile of ivory somewhere."

"Yes," I said, "quite a lot, but not even your trackers could find it!"

"We will see," he said, as if threatening me, and we laughed.

"Tell me," I said, "more about the privileges."

"Well," he said, "the Portuguese, in order to avoid paying money, will sometimes give people privileges otherwise unobtainable. And even if a successful hunt is not reported at the time, they usually find out all the details of the hunter who killed man-eaters."

I explained that I must take advantage of the recent events, and as Katasoro was well-known, I requested that he give me a letter of introduction and explain what had happened.

"It will have to be in English," he said.

"Yes, English will do," I replied.

I gave him an address and he promised to send the letter, which he eventually did. "I will exaggerate a little," he said, "but I know you can live with that!"

He informed me that he had gotten five man-eaters on the same night as my encounter with them. I asked him what effect our total numbers would have.

"Well," he said, "the human killings will decrease, but the remaining man-eaters will continue their attacks, only on a lesser scale."

In his experience, the lion would go back to game areas for a while and then in all probability they would go in Faanie's direction.

"I had planned to be out of here come early dawn," I said. "My only regret is that I would like to have hunted more with you instead of your excellent tracker—I must now fall back on my human jackal."

"There may be other times," he said. "These man-eaters are almost impossible to eradicate, and even if we do, others from the game areas that have learned to kill humans will eventually return. People to them are much the same as game, only easier prey."

Being with Katasoro had been an enlightening introduction to lion activities, and I much later learned more about lion and their ways. The following informative memories come to mind. Though lion, like all predators, will stoop so low as to scavenge on putrefied meat, in their natural habitat they are admirable, powerful, fast, and fearsome. In their organized unit, commonly known as the pride, they live within roughly defined territorial areas, which they mark by their roars of dominance and their habit of urinating on ground, trees, and other vegetation bordering their areas.

They have a ruthless attitude toward their own kind and a selfish indifference to weaker members, most noticeably their young, half-grown cubs, which have to stand on the outer fringes of the pride out of fear of the older cats. The cubs must likewise show caution around a kill, deferring a share in favor of the adults. Because the residual from a kill is often inadequate to satisfy the lesser animals' hunger, they must learn to assume the role of an adult; to hunt successfully and contribute to the pride, or decline and starve to death. This is the eternal pattern of survival of the fittest; it also keeps the pride strong and healthy.

I estimate that of every three cubs born, only one may reach full maturity. Cheetah losses must be at least double that because their young are very vulnerable to scavenger hunters such as hyena packs. So the sight of lion in the wilds bears witness to a lineage of survival of these superb hunting cats.

It takes more than average nerve to stand up to a charging lion, successfully bowl it over, and then finish it off. If two of them come at you simultaneously, your chances of survival are slim. When I had to hunt them, I usually reserved my initial shot for what I considered the dangerous females of the pride. Doing so seemed to have a temporary confusing effect, whereby I could go into action and get others. If armed with a dependable double-barreled shotgun with heavy shot, I could steel myself to face a charging male.

The principle of survival was to shoot the lioness first and then any other that decided to charge. As mentioned, the ideal weapon for this in my day was a double-barreled rifle/shotgun combination, one barrel chambered for a 9.3mm Mauser cartridge and the other a 12-gauge shotgun. If a male became aggressive, I would wait until he was at close quarters, then I would stop him with a shotgun blast to the face, reload as he curled over, and finish him off.

Patterns of action, however, were not always enough to keep you alive, and in my experience it was mostly the human factor that failed. One certainly cannot fault a reliable weapon for not placing its bullet or shot charge accurately at the critical moment.

To illustrate this fact, in a later episode a Mr. Stock, proprietor of the Sabi River Hotel in Southern Rhodesia, followed a lion and it turned on him in low scrub bush. As it charged, he braced himself for the event, but at the critical moment the lion swerved in full charge to come around a low bush and not over it as the hunter had anticipated. It cost him a mauling and disability. But he was one of the lucky ones who escaped the fearsome speed and strength of a lion. While he was being mauled, his courageous servant grabbed the rifle and shot the lion.

Circumstances such as numbers and dispositions of animals, vegetation, and your own personnel are vitally important. I preferred being alone or with a skilled, armed, and courageous tracker on whom I could entirely depend to share what disaster might follow. In other words, I tried to give myself a good chance to avoid a mauling! The real deciding factor, of course, is the hunter himself and his superiority in effectively using the right weapons. Man as a species is a very successful predator himself. But when man the predator has to match his efficiency against the great cat predators in their own environment, the balance changes to that of fearful man unsure of his environment, closing in on hunting cats that are disturbed, nervous, and sometimes fearful. Often enraged cats in such a state will turn and attack.

I have heard of and personally seen hunters unashamedly refuse to follow after wounding lion. Some of these men were important and held in hitherto high esteem, but the disgrace of being overwhelmed by fear made no difference. Putting themselves in danger beyond their abilities to cope was too much, and it made no difference to them what their own kind thought. In their desperation, they only wanted to see the sun go down again.

Men who react as described are generally not hunters by instinct, but are driven by the false value of prestige to acquire trophies for display. It becomes a symbol in their strata of society to have a trophy room to impress people. This facade only disgusts others—animal lovers and conservationists—and brings about in them an emotional abhorrence of all hunting people, primitive or otherwise. I should mention here that I also have game trophies on display at home in Harare. One particularly long, thin pair of cow tusks reminds me of the days when I hunted the Zambezi Ladies. They were cow elephant of a particularly intelligent, fearsome, courageous disposition that attacked the sound of rifle blasts, as is described in later chapters. But enough of men and their foibles.

In the society of lion, roars of the dominant males communicate to the lionesses the males' position of superiority within the pride. This dominance and the pride's internal social strata are conducive to maintaining mastery of the pride's territory. By promoting the interests of the pride as a whole, the pride system also promotes the interest of the individuals within it. So lion are superior, organized, collective hunters, but they suffer as individual hunters. In contrast, the leopard is mainly a loner and, as a result, is the superior overall hunter of the two cats. He depends on himself and, on occasions, a mate rather than a collective unit. Therein lies a major weakness of the pride system. Furthermore, while lion are wary of humans, they will turn on and drive off or destroy other lion entering their ranges. This is an unquestionable fact: Where lion are being exterminated, leopard continue to survive.

The pride usually consists of a few males and twice as many females with younger animals. But in Mozambique, with its profusion of game, we came across large prides with as many as fifty lion. It could only mean a coalition of prides into a super pride, and I don't profess to know how it comes about. Such a hunting unit can decimate resident game like impala and cause migratory movements of others out of their preferred ranges.

A large pride's invasion of another's territory may result in the survivor's acceptance, making the pride even larger. But a pride cannot remain very large for long because as their hunting activity is concentrated, they come under the stresses of a lack of game. Then the pressures of starvation, internal dissention, and loss of numbers will reduce the pack size to normal again.

Lion have a tactical skill whereby they will drive their prey into other waiting or stalking lion or any obstacles, including even other members of the hunted herd. The saying "survival of the fittest" doesn't always apply to a lion's prey, as I have seen lion pull down the fitter animal while lesser ones escaped. Much depends on the stalking position of the hunter relative to the hunted. Perhaps what is meant by "the fittest" with respect to a lion's prey is the most cunning, alert animal best suited to combat or flight.

I used to think that lion, leopard, and cheetah bypassed each other out of respect, but this is not so. It is of interest to note that leopard successfully kill the speedy cheetah with impunity and devour them, especially in scrub cover where the leopard can surprise them. Whereas leopard can be territorial like lion, unlike lion they remain loners and must be self-reliant in mastering their territory.

Lion tend to break into smaller groups in the rainy season as this is a hard period in their lives, with game scattered all over, thanks to the abundance of water and green vegetation. What is profusion to vegetarian animals is the opposite to predators. I always bore in mind that darkness stimulates lion to become bold and daring, even to the point of invading the campfires of hunters.

Lion cannot always match the speed and endurance of the hunted, but they possess great stealth and strength and are superb sprinters. They have an urgent need to kill at least once in seven days. The expression "a hungry lion" is accurate; under the duress of hunger they will tackle almost anything, including man, especially at night.

I sometimes used to amuse myself by closing in undetected on wild animals, hidden by vegetation in which I could view them through slight gaps that gave me enough vision. I found that if I concentrated my mind and eyesight sharply on them, a type of telepathy developed whereby antelope in particular would become suddenly uneasy and alarmed enough to inexplicably bound off, always away from my hidden presence. Buffalo were not that sensitive, but the moment I adopted a menacing attitude, some of them would turn in my direction, though I was, unseen. Puzzled and alarmed, they would ponderously canter off. Occasional individual animals would pause momentarily to look back in my direction.

However illogical, this seems to imply that animals sense human presence without sound, sight, or scent. I proved it many times, at least to myself. The unseen concentration of a hunter's eyes in particular gives off a form of threat whereby prey animals become uneasy or alarmed. I tried it at various distances, and the farther away I was, the less sensitive they became to my presence. But the best proof I had involved leopard; these hunting cats seem inherently bestowed with unseen instincts.

On one occasion in particular I was moving ever so slowly through a forest of mottled shade; occasional shafts of sunlight lit up the forest ground. The place was so intriguing, peaceful, and relaxing that it conjured up visions of mythical, dancing fairies. In this atmosphere and with these gentle thoughts, my hunting instincts receded and I was absorbed in the setting. I stood silently for some time, enjoying every moment. Then it all changed. I knew instinctively I was no longer alone and had come into danger. I could not at the moment detect the danger, so I peered into the vegetation around me. Suddenly I detected a movement in the mottled shade. It was the slight flexing of the tail of a leopard in a tree facing away from me. The cat was studying activities in my camp across a semi-open plain about four hundred yards away.

I leaned to one side to get a better view of the leopard, and no doubt my concentration sharpened on it. When that happened, the leopard, a large, broad-bodied male, in a flash jumped to a higher branch and in so doing swerved in midair to face me as only a true cat can. It fixed on me its penetrating, fierce, merciless stare of sharp, yellowish-khaki-coloured eyes, and its ears flattened in defensive aggression. In a second it landed on the ground and bounded away into the mottled shade.

Various elements had been at work here. I had penetrated a beautiful place in a relaxed and peaceful mood, but had come unknowingly into the presence of a leopard. With its concentration on my distant camp, the cat was unaware of danger—that was, until I came to concentrate on it. I am convinced this triggered its instincts, and it suddenly knew exactly where I was and then became defensive and bounded off.

These are some of the thoughts that came to me as I spent a pleasant last night around Katasoro's campfire. At dawn I had the carriers and tracker ready. There was a feeling in the air of storms coming, so mentally I prepared myself for some misery. Rifle in hand, Katasoro walked a mile or so with me. We both felt regrets, and I remember his parting words:

"We will see each other again—maybe you and the Dutchman will return." Then he advised, "For God's sake, don't neglect to place guards at your fires at night."

And so we parted in the slender forest.

We did not see each other again for thirty years. I stumbled on him in Salisbury, by then renamed Harare, and he often visited me on my small farm close to the city where I was breeding race horses. Just prior to that, my friend Faanie had shot himself in the head with a shotgun on the Angwa River, the place of his dreams of gold and glory.

But, returning to the story, we continued all day until late afternoon without seeing any game. That night, taking Katasoro's advice, I

I stumbled on Katasoro in Salisbury, by then renamed Harare, and he often visited me on my small farm close to the city where I was breeding racehorses.

placed guards at the campfire and did so for many nights until we reached an area we considered safe.

About five days later I entered a village and tried to trace Faanie, but had no luck. Locals told me of a very young Portuguese hunter who was shooting elephant successfully. He was a few days ahead somewhere. I pushed on and at another village gleaned information about a hunter who may have been Faanie.

Eleven days passed. We were miles from any villages but kept moving on. Finally in a village I picked up information. Faanie had passed through two days before with the truck and carriers, and I found him. He'd had success, having shot eleven elephant bulls, but nothing over fifty pounds a tusk. Still, under the circumstances it was good going and I was very pleased to see him again.

We brought each other up to date on our recent events, and Faanie added that he had met a mild-mannered hunter named Bromfield and had stayed a night with him. For reasons of my own, I did not want to be seen in the town of Nampula, so Faanie decided to go and get rid of all the ivory and resupply where necessary. But first he had to drop me about forty miles farther west in game country that I particularly liked. The next morning he did so and disappeared with the vehicle to Nampula. He was beginning to acquire a strong taste for liquor, especially the native palm wine, which was pleasant but quite potent. He was gone for four days and returned late one afternoon.

He told me I was known in Nampula by the name of "Wild Dog"—the man who had shot up the large herd of killer-cow elephant. I asked him if there was any unnatural interest in the amount of ivory. He said that no one was interested since he had sold it at different outlets. I had, in his absence, come across evidence of pilot bulls farther north and also spoor of large bulls. I thought we would now cross paths with the bulls from Tanganyika—and so it was that some days later we found and shot three large bulls ranging in tusk weight from about sixty to ninety pounds each. This was more like it, and the good fortune continued as we went onward. Faanie had found a good tracker who could shoot well, so I got rid of the human jackal by paying him off with money and some favoured goods.

With the new tracker, by name Chikati, we covered the adjoining areas, moving far and wide and wandering toward the Tanganyika border. There I hoped to contact Chirenge. I asked Chikati if he knew him, to which he replied, "No." I felt he was deceiving me but left it at that.

This new tracker was excellent, and we safely got more heavy ivory. Faanie had conditioned himself to hunting in less reckless ways. It made life easier as we could hunt in coordination according to the situations and circumstances. We had our ups and downs, with occasional dangerous moments. Coming closer to the Tanganyika border, we hunted elephant in large numbers in places of lush vegetation.

In these gatherings the younger bulls mock-challenged each other to test their skills and strength. It was all playful, but they were very rough. Animals lying down would not be left in peace very long as the youngsters rose on their back legs to trample them and then the mock fights started again. The drive to procreate, at times a rowdy affair, was no doubt one of the reasons so many elephant congregated there.

It was difficult to tell if the cows were in estrus, Except for the swellings of their temporal glands, which exuded fluid that oozed down their cheeks, there was no other sign. On such occasions large bulls appeared in *musth*, the violent, destructive frenzy also evidenced by the swelling of their temporal glands. These males were aggressive and possessive as they chased the cows in estrus, and, coming up to them, stretched their trunks forward across the cows' necks and shoulders to halt them. When a bull mounted a cow, he stood almost upright on his back legs. Elephant are at times great intimidators, from the massive bulls in rut, to the matriarch cows leading the herd, and on down the line. But in general they are considerate, especially to the calves, and they prefer the presence of comrades and friends.

We rarely saw large bulls fighting, as they accept others that are superior, but when they did fight it was an impressive exhibition of rage and power, with heads coming together, trunks intertwining, and efforts to find weaknesses from the sides so as to lunge with their tusks and cause mortal wounds. Here, as in other places, butterflies clustered, attracted to the remains of elephant urine on the ground.

We noted that calves gripped their mothers' back legs with their trunks when they wanted to halt them and perhaps scamper with favoured playmates. Calves would also trumpet in frustration as a form of protest. The cows tend to their young, but elephant mothers do not continuously search for their young because it is customary for the young to stay with their mothers.

Wet, lush seasons meant large congregations of elephant herds, which gradually broke into small groups in the dry seasons. If unrestricted, elephant will range over hundreds of miles. There is no doubt that they find pleasure in great herds, which also helps to promote selective breeding. In the great herds one could detect the dominant animals. On rare occasions we saw elephant in a bad state, weakened and succumbing to disease. The reason was not evident, but they were definitely not wounded and could have been the victims of internal parasites. Animals in advanced old age got to a certain level of malnutrition, then wasted away. I often wondered if people realized that old elephant, once their final molar teeth are worn, inevitably starve to death. I have come across large old bulls with excellent ivory in an emaciated state, living close to available water, usually in isolation.

The same age-related problem beset predators. I once awakened to a feeling of danger and saw the shadowy outline of a large lion scavenging on fish that the cook had caught and left near his head where he was sleeping. I had no option in the dark but to fire at it, as I thought the lion would kill the sleeping cook. The lion slumped to the heavy bullet with a deep moan and instantly died. When firebrands illuminated the scene, it was discovered that the lion was in a dreadful state of emaciation, with teeth worn down to stumps. It somehow had managed to avoid wild dogs and hyena.

It was during this period that I had a mishap. We were closing in on a large cow herd accompanied by some big bulls. A water carrier panicked and got separated from us during the process of trying to locate the bulls. The elephant got the water carrier's scent just as I was about to shoot a bull, and I heard the whole mass turn and stampede toward us. Chikati, Faanie, and I stood in their path as the carriers ran off, dumping their loads behind us. With his knowledge of such events, Chikati tensely uttered the words, "Beware of the chosen path," spoken in his own Naos language. In hunting terms this means the direction of an elephant escape or stampede: Once in formation, the mass does not deviate from the chosen path, and we were in it. At first we were aware of the snapping of branches and trees; then we heard the leading cows trumpeting and roaring. A mass of elephant came down on us. There was no hunting pattern to adhere to now, only fast and accurate firepower in the hope that the herd would split on either side of us.

They ran shoulder-to-shoulder in a mass. We opened fire, and at one stage I thought we would not be able to split the herd. The dead ones in front helped us as they formed barriers that the others had to pass. One particular elephant, as it veered, came to one side of me. I had dismissed it from my mind, believing its speed would carry it past us. I was conscious of it but concentrated my fire on oncoming animals. Prior to this incident I had lectured Faanie that the hunter must never allow an animal to get too close, as once the gap was closed, it was the inferior, puny physical strength of man against a powerful beast.

I had miscalculated. This elephant in passing struck out sideways with its trunk, catching me on my lower legs. I remember sharp pain and spinning in the air, an impact, and then nothing. I came to with the feeling of water running through my hair and down my face from a water bag held by Faanie. I had pain in my neck and shoulder and less in the leg. According to Faanie, the tracker Chikati had instantly recovered my rifle and taken a kneeling position next to me in order to reach the ammunition on my belt and bandoliers, continuing what should have been my firing position.

Faanie said Chikati was excellent and no doubt realized he was also fighting for his life, as all of us were. Despite the pain and discomfort, I was very much alive. Anyhow, what you don't know at the time does not bother you. My neck was the worst, and even now, after many years, it still troubles me when I do rough riding on horseback. I could hardly move for days, and recovery was painstakingly slow. At one stage I toyed with the idea of going all the way back to Salisbury for medical treatment. Eventually it eased off, but I experienced sharp pains each time I fired the rifle. It tended to make me gun-shy, but for the time being I had to learn to live with it. To make matters worse, most of our party came down with fever and dysentery—except for Faanie and the tracker and two carriers. For the dysentery we had sulpha drugs, but I panicked about malaria, for it seemed either our drugs were faulty or the malaria virus was new or stronger. Initially, I feared cerebral malaria as I had seen others die of it. There was also the possibility of sleeping sickness—the initial symptoms were similar—but time proved our malady was not deadly.

The sickness set us back two weeks, and in the last week Faanie suggested crossing the border to contact Chirenge. As I was in no condition to hunt and Faanie was going to take Chikati and a few carriers, I took Chikati aside.

"You say you know the Tanganyika border," I said. "How come you told me that you don't know the leopard hunter Chirenge? You are both the same type of man."

Without the slightest hesitation he said, "Bwana, I know him well; he taught me to shoot with a rifle."

I did not reprimand this wild man for having lied to me, especially as it had done no harm. However, I was curious and asked him why he had lied. His answer set me back for a few seconds. He said he lied because white men use such statements as evidence against them, to be followed by imprisonment. I knew this was true; I had heard of some isolated cases where tribesmen were tricked into saying certain things, and so I agreed with him.

He said he was afraid to identify himself at first, but since we had hunted together he no longer feared our knowledge of his background. He went on to tell me how he and Chirenge had many times poached together. We understood each other, and as I listened to his past, I recalled that I had enough of my own misdeeds to think of.

Faanie was gone a long time, and I wondered if he had perhaps had a mishap. I planned to follow him to the Rio Ruvuma, but he returned on the sixth afternoon with the tracker Chirenge. I was pleased to see them all—now we had two excellent trackers and men who could use rifles effectively. It turned out that they were not just skilled trackers but courageous hunters of deadly efficiency.

Faanie had an amused look about him, then said, "I shot the king's elephant in Tanganyika."

"And the ivory?" I asked.

"It is well hidden," he said.

"Son of a bitch," I said. "An Afrikaner who hasn't been in an English prison!" and we both laughed about it.

I asked which tracker he had used, and he said both.

"You won't get better," he said. "That faceless one (Chirenge) can run on the spoor."

We moved off the next day at a slow pace as some of us were not fully recovered. In late morning two runners came from the forest, saying that a Portuguese hunter had been mauled by a leopard and was close to death.

"How far?" I asked.

They indicated, by the sun, about an hour or three miles away. We had excellent medical equipment, but if he was that badly off he could be dead by the time we got there. On arrival my first sight of the hunter was a mop of raven black hair caked in blood. He was lying face down in soft sand with his back exposed to the sunlight and looked a mess of dried blood and long, open wounds on his backside, some deep enough to see bone. I heard his moans as he tried to roll over but could not.

He was lacerated all over, particularly on the buttocks and lower back legs. The top of one shoulder had been badly bitten and both shoulders severely clawed. I doubted that we could save him. We had to try, even though we wondered if he might be better off if we simply let him die.

We had water, but Faanie sent the Portuguese hunter's staff to find more. All they had were two waterbags—that plus our own might be enough to wash out the wounds.

Faanie said, "You are more adept at this, so I will assist by keeping the flesh open while you deep-wash the wounds."

Some wounds appeared clean, but they had to be washed and treated because of the leopard's germ-laden claws and teeth. Others had sand in them and would take care and time. I felt for this man lying on the ground. His pain must have been excruciating. Only after I had injected morphine did I manage to concentrate on the task. I did not think he would live to see the sunset, but we worked feverishly—eventually sewing him up in a rough fashion, allowing for the suppuration of the wounds.

Afterward we gently turned him over onto a blanket. On his front the damage was by comparison minor, but he must have lost a lot of blood. The pain receded and he muttered something in Portuguese, repeating it a few times. Not even the locals, some of whom spoke Portuguese, could understand him. Having worked on him personally, I did not want to watch him die. Faanie had fought in North Africa and Italy during the war and was used to this. He volunteered to drive him to Nampula. I suggested that we pack a lot of grass and a cloth under the hunter to absorb the shock of travel.

The hunter's staff reported water a quarter-mile away. We set up a camp there, and the last I saw of the young Portuguese hunter was his dark eyes watching me as Faanie drove off on his way to Nampula. I wondered what the medics would think of my crude surgery.

I now questioned the locals as to what had happened. Apparently the Portuguese hunter was the last in a line of men when a leopard dropped from a tree and mauled him. His tracker, another one of those human jackals, ran off, as did all the others. I got the faceless one, Chirenge, to help put the puzzle together and what with all the human footprints around, he took his time. Finally he then showed me where the leopard had climbed the tree hours before the attack and where it had reluctantly moved off afterward.

Next morning, after sending the carriers away with the loads to a camping spot, we took this leopard's spoor, which was leading off into thickening forests. The speed and accuracy with which Chirenge followed the spoor was almost unbelievable. At times I thought he was following nothing, and then within a mile or so I would get a glimpse of leopard pug marks.

The sun had passed its zenith when Chirenge started to slow down, saying the leopard might lie up here somewhere, and sure enough, within the hour we found where the leopard had come down to the ground from its lookout on some tree branches. It had loped off for a short while, then continued walking, and Chirenge was of the opinion that the leopard knew it was being followed.

In a spot easy to decipher he showed me how it had paused occasionally to listen to our approach. Should it make a stand, Chirenge said, do not look for spots but for the shine of its yellow-khaki eyes, which are more noticeable in comparison to its coat. When it knows we are approaching, its coat may be hidden but not the eyes. We were both well armed, and, as Chirenge explained, should the leopard land on one of us, the other was free to shoot it quickly. He further explained from his experience that a leopard cannot instantly kill a fighting man, as a lion can, and the seconds of delay would be the death of the leopard.

Watching this tracker at work would bring out the admiration of any man, even a leopard lover. We had hours of slow, nerve-wracking tracking, and given my weakened state following my recent illness, I was beginning to feel the strain. There was no way of seeing strain on Chirenge's face since it was a mass of mutilations, but his eyes were exceedingly bright and penetrating. He was in his element and keen to kill the cat. Being as tired as I was, at that moment I was almost sorry to have met the man. We followed the leopard until sundown without contact and then had to abandon it to get our bearing on our camp. We finally found it late at night. At dawn, to my dismay, Chirenge was ready at the campfire to follow the leopard again. I ached slightly and hoped the day's walking would free it up.

The tracker took a shorter route, going directly to where we had abandoned the leopard spoor. We found and followed it. With the previous nightfall, the leopard had eased its pace, and we saw where it had lounged at times.

"Not hungry," Chirenge said.

Chirenge moved fast, but we did not close the distance. It knew we were after it. Chirenge was hoping the leopard would make a stand, but perhaps it was too cunning for that. After tedious nonstop tracking, we had to abandon the spoor again in late afternoon.

The events on the spoor of this lone leopard were unusual. Leopard, more so than lion, are creatures of stealth and concealment and consequently when pursued use cover as a means of defense and/or attack. If wounded, they may or may not slink off and usually do not go far, but if pursued they can be depended on to make a stand with deadly ferocity. Being masters of concealment and having exceptional senses, they can surprise the hunter as no other creature can, exploding out of the vegetation and perhaps mauling the hunter, who hardly has time to effectively raise the rifle.

Their attacks are unexpected and deadly, sometimes occurring in places where you would not expect them to be. Anyone who alone follows a wounded leopard in dense foliage is either a fool or a highly skilled hunter of courage and ability, a master of the environment, and a man of superior senses and instant reflexes. Chirenge was one of the few of this class. I asked him why this leopard did not make a stand, and he replied that it had attacked people before and knew what followed; perhaps it was wise enough to know that distance and concealment were its greatest assets for survival. It would attack only when all circumstances warranted it, much as it had attacked the young Portuguese hunter.

We arrived late at the camp. Faanie was there, and he told me the young Portuguese hunter had lasted long enough to be put on a light plane piloted by a Greek-speaking Portuguese who had arrived a few hours previously and was returning to Beira on the coast. Faanie had given the pilot extra morphine and a syringe. It was all out of our hands now, so we could only hope for the best.

We spoke speculatively of the mauled hunter, whose equipment we still had in our camp. We would have to return it to the authorities in Nampula. That meant another motor trip and an excuse for Faanie to be drunk for a few days.

These outposts, especially those on the coastline, were enticing places, with good food, wine, and a wonderful feeling of relaxation—all in a lovely warm climate. But hunting is usually seasonal, and this was our season. Even so, after my illness I felt I could do with a break. But the best bet was to get the Portuguese hunter's gear together, list it, and send it with all his carriers to the administrator in Nampula. If Faanie insisted on motoring again, I would have to hunt the leopard for the third time. It was such an elusive bastard that I did not feel like hunting it anymore. Furthermore, I did not want to get caught in official enquiries about the Portuguese hunter. So we packed up as planned and moved on, the other carriers and goods going in the direction of Nampula.

That night around the campfire, we drank wine that Faanie had brought back from Nampula. I knew him well, and as soon as the wine went to his head, his humour came to the fore.

"Well, let us see," he said. "The Nyschens expedition has so far lost one man dead from cow elephant, one from snakebite, and a 'Pork' hunter who will probably die!"

We always referred to the Portuguese as "Porks."

"The Wild Dog himself took a flip from an elephant because he could not gauge distance. Pity he lived—think of all the ivory I would have had."

"And," I interjected, "you nearly became the murderer of the party because of a lion head."

"Englander," he said, "men have killed for less. It all depends on how you feel at the moment. Anyhow, murder is only an illegal form of warfare."

I knew he had done sniping duties in the last war, and he said it was impersonal—all you saw was a man drop at a distance. Since I had been sick, Faanie had organized our safari and did it very well. So, having got rid of the responsibility, I said, "This now becomes Faanie's Expedition—let us see what happens from now on."

"Oh, I can tell you all about that," he said. "You will either get killed or go to jail in Tanganyika."

"Killed would be better."

"Then one tracker will die, and the faceless one would be the last to die as I need him most. The carriers would not die just then as I need them to carry the ivory; then, if they like, they can also all die. I will, of course, report it all and live on the coast like a king. I might even go and get myself a good-looking tough wife from Zanzibar. You know, one of those that won't die of tropical diseases."

It was not so much what he said but the way he said it. We laughed.

"Well," I said, "so much for the workings of your mind—let's see how the Faanie Expedition goes."

At dawn we moved away and in late afternoon came across the large, fresh spoor of two elephant. I was tempted to take it but felt the sunset would be against us. Here we were well into the area of migratory bulls from Tanganyika. I told Faanie to be selective from now on and go for large ivory only. In the morning he decided to hunt the two bulls of the previous day while I went out to get buffalo meat for the camp. I got two buffalo and returned to camp late, having spent some time in glorious country watching the numerous herds of game. There was plenty of lion, hyena, and leopard spoor, indications of a well-stocked game country.

There were villages here, small family affairs many miles apart, and except for the crop-raiding, such a situation would be a perfect balance between man and beast. In late afternoon, as I approached the camp, a messenger came out to greet me. He was not one of our men, so I dismissed any possibility of mishap to Faanie. He said there was a loggers' camp, meaning a camp where trees are cut for poles, a few hours' walk from here. A Portuguese child had strayed, and they desperately needed a tracker to find it. Unhesitating, I took gear and water and left a message for Faanie to bring the other tracker. The messenger remained in camp as a guide for Faanie, and I took Chirenge to move on the messenger's spoor.

With a realistic analysis, Chirenge said, "If the child is small, the hyena will kill it tonight." We carried on, darkness fell, and Chirenge took a general direction until we saw campfires and arrived at the loggers' camp. At the edge of the clearing we paused and heard the wailing cries of a woman. As we got closer they turned into sobs of great grief. She was in a cabin built of poles, set off the ground. It was so pitiful to listen to that I did not want to see her and beckoned her husband from the cabin. He was disturbed but calmer, saying Jesus would answer his prayers. I wondered where Jesus could be this dark night in the forest around us. I was taught as a youngster that faith moved mountains, but in my later years I came to believe more in a faith in explosives for that purpose.

Obviously this man had come to the end of his tether. I explained that it was not possible to track on a dark night. He thanked us and ambled back to the cabin, offering another cabin for us to use and saying again in broken English that God would look after his child and all of us. From the wails and sobbing of the woman inside, I knew she was of a different opinion. In the dark I went with Chirenge to the spot where a guide said the child had entered the forest. Here we built a fire away from the disturbance of the loggers' camp. We had the necessary gear and slept around the fire. Much later Faanie arrived with the other tracker. I explained the situation, and we all got sleep while we could.

In the first light of dawn I saw Chirenge appear from the thicker part of the forest. He had found what might be the child's spoor. We all realized that time was of the essence and headed out, taking only a few water bags and no food as we did not expect to go far.

At the last moment Faanie snatched some pummeled biltong, saying that if the child was alive it would need nourishment. Well, perhaps, but water certainly. Chirenge and Chikati spread out to move parallel on either side of where the loggers had tried to spoor the child. The area was a confusion of many human footprints, but they moved through it quickly until it became less confusing.

Then the footprints milled around in large circles. Here Chikati said the loggers had lost the spoor. We heard a bird call from Chirenge farther on. He had the child's spoor. He said something to Chikati, and they both started running. Having rifles, bandoliers, and belts, it was harder for us to keep up. At the speed they were tracking, I honestly thought it impossible for them to keep the spoor without losing it. Faanie drew my attention to their pattern: Chirenge on the run spooring, while Chikati watched the sides in case Chirenge overshot the spoor or the child had moved off at an angle. No sooner had he said that than it happened.

Both trackers pulled up and after a glance started running on the spoor in a different direction. Chirenge continued while Chikati stopped to explain that the child had hurt its foot, which made spooring easier. Then another bird call came from a few hundred yards away. The spoor zigzagged, but we went straight to the sound. When we got there, Chirenge had already moved off, leaving some broken leaves indicating his direction and progress. Another bird call came from the side. The child had moved in a circle, so we cut straight across. Chirenge had left more leaves and finger marks circling hyena spoor in the sand. The hyena spoor became menacing as we followed in the direction of the child.

Chirenge was way ahead of us, continuing to bird-call from time to time, and we released the other tracker to aid him. The spoor indicated wide circles—the child was completely bushed and just wandered. I felt the heat of the earth increasing. There was a series of bird calls from one place. We got there, but both trackers had gone. Then through the forest came Chikati.

We followed him, and to my amazement I saw a child curled up sleeping on the sand next to a large low-lying bush. His face was stained with dirt and tears. We kept Chirenge away in case his face should startle the child, then silently woke the boy. He seemed dazed, so we gave him water and he began to revive, and eventually started crying. He was a Portuguese boy about seven years old with a bewildered look in his eyes. Faanie gave him some crushed biltong, and he slowly ate it and stared at us in turn. We sat around the child until he was used to us, and then Faanie told Chikati to carry him on his shoulders. Every so often, we let the child down to walk slowly with us. For a small fellow he had an amazing capacity for water. Eventually we reached the clearing.

The child had become talkative, but we did not understand him; the trackers said the child did not know what he was saying. Other people saw us, and then the child's father came forward. He spoke English of a sort and, with the muttering of many thanks, took his son off to the bungalow where his wife was. We heard the sounds of joy and moved off to our campfire site.

There was not enough shade, so we moved deeper into the forest. Here, in the heat of the day away from our base camp, I looked at our meager possessions. It reminded me of days gone by when I could barely afford bush rations, rifle, and ammunition. There is value in having to be humble, and sometimes when you become too mighty, a good shakeup can bring you back to normal.

I discussed with Faanie our two trackers and their outstanding ability to track and shoot. In our day it was a rare black man who had both skills so well developed, especially accurate shooting. I said to Faanie that if any one of us got killed now, it would be the result of misjudgment or carelessness.

"Don't talk," he said. "This is the Faanie Expedition. You have already hit the dust with the aid of one of these dangerous creatures."

After lounging a few hours we were about to move off when the Portuguese woman, her husband, child, and manservant arrived. The servant spoke Portuguese and Chi-lapa-lapa, the *lingua Franca* of the south, so we managed to understand them.

She was a different woman from the previous night. They were embarrassingly thankful, so I pointed at the trackers, saying those were the men who had found the child. The gratitude moved from us to them, and then she was struck with the face of Chirenge. We could not help a mild laugh at her reaction while Chirenge, without knowing the false values of civilization, stared at her. To us it was fast, excellent tracking, but to the family it meant the life of their child. We were invited to stay, but as communication was poor we preferred going back to our base before nightfall. We never saw these people again. In these foreign, wild parts of Africa we were always moving and hunting, and so isolation and secrecy were our way of life.

Within a few days Faanie and I started hunting together, going in all directions. Though I had been thrown by elephant, I still felt he was in greater danger than I. He had toned down, but he still occasionally treated oncoming elephant as if he were a bullfighter, so I refused to let him hunt without me. It was just as well—we were getting into large troops of big bull elephant where the advantage of more than one man was needed to exploit situations. Because of my previous experience with the large cow herd, I estimate that I could account for two elephant in five seconds, and this fast-fire rate later improved with the continued use of double-barreled rifles. It must be realized that once the contents of a magazine rifle have been fired, a double-barreled rifle starts to catch up with it in rapidity of fire because the double user doesn't have the longer pause to refill the magazine or the time delay of the bolt action. I mention this to explain how we managed to quickly kill large numbers of bull elephant, even in the anger and panic of their fast movements.

We so disturbed the elephant in the area that they crossed the border, and we followed them, only to find new herds. I was becoming apprehensive about the amount of ivory we had; the sight of this quantity in itself could attract attention and cause trouble. So we had more than half the ivory moved and sold through others, for a fee. Even with more than half of it gone, I could not shake the fear of being in a precarious situation.

An incident occurred that influenced me to move out of northern Mozambique for the rest of the year at least. The rainy season was over, and we had decided to aid some villagers who were being terrorized by occasional man-eaters moving across the Ruvuma River. It afforded us a change and Faanie was also keen to hunt them. Above all, hunting man-eaters would help us get additional permits from the Portuguese administration for the next year's season.

On the first night we both waited in the largest village, but no man-eaters appeared. It was a boring occupation just to wait, hope, and hang around villages. We decided to split up to increase our chances, and each of us slept at a different village. Faanie had Chikati with him, and as the sun set they watched a woman sitting next to the fire, gazing into the embers. I have seen the antics that were about to take place, but Faanie had not.

As hyena wailed their disturbing, eerie calls, the woman pulled a black cloth over her head and shoulders, and it draped well over her sides. In witchcraft this means that the woman is transforming into a hyena. It is done by a woman who wishes to instill fear into others, and this is quite impressive when seen in firelight, with the hyena wailing in the background. In such circumstances villagers disperse to their huts in fearful respect. Whole villages and sometimes districts can be dominated by such individuals, and you have to witness such events to credit them.

This was only one incidence of witchcraft; there were many others. Sometimes it was done for the benefit of poachers who shot elephant for ivory and rhino for horn and left the meat for the tribe. Sometimes the chiefs, the witch doctor, or the medicine men would let it be known, sometimes through example, that to discuss or reveal the presence of poachers or their activities would be to face fearful consequences. It had the effect of silencing the gossip of the whole tribe from the youngest to the oldest. I knew well of this because I used it myself through the chiefs, when necessary. Thinking back, I recall no repercussions, but in later years, when I fully realized what I had instigated, I was grateful no one had been hurt.

But Faanie, unseen and waiting in the village, had seen fit to test this particular woman transforming herself into a hyena. The people already had man-eaters to fear, so in anger Faanie moved in quietly and boldly threw the woman onto the glowing embers, holding her down until she screamed enough for others to realize she had not been transformed into a hyena. He then let her go, and she rushed off looking for refuge.

Sometime later that night Faanie shot three man-eaters from the underhang of a hut, managing this before the man-eaters could kill anyone. I had no luck where I was and returned to base. Faanie arrived that afternoon to inform me of his success. One of his lion skins had distinct rosettes, much like you see on an overconditioned horse, like rosettes of health, and if it kept this quality it would be an unusual skin.

I felt the season had been hard, both physically and on the nervous system, and was ready for a break. A break to me would be the pleasures of the

Portuguese coast, Zanzibar, or Mombasa—"wine, women and song," as the saying goes.

Because of the man-eaters, we had been leaving porters on guard duty. Sometime during the next night, I felt rather than saw that the fires were low. I always slept with rifle handy under my mosquito net, and as I raised myself slightly, I saw tribesmen disappearing into the night. I thought they must be raiding the camp for weapons or ivory, and instantly I was up, rifle in hand, out from under the net. I rekindled the fires with branches and then realized the two guards were gone. Perhaps the man-eaters had silently taken them, but I was perplexed because the tribesmen I had seen running off were unclothed. Raiders usually smear their bodies with animal fat to make it difficult to seize or hold them, and you can see the glow of firelight on their skins. I woke the camp. Faanie stood up and in so doing pulled a spear at an angle from the ground where he had been sleeping. His rifle was in the other hand.

I was trying to figure him out when he said, "I think that spear was meant for me."

More puzzled now, I called for firebrands to try to trace the guards. There was lion spoor. It was night and nothing could be properly observed on the ground. Unthinkingly I asked Faanie if he had been buggering around with women at the village, suspecting that a jealous husband may have had a go at him with a spear. He just stared at me, holding the spear in the firelight. It was the type with many small barbs used mainly to spear fish.

Then Chirenge quietly said, "The work of the hyena woman."

These trackers, because of their prowess and use of firearms, were mostly above the fear of witchcraft, and so we moved aside from the others and discussed it. There was the possibility of mistaken identity—that the spear could have been meant for me—but both trackers were adamant that it was the work of the hyena woman. Furthermore, there would be punishment for those who had failed to spear Faanie. In view of this, we ourselves stood guard in twos until dawn. At first light we were on the spoor of two would-be assassins. We saw where they had circled the camp looking for another opportunity and, having failed, must have been watching us. No doubt the sight of Chirenge, shotgun in hand, his sinuous body illuminated in the firelight, had changed their minds, and it was well that we ourselves had mounted guard. The assassins' tracks moved away from the hyena woman's village.

"Purposely," Chirenge said. "They will move from village to village to confuse spooring or even stay undetected in a crowd of people."

He also said the two guards had been intimidated and had probably gone off toward the village. We backtracked and confirmed that. By this time the heat was developing, and I reasoned that it was no good following phantoms, and even if we could identify the assassins—which we could not—I felt our only chances to locate them were if they stayed away from villages.

But even if we found them, we could not kill them out of hand—or could we? To hand them over to the Portuguese authorities would entail enquiries about ourselves as well as the large amounts of ivory we had. Officialdom in parts of

Africa was despotic, and could become tyrannical at the whim of any petty bureaucrat. I had heard horror stories of arbitrary rulings applied to other hunters, so when it came to officialdom I had always adopted the attitude of being mentally backward—dense, if need be—to rake in the ivory, to stash it away, and, above all, to stay beyond official reach.

Another attempt was made to distract our new camp guards, and it became obvious that we were to be continuously plagued by the threat of having spearmen, on instructions from the hyena woman, attack us at night while we were asleep. We moved from area to area, but this threat continued to follow us, so at night we took to disappearing in the dark to sleep elsewhere. Then an attempt was made on one of the trackers.

It was now a matter of thrust and parry, and we, at the risk of our lives, were doing the parrying. The time had come for the thrust. As far as I was concerned, this was the end, so on a lovely warm night I decided to get to the core of the problem by counterattacking and hunting the hyena woman. Chirenge and I arrived near a village where the hyena woman was said to have taken up temporary residence. We watched the village from the cover of the forest, not knowing which hut the hyena woman would be in. Then hyena started wailing in the distant darkness in their spine-chilling way, and to my surprise the hyena woman emerged from a hut with her black cloth draped across one shoulder. In the moonlight she crossed the open yard and sat close to the embers of the fire. I watched her for a while, trying to study detail—she was about forty years of age, of an upright carriage and in her semi-nude state well proportioned. The hyena again wailed, coming closer, and she moved the black cloth over both her shoulders as I advanced on her. Halfway in I took Chirenge's spear and he my rifle and we closed in. In the final moments she partly turned her head and cast large eyes on me, and in a flash I speared her.

Ivory hunting to me had developed into a science of survival. At most times it was an unemotional procurement of food. Having all these things in mind as well as a persistent, nagging premonition of disturbing developments to come, I told Faanie that it was just as well this recent event had occurred. He did not follow my line of thought, so I explained my fears. The dry season was upon us and officials would be freer to move about. With the use of the askaris, *cipias*, and *pedi* (the secret police), who were usually quite skilled, we would slowly be uncovered.

"So what," he said. "It's supposed to be legal to take crop-raiding elephant, and what of our good-Samaritan efforts with the man-eaters?"

To add to my anxiety, Chirenge adopted the hyena-woman affair as an example to solve his own past problems with his brother, a chief across the border in Tanganyika. Chirenge suddenly disappeared for days and later returned saying that he no longer felt disturbed or revengeful. His peace had been obtained by crossing the Ruvuma River and successfully spearing his brother in a hut at night. Even here in these isolated wilds, I could feel the pressure of events building up. But Faanie was keen to stay on. *Quite a switch,* I thought, *from gold to ivory fever.*

I was of the opinion that we should later take in the area adjacent to Rhodesia from the Rio Save to the Mwanezi River. I knew there were marshes and floodplains there—an ideal place during the Months of the Sun, which would develop about five months from now. In the meantime we could relax up the coast in East Africa. Faanie always had that bulldog tenacity to hold onto anything he enjoyed. Having reasoned things out to my mind's satisfaction, I lost patience with him. We parted, and it was the end of the "Faanie Expedition."

We had already sold ivory and paid the two trackers for their ivory, plus large bonuses. Other incidents occurred that caused officials to become suspicious, resulting in my having to leave northern Mozambique at least for the coming season. So I moved up the East African coastline, temporarily leaving Faanie behind. It was not long before I started to miss him, the trackers, and, above all, penetrating the great herds of elephant.

EAST AFRICAN COAST:

A PILGRIMAGE THROUGH HISTORY— 1951

Later, I told myself—I will return later when I feel more at ease. That word "ease" was on my mind as I boarded a not-so-good-looking boat that plied goods up and down the East African coast. It had the advantage of calling on islands unvisited by bigger and better ships. The captain was an adventurous man of Danish origin, Karl Larsen by name. For years we had both traveled the coastline without getting the opportunity to see the wilds of the hinterland.

I wanted to see the famed Serengeti Plains, the crater of Ngorongoro, and other places, and I invited him to join me. He was keen but also reluctant, as he would have to find another captain to relieve him of his ship. Trying to goad him into venturing with me inland, I asked him how this vast sea of nothingness could attract him, adding that the real jungle lies beneath the surface and he was floating over it. But he informed me that his life was profitable, thanks to smuggling on the coast, and because of this and his responsibilities it was hard for him to leave his ship.

He gave me names, addresses and letters of introduction to his friends, saying I would be welcomed by them, and it turned out to be that way. "In

Zanzibar," he said, "you will have a pleasant surprise." We were drinking, and he seemed smug in his secrecy.

While cruising on his boat, I was astonished to see dugouts on the sea, mostly when it was calm, some going to minor islands no doubt to ply trade. I could not picture myself in a dugout at sea, no matter how calm the ocean was. The occupants must have been familiar with the currents as they had only paddle power. I greatly enjoyed the company of the Arabs. I had always thought of them as men of the deserts only, but here they had for many centuries mastered the sea, its moods, and star navigation. Listening to them put me into the past of East Africa as they had learned it from their ancestors, as opposed to our European historical versions, and it greatly interested me.

There was no doubt in my mind that the European nations' scramble for Africa was only for mineral and other wealth—wealth was the inescapable word. This type of wealth was unwanted by Arab nations—they were not industrialized enough to use the minerals. Hence their interest in Africa receded proportionately with the banning of slave dealings. As slave trading waned, they lost their grip on Africa.

In Zanzibar, in the company of an Arab, I visited an address given me by Karl Larsen, and my knock at the door was answered by the most beautiful woman I have ever seen. She was Ceylonese, and at the mention of Larsen's name we were invited in. Her husband, also Ceylonese, was a doctor, and as we entered he stood close behind her. We were taken to an inner courtyard where we were entertained, having the option of sitting in shade or sunlight. The doctor had established a medical practice on the island. It was obvious that the luxury of their surroundings and home was too grand to have resulted from a medical practice, so I guessed they were associated with Larsen in the smuggling racket.

I returned to their house often and got to know this couple well. They came down to the beach where I relaxed, tried to surf, and enjoyed the company of the Arabs and the local fishermen. In this environment the Ceylonese and I would relax together, basking in the heat until sunset and nightfall cleared the beach.

The island of Zanzibar was many years later the scene of horrific slaughter, with people being driven into the sea and butchered. In later years I often wondered what had happened to this Ceylonese couple and whether they had managed to survive. It seemed inconceivable that one so delicate and beautiful as this woman might have been butchered. Many years later my worst fears were confirmed by others who had left the island prior to its independence—the Ceylonese couple had indeed been slaughtered.

I kept in touch with Karl Larsen, who eventually managed to hire a temporary captain for his boat. Together we moved through the vast Serengeti Plains and Ngorongoro Crater of Tanganyika. We viewed great herds of wild animals. After a while I became conscious of a "much the same" look to the open country, but the game in their vast numbers always remained impressive. I yearned to gallop amongst them with a good horse under me—I thought it would be exciting to see them racing away, instead of just grazing slowly across the plains.

Here the predators were easier to observe than those I was used to in the forests and bushlands, and on the Serengeti Plains we often witnessed their hunting activities, particularly their final killing strikes. There is a savage, merciless, sometimes unnecessary cruelty to the actions of all predators, especially wild dog, lion, and leopard, in that order. Even on these open plains they knew when and where the game was at their "mercy."

Lion in particular, with their great strength and dexterity are capable of breaking necks and strangling to shorten the suffering. I often saw them kill by biting the back of the neck close to the head, and wondered if the large fangs penetrating there, so close to the spinal column and brain, had a paralyzing effect. I also witnessed lion seizing their prey by the throat and exerting pressure to strangle the victim, while others immediately started to feed from the back, away from the kicking legs of the live animal. I suppose it makes no difference to a lion how long an animal takes to die.

It is easier to observe and appreciate the pattern and activity of wild dogs on the open plains. I had seen them in Zambezia and on the Rio Ruvuma following game. There, because of the higher grass cover, they would call to each other in their unimpressive, almost innocent noises, not at all indicative of the true killers that they are.

Sometimes temporarily confused, the wild-dog leaders would leap into the air while on the run to get a view of the game ahead of them in the long grass. They appeared to have a pattern of approach whereby the leader or leaders would take off after the quarry, allowing the pack farther back to take short cuts to the victim, which usually did not run in a completely straight line of retreat. At times I watched some wild dogs from the pack come "off the bench" in a fresh state to continue the chase—probably not by desire but because previous leaders had tired. At most times a quarry singled out by dogs is doomed, regardless of its speed or stamina. Closing on their running victim, the wild dogs leap at the flanks, tearing at the flesh of the back leg muscles and most times freeing the entrails. The unfortunate animal quickly loses the advantage of speed and in its last movements is literally torn to pieces by the pack around it. It is one hell of a death to be attacked by wild dogs. They are reluctant, possibly even afraid, to attack man, although I would hate to have them come around me if I were unarmed.

In Mozambique I had a large pack come loping up close to me and communicate with those innocent, yappy calls, almost as if they were asking each other what this creature was. By curiosity or design this pack became intense—why I do not know—and as they got too close I shot a few. The others stalled and looked at their dead comrades, obviously bewildered. The noise of the heavy elephant rifle disturbed them and they moved off, occasionally looking back at me—just as well, since they were many and the ammunition was expensive. They seemed, even at close quarters, innocent of their cruel hunting habits and looked inoffensive.

I could not associate myself with the wild dog and wondered why the tribesmen in Zambezia had named me after this creature. It certainly was no compliment and was considered a degrading name.

A hunter who lives long enough in a particular area will be given a native name by the locals, especially trackers. They find most European names unpronounceable, much as we do theirs. So, for identification purposes, they create a name for the hunter in their own language based on noticeable traits or deeds. That name may not only be something appealing, humourous, or condemning, but also a reflection of trait or deed surprising to the hunter. I have many times smiled to myself at some of these descriptive names. *Behrey*, meaning hyena, usually describes a gutless person who hides amongst others to scavenge or slinks in on a kill at the last moment. *Nalugwe* or *m'bada* (leopard) is someone who is unseen and unknown in his activities—treacherous and destructive to others. They often refer to plainclothes policemen as *nalugwe*. *N'gire* (warthog), with its large curved side tusks, looks, they say, like a native commissioner, who is usually also the local magistrate that sentences them for their offenses. *Mondoro* or *pondoro* (lion), is a name usually given to someone to be obeyed and feared, based on some powerful or bold characteristics. These are but some of the many animal names applied to people. We lived mostly in a hunting world, so it stood to reason such names would be chosen for hunters.

These names, however, were not always of animals—for instance *Katasoro*, meaning he who uses one bullet to shoot two animals, or *Kam cha cha*, the dancer or someone vigorous. Faanie Jooste was named *M'chena hoochie* meaning in direct translation, "tigerfish fearless," because of his great ability and fearlessness in water. Jeffrey, a later hunting companion, was called *Kamwendo*, he who drags a leg, because of his permanently damaged leg. A much later hunting companion of mine, John Conner, they named *Chipisa moto*, the grass burner, because he was always lighting the grass. I once saw the Zambezi escarpment burning for miles through his actions. In later years my own name became *Kaporamujese*, meaning penetrator of dense thickets.

Here on the Serengeti I had a particular interest in observing the speedy cheetah, and often watched them through the lens of a single binocular chasing game at great speed. It was a powerful scope and for proper visual effect had to be mounted on a tripod. I saw the cheetah chase and single out antelope but never actually viewed the detail of the final frontal strike, perhaps because most times the chase went away from me or across my vision. Had I managed to get a cheetah coming toward me to make a kill, I may have seen the final contact.

From my observations I got the impression that cheetah prefer reaching for the shoulder or front leg of a victim when running parallel to it, but if a rear attack was necessary, the cheetah was equally adept clawing at its prey from the back. Then there would be a collapse in the dust and no more clear vision until it was too late to see details. The cheetah was impressive in its speed. It never behaved or looked like a true cat to me and certainly had no leopard characteristics that I could detect.

The charm of East Africa is its openness. Here, it seems, the African wilds are exposed for all to see. Lying astride the equator, it does not have a harsh climate and is an invitation to relaxation. But the high elevations become cold at night. At Karl Larsen's suggestion we combed through historical records in Dar es Salaam, he being able to speak and read German, and I found them very interesting. The area was known early on as German East Africa, and it amused me to hear Mount Kilimanjaro referred to as the Kaiser Mountain. East Africa so impressed me that I reached the conclusion that there could be no greater game concentrations and thus no greater place of beauty.

I felt Tanganyika a fitting place for Selous, the hunter, who was shot while fighting the Germans toward the end of World War I.

I visited many other places of interest in Central, North, and East Africa and hunted in some of them, but those events are not relevant to this book. I eventually arrived back in Zanzibar. Faanie was there living it up as if there was no tomorrow. He too had moved around some. I had a hunting permit to reenter Mozambique from the Zambezi to the Rio Ruvuma, but Faanie informed me that the Portuguese authorities in Niassa were looking for me with a warrant of arrest. Faanie had obtained information that hunting permits were available without limit in Southern Rhodesia for elephant in the tsetse-fly areas. I doubted this information and thought instead of the Portuguese. I would not return to Zambezia at present—but there were other ways.

They could not keep me away from the wild waters of the Zambezi River even if I had to enter Mozambique via Mupata Gorge. In fact, there were always wild borders where the whole of northern Mozambique could be reached—across the British territory from Lake Nyasa, for example, as Katasoro had done. If need be, I could use him as a contact point on the lake. My hunting areas could also be reached via Southern and Northern Rhodesia on the river, and this prospect was inviting as I had as yet not penetrated the Luangwa Valley from the Zambezi.

The success of any such schemes would depend on knowing who the human hyena and leopard were, since eventually I would have to return to this element of humans. We parted again: Faanie remained to continue living it up in Zanzibar and Mombasa. He said he would follow me later.

To savour history, I arrived on the Rufiji River in southern Tanganyika, where I saw the remains of the old sunken German cruiser *Konigsberg*—the boat hunted down and found by the great hunter Pretorius in the 1914-1918 World War, as described in his interesting book *Jungle Man*.

I also visited the grave of famed hunter Frederick Courteney Selous near Beho Beho, where there were many species of wildlife. Tanganyika, from what I saw of it, was probably the greatest stronghold of wildlife in Africa at the time. This was a fitting setting for Selous, who was shot while fighting the Germans toward the end of World War I.

This change of atmosphere had restored my nervous system and physical energy and I felt healthy again, though I sensed I was becoming soft and not as fit as usual. My mind turned to hunting and other places: Always reserved in my memory, for example, was the story the old Portuguese hunter had told me at the village of Espungabera in Mozambique of the large bull elephant between the Sabi and Wanezi Rivers. It so happened that I never got there. In Zanzibar Faanie had spoken of his intention to hunt crocodiles in Mozambique and the Rhodesias, so with this and the Sabi-Wanezi River elephant areas in mind, I moved south.

Zambezi Crocodiles:

River Adventures and a Parting of the Ways—1951

From Tanganyika I motored the long, slow, overland route across Northern Rhodesia, eventually arriving at the home of Kam Cha Cha, the dancer, Nic Vlahakis by given name, a man of Greek descent living near the junction of the Zambezi and Kafue Rivers in Northern Rhodesia. On arrival I was surprised to learn that Faanie had come and gone before me and had been active on the Zambezi in the enterprise of shooting crocodiles for their skins. I was pleased to hear this and consequently borrowed a dugout and, with the help of a paddler, drifted lazily down the Zambezi River in the current of the west bank. It was a good, relaxed feeling to be home again on the mother river.

The current speeded up as we passed the Kafue River junction and within a day I found Faanie and George Jeffrey, a hunting companion, at Chief Chiawa's village. They had already hunted crocodiles, whose skins were on display, kept damp, stretched out one on top of the other, and stored in shade. These would be delivered to the market at Lake Industries in Tanganyika. Faanie had obtained legal permits for his enterprise in Lusaka, capital of Northern Rhodesia, giving us all access to anywhere on the Zambezi River of that country. He and

The home of Kam Cha Cha, the dancer, Nic Vlahakis by given name, living near the junction of the Zambezi and Kafue Rivers.

George Jeffrey, a half-caste resident on the river, had formed an enterprise and I became the third partner.

They complained that they were not getting enough skins. The crocodiles were plentiful, but daylight shooting had quickly made them wary. Crocodiles have amazing eyesight and sharp hearing; on being persecuted they soon became elusive. Their ears consist of small apertures over which fits a shutterlike mechanism that closes as they submerge and opens to listen when on land. In addition they have transparent film coverings over their eyes. This filmy lens gives them clear, undistorted vision underwater and, when rolled back, sharp eyesight on land.

With a persecuted creature of such good senses, it became increasingly difficult to get within rifle range, especially as the crocs lingered so close to the water's edge that they could disappear into the river in seconds. We decided to use torches to detect their eyes at night, drifting up to them in the dugouts. Essentially, we had to shoot to hit the brain at close range so that a second person could reach out and catch a leg to tie or haul the dead crocodile behind the boat.

Dugouts, even large ones, are not stable enough for tackling crocodiles—they served mostly as our river taxis. Any shot missing the brain could cause considerable danger as the croc would either submerge and be lost or, worse still, thrash violently as you reached out for a foot at that critical moment. Occasionally a wounded croc's tail would hit the dugout with tremendous force, making the craft shudder. If you lost balance, you had to hang on for life to rebalance the craft as there were other crocs about in the dark waters of the night.

We needed a more stable boat, and this we got from Kam Cha Cha. The work was better now, but still we had some close, dangerous encounters. In desperation Faanie sawed half the barrels off a shotgun and firmed them. This gun proved successful as the enlarged area of heavy shot or spray allowed for human error, immobilizing the crocodiles because it virtually scooped out the brain cavity. With a stable boat, an outboard motor to traverse wide waters, shotgun, torches, and paddles, we were successful. It was not a type of hunting to my liking, partly because of the mosquitos and other insect pests that were attracted in great numbers by the lights. But Faanie, a man of great ability in water, was content to carry on with it. He certainly deserved his native name *M'chena ahooche* (fearless tigerfish).

Jeffrey, well known for his hippo hunting activities, added to our success by shooting, lacerating, and staking hippo in the water next to the islands: They were irresistible bait to the crocodiles. In an hour on the first night of this strategy we shot more crocs than we had in a week on previous hunts.

This was more like it, so we placed two more dead, lacerated hippos close together in about four feet of water. We gave the crocs plenty of time to congregate as we sat around the campfire a considerable distance away, listening to their activities. It was a dangerous experiment since Faanie and Jeffrey had decided to tackle the crocs by standing in the water and blinding them with torches. When we got to the bank, I was amazed to see so many croc eyes in such a small area. I had hardly taken in the scene when Faanie began shooting, using the torch to aim at crocodile brains. There was no current here, and as the reptiles sank slowly Jeffrey and I grabbed legs to pull and float them ashore. In the commotion some crocs in their hunger were still seizing and twisting off pieces of hippo carcasses. We got about fourteen this way until most became wary, submerging into deeper water.

Jeffrey and I were standing in about four feet of water, more than deep enough for a crocodile attack. Faanie had moved even farther and deeper, expecting us to follow, and was shooting faster than we could grab them. Up to then Jeffrey and I had acted in silence, remaining mostly behind and to the side of the light. Now I could feel the situation getting out of hand.

My instincts of self-preservation took over and I shouted at Faanie, "Slow down, or I leave the crocs," meaning the dead ones.

In the fever of his excitement I heard him say a few times, "Grab, Englander, grab."

Jeffrey and I both had short spears, and as our eyes had become accustomed to the dark we could at most times see any water disturbances. Our safety seemed to be in Faanie's firepower, and it helped to stay out of the torch light. The crocs were giving way now, and the light revealed some a distance off in the current. I thought it unlikely with the almost constant explosion of the shotgun that they would submerge at that distance and attack underwater.

As a youngster I had swum many miles on large lakes, but that did not qualify me here in four feet of water with these crocodiles. This crazy night hunting was working, but it was also becoming too dangerous.

I did not want to abandon my companions, so I shouted, "OUT, all of us out!"

At that moment I saw a large croc head coming over the water in a straight line for Jeffrey. I shouted a warning too late; at the last moment I saw Jeffrey thrust his spear at it and shout, "Oh, my God!" He fell over backward and disappeared under the dark water, the croc above him on the surface. It all happened in seconds. As the croc passed me, I stabbed my spear into it from the side.

Unarmed now, there was no way I would stay in the water. I shouted, "Jeffrey has gone under—get out, get out!" and waded and splashed toward shore. Then Jeffrey rose out of the water and Faanie and I both dashed back to grab and haul him, safe and sound, out onto land.

It should be mentioned here that Jeffrey earlier had damaged a leg in a hunting accident and could hardly bend it. I know of no other man who would stand in water hunting crocs with such a leg, and though it was senseless, I had to admire him.

Faanie shone the torch around. We had beached twenty-one crocs, and I was amazed that they had lingered so long to be shot at. Others were no doubt lost underwater. Then I saw the one with two spears in it. It had apparently been stunned as it came at Jeffrey and continued on to beach itself. To make sure it was dead Jeffrey speared it in the brain. Considering our success and what had happened, I felt lucky to have emerged intact from Faanie's watery lunatic asylum. We were elated by the haul, but for my part, I knew my nervous system could not take this experience every night. Thank God the time needed to hunt and stake the hippos gave me breaks.

Looking over the kill, Faanie said, "You must admit, I looked after you children, since no live croc got near you."

"What about the one that came at Jeffrey?" I asked.

"Well," he said, "I don't know what happens under the water—maybe that's where he came from." Then he said, "Don't worry, Englander, this idea works and we are all alive and in a short time we will be back in Zanzibar living it up again."

I asked him why he always had to tackle a chore with such zest, fury, and disregard for others. His usual answer was something like, "Don't worry, Englander, one day you might adjust to Africa." Or, "You're just neurotic, Englander." We staked the crocs, knowing from past experience that although dead they at times moved enough to reach water. It must have been some kind of reptilian reflex.

In the early morning Jeffrey hailed the locals from the mainland and they came over to do the skinning and later the treating of skins, under supervision. Here on the large sandbar island it was shadeless and would become increasingly hot. So the skinning came first, and then we camped on the mainland to do the skin treatment. Before leaving the island, Faanie got our labour force to pull the croc carcasses into the current saying, "Have a feed, brothers, have a good feed," addressing the fish and other crocodiles.

We examined Jeffrey's crocodile. It was about twelve feet in length, and we saw where Faanie in his feverish shooting had missed the brain, semi-paralyzing the croc with a spread of heavy shot along the neck. The brain of a croc lies under a thin, bony plate just behind the eyes. The largest we ever shot was sixteen feet long and had tremendous girth and weight. I doubt whether any creature, with the exception of elephant and hippo, could physically resist such a large reptile, particularly in water.

Crocodiles are not only deadly in the water. We at times tested them on land, while we lounged in the winter sun near the banks. If the crocs were far enough from the water, we ran to cut them off—it sometimes became a game and I estimated that a middle-sized croc had the speed of a fit man on land. Once, in a humourous mood, I chased one, shouting. The croc was large and heavy and did not have my top speed. Finally, just by the shoreline, it spun around and faced me. I was naked and unarmed. His open jaws were hugely impressive, and as a man tends to be realistic when naked and exposed, I gave him the whole of the Zambezi Valley. (It is perhaps not widely realized that running crocodiles raise themselves well off the ground on their powerful short legs, giving their bodies clearance for speed.)

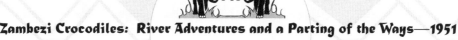

Many times I watched leguans (monitor lizards) hunting for and finding places where crocodiles had laid their eggs under the sand for the heat to hatch them. At times the croc would be close by guarding the nest, but the patient leguans eventually dug under the sand and consumed the eggs. The leguans would lay their eggs in hidden places, including anthill nests.

We had on occasion entered the large Ka Koma Marara, Chipara, Nyakasanga, and Chipandehoure swamps, favorite breeding and mating places for crocodiles. It was in the days when the Zambezi River broke its banks, before the great dams. These swamps were dangerous places, with big game feeding in the reedbeds and the crocodiles partly visible, half covered in mud and ooze. The crocs would make their nests on the few dry patches of land and lie close enough to guard their eggs.

Crocodiles are unpredictable. Should an intruder rob their nests of eggs, they seem more concerned for their own safety, for not only do they fail to protect their eggs, they will slip into the water for sanctuary. But there are frightening records of their bold, unexpected attacks, and I personally knew one that had the reputation for listening to human activities on the banks and then rushing across land to speedily seize the victim and escape back into the water again. This crocodile became so bold that it was eventually shot with a muzzle-loader and later found washed up on a sandbar.

It should be understood that a crocodile is usually the victor when it seizes a victim. A man armed with spear or knife has a chance, but even then the croc often wins. In water crocs are absolute masters of attack. Crocodiles are even known to take full-grown rhino into watery graves. With such deadly power, an unarmed human has no defense. I know of some Europeans and others, especially women and children collecting water at the rivers, who have been seized and carried to a hideous end.

One such European man, named Rankine, was either fishing or birdwatching on the banks of the Sanyati River where it ran into the Zambezi, above and prior to the building of the giant Kariba Dam. I am going on hearsay, but Rankine was seized on the bank and pulled into the water by a crocodile. He fought it off, probably with a knife, but on emerging near the bank was seized again, by the same croc or another. He again fought it off and managed to emerge on the bank. Although he won the fight for his life, the episode cost him a hand and a leg. He must have been a man of courage and determination to have survived such attacks. I met him after that, but, having gotten the story secondhand, I did not question him on it. I record these happenings to emphasize the risk of crocodiles. I have a natural fear and loathing of them, particularly in water, where they are in their element and I am out of mine.

Crocs are hard to study because most of their time is spent away from human vision, under the surface of the water. An observer begins his study, however, by viewing them basking in the sun close to their sanctuary, the water. They have keen eyesight and most times see you before you spot them, after which they will glide into the water, giving you the impression that there is no danger.

On close scrutiny, however, if you remain still long enough, they emerge, showing nostrils and eye sockets on the surface. In the sanctuary of water they take in all details of what is on the surface, the banks and vegetation, and little detail escapes their eyes. They have a good sense of direction above and below the surface, and I have even seen crocs fool baboons drinking at the waters edge. The croc will swim away from them, showing only a tip of nose, but then suddenly it will emerge amongst them, seize one, and quickly move back into the water before any counterattack could take place. On other occasions they lie still just under the surface and suddenly emerge vigorously, as if from nowhere, and seize a victim on the shoreline.

A most distinctive and frightening feature of crocodiles is that they cannot be anticipated or identified, even just a few feet under water. In the Zambezi River their coloring so blends in with a rippling water surface and the mottled reflections of the sand underneath that they remain unseen until they move their tails.

There seems to be a certain familiarity between men and crocodiles. I would say that humans, despite all their intelligence, are less wary of crocs than many other animals. I think it is because people see them so often while boating on the rivers, whereas game animals mostly see crocodiles only when they strike. For this reason, game would prefer to drink from dirty-looking shallow pools close to the Zambezi rather than the river itself.

The actual attack and/or retreat impulse of crocs is hard to define. In the Months of the Sun I have at times seen tribal children playing in the shallow water's edge with crocodile noses and eye sockets protruding nearby in the current. On those occasions I was well hidden in vegetation on high banks, with the advantage of waiting for an attack. Should the children be in danger, I had the time to shoot just under the surface at the crocodiles. Most times the crocs would lie there, hardly moving at all. If they so much as dropped out of sight, I would immediately yell at the children to clear out. Children are certainly easier to catch than baboons, and yet on most occasions the crocs would leave them alone. On other occasions they seized them unexpectedly.

One can travel for many miles on the rivers without mishap and then hear of some unfortunate person being taken by a croc as he stepped out into shallow water from a boat or dugout. I have on rare occasions had crocs come up to the dugout on the surface and reluctantly submerge only when we shouted and beat the paddles on the water.

They are cunning and patient and yet at times appear to have hyena cowardice. On other occasions they become inexplicably bold and deadly. Their attacks come in a flash, and I often wondered whether they were triggered merely by hunger. Whatever the reason, woe betide the creature caught by a crocodile in the water.

We continued our pattern of crocodile hunting, learning how to operate in safer ways, and were so successful that the crocs became quite wary. They relished the hippo bait but also realized it meant their end. Eventually they became cunning enough to float at a distance in the current at night to observe us, not coming to the bait anymore. We would retreat for a long time and slowly come back, but they knew what our presence meant and submerged to move away from the carcasses again. We then changed our habits, not wading into the water but rather using the boat near the carcasses, but the crocs caught on to that ploy and moved out into the wide waters and stayed there. We had obviously overshot the area and had to give it a rest.

Crocodile hunting had no real appeal to me, but we were in partnership and I had to carry my weight. As they diminished in numbers, it pleased me to know that eventually they would lose their value by becoming so widely dispersed over large areas that it would not make business sense to pursue them.

It was noticeable now that these crocs no longer lingered around human watering places. The hunters had become the hunted, and so we lounged and swam in the river, but always with one of us armed and watching from a high bank for protection. It is said that crocodiles in their present form have not changed in millions of years. The thought struck me that never over all that time had they been so intensively hunted as in our era. As a result, they had become positively shy and always alert to escape. I felt confident that we could travel the waters freely, thinking of them as a less dangerous menace.

We switched to hunting crocodiles in the dense swamps of the Zambezi and river confluences. I was apprehensive about the swamps. We all had entered some of these swamps and knew of the mixed danger imposed by the variety of animals feeding there, especially at night. Elephant cows in particular, plus buffalo and lion, were concerns, and we would be firing in thick vegetation where big animals could stampede over us. There was little room to maneuver and no trees for protection in the dense reedbeds. It must be realized that the Zambezi, in those days before the building of the Kariba Dam, used to overflow its banks periodically during the annual floods, its waters feeding the vegetation for miles inland and then slowly receding. As a result the swamps remained well watered and thick with mud, stagnant surfaces, and massive, dense reedbeds.

Jeffrey, our hunting companion, was one of those rare uncommunicative people, but when called upon he was a man of action. He had been named *Kamwendo* (he who drags a leg) by the tribesmen. There was no doubt his heart was in the right place. He was a half-caste, having Malay and white blood, and was wiry and of great strength and determination. I had learned this while hunting elephant with him in the foothills of the west-bank escarpment where he temporarily resided.

He was possessed of great stamina and could walk most hunters into the ground on a safari, even with his damaged leg. He never showed signs of physical fatigue or discomfort—except in rough terrain in the hills, where his almost unbending leg gave him trouble. It was because of his leg that we avoided the rough terrain of the Manyanedzi Pools, meaning "the pools of reflecting stars," a beautiful place on the Kafue River at the base of the western Zambezi Valley escarpment. It must have been very close to where Livingstone stood viewing the Zambezi Valley when he saw the greatest concentration of big game in Africa.

Jeffrey was dark-skinned, with curly black hair and penetrating black eyes. His incredible eyesight could pick up distant details on the open waters of the Zambezi River. By nature he was a decisive and violent man, not one to stir up. Yet in other respects he was likable, though I didn't really know why. Perhaps it was his guts, determination, and ability to silently cope with harsh conditions. He was the opposite to Faanie in some respects, being distant and uncommunicative. I sometimes studied Jeffrey from the side as he watched and listened to other people gathered around in the camp. After a while he would rise and move away, usually to the banks of the Zambezi, where he would gaze out across its great length and width, seeming to find himself again.

On some of those occasions, after leaving him to himself for a while, I would sit with him. Once I asked him why he so abruptly left the company of others. His reply was not without humour. After much thought he said, "They talk for hours, saying nothing, and they tire me. It's like hunting cow elephant—they work on my nerves and there is no reward in having to listen to them."

I often felt something like that myself, so I understood what he meant. His great weakness was European liquor, especially gin, and having it available in camp was dangerous, given his violent, aggressive, and murderous nature. I was probably the only man he could tolerate under such conditions. He seldom spoke in English but made himself well understood. When he did speak, every sentence was to the point and no arguments. He was a man of simple fact. He never spoke to me by name until one day he saw a tin of *Milo*, a type of chocolate drink. I made him a drink and he liked it. He picked out some writing on the tin and said, "Baby food," and from that time onward he called me "Little Boy."

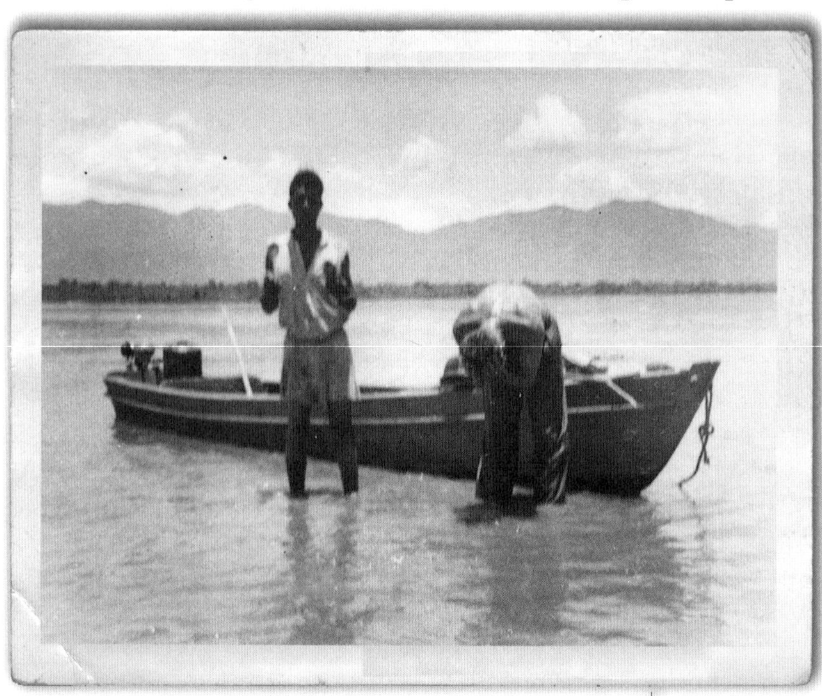

Jeffrey was dark skinned with curly black hair and penetrating black eyes.

At times Jeffrey was unfathomable, and to enquire

into his background at those times would bring about that fierce, penetrating stare. It was unfortunate that this man with his mysterious character was a natural cause for curiosity. He loved being on the river hunting hippo, perhaps because that kind of hunting kept him off his bad leg. Or the hippo may have tipped him from his dugout at some stage, making him revengeful, for he showed them no mercy. For whatever reason, he had a passion for hippo hunting. At times he would go in amongst them, taking them from dugouts in the open waters. Such close-quarters hunting posed great risks from both hippo and, if the boat was capsized, from crocodiles.

Jeffrey was outlawed on the eastern banks of the Zambezi River in Southern Rhodesia, but because he knew the country and the chiefs well, he crossed over when convenient. He impressed me as a man who took only what was necessary to maintain himself on his beloved Zambezi. It was noticeable that the tribesmen were in fear and awe of him. I gathered from his knowledge of certain elephant and rhino haunts that he was a poacher, though he seldom spoke of his activities. At times, when drunk or disturbed, he would boast that whole of the Zambezi Valley lived in fear of him. This, at the time, was all the background I had on Jeffrey.

I always felt that the heat of such men as Jeffrey could not burn out of them while alive—and so it happened. When Jeffrey was eighty-four years old, in 1982, he and three others were arrested while poaching in the Zambezi Valley below Mana Pools. In my mind, such a man, even in old age, could only be taken if caught unaware. Because of his advanced age, it was thought that he might die on the arresting authorities' hands, and consequently they later released him to cross the Zambezi River into Zambia. There he was attacked by relatives of the other captives, probably because he was released and they were not. In any event, it was said that he either shot himself or was struck down by a chopper to the head. I sincerely hope that the blade went straight to his brain.

There were discussions about whether we should hunt the swamps during day or night or both. Faanie was outvoted, and we took to the swamps during daylight hours. I thought this croc hunting would only last a few months, and then we would be back amongst the elephant during the Months of the Sun.

On the first early morning that we entered the swamp, we heard straggler elephant families and buffalo that had not yet vacated it. Other large herds had left to go inland to their daytime bush sanctuaries; they would return at night to feed in the swamps. The daylight stragglers, which remained unalarmed, were an indication that humans almost never entered the swamps. We came across the marks of crocs' slithering tails and clawed feet. Here, of necessity, we were heavily armed with defensive weapons. The smallest-caliber rifle was Jeffrey's 9.5mm Mannlicher, a beautifully fashioned weapon but in my estimation lacking penetrating power when used on big-boned bull elephant.

Being used to his own rifle, he refused one of our other weapons, a .404, and so we left it at that. The swamp reeds were frighteningly tall and thick, and I told Faanie that we must always be upwind before shooting as

I was fearful of elephant stampedes here in the dense reeds. Our vision was limited, sometimes a matter of a few yards. While meandering over and wading through mud shallows and occasionally dry ground, we sighted the first bunch of crocs, a dozen or so, half-lying in shallow mud. Because they constantly heard much animal feeding noises around them, they were not alarmed and moved only when we got close and they saw us. It was too late—we opened fire.

Since they were hampered by the reeds we got them all, except for one that ran off. This was the croc's environment, but not when they had to crash their way through the reeds. I followed this one close to where it lay thinking it was concealed, much as it would have in water. But land is man's element, and there I shot it in the only visible place, its shoulder formation. It was large enough, about eleven feet, and as I approached from the back, it lashed out with its tail, smashing the reeds around it.

I could hear Faanie and Jeffrey behind me as they looked at the dead crocodiles and in the distance heard the neurotic trumpeting and squeals of cow elephant disturbed by our gunfire. The usual Zambezi wind was blowing, but we were safe enough for the moment because we were downwind of the herd. I called my companions to come see this croc that did not act like a hyena but stood to fight. Jeffrey was the first to realize that my bullet had smashed the shoulder, immobilizing it, but they could see from the smashed reeds how dangerous the tail was.

"I prove to you, little boy, that he cannot hurt us now," said Jeffrey as he approached. He stood directly in front of the croc, extending his rifle until the croc snapped at it. The proximity of those large jaws was frightening, but Jeffrey was confident.

"See," Jeffrey said, "he cannot reach me; we have learned something today—better than listening to all the rubbish people speak."

And so it was that we learned to immobilize crocodiles by a shot to the shoulder. Had we previously used this technique, instead of other body shots, our losses would not have been as great. From then on we used this shot extensively, then hacked them in the brain with a chopper to save ammunition.

By now the elephant cows were cutting up roughly, and as we had the first day's prize we temporarily postponed hunting in hopes that the elephant would leave the swamps during the day. Upon traversing the area to get the skinners, we passed three medium-sized crocs partly hidden in the reeds. We all knew we were now close to the elephant. No longer disturbed, the herd had quieted down, but Faanie, unable to resist the temptation to try the shoulder shot, fired at a croc without warning. I had placed myself behind Jeffrey because of his leg, and Faanie was behind me. We all knew the elephant were near. When Faanie fired all hell broke loose, with angry elephant trumpeting and roaring. Even amidst these danger signals, Faanie shot still another crocodile.

With two having been immobilized, Faanie was attempting to follow the third crocodile when Jeffrey, his bad leg nearly immobile in the reeds and shallow mud, shouted, "They are Chirundu elephant!" meaning they had come from the five-mile strip on either side of the main Chirundu Road. This had been set aside as an extermination area for game.

The government in its backward stupidity had hoped to eradicate tsetse flies, but its extermination edict had resulted in many wounded animals, and worst of all, the strip cut across the elephant migratory routes so that the animals had at times to run the gauntlet of rifle fire while passing through it. We were all veteran hunters and between us had the skill for deadly accurate firepower. But here vision was limited to only a few yards, and the rifle shots had given the elephant our exact position.

The frightening sounds of reeds snapping under large feet indicated the speed and direction of the oncoming elephant, and we stood right in their path. The stupid Dutchman Faanie had caused them to come stampeding onto us. The sound of the stampede reminded me of hail I had heard as a child coming down on tin roofs. That staccato sound of snapping reeds increased in intensity.

We then hacked them in the brain with a chopper to save ammunition.

"Impulsive son of a bitch!" I shouted.

Then Jeffrey said, "These elephant have been to school," meaning that they were educated in the ways of man. It is absolutely terrifying and demoralizing to stand in front of stampeding elephant—much worse than a series of charges—and there in the reeds it was worst of all. There was no escape. Above the rapidly approaching noise I shouted at Jeffrey and Faanie to be reassured of their readiness. Then, all at once, I started losing hope and shouted to Faanie, "Son of a bitch, you'll get us all killed!"

Suddenly I realized Jeffrey had the lesser gun, so I moved to his side, placing him in the middle as we stood close in a row. Faanie, in fear but still possessed of humor, shouted, "Don't forget to shoot, Englander," as if there was an alternative.

In those moments of impending death I had disturbing flashback thoughts of when I had annihilated the troop of elephant bulls in the tropical storm. It brought about the same guilty feeling inside me, a foreboding that too many elephant were coming too fast, a feeling of intense fear that the odds against us were too great and that I would not survive the day. I thought, Nyschens, you bastard, your time is up, this is your end. I mentally accepted my fate, rationalizing that at least it would be better and certainly quicker than dying in a bed.

Then the elephant broke cover at speed, their nearness making me believe they could reach for me. Jeffrey, with his keen eyes, was the first to shoot through the reeds at oncoming heads. I had glimpsed the reality of the situation and fired before the terror got to me. The speed with which they came at us was unnerving, and I was conscious of nothing other than elephant heads and the rifle pounding my shoulder. Hasty but effective fire was our only hope to avoid being trampled and flattened into the earth. The huge animals dropped as rapidly as they came at us.

Miraculously the main body of elephant passed, and we survived the onslaught; the death of any one of us would have lessened our firing effectiveness and almost certainly caused the deaths of the other two.

As the firing diminished, I saw many dead elephant forming a wall in front us as the others tore past on either side. Thankful to have survived, I listened to the elephant continuing on like hail receding, waiting to hear if they would regroup. But by the sounds they did not, as we heard them careening off in the distance. Their attack and panicked speed had carried them running downwind, contrary to their normal habit of running into the wind so they could learn what lay ahead. No doubt the leading cows had attacked by sound only, carrying the others along in their wake.

We experienced the usual short silence that follows a serious shoot-up when men are at their lowest ebb. Then I stepped forward. Four paces brought me to the first line of dead elephant, closer to Jeffrey than me. I leaned against one that had crashed upright with its head on another, and I turned, looking in disbelief at Faanie. I had enough adrenaline left to feel murder in my heart.

Beyond the dead elephant, the reeds had been flattened into a tunnel by the force of the stampede. In the face of this monumental folly I realized no single man could have fired quickly enough to prevent his own death. I ran up on a dead elephant. Others lay beyond the first line, probably another dozen.

Unconsciously I said, "*Machende pamusoro*" (testicles raised in fear), but it no longer had its humorous appeal. This close call with disaster wasn't just a matter of Faanie being fearless in character; it was much more than that: His moment of amateurish stupidity had needlessly risked our lives—and for what? Mounds of meat would go to the scavengers, we had wasted expensive ammunition, and measly cow tusks were the only tangible result. The audacious impetuosity of Faanie to have gambled with my life! It meant I had virtually no control over this menace to our lives. No one had control over this man, not even himself. Was it stupidity, conceit, overconfidence, or madness? I was convinced it was a form of uncontrollable madness, and so I made a decision. Faanie said something that must have been very humorous, for I saw Jeffrey smile, something he seldom did.

"You and I," I said, "we don't hunt anymore. It's a dead deal."

"You will feel different," Faanie said.

"Look at all the crocodile bait here in the swamps!" I said. "Crocs are your business, and elephant mine. You still have not learned elephant; otherwise, we would have been able to move out of the swamps undisturbed, not having to fight for our lives. This was more in your line, like a stupid war, not hunting. Son of a bitch, my life is mine, not yours!"

He called out, "You will feel different tomorrow." But I did not. Our parting of the ways there and then in the swamp was the right decision. I felt Jeffrey's penetrating eyes on me and said as I left, "Watch yourself—that bastard will get you killed."

There was high humidity in the swamp. My clothing clung to my body from the excessive sweat, which did not diminish until I reached the higher ground. Furious at the circumstances that found me sloshing through a dangerous swamp, I was forced to concentrate on my way through the dense reeds—my anger was temporarily diverted to the task at hand.

Above the swamp at the main camp I collected my gear, loaded a dugout, and summoned a helper. Not until I was finally on the waters of the Zambezi did my anger begin to abate. As the river calmed me down, I was reminded of days gone by—alone on the mother river and in control of my own destiny again. That night we slept on a sandbar downriver, where I felt relieved of the responsibility and risks of other people's lives and knew that I was better off alone, at least for the time being.

I had decided to go downstream to the Chewori River junction, close to where I had hunted the elephant bulls in the tropical rain storm. It was pleasant and relaxing to travel downstream and see the occasional reedbeds, the high banks, and trees passing by. I stayed along the north bank, where usually the current is stronger and faster from the effects of the Kafue River spilling into the Zambezi miles upstream. This was the country of Chief Chiawa. His second village could not be seen from the river, so I paddled in to a landing point where there were many dugouts. I had the memory of Kampari and his family, who had befriended me in the Mupata Gorge in my moments of loneliness and despair. His wife had come from this country of Chief Chiawa, where they had said they would settle. I followed a path through a minor reedbed and emerged on the bank, where I spoke to a few tribesmen. They did not know of Kampari or his whereabouts. Not satisfied, I proceeded to the village and found Chief Chiawa himself. He knew of no one named Kampari. I was disappointed, for I had anticipated spending a few nights around the fires with Kampari. Where the hell could he disappear in the wilderness of this valley, I wondered.

After a few hours of futile questioning of others I returned to the dugout and continued downstream. We passed the Chongwe stream confluences and from here on we were in the endemic sleeping-sickness area, a large section unpopulated by people, where I was hopeful of getting a few elephant bulls. Much farther downstream from the confluences, a full day's travel, I found spoor, but not recent enough, so I camped and looked around.

There was thick, frightening bush with much feed for elephant, and after a few days we eventually found fresh spoor and followed it. These elephant had been hunted previously and were masters at hiding in the thick bush and using the wind to their advantage. Upon being disturbed or approached, they would rush off a few hundred yards and take sanctuary again. They never gave me a chance to close in on them, but played us out all day.

The tracker, Furese, an employee lent to me by Kam Cha Cha, was doing his best and spoored reasonably well, but his nerves were going to pieces. I was conditioned to this reaction but felt helpless and frustrated. Day after day we persisted in following, and on the third day these elephant, finding no peace in the thick bush, left and headed across the beautiful parklike country to the western escarpment. All we got from this hunt were the bites of many tsetse flies in a sleeping-sickness area. Insects had killed tens of thousands of people in Africa, possibly millions, but that was just another occupational hazard associated with getting ivory, and luckily we suffered no ill effects.

Next day, it was back to the river and the relaxed life again. That afternoon, while passing a reedbed, I saw the backs of two elephant feeding, their bodies mostly hidden by the reeds. We pulled up on the bank below them, but because the wind always comes upstream on the Zambezi, I thought they would certainly scent us. I approached the reeds and heard the animals deep within. I cautioned Furese, saying that although we had seen only two, there could be more. We entered the reeds, moving in on the sounds as the elephant thrashed and fed. In their noisy activity they did not know I was there until the last moments. To get close enough in the thick reeds, I moved in until the first bull saw me. He raised his head and ears, and as he began the dip action of his back legs preparatory to a charge, I shot him. The other, now alarmed, also saw me and turned, and as he did so I put him down also. We heard others running inland through the reeds. The ivory was not much, about forty-five pounds per tusk, but it would pay my costs here.

We stayed on a sandbar for the night and established a camp on the riverbank early next morning. I left Furese to remove the ivory and walked downstream, where I found old village sites with the remains of round rings on the ground indicating that huts had been there at some time, probably many years back. I returned to the previous hunting site, where I assisted Furese in removing the ivory.

From here downstream along the river there were floodplains much as one sees at Nemana Pools, but smaller. It became obvious—as I was later to experience while traveling in the floods—that the confluence of the Zambezi and Rukometje Rivers in Southern Rhodesia at high waters caused floods to sweep across the Nemana area, aided by rain catchments inland. The torrents then swept much farther downriver to where the Zambezi would again break its banks, flooding inland on the west bank in Northern Rhodesia as far as and beyond the area of Chief M'baruma. This was the center of the deadly sleeping-sickness section of the Zambezi Valley, but a place of impressive vegetation and watered areas, with the escarpment mountains looming in the background.

The word used to describe the floodplains in Southern Rhodesia, when I first heard it spoken by the KoreKore tribe, was *nemana.* Later they used the word *mana*, but when I spoke to old Chief Mudzeemo, he always referred to it as *tamana*, meaning a place so full of wild animals that man could escape from man there. It could also mean danger from man or beast. I can only surmise that it may have been a place of retreat when the warring Matabele armies penetrated into the KoreKore country in their raiding activities.

On the second day we took to the river again for a few hours, then crossed to the east bank so that I would not miss the Chewori River junction. We at last found it and camped where there were signs of old huts but no people. Here the scenery had a rugged, enticing atmosphere with inhospitable stony hills, slopes, gullies, and flat land suggesting a rainy-season runoff. The unusual landscape had a combination of forest trees, grasses, and bushlands and was particularly intriguing as the African sun set and the harshness left the sky, causing feelings of isolation and loneliness. Such scenes always held me spellbound for a while, especially when I could view them from higher ground.

That night I told Furese I intended to visit Chief Chundu at the base of the eastern escarpment, probably a two-day walk. He had the option of coming or staying in camp. He preferred coming with me, so the next morning we hid the dugout and, with a few provisions and water, proceeded overland, following the dry Chewori watercourse. We soon learned that the river meandered a lot, doubling the distance, so I moved away from the Chewori and walked in a straight line to where I thought Chundu's village would be.

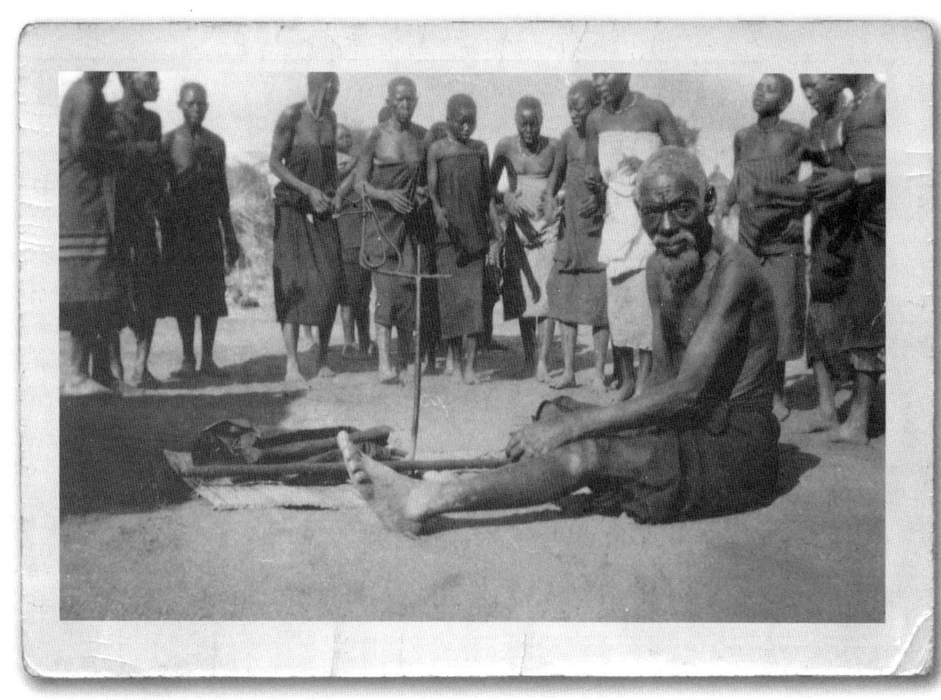

The metal god named Chimombe Kasimbe.

The place was wild and isolated, with the rugged Wadoma Hills in the background. We came across large numbers of undisturbed game but also large areas with no life at all. We could not reach Chundu's village the first night, so we searched for and found water under the sand of the dry riverbed, ate, and slept around a fire. We walked out before full light and arrived at Chundu's village about midday. He was not an impressive chief and was at first wary of us, but thanks to Furese's talkative and pleasant nature he eventually relaxed.

Chundu had the typical look of tribespeople resident in tsetse and malarial areas—lean body, muscular, but frail looking with the whites of his eyes

Chimombe, a metal image looking somewhat like a praying mantis, was placed in the center of a reed mat.

discoloured by a slight yellow-cream tinge. No doubt many generations of living under these conditions gave them partial resistance to tropical diseases, and perhaps gave them that look. I thought this would be a good place to take elephant since we had seen some herds and the spoor of bulls, but it was probable that this chief would crack under official pressures, so I had to dismiss the idea from my mind. Besides, this area seemed too far from the Zambezi; the lower portion of the Chewori and Wadoma was probably better.

We stayed a few days near Chundu's village and witnessed a ceremony involving a metal god named Chimombe Kasimbe. Although pagan, the ceremony was impressive with much palaver and the beating of drums, the type of ritual that appealed to my primitive senses. Chimombe, a metal image looking somewhat like a praying mantis, was placed in the center of a reed mat, which was covered with black cloth, and surrounded by magical talismans with some unimpressive ivory to show it all off.

In the Sudan I had witnessed the grip religions such as Islam and Christianity had on millions of people. Regardless of how sophisticated or primitive, this one seemed no better or worse in fulfilling its purpose—to feed the soul of man. It is of interest to note that as of 1987 this same metal image was still worshipped in the same paganistic rites where it was kept by the new Chief Chundu, who, by that time, resided away from the valley in the escarpment. It must be understood that residing in the metal god Chimombe Kasimbe is the medium to communicate with the spirit world of ancestors.

Two days here were enough, so we headed back across the valley floor toward the Zambezi, occasionally touching on the curving Chewori River. There was abundant game big and small, including many rhino and masses of biting tsetse and mopane flies, the latter going for the liquid of the eyes and forcing us to use branch leaves to chase them off. We traversed open areas, thick bush, mopane forests, and thickets, and saw lion, leopard, and wild dog spoor, occasional bull elephant and many cows, buffalo in medium-sized herds, and always antelope and zebra. It is amazing how zebra survives over most parts of Africa.

On the second day, about ten miles from the Zambezi, we walked the sands of the Chewori riverbed trying to find water. Coming around a bend, we saw three short tribesmen, two armed with spears. Attached to one spear was a large, dead lizard with bush bark strapped along its length. I had never seen these people before but knew them as the Wadomas (Vadomas), a small clan living in the broken country of the Wadoma Hills, different in their ways and isolated from other tribes. Having heard stories, I was curious to meet them, but on seeing us they ran off down the sandy bed.

I gave chase and in a short time closed in on them and flung one to the ground, sitting on his back so I could get my breath again. While the others ran off, Furese came up with my rifle and gear. We questioned our captive, but he did not understand or did not want to communicate. So we tied him up with bush *tambo* (bark-strip rope). In the shade I tried to get some sense out of him but got no response. He eventually started wailing and muttering something insensible. He seemed dim-witted and backward, so we released him then watched him take his spear and sit on the opposite side of the dry river bed on the bank. I had wanted to test the truth of the rumour that his people had splayed feet and thus were known as the two-toed tribe. His were only broad, so we slowly approached and questioned him in KoreKore again.

He looked dense and did not seem to know what we wanted. Throughout my travels in Africa, I had found that most backward tribes had some form of intelligence, but this man here had none. I thought perhaps that these isolated people were inbred. It was useless, so we left him and moved off, but he kept following us at a distance, much like a dog I once had. This lasted a few miles and then we noticed he was no longer there.

We camped that night near the Chewori confluence and in the morning started the long upcurrent journey in the dugout. For days we battled upstream on the Zambezi, staying in the slower waters close to the shore. We eventually arrived at Chikwenya Island, the top part having shade trees and the

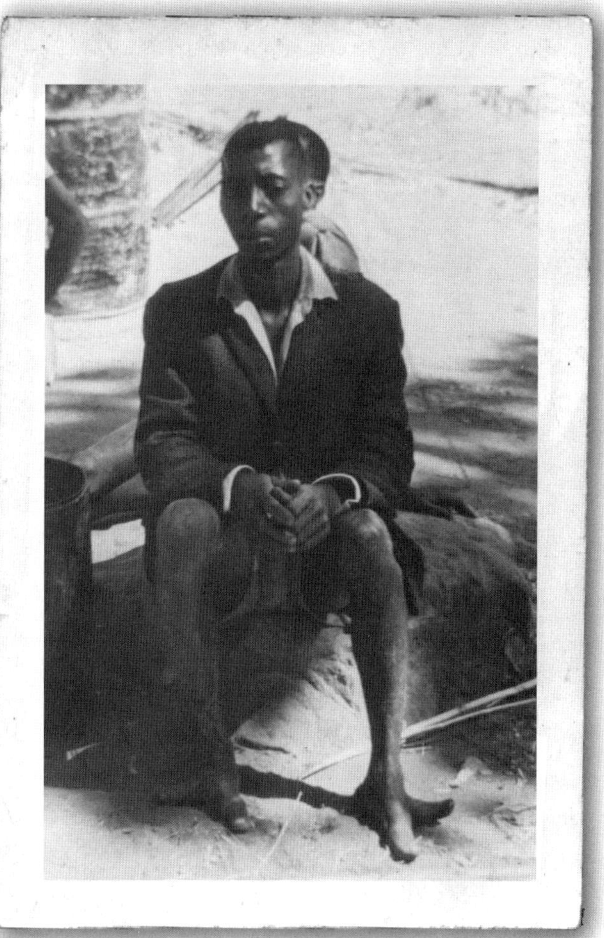

I had wanted to test the truth of the rumour that his people had splayed feet, and thus were known as the two-toed tribe.

We eventually arrived at Chikwenya Island . . . because of my meager possessions, I humourously named myself the Count of Chikwenya.

lower, downstream section covered with reeds. This pattern of vegetation was evidence that past floods had covered most of the island except for the upper treed part. We camped and looked around. Because of my meager possessions, I humourously named myself the Count of Chikwenya. Kam Cha Cha had given us line and hooks, and between our fishing skills and my supplies we lived well enough—certainly many times better than when I had experienced hunger and deprivation years earlier on my original penetration of the Mupata Gorge.

I ventured inland on foot up a dry watercourse (Sapi River) opposite our island, and found much evidence of elephant spoor in the sand bed of the river. It led through patches of forest and thick bush. That night we heard lion roar as if they were in competition with each other. In the morning we crossed again from our island and took the lion spoor, discovering where they had left the remains of two buffalo, mostly eaten. The marabou storks and vultures were already there, some on the ground and others perched in trees. As none of them had gone right up to the kills, I thought the lion might be lying close by in some cover, so I scouted around.

We disturbed hyena, and as they moved off I heard a few lion grunt, and they too moved in dense thickets, no doubt with full bellies. I left them because I wanted to see what game was in the area of their influence. We walked inland a mile or so and then parallel to the river. The vegetation began to thin out and give way to large *musango* trees (a forest tree, *Acacia albida*), which gave a beautiful parklike effect. In most places grass covered the ground as far as the eyes could see, even under the trees.

Antelope were there in impressive numbers—eland in particular in large herds, tame and staring at us. On approaching closer I wondered why they did not run off, merely parting and allowing us to walk through them. Strangely enough, they were not browsing as they usually do but feeding off the prolific grass growth, chewing and staring at us as they gave way to our progress. The same happened with the large buffalo herds and, farther on, hundreds of impala, waterbuck, many kudu and sable, zebra, and occasionally bushbuck

Now and then we could hear the grunting of distant hippo in the Zambezi.

and warthog. All the time we were within the sound of fish eagles calling their haunting cries along the river, probably a mile or so distant, and the cooing of the spotted wood doves.

I was taken by the sheer wild glory of this place. Eventually the giants themselves appeared, family herds of elephant feeding on the grasses and occasionally reaching high into the branches for the pods of the *musango* trees. Now and then we could hear the grunting of distant hippo in the Zambezi. We saw no lion or leopard, but their spoor were evident, and we came across hyena curiously staring at us from a distance. Everything looked so well fed, tame, and contented in such beautiful settings that it was like a mythical paradise, and I envisioned the Garden of Eden. The only threat I could see here was that at night the abundant wildlife might stumble upon me.

In the distance through the trees, the light and skyline indicated clearings, and we soon emerged to find depressions with large, elongated pools. Some were draining or receding because of both evaporation and the drinking of many animals. Crocodiles there were hesitant to move into the water and were still alert and watchful. They numbered in the hundreds. When we came very close they reluctantly slid into the water, and after a while, their nose tips appeared unobtrusively and they lay that way almost unseen for long periods.

We continued walking through alternating forest and grass-covered country, from pool to pool, among elusive crocodiles, until we decided to change our heading, moving farther inland. Tsetse flies continued to bite

The giants themselves appeared, family herds of elephant feeding on the grasses and occasionally reaching high into the branches for the pods of the musango trees.

us, mostly when we moved through thick bush or deep shade near water. Eventually we reached a particularly large pool with sparsely populated tree cover on its banks. In the distance, to the east, in ugly contrast, an anemic-looking scrub mopane forest rose on higher ground, suggesting an end to this well-watered fertile country.

It was evident from the spoor that the game also moved inland at times. From a high bank we saw shoals of fish in the large pool and, to my surprise, a dozen or so hippo, even though we were miles inland from the Zambezi.

In all my years in Africa, I had never seen a place nearly as beautiful. It was an unspoiled wilderness, the world as it once was. But even as I stood there, politicians and technocrats were planning its destruction: Waters behind the giant Kariba Dam, to be built upstream on the Zambezi River, would enshroud this place forever.

From our vantage point we could see where the Zambezi had overflowed, extending possibly three miles inland. It appeared that this complex lowland delta was created by tributaries of the Zambezi, irrigating the area and draining back into the river close to where we had left it. There was much evidence of alluvial deposits from past floods, enriching the earth with decayed matter that acted as a natural fertilizer. That is how this area replenished itself: The mighty Zambezi occasionally broke its banks to flood inland.

We felt loathe to leave this wonderland but did not like the idea of being here among the large game numbers at night. So we moved off back toward the river. The sun was already low, and I realized we would get back to Chikwenya Island in the darkness of night. On the return trip, we again passed through large animal herds. The elephant in particular were more numerous, and we had to circumvent one herd after another.

Now, near sunset, crocodiles were in the water, no doubt hunting fish or waiting for unwary animals to come to the pools to drink. I had unknowingly entered the paradise of Nemana, known as Mana Pools prior to the building of the Kariba Dam. Although enthralled by this place, I was glad to emerge from the herds to reach Chikwenya Island that night. Next morning we paddled upstream a full day, landing at a place I thought was well into the Nemana Pools area. We camped, ate, and slept on the banks under large trees. But it was a disturbed night, there being too much game activity around us.

In the morning we walked inland again, Furese carrying fishing tackle and bait. Here too were large herds in beautiful country, everything so pleasing to the senses. Furese caught many fish, until I stopped him from wastefully catching more than we could eat or carry. I made sure this time that we got back before dark, and then we crossed the Zambezi River to sleep on the west bank in Northern Rhodesia, where I could get a good night's rest.

We spent about ten days exploring, walking first to Chief Dandawa's village on the Rukometje River. Habitation here consisted of family villages spread at intervals in the forest along the dry river's course. I spoke to the chief, who used the opportunity to complain of crop-raiding elephant and baboons during the crop seasons. This area was known for its witchcraft activities. Most of these small villages were in well-wooded, shady country, so I traversed them to reach the escarpment and the Nyakasanga River, and eventually went back across the valley floor away from the Rukometje River through dense thicket areas to reach the Zambezi again.

We paddled upriver again. Days passed before we reached Ka-Koma-Marara (the hills of the palms), eventually landing on Kanyemba Island and thereafter heading back to Kam Cha Cha's. Somewhere behind me I had passed Faanie and Jeffrey, still hunting crocodiles in the swamps.

While paddling upstream, subconsciously aware of the slow, strenuous pace—hour upon hour, day after day—I thought often of Nemana, that wonderful parklike country, and tried to visualize this country millions of years ago when prehistoric monsters had likely roamed the Zambezi Valley.

Mana Pools, as it is now known, strangely enough made me think of Cecil Rhodes, who imported the Mafia to Africa. He made a fortune in the Boer Republic of South Africa, only to use it to try to undermine that country. Failing, he concentrated his efforts on the Rhodesias because he thought there was great mineral wealth to be had there. He focused on gold, and the stronghold of that precious metal was close to Johannesburg and the power it represented. His visions of gold were tarnished, but his inglorious goal did not stop the English government from manipulating the Republican Boer government into a state of friction, causing the Boer War. The prize, of course, was the Johannesburg gold mines.

At the time the British Empire was strong and its war machine could back up enterprises. It took them three long years to defeat the uneducated Boer farmers. Their women and children were hounded and killed by starvation, exposure, and disease, and finally the Boers, in rags, had to surrender. An inglorious victory, but the British acquired the indirect control of the Johannesburg gold mines.

All this was done for gold, and Cecil Rhodes was a major part of it. At Mana I wondered if Rhodes, the founder and so-called father of the Rhodesias, would have raised himself from his chair to journey to see this wonderland, as all this land had been his, including the Mana wilderness.

The crocodile that attacked Athena.

After paddling in the bankside waters for days we arrived at a small village on the banks of the Zambezi River near Kam Cha Cha's. It was here that I learned the meaning of the word *"manderegerera."* This happening was pathetically disturbing; people were washing and others filling calabashes for drinking and cooking purposes. Amidst this domestic scene, a crocodile suddenly emerged and seized a woman, throwing her off her feet and pulling her into deep water. In fear and pain, fighting it alone with her bare hands, the desperate woman pleaded to her companions for help, but her cowardly friends abandoned her to the crocodile. In those last moments of her life, as she was dragged into the depths, she desperately called out, *"Manderegerera!"* meaning "You are leaving me to die."

On another occasion Kam Cha Cha's sister Athena was also attacked by a crocodile. In those days prior to the building of the Kariba Dam upriver, crocodiles were numerous, thanks to the area's abundant fish and other prey. Athena was a young woman (*musikana*) fishing with companions using a bulbous plant, known as *m'kondi*, to stun fish in a pool. The fish would rise after being struck and were gathered and thrown onto the bank. A crocodile seized Athena by a leg, fortunately in shallow water and, like the woman in other incident, she desperately fought the hungry reptile. Athena survived only because the others came to her aid. Her father (Jim the Greek) eventually managed to attract the crocodile from the water by using a goat in a cage as bait, and shot it.

Man-eating crocodiles follow definite patterns, very much like those of man-eating lion. Some crocodiles venture near villages to lie in wait to seize people, and, like lion, they are particularly deadly during the hours of darkness. I once lost a camp cook who disobeyed orders by collecting water at night. He did not return, and after a while I became alarmed. Upon lighting firebrands to illuminate the scene, I saw the ground signs where he had been seized by a crocodile.

At our base at Kam Cha Cha's, there were permanent abodes of sunburned brick on the west bank of the Zambezi River a few miles below Chirundu, which is the narrowest part of the river. Kam Cha Cha's father was known as Jim the Greek, one of two brothers who had arrived from Greece and settled at Chirundu in the early days. They were the Vlahakis brothers, Demetris and Nicolas.

Around the firelight Kam Cha Cha, the son of Demetris (Jim), related the story of how a lion had killed his uncle Nicolas. Apparently lion had swum across the Zambezi, which I have seen them do. They arrived in daylight at the Vlahakis's place and started to kill and maul the sheep herd, apparently knocking them down with their powerful paws. The herd boy, who had run for his life the half mile to the house, called the Vlahakis brothers to tell them their sheep were being preyed upon.

The brothers immediately armed themselves and arrived at the scene, by which time the lion, having had their fun, were feeding on the sheep in the shade. The two brothers managed to shoot some lion but wounded one. It is hard to say accurately what happened, but as they closed in on the wounded lion it charged and knocked them both down, guns flying, and then started

The Vlaharis Brothers

Buffalo in the minor reedbeds.

Demetris Vlahakis with eland bull.

Nicolas Vlaharis who succumbed to a lion mauling.

Buffalo hunted either by the Vlaharis brothers or the tracker.

mauling Nicolas. Demetris scrambled unarmed up a tree, where he had to witness the scene below of his brother fighting for his life. Nicolas eventually managed to locate his rifle and finally shot the lion. But he was in a bad state. He was taken to the district commissioner on the escarpment, but succumbed to poisoning caused by the lion's claws and teeth.

We spoke about Jeffrey, whom Kam Cha Cha knew well, and I found out more about Jeffrey's audacious and humourous exploits. He apparently dressed up properly only once a year when he would go to Lusaka, the capital city of Northern Rhodesia, to visit the district commissioner, who would renew his hunting license. This seemed to be his greatest anxiety each year. Here the stories of Jeffrey came together. Nowhere else was there information to be had, as the tribesmen feared him too much to talk of him. It amused me to hear him spoken of as *Kamwendo* (he who drags a leg) or Bwana Jeffrey, in his case meaning Lord Jeffrey.

I had been gone a long time from Salisbury and impetuously, past midday, decided then and there to motor back. The sun was setting as I crossed the steel bridge across the Zambezi River at Chirundu and motored from Northern to Southern Rhodesia. In the gloom of dusk I crossed the Zambezi Valley floor, then in darkness drove up the eastern escarpment where I made a camp in the foothills of the mountains. It was noticeable that there were hardly any animals, not even their usual sounds at night. In the morning I passed a place called Kent Halt and then entered the farming areas of the plateau on the long journey to Salisbury, where the air was even thinner and colder than in the escarpment mountains, so unlike the comfort and warmth of the great Zambezi Valley.

Zambezi Valley:

Paradise of Adventure—1952

The Southern Rhodesian portion of the middle Zambezi Valley is a place of wild charm with its bushlands, riverine areas, jess bush, and mopane forests. At the coming of winter I stood on the edge of the escarpment and gazed out on the magnificent panorama of this intriguing valley. It is a distinct valley—about sixty miles wide, with the Zambezi River flowing through it and impressive escarpments rising from plateaus on either side, both east and west. Thanks to the rains that clear the air, one can see the details of the valley floor and mountain ranges at great distance.

In the winter, because of the drying out of vegetation, burning of plateau grasslands, and the seasonal heat, a smoky, blue-gray haze hangs like a mysterious veil over the Zambezi Valley. The prevailing wind at most times comes from the east, the direction of the Indian Ocean—healthy breezes, oxygen laden from blowing through millions of trees on its journey. The breeze, in my opinion, is one of the reasons for the relaxed atmosphere in central Africa. The ambiance is especially noticeable to newcomers, though the reason for it may not be.

At most times an air movement comes up the Zambezi River against the current, sometimes penetrating into the riverine areas. Looking down from the escarpment stirs feelings of adventure. Green webs of flood rivers and their riverine vegetation, fed by rain storms on the plateau, meander across the valley. A few large rivers reach the Zambezi, but most peter out after traversing the valley floor. In the dry seasons when the bush is stark, water can be found in a few places by digging under the sandy surfaces of these dried-up streams. Animals, however, must rely for water on the Zambezi River, swamps, and isolated river pools at the base and in the foothills of the escarpment.

For the hunter it is a land of intrigue, excitement, and danger, loaded with big game. In contrast, the valley is also much like Mozambique, a land of malaria, sleeping sickness, and other tropical diseases. To me, as an ivory hunter, the valley reminded me of experiences I'd had in similar low-lying wild country, though its size did not compare with Zambezia or Niassa.

I had obtained a tsetse-fly permit to shoot here without limit. Those permits, issued to the public in Salisbury by Archie Fraser, the game officer, allowed the hunting of wild animals to further the so-called eradication of the tsetse fly. The eradication zone, in the northwestern part of the country, included a strip on either side of the Chirundu/Zambezi Valley road and higher escarpment, and the Kariba portion of the Zambezi Valley. These permits were slips of paper costing one pound or two dollars today, and issued under the Tsetse Act of 1930.

It was disturbing how the Southern Rhodesia government displayed no sense of game conservation. But that was not all—the act resulted in large-scale government hunting operations over vast tracts of land. From 1940 to 1950, government hunting campaigns alone resulted in the death of 551,000 animals, with probably at least one animal wounded for every one killed. It is anyone's guess what the totals might be subsequent to 1950. This is not to imply that man's indifference and negligence to wildlife resources is limited to Africa. The world's largest animal massacres were probably the decimation of the great bison herds of America. In my own country of Southern Rhodesia, government destruction of wildlife through dogmatic policy, indifference, and

Rukometje River in flood traversing the Zambezi Valley to spill into the mighty Zambezi River.

ignorance of its people was accepted as normal. The government wanted to control the land at any cost, even just to dominate vast spaces sparsely occupied by humans, and so man's greed triumphed over his reason.

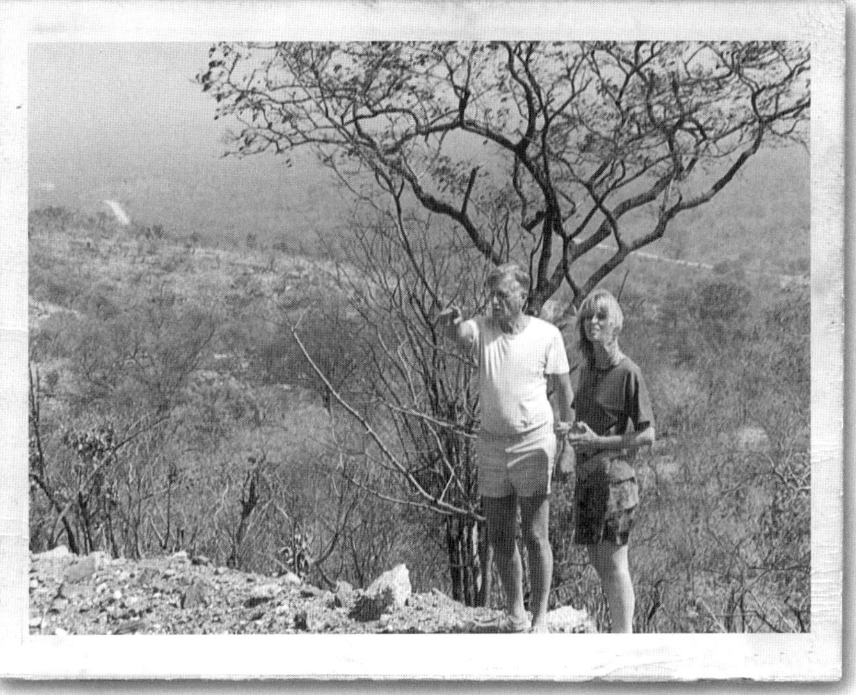

Across the valley floor was a slender road connecting Southern Rhodesia with Northern Rhodesia.

Southern Rhodesia had no effective game regulations concerning wounded animals. In fact, though it is hard to believe, in the early 1950s there was not even a game department. Wild animals in those days lived in balance with the tribes, except crop-raiding elephant, which most times devastated the lands. All wilderness areas and tribes came under the control of native commissioners stationed on the plateaus who had the responsibility of controlling crop-raiders. Some were entitled to the ivory, which augmented their meager salaries. I knew of a few who managed to educate their children abroad using this source of income.

At my vantage point high on the escarpment I gazed spellbound for hours at the valley below. As I left, I saw a sign on a tree that read, "Hell's Gate." No doubt it was a bitter inscription were put there by someone who had suffered in the Zambezi Valley.

Across the valley floor was a slender road connecting Southern Rhodesia with Northern Rhodesia. On our side in Southern Rhodesia the Tsetse Fly Department had seen fit to eliminate the wildlife in an area five miles on either side of this road. Some high-up idiots in Salisbury had drawn lines across a map and issued permits to people, especially farmers, to shoot out the game. There was no limit on the kill. For the farmers it meant cheap meat for their labour forces. Other vast areas of the country were also set aside for game extermination, based on the simple principle that killing game would deprive the tsetse flies of their lifeblood. In all fairness, I think our African chiefs would have made more realistic decisions.

To make matters worse, the five-mile strip cut across old elephant migratory paths. In addition, all these areas had *magotchas* (indigenous hunters) employed by the Tsetse Fly Department to exterminate game. A lot of these people were inaccurate shots. So many wounded animals were left to a lingering death, and wounded, enraged big game pose great danger to unwary humans. Consequently most of the hunting fraternity was in fear of and avoided dense bush areas.

Today I am still baffled by it all. As a matter of present-day interest, all these extermination areas were eventually allowed to rehabilitate themselves and today have been converted into sightseers' and visitors' reserves and controlled hunting areas. The tourist and other revenues from these areas, if it increases, could mean the survival of this wonderful wild and unique place of Africa—but in the long run man's numbers will overwhelm the land and the tremendous water resources of the mighty Zambezi River, which contains more water than all the rivers in South Africa combined.

Well, I told myself, *if this is "Hell's Gate," enter, hunter, and see what "hell" is like.* And so it was that I descended the foothills and traversed the valley, which I came to consider one of the most intriguing places in wild Africa with its variety of fauna, flora, and people. On motoring a few miles on the main road I recognized some of the Mozambique-type vegetation. Then I entered dense vegetation commonly known as *jess* bush. This was the land of the KoreKore people, and they spoke of the *jess* as *machesse.*

I took a rifle and some water, then entered the *jess* bush to get the feel of it. It was early season and there was still considerable leaf cover so I moved cautiously on the elephant paths, there being no other way to traverse the dense bush. The labyrinth of paths reminded me of a board game called "snakes and ladders." Only the occasional tree and rarely the giant baobab trees with their massive trunks offered shade.

In a thicket I closed my eyes, spun around a few times, then opened them to test my sense of direction. I did it a few times, always able to calculate the direction of the Zambezi River. There was no way an experienced person could get lost here with the river to the west, the escarpment to the east, and the road to the north. I tried to picture elephant bulls treading the paths to their sanctuaries. No doubt because of its density, the harsh vegetation would scrape their sides.

I sat and listened to the great silence of the *jess*, even feeling it—it was as if time stood still here—and occasionally I was conscious of the air currents well above, coursing over the tops of the vegetation. I kicked up some dust, and there were slight swirls of air. Not encouraging, I thought. On my return, it took me a few hours to locate the road and then my vehicle.

I motored on, and eventually the dense bush thinned as I moved through mopane forest. Much later a slight rise indicated the Chirundu Hills at the Zambezi. There was an indistinct track, and I followed it to a hill to see a glorious view of the Zambezi River wending its way for miles. Across the river stretched a steel bridge, which seemed in complete contrast to the magnificent wilderness. Time meant nothing to me, so I camped a few days until my soul had been fed enough of this wonderful view.

From here I could see the riverine vegetation running parallel to the great Zambezi—islands, sandbars, diverting currents, and below me an uninviting swamp of reedbeds a few miles wide. Looking at the reed fronds waving in the currents strongly reminded me of biblical colour pictures I had seen as a child of "Moses in the bulrushes." On an island I saw a few tribesmen pulling nets into their dugouts. I hailed them, but on hearing me they paddled off to the west bank.

The following day at sunrise, amidst the harsh cries of the *chikwaris* (red- necked francolin), I took a long walk circling the swamps, then changed direction to pace the riverine vegetation upstream to the river. There was game spoor from night activity: kudu, waterbuck, occasional sable, and elephant and buffalo where they had emerged from the swamps. Then, farther on, parallel to the river, I found large, elongated overflow pools from the Zambezi floods, with good vegetational cover everywhere. Old lion spoor showed where they had lingered in tawny-coloured, fading grass. There were signs of wild dogs, two cheetah, and large packs of hyena. In the distance impala ran off as if I had fired at them. The game here was quick to take flight at the sound or sight of man. Walking under beautiful *musango* trees to the banks, I saw spoor of a grown rhino and calf and, coming cautiously to look over the high river banks, saw crocodiles lying on sandbars and hippo in a school, some lying with their large heads on others' backs. Apparently this aquatic life was undisturbed. The crocs saw me and slowly submerged in a few feet of water.

A glorious view of the Zambezi River.

Much later I came across evidence of people, old fireplaces of campers under sausage and Natal mahogany trees. I pushed on. In places I had to cross elongated depressions partly filled with water from past floods to gain firmer ground. Inland, tsetse flies alighted on me, but otherwise it was pleasant country with occasional thick bush in the open forests.

I was well out of the five-mile eradication strip now and started to hear the constant calls of my favourite birds, the spotted wood doves, plus occasional cries of fish eagles far off at the river. I was completely at home here, walking slowly enough to read the ground and absorb as much knowledge as possible. With the sights, sounds, smells, and ground signs, it was like reading a book in ideal, relaxed conditions.

On an elephant path I came across prints of bare human feet, that had slightly disturbed the trampled leaves. I traced their direction. Unlike game paths, which were mostly to and from watering approaches on the river, these human prints led parallel to the river. From the tracks, it seemed like five men, but that number was difficult to determine accurately with so much dead, trampled leaf on the ground. Then, ahead in a clearing, I saw that there were actually seven of them. They had been walking unhurriedly in single-file, but stopped to allow one of them to urinate. *So, KoreKores, where are you going?* I wondered. There was evidence of tree cutting, so I reasoned they must have been from a local village. I was hoping the village was not too far because I did not want to make my return through the swamps in darkness, and thought I might be able to stay there for the night.

Then I heard the thud, thud, thud of maize being stamped in large wooden pestles. I saw naked-breasted young women pounding corn in rhythm opposite each other on the edge of a village—a common and natural sight in the wilds of Africa. A half-grown child gave the alarm and ran off to disappear in the center of the village. The alerted women stopped pounding to stare, uneasy as I approached them.

I greeted these women as men, but they did not respond. Then I asked, "Whose village is this?"

They appeared afraid and nervous, perhaps shy. A middle-aged woman came from a hut, greeted me pleasantly, and said, "This is the village of Mudzeemo, a chief of the KoreKore tribe."

She led me through the village, under large, spreading, shady trees, and walked behind a hut to where some men were sitting on low carved wooden stools. Seven of them were the men I had tracked: I recognized their spears with goods attached. Their greeting was that of wild people—gentle, lengthy, and respectful. "*Kuombera*," the slow clapping of hands; "*Magadee*?" (How are you?); and so on. Then they looked at the large cartridges on my bandoliers and belt, saying, "*Humba rumi*," meaning "A man who hunts to live."

A portly, pleasant man came forward, saying he was a headman. Jokingly I asked for Chief Mudzeemo.

"Where do you keep him?"

The fat one indicated an elegant, lean, gray-haired old man approaching. Like the others, he was dressed in black loincloth around the waist, much as I myself wore in the Mozambique lowlands. He took his time to stare and read me, then greeted me much the same as the others had. There was an air of authority but none of the unrealistic self-importance and attitude of so many other chiefs. I detected something masculine and at the same time refined about him. At his side stood a young man carrying a short spear. Mudzeemo was tall, old—about eighty or so—and still muscular. As a gesture of goodwill he took the spear and handed it to me as a present. I envisioned his appearance and demeanor as a young man and imagined he was no less formidable to contend with at eighty. I took an instant liking to him—in admiration of his self confidence and quiet sense of independent dignity.

I had nothing to give him in return, so I said, "I will hunt elephant for your villages."

"White men come here and take the meat away—so, we will see," he said.

I asked him about game populations and movements and told him of my need for good trackers. He sent for three men—two were lean and small, but the third had a magnificent build. We greeted each other and they stared at me from where they sat on a log. The well-built one was named Joram, the other two, Jacoba and Micheck Zaratina. They track, said the chief, except Jacoba, who was a reliable water carrier and, the chief added, would not run away in the face of danger. I was satisfied with the well-built Joram and now questioned Zaratina (also named *Kamuchokomuchoko*, meaning "a fish with spikes that a croc raids to swallow").

"What can you do?" I asked.

"What is required?" he answered.

There was an almost antagonistic arrogance about him. Perhaps the elephant would change that, I thought. He was a small man, unimpressive and frail looking, except for his black, burning eyes. I expressed my doubts about whether to stay in the village or go back to the comforts of my own camp at Chirundu, using the swamps as an excuse.

Mudzeemo said, "Stay if you wish, but the small one, Zaratina, can take you around or even through the swamps at night."

I laughed—swamps at night can become hellish places where one has to move mostly by the sound of the surrounding animals.

"It makes no difference," Mudzeemo said. "I have hunted with Zaratina—he will easily take you back around or through the swamps. He knows all the game and human paths."

Then Zaratina cut in boldly and said in a quiet voice: "If we go, we go, or if we stay, we stay!"

He had hustled me into a quick decision.

"We go!" I said.

In a short while the three men had their few belongings hanging from spears over their shoulders and, after I thanked Mudzeemo, we departed. We had about an hour of daylight left, and I noted the tracker Joram had a good direction, heading in almost a straight line as the paths and floodplains allowed. It was dark before we reached the swamps, and here the men were cautious of the large animals and cats that came from inland to feed and hunt in the swamps. On my left were great reedbeds unseen in the dark and on my right were trees and paths giving partial vision as our eyes accustomed to the dark. I heard the elephant and buffalo pushing and feeding their way through the dense reed vegetation. Here Zaratina took the lead. Higher up we crossed the stagnant Chipandehoure Pools and moved into easy country of better vision. Eventually the slopes of the Chirundu Hills appeared and soon we found my camp and vehicle in the dark. Easy enough to get through when guided, I thought. These men knew the place and what they were doing.

Now for fire, food, and the restoration of the body by sleep. Hyena howled during the night, no doubt expecting the camp eventually to have meat. In the dawning light I sat at the campfire waiting for the earth to take shape. Every second ghostly shapes and forms materialized until at last the mighty Zambezi River was visible in the daylight—its massive flow, circumventing islands, slightly veering in its great course to reach the distant sea at Chinde. I had traveled so much of it, but this was the first vantage point from which I was able to appreciate its enormity and wild, alluring beauty as it disappeared into the distant haze.

Bird noises reached me from far off, and I saw flocks of ducks wending their way to unseen feeding grounds. To the south below me the great swamp seemed silent, but I knew large numbers of animals had been there last night. There were probably stragglers there now, but it was so dense I could see no movement, even from our elevated position. Zaratina appeared at my side, gestured at the country below, and said there was enough *nyama* (meat) and excitement down there for any man.

Then he said, "We must camp near the pools of the floodplains halfway from where we crossed last night. We can negotiate the vehicle above the Chipandehoure watercourse, and there we will be in the center of animal movement to check spoor parallel to the river."

In a few words this small man had made me realize how greatly improved our possibilities were. I nodded and thee three men packed my gear into the truck. I checked after them and had a long, parting look at the savage grandeur of the Zambezi and surrounding country. No artist could do it justice. It emotionally charged me.

Zaratina came to my side, saying, "We are ready. It is early, and we may yet find bull spoor."

I turned to go, but he hesitated for a while, looking back in lingering admiration of his homeland. It was unusual, I thought, for a local to appreciate such wild beauty. They normally take it for granted.

We traveled roughly parallel to the river a mile or so inland. It was easy country in which to find spoor as most game during the day moved inland to thick bush sanctuaries. The animals included mixed herds of elephant, as well as buffalo, antelope, occasional zebra, and many hyena. We had to make our way cautiously, driving over water depressions, to reach the shade of many spaced-out sausage trees (*Kigela africana*), where we established an open campsite on the floodplain. I warned the men not to take water for me from the pools as there was cleaner water in the Zambezi River close by. We ate, then abandoned the camp to walk upstream and cut inland. They talked of a *jess* forest called Nyamaque and were trying to locate spoor between it and the swamps.

We saw much evidence of cow elephant and then the spoors of three bulls separate from the herds. Joram took the bull spoor and after a few miles we entered the Nyamaque *jess*. It was not as dense as the other *jess* I had entered near the main road. I mentioned this to Joram, but he did not answer so I assumed he had never been there. He eventually showed signs of nervousness and kept losing the spoor. Even the water carrier indicated the spoor to him. All this time Zaratina walked at the rear. I had been through these antics before and was becoming agitated; I knew Joram could track well, but when he got close he no longer wanted to.

They were men of the forest, and I was on the verge of driving my rifle butt into Joram's throat—the usual procedure under these circumstances—when Zaratina came forward between us and removed the *rota* (ash bag) from Joram's hand. He took the spoor, sure of himself, and we continued at his pace. With occasional glances down at the spoor, I knew we might catch up to the elephant. My murderous mood faded from me. It was more like being with Chirenge or Chikati, the great trackers of Mozambique.

There was a carpet of flat, trampled leaves on the paths, and the elephant walked at their leisure, leaving little evidence of their progress. Eventually fresh dung droppings appeared, and later we heard the breaking of branches ahead. I turned to check the others and saw Joram disappearing down an elephant path behind us—he had turned coward. That magnificent Hollywood specimen was a human hyena. We continued, but cautiously, and then I began to appreciate the excellence of this tracker Zaratina. He said the elephant were moving slowly, taking a branch here and there. It meant they might be spread out a little. I questioned him on this, and he said he was following a center spoor, the two other animals being to the sides on adjoining paths. The *rota* indicated the air currents were swirling, and, because we were close now, Zaratina tried to make visual contact. He came in at two angles, both unsuitable, so of necessity we stayed back, letting the bulls get ahead again.

The wind was so unreliable that we had no alternative but to be cautious. Most of man's success as a hunter comes from his stalking: In this respect we have much in common with lion and leopard in the intense moments of closing in. The only difference is that sometimes elephant attack men, but with cats, combat comes when the hunted stands at bay.

An hour or so later we came up to the elephant again—unseen somewhere close ahead. The wind was right, and the elephants' silence indicated that they had stopped in the midday heat. Zaratina paused for quite a while, hoping to hear some indication of their immediate whereabouts, but there was none. I felt the tension in the great uncertain silence of the *jess* bush. It sounded as if there were no living creatures here. Zaratina indicated the elephant were about fifty yards ahead. He had finally heard them, though I had not. I could tell by the tense muscles on his face that he was sure.

He stood close to me and, in a near whisper, said, "I will do my job, so let us see if you can do yours!"

He then noiselessly moved on, and we followed. Very cautiously he brought me into position. I could see an elephant chest and nothing else. As he tried to get me into a better position to where I could see the head, the elephant's chest moved forward. But I still could not see its head, so I fired at the V of the chest. I knew he would come closer, hopefully parting the bush, and I could use the second bullet from the double-barreled rifle for a head shot. But instead, on receiving the first shot he sped forward with his head still covered. As he passed, barely missing us, I gave him the second barrel through the *jess*, to his shoulder. He carried on a few more yards, and I heard a crash of bush, indicating that he had collapsed.

Another one trumpeted and came crashing through the *jess* bush in my direction. Coming at speed, the trumpet changed to murderous roar. In a flash I realized the gun was empty, and I barely managed to reload one cartridge as his head burst out on us. A snapshot, and he was down.

Instantly I reloaded and waited, listening intently, but there was no sound. Zaratina ran up to the second dead elephant and stood there for a while looking and listening while we all remained motionless. Eventually the tracker came to me and said the last elephant had run off during the shooting. I needed rest to let my nervous system recover, so I sat leaning against a tree for some time. Eventually I rose to check the ivory. It was unimpressive, about forty pounds per tusk. Zaratina showed me suppurating sores on the second bull where it had been previously wounded—no wonder it had roared with such rage.

I mentioned the light ivory and Zaratina said, "Where do you get bigger?"

I said, "In Mozambique and Tanganyika."

He did not know where that was, so I said, "Far away," indicting northeast.

He said, "There are sometimes big tuskers here but not often."

Then he asked me why I had fired the second shot at the passing elephant.

"Because it came partly toward us," I said.

"You could have let it pass," he replied. "It already had a dead heart shot."

It dawned on me that this little bastard knew the dangers of this game. Being new here, I had made what could have been a fatal mistake—firing the second barrel at close quarters, with the risk of being caught with an empty rifle. I was glad Faanie was not here as he would have derisively reveled at a man of my experience making this stupid mistake. For those few moments I had lost my self-discipline—a fatal mistake made by some of the best hunters.

My first hunt with Zaratina in the Zambezi Valley.

We had some daylight hours left so I suggested we take the third elephant's spoor. Zaratina said it would move out of the *jess*, cross a large mopane forest, and enter the great *jess* bush called *Naukaranga*, an ominous name meaning, "Your feet marks go in, but do not come out." I worked on the theory that the bull would circle to stay in this Nyamaque *jess*, but Zaratina proved to be right. The bull had taken off at speed in the mopane forest, heading for *Naukaranga*. It did not seem logical for him to cross the semi-open forests to reach a greater sanctuary when there was one big enough here, but that is what happened.

We returned to camp, and on the way I began to think of this insignificant-looking little man. He had tracked with unusual skill and speed, and his heart was in the right place. He had the instincts of a professional, and his question about firing the second shot showed that he knew the mental, analytical, and emotional weaknesses of hunting. No doubt he was a man of skill, courage, and knowledge, and if there were enough bulls, I would most likely have future success with him.

This was my first hunt here and already news had penetrated through the bush telegraph both ways. One message was that hunting conditions in the *jess* bush did not bother me. Another, coming back from the distant villages, was that the Chiefs Dandawa and Chundu, as well as Chief Chopota, across the Kapsuka Range of the Mupata Gorge, had had a bad crop year with elephant raiding at will, and they were short of maize supplies.

There were many guns on the opposite west bank seeking limited amounts of game. This was because of the old Queen Victoria Hunting License, as it was known, costing (if memory serves me right) two shillings and six pence (twenty-five cents) annually, allowing anyone to shoot game on the west bank and in the Northern Rhodesian territories. As a result, in a few decades the large herds of big game there were decimated. Only the fastest game survived.

In addition there was a "hut tax" of one pound sterling, forcing the Africans to work in the white man's enterprises, at least temporarily. As Cecil Rhodes said, "You must teach the natives to want."

It was common in Northern Rhodesia to come across large groups of locals with muzzleloading weapons. These primitive guns were a curse: Nine times out of ten they wounded animals, most of which died a lingering death. What was beginning to annoy and sadden me most was the European influence, particularly here in the Rhodesias, whereby the Africans were beginning to discard their traditional loincloths. As civilization advanced into the wilds, it became noticeable that the tribes were struggling to maintain their culture and the memories of their ancestors. But the arrow had already flown from the bow and industrialized society was having its effect; many of the younger generation were seeking lucrative employment on the plateau. I discussed this with Chief Mudzeemo, and it was obvious that he was disturbed, realizing that his people wanted the benefits but not at the cost of losing their tribal identities.

In the warm country of Mozambique, I used the loincloth extensively for years. It was easy to merely wrap a piece of cloth around the waist; in addition to being comfortable, it allowed the body to breathe. Another loincloth was used on the head, draped over the shoulders when necessary. At times I hunted other fully clothed Europeans into the ground simply because they would not realize that their clothing exaggerated the effects of the heat on their bodies.

Like most tribes, the people in the Zambezi Valley were poor, not so much by their standards but by ours. It struck me as unrealistic and shortsighted to think that any occupying force could continue to rule indefinitely without

What was beginning to annoy and sadden me most was the European influence, particularly here in the Rhodesias, where the Africans were beginning to discard their traditional loincloths.

enlightening the poorer classes. It was the basic reason why Rhodesia became Zimbabwe—that and a rising emotional nationalism. Money, however, is the real master—even today in Zimbabwe. Africans have never had money of any consequence. They have always been the labour forces of the white man's enterprises. Consequently, people in the Zambezi Valley and elsewhere, if their crops failed or were raided by elephant, had to seek work on farms or in towns on the plateau. Such was the lure of the white-man's economy.

In the African wilderness, one had to live in primitive conditions to appreciate the lifestyle of others—both rich and poor. I have had the opportunity to sample both ways, and for me, primitive and wild is best.

A few days after my first hunt, a bull elephant crossed the Zambezi to raid the remains of old croplands on the west bank. It was driven out and shot at with muzzleloaders and returned to Southern Rhodesia. We found it still alive in dense thickets and finished it off.

Around the campfire I learned from Zaratina and Jacoba that hunters from time to time descended the escarpment, mostly from the tobacco farms, to hunt any living creatures for their pleasure and above all for meat for their farms' labour forces, of which there were many. In Rhodesia tobacco is the main farm crop, the biggest export, and the mainstay of the economy. Consequently tobacco production is a priority over most other things.

The campfire in this new area was alive with the happenings and people of the past. One, Kanyemba by name, was a tyrant who dealt in white and black gold, meaning ivory and slaves. Apparently Kanyemba was clear of mind but mad of soul, using eunuchs as bodyguards to raid villages up and down the Zambezi River for slaves, who were sold to Portuguese traders along with ivory, when obtainable.

A tyrant's rule in Africa demands three things: The first is to have a long, powerful life; second is to be a ruthless, physical exploiter of other people; and the third is to aggressively eradicate all real or imagined enemies and opposition. Kanyemba was greatly feared. He was also reputed to have reached the gorges below the present-day Victoria Falls. Near the Zambezi/Kafue River confluence there is a large, well-shaded island named after him, where he often had his headquarters when coming upstream from Mozambique.

At times I searched this island to try to find evidence of his occupation, but without success. After the European occupation of the Rhodesias, this cruel, ruthless tyrant alternately exploited and operated from both countries. Eventually he expanded his operations to include Mozambique. He and his army of eunuchs were feared far and wide, and his cruelty was legendary. According to lore, if a man set eyes on any of his wives, he would immediately be flung to the ground and castrated. It is difficult to verify the accuracy of spoken African history, because prior to western occupation there was no written word. But considering Africa's wild, untamed nature, there is no doubt that these and other savage stories have at least some truth, the degree of which depends on the source.

Another story involved an ancestor of Chief Chundu at the Chewori/Zambezi River confluence. It is told that the warlike Matabele nation were living in the Bulawayo area and used to raid in all directions for young women and cattle. During these raids, everyone other than the female captives were put to the spear. So contemptuous were these fierce, brutal people—descended from the Zulu nation in Natal—that they referred to other tribes as *masweenas*, meaning "the gut containing the dung of cattle." These Matabele *impis* (armies) had penetrated and terrorized the distant tribes of the Zambezi Valley as far as the land of Chief Chundu's ancestor on the Chewori River in the Zambezi Valley. But this KoreKore chief had permanent lookouts on the escarpment to warn him of any approaching Matabele. He also planned defensively for the inevitable raid: He maintained many dugouts on the east bank of the Zambezi River. When the Matabele with their short stabbing spears arrived, they were disappointed to see all the livestock and people had simply moved to the opposite bank of the Zambezi. The Matabele in their haste for blood and plunder took to dugouts left for them on the shore. When they reached midstream, and were trapped in the current, KoreKore bowmen attacked from hidden positions on islands and other dugouts. The Matabele, with their feet off the ground (in boats), could not use their dreaded short stabbing spears (assegais), and were defeated. Jacoba delighted in telling me how the KoreKore annihilated the Matabele.

The story went further: After this tribal war, the chief whose leadership had caused the Matabele retreat disappeared at the river one day. In primitive African logic that means he was murdered. A few seasons later a strangely shaped, twisted piece of metal was found in the Zambezi River after the floods. It was taken to the main village and has been worshipped ever since as the spirit of the murdered chief. Villagers called their new god Chimombe. These were the ceremonies I witnessed in which it was placed on black cloth to the beating of drums, and surrounded by magical talismans and ivory.

P. J. Pretorius, a big-game hunter from the turn of the century to the 1940s, wrote *Jungle Man*, a book that has had a profound influence on me. Many times I had visited the places Pretorius mentioned. In fact, he stayed some years in the Zambezi Valley and describes how a wounded lion killed his companion there. To my amazement, I stumbled upon a stone mound, an apparent grave, at the exact site where Pretorius said the incident occurred.

On another occasion, Chief Mudzeemo visited me in my camp, and I asked if he knew of a man named *Matanda wantu* (he who likes people), Pretorius's native name. Mudzeemo's eyes enlarged and he showed great interest, wanting to know how I knew this man. I told him as best I could, and he went on to verify what Pretorius had written of the Zambezi Valley, describing how these very trees where we sat were part of Pretorius's old camping sites. Here, he said, the hunter kept cattle traded from both banks of the Zambezi Valley. Apparently he traded an ox for a length of cloth (*limbo*) measured from the ox's head to its outstretched tail. Two of Pretorius's main concerns were swimming his oxen across the crocodile-infested Zambezi into Southern Rhodesia and guarding them at night against marauding lion.

"And what of the tsetse flies and the cattle?" I asked.

He said, "There were no tsetse flies in those days, and we all had cattle. The flies only came after the *murungos* (white men) occupied the land."

What happened was that within a few years, large herds of buffalo had continuously migrated to the Zambezi Valley, causing the fly to move with them from the Munuati and Mupfuri River districts. Astonishingly, the fly is now resident in the whole Zambezi Valley.

Finally, I asked Mudzeemo, "What of *mahachi*?" meaning horses.

"No," he said, "we had no horses, but Pretorius had two, which he kraaled at night because of the lion."

There was no doubt in my mind that Chief Mudzeemo had known *Matanda wantu*, P. J. Pretorius, as all these events and animals were mentioned in his book. To explain for those unfamiliar with the domestic stock problem in the Zambezi Valley, no domestic stock can survive where there are tsetse flies: Stock bitten by the flies become infected with the disease trypanosomiasis (sleeping sickness)—known as *nagana*. In later years I mentioned all this to a friend of mine, a glossinalogist whose work centered around the extermination of the tsetse fly. He was skeptical, so I managed to obtain the book of Pretorius' wanderings in the Zambezi Valley. After reading it—and hearing of my own experiences with Chief Mudzeemo—he did not know what to believe about the history of the tsetse fly, and I think he is still confused. It shows that the past soon enough fades into oblivion in a land that knows no written history.

The ten-mile wide extermination strip, five miles on either side of the Zambezi Valley Road, is a casual stroll to an elephant. When pressed, they can do fifty miles a day, but fast travel increases their hunger, causing them to slow down to feed. On the strip it became evident that there were many wounded elephant and buffalo, probably the area with the highest incidence of wounded animals in Africa. Because this area was their old haunt, some of them stuck to their habits, feeding at night in the swamp, and finding refuge during the day in the dense *jess*. Because of persecution, cow elephant had become notoriously aggressive.

In midwinter other European hunters appeared, some from as far away as the eastern districts on the Mozambique/Umtali border. There was a family—the Grobelaars—who most times had salads and fish in their camp, which was for me a great pleasure.

Mrs. Grobelaar was a keen fisherwoman, and twice a week they sent their truck up to the plateau for supplies—butter, bread, and vegetables—body needs such as I seldom got. One day Grobelaar, whom I had not seen before, passed close to my camp on the way to his own. He paused where two lion often slept at night near where they had recently killed and eaten their quarry in the swamps. On seeing the spoor where they had lounged for hours, he was astonished and came up to tell me the news. I assured him I knew of this, having seen them often from the cover of my mosquito net at night. They were a pair of large males and were obviously hunting companions, which I thought unusual. In the first such occasion, I could see the lion in the bright moonlight, licking and pawing the blood stains around their heads and paws. But I didn't care and went back to sleep. Thereafter these lion would occasionally lounge, sometimes visible, just within the light of my large fires, eventually lying down to sleep. Contrary to wild lion behavior, they behaved like tame lion on the loose.

I had just come back from the river, where I had bathed using the fine sand just as others use soap, and was wearing an old loincloth—Grobelaar gave me a perplexed look. Whites, I thought, were carrying their prejudices to the very banks of the Zambezi. It is a mystery to me why they are so intolerant. If the lion had not visited so close to my camp, and I had worn a towel instead of a loincloth my behavior would have been "acceptable." I told him my thoughts, and, by way of embarrassment, he invited me to his camp for drinks and supper. Grobelaar was short of stature but thickset and probably strong. As he was leaving, he glanced at my meager possessions and said with humour, "I can see why they say you are wild." We laughed and he moved on back to his camp.

That night toward sunset I took the double rifle and cartridge belt and walked the few miles to Grobelaar's camp. En route in the dark I had to circumvent a herd of neurotic cow elephant that may have got a smell of me. They were trumpeting, roaring, squealing, and smashing the bush. I felt fearful, so I speeded up to get away from them. The angry, nervous disposition of these Chirundu-strip cows were a reminder that they were always dangerous. How unnatural, I thought—game so persecuted as to make one apprehensive of what lay ahead.

At their camp, the Grobelaars expressed anxiety, having heard the cow elephants' trumpeting only a mile distant in the warm, clear night air. Mrs. Grobelaar had prepared an impala stew, which did not interest me, but on seeing green vegetables I asked her for some. After drinks, we dined, they eating their impala stew and I the green vegetables as a salad. I was starved for such foods, and that night, when I felt the positive effect it had on my system, I wondered how much my hunting performance would improve on the balanced foods the Grobelaars took for granted on their holiday. My hosts were concerned about my intention to return to my camp that night and asked me to stay until morning. I thought it unnecessary and explained that I was accustomed to crossing game country alone, at night.

"Yes," said Mrs. Grobelaar, "but this is the strip country."

I countered by saying that at this late hour most dangerous game would be feeding in the swamps. I left close to midnight, assuring them that I would be all right. It was only a few miles across the floodplain and through occasional bush. Before I got to my camp I scented a big beast ahead of me. It turned out to be a rhino that snorted off in alarm.

Just before entering my camp I picked up the unmistakable odor of lion. Hearing my return, Zaratina woke to say the lion had visited again. After that we did not see them for a long time. Perhaps they moved to other swamps much farther down the river out of the strip, probably returning to their pride.

With Zaratina's help, I managed to shoot other bull elephant without dangerous incident. Once, when we had temporarily lost elephant spoor, I found myself practically leaning over a sleeping rhino. Silently I retreated, puzzled why it had not smelled or heard me. Suddenly, at a distance, we heard it rise and charge off, probably having finally gotten my scent.

A few mornings later, we found the spoor of a large bull in the company of about thirty cows. The bull occasionally wandered away to feed, but always returned to move with the herd. They crossed through *jess* above the Chipandehoure Swamp and then headed toward the escarpment. Zaratina said they were sure to enter the dense thickets of Naukaranga. We paused and Jacoba turned to me quietly, laughing and saying, "*Lapa nasi teena heenya*?"—"There in the *jess* we will s--t ourselves in fear." Not funny in our language but hilarious in theirs.

We crossed miles of forest to enter the *jess*. As we progressed, the spoor indicated the elephant were more relaxed but were seeking the sanctuary of dense thickets for their daylight sleep. The wind had been unreliable most of the day, and here in the thickets it decreased. Parts of this bush were more dense than others, and in one section I estimated vision at two yards maximum—not encouraging when you consider the length of an elephant's trunk and the fact that we were the aggressors. If we fired, these Zambezi Ladies would certainly attack toward the sound of our shots. I cursed the cow elephant and wondered how the bull could be so amorous as to surround himself by so many of them.

Zaratina was fearful of losing the element of surprise, and consequently it took us more than an hour to do a quarter-mile. Eventually Zaratina got a break, hearing an elephant squealing. The wind was uncertain but not against us, so we closed in. The bush was dense, but the sound of the elephant led us on.

Zaratina paused, saying, "*marire*," meaning a tuskless bull. These animals are usually at a disadvantage as they cannot dislodge tree bark that is necessary to their digestive systems. Consequently they are irritable and truculent and usually have large, wide, and strong trunks. Elephant were ahead and spread to our sides as Zaratina closed in on the squealing, trumpeting sounds.

We were almost up against them, perhaps too close, when the tracker parted the bush to give me a small window. From about three paces I saw the large head of a tuskless bull waving his trunk to reach above his head, each time squealing in a neurotic way. Curse the bastard. If I shot now, the cows would attack and the hunt would turn into a war. If I did not fire, we might again follow this bull, thinking he had ivory. I was on the verge of taking my chances when Zaratina touched me on the arm, indicating that we must retreat. Silently we did so, and at a safe distance I questioned this action. The tracker said he felt the cows were spread to both sides in an ideal position to attack, and opening fire there was against all his instincts. Reluctantly we had to accept it and, having failed, moved off.

The Months of the Sun were now almost on us, and the Zambezi River was about fifteen miles off. After a long walk, we arrived there late at night.

But this incident was not finished: It continued with the unfortunate hunter Grobelaar. Some time later he also took the spoor of this herd, where they had vacated the swamps at predawn. After many miles they all entered the lower portion of the Naukaranga *jess*. The details of what actually happened will never be known, but it seems that after Grobelaar fired at the tuskless bull, he was attacked by the cows. Amidst the panic of probably too many helpers, he managed to shoot a half-dozen or so cows to ward off attacks, allowing myself and the rest time and opportunity to scatter and escape.

In those days, we jokingly referred to these Chirundu elephant as the "Zambezi Ladies." But they became fearfully dangerous. As the main body of the herd attempted to scent or see you, others swept the bush with their trunks, trying to make physical contact. Those that found your spoor went into action following your scent. Then the herd leadership encouraged the entire herd in a fearless and relentless attack, unified to hunt you out.

In those years few people penetrated beyond the outer fringes of the Naukaranga *jess*. It is a large area of hellishly thick, dried, elephant-coloured, leafless thicket. Deep inside, especially toward the base of the escarpment where perhaps the soils are richer, the bush was so thick that vision was often limited to a couple of feet. Under these conditions, absolute skill, nerve, and indeed some luck decided whether you lived or died. Elephant learned to attack in the direction of rifle shots, and the intensity of the attack was proportional to the proximity and location of the sound. It became habit for elephant to react in this defensive manner. In such close cover you had to wait until they were a few paces away, coming at you. Then it took quick, accurate firing to ward them off.

We often stripped and smeared our bodies with elephant dung to disguise the human scent and tried to camouflage ourselves with branches held closely in front of us. Fear makes you take what may seem to be ridiculous steps, but these tactics did help, and probably even saved our lives.

The first time we did this it worked well. Our fear was so great that, having access to fresh dung, we stripped and covered our entire bodies, including our hair since elephant often looked down on us. This resulted in much laughter and discomfort when we looked at each other afterward, in addition to some hilarious but unrepeatable remarks. One mild one was "*Machende wa buda,*" meaning "Your testicles are gone," in this case covered with dung. There is a unique style of humour and a depth of mirth possible with African language that does not easily translate in our own.

The laughter did not last of course. Each time, as we dried out in the heat, the dung acids began irritating our skin. I used soil to remove the dung, but often it had already settled into the skin pores, and we were conscious of it as we made the long walk back to the Zambezi River, often without water. It became a matter of determination and stamina to reach water.

Hunters do not always have it their own way, and many have been killed by animals. I had heard of the Patterson brothers, one of whom was killed when a wounded elephant—supposedly just about to die—lunged forward on him. On the west bank I saw a tribesman smashed against a tree by an elephant. He seemed to break up on impact. I shot the elephant, but I was too late to help the tribesmen. Such occasions illustrate the fact that if you allow a dangerous animal to close the gap and seize you, all is lost. Grobelaar, who probably had more guts than experience at the time, was lucky. Two of his staff never returned. When attacked, they deserted him to flee for their lives. Grobelaar himself was in a bad spot but survived, no doubt by virtue of determination and toughness. I once came close to death from thirst after a water carrier deserted because of attacking elephant cows. I barely managed to reach Chimba, a picturesque watercourse coming down from the escarpment. It held small pools of water in the low hills and one at the base on the valley floor. I was so dehydrated that I had to stay for days eating meat and drinking water to try to regain some of my strength. I had pushed myself too far, and it took many days and what little stamina I had in me to cross the valley floor to the Zambezi River.

Now, in the Months of the Sun, after the Grobelaar incident I had to speed up and concentrate my efforts to get ivory. Most of the hunters left the valley at this time because of the discomfort of heat and the threat of thirst. I got a reasonable share of heat and thirst, but fortunately the elephant had by now learned to feed and drink inside the strip mostly at night and to leave during the daylight hours. We knew our Cordite-loaded cartridges were sensitive to the excessive heat, which caused more violent explosions and increased velocity, resulting in more severe recoil. Shooting bruised our shoulders. Zaratina, although he used the lighter .404 magazine rifle, suffered more than me because of his lightweight body. On the plus side, the .404 bullet's penetrating power increased, giving the user more confidence on the large heads of bull elephant. With this increased velocity, the bullet also seemed to keep a truer course on impact.

The best successes occurred when I reverted to the simple practice that Faanie had devised in Tanganyika and Mozambique of shooting the bulls at night. It is a risky affair, calling for concentration and nerve. Using a blob of white toothpaste on the front sight to make it visible, I would wade into the water where the elephant were drinking. With the wind in my favour, I would get up close in the dark, wading silently in about three feet of water. They would be rowdy, drinking or splashing and bathing, throwing water over themselves with their trunks. Depending on the angle at which each animal was standing, I would go for either the brain at close quarters or the shoulders. It required sound concentration because visible details were limited; sometimes I could see only large slabs of shoulders at a few paces.

An elephant shot in a shoulder usually runs in the direction it is facing, but on the brain shot, even if it drops for a few seconds temporarily stunned, it can rise, become suddenly conscious of you, and turn on you at close quarters. I came close to being killed a few times. Elephant at night are bold, at times even aggressive to foreign sound and smells. I always tried to keep my scent from them. Several times they tried to flush me in the water, but the hunting gods were with me.

Near the base of the escarpment, at a sulphur spring that fed a pan of water, we found the spoor of large bulls and decided to have a go at them at night. We camped a few hundred yards downwind and in the night heard them splashing and gurgling their elephant sounds of pleasure. At the time I had a borrowed double-barreled .600 Nitro-Express rifle. Death had been knocking at my door too often of late, so I armed myself with this powerful weapon before entering the water pan to approach the elephant. There was some cloud cover over a half-moon, so I waited for it to clear.

Seven bulls were splashing in about four feet of water. My vision was limited, but I could see the outlines of great backs and dull white tusks. Confident with this rifle, which I had tried elsewhere in the daylight, here at night I slowly waded into the pool, bandolier across my

Zambezi Ladies (cow elephant)

chest. The largest bull was my first prize, and I was moving cautiously toward him when a cloud came over the moon and it got darker.

The elephant continued splashing and making other noises when I suddenly realized the big bull was just about on me, passing by my side. In surprise, haste, and fear I fired at his shoulder, there being no time to fully raise the rifle. The forceful recoil of the .600 drove me under the water. I heard a tremendous splash as the bull fell toward me, landing within a foot of me with a smashed shoulder and a bullet through the heart. (I had fired at a slightly forward angle as the bull came up to me.) It is amazing how quickly the human brain assesses probabilities, especially if stimulated by fear. While under water I had not really known what had happened. Fearful of rising above the surface, I stayed down. For a while I struggled to free the rifle, as the barrels seemed stuck. I panicked, believing they were under the elephant, but when I yanked they came free. Upon rising, only my head above water at first, I looked into the mass of a dead elephant's back and large spinal column.

There was drama here, with angry elephant in the water and on land. I had never had such an experience at night, and, instead of taking a chance on the soaked ammunition for defense, and using the dead elephant as a shield, I lost my determination and nerve and retreated. It seemed the better part of valour.

This escape was a rather clumsy affair, with me struggling through the water trying to work up speed, only to lose it on the slippery mud bottom. When I did reach dry land, I raced at top speed down the elephant paths. It was just as well—a morning inspection revealed that the elephant had tried to locate me on my side of the pool. The ivory from this bull was about ninety pounds a side, certainly good for Rhodesia.

On another occasion, also at a water hole, I had an eerie experience with a bull elephant. In moonlight Zaratina and I waited under the moon-shade of some trees, downwind of but close to a pan. We observed a few nervous antelope and zebra drinking. Their approach had been cautious, and having quenched their thirst, they trotted off back to the forest. We sat leaning against a tree and from time to time dozed off, but one of us was always alert.

We had come here because we had seen the spoor of a large bull at the water's edge. Past midnight I woke to see Zaratina listening to the approach of a bull on the opposite side of the pan. The animal was in the forest and branches scraped against his sides. I planned to give him time to settle to the pleasures of the water, but this bull would come no closer than the last shadow of the trees. Zaratina and I were absolutely silent with the wind strongly in our favour. It was the time of year when all animals had to have water frequently. The bull must have been thirsty but refrained from leaving the moon shade of the trees. Why did he not come to the water? Perhaps he had drunk elsewhere or was waiting for other elephant to come up behind him.

We waited a good half-hour, then I became perplexed. The bull on the opposite side of the pan remained absolutely silent and immobile, an indication that he might be aware but was not afraid of our presence. I thought perhaps he was not a Chirundu elephant. Then, after another long period, Zaratina gestured, and I saw the bull' s bulk come very slowly forward. Tusks, trunk, big head, and ears faced us in the pale moonlight. After a few seconds, he shook his head vigorously, showing suspicion and/or disturbance, his large ears slapping against his neck or shoulders. He then quickly withdrew his head from the moonlight and stood back in the shade again, almost unseen.

In humour Zaratina said, "Why did you not shoot him then?"

The impossibility of an accurate sixty-yard shot at night made us laugh a little. There was no way he could detect us. But still he was aware of something. He retreated farther back, and we could no longer detect him. I thought if the mountain won't come to Mahomed, then Mahomed must go to the mountain, and since there was only one elephant, I thought of putting a large blob of toothpaste on the rifle's front and stalking him in the moon shadows of the surrounding forest.

Foolishly I left Zaratina where he was, working on the theory that one man is harder to detect than two, and slowly skirted the pan in the shadows of the forest, always aware of wind direction. It took caution, skill, and a long time. When I eventually got to his position, there was no bull. I could not detect spoor because of bad light, but did see some ground disturbance where the bull had stood a while. He may have gone deeper into the forest, but I continued to skirt the pan under the trees.

I heard a nightjar call and knew Zaratina was coming up behind me. He said the elephant had come close enough to disturb him so he moved after me, thinking the bull was actually stalking him.

"No," I said, "you are unarmed—that is why you think so."

"No, bwana," he said, "this elephant is different—it was close and dangerously coming into my wind when I silently flitted off into the forest to come up to you."

I knew Zaratina well enough to believe what he said must be so. Then we went on to complete the circle around the water pan, reaching the place where we had originally waited. Zaratina indicated that the bull had just recently been here and could be standing close by now. *I can't see how,* I thought. *He would have scented us many times from here.* I whispered this to Zaratina.

"I don't care what you think, bwana—he is here now and is possessed of the spirits of his ancestors (*Mudzimu ndzou*). He is wise to the ways of man."

If it were not so serious and dangerous, I would have laughed at the situation.

Persecuted elephant always react upon detecting man—so what was with this one? Perhaps he was a freak or had been damaged or had lost his sense of smell. If only we'd had enough light we could have determined the situation by spooring. It was about two o'clock in the morning, and we had had little sleep. I felt stupid and inadequate. No elephant has the hunting sense of the human brain, but on the other hand we could not continue trying to locate or be tracked by a phantom elephant. We could be taken unawares by this cunning bull if we got sleepy.

Zaratina said, "I will choose a direction to retreat from here."

We moved off into the forest, feeling our way for some distance, and returned to the camp a few miles off.

I left instructions for the pan to be scrutinized in early morning. Helpers followed the bull spoor to determine the events of the previous night. The bull had fully circled the pan from where it originally had stood, but first it visited our waiting position and then stood in thick bush close by, having scented, seen, and possibly heard us—but it did not react. The spoor showed where it eventually drank, stayed around the pan, and moved off at early light. Perhaps it was one of those elephant that only attack sleeping camps—who knows. Anyhow we were glad to be away from it and never saw this bull again—unless we unknowingly shot it amongst others in daylight.

The ability to think like elephant can come about only by being among them and observing their habits. I often did this and learned much in their presence. Once, in the semi-darkness of predawn, I watched a lone bull standing at the water's edge, having his final drink just prior to the rising of the sun. I could sense his insecurity as the sky started to light up, and as he turned to enter the adjoining forest, I followed him. His timing was perfect. As the sun started to rise, it gave him partial cover in the semi-open forest.

He was ponderously silent, moving like a phantom, and he knew his environment well enough to select thicker vegetation. Though the sun rose, it was almost as dark as predawn in the thick bush that now gave him cover. In absolutely silence and with the wind in my favour, I followed him alone. At times he would test the air currents ahead of him, I think mostly to detect vegetation of his choice. He fed occasionally but did not linger as his instincts were directing him to the sanctuary of denser bush as the brilliant sky lit up. He got there in less than an hour. Here he occasionally lingered to feed, sometimes standing for moments to listen, trying to detect foreign signs other than the birds or occasional animals. This now was the domain of elephant, and from here on he selected certain elephant paths, trying to avoid making noise until he reached the densest vegetation. Here he felt secure enough to be noisy despite the brilliant sky, at times pushing off the paths into the very dense bush. This was his daylight element and he fed at will, even though he had fed extensively most of the night in his other sanctuary of the darkness. I spent hours spooring, occasionally seeing him from the back and hearing him ahead. As the sun increased in intensity, he selected beautiful areas of shaded trees. He was unknowingly showing me the secrets of the forest. Occasionally I heard his rumblings and at these places detected the spoors of other elephant, but they were not recent—he was merely acknowledging their presence.

The heat of the day brings about a type of silence that can be felt only in the bush; besides the occasional calls of spotted wood doves, most creatures are silent. Generally the air currents are slight, sometimes proved only by using the *rota*. At other times stronger air movements can be heard coursing over the dense vegetation at higher levels. Such an incredible atmosphere can exist only in the wilds of Africa.

From the signs I could see that the bull was beginning to search for his own kind. Restless, he kept ponderously on, and eventually I heard growls of recognition and knew he had joined a herd. I found them in a shaded forest. I approached carefully and saw that he was in the company of some of the infamous Zambezi Ladies. Because the bull's ivory was poor, and because one does not linger in the presence of persecuted cow elephant, I was content to retreat.

It was so hot now in these Months of the Sun that all other hunters had cleared out for the cool air of the plateau, leaving me the whole valley. Before the coming rains, I wanted to renew energies and stamina to cover as many watering places as possible. I mentioned to Zaratina that instead of these long, thirsty treks from watering places to the elephant sanctuaries, we should carry what water we could to enter the Naukaranga *jess*. He warned me of thirst, saying he had personally seen men go down within hours of entering the *jess*. A single day could mean death.

Nonetheless, with a rifle, *rota*, dried crushed meat, rice, a pot, and water bags between us we entered this place of elephant bulls in the hope of finding fresh spoor. We knew that once elephant were here, they did not need to venture far as the density of the *jess* was sanctuary to them everywhere. We estimated we could possibly stave off thirst for two days, after which we would have to head for the pools of the Chimba River at the base of the escarpment. Here in the *jess* the silence was almost tangible, occasionally broken by slight sounds of our footsteps on the decayed, flat, trampled leaves on the many elephant paths.

Occasional ancient baobab trees seemed to hang upside-down as if their roots were pointing at the sky. In the vast areas of dense *jess* they stood out, towering massively high above the thickets. Their wide trunks gave some shade, depending on the angle of the sun.

Far inside, surrounded by walls made of thousands of dried sticklike branches around us, we listened to the intermittent slight wind disturbing the upper branches. When the wind stopped, the silence was so great that I felt it was a palpable part of the Creator's presence. Then a distant hum steadily increased, and we looked up and saw a wide tunnel formation of migrating bees. We were pleased that they had passed over and gone.

This wilderness, untrodden as yet, could be a hunter's paradise or his hell. I asked Zaratina why this vast mass of dead-looking, leafless thickets for many miles in all directions was such a sanctuary for elephant. He said that in the rains it was a virtual paradise of dense cover for elephant herds feeding on the millions of leaves. Elephant were drawn to this *jess* from as far as the Rakuti, Marongora, Chimutsi, and other sandy watercourses. The select feeders, of course, still emerged from the Zambezi River swamps also to enter Naukaranga. He went on to say that he thought it was too dense for cows with small calves, which would have to walk at their mothers' feet in the dense thickets and thus risk being stepped on. That, he felt, was why the cow herds fed mostly in the outer fringes of the *jess* bush.

"I have a place, bwana," he said, "where we can store hunting equipment."

"What sort of place could anybody have here—a few huts and running water?" I jokingly said.

"Watch yourself, bwana," he said, "this place has a way of making people go *penga*," meaning mad.

The wind swirled as I tested it with the *rota* bag. Not so good, I thought. Zaratina took in my thoughts and said wind direction also depended on the time of day. In the excessive heat of midday, the air slowly rises, causing the ash to fall straight down to earth. This little jewel of a tracker knew his environment well. "What's this place you have?" I asked.

He replied, "It is a large, hollow baobab tree trunk—big enough inside to hold four sleeping men. It is here somewhere close by, but as all the paths and bush look the same, it will take time to find it."

How he would find an isolated tree in this wilderness was beyond me, but knowing his prowess in the thickets, I followed him. Within the hour he took us off an elephant path, and we forced our way into the dense thickets. There it was, a large baobab tree with a hollow trunk. It was about eight feet wide and taller than a man inside.

"We stay here in the rains," he said. "We, meaning who?" I asked.

"Jacoba and I," he said.

So this was part of the bond between these two men. They sometimes shared the dangers of the *jess*. It dawned on me how great their bushcraft must have been to penetrate the dense lushness of this *jess* in the rains.

The tree was big enough to hold four sleeping men.

We kindled a cooking fire and used the water sparingly as it was our lifeblood. It was an eerie feeling, sitting in the firelight with the *jess* pressing in on us as the black mask of night fell. It took quite a while for me to learn my way in the frightening sameness of the *jess*, but by following elephant almost daily, twisting and turning on their maze of paths with such limited vision, it came to me. Eventually the only times I temporarily lost direction were when we closed in on bulls.

Considering the conditions of the *jess* and the numbers of wounded animals there, this period became the hardest, most nerve-wracking, most dangerous of my life. To offset it somewhat I had the courageous, skilled little tracker Zaratina and the plucky watercarrier Jacoba. Both were small, insignificant-looking people but far superior in hunting ability to the thousands of KoreKore of their tribe.

We heard that a skilled Tsetse Fly Department hunter had been killed following a wounded buffalo into the *jess* bush. Zaratina stumbled on both his and the buffalo's remains. Others were killed at various times, and the deciding factors here were thirst, skill, and fear. If I stayed alive here long enough, the *jess* with its abundant bull elephant would become my home.

I hunted successfully, but at a cost to my nervous system, and I occasionally came close to going to the mythical hunter's heaven. The elephant knew where they were safe, even at a few yards, and would not move other than sometimes to lash out with their trunks or make short rushes to reach us. The drill was always to take a quick snapshot at their heads, then try to anticipate other targets.

Ancient baobab trees seem to hang upside-down as if their roots are pointing at the sky.

Each man is different in temperament, and so were the elephant. Some would stand perfectly still in dense thickets at only a few yards, forcing us to manually post the thicket gently to get vision for a vital shot. Others would come from a short distance like express trains to emerge almost on top of us. Besides the skill to locate them, it was always a matter of nerve and quick, accurate firing in the final moments that brought us through. I was lucky to have had the experience of many previous hunts. Otherwise I doubt if I could have hunted successfully there.

One morning we followed two large bulls. We thought they had come from the direction of the Chimba Pools at the base of the escarpment. We continued on their almost unseen spoor over the many-times-trampled leaves of the elephant paths. Toward midday in the intense, shadeless heat they came to halt in particularly dense *jess*, having left the elephant paths and pushed their way through the dense thickets. These thickets were not broken by their slow progress, springing back into their original positions after the animals had passed.

We located the bulls but were unable to make contact, the bush being so dense that we could not even see a patch of their skin at two paces. They had all the advantages of invisibility. It was incredible—we could do nothing as they stood stock-still and we had to do the same, just hoping they might move to give us some idea of what part of their bodies we could shoot at through the scrub. I tried to approach from what might be the back of an elephant in the hope of immobilizing it with a spine or hip-socket shot, but these elephant had selected an ideal place, and there was no way we could get safely through this patch of almost impenetrable thicket. For the third time in my life, elephant had me truly buggered. We carefully retreated out of that impossible place.

That incident was the first of many times we lost elephant because our vision was so limited in the gray thickets, the same colour as the elephant. It struck me that since the animals were so wonderfully camouflaged and confident of their environment, perhaps I should expose myself in the hope that they would see me, and either turn to move off or attack. Charges—really lunges toward us—were common, and then it was a matter of snapshooting accurately enough so we lived for yet another day. By now I had conditioned myself to this fact of life.

I was not sure whether the elephant's eyesight could define colour in addition to movement. So at the first opportunity I secured three hats—I generally wore a light, short-brimmed straw hat in the hot months—and painted them with glossy white paint, hoping to help the elephant detect our presence. We reentered the *jess* and within days put these hats to the test. Imagine these thickets if you can, dense stems—much higher than the elephant—all growing from central clusters. The higher they grew, the more they spread and let in the daylight.

We walked along the elephant paths and found fresh spoor. While Zaratina was determining when they had passed, Jacoba quietly said something funny and we all laughed, but I could see the signs: stress was building up inside us all but was more evident in Jacoba.

Prior to my knowing him, Zaratina had learned to shoot buffalo with a muzzleloader. He was a poor shot, but the closer an animal was the better his shooting became. His success was probably a matter of his wonderful courage and self-control—the opposite of some accurate long-range shooters who miss an elephant at close quarters. I had seen my share of those.

I had of necessity armed Zaratina with my spare .404 magazine rifle and myself with the .450 double rifle. I usually carried two chest bandoliers and a belt, giving me the security of seventy rounds of ammunition, but here so much firepower was unnecessary because of the smaller bull numbers, so I carried a belt around my waist holding thirty rounds plus two in the rifle.

Elephants crossing the road in the jess.

We followed the spoor and saw that the beasts occasionally broke off and chewed dry sticks, then released the remainder from their mouths—roughage no doubt. We saw the rearmost bull's backside as it walked on the elephant path in front of us. I stepped past Zaratina to come up close to it on the open path and then made a human sound. The bull spun around, crashing some bush, and gazed down on me.

In a flash I shot it and heard another one run off down the path, roaring. Then it stopped. We continued, hoping that it would make a stand—which it did. No doubt this elephant saw the shining hats approaching it. It hesitated, and as it spun to dash off again a quick shot to the hip disabled it. The bush was so dense on either side of the path that I could not get around to have a shot at the brain, so I took the second hip joint. Its back collapsed, giving me a raking shot from the back of the neck at the brain, which I took.

That encounter proved only that the painted hats were more noticeable. We continued to wear the hats. Jacoba seemed to regain some confidence as he thought the hats had *not* attracted attention—he did not want to be more noticeable.

It seemed we were coming to the end of our tether. A few days later we spoored another lot, and they played hide-and-seek with us most of the day. Under these trying conditions we were wearing down in stamina and nerve. In late afternoon these elephant slowed down and eventually took a position in thick bush. We stopped close by. I thought about it for a while, then went in after them alone on my instincts. Twenty paces brought me to the nearest one. I purposely made a noise by pushing my way through the scrub, knowing that the elephant would hear me coming. Halfway there I stopped to listen to its reactions to the painted hat, which I knew it must be able to see from its higher position. I could make out only a darker patch amid the mass of sticks, but no detail. I stood there, rocking on my feet, ready for it. It must have been at an angle because I heard its body thrash the vegetation in a quick spin and then the snapping of sticks as it came toward me. As its head partly cleared, I shot it.

Another bull came crashing past unseen, then stopped to listen and scent. I climbed onto the dead bull to try to see the other bull and could faintly make out its large forehead facing in my direction. The bush was so thick that elephant felt secure

In a quick spin and then the snapping of sticks it came toward me. As its head partly cleared, I shot it.

surrounded by it. Upon seeing you, they usually made a rush in your direction. This one must have seen the white hat and the upper part of my body as I deliberately moved to attract it. The ploy worked, and it came at me with a roar. I put it down as soon as I could see its forehead.

Other elephant now rushed off through the *jess*. It was impressive to hear them crash through the thickets trumpeting and then recede in the distance. We usually heard rather than saw them smashing through the bush. When we did see them, it was awesome, full of power and majesty. I felt sure the painted hats had caused them, to hesitate and stare for seconds to locate me. If this was the case, those few seconds gave me valuable time.

Hats were an encumbrance in the thickets as the branches were always moving or dislodging them. With gun in the right hand and hat in the left, we pushed through the thickets. But the heat and sunlight were so intense that we had to put them on again. On the elephant paths it was better for we could duck here and there to avoid the overhanging branches.

Eventually we neared three bulls that I thought might be facing me. As I pushed my way through the thickets toward them, they faced me square on. When the nearest one saw me moving under the bright hat, it extended its ears in alarm, head raised. Then it lurched at me as its ears flattened on its sides. I put it down and instantly ran up its shoulder exposing myself to the two others. They gazed at me and my bright hat in alarm, their ears out and heads raised, not knowing whether to bolt or charge. Before they could make up their minds, I got them. I was pleased that the shiny hats were working, giving me the necessary time to go into action. I later also used a white shirt, which proved even more effective.

We continued hunting like this and accumulated average ivory. But because of the frightening conditions, we were wearing down. Jacoba in particular showed signs of nervous stress. Then I started seeing elephant where there were none. It got worse, and every few hours, when under duress, I imagined I saw elephant and would indicate so with my eyes, but they were purely imaginary. I knew this was a danger signal of the "bush tap." Poor Jacoba was the worst off—every time we got near elephant he started to shiver, brave man though he was. We ceased hunting for a while and later resumed. Then Zaratina showed signs. This was the end; we had to vacate the *jess*. We lounged in the clearing we had made around the hollow baobab tree, using it as a storage place for ivory. Some days we could see the distant dark skies over the plateau, indicating rain, and sometimes flashes of lightning above the escarpment.

Our first need, in or out of this dense wilderness, was water, so we decided to go back to the Zambezi River but first to visit the Chimba Pools at the escarpment. We organized and carried our gear, leaving the ivory in the hollow baobab tree. Chimba was a day's walk in tremendous heat. Eventually we emerged on a small hill above the large pool and camped on a slope away from it.

Around a fire that night we heard rhino grunting and snorting at the water. Sometime during the night elephant cows squealed and splashed about, and we heard the familiar calls of the hyena below us in the valley and the grand sounds of lion roaring. It was a welcome change from the wilderness of the thickets. In the morning I examined the pools to see what had drunk during the night: A few antelope, some cow elephant—plus lion, leopard, and rhino. I discovered a place close by where rhino had rooted a tunnel into a hillside, no doubt feeding on mineralized soils.

We stayed two days at the Chimba Pools a little above the valley floor in the escarpment. Then I changed my mind, so instead of heading across the valley floor to Mudzeemo's on the Zambezi, we dropped down to the base of the escarpment and headed for Nyamando's village farther north, also near the escarpment. I knew of an isolated pan there and thought we might find elephant. We heard drums beating for miles before we got to Nyamando's. It meant that any elephant that had been persecuted would likely stay out of this area. We climbed the gentle slopes to the village just as the sun was setting

Amidst the pounding drums and the calls and yells of drunken, dancing tribesmen, I watched the sun turn red. The whole valley had a glow for a few minutes, and then the sun sank below the distant western escarpment. The darkness spread, but the fires were large and threw light on the shining bodies of dancing men traditionally clothed in their loincloths and animal skins. I stood next to the two main base drums and watched the drummers in their state of ecstasy, pounding away with what looked like large rhino or small elephant rib bones—the curved part making contact with the leather skins stretched over the wooden bodies of the drums. There was a large gathering of people, visitors having come from distant villages. Every now and then one of them dashed off beyond the firelight to urinate, returning quickly to avoid missing something. They had no doubt planned this event as they had large quantities of beer.

An uninviting gourd was thrust at me. I drank half of it to please them, but it tasted foul and I threw the remainder onto the fire. I saw the dancers throw out their arms, gesticulating in the air, but never ceasing to stamp their feet. One came over to me shouting: "*Kaporamujese!*" They all took up the cry. He danced in athletic rhythm, using physical expressions to indicate that he wanted my rifle. I know wild men's dances and thoroughly enjoy watching frenzied men move to the drums, but I was not going to hand over my beloved double-barreled rifle. Zaratina, also armed, thought I was going to shoot and quickly cautioned me, saying the dancer wanted to indicate the hunt and needed the rifle. I said I knew what he wanted. Another man came forward, pounding his feet with the same physical request. Zaratina, having had his share of beer, was in the spirit of it all. He asked me if he could hand over his own .404 rifle.

"Yes," I said, "but remove the shells and bolt and give it to the original one who came forward."

That dancer was particularly athletic, and, having heard them chanting my bush name, I knew they were going to give their impression of a hunting act on the firelit "stage." There was a change in drum intonation, and about twenty men came together dancing, representing the thick bush. Then two from outside danced into them as they slightly parted. These two were the tracker and hunter. The tracker then leaped in short jumps into the air, and the hunter emulated a man shooting a gun. I doubted if this tribesman had ever had a gun in his hands as he seemed to point it at his own body. As the dead "animals"

I was pleased as the shiny hats were working, giving me the necessary time to go into action. I later also used a white shirt, which became even more effective.

were shot, they dropped and crawled to the outer circle of men around the tracker and hunter. The tracker shuffled and bobbed his hands up and down, indicating he was using the *rota*. Then the hunter leaped into the air and, at his peak height, pointed the rifle forward. We started to laugh, knowing there was no way we ever hunted like that.

Zaratina explained to me: "He is imitating you—he is either jumping to look over the bushes or to attract the elephant."

Although the dancer leaped high and landed well, I was concerned in case the rifle stock should be broken. I was grateful when he tired, then went through the antics of warning the imaginary elephant, swearing at and challenging them, and finally kicking to make sure they were dead.

When the drums beat and primitive men are liquored up and dancing, they have a talent for relating past events. It was their version of what they had heard or imagined. Eventually Zaratina got the rifle back, and we parted to sleep in the forest close by. It was lovely and warm, so we lay exposed to the night near our own fires.

Both Jacoba and Zaratina had had their fair share of beer and were comparatively useless the next day. The day after that, we moved off to camp at the Chimutsi, a small, dry, floodplain river. We found a water hole but no spoor other than the occasional rhino. Toward sunset hundreds of partridge watered there. We moved farther up the dry riverbed and slept where a sulphur spring formed a watering place. Here there was evidence of elephant and rhino occasionally drinking. Upon tasting the lousy water I wondered how it could attract them—all it did for us was cause minor dysentery.

During the night at the spring I woke with fear in my stomach and stared into the darkness. Then I detected a movement close to the earth—a man crawling in my direction. I recognized the small body of Zaratina and realized there was danger. On looking away from him and ahead, I indistinctly saw and at the same time heard the snort of a rhino as it came down on me.

I barely had time to grab the rifle and roll to one side as it lowered its head in its rush and pitched my grass bedding on which was a light ground sheet. It somehow got tangled: Its larger horn thrust through and its front feet caught on the material, causing the ground sheet to tear. Then in a state of fury it tried to rid itself of the ground sheet. It turned in a half circle, and as I got to my knees it sensed and saw me and in seconds charged. It looked particularly menacing from my position on my knees. I knew I might have only seconds to live, so I concentrated on firing past the second horn in the poor light. The heavy bullet put the rhino down, but it thrashed in a daze until I put a final shot into its lower shoulder.

Caught off guard that way, I was both fearful and then angry at the thought of the rhino thrusting me while asleep. Had I not awakened, it no doubt would have smashed my spine.

Next morning Zaratina mentioned a cave entrance he had once seen at the base of the escarpment. I suggested we have a look at it. He said the ground around it consisted of masses of flat rock, so it would be impossible to see signs of what might have entered it. Spoor was impossible to find at the entrance, so we gathered and lit some firebrands and moved into the cave. The silence was awesome. I did not feel secure in the cave, as our primitive forefathers must have. I was beginning to feel the venture was a waste of tune when we heard a warning growl from the interior. It was a leopard. Jacoba, at the back, yelled something unintelligible. Then we heard many soft squeaks and hundreds of bats came flying past, just missing our faces.

Realizing that we should not be here in the first place, we urgently moved as one to get out of the cave. We climbed a short distance above the entrance and sat there, hoping to get a glimpse of the leopard should it emerge, but it did not. I asked Jacoba about that noise he had made in the cave, and he said he just had to yell something to feel better. We all laughed about our stupid venture and returned to Nyamando's village.

The next morning, with about twelve others and carrying water, we crossed the valley floor to reach Chief Mudzeemo's village on the banks of the Zambezi. In our party were two barefooted, semi-naked women. Tough and gallant, they walked with us all day long in the intense heat and into the night. I thought of these women often in later years when I saw white men fussing over their own women, trying to protect them and make life easier when, in actual fact, women put to the test may prove tougher than the men.

In days to come we walked the Zambezi River Valley about a mile inland from Mudzeemo's to the bottom of Kariba Gorge past Namomba Island. The elephant there, mostly cows and a few herd bulls, were still very much disturbed. To tangle with the cows was a waste of ammunition as they could always be counted on to come at you, and we had to run off a few times. We had hunted the elephant in the *jess* and thereby had made them even more dangerous than ever. Our nervous systems needed recuperation, and the only way to get it was to stay away from the *jess* until the next season.

Walking parallel to the river, we camped in the much-appreciated shade of the *musango*, sausage, Natal mahogany, and pretty yellow-flowered cassia trees. The nights were hot and sleep was impossible if clothing was worn. Fires at night were always part of our lives, but in this climate we had to stay away from their exaggerated heat. At nine in the morning on the final days of the Months of the Sun, I estimated the temperature to be about 115 degrees. Imagine what it reached from midday to late afternoon!

Besides us, other hunters had disturbed the game, and, control measures being poor, there were many wounded animals. Our main concerns were the wounded elephant and buffalo. Shooting predators was prohibited—the government wanted those animals to help destroy the wildlife that harbored the tsetse fly. It was a policy I failed to understand then and still do. It could only have been instigated by ignorant, inexperienced persons—certainly not men of nature.

Late one night we camped under shade-giving trees above the Chikomba, a dry watercourse entering the Zambezi River. We had the usual fire but slept a little away from it because of the heat. During the night a crazy rhino snorted us awake as it charged the fire, scattering it all over the place. It then spun around and had another go at the remains of the fire while we all took refuge behind the trees. It seemed confused, not knowing which of the scattered burning branches to attack again, then attacked them all. Apparently feeling satisfied with its efforts, it trotted off but, unknown to us, halted close by. We laughed, and Jacoba said I should have sent it on its way with a shot up the backside. Then all of a sudden the rhino reappeared, and we had to take refuge behind trees again. It looked and listened, trying to find something or anyone to charge at.

Our laughter ceased abruptly as we stood hidden, waiting for its next moves, but all it did was repeat its crazy antics of spinning, snorting, and mock-charging the remains of the fire. It occurred to me that there might be more than one rhino, and I turned to watch behind me. Then the rhino trotted off. We remained silent, so as not to attract the rhino back again, and collected the remains of our fire and put more wood on it. Eventually we fell asleep, but some time after that we hastily rose again to another snort. The crazy rhino attacked the fire again, preferring to do so even when it heard Jacoba laughing. It spun a few times, challenging in different directions, then trotted off again. At this stage we were no longer sure of what it might do next, so we stayed quite a way from the remains of the fire, sitting in darkness and listening. Eventually Jacoba said, "I told you, bwana, to shoot it up the backside!" I wished I had.

It would have been a good time to go and sleep on a sandbar, but we had no dugout. The rhino did not return, but our sleep was not sound and just before dawn we heard lion roaring in the distance, inland away from the river. In the morning Zaratina spoored the crazy rhino and found places where it had charged off, finally stopping three hundred yards away. Here it had defecated and, as is customary for rhino, kicked and scattered the dung and tried to savage it by gouging the ground with its horns. Jacoba said that since there are mad people, there must also be mad rhino. We moved down the riverbank some miles for we did not want a repeat of this performance.

I sat in the shade on the high banks overlooking the magnificent Zambezi River scene. As always the lazy hippo schools were somewhere about, and I occasionally heard their grunts coming across the waters. Amidst these and other natural sounds, broken by sometimes incredible silences, one is always conscious of the mighty river with its sandbars, islands, high banks, and reedbeds. The brilliant sun causes the smooth waters to shimmer for miles. Far across the river I could see occasional fires, their spiraling smoke indicating human activity.

These settlements, in what was now gameless country, were becoming more numerous. I wondered why the colonial powers had allowed the western half of the Zambezi Valley, of all places, to be raped of its wildlife and vegetation when there were far better areas for human occupation, especially on the more suitable plateaus. Northern Rhodesia is an area of great agricultural potential—why did they allow the destruction of their half of the Zambezi Valley? It can only be that the governments of Northern Rhodesia and England had no vision beyond the copper mines, which gave immediate profits, and cared about neither people nor beasts. To the big boys at the top, the wilderness of Africa meant vast areas on maps to be exploited to meet their own needs.

I was brought back to my immediate surroundings when I heard Zaratina and Jacoba talking to a tribesman in a loincloth standing with two bare-breasted women, one with a child on her back. They were exhausted by the heat, and Zaratina asked me if he could give them some meat and let them cook it at our campsite. He did not have to ask, for as long as we had meat, visitors could always have some.

While the locals were eating, Zaratina and Jacoba came up and looked out over the river for some moments as if there was something I could see and they had missed. Then Zaratina said, "These people have seen the spoor of a large elephant where it came out of the Chipandahoure Swamp. It has gone in the direction of the minor *jess* above the dry Chipandahoure River." He said its spoor suggested it was wounded or damaged as it was dragging a leg.

On receiving this news I beckoned to the male visitor. He came over with hunks of meat that had been previously dried and now were cooked. He greeted me not as *Kaporamujese* but as *Humba rumi* (he who hunts to live). He was a

KoreKore on his way to Chief Mudzeemo's. We all sat close on the banks, and in the quiet voice of wilderness people he told me of the bull elephant spoor. He volunteered to go back and show us, but I said it was unnecessary as the trackers would find it in the morning.

That night the visitors stayed in our camp, and we spoke of this and that. As always I was impressed with the quality of the tribespeople's teeth; they eat no sugar other than seasonal coarse sugarcane. Perhaps their black skins emphasized the whiteness of their teeth more so than our white skin does.

Zaratina greeted me not as Kaporamujese but Humba Rumi (he who hunts to live).

I thought that we might as well hunt this elephant, and Zaratina and Jacoba were keen to do so, the area being close to their village, which would facilitate the cutting and storing of meat. In the predawn Zaratina and Jacoba made arrangements with the tribesman to have his family and friends come to the top of the Chipandahoure Swamp in case we got this bull elephant. Zaratina and Jacoba already had stored some meat in Mudzeemo's village, but this would give them more to barter with for other goods. I was going to leave the Zambezi Valley soon as we were well out of the season. Christmas and my birthday, 31 December, had passed, and I had been away too long.

We used the truck and got to the top of the swamp at sunrise. Sure enough, we found the spoor of a bull elephant where it had fed at night and left the swamp at predawn. It occasionally dragged on one front foot, not necessarily because of a wound. The spoor led us to the *jess* forest above the dry Chipandahoure River. Portions of it near the dry watercourse were shaded. We walked warily on the spoor, not so much because of the elephant but because of the buffalo-bean creepers that flourished there. When disturbed, this vegetation gives off fine hairs that inflame the skin and make you itch hours after contact. It is particularly disturbing when the hairs get into your eyes. Medical treatment is required for the eyes, but a mud bath, allowed to dry, usually removes the skin irritation.

We tracked the bull to a shaded spot in dense vegetation, and as we closed in it moved off silently ahead of us, crossing behind the Chirundu Hills into the mopane scrub country and crossing Chirundu Road. It was early morning, but already we could feel the heat increasing. As we were crossing the road we saw two Humber motor cars come to a halt a hundred yards off. Families emerged and unpacked blankets, picnic baskets, and bottles under some sparse shade of mopane trees.

Jacoba said, "*Murungo una penga*," meaning "White people are mad."

Amused, we walked up to them. They were obviously from the wealthy Copper Belt Mines area in the north and were jolly "English types"—"mad dogs in the sun." They displayed a spread of delicious cold meats, salads, and liquor. I thought if I spoke nicely to them I might be invited to indulge. I must have looked like a wild bandit as they greeted me cautiously, unsure of themselves. I was about to try to put them at ease when one of them asked me what I was doing here.

I said, "Hunting an elephant that has possibly been wounded and recently crossed the road before your arrival."

They did not like that part of it. Hoping for a feast, I said that for their safety I would stay with them while they ate. In their ignorance they became alarmed and questioned why the flies bit them so instead of going for the food on the spread blankets. I said the flies were not the common type but rather tsetse flies.

"You mean the insects that carry the dreaded disease?"

"Yes," I said, "but it is only one in thousands."

The twin threads of bull elephant and tsetse flies were more than enough for them, and without even discussing the details they lifted their blankets from the ground, dumped all their goods and food into the back boots of the two cars, and rode off without so much as acknowledging that I had even spoken to them.

We watched the cars disappearing down the Zambezi Valley road toward the eastern escarpment plateau. My hunting companions could not understand English and were puzzled by the quick disappearance. I was disappointed but started to laugh.

Then Jacoba, true to his style, said, "All white people are mad, unpredictable, and confused like rhinos. The only thing they know is money and what it buys." Even *Kaporamujese* goes mad when he meets them."

Then they had a joke about Faanie as a tigerfish and a crocodile chasing him. Zaratina added to it by saying, "*Kaporamujese* has had too much sun and not enough Zambezi water." We laughed at it all and then took up the bull's spoor again. In broad daylight this persecuted elephant walked past an open sulphur bog that had almost dried out, on into leafless mopane forest, then into some minor *jess* bush where it took sanctuary.

Zaratina no doubt wanted the bull badly that day as he closed in. The bull died from a brain shot without sensing our presence. It fell on the side of its damaged leg, but we could smell the rotting flesh of its infection and assumed it had been wounded high on the leg or shoulder. I thought this must be the last hunt of the season. After Zaratina had cut off the tail, we walked back across the road to the Chipandahoure forest and then to my truck above the swamps. By now it was close to midday and hot as hell. So we parted—they to wait there for the promised labour for meat cutting and I to motor across the valley floor to the escarpment. Within a few miles I came into the rain belts upon the plateau. It poured heavily, and I knew those rains would eventually water the vegetation of the Zambezi Valley. I arrived at a small village called Karoi (the tribesmen call it Chikangwe, after a small watercourse there). At a store I ordered powdered milk and ate a pound of butter and a loaf of bread "like a starved wild man," as the store owner said, sitting on the pavement. For months I had had a craving for butterfat and vegetables.

I then motored on to Salisbury, where there was every amenity. There I was again in the thin air of the plateau in the full rainy season, and I would have to reside there to await the drying out of the country for the season yet to come.

DISASTERS:

WILD RIVER SETBACKS—1953

In the midsummer of 1953 I found Faanie in Salisbury, sitting at an outside cafe, where we brought each other up to date on our recent activities. He had made a good profit from the crocodile venture, and consequently paid me my share for the time I was with him and Jeffrey before we parted in the swamps. He had plans to buy and erect a stamp mill to mine gold-bearing rock on the Angwa River.

I asked him about the legality of it and he replied, "You, with your elephant hunting—how can you question me on legality?"

I was concerned because poaching activities take time to surface; I was wondering whether problems might crop up on his return to the Zambezi River.

"Anyhow," he said, "these places are part of the river system, the swamps and all that." And so we left it at that.

He told me they had hunted Nemana Pools, and with his efficiency in water, they must have shot many crocodiles there.

"So, you have money now," I said, "and are determined to blow it on the gold fields?"

He told me they had hunted Nemana Pools, and with Faanie's efficiency in water, they must have shot many crocodiles.

I then told him of my plans to again hunt the Zambezi Valley in the dry season, meaning the winter and spring. Don't be misled: Spring is the period when heat is at its worst and inland water scarcest.

I also had in mind the Kariba Valley Basin, the large tract of land that was open on tsetse-fly permits. Here, too, game extermination to help eradicate the tsetse fly was encouraged by government policy.

While on the plateau during the rainy season, I did odd work here and there, feeling the pulse of industry. It was not to my liking, and I was thankful that I had a better way of life. I reasoned that I would rather risk life and suffer thirst than be regimented into an imposed routine of dull commercial or industrial programs. By many people I was considered a "crackpot," but when they had cold, miserable conditions in the winter, especially at night in the high altitudes, I would be down in the low, warm country hunting and lazing around in rivers. People thought I was living a life of self-imposed hell. No doubt residents of the plateau knew little and cared less about the country to the northwest, since it was visited only by the occasional farmer, hunter, or native commissioner.

We both had extra cash now, so Faanie and I, while waiting for the hunting season, started up a reclaimed battery business. We collected the battery scrap from farms and processed it to sell to a company in Johannesburg. The venture worked well enough, but eventually we exhausted our sources of supply. In this enterprise I got to know the farming community of Rhodesia, including some who went hunting. I found them distinctly different from the city folk and enjoyed their company. We had much in common: interest in crops, livestock, and horses. I had spent much of my life on horseback, having had the privilege of playing polo at Roberts Heights, a military base outside Pretoria where my father was an officer. On the northern plateaus I'd also had the exciting experience of hunting lion, buffalo, and elephant on horseback. Hunting astride a fast, although sometimes a frightened horse called for a totally different approach; it was quite different from hunting on foot. Besides shooting, the emphasis was on maneuverability and control, and I always felt confident and exhilarated on the back of a well-schooled horse.

The mainstay of the economy in Rhodesia was tobacco produced on farms. Soldiers returning from World War II had been given the opportunity and support by the government to open up vast areas of virgin lands to this golden crop. Large tracts where wild animals had recently roamed became human communities. Before the farm occupation, government campaigns resulted in game being slaughtered out of the areas. Responsible, of course, was the Tsetse Fly Department, known at the time as the Department of Research and Specialist Services. It always had in mind the need to eradicate game in the fly areas so they could become croplands and ranches. Whenever man and his greed emerged, the wild animals were decimated.

Africa was again and again experiencing the unrelenting encroachment of the white man's enterprises, which took up the land at great cost to anything wild. I often thought of it and reached the conclusion that all of us were hypocrites: The government and its policy of extermination, the game conservationists with their sentimental "conscience," hunters, farmers, and fishermen. Fishermen especially have always amused and amazed me. They are of the belief that they do not kill, that fish feel no pain, that they only hook the fish in the mouth under the water and haul them into the air, where they slowly strangle to death. The worst is when they force a hook or spike through a living fish and use it as bait to catch predator fish.

The unfeeling attitude toward certain species of life also applies to chickens, cattle, and all domestic meat animals. To me a chicken is a beautiful fowl, especially bantams with their bright plumage and miniature chicks at their feet. I have seen cattle brought to prime condition, healthy, heavy, and glistening as no buffalo ever could be—only to be sent to the slaughterhouse for the consumption of humans.

So what is the difference between domesticated and wild animals? Is one the creation of man and the other of God, or is game killed because we cannot control it as we can domestic stock? As game becomes scarce, perhaps humans will develop a conscience concerning it. Above all, if wild animals can be commercialized so they can be controlled for profit, they may be spared for posterity. To me the most inexcusable hypocrites are the meat-eating people who preach pathetic, unrealistic sentiment about game animals.

Here on the plateau I had an acute sensitivity to weather changes and was always conscious of the climate. In Salisbury I waited and prepared for the signs of the changing seasons. Finally autumn was close at hand, and I ventured forth to the Zambezi Valley and the Kariba basin, motoring from Salisbury and camping alone the first night in the foothills of the mountains. Here a large fire was necessary for warmth. In the early morning I traveled to the last hills of the escarpment base. It being early in the season, the air was clear and I gazed out across the great Zambezi Valley. Somewhere below, unseen and far off, flowed the great river with its islands and sandbars, riverine areas, and swamps. My eyesight moved over the mass of the *jess*, which I had penetrated before. Only God knew what would happen in the coming season or seasons—that is, if there were to be any future seasons.

In the far distance I could see the western escarpment, mauve-coloured across the valley. To the south the mountains of Kariba jutted into the great Gwempe Valley of Northern Rhodesia, and directly below me the foothills of the eastern escarpment descended to seemingly impassable thickets.

The details of the bush below me were partly obscured by distance. Because it was early in the season, the fingers of the minor rivers showed their riverine belts of vegetation in distinct green as they spread across the valley. I experienced the old, exhilarating feeling as I motored down to the valley floor. Here was primitive Africa appealing to my very soul, and I wondered what gave this land such a hold on me? I'm sure it was the river, the bush, the wild animals, the tribes, and everything that goes with them.

My ears rang and my hearing was dulled because of the drop in atmospheric pressure, and the heat rushed up to meet me as I moved across the valley floor. The bush was thick because of the early season, with green and fawn-coloured leaves. The different leaves indicated the approach of the season when all greenery would shrivel from the branches to carpet the land in its dead, decaying pattern.

I knew that if nothing had happened to prevent it, Zaratina and Jacoba would be waiting for my return. They and their tribe had benefitted from my presence, especially the meat I provided. I camped on Chirundu Hill overlooking the mighty Zambezi River—at the same place that had held me spellbound when I first saw it.

Below me was the great Chipandehoure Swamp. I listened to the evening stillness of the marshes, soon to become the feeding place of many wild animals. The swamp would erupt with their calls, with the roaring and trumpeting of feeding elephant and the added sounds of reeds smashing under their large feet. I stayed there to listen to it all, and heard in the darkness the wails of hyena close to my camp and the occasional rasping grunts of hunting leopard moving like phantoms in the night. I was home again and a great calm came over me. I woke in the morning to the harsh cries of the *chikwaris* (red-necked francolin), their piercing shrieks making further sleep impossible.

I drove off, but it was difficult to stay motoring on the old track, which had become overgrown in the rains. Had I been walking instead, it would have been a simple matter. Eventually I reached the floodplains and my old camping site. It had a different look at this time of year. The pools were much larger and the vegetation denser under the large *musango*, sausage, and Natal mahogany trees. Crimson creepers grew here and there in the higher branches, and the flame bush lianas added their bright red to the greenery.

There was time enough, so I took a rifle and gunbelt and strolled upriver to Chief Mudzeemo's kraal. On arrival I was disappointed to find the village deserted. Puzzled by the tribesmen's evacuation, I walked between the pools to arrive at the Zambezi River. There were dugouts well beached, pulled up to high places beyond the recent floods. Then it dawned on me: Zaratina had said that during the rains his people stayed at another village about ten miles inland.

There was no evidence of the village's direction, and the past rains had altered the look of the country. To find the village I would have to scout the country inland. Then I remembered Jacoba saying the village was close to where we had hunted previously, so I had a hazy idea of where it might be. Disappointed, I returned to my camp. There was something missing here without Zaratina and Jacoba around the campfire at night, so I determined to find the village in the morning.

In the first moments of predawn, just before the harsh calls of the *chikwaris* began, I moved inland with rifle, cartridge belt, and waterbag. Given enough time I would find the village of the tracker and water carrier. I followed the large elephant paths inland, found fresh spoor, and passed patches of *jess* still in leaf. Visibility was limited until I passed into the open mopane forests. Having found nothing by midday, I decided to walk at an angle to the river and came across spoor of kudu. Two bulls with well-developed spiral horns rose, stared, snorted at me, and ran off, bending their magnificent horns back over their shoulders to allow themselves easy access through the bush.

Then I heard the unmistakable sound of choppers cutting into wood, so I advanced and found four tribesmen cutting a tree. They informed me that there was a beehive in the upper trunk, far out of their reach, and because these particular bees were vicious they were attempting to cut down the tree, smoke the bees out, and extract the honey. I had come across them just before the tree was about to crash.

My respect for angry African bees is great, and as the tree came crashing down I ran off a safe distance, watching the tribesmen dance from the bee stings while they moved the already prepared fire and smoking materials toward the tree. This type of enterprise was not for me. I remembered one bee attack in particular when I jumped off a high bank into the Zambezi River's deep current, swimming underwater and risking death by crocodiles to escape the stinging bees.

The tribesmen eventually came to me in the shade, carrying honey in yellow combs on stripped bark slabs that acted as homemade trays. We had a feast of it, and I asked them of the whereabouts of Zaratina and Jacoba. They informed me that they were in the *jess* from time to time but might be at the village. I said nothing but suspected my two companions were storing water and snaring wildfowl around the hollow baobab tree where we had cached ivory.

Accompanied by the honey seekers, I came to the inland village in late afternoon. I walked up and greeted Mudzeemo. There was a bond between us. That night I was engrossed as I listened to the unwritten history of the Zambezi Valley. Zaratina and Jacoba were not in the village and had been gone for days. That night at the campfire Mudzeemo told me that black spies had been sent from Miami, the control center on the plateau, to investigate my successes of the previous seasons. The spies were particularly interested in any contacts I had made across the Zambezi River in Northern Rhodesia. It did not worry me, since that country, although British, had laws similar to Roman Dutch law: In principle a man was innocent until proven guilty. Besides, there was no way any man could stay on my track to obtain evidence as I had the advantage of being able to leave false trails and the night was my friend.

I could not visualize the authorities being able to prosecute me other than by breaking down human witnesses. The chief would silence the tribe, and that left only Faanie, Jeffrey, myself, Zaratina, and Jacoba. The last two I knew would succumb under pressure, but at the same time they would use their cunning to lie enough to cause total confusion, for such is their defensive nature.

Hospitality was good, as always, in this village of Mudzeemo, and, being well fed, I slept in the council hut, which had an opening all around from about three feet above the ground.

In the morning, to my surprise, I rose to see Zaratina and Jacoba sitting around the campfire in the dawn. We were pleased to see each other. I learned that they had stored water in the hollow baobab tree in the Naukaranga *jess* forest, but Zaratina warned me it was too early in the season and the *jess* had too much leaf; it would be extremely dangerous to hunt there.

This I had to see to believe. That night we slept on the fringes of the Naukaranga thickets and next day entered them. It was as he had said. The elephant paths were crowded by new lush vegetation, and vision farther than a few feet was impossible. Perhaps, I said, it will not be so bad; at least the gray of elephant skins would show up well against the green foliage, even if at only a few feet. We penetrated along some ancient elephant paths, and it was tough and irritating always to keep an arm in front of the face to protect the eyes from the vegetation closing across the paths. Where before this *jess* was fearsome, it was now terrifying.

Zaratina was adamant, saying we must hunt elsewhere until the leaves fell from the *jess* forests. Perhaps it was just as well, I told him, as I had a permit to hunt the Kariba-Zambezi basin.

"Do you know it?" I asked Zaratina.

"No," he said, "but it can't be worse than this."

On our return from the Naukaranga, we cut straight across the valley floor, which was most pleasant because of the season. We walked in comfort, there being much shade and a few pans of water. We came across the spoor of buffalo and a lot of elephant cows—the infamous Zambezi Ladies so prone to attack on sight, sound, or scent. We were in no danger from them here and joked of their dangerous attacks.

Zaratina told me how these cows had completely discouraged white hunters from coming to the valley. The locals here referred to cow elephant as "the pigs"—not because they lounged in mud but because of their unexpected habit of attacking humans. They said the cows had no manners, or the manners of a pig. We derived much pleasure from the stories of how the many hunters had had to shoot and run for their lives. Indeed some non-hunters were killed simply because they were smelled or heard by the cows.

It was noticeable that the tsetse-fly campaign was having the desired effect of eliminating wild animals, with the exception of what had now become vicious elephant. But the tsetse-fly numbers were still astronomical; no doubt, the flies adjusted their bloodsucking needs to the many minor animals untouched by the shooting campaign—such as birds, lizards, squirrels, and badgers. As always, the stupidity of this extermination policy disturbed me.

Toward sundown we arrived at my camp, where I was pleasantly surprised to see Faanie. He had acquired a new vehicle and had boats on display.

"Going posh," I said.

I asked him how he'd found me and he said, "Your reputation stinks and all I had to do was follow the smell." *Son of a bitch,* I thought—*still full of bull.* He explained that he had erected a mill to crush rock for gold extraction on the Angwa River, but the reef had petered out. I reminded him that I had read of the Rhodesian reefs having this characteristic.

"Anyhow," he said, "it is no problem as I can recoup most of the money from the resale of the mill."

I told him he was like some people with religion, going overboard about something he could not see, meaning the yellow mineral under the earth.

In reply he said, "Not everything has to be coldly logical."

"And now what are you doing in the valley," I asked, "having a holiday after breaking your back on the gold fields?"

"No," he said, "I have come for a while to hunt with you."

For a moment fear struck my heart at the thought of hunting again with my lunatic friend. But I brought him up to date on the cow elephant here.

"Don't worry," he said, "we will cut them down to size."

Still the same, I thought.

"Anyhow," he said, "why waste time with these trash elephant? Let's have a go at the crocs again. They paid well; that is how I could afford the mill and the new truck and boats."

I thought for a while, not liking the idea of crocodile hunting.

"You usually make up your mind fast," he said. "Are you confused, Englander?"

I said, "I was balancing my chances of survival with you."

"Don't worry," he said, "I have changed for the better. The hard work and sweat of mining have made me think like you."

"Lying bastard," I said.

"Well, anyhow," he said, "let's give it a go. Nobody but you and I have mental telepathy in danger—don't worry, Englander, together we will always survive."

He was an excellent companion and a persuasive liar.

"If we take to the river," I told him, "I will leave later in the Months of the Sun to hunt the bulls in the *jess* ."

He said, "We will both take them in the Months of the Sun."

I shook my head and said, "To have you with me in that *jess* would be the end of both of us."

"Don't worry," he said, but he went no further.

"I will hunt crocs with you," I said, "but the moment you become insensible I will desert you, wherever we are or whatever we are doing. These are my conditions. But first I must hunt cows for Chief Mudzeemo. How many crocs do you think will be on the river?

"Plenty still," he said. "They are mostly hiding. I know where they are. Come with me and find out."

Faanie was always good at organizing; he had a boat turned upside-down on a rack on the truck with a smaller one inside it, plus outboard motors. It was the sight of these boats that had made me ask him if he was on a holiday. In anticipation of things to come I examined his equipment—good, light boats and motors; rifles—a double-barreled .600 and a .416 bolt-action Rigby; sawn-off shotgun; lamps; and batteries. The .600 we had both hunted with, especially elephant in the water holes at night.

"The .416 Rigby you will like," he said. "It is your type of weapon."

I replied that I knew this caliber from experience; it and the American .375 and the English .404 were probably the most dependable magazine rifles I had so far used—that is, if a magazine rifle can, like a double rifle, be completely dependable at all times. I considered the .416 to be on the light side. I told Faanie this, and he said a lot has to do with the man behind the gun.

I said, "Be that as it may, there is no way I would want to go into the *jess* with anything below a .450." Even then, at times, I felt it was taking a risk—though perhaps it had been fear overruling reason since I had so far always managed to survive. I told Zaratina and Jacoba that instead of hunting elephant I was going downriver with Faanie to hunt crocs for a while, giving the leaves time to fall. Then we could go to the Kariba-Zambezi basin and finally, in the Months of the Sun, into the Naukaranga *jess*.

I invited them on the river trip, but Zaratina only reluctantly agreed, staring at Faanie with his burning eyes. He said, "I know he stands up to anything on land, but in water he thinks he is a tigerfish. Crocodiles eat tigerfish, and we are not even fish. What will happen to us if we follow him into the water at night?" He added that once Faanie's feet touched the water it went to his head, and he went berserk. We laughed hilariously—except Faanie and Zaratina, who stared at each other over the firelight. Still half laughing, I asked Zaratina where he got his information.

"I know all of this valley," he replied, "even where the mad people hunt."

I later warned Faanie in English not to be verbally abusive with Zaratina.

"Of course not," he said "I admire him—he is an independent, courageous little bastard and does not give a stuff about what any man thinks. No doubt he is a master of his environment and arrogant about it too."

I told Faanie that Zaratina had been made wise and developed an attitude of survival because white hunters had left him in the lurch, and he'd had to dodge, hide, and run for his life.

"I think he has learned the hard way and because of that is quite capable of reading men."

"Well," Faanie said, "Zaratina says I am mad, so let's be kind and just say he is a survivor."

"You will change your mind," I said. "He is a jewel in the *jess* ."

Faanie was for using Kam Cha Cha's place on the opposite west bank, farther downstream near the Kafue River confluence, as a base to hunt the waters of the area. He had his mind on certain places farther down the river. With

Faanie, "farther downriver" could be a few hundred miles, well into Mozambique. I thought we should go up the Zambezi into the Kariba Gorge and particularly to its end where it entered wide waters. I had seen many crocs there. The junction of the Sanyati, too, was known for its aggressive and cunning crocodiles.

Zaratina and Jacoba went to their inland village to fetch their families and then returned with the rest of Mudzeemo's people to their huts on the banks of the Zambezi River. This annual occurrence took a few days, and then we all went after the elephant cows for Chief Mudzeemo. Faanie was mentally bright and had acquired professional hunting knowledge of a high standard and knew how to use it. But he still had suicidal tendencies and an over-abundance of reckless courage. Again I warned him that if he turned into a matador, I would abandon the croc hunting. Blackmail, arm-twisting—call it what you like—but it had its effect.

We followed a large herd of elephant cows as they entered the Nyamaque *jess*. This *jess* was not as dense as Naukaranga but was dense enough, considering we were following cows, and we had to be careful to keep the element of surprise since the cows had that frightening reputation for attacking. Here Faanie saw the skillful tracking and maneuvering of the tracker Zaratina.

"Impressive little man," he said "Reminds me of the courageous and skilled trackers of Mozambique. They are just a handful in the thousands of tribesmen we have known."

"Lousy stuff, this *jess*," he added. "How the hell do we know where we are going?"

"Let's see what you can do in it!" I said, and gave him the lead. "Just remember, there are other people dependent on you."

"Don't worry, Englander," he said, "these elephant are my friends and besides, I don't stink in their trunks like you do."

Incurable, I thought, and warned him again: "Be serious or the elephant will make you so, and above all, use the proven pattern of hunting. Remember now, no matador stuff."

Sometime after this we heard the herd in front of us slowly move through the dense scrub and thickets. The noisy conditions were ideal; we should be able to get in close before they became alarmed. Occasionally we saw parts of their backs moving forward, and Faanie said, "How does a man hunt elephant off the paths?"

"Forget it in these thickets," I warned, "If you are off a path, the *jess* will throw you back or trap you in its mass."

Our positions on the elephant paths were: Zaratina first with the *rota*, testing the wind; Faanie; then me; and finally Jacoba, the water carrier. Zaratina indicated that at the rear of the herd were what we call "brush elephant," old cow leaders that take up positions following the herd. The herd was not compact but spread out, judging by the sound of their movements. I could tell by the tenseness of Zaratina's facial muscles that we were going to close in at any moment.

We came to a V in an elephant path. Faanie was for going one way and Zaratina the other. I stopped Faanie with a hand action, and he followed Zaratina. Then Zaratina halted, causing all our senses to be alerted. He indicated unseen elephant facing us in the dense thickets. It meant they had turned and were suspicious.

We saw nothing, only felt their presence and heard the sound of others farther away. I could read Faanie's mind like a book: These elephant were a few yards in front of us, and he was not going to try to move through the thickets. Then Faanie put his left hand to his mouth in an action similar to a good-bye kiss, raised his rifle, and yodelled. The elephant's reaction was almost instantaneous. With piercing trumpets descending into roars, the whole bush seemed to move toward us and the foreheads of cow elephant appeared high up. I saw Zaratina drop, turn, and swing, avoiding any physical contact with Faanie. The elephant heads were almost above us. Accurate, fast firepower put them down, but because of their numbers and closeness, both Faanie and I had to fire. The rest of the herd went berserk ahead of us, and we deduced from the crashing bush that some were moving away and others had turned in our direction. These were tense moments of indecision for us, as we had to wait stationary to determine elephant positions by sounds and guess at their distribution and numbers. Such conclusions can come only with much experience.

Faanie finally realized this was a different hunting environment. I sensed his uncertainty about the elephant's closeness in the thickets and indicated with my hand, "Paths only." He understood and looked back at Jacoba, who was shivering. I stood next to him, pressing my hand on the back of his neck to reassure him. It was done in fondness and pity but was not necessary as we had been through this before, and I knew that despite the fear overtaking him, he would stand to the test that was yet to come.

He took no notice of me but gazed fearfully toward where the cows were grouping, regrouping, and spreading to search for us. Then the situation got out of our control for a while as cow searchers were on both sides of us. Because of a change in wind direction, we had only one course—to continue forward into the elephant and shoot our way through them. I could tell Zaratina had the same thoughts. He looked back to me for approval. I gave the slightest nod, and he continued along the path. It is one hell of a task to move into elephant from which you feel you should be escaping, but the professional has to overrule fear with coolness and intelligence.

We neared the performing Zambezi Ladies, while other elephant on both sides vented their fears with angry trumpets and low, rumbling roars. Both men and beasts thought only of fear and attack. I thought to myself, *Faanie, you are a man of war; well, you will have it now if only for a short while.* The elephant smashed around us, then contact was made as the guns went off. Zaratina never hesitated but continued forward, knowing his protection lay in the guns immediately behind him. I was the third in position and had to take care not to fire close to Faanie's eyes.

The cows plowed toward us as if the thickets didn't exist. There was great relief when we realized no more elephant were in front of us. Behind and to the sides they still sought us, but we were escaping. After a half-mile we sank to earth in a little opening. I poured water into Jacoba's cupped hands and had some myself. Zaratina and Faanie did not need it as yet.

"Strange place," Faanie said, meaning the *jess*. "Restrictive and nerve-racking having to walk into them or have them come at you. It is better when the elephant come at you."

He was reaching the conclusion that we had arrived at with the help of the white-painted hats, and I explained it to him.

Then he asked, "Is this the first time you have tackled such a large herd in the *jess* in the full leaf season ?"

"Yes," I said.

"So, you bastard, you used me," he said.

"No, it just happened that way," I said "The bulls are easier, but the Naukaranga *jess* is much thicker."

"It's hunting only up to the first contact," he said, "and then it is just a fight in there."

He pleased me as he continued, "We owe our lives to the pattern of hunting we use. This tracker kept moving into the herd even though he was unarmed and closer to the cows than us. An unusual little man."

I asked him if he would do the same.

"No," he replied, "not without a rifle in my hands." Then he added, "This is the place for the .600 Nitro Express."

"For bulls, yes," I said, "but with the large numbers of cows, a man's shoulders could not take the punishment of the recoil."

"And you, you shaking little man," Faanie jokingly said to Jacoba.

"Hmmmm," Jacoba replied, moving his head gently and staring at the ground. "*Ko heenya*," meaning "to sh-- in fear." We all laughed.

These two black men were very small of stature, by our standards. I told Jacoba, "You have no real problems in the *jess* as elephant always kill the bigger people."

He looked at me in disbelief, then said, "The elephant do not know that yet, so next time I will tell them."

I asked Faanie if he realized how brave this little water carrier was. Every time Jacoba had had contact with elephant he got into a state of shivers and yet was always ready to hunt again and again.

"Can you imagine yourself under those conditions of fear forcing yourself to penetrate the herds?"

"No," he said. "He is a plucky little bastard."

As was customary after a serious shootup, we relaxed for some time and I took a brief nap to restore my nervous system. I woke to hear Zaratina and Faanie talking in low tones. Jacoba was still asleep. I joined them and Faanie said, "I have been thinking of you and the first time we canoed above Victoria Falls on the Zambezi River. You were a weakling then, not even croc bait, but look at you now. You are robust and have great stamina."

I told him I had often thought of my health and always reached the conclusion that I had become robust because of my life amidst nature. It was either survive or die, and I survived because of nature and my youth.

We returned to our camp, and Zaratina and Jacoba left for their nearby village to inform Chief Mudzeemo of the dead cow elephant. They would be gone for some time, and the villagers would go into a meat-cutting orgy.

In the meantime we rigged up Faanie's gear and adjusted the boats to our needs on the Zambezi River. Then we crossed to the west bank and went upstream to a small isolated village, where we procured labor for skinning. These west-bank people were decadent, and I never felt relaxed unless I had them on an island where they could not escape or rob us. This trip was a test run to see how the equipment operated, and it was sheer pleasure going up against the strong current and watching the banks pass by.

I suspected that the motors would scare off the crocs, and as we approached sandbars and likely places on the shoreline we could see the crocs at a distance disappearing into the water. Anyhow, night hunting would prove how many crocs lurked under the surface. The idea was to penetrate the Kariba Gorge in a trial exercise to see what crocs were available.

A few days later we were well within the gorge; we floated silently downstream, using paddles to maneuver quietly. On sighting the pink glow of a croc's eyes in the lights, we would maneuver up to it, take a shot at the brain, and immediately pull the croc in. Away from the swamps, the insects, especially the mosquitoes, were few, making it pleasant to travel across the water at night. We seldom got small crocs in the gorge—mostly medium and large ones—and we got only about half of what we saw, but their abundance gave an idea of how dangerous it was under the water even though crocs were not often seen during the day.

Eventually we left the gorge, drifting silently downriver and sighting large numbers of crocs on both sides of the spreading Zambezi, but particularly on our side. We camped among the crocs at night and achieved excellent results, taking over thirty of them. We stayed a few days, and then, because I was reluctant to continue using helpers from the west bank and because we had enough skins temporarily treated, we decided to go back downstream. It was a lazy trip, with the paddles keeping the boat straight in the current.

After unloading the results of our labour at the village, Faanie opened the throttle of the motor, and we skimmed along at a good pace, well loaded. I felt uneasy because I knew a place on a bend in the river where there were large rocks just below the surface and where big schools of hippo resided. It was a dangerous place. We passed the rocks to one side, though we must have come close to some. A large crocodile heard us coming and ran front of us to get from land to water. I shouted at Faanie above the roar of the engine, but he took no notice. Luckily we missed it.

We rounded the bend and there in front of us was a school of hippo stretched across the water. We were traveling at speed—to turn back would have entailed doing so in amongst the hippo. There was only one way, right through them, and Faanie opened the throttle to maximum. The hippo, only their large heads showing, saw us coming and submerged, but there were so many that we were lucky one did not surface under the boat. But I did hear a distinct dull noise and a hesitation of the motor as the prop cut into the back of a submerged hippo.

Faanie, the bastard, was at it again. I shouted at him above the roar of the motor. He took no notice and continued at speed, so I worked my way from the front to the back of the boat and tried to take control. He resisted me. My nerves had taken enough of these man-made dangers. Anger rose in me, and I hit him and knocked him off the boat. Then I turned it in a circle, back-throttling the engine so he could pull himself aboard in the bow.

We were both angry, and he yelled, "Africa will have you when I decide it's your time to die."

To be endangered and then threatened again with death infuriated me and I shouted, "Why wait, try it now!"

I grabbed the shotgun, saying, "I have always wondered what this could do to a human body." He was a powerful man, probably a little heavier than me and at least twice as strong. But he knew I meant it, and if he had come the length of the boat, I would have murdered him. He stayed where he was, then stripped and dried himself in the sun. I started the motor, and we cruised downstream again at low throttle.

Much later he complained in an aggressive way, "You are like a *munt* (a black-skinned person)."

"Swear at me as much as you like," I said, "but stay your distance. Many people have died on the Zambezi."

We motored for hours, Faanie watching the water ahead and taking in the sun. Eventually he turned and said, "How are you doing, Englander—are you normal now?"

"Don't give me that," I said. "Any man would get high blood pressure with you around."

Then he became humourous: "It's funny, but no woman ever spoke to me like that and they can hate even more than you."

I no longer answered, but eventually his wisecracks made me simmer down. It took a long time.

We reached our camp near Mudzeemo's kraal, where a tribesman named Furese had been left in charge. Here we heard bad news: A crocodile had seized one of Zaratina's children among a group of others. I tried to picture how I might feel as a father under such circumstances, and it disturbed me deeply. I sat on the high bank overlooking the wide Zambezi while Faanie and Furese unpacked the boat, laying the damp croc skins in shade for further treatment with formalin to preserve them. I thought of how easy it is to lose or take a life in the wilds. Life is of little value—unless it is your own.

On this side of the river was the KoreKore tribe, a reasonable people, while across the river lived a bunch of soulless degenerates. The two groups sometimes had contact, but their mentalities were different. The death of Zaratina's child made me think of past fatalities: waylaying and murder, hunting fatalities, the terror of past slave raids, the Matabele marauders, and injustices at the hands of tyrants. Diseases—leprosy, malaria, dysentery, bilharzia, sleeping sickness—and especially tick-bite fever, no doubt the greatest killer of all the insect pests, decimated millions of people in Africa. Some of these illnesses I had seen and others only heard of.

Human populations, however, always increase, especially now since the whites have brought medical attention and reduced malnutrition. As the standard of living rises, Africa moves from its primitive past and in the process is bound to overpopulate itself. It will, in time, become grossly overpopulated.

The mighty Zambezi River will ultimately be tapped for irrigation, and all wild vegetation will disappear in favor of food crops. The riverine areas, bush, and mopane forests will disappear, hacked down for fuel. The escarpment will be used for grazing domestic stock. I thought to myself: *Maybe not in your time, but it will all happen. Nothing can change the march of time.*

You learn in life that everything changes and passes, eventually your own life itself. I thought, *Live it now while you can. Future generations won't even be able to visualize primitive Africa—their lifestyle will be different; it will be another world.*

In late afternoon, after bathing in the river, I climbed the bank to see Zaratina and Jacoba approaching through the riverine forest in their black loincloths. I stood waiting for them and leaned my rifle against a fallen tree. We had to talk about Zaratina's child.

The child had been playing with other small children in a few inches of water in the Zambezi, waiting for their mothers to arrive to collect water in their calabashes, which they balance on their heads. Just before the women arrived, a crocodile emerged and ran across the shallow water, seizing the child. No doubt the noise of the children playing had attracted it. The child obviously had moments of horror and pain as the crocodile dashed back into the deeper water, where the child was drowned. Although he didn't show it, I knew Zaratina was disturbed and vengeful, and I felt compassion for his plight.

The time of day had arrived when the setting sun would bring a colourful orange and red glow to the river's surface and surrounding vegetation, and a great peaceful feeling of belonging would descend. Then the light would fade into darkness and we would hear only the soft sounds of the mighty Zambezi flowing by. It was only a temporary peace, as the sounds of nocturnal life would soon intensify. In these last moments of dusk, Zaratina looked into the waters and said, "I will hunt now with you and the bwanas."

For days Faanie, Zaratina, and I plus two skinners hunted the areas above Chirundu and into the Kariba Gorge. We got many crocs, but the remaining ones became wary. I sensed Zaratina's hatred as he vengefully drove his spear into the crocs, sometimes damaging the skins, though mostly his thrusts were to the head. Their deaths seemed to relieve his sorrow for a while.

Not far from our camp, new hunters had arrived from the plateau. They were farmers—Fergus du Toit, his father, and a hunting companion, D. R. Smith, from the Selous farming area about sixty miles from Salisbury.

They sent a message inviting us to dine with them. We found them to be jovial, relaxed people. We needed laughter after the death of Zaratina's child, and we enjoyed good food, wine, and liquor. Farmer types like their luxuries, and we, being starved of them, enjoyed them more so. Fergus, known as Gus, was anxious about his elderly father, called Pop du Toit, who insisted on hunting elephant with them. It meant a probable go at the Zambezi Ladies in the Nyamaque *jess*. They had heard from the locals that Faanie and I had just recently shot a large number of them for Chief Mudzeemo.

Gus asked me what my name *Kaporamujese* meant. I said it meant "the penetrator of the dense thickets." By this time we had all had a few drinks, and Gus said, "This is the man we need to counterbalance old Pop's company on the hunt."

Old Pop, though mostly deaf, was a large man of magnificent frame and probably had been a physical force to contend with when younger. He was a defiant individual, sticking to the proven ways of his earlier years. Because of his deafness he had a curved horn that he inserted into an ear when he wanted to hear what was being said—which was not often as he believed all people around him talked rubbish. He was a likable sort who felt that he was the product of a more manly, intelligent, and adventurous era than ours. He was no doubt quite experienced in hunting, so I tried to explain to him—a feat in itself—that these Zambezi Valley cow elephant, because of constant persecution, were not normal and were considered fearless, aggressive, and dangerous. He would have none of it.

"The problem," he said, "is you," meaning that everybody but himself was afraid and inexperienced. I looked at him in amusement.

"You will see," he said. "When the going gets tough, you will all run away."

I told him the only places to run were elephant paths.

"Well," he said, "you will fight for positions and run down them."

Once this character had made up his mind, it was final. Faanie said the hunt would be a charade, and he wanted to go through the croc gear and tune the motors. For my part I wanted to see how this party would tackle the Zambezi Ladies.

So next morning we followed a herd of about thirty cow elephant where they had come from the swamps. Eventually they entered the Nyamaque *jess* and came to a halt. I had no staff with me and hung around the back of the party like someone in an audience watching the stage. The party knew what they were doing, all right. They came up closer to the elephant, still visually undetected. Men and beasts were about thirty yards apart, unseen by each other, and everyone stood still to listen. At this critical moment old Pop saw fit to ask why this bush was so thick and why we had stopped to listen. Unknown to him, his voice stirred the elephant herd into movement, and we heard shrill trumpets and the breaking of branches. There was a look of fear on everyone's face except old Pop, who could not hear the elephant. Instead of being silent, he then demanded to know what was going on. The elephant again heard him, but this time they moved en masse toward us, smashing the bush down in front of them. I looked in wonder at the old man with the listening horn in his ear, trying to determine the elephant's direction.

For a few moments I thought there was going to be another war here, but then the fear was turned into action as we all started running down the interspersed paths in the hope of evading the oncoming elephant.

The old man shouted, "Why are we all running?" But it did not stop him from running with us.

The wind was in our favour, and luckily the old man stopped talking, giving us a chance to open the distance. This old character thought we should go back again to the herd. His courageous stubbornness and lack of hearing were a lesson to me, revealing how less fearful a man was when he could hear no sound from an elephant herd. When safe enough, we all laughed at our performance—except the old man, who refused to believe what he had caused. Indeed, he was annoyed, accusing us of being the new generation of two-legged jackals.

"This *Kaporamujese*," he said, pointing at me, "got so fit running away from elephant." Trying to explain to him would only have annoyed him more.

In later years I loaned old Pop a good tracker—one who could handle a rifle for Pop, who was getting very old. The tracker told me he was hell to hunt with since he could not see impala until he put on his glasses; by then the impala had run off. He would then accuse the tracker of seeing imaginary animals. This also happened with a rhino and kudu. Pop du Toit later told me the tracker was useless. This particular tracker had hunted and shot elephant in Mozambique—but whatever his experience, it was not good enough. These hunting events merely reflected the rigors of old age and intolerance and were humourous and appealing.

Just past midday we returned to Gus du Toit's camp, where everyone swore they would no longer hunt with the old man. The more they drank that night, the more determined they became. In the predawn they left to go hunting inland, leaving the old man in the camp without his knowing they had departed.

At the camp I took my time, then left. I had decided to go back to Faanie a few miles downstream. After I left, the camp cook told the old man he had seen a bull elephant passing some distance out. The old man followed and shot it a quarter-mile from the camp in ideal open conditions. Gus and his party returned that afternoon, having had hell again from the Zambezi Ladies, shooting some of them to escape. One can imagine old Pop du Toit's attitude when he informed the exhausted party that he had shot a bull close to camp.

At our own camp Faanie said we must tackle other croc hunting areas. So we left Zaratina and Jacoba at Mudzeemo's village and crossed under the steel bridge at Chirundu, going downstream. The steel stretching across the Zambezi was a sign of the penetration of civilization to come. Faanie was in good humour, jubilantly reciting a German warrior's poem.

Feeling good on the water, we traveled at low throttle, Faanie at times telling me he was a "river boy." We reached Kam Cha Cha's in the morning and mounted the high riverbanks. There were two bush houses, the first at Kam Cha Cha's just below Chirundu and the other farther down belonging to his brother. This place acted as a nerve center for us, and we relaxed under a large tree and listened to what was taking place in the Zambezi Valley. Kam Cha Cha told us black spies were active, trying to get information about me.

"Lie to them!" I said, "Tell them anything unreal. Get your people here to cross the river and spread false information, and above all find out who the spies are and where they move around and where they come from. No white man alone could ever uncover this information."

I got a message to Zaratina, bringing him up to date on this spy business. I knew he would do counterspy work. He could move like a phantom, had the contacts, and knew how to obtain information for our survival.

Here on the west bank I had nothing to fear and could move anywhere on the river, it being an international waterway. I laughed at the thought of being apprehended on the river; how would anyone know where the boundary was on this wide river? Jeffrey, the other possible witness to spy activities, was downriver, having been gone for a long time—God alone knew where, as he was always hiding on the banks in dense vegetation. Kam Cha Cha knew only that Jeffrey was armed for both crocs and other animals. Well, I thought, perhaps the hippo would give us a clue. If they were skittish or nervous, we would know Jeffrey had shot some of them.

We spent a day or so with Kam Cha Cha, and the last night my curiosity got the better of me. I crossed the river in a dugout to visit a tribesman friend of mine on the east bank, the Southern Rhodesia side. His name was Dicka, probably taken from the European name Dick, which he fancied. He told me three men had made enquiries about me. Two of them, he said, were not valley tribesmen and were dressed in khaki clothing and boots.

"What did you tell them?" I asked.

"*Kaporamujese*," he answered, "we always say you are across the river or in the Matonga country above Kariba."

"Where else have these people made enquiries?" I asked.

"In most villages and close to Mudzeemo's," Dicka told me.

"Who is the tribesman with the two others?" I asked.

Dicka hesitated, then told me he was from the west bank above Chirundu in Northern Rhodesia—the same side as Kam Cha Cha's, where we always felt safe, but much farther upriver opposite Mudzeemo's village. This news disturbed me. So then, investigating my activities were two police, probably from the plateau, using a tribesman from the opposite bank.

There was a half-moon, and I felt energetic in the warm air. I walked a few miles to the village of Zekoni, a man I knew and trusted as he had helped me before. He was powerfully built, having spent much of his life rowing dugouts, but his eyesight was failing. The village, a few huts with dying fires outside them, was silent, so I gave the call of the nightjar bird next to Zekoni's hut. I kept calling at intervals, then did so in short bursts unlike any living nightjar so that Zekoni would become suspicious.

Inside, he softly called, "*Indianie?*" meaning "Who is it?"

I answered, "*Kaporamujese*."

He emerged, at the same time tying a loincloth around his waist. Plainly he was puzzled. We walked inland to the forest fringe, and here I questioned him.

"The three spies are here now, sleeping in the village," he said.

"What is it they really want to know?" I asked.

"Everything," he replied. "All the people you contact, the chiefs and headmen. What you do in the villages and on the river and the people you have used in the past and are using now in hunting. Two of them are of the KoreKore tribe. One knows you; his name is Kapessa from the plateau. The third one is from across the river—maybe one of Chiawa's people."

I faintly remembered Kapessa as the man who was with Guy Patterson when he was killed by an elephant.

"Where are they sleeping?" I asked.

"In the open council hut," he replied. Zekoni always had a calming effect on me and now he said, "No blood."

"No," I said, "but I will question them as they question everyone else. Go back and stay away."

"No blood," he repeated and moved back in the direction of his hut. The night was silent except for a few insects and the distant wail of hyena. I walked over to the council hut and entered. The three sleeping men had a short spear, a Martini-Henry single-shot rifle, a waterbag, and some food and other gear, plus two pairs of boots of the type supplied by government and a short skinning knife. Quietly I raised the Martini-Henry, removed the cartridge, and leaned the rifle on the outside of the low mud-and-pole wall.

I looked at the men for a while until my eyes were accustomed to the dark interior of the hut, then woke Kapessa by tapping my foot on the side of his neck. He was slow to awaken and then sat up, looking toward the place where the rifle had been.

"Who is it, what is it?" he asked, uncertain of himself.

"*Kaporamujese*," I answered.

He stood upright and faced me and as the others were awakening. He told me the whole story as I had previously learned it from my own enquiries. I questioned him some more.

"What is it that the governments really want?" I asked.

"They just want to know everything about you," he said. Not quite sure whether to trust Kapessa or not, I asked him how many shells he had for his rifle. "Four rounds," he said.

I gave him the one I had extracted and told him where the rifle was but to leave it for now. The other men I did not know. As one of them cautiously moved toward the entrance, I warned him not to. He hesitated, but I could feel he was ready to take off like a hare. Kapessa warned him also, and he came back. *At least we were not trying to kill each other,* I thought. I ordered them to feed the outside fire, and as it glowed, spreading its heat and light, we sat around it, me with my back to the forest and the rifle across my lap. In the firelight I took in all the physical details of their faces and bodies. Two wore European clothes. I could understand why the two government men were here, but the tribesman from across the river puzzled me. So I questioned him. He was fearful and evasive. I tried to identify this man but could not remember him. I wondered why he should be so afraid and uneasy.

I questioned his origin, and he said, "Chiawa's village."

"And recently?" I asked.

He said again, "Chief Chiawa's village."

I knew he was lying, but why? I had to resist the urge to drive my rifle into his throat. I did not want witnesses to violence here in the east part of the Zambezi Valley. I knew this portion of the valley was controlled from Miami on the plateau by the native commissioner, with a police force for backing.

"Well," I said, finally having got information from each individual about the number of people in Miami, "tell them I am also investigating them. It may give them something to think about."

It was a queer setup, I thought—Kapessa and his friend open to questioning but the tribesman evasive and fearful.

I left them at the campfire and trotted a half-mile or so into the forest to open the distance in case of treachery. A few hours before dawn and much farther upriver I crossed the Zambezi to Kam Cha Cha's. In the morning I explained to Faanie what had happened. We stayed an extra day, then proceeded downriver in the boat, well loaded with the gear for a long croc-hunting expedition.

We passed schools of hippo and occasional crocodiles, the latter wary as they ran off the sandbars to disappear quietly into the river. We bathed and lounged in the water, then past midday landed on a sandbar that held what looked like temporary structures of branches and abandoned fish-drying racks. I was in the front of the boat, barefooted. As we eased into a landing bay, I was about to jump from the boat when my eyes detected what looked like sharpened wooden stakes about eight inches long, driven into the sandy bottom and just visible under the water's surface.

Leaping from the boat would have impaled both feet, and to have fallen over would have further impaled me through my hands. I warned Faanie, and we went farther downstream, landed, and walked up to the staked area. No doubt tribesmen from the west bank, probably from Chief Chiawa's, had gone to the trouble of laying this death trap. I felt anger rise in me. What manner of men would do this and for what purpose? I was always cautious thereafter when leaving a boat in shallow water.

Whenever I was puzzled by inexcusable human behavior, I used to fall back on the well-known words, "It takes all kinds to make a world." But the trouble they had taken to set their merciless traps still puzzles me.

We stayed on this sandbar island and looked around. I found human footprints six days old and the remains of fish here and there. It was evident that the landing was used often.

The next morning at dawn, we pushed out into the current again. After I warned Faanie again to ease off the throttle, we proceeded past a long run of thick, appealing vegetation growing along the water's edge with a deep current rushing by. Here we saw a medium-sized crocodile lying on an extended branch about six feet over the water. As we approached, it dropped off into the water and disappeared. I wondered how it had managed to get out there. On the banks we could see where crocodiles had scooped the sand to lay their eggs.

Faanie was right, there was evidence of a lot of crocs, but they were for the most part unseen.

He suggested we look at some small, isolated swamps on the west side above Mupata Gorge and some much larger ones below the gorge. It was way off to hell and gone, I thought, but we had the motors, an extra small boat, and adequate fuel, so I thought it all right. We were cruising a few hundred yards from the west bank, looking ahead for hippo, when I saw about seven crocs lying in the sun on a small sandbar.

I was about to signal Faanie when I felt a thud underneath us and the boat leaped sideways, throwing all our gear into the powerful current. We had hit a rock shelf about a foot under the surface. Normally we could spot obstacles close underwater by the altered colour and surface disturbance, but in this case the rock shelf was too far down to distinguish. Faanie and I landed on this rock shelf—me with my .404 rifle in hand; I had grabbed it thinking the disturbance was a hippo. The rock had ripped a hole in the boat, which floated down a bit and then submerged in the adjoining deep water. Faanie stood near me, the rope in his hand attached to the boat somewhere under the water.

The other, smaller boat was also somewhere under the surface. All our goods had sunk except the .404 rifle with three shells in the magazine. That, the clothes on us, and our footwear were our only possessions.

The disaster had struck in a matter of seconds. I thought of the thousands of miles I had traveled on the Zambezi—this was just not our day. We stood in a foot of water on a rock shelf about the size of a small room. Imagine this small area in comparison to the width of the mighty Zambezi River, and it had been our amazing luck to have hit it. Gazing into the fast, powerful current, I regretfully thought of our specialized gear lost forever, especially my beloved .450 double-barreled rifle and expensive medical kit including snakebite outfits and all the equipment needed to do emergency operations in the wilds. Then I realized the greater loss was Faanie's—his double .600 and .416 Rigby rifles, a shotgun, his boats, motors, and other equipment. I looked at Faanie, who was slackening and pulling the rope, meaning that the boat was jammed somewhere, or held by the current. All our treasured possessions were gone underwater; there was no sign of anything except two bags of maize meal floating far down the river.

I doubted it could have happened in a dugout. I reflected that the more sophisticated man became, the greater the tragedy when things went wrong. The loss of my .450 rifle disturbed me so deeply that I was not at the moment concerned with the crocodiles, which could view our plight from their sandbar below us. This rifle had given me the confidence to penetrate thick bush where no other hunters had dared. It had fit my hands and shoulder as if it were part of me and was an extension of my physical power that had enabled me to survive where others had failed.

Against the reeds on the west bank I saw a dugout moving slowly; the owner had seen our plight and had come through a path in the reeds to pole and paddle his dugout to our rescue. I hailed him to make sure, and he waved back as he headed upstream so that he could use the current when crossing to come down on us. The crocodiles, on hearing me, moved into the water, and I regretted having hailed across the river. I was armed with the .404 rifle but had to keep a sharp lookout now that we were stranded in the middle of the Zambezi. Eventually the dugout reached us, and Faanie pulled it close to the rock shelf. It was badly made, not even straight, and could hold only two people—but at that moment it was more important than the *Queen Mary*. As I had the rifle, I advised Faanie to go first. I watched them cutting across, being taken downstream by the current—knowing I must be more vigilant now that I was alone. It took a long time, but eventually the tribesman in the dugout cut across the current again to collect me. He mentioned the crocodiles, and once I was paddling in the dugout I realized again how dependent I had been on these primitive craft with their ability to glide over the waters in comparative safety.

Eventually we reached Faanie on the bank. The two of us were still alive but were beggars in the wilderness. I said so, and we both started laughing—why, I don't know, but it was deep mirth—and the tribesman no doubt wondered about the madness of the white men.

Eventually I said, "You know, I don't give a damn about the rest even though it is a financial setback; but the loss of my .450 rifle haunts me!"

We allowed some time to gather our thoughts. Then, with the words "*Handey a tiendey*" (Let's go), we started walking to try to reach Kam Cha Cha's, about fifty miles upriver. This entailed having to cross through an area where the locals were known as hostile to white hunters. The tribesman who rescued us had a panga (machete), and Faanie used it and a branch to make a stabbing spear. I asked the man his name so that if the opportunity occurred, I could send for him and reward him with elephant meat. We were more grateful than he could realize but had nothing to offer this poor helpful man for his lifesaving services. That's how true and simple it was.

After getting directions to major paths from the tribesman, we proceeded upriver, inland from the banks. After a while I turned to see him still watching us, and he shouted, "You must be *Kaporamujese*."

I signaled, and we moved on.

Faanie said: "The dense *jess* must be one hell of a place if people know you so far from it."

It was midday, and we had to stay within reasonable distance of the river for water. If all went well, it would be another two or three days' journey on foot. Exposure was not a problem, for the country at this time was comfortable, with warm sunshine during the day, and we could obtain fire from some of the villages ahead.

It can be fatal to move through parts of primitive Africa if people think you are desperate and weak, for it is generally in their nature to see weakness as a reason to dominate, bully, attack, and rob. And good luck to anyone at their mercy—especially this lot on the west bank of the Zambezi River. It worried me little, however, since we had a rifle, though admittedly with only three rounds. We pushed on until almost sunset, having passed two villages, where we were refused food. We took some fire from the last village and a few miles farther slept next to a good blaze in a comfortable climate. Because of the many muzzleloaders on this side of the Zambezi, there was almost no game except the elephant that sometimes crossed the river from Southern Rhodesia.

I had made up my mind that if we saw game I would shoot, to have the meat to eat or to trade for other food. We moved the whole of the second day, sighting nothing other than old bushbuck spoor. Late that afternoon at a village, I asked the headman for some food, saying that we would reward him from Kam Cha Cha's across the Zambezi/Kafue junction. He refused, so I gave him the option of giving me some or I would take it. He haggled, drawing attention from others who were starting to surround us. I told Faanie to take what we needed. In these moments, had they resisted or attacked, I would have shot the headman at least. We left with them grumbling aggressively, some armed with muzzleloaders. That night I selected a spot in dense bush, where anyone trying to get near us would have made noise in the scrub and fallen leaves, and we spent a comfortable night.

Next afternoon we arrived at the Zambezi/Kafue River junction. Kam Cha Cha's was only five miles from here, but we had to get across the Kafue River, well known for its crocodiles lurking in the deep waters under the overhanging vegetation on the banks.

Two dugouts were tied in the reeds, and as I examined them for their paddles some tribesmen emerged from a path through the reedbed. I appealed to them to take us across the river, a matter of two-hundred yards over the deep waters where the Kafue converged with the mighty Zambezi River. They sensed we were desperate but underestimated us. I identified the man who had the first dugout, handed the rifle to Faanie, and then flung the owner into the deep water. We took over the dugout, and as he emerged in the water, swimming the pathetic dog-paddle stroke, I hit him on the head with the paddle and told the others to retrieve him, which they promptly did. Perhaps he was a headman, for they unhesitatingly jumped into the water to aid him.

We paddled across the Kafue to the opposite bank, and then, still full of venom at the thought of the locals taking advantage of us when we were down and out, I released the dugout into the current and watched it flow to the Zambezi confluence close by. There it was taken up by the major stream and quickly disappeared around the bend.

It was only a matter of five miles now until we would have food and shelter and the loan of rifles and ammunition. We rested a day at Kam Cha Cha's and then, with the loan of his boat and labor, returned to the rock shelf. It was an underwater feat by Faanie to raise the boat from where it was jammed in place with the current sucking to keep it in that position. We got both boats out, with one motor still attached to the larger one. It had a large gash, so we patched it as well as possible and towed it back to Kam Cha Cha's. Faanie later took it to Lusaka for repairs and at the same time acquired more gear, rifles, and supplies for another attempt at the crocodile venture.

After a week we were ready to go croc hunting again, only this time not so well equipped. I had the .404 from my early days and ammunition that Faanie had purchased, plus another .404 rifle borrowed from Ling Ah Toy, a Chinese, plus an additional shotgun and lamps.

In order to reequip ourselves to where we were prior to the disaster, we would have to hunt the crocs consistently and with determination. After a ten-day delay we were back on the waters again. Cruising slowly on the first day above Nemana Pools, I took a shot at a large crocodile basking in the sun. It was a chance shot as I stood up in the boat. I knew I had hit, but it managed to reach the water, and we lost the skin. We continued downstream, and the motor started misfiring, so we pulled in on a sand bank near Nemana Pools.

In those days this was all wild country: No one other than an occasional official went there. Unknown to us, someone was there now. The motor simply needed resetting and timing and clearing of the fuel system, at which Faanie was proficient. I left him to it and went farther on to select a washing place. I heard a motor and, puzzled by it, returned to see Faanie standing staring at me as I approached.

"You will never guess," he said "I was caught off-guard—they have taken the firearms."

I still had mine with me, so I queried him.

"No," he said, "the other firearms from the boat."

He explained that as he was repairing the motor an armed white man approached him and another took up a position in some trees, covering him with a rifle. They questioned him, and he explained that he intended to proceed downstream to hunt crocodiles, for which we had a permit from Lusaka in Northern Rhodesia. They did not believe him, and consequently the questioner, who turned out to be the district commissioner, removed all the firearms from our boat. I was disappointed in Faanie for letting them get our guns.

We needed the shotgun for night croc hunting; without it our expedition would be unsuccessful. It was especially maddening given the large crocodile population. In Mozambique I had learned the power of officialdom and had also learned how to evade, sidestep, and stay hidden from its powers.

Had Faanie not been so unsuspicious, he could easily have repaired the motor on a sandbar, an island, or on the west bank in Northern Rhodesia. It was just bad luck that the motor gave trouble as we were passing Nemana and that the native commissioner was there at the same time. From a legal point of view we were wrong because in this territory we were too far from the Chirundu five-mile strip.

I could still hear the drone of the commissioner's vehicle disappearing in the depths of the Nemana forest. Paramount now was recapturing our weapons, so I found the vehicle tracks and started running on them, carrying a belt of thirty rounds and the .404 rifle. From time to time the drone of their engine filtered to me through the forest. The numerous game caused me to lose time, especially the elephant herds as I had to be cautious in case there were any Zambezi Ladies among them. I ran a few miles parallel to and then away from the river and was hoping that the drone ahead of me would cease, indicating that the party had camped at Nemana for the night. If they did, I was confident of attacking them in the darkness and retrieving our firearms. Then a shot rang out miles ahead, followed by two more. I hoped they were in trouble with elephant, so, being very fit, I sped up.

It was simply a matter of running on the tire marks, for the driver picked the easiest way through the beautiful *musango* forest and grassland. The grass in places was dangerous to a running man, but being well armed I felt I could defend myself in a flash if the need arose. My main concern was lion, and I hoped that on hearing me coming they would stay clear. I kept up a good pace. This was the first time I had run miles through a wildlife paradise, with the game parting to escape in front and to the sides of me.

I saw many animals—elephant, buffalo, waterbuck, eland in large numbers, kudu, sable, impala, warthog, occasional bushbuck—and then a lone leopard in the fork of a tree. He jumped down and slunk off in the grass. The animals were mildly curious, giving way but staring at me. This man-creature was something new, a diversion breaking the pattern of their lives. I must have covered three miles and saw ahead some scrub mopane trees. The vegetation was changing, and I knew there was a large pool here—perhaps my quarry would camp there. Suddenly I came upon human footprints next to the tire tracks. The prints of three men and that of the vehicle turned at an angle, and then I heard the distant drone of an engine. About one hundred yards to the side I saw the carcass of a young buffalo half hidden in the grass. Its back legs had been butchered and taken away. It would be only a matter of hours before predators and scavengers would close in on the remaining carcass. I saw where wheels had circled to pass the large pool and head onto the higher shelf of the mopane country.

Obviously these men were not going to camp here, and I lost all hope of closing in on them. I was disappointed but thought perhaps it was just as well; in my frame of mind I would have shot them for our firearms had they proven defensive or unreasonable. Lucky fellow, this native commissioner, I thought—lucky he did not linger here at Nemana. The officials, now well ahead of me, must have been going to stay the night with Chief Dandawa on the Rukometje River. Their ultimate destination would be the control center at Miami on the plateau.

I looked at the vast, open country, which bristled with food and cover for game. Some elephant in the distance disturbed the *musango* trees to get at the curled pods. One large elephant raised itself on hind legs to reach into the branches with its trunk. So much, I thought, for trying to hide in a tree from an infuriated elephant!

Here in the peace of this forest it was hard to maintain murderous thoughts. I resigned myself to thinking that we would now have to go all the way back up the river, about sixty miles against the current, then overland up to the plateau to negotiate the return of our firearms. What a waste of money, time, and travel. I wondered what sort of chap the commissioner was to be so high-handed.

I was wet with sweat, so I took my time and cooled off by walking leisurely to recross the Nemana Pools and return to the Zambezi River. I passed through *musango* forest, where bright scarlet creepers sought light through the canopy and gave out a pleasant scent. I moved through and around impressive numbers of wild animals, which were aware but not frightened of me, and I thought this might be the closest I could get to the mythical Garden of Eden. Even for a hunter, it would be sacrilege to disturb it. I pondered why previous hunters and explorers had never mentioned Nemana. Surely some must have seen it. Perhaps it was not worthy of mention because in the past the whole country was as well stocked with game.

Lion were lying in the pampas grass through which I was walking. In Mozambique, this type of vegetation was the lion's favourite when they wanted to become invisible.

I came to a depression filled with pampas grass, its colour fading because of the season, and visually searched it. It consisted of thick, large, chest-high clumps, with small openings here and there to allow for walking. Ahead of me on a rise was a magnificent herd of some two hundred sable antelope with their curved scimitar horns. Their attitude, alert and not feeding, indicated that lion were lying in the pampas grass through which I was walking. In Mozambique this type of vegetation was the lion's favorite when they wanted to become invisible in front of your very eyes. No other vegetation gives them such perfect blending for camouflage.

I was almost halfway through it when I realized my mistake. It was possible that I had already passed lion, so I did not hesitate and moved forward, keeping the rifle in a ready position. A little farther on a lioness slunk off close in front of me and turned slightly—so well camouflaged was she that in seconds I lost sight of her, so I veered off. They say the female of the species is more dangerous than the male. I think it is because they are sometimes neurotic and thus prone to attack.

In this situation I was worried about moving away from the lioness, only to walk into another. Consequently I felt my way slowly, making noise so that any cats in front of me would move off. I knew what could happen and was tense. When I had almost cleared the depression, a large, magnificent male with yellow mane emerged from the pampas grass onto the higher ground between me and the sable herd. The sable snorted, but he took no notice of them and turned to concentrate on me.

I was clear of the pampas grass now. As the lion had already gazed into my eyes without wanting to attack, I kept walking toward him—watching in case he should spin around or raise his tail to twitch the black tassel on its end, which I knew would signal a charge. Defense in close quarters is not always a matter of action or reaction but often instinct, and I relied on my instinct heavily. I was in no immediate danger and kept walking toward him. He trotted off and entered a small patch of thickly clustered, thin-stalked bamboo cover. I passed close by, the mottled sunlight and shade giving me some view of his presence and shape. I felt an emotional appreciation of him. Finally he growled, as if warning, "No farther, hunter—I have my pride and position here. If you enter I will charge you." I gave him his territory and moved on.

Some of the sable were looking at us and probably had been all the time. They did not move away, possibly because the lion had been following them all day. Lion may attack in the day, but it is more likely to occur at night. I counted my blessings; it felt good to be not a sable but a man, the most intelligent animal on earth and with a rifle in my hands. For all the alert senses and instincts of the hunted, some of them must fall prey to the predators, man or beast.

It was getting dark under the tree canopy of the *musango* forest. In the far distance I could see some brightness indicating the open waters of the Zambezi. The river being close, I felt relieved, for I knew full well that walking through this game-stocked paradise at night was risky. I emerged on the high bank of the Zambezi River and was treated to a breathtaking sunset of yellow, orange, and then red.

I could not see Faanie, but knew I was close to where our rifles had been confiscated, so I called out across the open expanse of the river, my voice traveling well across the water. I called a few more times and waited. Eventually I heard the outboard motor start downstream, and in the fading light the boat slowly emerged, with Faanie searching the banks for me. We needed to sleep on a sandbar to get away from the animal activity of the night and in anticipation of that I had collected dead branches for firewood. We loaded up, leaded out to the mainstream, and landed on a sandbar to camp.

I was depressed by our misfortune, but Faanie took a lighter view, saying it might have happened for the best and perhaps we had come to the end of our bad luck. We decided that Faanie would go to Miami on the plateau to negotiate the release of our firearms, because I did not trust myself to be in the commissioner's presence. I could only hope that all would go well with Faanie; in the meantime I would visit Zaratina and Jacoba until he returned.

That night we heard the activities of the wild animals of Nemana right up until early morning. The trumpets of elephant and their low rumblings of pleasure sounded across the water. Mixed in was the hyena's wailing calls and the roars of lion. No doubt the sable antelope lost some of their numbers that night to the great stalking cats with their superior eyesight, their tense muscular bodies, their quick rushes, and their ability to kill with powerful jaws and merciless grips. Such is the pattern of their creation.

Normally we would have unloaded and hidden our gear while we returned to sort out our problem, but, fearful of more setbacks, we carried it all in the boat—an added load on our journey upstream, sixty-odd miles with the motor constantly fighting the current.

There is a monotony in going upstream with the motor roaring all the time and the noise causes the animals to move off. Two days' full throttle with the load, and we again reached Kam Cha Cha's. From here the rest of the trip was easy with the interconnecting roadways from his place. We told Kam Cha Cha our tale of woe. He was Christian in his upbringing but had a pagan slant that I found appealing. He told us the "river gods" are sometimes against you, but when they relent, you may again achieve the purpose of your efforts. To me gods had nothing to do with—it was all the work of mortal men. But his words rang with promise, so we were encouraged. I reclaimed some .404 ammunition that I had left there.

By arrangement, Faanie left me with the necessary supplies at my old camp spot under the giant sausage trees on the floodplains near Chief Mudzeemo's village. He would return after trying to retrieve our guns. Failing that he would try to buy a shotgun and heavy rifles farther on in Salisbury. I listened to the sound of his motor vehicle disappearing until finally I heard it no more.

I felt the atmosphere of the valley closing in on me like a welcome, warm blanket on a cold night. This was my country. Some of us are almost as wild as the tribesmen and animals. Although wild, I had acquired much practical intelligence, and it made me feel even more at home.

That night I camped alone, nodding off to the wails of hyena. In the first light of early morning I saw two men approaching. It made me feel good to know they could only be Zaratina and Jacoba. Zaratina was not one for greeting in the native custom, but I could read welcome in his eyes, if only for a few moments. He patiently waited for Jacoba to finish the palaver of greeting. I asked them how they knew I was here.

Zaratina answered, "The gods of the winds whispered to me," and added with the slightest smile, "We heard a faint distant motor and knew someone was here."

From this camp to Chief Mudzeemo's was a good three miles, and I wondered at the hearing of these people. They asked me why I was back so soon. I told them, and Zaratina asked, "And the one that swims like the tigerfish?"

"He has gone to Miami and probably to Harare," I said.

It is interesting to note that although these tribesmen had never seen Salisbury, it was always, even long before independence, referred to as Harare, probably meaning a place of bad dreams.

The *jess* still had much of its leaf, and because I was limited to the .404 rifle I told them such places were out of bounds for the time being until it thinned out. With this medium-caliber rifle, hunting would be more dangerous than necessary.

Zaratina said, "Some bulls have come into the area since you left, and they seem to favour the Nyamaque *jess* ."

"Well," I said, "in the Nyamaque and with bulls only, it may not be that bad."

The next morning we found fresh spoor where bulls had left the swamps. Just as Zaratina had said, their tracks took us to the Nyamaque *jess*. The thickets were still dense, but in places the leaves were falling in masses and began to carpet the ground and the elephant paths. My rifle was not heavy enough in caliber, so I had to be cautious. No wars in here—I had to hunt to survive, and it was safer to work on bulls rather than the aggressive Zambezi Ladies.

I cautioned Zaratina: "I am not armed for elephant that come crashing through the bush down on us, and so we must use extra precaution to hunt safely."

He joked, "Maybe if *Kaporamujese* dies, I will have a good gun and will not complain about it like him."

I returned the joke, offering him the gun to do the shooting. Zaratina was not one for outright laughter, but he had a look about him of deep humour.

"No," he said, "I can see that *Kaporamujese* is getting old and frightened. He has had too many contacts with people and not enough with the pigs (meaning the cow elephant). Soon you will be too old to drag your feet along the elephant paths and then the pigs will have you. When they are finished, which will be days later, you will be a mixture of branches and sand. Before you die you must throw the rifle aside so that I can come afterward and collect it."

Judging by the look of them, Zaratina and Jacoba were at least twenty years older than I. I asked Zaratina how old he was, but neither knew their age. "Just younger, wiser, and blacker than you," he said.

We all laughed, and then Jacoba said, "Ahead of us is no laughing matter."

So we eventually sobered our thoughts and then continued to follow the spoor. But laughter is good for the nervous system, and we followed the elephant less fearfully than before. Eventually we heard them, and Jacoba said anxiously, "Let me see those bullets that will not save us."

I gave him one from my belt. He examined it with a knowing look and said, "Hmmmm. So the pigs will kill you because you are the biggest amongst us. Are you sure they all know that, even the stupid ones? Perhaps they don't know that these bullets cannot stop them."

He was having a humourous go at me. Finally he said, "These elephant may be stupid, but they are big and very strong and are not afraid of Jacoba."

Luckily the bulls were spread out in a semi-open clearing. There were five, carrying medium-sized ivory. Zaratina put me into the right position, and because of the open bush, I fired confidently.

I put them down with brain shots from all angles, trying to get the lot, but in my haste I wounded the fifth one with a high head shot above the brain in the porous bone formation. I cursed myself as the bull temporarily slumped, recovered, and spun in seconds to be swallowed up by the surrounding thickets. With a head shot like that an elephant can live out the rest of his life, though he'll probably have a headache for a while.

My speed had made me wound an elephant. It would have been better to let it run off unwounded. A single wounded elephant was of no frightening consequence, but if he went into dense thickets and I had to follow with the medium-caliber rifle, he might push the bush down on me unless I got him in time. We immediately followed. He was traveling three times our speed on the elephant paths and at this pace could go all day. He was carrying about fifty pounds of ivory a side. That and the thought of us one day stumbling onto him wounded urged us on. Then Zaratina slowed on the spoor. He said the bull was dragging, meaning he wanted to stop, so we slowed down and saw a place where his spoor indicated that he had waited for us but had changed his mind and continued. Then unexpectedly we heard a rifle shot ahead, the roars and grunts of lion, and then another rifle shot followed by what sounded like the moaning of a lion in distress. It was in the direction of our wounded elephant, and at once I made up my mind that I was not going to follow a wounded elephant and risk coming upon a wounded lion.

Puzzled, we waited on the elephant tracks, then sank to earth to relax and try to fathom the situation. Ahead of us was a not particularly dense area, and Jacoba stood to peer there. We then all distinctly heard a mechanized clanking noise coming toward us. *What the hell could that be?* I wondered, thinking I was getting a touch of the "bush tap." It got louder, so we stood up to wait for its appearance. Coming around a slight curve on an elephant path we saw a black man armed with a .303 rifle and peddling a bicycle. Upon seeing us, a look of pleasure lit up his face. Calling greetings, he passed us and crashed into the vegetation—he had no brakes. His face was flushed with excitement. We broke out in laughter as he pulled himself free of the thickets. We could see where these and other thickets had lacerated his arms and torn away half his European khaki clothing. He was shocked but happy to see us, so we all settled down, laughing, to await his story.

He worked for a ranger in charge of tsetse-fly control, a European known as Lofty Stokes. Stokes resided on the plateau and had a large staff of African hunters armed with .303 rifles to exterminate game for fly-control purposes. To curry favour, Lofty Stokes had promised someone, probably a woman, a lion skin, and this *magotcha* (hunter) on a broken bicycle had been used to do the hunting. I knew Lofty Stokes, and he was quite capable of shooting his own lion, but it was a matter of opportunity. Lion hunting at this stage was forbidden—the authorities depended on lion to help kill off the game for their tsetse-fly campaigns.

This *magotcha* had come across a pride of lion ahead of us in the *jess*. He shot a big male as instructed, and then a lioness charged at him. He said he managed to hit her in the chest, and as she veered he grabbed his bicycle and peddled for his life on the elephant paths, only to have his face, arms, and clothing lacerated. We all laughed at him, but he was too shocked to join in, though he seemed to get relief by talking about it. We told him of the wounded elephant and our decision to abandon the hunt. Because of our company, his confidence returned and then his true comical, cocky nature asserted itself.

Examining his rifle and bullets he said, "This gun is magic—only recently has it not killed outright. Bwana," he said, speaking to me, "I know the big lion is dead and the other cheeky one must be dead by now. Come, let us collect my skins. I have been promised one pound sterling for a lion skin."

I asked him if he would shoot a lion in the *jess* for his wife or girlfriend. He looked at me as if that was a stupid question and said, "No, for none of them have a pound."

I was the only one who laughed—the others did not know of the concept of favours to the female sex. It made me realize how realistic these people are when it comes to monetary gain and risk of life. I asked him why he thought a white man wanted him to shoot a lion for his girlfriend. He did not know but guessed that his master must owe this woman money and was going to pay with the lion skin. It made me laugh again, and I could not but think how stupid is our customs of currying favour with the fairer sex. White men have died tackling dangerous game to make a present for a woman, but black men have only died trying to make a profit. What a world we live in!

We abandoned the hunt despite the *magotcha's* efforts to get us to go back to recover his lion. As we returned down the elephant paths, I turned to see the *magotcha* staring back in the direction of his hunt. Losing that £1 worried him, but his experience with the lion had robbed him of his courage. A little while later we heard him clanking toward us on the elephant path, one pedal knocking against the bicycle's frame. He stayed a few days in our camp, and I found him to be good company. Although he was a government employee, we were quite confident of him and gave him food and our fireside hospitality. This *magotcha* was killed later that season by a wounded buffalo in the*jess*, and because of this I often thought of him and what he considered his "magic rifle."

Sometime after this Faanie arrived, having got the rifles back from the native commissioner at Miami. He said the commissioner was friendly in that stupid way that said we should be grateful for the return of our possessions. So it was that we moved back to Kam Cha Cha's on the opposite bank of the Zambezi and eventually were equipped again. We took to the water again for the crocodile hunting expedition, and damned if something else didn't happen.

We traveled past Kanyemba Island and the Zambezi/Kafue junction and then on to Chiawa's village. Here there was a large, elusive croc that had killed many of the locals. It sometimes lingered in the deep waters of the Kafue River under dense vegetation overhanging the banks. It could be anywhere in a twenty-mile range from the noise of villages. The Zambezi below the Kafue confluence speeds up because of the combined flow of the two rivers. We cut the engines to save fuel and floated in the current for miles, keeping the boat straight with the motor rudder. We traveled silently, not too close to the banks, listening to the movement of the mighty waters and viewing the banks from time to time.

Relaxing in the hot sunshine, I suddenly realized I was looking at a large crocodile slowly moving across the shore to the water. We had developed the art of shooting crocodiles in the shoulder while standing or sitting in a moving boat. I realized this could be the man-killer crocodile and speedily took a shot at it. I hit and immobilized it but heard the heavy bullet whining off somewhere. We had skinners along, so we pulled up on the land. The croc was still very much alive; under normal circumstances I would have chopped it in the brain with one of our local axes, but because this croc had such a frightening reputation I thought it unwise to chance that. As I approached, it managed to turn and snap at me, even with the damaged shoulder. It was a very thickset specimen with wide jaws, reminding me of a massive bull terrier. This croc could rip almost any flesh apart by its usual tactic of grabbing and spin-turning.

A crocodile's jaws are structured for seizing and holding on; then it drowns the victim or renders it senseless by spinning. Faanie put a shot into its brain, and we examined and measured it with our footsteps. It was fifteen feet long, and its wide girth, weight, and heavy jaws and neck made it look especially impressive.

The helpers skinned the reptile and scraped the inside of the skin for treating. We moved away until they had finished. Then they called Faanie, showing him the bangles and ornaments they had taken from the croc's guts. Faanie shouted to me that they had also found decayed fish and large stones inside it. I had seen this type of thing before and did not enjoy looking at it.

I shouted back, "What kind of fish?"

He replied, "I don't know, maybe *vundu*, bream, tigerfish."

I walked halfway up to him and said, "Well, now you know what Zaratina meant when he said you think you are a 'tigerfish' and crocodiles sometimes eat tigerfish—so don't get too cocky in the water."

"I give you my word," he said.

Obviously this large crocodile and the contents of its stomach had some effect on him. I saw Faanie struggling to open the croc's jaws, and he said, "He doesn't seem to have any interest in me."

We loaded the skin and motored across the water to the landing at Chiawa's village. A number of tribesmen were waiting for us, some with muzzleloaders. Faanie, unarmed, stepped from the boat, and they grabbed him. He was far too powerful and knocked a few of them into the deep current, but the remainder faced him with their muzzleloaders. I was still in the boat and could see the situation getting out of hand with all the firearms. I fired a shot and they paused; Faanie in that instant jumped back into the boat and grabbed a gun.

In these seconds I realized how difficult it would be to fight him with a gun in his hands. Given his warrior nature, there was danger that he would use the situation as an excuse to shoot the tribesmen, armed or not. Sometimes it is better to talk than fight. I saw Faanie's body tense for instant action and knew it would take only a false move for all the guns to go off.

I shouted, "I am a friend of Chiawa. What is wrong?"

One spokesman came forward, muscular and emotional, the large blood vessels pulsing on his temple. I could feel Faanie looking for an excuse for war, so I moved in front of him. The disturbed tribesman shouted, "You have killed one of our people," pointing at Faanie.

"So?" Faanie said. Then he yelled to me, "Goad them into shooting so we can clean them out!"

I was tense, because of the tribesmen and because of Faanie. I asked how we could have killed anyone when we had just come from the river.

"Your bullet came out of the sky—we all heard it—and it killed a woman who had come here to get married!" he shouted.

Puzzled, I lowered my rifle and went up to them, knowing that Faanie was covering me.

"What are you talking about?" I asked.

The tension was easing, but the emotional one shouted, "You fired on the river and killed one of our women."

Faanie then said, "Englander, your bullet ricocheted off the croc and landed in the village."

This possibility struck me, and I had to accept that it could have been me. They all looked at me except the emotional one, who watched Faanie. I told him, "I am not afraid to face Chiawa, but you are not Chiawa."

"I am the uncle of the woman," he said. "She had no other family. You killed her."

Here's a man with his blood up, I thought, *and I may well have shot his niece.* There were two alternatives: Either he calmed down or I would take the muzzleloader from him. If I used force, the anger of the others would rise and Faanie would start shooting. I informed the disturbed one in front of me that I had shot the killer crocodile.

"You should be pleased," I said. "Ask the skinners—they have the bangles and ornaments from its stomach. It is not my fault if the bullet continued into the village. We cannot even see the village from the water. I only shot the croc because his size told us we knew he was the river killer."

We faced each other in silence. Then he said, "Maybe."

He lowered the muzzleloader that had been pointing at me and said it was for Chiawa to decide.

We walked on the path through the reeds with the emotional one leading, Faanie at the back, and about nine armed men and the beaten ones in between. The village was about three hundred yards inland, and as we entered, to my surprise I saw Jeffrey. He was armed and coming through the trees, bareheaded as usual and slightly dragging his one leg. He went ahead of us up to Chief Chiawa and said, "I know these men."

Chief Chiawa looked at all of us and the armed men. "I know this one," he said, indicating me. "He has hunted with my son. He is *Kaporamujese*! Who killed the woman?"

Jeffrey moved aside to be free of the crowd.

I answered, "I shot the killer croc, and the bullet must have reached here."

There were too many people talking, and I could see Chiawa was getting agitated. He spoke in a dialect I did not understand, silencing all. Jeffrey came forward and asked me to explain to him and I did so. He then told Chief Chiawa. Words were flowing here and there, and a sort of control came about.

"All this trouble for one dead bitch," Faanie said.

He then asked where the dead woman was. On Chief Chiawa's instruction the tribesmen remained and Jeffrey took us to the woman who had died at the entrance of a hut.

At a glance Faanie said, "She sure as hell is dead." But I was not satisfied and felt for a pulse. There was none. She was young, a *masikana* (a young woman of marriageable age).

"What now?" I said.

"Englander, you surprise me. This is Africa. Throw her in a hole before she starts stinking," Faanie said.

Men of war are hardened people and have no compassion except for their own kind. Jeffrey said, "Have you any liquor in your boat? We must drink to this occasion." It was all very well for them, but I was the one who had shot the woman.

Jeffrey said, "Chiawa will see you in the morning, and you will have to report this to the police."

Deep in thought at Jeffrey's camp, I wondered about this string of disastrous events that were stopping us from going downriver. Jeffrey told me that my bullet had been out of balance as they heard it coming down. Most people knew what it was. The woman was sitting on the ground when the bullet struck her at an angle, penetrating her chin and going down through the heart and, as Jeffrey put it, churning her guts up.

I told them there was no way I was going to sleep near this village, given the smouldering emotions of the people. There were far too many muzzleloaders here.

"Don't worry, Englander," Faanie said. "We will eat and drink here; then we can take some bedding and disappear into the bush for the night."

I knew Faanie had gin or something that looked like it in a jar on the boat. I said, "You are surely not going to give Jeffrey liquor while we are here? Let him have it when we go tomorrow."

"Why not, little boy?" Jeffrey said, "We can drink what you do not want."

One drama on top of another, I thought to myself. I told Jeffrey, "I do not want to drink with you."

"Have your man make some food and I'll be off," he replied.

Jeffrey and Faanie went down to the boat with a few helpers and brought back the necessary items, including the jar of liquor. I took a stroll before sunset and found a suitable place to sleep in dense bush, off the beaten track. That night after eating I waited for Faanie to come with me, but I could see it was going to be a liquor session, so I took my light bedding and rifle to sleep away from the village. I had a disturbed night, with hungry hyena coming close. With so little game left in this area, they might have been hungry enough to tackle a sleeping man.

During the night I had made up my mind that to be rid of this event I would have to go upriver again and report the matter. I did not want to interfere with the crocodile hunting enterprise, so I volunteered to take my hunting equipment upstream in a dugout borrowed from Jeffrey. He made his own dugouts, and they were far superior to those of the locals. We parted, thinking it would be only temporary. I went upstream to Kam Cha Cha's at Chirundu and then overland to Miami, the control center on the Southern Rhodesia plateau.

Officialdom can be irritating, and for me it was worse. At Miami they were surprised to see *Kaporamujese* for the first time in the flesh. They were delighted that I was suspected of intentionally killing someone, thinking that it would put an end to my days in the Zambezi Valley. The police officer said, "You were bound to kill someone at some time, but since it did not happen on our side of the river, you must report the matter in Lusaka."

I had to motor back across the plateau, recross the Zambezi Valley onto the Northern Rhodesia escarpment, and report at Lusaka. There I was treated properly, and I gave details of what had happened.

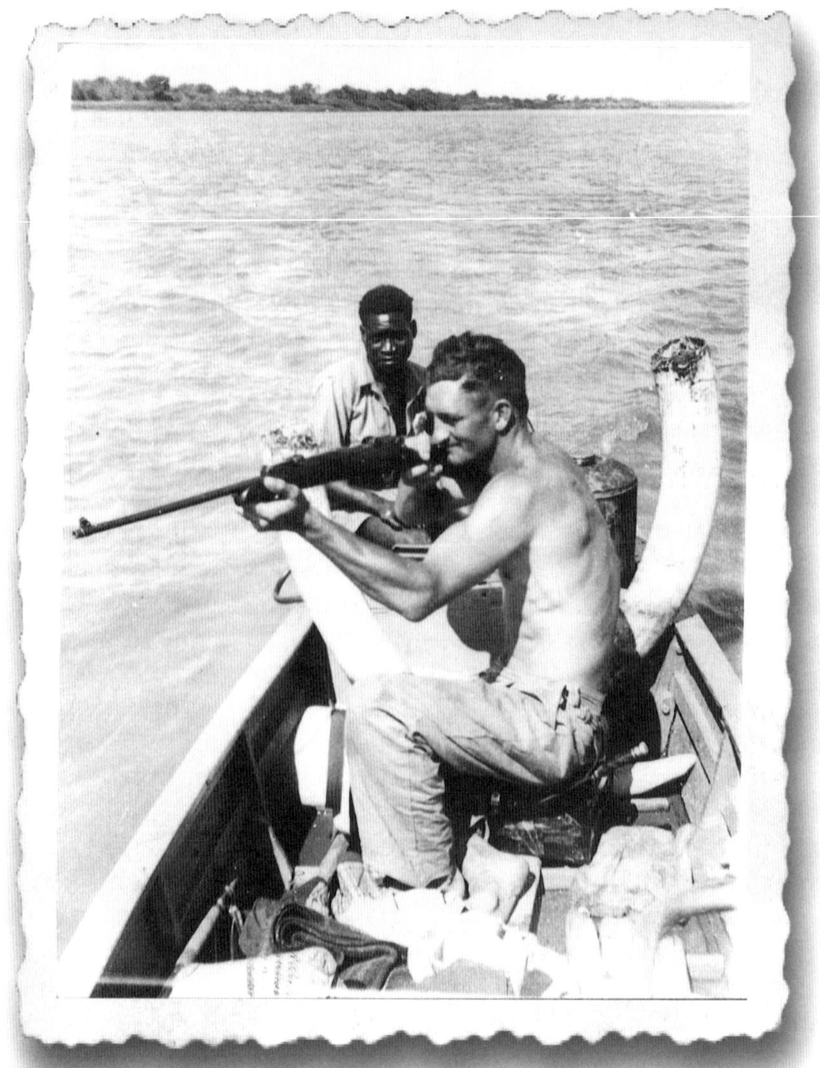

We had developed the art of shooting crocodiles in the shoulder while standing or sitting in a moving boat.

The policeman heard my story and to my surprise said, "When you shoot people, why don't you shoot them on your own side?" meaning the opposite bank of the Zambezi.

He then sent me to the Kafue police station, a small control center about thirty miles back on the road toward the Zambezi Valley. It must have been an unimportant place, because the police officer in charge lacked character and drive. He gave the impression of being a degenerate civil servant doing the least amount of work for minimal payment. He took a statement from me, then phoned through to Lusaka. He was instructed by his superiors that the body of the dead woman must be brought in for a postmortem and rifle-bullet identification. This whole scene was becoming a drawn-out procedure.

It was police duty to recover the body but I volunteered to assist by showing them the country and pointing out any witnesses they might need at Chiawa's. I returned to Chirundu to await the enquiry and was followed there by the European officer-in-charge and an African constable. They stayed the night with the customs officer, whom they obviously knew. The next day we proceeded in their truck twelve miles downriver through the mopane forest, and then stopped to see my old friend, the physically powerful Zekoni, who was going blind.

We were at Ka-koma-Marara (the small hills of the palms) near the Chipara swamps. The road ended here, and we would have to use dugouts either to go downstream about twenty miles or to cross the river and then walk the twenty miles on the opposite bank. Either way, getting there and back would be an effort. The officer alighted from his truck and, after gazing around, took on an air of pompousness quite unrealistic for the surroundings. He behaved as if he had just acquired the place. I watched him, not wanting to believe what I was seeing and hoping he would change so that we could get on with the program. But he seemed incapable of temporarily adjusting to the environment and became childishly aloof, as if to protect himself from the surroundings of a few village huts and the expanse of the great river. I wondered what this was about. Perhaps the sight of the river had gone to his head, making him feel important. It reminded me of the silly jokes about "Doctor Livingstone, I presume." I guessed that he was not used to anything other than tar roads and concrete pavements. In any case, his attitude and demeanor were ridiculous and he was unresponsive to the need to collect the body.

He had the only rifle in our party, a .303 Enfield, and seemed uncertain about moving away from the clearing and the few huts. A crocodile basked in the sun about two-hundred yards downriver. As we stood aside waiting for the officer to come to reality, he sent his African constable to get me—although I was within hearing distance of him. I thought we would now all take to the dugout to cross or travel the river, but instead he questioned me on the estimated distance to the crocodile. I said it was about two-hundred yards.

He replied, "I would have thought so too."

He wanted to shoot it, and after he had raised the rifle several times I advised him to use one of the trees for a rest. He did this but missed the crocodile, saying, "I am certain I got him."

I could see by the way the croc went into the water that it was not hit. We still had time to reach Chiawa's before nightfall, but when it was time to step into the dugout with his black constable the officer point-blank refused to do so. I paddled into the current and back to demonstrate that it was safe, but under no circumstances was he going to get into the dugout. It was unreal—even a schoolboy would have had a go at the dugout. I explained to the officer that if he crossed the river now we could all be at Chief Chiawa's village by nightfall and could have the body exhumed and brought back here by the following afternoon. It would then be a straightforward motor trip of a hundred miles to Lusaka. He obviously was afraid of the river and stated that it was not part of his duties to get into a dugout.

I asked him for the rifle since he did not need it if he were staying in the village, but he refused. In desperation I said I would do his job for him. So the constable and I paddled across the river. The dugout was ill-made for distance travel, having a bend in it, so I decided to cross the river directly and go overland. We disembarked and proceeded to Chiawa's. In a while I realized I would be among people who would be hostile to me. I hoped the uniform of the constable would act as a restraint. On coming down to Chiawa's village, I skirted it and was pleased to see Jeffrey still at his camp. Faanie was also staying there but had gone across the river to check some swamps.

I told Jeffrey I had been charged with manslaughter at the Kafue police station on the plateau and also explained what an idiot the white policeman was and that, like a fool, I had come down here unarmed. I requested a rifle, and Jeffrey gladly gave me his 9.5 Mannlicher and a belt of thirty rounds, saying it was just as well because he would now have to use one of Faanie's more powerful rifles.

He told me a conspiracy was developing, and I must be out of here before dawn. He would have the body exhumed and sent upriver to us. Jeffrey was often truculent, but in times of need he always rose to the occasion. In the predawn I heard him calling, "Little boy, you must move now."

I woke up the black constable, and we disappeared into the night, skirting the village and proceeding overland to go upstream. An hour or so after sunrise we came across a herd of elephant in thick scrub. They had no doubt come across the river to feed. As there may have been some Zambezi Ladies among them, I gave them a wide berth. We reached Ka-Koma-Marara just before midday, and I was informed that the officer had gone back to Chirundu to stay at the customs post. He apparently did not care about anybody but himself, knowing that I had neither rifle nor food for myself and his constable. If it hadn't been for my friends, we would have had neither.

Zekoni gave us food and the hospitality of the huts and that night brought me a mosquito net that I had previously given him. I told Zekoni that I had had enough of this *murungo* (white man) and, whether he was a policeman or not, something would happen when he returned. Zekoni had a sensitivity to others, and perhaps because he was going blind it had become more pronounced. In the early morning, as we sat around the fire overlooking the river, he explained how over the years his eyesight had changed for the worse.

"I could see," he said, "clear over the river—miles into the distant trees but now only to the water's edge." I wondered about this good man and determined that at the end of the season I would take him to a doctor friend of mine, Tom Williams, who wanted to see wild Africa.

I sat for some time enjoying Zekoni's company. The temperature started to rise and the constable and three tribesmen accompanied Zekoni to the river where fish nets had been stretched out. As they pulled the nets in, I noticed a heavy shape among the fish. It was a crocodile. To prevent net damage, I shot it. The fish were not big, but there were plenty of them, and they were edible enough, and Zekoni gave most of them to the constable to take back with him.

It was getting to midday as we split and cooked some of the fish on sticks near the fire. Then I heard the beating of a drum and later singing and chanting downriver. It would be the work of Jeffrey, and I rightly guessed he had sent people up in dugouts with the body, the breeze traveling upriver bringing their sounds intermittently to us. Eventually they reached us. It was primitively appealing watching them sweating to fight the current, their black bodies in loincloths, the drums thumping and some of the men chanting. Men of the river are usually well developed with good torsos from constant paddling. They landed below the high bank and called out greetings to Zekoni and others. I could smell the body, a sickly, penetrating odor unlike that of dead animals. It was encased in limbo cloth and tree bark. They brought it up to the bank on a bush-made stretcher and were keen to get downriver again.

I watched them paddling quickly away down current, the drums beating. Then they cut across the river to their own side. The stench from the body was bad, and we had to move away. I wondered what we would do with this body if the officer did not come back today. I was thinking of getting away for a while to shoot something for Zekoni, even though we were far from the five-mile extermination strip. As I contemplated this, I heard the drone of a motor vehicle. It could only be the officer coming back from Chirundu.

As the drone increased so did my anger, and I tried to contain it. Because of his cowardice and attitude and my anxiety, I had to do this policeman's duties. He should at least have been with me to question the witnesses at Chiawa's village. I wondered what sort of halfhearted investigation this was going to be? Eventually the officer alighted from the truck. He had another European with him, the customs officer from Chirundu.

They picked up the smell of the body as I got Zekoni's people to load it. Surprised to see me with a rifle, he asked where I got it. I did not answer him.

Then he said, "The place where you got the body must be really close. If I had known that, I would have gone with you." The bastard was giving the impression of being dutiful in front of his friend.

I said, "Why don't you just keep quiet and let's get the body back to Chirundu, so you can be on your way."

This man was like a chameleon. Now he became pompous with an exaggerated air, apologizing in that hypocritical English way, saying, "I am sorry, but there is no room in the front of the truck. You and my constable can get in the back. It is not my fault that the body is there."

There was a limit on how much of this attitude I could take, and for seconds I struggled to contain my rage. But it got the better of me, and then I felt the sheer pleasure of physical action. I was not afraid of authority, and I did not feel guilty. I believed he was trying to intimidate me into a state of cowardice. He saw my rage rising but continued to bluff his way—I can't remember what he was saying at the time. He was beckoning to his friend in the front of the truck when I gave him the bush treatment—a lunge to his throat with the butt of Jeffrey's rifle.

He was a large man but soft—I could tell this by his exaggerated gasping as he fell back on the truck and then to the ground. His friend shouted that he was going to arrest me and called for the African constable to assist him.

I knew of this white man; he had come from South Africa to take over the customs post at Chirundu. Men never frightened me, but firearms did, so I leaned into the truck to get the .303 rifle. As I did so, he grabbed at it, but I got it first. The African constable was behind me, in an easier position to attack as I leaned into the truck, but he did not; instead he walked away to join Zekoni and the others. He obviously was contemptuous of them and showed it. I grabbed the customs officer's hair and pulled him from the truck. He got the same bush treatment right through one hand as he tried to protect his throat.

As the man staggered, Zekoni appealed to me, saying, "If you kill them, where will you live?" He meant that others would hunt me because of these men.

I left the officer alone, though I was sorely tempted to smash him some more. So there I was with a dead body in the truck, two damaged law officers, and an African constable who would no doubt be punished for not trying to apprehend me. I spoke to the constable about it, and he said he did not care. It took the two injured men some time to comprehend what the circumstances meant.

A rifle thrust to the throat is more damaging than people realize. It brings pain and shock to the spine and if done too often or drastically it has a bad effect on the larynx and the breathing muscles. It was an act an old professional hunter had taught me. While the officials were trying to recover, I told them to climb into the back of their truck. The customs officer aggressively refused, and as he protested I gave him another thrust and heaved him into the truck, where he thrashed next to the woman's body. I knew that in a short time Jeffrey and Faanie would know about this.

As I drove through the beautiful mopane forest, where a few buffalo stared from a distance, my anger receded. It was a bad road all the way to Chirundu, where I had left my own transport. As they alighted from the back of their truck, I noticed that the officers were still incapable of attacking me. Those throat thrusts have long-lasting effects. I knew that previously in Kafue officials had taken a fired bullet from my rifle to use for ballistic purposes. I gave the .303 rifle with the magazine removed to the African constable and walked up to the officers. They did not look at all lively. I said, "You jackals, I am looking forward to seeing you in court. I have a case that can be put over well, and I will be there."

Unarmed and with the clout of their authority gone, there was not much man left in either of them.

ZAMBEZI KARIBA BASIN:

SHADOWS OF PROGRESS—1953

Having had more than enough of the recent man-made disasters and dramas on the Zambezi River, I decided against croc hunting and abandoned the enterprise to Faanie and Jeffrey.

In addition to being able to hunt in the five-mile extermination strip of the Zambezi Valley, I had acquired a tsetse permit issued by Archie Fraser, the game officer in Salisbury, to hunt the land known as the Zambezi Kariba Basin. Its area lay roughly from the main Salisbury/Lusaka road down the Charara River track to the Bawamombi range at the Zambezi Kariba River gorge, then east up the Sanyati River close to the Matussadona range and Wamira Hills, then north back to the main road.

There were other rivers traversing the valley, but except for the Sanyati and Zambezi they were dry watercourses that flooded during the rainy seasons. In the hunting season these rivers eventually dried out, but in places water could be found in isolated pools or, better still, by digging under the sand beds of the rivers—but only at certain isolated places, and even these eventually dried up in the Months of the Sun.

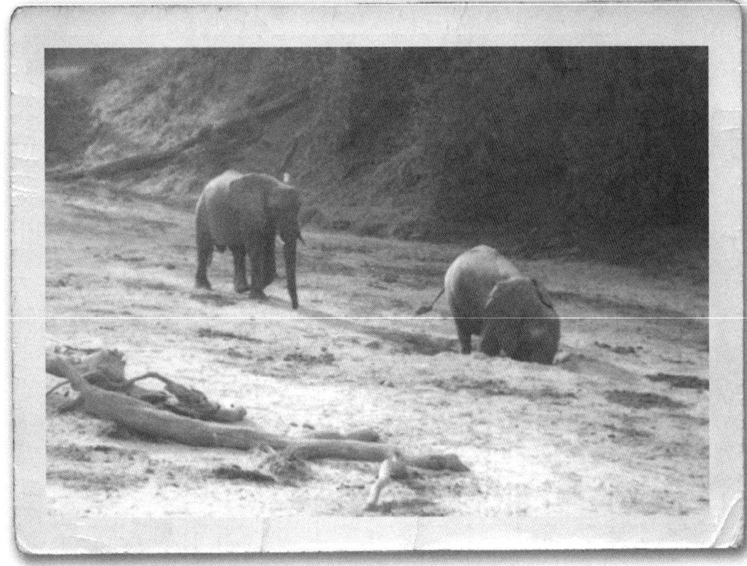

We spent a half-day scouting along the Charara sand river to find drinking places, perhaps dug in the sand by elephant bulls.

These major dry rivers were the Charara, Naodza, Gatche-Gatche, and Urange, and all had shaded vegetation on their banks, making them ideal places to camp. The other watercourses were minor. The area was accessible from a track leading off the Zambezi escarpment in the range known as Macuti.

I motored to my old campsite on the floodplains near Chief Mudzeemo's village in the Zambezi Valley, and in the afternoon the two tribesmen, Zaratina ad Jacoba, appeared. After discussing future events, we motored across the valley floor in the early morning to climb and reach the eastern escarpment. We were heading for the Macuti turnoff to find the Kariba Basin. We searched for some time and eventually found the track that led off to the dry Charara floodplain river and proceeded roughly parallel to it. It took a full day to reach Chief Nyamunga's on this dry river, a distance of some forty-five miles.

This undulating bush country was a good place for human habitation because the topography allowed for a quick runoff of rainwater, preventing stagnant pools where malaria-breeding mosquitoes could flourish.

We arrived at night, slept near the village, and in early morning listened to the greatest chorus of *chikwaris* that I had ever heard. It seemed they wanted the world to know they had awakened to the new day. Their screeching, piercing cries continued for almost half an hour and then slowly receded.

From time to time we saw them running through openings in the scrub. I always liked Jacoba's bush version of events, so I asked him why the *chikwaris* were so noisy. He said the dawn is theirs and we humans are intruders with our human voices, long steps, and fires. He said we had disturbed them during the night, so now it was their turn.

I spoke to Chief Nyamunga with Zaratina and Jacoba present. He was very conscious of being a chief, but other than that there was not much to him. He had conditioned his people to secrecy as far as hunting was concerned, and he wanted to be paid personally. I brushed this chief aside and left him to his self-importance. Consequently, our questioning of the locals about the whereabouts of bull elephant was unsuccessful.

We spent a half-day scouting around—Zaratina going upstream and Jacoba going downstream along the Charara sand river—to find drinking places, perhaps dug in the sand by elephant bulls. I took to some *jess* cover and looked for spoor.

We regathered in the midday heat to compare our findings. No one had seen recent spoor, but Zaratina had come back with a tribesman from farther up the Charara who lived with his family away from the village. So typical, I thought, of individualists who, because of their superior skills, isolated themselves to continue their chosen lifestyle where possible. Zaratina said this man had been following our truck tracks to try to join us. They had met at an old elephant water hole. I knew this man would be above average, and so he was.

Next morning we motored on to a dry watercourse named the Reefa. We camped, and two days later I shot three bulls. The new tribesman, under whose guidance we were moving, knew the country. His name was Chakadama, and he had sharp features, reminding me of the Dinka tribe I had seen on the Nile River in the Sudan. The meat from these elephant went to the scavengers; I hadn't cared for Chief Nyamunga and didn't bother to notify him of the available meat.

However, later that afternoon, when I was alone in camp with the others many miles away, a lone tribesman entered the camp. His name was Juda, and he turned out to be a *nanga* (medicine man). Similar to Chakadama, he had good features. His manner of speech was direct, and his logic and basic honesty impressed me. His had one physical drawback—one leg was bowed backward in a fixed position, which put him at a disadvantage. I advised him to stay, for I knew the others would bring back elephant meat, and he could have some. Later we all talked around the campfire about the area, which was new to me, and through the descriptions of Chakadama and Juda I got a hazy idea of the places we would be visiting.

Chakadama had sharp features, reminding me of the Dinka tribe I had seen on the Nile River in the Sudan.

In the morning I woke to find that Juda had taken his share of meat and gone. I checked his tracks to determine his general direction. I was hoping he might stay on for a while to act as a camp guard, giving me three good men to range with. This country, although low in altitude, was unlike the mile-upon-mile of beautiful forests and mixtures of bush scrub and plains found in Mozambique. This country was rugged, and every time we slowed down in the truck to negotiate the drifts and small dry watercourses, the tsetse flies would swarm into the vehicle, biting and making life miserable. We carried short, leafy branches and swished them, but the flies took refuge in the truck and eventually got their share of our blood when we were otherwise occupied.

Our immediate destination was the Naodza, a dry watercourse with forest on its banks, and we arrived barely in time to see our surroundings in the setting sun, whose orange glow silhouetted the stark, inhospitable-looking dry bush on the horizon. We listened to the wails of the hyena that night as Chakadama told us about this and other places. He had a good knowledge of the area.

In the morning I took him with me upriver, where rare pools still existed in depressions along the riverbed. There was spoor of elephant cows and a few herd bulls. Some buffalo, kudu, sable, and impala were seen running off. Plenty of baboons lived along the river, and on our way back we came across fresh lion spoor.

I knew by the nature of this country that elephant would have to range over long distances to obtain the nourishment they needed. It was coming to the end of winter, and the sun's heat increased almost daily here in the low country. I asked Chakadama why the game was so skittish, and he said the white farmers and hunters had already worked this area the previous year in the campaign to rid it of the tsetse fly. From the fly's abundance and the amount of bites we had, I knew they weren't succeeding.

There were not enough elephant prospects to keep me here, so we moved on to the Sanyati River, above where it flows into the Zambezi at the entrance of the Kariba Gorge—pronounced "Kariwa" by the tribesmen. The Sanyati had large, long pools with cascades of water between them. These pools were all well stocked with fish and large crocodiles, and if I had not been on the ivory trail I would have shot some of the crocs for their skins.

This was the place where Rankine had been seized by crocodiles and fought for his life at the cost of an arm and a leg. He was well known for his ornithological studies of birds in the wilds.

Resident on the Sanyati River was a headman by the name of Rice. He no doubt liked the food or the sound of the word in English. He was in the process of making a dugout from a large sausage tree he had felled. This was a long, drawn-out job that required chopping out the inner section. He said it would take him a whole season. The large, elongated fruit of these sausage trees is eaten by baboons, rhino, and porcupine. The beautiful dark red flowers are also eaten by baboons, impala, and at times bushbuck and kudu.

Rice told me they had lost some of their people to the crocodiles, and they were pleased when I shot a large one measuring, by my footsteps, sixteen feet! As is usual with these old monsters, it was wide of jaw and girth and looked particularly heavy out of the water. This one had the usual indigestible bangles, ornaments, and stones in its guts.

I advised the villagers to build half-circles of stakes at the watering places to prevent further fatalities. Apparently the energy needed to do this was not worth it as everyone felt the crocs would seize somebody besides themselves. So they continued to lose people to the crocodiles.

Eventually the trackers located elephant bulls that had come across the Sanyati River from the district known as the Great Sebungwe, which is the large tract of land sparsely occupied by the Matonga people, supposedly the most backward and isolated tribe in the country. I later learned that this was an exaggeration caused by the different habits of these people. For example, the women, smoked large-bowled water pipes, drawing the smoke across the water as they inhaled. The other custom was disfiguring, whereby the witch doctors and medicine men knocked out the front teeth of the women to make them unattractive. This had been the practice in the days of the slave raids. The slavers had long since disappeared, but in my days these backward customs continued in some places.

We took the spoor of four large bull elephant where they had crossed the Sanyati River into our area. It led through bush and forest and eventually into *jess* previously unknown to me. It was leafless but thick with thorn, making progress through it uncomfortable and at times painful.

I was ill-equipped in these dense thickets; armed with the .404 rifle, I did not feel at all confident, but as the prize was ivory—which we needed to sustain ourselves—we continued on the spoor, hoping for a break in the vegetation. It was not to be—the elephant eventually came to a halt in thickets where vision was only a few yards. Here I fully appreciated Zaratina's value, for he would slowly and silently open branches so I could get killing shots.

I brought down two bulls by this method, and then the others wised up. In the fearful denseness I had too much to concentrate on. Chakadama may have ignored the air movements, for suddenly the remaining elephant came crashing down on us. One appeared right in front of me in dense thorn thickets. I was barely able to move, so I had to wait for the last moment to fire up at an angle at an elephant's brain, a "do-or-die" situation. We took cover behind this dead one while the remaining elephant continued past, crashing through the bush. We listened to its progress, hopeful that it would not stop and return, which it didn't. The bush density plus the thorns made hunting here particularly dangerous.

The Matonga people were thought to be the most backward and isolated tribe in the country.

As in Mozambique, the elephant we met at close quarters were formidable not just from the front—their widespread feet gave them remarkable balance,

The women smoked large-bowled water pipes, and witch doctors and medicine men knocked out the women's front teeth to make them unattractive, a holdover from slave-trading days.

speed, and the ability to reverse onto us. It did not often happen, but in the thick bush we felt almost defenseless as their bulks forced the vegetation down onto us. Most times the shooting was a desperate attempt to immobilize animals with a hit to the spine or ball-and-socket joint.

When the animals made their inaccurate, slower charge in reverse, the lighter-caliber rifle was inadequate, by comparison to a heavy caliber rifle for immobilizing elephants from the back through the vegetation. Not easy, and certainly frightening and demoralizing as the mass of dense vegetation came down on you.

Over a period of time I managed to shoot some bulls under these conditions but considered the risks from a medium-caliber rifle too high. When closing in on elephant I cursed the fate that had robbed me of my beloved .450 double-barreled rifle. Even with that rifle the risks here would have been high, but at least such a weapon, if I waited until the last moment, would have kept the elephant off us. Thank God for past experience, bushcraft, and nerve.

I met various hunters in this country, some of whose names I no longer remember. There was Norman Payne and Sunny, his nephew, farmers from the plateau; Jackie Waddell; and the Meyer family also come to mind. I named Meyer the "Roman Road Builder" because he made roads quickly and with much skill to access the elephant meat that I had shot. I was later to learn that Meyer acted as an informer to the newly formed Game Department in Salisbury.

Many years later Norman Payne became a game officer in the Department of Parks and Wild Life and in that capacity considerately arranged for my son and me to hunt elephant in the Chireza and Omay areas of the Great Sebungwe district. It is because of him that my son, Clive, had what was considered then to be "privileged elephant hunting."

(I remember the occasion clearly, partly because my wife, Joan, became almost frantic at the thought of her thirteen-year-old son hunting elephant in thick bush. On this occasion Clive stunned a bull and, when it quickly rose, put a second shot into its shoulder. It instantly turned on him at close quarters, but he was armed with a magazine rifle and was able to dispatch it with a frontal brain shot. I watched him, mostly unconcerned, as he extracted himself from the dangers of the situation. The magazine rifle gave him an advantage over the double—more cartridges in reserve. That is about the only good thing I can say about a heavy-caliber magazine rifle. Perhaps I am biased, but I feel more confident with a double-barreled rifle in my hands, and Clive would later experience the same feeling. I could see Clive developing elephant fever, so I slackened off on his hunting adventures.)

Eventually a hunting companion of mine arrived from the plateau. His name was John Connor, a tall, ginger-headed, freckle-faced man whose skin was a disadvantage in the penetrating sun. He protected himself, but his lips, even with a hat, swelled and cracked from sun exposure. He was a good hunting companion—intelligent, jovial, and stubborn—but his Irish blood was at times a distinct disadvantage.

We had many good hunts together. I distinctly remember the first time John shot a bull in amongst a cow herd of about thirty animals in some *jess*. It was one of those occasions when everything went wrong. As the bull collapsed, the cows ran off to regroup in the thickets. With undue excitement and danger we took a position between the dead bull's legs, expecting the cows to come back at us. I noticed that John was quietly upset, his freckles standing out on his pale countenance. Prior to this I had ragged him about religion. Now we needed each other's firepower, and I goaded him into action, saying, "You either die here depending on the Virgin Mary or give me a hand in the shooting." I must say that John forgot all about religion and reacted well. From that moment on he changed, and we thereafter had some interesting and exciting times together.

I remember him wounding a lion in dense cover where he and my tracker Zaratina had to follow it with other lion moaning all around. Once, when we had lost bulls in the Zambezi Valley, John complained of the tsetse flies, the heat, and thirst. I told him we were privileged to enjoy it—even the worst—and that one day it would all be gone. There was something manly, jovial, and likable about him—thereafter I never heard a complaint from him, even when thirst was drying the backs of our mouths and throats.

On another occasion Jackie Waddell, John Connor, and I were trying to close in on a large herd of elephant. The bush was in full leaf, and I felt there would be a war when we reached them, but we never did catch up with them because they kept moving ahead of us. Then Jackie Waddell, as if to finalize it, showed me how his magazine rifle kept jamming. I said, "God looks after the Rhodesian farmers," for that is what he was.

When John Connor came back from the coronation in England, he brought with him a double-barreled .470 rifle. It was a good stopper but useless if it was not in the man's hands at the critical moment. I had warned him about not carrying his own rifle, particularly when vision was limited by thick bush. He had a servant called Sinoia, from the plateau, who carried his gun. One day we penetrated a swamp to see if there were any elephant bulls. A day or so prior to this and unknown to us, some hunters from the Hartley area on the plateau had lined up in this swamp when they heard buffalo feeding. They must have been afraid to try to close in, for they all—probably four of them—fired into the reeds at the buffalo. Assuming each man had four rounds in his magazine and chamber, sixteen shots were fired. They killed none of the buffalo but naturally wounded some. Then along we came looking for elephant in the swamp, Zaratina in front of me, then John, like "Lord Muck," with Sinoia carrying his heavy double-barreled rifle behind him, contrary to what I had tried to instill in his mind.

Without warning I heard Zaratina shout, "*Nyati!*" (buffalo), and it came at him in a peculiar gait. To draw the buffalo away from him, I shouted at it, and it turned slightly to come at me. My beloved .450 rifle was by now rusting somewhere under the powerful current of the Zambezi River, and I faced the oncoming buffalo with a medium-caliber .404 magazine rifle. I knew there was no chance of dropping it instantly, so I hastily fired at its chest, hoping it might not get me before it died—but this was wishful thinking.

I know of no other animal so tenacious as the buffalo, and as I stepped back to try to avoid it, I tripped and fell on my back—now the buffalo actually stood over my legs. I have always admired buffalo more than any other species, mainly because of their courage. I remember reading in my childhood of early civilizations that honored and worshipped bulls. But here and now, with this buffalo glaring at me, it was a different setting. I will not forget the expression in that wounded buffalo's eyes. If the lion had the heart of a buffalo, few hunters would be left alive. As the buffalo lowered his head to get me, I noticed that it had a broken front leg. Without this handicap it would have had me with on horns in seconds.

Feeling that life was about to leave me, I shouted for John to fire, dismayed by the fact that he had not done so long ago. "For Christ's sake, John, shoot!"

But there was nothing except the silence, the buffalo, and me. Because its broken leg was a disadvantage, I thought as it came down to gore me that I might hang onto the mighty horns to keep them from gashing and ramming me. It came down to lunge at me and then swayed slightly. In that instant I realized its lung or heart, whichever I had shot, was collapsing. Instinctively I pulled my feet in and the bull dropped, bawling in its last moments before death. That bawl suggested a lung shot. I spun around to fire into it again to make sure and then turned to John, who was standing behind me unarmed—his servant had run off with his heavy rifle. Had this buffalo not had a broken leg, it would have cost me my life. I do not want to mention what I said to John, but this is what I meant about his having Irish blood and being stubborn.

As I think of those adventures today, I can see that my companions and I were among the last generation of the wild era of hunting and adventure in Africa. Even the tribes have changed, seldom adhering to their traditional ways. The loincloths, stabbing spears, bows, arrows, and axes represent securities of the past, subsumed by a mixture of European and African mentality.

There is a great gap between the rich and the poor, the privileged and the underprivileged. It was bound to happen as advanced civilizations penetrated Africa for prizes of mineral and other wealth. The white man with his enterprises showed the way.

Today there is a struggle for power throughout the continent. To me the AK rifle is symbolic of this new dawning of power. From the game's point of view one can only hope that as African countries obtain independence, they will settle down enough to rehabilitate themselves and, above all, set aside land for the wild species to survive. Land needs and looming problems of corruption, inefficiency, and overpopulation will no doubt be deciding factors. I feel that the elephant, because of the great range he requires, will be affected more than other species. Time will tell. But let us return to my adventures with Zaratina and Jacoba in the thick thorn bush near the Sanyati River. The elephant had wised up, and it became an all-day, everyday affair of trying to make contact in the dense cover. They used every element of their surroundings against us, plus sight, sound, scent, and instinct.

Eventually they became cunning enough to move all day for days on end, pushing with ease through the dense thickets where we puny humans had to force our way and protect our skins and eyes as much as possible. After this the only elephant we managed to get here were newly arrived ones from the adjoining Sebungwe. The resident animals were masters of the situation, and most times when they attacked, I barely managed to keep them off us. Many times we stood in fear listening to the great silences.

Occasionally we expressed our doubts in low tones. Listening to the others confirmed my own thoughts about what we should or should not try to do. The swirling air currents seemed to bring the greatest uncertainty of all, reminding us that we were mere men in the kingdom of the elephant bulls. These elephant would push their way into the densest vegetation and stand for hours totally silent, as if they were not there, despite our proximity. I was constantly amazed by their great senses of detection and their ability to remain as silent as the bush itself. In these unnerving silences we would try to contact them, always fearful of their close presence.

On watching the wonders of Zaratina's bushcraft, I thought of how—even after long periods of painstaking stalking to gain the advantage of surprise—the thick bush a few yards from us would give way beneath their mighty feet as the elephant surged toward us. At such moments I seriously questioned my ideas of human superiority.

Zaratina felt his gods were punishing us, not only by making the thickets practically impassable, but also by trapping us to the advantage of attacking elephant. I realized that only an ignorant fool would continue hunting elephant in bush so dense you could see only the sky above. Some or all of us would eventually be seized and trampled if we persisted. I expressed my fears to Zaratina, who said something revealing of his background: "We may perish, but I will continue to live, as my spirit will enter my eldest son and guide him in life to the benefit of my family." So this was an additional explanation for why this man had so much courage. This wonderful belief, I was later to learn, is part of his culture, and I thought of how comforting it would be to be brought up to believe it.

So we had to honour the elephant as the victors. From here we explored the area of the Gatche-Gatche River, penetrating up to the Matussadona mountain range and farther northeast to the Wamira Hills. Here many rhino were being shot.

If the powers that be had known of the rhino's vulnerability and poor reproductive rate, I doubt if they would have sanctioned its destruction. However, it was all part of the policy of game destruction in the name of tsetse-fly control—all living animals had to be wiped out of existence to make way for man's needs. What man's needs were here in this isolation, God alone knows. As useless, unthinking administrators were eventually removed from decision making and thinking people were appointed, the trend was reversed, but almost too late. Much later, as man's interference was reduced, the area was rehabilitated.

In the mopane forest and scrub we came across large herds of sable antelope and buffalo. Unless they moved out of this area, they would also eventually be killed by the meat-hungry hunters from the plateau. Those hunters would commonly turn the meat into dried salted rations commonly known as "biltong." It thus lost much of its weight and could more easily be carted onto the plateau for use on the farms or sold elsewhere. The farming community has always been a major influence in Rhodesia. Tobacco production was the mainstay of the economy. Consequently efforts were made to boost the golden crop—another reason for the saying, "God looks after the Rhodesian farmers."

John Connor returned from the plateau, and we made a camp on the Naodza dry riverine forest, thinking of hunting up the Charara River and down close to Kariba. During our wanderings, while walking home one night we passed a well-organized camp at the Gatche-Gatche River. It had been established for D. C. Lilford, a successful tobacco farmer turned financier. Lilford had not arrived yet, but two employees offered us drinks and food. They informed us that all our hunting activities must cease because Lilford, who was the chairman of a newly formed Hunters' Association, was coming down from the plateau to hunt. I had legal access to this place, and I wondered why we were expected to move aside on the arrival of this man. Not one to be subservient, I decided to welcome this new "god" by disturbing as many elephant in the area as possible. Consequently, we covered the area doing just that.

After this I managed to get Zaratina and Jacoba back to Chief Mudzeemo in the Zambezi Valley. The Months of the Sun were coming, and I needed them to check elephant haunts and bull movements in the Naukaranga *jess* forest. I would join them later on in the season. The only reasonable trackers we had now were Chakadama, who would stand up to anything, plus two particularly brave men from the Sanyati River—Rice and his friend, Kamptapere—plus Sinoia acting as water carrier. Sinoia was the man who had run off with John's .470 rifle during the drama with the buffalo with the broken leg in the swamps.

In early morning we found the spoor of a large herd of elephant and followed them hoping for bulls. They were spread out and moving through some scrub and mopane forest. Any bulls must have been at the front of the herd, as no large bull tracks were visible with all the cows obliterating the spoor from the back. Eventually the bush changed, and the elephant moved along many well-trodden paths that intertwined here and there.

I was up against the stubbornness of Irish blood again, for John had veered off after a different section of the herd, taking all the staff with him. I had only Sinoia with me. He had a water bag, so I kept him with me as I followed on the elephant paths, thinking that John and the trackers would eventually merge to meet us. I was sure that if there were bulls, they would be in this section of the herd that I was following. Sinoia was fattish with a round face and large eyes, not at all lean like most tribesmen.

To one side of the path I saw part of the spoor of a large elephant, so I knew bulls were in front of us. Satisfied, I put Sinoia on the path in front of me, and after a while, to my surprise and delight, he left the path, saying the bull spoor had veered off. I came up behind him and, sure enough, he was right. We followed for a while. It looked like five or six bulls, their spoor crossing each other. I casually asked Sinoia how many, whereupon he raised his hand and opened all his fingers. This man, his first time at it, could read mixed-up spoor, though I thought perhaps he had guessed. A little farther on the spoor rejoined the large herd. Here we waited, hoping for John to come up with the trackers. We halted a long time, sitting and leaning against trees in the shade as the heat had already set in. But there was no sign of John. I became agitated and angry, wondering where this man could be.

The only reasonable trackers we had now were Chakadama, who would stand up to anything, plus two particularly brave men from the Sanyati River—Rice and his friend, Kamptapere.

It was hard enough to locate elephant bulls without worrying about where the rest of your party was. I asked myself, *What goes on inside John's head?* We waited for hours, and eventually I did not care any more. So I put Sinoia on the spoor again, double-checking him myself. In a short while I realized this man was gifted concerning elephant spoor.

He was sharp-sighted and sure of himself, managing to maintain vision of bull spoor in the mixed herd. A few times I checked, thinking the bulls had moved away from the herd, but he was always right on them. We carried on for hours. The sun passed its zenith, the bush thickened, and after a few more miles we knew the herd would halt in thicker cover. Eventually we reached a place in open forest with thick surrounding bush. By sound we could tell the herd was well spread out in the adjoining thick bush.

The elephant were about two hundred yards off. So as to maintain the chance for surprise, I climbed a mopane tree, hoping to see the big backs of the bulls. I could only see sections of cows here and there and occasionally heard an animal break branches halfheartedly in the heat.

I was sure the bulls were to one side, separate from the herd. In order to determine this, I thought it necessary to stay up the tree for some time to see if they would give their position away by noise. I pulled the rifle and Sinoia up the tall tree after me and climbed high to try to see farther. Then two large cows came strolling from the thick bush, passing amongst the trees and eventually halting under our tree. We were well up above the air currents, and I found it interesting, feeling safe and looking down on them. They stayed there some time, and eventually we became uncomfortable up in the top of the tree.

Then, to my dismay, one cow started to rub up against the tree so strongly that the trunk swayed back and forth. We had to hold onto tree and rifle for dear life. There were hundreds of mopane trees, but this cow had chosen the one we were in! I thought she would shake us loose or dislodge the tree from its root system, and in desperation I clamped my legs and knees around the trunk to get a good grip so that I could shoot down at her. She suddenly stopped, and they both strolled back to another section of the thick bush. Badly shaken, we watched them enter it. One of the cows broke a branch, and after that we heard the crack of another branch on the opposite side of the forest, likely indicating the position of the bulls.

We scrambled down the tree, happy to be on the ground again and, after a pause to collect our wits, tested the wind and moved off in the direction of the bulls. It was amazing that we had not been able to see them from the tree, for here in the semi-open forest we easily sighted them. This portion of the country was too open for a close approach, so I had to take them from about forty yards.

These conditions were ideal for the .404 magazine rifle. I managed to get off four quick brain shots. Interestingly, two of the bulls fell in an upright position. Hastily I loaded a single round and got the fifth bull in the shoulder as it turned to run off. I heard the bush crash as it collapsed from the heart shot. After the hell of hunting in the thick Sanyati bush, this was like shooting on a tennis court.

The herd opposite split up now, with most stampeding impressively through the adjoining thick bush. A few turned angry. Judging by the sound, the matriarch cows were trying to locate us. As I had what I wanted, we moved away from them hurriedly and continued for a while, then rested in some shade and had water. Refreshed, we ambled along a path in the general direction of the Tsororo, a dry, sandy watercourse that led close to our camp. We had ranged far that day and knew we would not get back until night.

Toward sunset, tired and inattentive, we almost stumbled into a herd of about thirty cows with a large bull standing in their midst. Without considering any consequences, I immediately took the fatal shot at him, and he dropped.

The cows turned on us, first spreading and then converging on our location. As the leaders got our position, I put some of them down and was thankful that others passed on our sides. About half of them made a determined rush to get to us, and I was grateful that Sinoia never lost his nerve. I depended on him, and he removed the bullets, four at a time, from the back of my belt and neatly passed them into my right hand each time I had finished firing so I could top up the magazine again. His intelligent, calm action was the deciding factor here.

I distinctly remember the last cow as she veered in a slight circle, coming around a large tree. I almost underestimated her as I thought she would pass, but at the last moment she turned and nearly got me; I barely managed to shoot her at an offset angle to the brain. She was the last and most intelligent one to attack, and then we wind-tested and moved out of the place.

Two of the bulls fell in an upright position.

I was impressed by Sinoia's activities. Considering his previous desertion with John's rifle in the swamp, his action here was a noble effort. He seemed to know that it was just him and me, depending on each other for our lives.

Because I had started off with John, I had limited myself to a belt of thirty rounds. Now I was running short of ammunition. The sun had set, and we now had to proceed with caution to make sure we did not blunder into dangerous animals. Here, as in all tsetse-fly-control areas, there were numerous wounded beasts, and we

After the hell of hunting in the thick Sanyati bush, this was like shooting on a tennis court.

could expect to come across them anywhere at any time. I left our direction to Sinoia and soon realized he was lost in the dark. His homing instincts had not yet been developed. I instructed him to take a particular course, knowing we would eventually come to the Tsororo watercourse that way. Our water was finished, and although we were thirsty, there was no urgency as we no longer experienced the blazing heat of the day.

The frightening cow attacks had impressed upon Sinoia the need to be alert and to sense ahead. The dark African night soon allowed limited vision as our eyes adjusted to it, but the real danger was walking into a wounded animal and not being able to see the rifle sights to defend ourselves. We had miles to go and tried where possible to move in the more open areas to avoid heavy bush and possible ambush. We heard lion roaring off in the distance, and I thought perhaps they had made an early kill.

I was grateful that Sinoia never lost his nerve. I depended on him.

After a while I became anxious—by this time and distance we should have come across the Tsororo watercourse. To avoid two dense patches of bush, we had to pass between them. I slowed Sinoia down. The thickets on both sides came closer, and eventually we were on a path between them. I took the front position. No sooner had I done that then there were a few snorts and crashing of bush on both sides of us. In the darkness we had stumbled into rhino.

These creatures in some respects are different from buffalo. Buffalo can precisely pinpoint their antagonist by sight, sound, or smell; if wounded, they can make a deliberate and most determined attack. Rhino, on the other hand, tend to fluster themselves. They will, if disturbed—and they seem to disturb easily—rush in a general direction and, if they miss their opponent, are likely to continue on or swing around to have a few lunges at anything handy. They can usually be avoided if the hunter is quick and skilled enough.

We froze, hoping they would crash off, but on the path ahead I heard a snort and, to my dismay, could hear a rhino coming along and closing in fast. It was probably rushing to join the other rhino in the thick bush on both sides of us. I did not even have to think about it—as the creature appeared in the gloom, I fired as best I could past the second horn to try to immobilize it. It dropped, but there was a chance it was only stunned. Sinoia, instead of being silent, was saying something, trying to warn me. Then the bush to my right suddenly parted and a rhino head and neck appeared. It lunged at me, but I managed a shot from the hip at its head, and it fell. I felt this second one was dead and so took refuge next to its shoulder as the back part of it was still covered in the bush. There was silence all around, and then the first rhino started struggling. I put a raking shot to the point of its shoulder, as best as I could guess it in the dark. Its struggles ceased.

The other rhino—for there were more—crashed off away from the path, then paused. I heard distinct thuds as if they were butting at each other, and then they crashed off again. We waited where we were in case either of the downed rhino rose, but they did not. We moved off along the path to get out of there.

Rhino were not really my scene, but I had a Chinese friend in Salisbury who had lent Faanie a camera that had gone down with our boat when it overturned in the Zambezi. My friend had four daughters but no sons who could carry on the family name. The Chinese believe that rhino horn acts as a sexual stimulant that can help produce a son. When you consider the millions of people who inhabit this earth, especially in China, what is a family name? I suppose it must bring a feeling of identity and perhaps some sense of being immortal. I laughed to myself at this thought—here in my world man and beast were anything but immortal. Anyway, I decided to give my friend the rhino horns in exchange for the loss of his camera.

More anxious than ever, thinking of how few rounds of ammunition I had left, Sinoia and I walked on and eventually reached the Tsororo watercourse. Because of all the upset during the previous day and night, I was not quite sure whether the camp was up or down this watercourse, but as we tried to follow in the dark it seemed that it was wider here from past flood waters. So we proceeded "upstream" in the dry, sandy bed.

Occasionally we tried to find water by digging, but it was too far down under the sand. A few miles of tiring walking in the sand and we came to a sharp bend. Here I got the whiff of water—and lion. We found water in a well-dug elephant hole where the smell of lion lingered in the surrounding bush. In the darkness I watched the bush on either side of us as Sinoia leaned down in the hole to clear it enough so that we could have a drink. Eventually we had our fill and continued up the watercourse.

The intensity of darkness varies, and here on the sandy watercourse it was of a lighter shade. Tired but alert, I thought I sensed something ahead, and as we approached, a lion raised itself from the sand to growl and move off, taking what was probably its pride with it.

I was down to three rounds of ammunition, and even if I'd had a full bandolier I did not want the drama of dealing with lion in the darkness. Quite fearfully I had to make the decision to leave the open sand bed and move through the bank of bush opposite the lion. Lion can become quite fearless at night, and there could have been others in the bush we had to go through. We took our chances and heard the lion on the sand near the opposite bank. I was thankful and relieved when we moved on past them. Within a mile we came across our own water hole and the camp close by. No one was there.

Exhausted and hungry, we cooked, ate, and relaxed lying next to the fire. I wondered where John was and if anything had happened to him. We fell asleep, and when I awoke the embers of the fire had died down. I was concerned about John, wondering if he was alive or where he could be at this time of night in the bush. I took Sinoia, a water bag, and more ammunition and started down the watercourse, firing the rifle every two miles or so in the hope that John might hear and reply with rifle shots. About five miles from the camp I heard his answering shots.

They could only have been lost and walking around in the bush and had probably missed coming onto the Tsororo watercourse. We stayed in the Tsororo but moved farther down. John fired his rifle occasionally and I answered. In this way we closed the distance and came together. He and his crew were exhausted, having walked the whole day and half the night.

I asked John why he had branched off from me, and he said the tracking had confused him and he felt sure he was on bull spoor. When they eventually realized it was only cow spoor, it was too late. The sun set and they became lost. All I could do was shake my head in the dark. They would have made it without us; after the sun rose, they would have found the Tsororo riverbed.

We continued hunting elephant and "disturbed" the area, making it difficult and decidedly dangerous for others. Prior to this I had told John of my skirmishes with cow elephant herds and emphasized the need to avoid these Zambezi Ladies at all times. He was to experience their truculence himself. One day as we crossed the dry Reefa watercourse and were moving through scrub vegetation, the tracker heard elephant feeding toward us. We knew it was a cow herd and sped up to reach the top of a high flood bank.

On reaching it, I called a halt so John could see for himself the cows' reaction as they crossed our spoor with their highly developed sense of smell. We were far enough away to feel safe. When they got to our spoor, all the cows instantly reacted—some with raised trunks and others with trumpets of fear and rage. A few leaders took over, picking up the scent of our footsteps and then actually running on our spoor, encouraging and leading the herd to seek and attack.

It was incredible to see them getting into a run to follow us up. To avoid an elephant war and a waste of ammunition, we ran off to escape them before they reached the bank. We then heard them in dense vegetation there, seeking us out. We sprinted off and left the area and then later, almost out of breath, laughed at the happenings.

Some time after this we had occasion to pass Lilford's camp at night. We were in a truck, and they apparently heard us coming, for when we got close Lilford was standing on the track with his long, lean body and arms upraised to stop us. I wondered what the chairman of a Hunters' Association would want with ivory hunters, but he was friendly and unpretentious. In fact, I could not imagine him to be the powerful figure he was. With him and Tommy

Ferreira, his farm manager, we enjoyed the hospitality and luxury of their good food and liquor.

Afterward Lilford brought out two double-barreled rifles, a .465 and a .450 caliber, well made by reputable firms in England. My eyes fell on the .450 double, my favourite caliber, ideally suited to my weight and shoulders. This weapon was not the same as the one I had lost in the Zambezi. It had a shorter cartridge case with a higher chamber pressure, but on looking at and handling it I felt it was a suitable weapon. Those who do not depend on rifles for their lives find this hard to believe, but there is a contact between man and rifle the moment the right weapon is placed in your hands. This was such a weapon, and although the .465 double was a more expensive rifle, I preferred this .450 Rigby. In the firelight I admired both of them.

D. C. Lilford in1972. I've always remembered that this man helped me in my time of need, and it is probable that without his rifle I would not be alive today.

I asked Lilford why we had been invited here—the chairman of a Hunters' Association and a couple of ivory hunters were poles apart. He said the members of the Hunters' Association had heard of my exploits in the *jess* and he wanted to see what manner of man would tackle this bush for ivory. I said there was not much difference between me and his fellow members, only that I had a need of ivory where they did not, and if their hunting became difficult or dangerous they could always pull out and abandon the hunt. In my case, abandoning the hunt would mean I would starve or have to change my way of life—lose my soul, so to say, by joining commerce and industry. I had little tolerance toward other hunters because they did not have much in common with me, seldom having to face desperate situations as a mater of daily survival.

I was interested in Lilford's pack of mongrel dogs, which had been injected against the disease of the tsetse fly. It took but a few minutes for me to realize that one in particular, a rangy crossbred Irish wolfhound, was the superior hunter in the pack. This dog, like most true hunters, was a solitary creature that, when the pack crowded him, would turn on them and drive them away. Lilford saw me admiring this dog in the firelight and asked me what I was thinking, so I told him.

I added some thoughts about ivory hunters and finished off by saying there were only two elements I admired in his camp, the rangy dog and the double rifles. He was astounded by my frankness but did not take exception to it. I detected a certain disregard in him and an aura of powerful ruthlessness. I imagined that circumstances would determined how his emotions would rule him. When I voiced these thoughts as well, to my surprise he placed the .450 rifle in my hands and said, "Here, you use this so that we can be assured of your presence in the future and hear your opinions again." I thought he was kidding, so I placed it back in its position on a bush-made table.

Lilford had a movie camera and was keen to capture an elephant charge. He asked me if I would oblige while he did the filming. I reminded him that he could be in greater danger than I, but he said he would take his chances.

I then had to tell him of how and why John and I had intentionally disturbed the elephant to make his hunting life more difficult here. He was annoyed to hear that one of his men had tried to intimidate us by using his name and position.

Lilford and I followed two bulls for almost a day, and eventually they crossed the boundary of the tsetse-fly-control area. Here Lilford had to stop to avoid hunting illegally, and I laughed at him, saying, "That is the privilege you get from being the chairman of the Hunters' Association."

I offered to buy the .450 rifle. He did not want to sell but said I could use it for a few seasons. I drew his attention to the fact that this rifle could land up somewhere else in Africa, but he was unconcerned. There was also .450 ammunition available, so I was grateful. It meant that I could tackle the bulls in the Sanyati and the Naukaranga *jess*. I would again be equipped to penetrate the kingdoms of the elephant. I've always remembered that this man helped me in my time of need, and it is probable that without his rifle I would not be alive today.

Many years later Lilford was lured from his farmhouse at night, attacked, and murdered with his own sidearm.

The time had come for me to attend the inquest into my shooting of the woman at Chiawa's village on the Zambezi River. En route to the Kafue station on the Northern Rhodesia plateau, I stayed at Kam Cha Cha's, on the Zambezi about five miles above the Kafue confluence. He was not there at the time, but Faanie, who had been downriver all these months hunting crocodiles with Jeffrey, was there to greet me. He had previously learned of the hearing and was going to accompany me. The Months of the Sun were nearly upon us, and if everything went well I would be back in the Zambezi Valley in days.

As we waited on a bench outside the Kafue police station in Northern Rhodesia, where the inquest was to be held, a large Bentley motorcar arrived. It was the magistrate, who had come from the capital city of Lusaka to pass judgment at the hearing. As we filed in I recognized the officer I had assaulted—he was to act as prosecutor. The charge was manslaughter. The magistrate was excessively fat and could only move slowly in small steps.

As the official took a seat and gazed around with his bullfrog appearance, Faanie said, "You'll be lucky to get away with thirty years here."

It was typical of his humour, but I did not appreciate it at this moment. Witnesses were called in. I was surprised to see how many people had come from Chief Chiawa's village. In typical fashion they exaggerated and lied about the shooting incident until the magistrate warned them of perjury, but they continued to do so, and then most of them were removed. This fat magistrate, who most of the time sat looking out the window, was nonetheless wide awake to the details of what was going on. The hearing continued, and the facts were eventually revealed.

The officer in charge of the investigation was the other man I had beaten with the rifle butt. He at no stage brought this incident up, so I said nothing, thinking it might come later as a separate charge, but it did not.

I doubt I was asked as many as ten questions, all by the magistrate, and then the hearing came to an end. I stood in front of the magistrate, and he put a printed form in front of me, indicating that I must sign it. I asked him what it was, and he said, "Sign—it is a document recording that you shot the woman by accident—this form states that death was by 'misadventure.'"

I signed and felt quite relieved by the verdict but also because I had not been charged with two assault cases. As I was walking out, the officer stopped me. "Here it comes," I thought, but he said, "Through your friends Kam Cha Cha and Jeffrey we found reliable witnesses who cleared you."

I asked him about the other witnesses, and he said they were being charged with perjury. So now one of my main bases, Chief Chiawa's village, could be visited only at night and could no longer be considered a refuge as I had too many enemies there.

Faanie and I did some shopping to replenish stores. It was our intention to go on to Lusaka, which we eventually did, and there I was pleased to be able to procure 400 rounds of .450 ammunition for Lilford's double rifle, which I had with me.

Before leaving the Kafue police station, however, we watched the fat magistrate who, attended by a uniformed chauffeur, struggled to cross an open space. He held a leash that had three tethers to the collars of three silly-looking miniature Yorkshire terriers (we called them "spider dogs"). I wondered how anybody could get so fat. I had started my hunting career with a faulty heart valve, and here was this man, probably with a sound heart, barely able to reach his car. He was as likely a candidate for a heart attack as anyone I had ever seen. The *jess* would melt the fat off him, I thought. As we passed he beckoned to Faanie, so I walked on to our trucks. They spoke for a while, and then the magistrate rode off to Lusaka.

On motoring off Faanie said, "Englander, you have a friend in high places. The magistrate knows you assaulted the police officers, and his message is 'Don't live on your luck.'"

Sometime after this, in the Zambezi Valley, I thought of this magistrate and how just he had been to me. No doubt under that fat exterior was a real feeling human being who had the gift to see into the lives of others.

We motored back to Kam Cha Cha's on the Zambezi. Here I was pleased to see Jeffrey again. He had just come upriver from where he and Faanie had successfully hunted crocodiles. Together we sat on the bank overlooking the river. Faanie was busy with the final treating and packing of crocodile skins of various sizes, of which they had a full truckload. They had to be kept damp and protected from sunlight. We spent a pleasant night together, and in the morning Faanie departed with the truckload of skins to the distant market at Lake Industries in Tanganyika. He said he would come back in a week and trace me through Chief Mudzeemo. Jeffrey and I crossed the river in a dugout to find out what human and game activity was going on. At Dicka's kraal we learned that bull elephant had crossed the Zambezi into the endemic sleeping-sickness area on the opposite bank below Mana. The news had come through Chief Dandawa downstream. Such information would have been broadcast only because they wanted elephant meat.

In the early afternoon, as we were about to recross the river, we heard the beat of drums coming downstream and sighted a large barge loaded with goods and about twenty paddlers with a European in charge. It unhurriedly approached in the current and eventually passed from sight miles downriver. This was a remarkably romantic scene, the drums pounding, the tribesmen chanting, their sweating, shining loincloth-covered bodies paddling in rhythm to keep the barge going faster than the current. Their destination was about sixty miles downriver.

Jeffrey's bull elephant, a single tusker from Chikwenya Island.

For the next few days we too paddled downstream to where the bull elephant were reported. Past the Chongwe River confluence there was a deadly sleeping- sickness area. Here we had to search for miles to try to locate the reported bulls, which could water almost anywhere along the Zambezi. We came down in dugouts because Jeffrey wanted to check the country between the Chewori and Rukometje Rivers in Southern Rhodesia, and I was to return alone with some of the paddlers. To give us a greater chance of determining the bulls' whereabouts, we moved about independently, and eventually I came across their spoor a mile or so inland.

I followed them and put three large bulls down in a shady forest, known as M'baruma, named after a chief. I posted a lookout in a tall tree and with the others started chopping out the ivory. One of the bulls was very old and emaciated and carried about one hundred pounds a side, so we removed those tusks first. We had no sooner got them free when the lookout signaled that he had seen the bush movements of men coming. Together we shouldered the ivory, but it was too large and bulky to carry while running from pursuers. I gave the word, and we dumped it. Now we ran for the dugouts, got aboard, and paddled vigorously. Because I was not thinking calmly at the time, I allowed them to paddle upstream instead of down.

Once on the water I felt better, so we headed for the cover of a small island, but before we reached it I saw numerous figures up against the reedbeds on the banks, and they started firing at us. Some of the bullets skimmed the water, and a few thudded against the dugouts. Damn it, to be caught on the open waters under fire! Whoever they were, they were poor shots, but there was the chance we could be hit. I felt responsible and, in turn, angry. Here in this wild country it could only be an official.

We reached the island and rushed behind some vegetation, through which we could see the men in the distance up against the reedbeds. I lay down, dug myself into the sand, and fired a few shots at figures. The heavy rifle was a disadvantage at this range, and it pounded the top of my shoulder because of my prone position. I realized I had to look for a white man's skin, and I found him among the others. I sighted him and let fly, but the range was too far to give the needed accuracy. I raised the rifle slightly, and my bullets must have crashed into the reeds near the men because they soon retreated down the paths into the reedbeds. How I would have liked to have faced them with a medium rifle. A .375 would have been ideal.

In times of trouble I normally would have crossed the river to the west bank; now I had to cross to the east bank into Southern Rhodesia. There were no more signs of human activity, so we continued to paddle across the river, keeping the island between us and what had been our pursuers. On reaching the east bank we paddled upstream, hoping to get to Chikwenya Island before nightfall. This was the place where Jeffrey and I were to rendezvous. The paddlers and I arrived, but Jeffrey was not there.

On Chikwenya Island I woke at dawn in the gentle, warm air currents from the east, watching the earth and the mighty Zambezi take shape. I had a disturbing feeling in my gut as I realized the shooting incident was a sign of the times. The penetration of civilization was increasing. The earth would continue to turn and the sun rise and set in this wild land. But our era of hunting and adventure would surely recede into oblivion, and even the memories would fade.

On the second night Jeffrey arrived. Always stealthy, he came unseen, appearing with four tribesmen in the firelight. He had shot some elephant bulls much farther downriver and was particularly concerned about a friend of his named Arnold and a tribesman who had been killed by a buffalo in the Luangwa River area. The full details were not known, but Arnold apparently had wounded a buffalo in some thick cover, and it had surprised them. The buffalo smashed Arnold against a tree, and his chest caved in as the buffalo rammed him with its horns. At that moment the tribesman, who was probably the tracker, thrust his spear at it and the buffalo swung around and killed him also.

Having shared high danger with such brave men, black and white, I find it deeply disturbing to see a hunter or tracker covered in a mixture of blood and sand and perhaps even grotesquely beaten into shapeless pulps—men who were active and coordinated and capable, likable, and appreciated for their courage and skills. Death is a natural part of the cycle of life, but to me those who challenge the African bush on its own terms will always be as magnificent as the wild animals they seek.

Elephant seem to feel the same way about death. This species in particular has an incredible communication system that includes expressing concern for each other. As described earlier, I sometimes suffered attacks of conscience in the aftermath of my destructive inroads in the large herds. When an elephant was down, dead or struggling to rise, others would rush up to place their tusks under their fallen comrade, trying to help it rise again. Their rage increased as their efforts failed. It struck me that the bulls were more affected by the loss of their companions than the cows were. Losses among cows are apparently softened somewhat by their ability to bring their instincts and emotions to bear on their young instead.

Elephant communicate in low roars, gentle rumbling calls, and almost inaudible blurps, and even when not making sounds they are fully aware of each other, even at distances. They feed and move, crisscrossing each other's spoors, and yet always maintain contact with one another.

At times I have seen from the spoor where bulls had come across the remains of long-dead comrades. The ground signs revealed where they had moved around, touching the skulls and bones and trying to make contact. At such times elephant seem to be unaware of danger as their whole being is concentrated on trying to make contact with their dead friends. Sometimes this sight so greatly disturbed me that I left the animals unmolested, though I could easily have shot them under the conditions. These feelings of conscience were not a good state of mind for an ivory hunter, though they were at times overwhelming.

Young bulls growing up in the herd become irritating to the cows, which lose tolerance and drive them off. Or perhaps the young bulls become bored enough to leave by themselves in groups. Whatever the reason, young males leave their families, just as in human society, and one saw young and old bulls together in their wanderings. A troop of bulls can consist of all old giants or a mixture of young, old, and middle-aged animals. The mingling of major bulls within herd is a temporary condition brought on by the breeding urge. Elephant bulls at most times prefer their own sanctuaries away from the herds.

Large gatherings are the rule during migratory movements and when the living is easy, but in these conditions elephant, particularly cow herds, come under duress and have to range in smaller numbers to obtain their feed. They go through phases of hunger and in such circumstances are more prone to attack humans. In their wandering searches for food they are tolerant of each other. Under the stress of the Months of the Sun they try to conserve their energies until the seasonal rains can give them sustenance again.

Wild animals in advanced age usually die of malnutrition and starvation. Elephant have six replacement molar teeth with which to masticate their food, and when the last set is worn down, they slowly die. We occasionally found large old bulls in an emaciated state.

Elephants' method of attack are varied, and you know you are in trouble when an elephant's facial expression becomes a wide-eyed, fierce stare, sometimes with raised trunk to aid in identification of the enemy. This means a disturbed, aggressive elephant that has the hunter positively located. Under these circumstances a charge is likely, even imminent.

A blow from the trunk will smash a hunter to the ground, where the elephant then tramples him or tears him apart with trunk and feet. It may also kneel down to gore the hunter with its tusks, but most times the damage is done by the wide-based trunks. Rarely do elephant pick up a man on the run, but when they do, they usually impale him with a tusk and fling him aside, sometimes turning back to trample him.

Elephant will charge unexpectedly and noiselessly, their ears at their sides and trunks curled to the chest, deadly in their silence. Such attacks I considered the worst. The most impressive and frightening ones are those accompanied by trumpets descending into low roars of rage.

I have had elephant sort out my spoor a considerable distance away, then deliberately rush along my scent line to suddenly and silently emerge at speed in the hope of catching me unaware. Such events are unquestionably premeditated. They make me wonder at the unusual senses and intelligence of these extraordinary beasts. Jeffrey, my hunting companion, had an enraged elephant seize him in dense cover and run on with him, no doubt planning to impale him on a tusk. Jeffrey had the nerve, control, and presence of mind to fire his rifle while held in that position—and the accuracy to reach the elephant's brain. In so doing he was flung ("flicked" was the word he used) among branches and consequently badly damaged for life, hence his name *Kamwendo* (he who drags a leg).

It also comes to mind that Commander Blunt, an old-time hunter, managed to survive being tusked by an elephant. Such were my sunset ruminations that night on Chikwenya Island. Jeffrey later asked me what our chances were of recovering the ivory after the shooting incident at the reedbeds.

"Nil," I said. The discarded ivory and dead elephant would be easily found by others.

He had liquor with him and got drunk on the higher, upper part of the island, shouting defiance at both banks of the Zambezi River: "All white men are dogs, and blacks are worse." Since he was in between, I assumed he believed himself to be all right.

He shouted: "I am master of the night, and from now on you will sleep in fear of me," pointing with his Mannlicher rifle as an extension of his arm at the opposite bank.

I asked him who had been shot at, him or me, and he said, "It does not matter, little boy, they must not enter here," meaning the whole of the Zambezi Valley.

Later he settled down in the comfort of the campfire and then told me what he had known for some time about two enemies I had in the Zambezi Valley (as they say, liquor loosens a man's tongue). One was the customs officer I had assaulted, and the other was a half-caste man living near Chief Chiawa's. I had befriended the caste, pulling him out of troubles with the chiefs when he had abused their women. Faanie and I had teamed up to shoot a wounded buffalo that had been about to gore him. He had shared our hospitality and the security of our campfires. I had previously thought of him as a comrade, and it disappointed and disturbed me to think he could have lived with us in a state of false friendship. It now became apparent that the caste was the cause of my having been arrested and held in Lusaka pending trial for poaching activities in Northern Rhodesia.

My tracker had been badly beaten by police authorities trying to get evidence against me, but he had lied to the last, and eventually we had been released. It was strange to have been arrested so far from the scenes of the supposed crimes, so it must have been the result of a conspiracy. Was I just young or young and stupid at the same time? How could I have been so trusting ? Then it occurred to me that I had been neither stupid nor overly trusting. How can the leopard be seen at night? I pondered how such treachery could benefit a man.

I could not find the answer, so I asked Jeffrey, who was still drunk but no longer challenging enemies. He said, "Don't be stupid, little boy. You are not dealing with wild animals. They are incorruptible. You are dealing with men, and wherever you find them there will always be intrigues."

In these few drunken sentences he wised me up to the situation. Time was on my side, and when circumstances were right the caste would be brought into the light.

The next morning we parted, I to go upstream and Jeffrey moving downriver to range the area between the Chewori and Rukometje Rivers. On the second day, battling against the current, my group turned to hear the drone of an engine coming from far downriver on the air currents. Eventually we saw the boat, its bow out of the water and seeming to make effortless progress against the current. It was painted a mottled, dirty gray-black, obviously to make it inconspicuous.

Eventually it came parallel to us about a half-mile across the river near the west bank and then cut straight across toward us. I saw a lone white man controlling the motor and was impressed by the way the boat glided over the water. It was the time of day for us to have a break anyhow, so we pulled up and beached the dugout and then climbed the bank to eat under some shade trees.

I stood on the high bank watching as the boat headed for our shoreline. The motor was cut, and the boat drifted gently to the edge. The man ran its length and jumped off. Like us, he pulled it up and tied it, using a short spear driven into the earth to anchor it, then reentered the boat to get his rifle. He looked up and greeted me. Immediately I knew he was Northern European, probably German. He athletically climbed the bank, and we shook hands. I was curious to know how he had gotten here as we knew most movements on the Zambezi River.

"From below Mupata Gorge," he said.

This lone traveler was an efficient man to have tackled the gorge single-handedly. The gorge required drive, determination, and knowledge of the waters. I later discovered that the Kraut—for that is what I must call him since he had a shady background—had been in the French Foreign Legion after World War II and had then moved through French Africa, the Belgian Congo, and into Mozambique. He had hunted some time in Zambezia and, like me, had come up the Mupata Gorge—only he was better equipped, using a motor. He had crocodile skins, ivory, and rhino horns.

I knew the only places where he could hunt such products and realized this loner must be a man of exceptional quality to have hunted the animals and extracted the ivory by himself. He questioned me on this part of the valley and about the authorities and personalities living on the river, and I told him all I knew. I liked his cold frankness, but I also sensed this man could be dangerous. How, I did not know, but my instincts told me so. If I had not been about to hunt in the *jess* in Naukaranga, I would have invited him to join me. I could feel his ruthless courage, intelligence, and cold openness.

We spent the night there on the high bank, sharing the campfire and exchanging experiences. His life had not been without adventure, especially the man-made kind. He had many of Faanie's qualities but with practiced German analysis and calculation. He was impressive, and I felt that he should never be underestimated.

I wondered what would happen should Faanie and he be thrown together. Faanie hated the German race—the soulless people, he called them, because of his war experiences. This was not war, however, and certainly not Europe, and in hunting country one had to try to live with all races and personalities.

In early morning the Kraut, at his own suggestion, towed my dugout past the strong current of the Kafue River junction. Then he disappeared upriver, on my advice, to Kam Cha Cha's. I also proceeded upriver, much slower and on the Southern Rhodesian side. The heat was intense, and we sweated excessively at the paddles to move against the current. To avoid the heat we traveled many miles in moonlight. My destination was Chief Mudzeemo's village, where I planned to collect Zaratina and Jacoba, then enter the Naukaranga *jess* forests. It was a dugout journey of a few days.

At the village I spoke to Chief Mudzeemo. He was pleased to see me again for he thought I might have been sentenced and imprisoned in Lusaka. He greeted me as *"Jegede,"* provider of food, and advised me that Zaratina and Jacoba were away in the forests with the honey hunters.

I lounged around the village, speaking to some men, women, and children whom I had not noticed previously. I watched them grinding the corn and preparing a mixture of *munga* for brewing beer. Others were hand-curing skins, and I noticed a pile of croc skins. I questioned them on these, and they told me the reptiles had been trapped and speared by Zaratina. The traps were wooden cages inserted into the water and baited with fish and animal flesh tied around crude carved wooden hooks shaped like small boomerangs. To each hook was attached a plaited rope, tied to a flexible branch that acted like a fishing rod.

When the baited hook was ingested, the wide boomerang shape caught behind the crocodile's throat. The croc was then hauled out by others and speared by Zaratina. I was much later to see this venture, and it was really risky, especially if the haulers slackened off on the rope, giving the crocodile the advantage of rushing into attack on land.

It was apparent that Zaratina was still having his revenge on the crocodiles. He and Jacoba arrived that night. I questioned him on this, and he said that from now on he would hunt crocodiles so as long as he was capable.

Zaratina, the tracker, is on the left; Jacoba, the water carrier, in the middle; Kari Kinki is at the back.

This was some time after the loss of his child, and Zaratina was more like his old self again. Jacoba had regained control of his nervous system, and I had acquired a .450 rifle. It was hellishly hot in the thickets, but in the past rains they had stored water in the hollow baobab tree. At least our throats would get water. Silently we padded along the many elephant paths, overwhelmed again by the sheer gray mass of the *jess*. The only sign of life was the whispering air currents in the higher branches, traceable only with the aid of the *rota*. The overbearing density of the vegetation and the lack of vision were the hardest elements to get used to again. And once again I was absorbed into the silence and immensity of the place.

Occasionally we stood in the much-needed shade of giant baobab trees with their massive trunks, probably hundreds of years old. I got the feeling that these places had never been visited by man. I visualized modern man bulldozing this dense vegetation to make way for farmlands. It did not seem possible, but even then I realized it could eventually happen.

We slept the first night at a junction of elephant paths, the bush being too dense to camp anyplace else. The next day we came across elephant spoor, but because our water was running low, and the heat was great, we abandoned the elephant to seek our base, the hollow baobab tree, and luckily we found it just before sunset. Zaratina and Jacoba had remade a small clearing around it, and here, with adequate water and food, we relaxed away from our campfire, the air near it being unpleasantly hot.

In early morning we heard the crash of bush and the trumpeting and answering calls of elephant. They had no doubt entered the thickets early, having come from the swamps, distant water holes, or, more probably, Chimba, the beautiful watercourse in the escarpment hills. We knew we would be able to trace them in the coming daylight.

At first light we found their spoor where they had moved along the elephant paths in the darkness of night. As the sun penetrated the *jess* they moved to a thick patch toward the escarpment. I would have liked to have enjoyed a few hunts with a bit of vision to break the monotony, but this was not to be. For hours we struggled to catch up to them. When we did so, I was confronted by a wall of dense gray vegetation and could not see elephant although they were only a matter of yards away. It then remained to try to silently open the thickets to obtain enough vision for a shot.

The elephant must have known we were there but remained immobile and deadly silent. I had a white hat, but either the bush was too dense or the elephant were not aggressive. I was not prepared to work my way up to them "to shake hands," as Jacoba said. That would have been my last act of friendship here. So we adopted Faanie's method of yodeling, and they came to life—faster than I had anticipated. In no time a miniature war was going on.

The .450 rifle gave me the necessary stopping power, and I got three of them. The others cracked off through the thick stuff and then moved away almost silently on the elephant paths.

We followed quickly, hoping for a hip shot on the last animal. There was a twist in a path, and as we came around it we almost ran into a giant bull ambling along as if in slow motion. Opportunity must be taken when it is offered or it can turn against hunters. I took two shots from the hip at the ball-and-socket joint. The elephant's hindquarters collapsed, giving me an opening to rake the brain from the back of the neck. The bull dropped dead instantly. I ran up its back, gazing to see if others were perhaps standing in the thickets. After listening for some time, we abandoned the effort.

"He is a *garonga*," Zaratina said, meaning a giant mythical elephant described in tribal language and beliefs.

Removing the ivory without tribal help meant lots of hard work. So we decided that for a while we would leave all dead elephant where they lay and concentrate on hunting. There was no chance that anyone else would enter the Naukaranga *jess*, let alone find our ivory. In this intense heat, reaching 120 degrees at 10 A.M., the sockets and cartilage that held the ivory in place would rot in less than a week, and then it would only be a matter of jerking the tusks loose.

Sometimes a well-trampled elephant path became less distinct until it eventually petered out. It then became a matter of forcing your way through the dense and at times thorny vegetation until you again found a well-worn path going roughly in the right direction. But most times they veered and changed, confusing your sense of direction and sending you off course.

It was here that the civilized white man, his senses dulled by life in the concrete jungles, becomes unsure, confused, and at times useless while the black man's uncanny senses take over. I proved it to myself, trying but always failing to match the instincts of Zaratina and Jacoba. They always had that edge on me. Certainly I could penetrate the dense *jess* alone and return, but they could do it in half the time. They also instinctively knew which paths to take. In admiration I tried to develop my skills to be like them but had to accept the fact that they simply were closer to the earth of wild Africa.

And so it was that we moved along the elephant paths, searching for and at times finding bull elephant. They always became aggressive after sighting the white hat, and they always crashed to earth before reaching us. But it was telling on our nerves. I watched Jacoba and listened to him having nightmares. Later my own and Zaratina's nightmares started, disturbing our sleep.

We had been in the *jess* about seven weeks, having contact with elephant at least every second day. It was time to have a break or we would all be seeing imaginary elephants. So we started collecting ivory and labouriously carried it to selected places near a track that ran from the escarpment back to Namomba and to the bottom of Kariba Gorge. Eventually we completed this task, working mostly at night to avoid the devastating heat. We had to be careful because if we became overexhausted in these conditions it could take a full month to recover.

Some bulls were still coming into the *jess*, and, partly because our labours had been a diversion from our fears, I decided to do a few more hunts. One late afternoon we were nearing elephant that we had been spooring all day. We could hear them close ahead of us. To our surprise we came across the skeletons of two humans at an intersection of elephant paths. The two skulls and pelvic bones were intact, with other bones scattered here and there slightly off the path. We seldom saw any life here other than elephant bulls, so I wondered whether hyena had perhaps found these skeletons and dispersed the bones.

Zaratina and Jacoba took it as an omen of impending death, and for the first time I saw them falter on a spoor. It is strange but true that when you live a primitive life amid paganism and its omens, fears creep into your own beliefs. I did not feel very confident about this whole situation myself, so we left the elephant alone.

During my wanderings, I had reached the conclusion that the government's game-extermination policy had had its effect—on the game if not on the tsetse fly, its ultimate target. Many armed hunters had killed and wounded game in great numbers. The remaining animals had learned to hide and flee for their lives or had moved from the extermination areas—which were now almost faunal deserts, though the tsetse flies were still resident. The whole campaign was a failure as the game was being exterminated and not the fly. It was a sad reminder of the stupidity of man. The land's beauty was still here, but without the wild animals it was losing its appeal.

With these and other factors in mind I decided that my wife, Joan, should experience this atmosphere before it was too late. In my ignorance I thought she would appreciate it. I had to be wary, needing the right tracker and water carrier more than ever to assure success and her safety. The KoreKore tribe had the belief that if a woman was in a hunting party, some of the hunters would be killed by their quarry. This was a fearful belief to overcome. I informed Zaratina and Jacoba of my intentions and asked if they would hunt with me and my wife in the *jess*. I watched their faces in the firelight, knowing of the conflict going on inside them.

"We will both be armed," I said to Zaratina. "If the situation gets too dangerous, we can leave our quarry for some other time."

Slowly and reluctantly Zaratina indicated approval with his head and then said, "Yes."

"And you, Jacoba?" I said.

"I go where he goes," he said. It was gratifying to know that we had enough faith in each other that they would put their superstitions and beliefs aside.

This decision changed my plans—I would now have to go to Salisbury on the plateau to prepare and bring my wife back to the Zambezi Valley. I was gone a week. We arrived back at Kam Cha Cha's, where I gave Joan time to adjust to the heat, if possible. Here she had the luxury of boating pleasures on the river and a hut for sleeping. Later I gave her a trial walk from the Zambezi River to Mudzeemo's inland village, where half the people had gone to prepare for the coming rains. It was about seven miles from there to the start of the Naukaranga, which would make access to the *jess* easy.

Joan found herself in an unsuitable environment with the heat and the tsetse flies, and she became restless. I had made the mistake of thinking she would be interested in the trials of the hunters' world. Her dislike for the primitive environment and people created an urgency for me to get this hunt done as soon as possible. She was in that unfortunate mental state whereby she accepted only her own world. She excelled at being attractive and vivacious, had an appealing personality, and was at most times a confident extrovert in her own circles. I stressed the need for her to try to adjust, if only for the week she would be here. I was of the opinion that anybody would appreciate what to me was another world.

I was later to learn that most people lack a sense of real adventure and don't yearn for a chance to leave their own world behind, even if temporarily. For a modern hunting safari, sportsmen arrive in Africa with all sorts of unnecessary paraphernalia, including lighting and water-filtration plants. They seem apprehensive of any new environment, bringing with them what they can of their own.

Joan was down to our minimum: light clothes, hat, soft shoes, rifle, water, and food. We also carried a snakebite outfit and medical supplies. These we had carried for years and rarely had to use, but they had to be handy in case of mishaps. And so it was on hard rations and water that we entered the *jess* bush. I had warned Joan of the thick, restrictive nature of the bush, hoping it would not overwhelm her. We padded along the elephant paths and periodically stopped to let her get used to it. She never did, repeatedly asking how we knew where we were going, given the lack of vision ahead and the twisting elephant paths, some sunken beneath the surface of the adjoining ground from centuries of pounding by huge feet.

Though small of stature, Joan was strong and tough, but the great silence, lack of vision, and heat were getting to her. "It's like being in a frightening void," she said, "no life or sound other than ourselves." I actually had a feeling of belonging in the *jess*. I had grown to miss this world; to me the only dangers were the elephant and thirst, which from time to time also wore at my nervous system.

Soon Joan would confront the greatest land mammals on earth. We headed for our base in the hollow baobab tree. On the way we had to sit down near other baobabs to give her shade. I did not like the change in her and consequently tried to impart my knowledge and liking of the place. On those occasions she would stare, mostly at me and then sometimes at the others, as if we were aliens. I could sense this woman was losing contact with us. Anyhow, she was capable of shooting, and that seemed most important at the moment. Thankful I was when Zaratina brought us up to the hollow baobab. Here we made a fire and prepared ourselves for the night. The sight of this massive tree, its tapering, leafless branches reaching skyward like the arms of a giant distorted corpse, also had an effect on Joan.

In early morning Joan heard for the first time the sounds of bull elephant roaring and trumpeting in the distance. I told her we would be after them at first light. Later, on the spoor, the tracker and water carrier were fully occupied in their tasks and took no notice of us as we walked behind them at their pace. After a few hours they slowed down. The country had thinned out a little, with large trees here and there, but the surrounding *jess* still dominated. Even so, this was a welcome change from the hell of the thickets. It was by comparison a beautiful, shaded place. I thought it would make a more livable base.

Here we came across the bulls, about ten paces away—backs, heads, and some skin visible. To us this was a great opportunity. Zaratina got us into a suitable position, and I indicated for Joan to fire at a bull facing her. She hesitated, then finally fired. The bull dropped, but the others went mad with their frightening trumpets and roars. We were conditioned to this, but under the circumstances we took no chances and opened fire. Some bulls dropped, but others took shelter in the adjoining dense mass. Some of those would run off; others might attack.

Then the crashing of bush increased and two elephant came at us together. We put them down, then a third one crashed out close to one side, and as it passed Zaratina drove a shot into it. It ran on, then swung around to attack, and in so doing sprayed blood from its lungs on us. Zaratina took it head-on and it crashed over, never to rise again.

The other elephant rushed off, plowing through the thickets, their impressive sounds receding in the distance. I turned to Joan behind me and saw a glazed look in her eyes. I spoke to her, but she did not answer, only continued to stare blankly. I shook her, but there was no response. So I took her hand and sat her on a dead elephant's leg. Still no response. These were not good signs—people on an elephant hunt fought, cringed, or stood inactive but did not mentally blank out. I left her for a while, then gave her water. Some of it trickled from the sides of her mouth. Enough is enough, so I gave her a clout, without effect—not even a wince or whine. I gave her a very hard clout; still no response. Then the tracker restrained my arm, saying, "Her mind has turned; she has the silence of fear."

I watched her for some time, occasionally calling her name, but she just sat impassively. It alarmed me, and I felt I had to get her out of the thickets. I led her by the hand for a while as we moved off to head toward Mudzeemo's village. From there I would be able to transport her back to Salisbury. We walked along the elephant paths, and I suddenly became aware that Joan was no longer behind me. My two companions and I ran back, splitting to cover the numerous paths, and I found her slowly wandering around.

"Hell," I thought, "what a setup." We laced together some bush bark to use as a *tambo* (rope) and tied one end to her hand. Jacoba was the gentlest, so we gave him the task of leading her. She was no longer capable of walking fast, so it took us considerable time to clear the thickets.

Just as we were emerging from the fringes we heard the sound of an elephant in deep slumber and saw a bull lying on its side on a large ant mound. I left the others slightly behind and approached it, but by some instinct it rose and towered, roaring, in front of me. I quickly shot to the brain, and it crashed.

I took Joan's hand and sat her on the dead elephant's leg. Then the traker restrained my arm, saying "Her mind has turned; she has the silence of fear."

The others came forward with Joan, but there was not the slightest reaction from her. The blank stare was still there as if this recent event had never happened. We moved off, and as the sun set I took the last position in our line to stay behind her in case she slipped the bush rope and wandered off in the dark. We could only move slowly, and it had been dark for some time before we reached Mudzeemo's village. Here they gave me the council hut and we made the most of it.

I settled her in and left Zaratina to sleep armed at the hut entrance. I intended to walk another ten miles to the Zambezi River to get the truck. I explained this to her, but she did not understand. I left her lying in the semi-open hut and proceeded to the Zambezi with Jacoba and another volunteer tribesman. Tien Dieni was his name, meaning a man with a faulty eye. He was fresh, but we were tired, so we didn't reach the Zambezi until about midnight.

The vegetation looked shrivelled and lifeless, as if it had not had water for years. In fact there had been just one season of great heat.

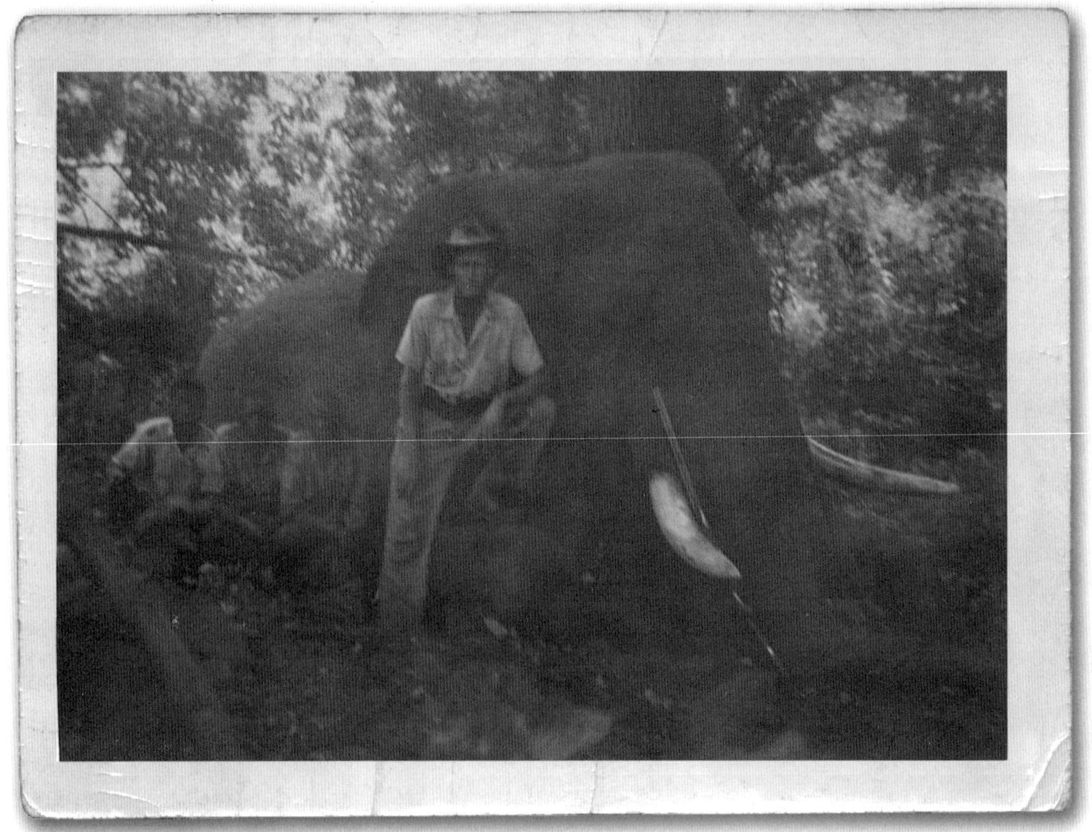

John shot some on his own near Chimba. It made no difference as we pooled the ivory.

We built fires and loaded the gear on my truck, driving to the Chirundu road and arriving at the escarpment. We then motored on the track leading to Namomba, toward the Kariba Gorge, and back toward the river to Mudzeemo's village.

With the tribesman's sense of direction we managed to arrive at sunup. Joan was still in the same state, so after a short rest I motored with her back to the Chirundu road again, heading to the plateau and Salisbury. We arrived there in late afternoon, and I contacted her doctor, a man named Riley. He examined her and said she was suffering from shock.

Still none the wiser and irritable, I asked him why she had to be so stupid about it. He explained that it was a mental process whereby people protect their sanity by blocking off the mind. I told him I had clouted her without success. He smiled in his knowing way and said that such treatment is only for hysterical people. It took Joan about three months to recover her normal personality. The life I thought I was losing, and so desperately wanted her to see and experience, was what had caused her to go into a state of shock.

Many years later, when I was writing this book in 1987, I got my daughter to have Joan read my version of these events. All she remembered was closing in on the elephant, the firing, trumpets, and roars of fear, rage, and attack. Interesting it is how the mind under stress sometimes works and at other times no longer functions. There must have been times when I was close to shock myself. Imagine mentally blanking out while facing up to elephant. It would have been the end of me and you would not be reading this.

I was never able to understand the complex workings of the female mind, probably because I thrived in the wilds of Africa rather than the civilized world. Joan is now remarried and, after a spell in the demoralizing climate of England, is now resident at Walvis Bay in Namibia. It pleases me that she is back in Africa again. I eventually realized how difficult it must have been for a woman to be married to a man who was seldom at home, spending most of his life following elephant.

In Salisbury I had occasion to go to the Game Department with John Connor. The man in charge was Archie Fraser, the newly appointed game officer. After a few moments of small talk Fraser offered me the job of overseeing the control of dangerous game. It involved becoming a game ranger, the first one in the country. Because of my lifestyle and past it did not really appeal to me. I suggested that John Connor was a better bet, but Fraser said no, he wanted my experience. It appeared that they had followed some of my activities.

"If you go to work in the Game Department," he said, "it will come as a shock to certain people."

We all laughed, realizing what he meant. To laugh was one thing; to be a part of the forces that had tried to catch and hound me was something else. I thought about it for a while. The rains were imminent, and by now the Portuguese in Niassa had a price on me. Fraser was decent enough to say he would give me a permit to hunt into the start of the rains before expecting me to appear in his office to work as a game ranger.

I was not suspicious but rather puzzled by the offer and asked why he had chosen me. He said, "We want you where we can use you and have some contact and control over you. Take your time and think about it. You must stop sewing your wild oats some day."

I thought about it for a while and said, "If I come back here as a game ranger, where will you station me?"

"In Salisbury, to travel to places where you're needed the most," he said.

"I had planned to explore the area of south-central Mozambique from the Rio Save to the Wanezi Rivers next season," I said. "If I come back, it must be understood I am not a policeman and I don't build roads."

He laughed and said, "Yes, go and do your hunting, then come back."

It would be a drastic change. Quite frankly I was still so puzzled that I put it out of my mind.

Within a few days John Connor and I were back on the banks of the Zambezi. I sent feelers out. Faanie had not returned from Lake Tanganyika, and Jeffrey was still down the river. We hunted the Nyamaque *jess* and Chipandahoure Swamp and got a few bulls. John shot some on his own near Chimba. It made no difference as we pooled the ivory. Every day there was a fierce buildup of heat as if it would rain, but it did not. In these circumstances we had to watch for heat fatigue and the signs of depressive headaches.

We traveled down to the Sanyati River area of the Kariba Gorge and en route got more bulls on the Reefa dry watercourse. Then I got others in the thick stuff near the Sanyati. We walked in oppressive heat from the Kariba Gorge to the Matussadona Mountains and Wamira hills. Here a rhino cow rushed us, and I had no option but to put her down. She fell more or less upright, and then we saw a small calf on her other side, butting its mother as if to say "Rise, something is here." This disturbed us, and we toyed with the idea of trying to save the calf but decided that under the conditions it was impossible—when the calf got weak the hyena would tear it to pieces. So we spun a coin to see who would have to shoot it. I lost, so I had to raise the rifle and put a bullet through its brain.

We moved on, not saying anything but feeling lousy. Later we came across a herd of sable antelope. They ran off a few hundred yards into the mopane forests and scrub, indeed blending so well with the background that they could be seen only when they moved. It was incredibly hot, so on reaching the Sanyati River we lay naked under the waters cascading between the large pools. It was pleasant, but too much water rushing across the human skin surface seems to sap the body of energy.

At the cascades we crossed the Sanyati River into the great Sebungwe district. We found the nest of an Egyptian goose on a dead tree that must have been moved by previous floods and was in the water well away from the bank. We waded in to reach the nest and got four good eggs, which we relished in our camp that night.

Within days we pulled out onto the escarpment. Here John and I parted, he going to Salisbury and I down to the Zambezi Valley again. When I entered it, the vegetation looked shrivelled and lifeless, as if it had not had water for years. In fact it had been just one season of great heat.

I met Zaratina and Jacoba near Chief Mudzeemo's village. In my absence they had checked out the area. The bulls were few and spread, moving great distances during the day and feeding in the swamps at night. It seemed that between the intense heat and the lack of bulls, my hunting season was over. Then Zaratina told me a story of interest.

It was midmorning and the air coming across the Zambezi River was already suffocatingly hot. Zaratina said that when he was a boy living at the Ruwee Pools of the escarpment mountains, a strange type of flu (*chifuya*) developed in their village, causing the deaths of many people. It must have been devastating indeed as the tribesmen were sometimes so weak that they could not bury their dead. After this they experienced the terror of lion feeding on the dead and, in turn, becoming man-eaters. The lion became increasingly bold, pulling the tribespeople from their huts and feeding on them.

Although some of the lion were shot at with bows and arrows and others were speared, it did not deter them, and the lion finally devised a method of getting into the huts, jumping onto the grass-thatched roofs. Using their claws and weight to enter, they would proceed to kill and devour the weak and sick inhabitants. The people's terror must have been great, for the remainder of the villagers, having no choice, vacated the area with their meager possessions, still being followed and harassed by the lion. Some of them managed to reach the Zambezi River, where they settled. One such person was my tracker. I concluded that the great flu epidemic of 1918 might have reached even this remote village in the mountains.

Intrigued, I listened closely as Zaratina continued: "There were always large bull elephant at the Ruwee Pools. As a child I could hear them drinking and bathing at night. Many times I saw their large spoor where they had left the pools in search of sanctuary in the thick *jess* bush."

I asked him if he thought elephant could still be there, and he was adamant that they should be. The cover, the feed, and the water were still there, and no human beings, so why not the elephant? I proposed going there. Zaratina was seriously concerned about water. In humour I asked how we could be short of water, gesturing at the mighty flowing Zambezi River.

His reply was, "Bwana, by the spirit of my ancestors it is not lion that I fear, but thirst in those hills before we reach the Ruwee Pools. It is the last of the Months of the Sun and all animals in that area will depend upon the Ruwee Pools for water."

Impulsively I told them of my intention to reach the pools. We discussed the journey and planned to penetrate the escarpment from the valley floor to try to reach the Ruwee Pools. Water was our main concern, and I planned accordingly by having the two men carry six water bags between them. We curtailed supplies to the minimum. I would carry a rifle, ammunition, a snakebite outfit, some pounded dry biltong mixed with rice, a small pot, and matches. It was to be my last hunt of the season and—unknown to me at the time—my last hunt for ivory.

The trek to the base of the escarpment was easy enough, and we arrived at Namomba. I waited in a crack of the hills at dawn while the trackers went off to the nearby Zambezi to collect water. Then we concentrated on making headway into the looming escarpment. We marched mostly over rough footing, and because of the season it was soon an inferno of bare, sun-baked hills, gullies, and slopes. We managed to last until the afternoon, when we halted and had water. Our thirst was monumental. After we'd had our fill, I climbed a hill and was amazed to see how the heat caused the sky and the barren mountains to blend and become one.

We moved as much as possible that night but at dawn realized we had gone off course. We were losing time, direction, and energy, so we switched to daylight travel again. Our sense of direction had become obscured by the continuous hills we traversed, most of them too steep to climb so we had to circumvent them. Our small caravan became silent, eating little, sleeping when possible. On the third day we consumed the last of our water.

Although we were all fit, weakness was now inevitable, and the use of salt seemed to make little difference to the now familiar discomfort of dehydration. Our throats were parched and painful, feeling cracked, and speech and breathing were difficult. The only temporary relief came during the night when a slight coolness settled on the parched trail. Despite the soothing night air, restlessness prevailed in our camps after dark, and often the distressed sounds of our nightmares jolted others awake. We could not possibly return now, so we had to make as much progress as possible.

Jacoba in particular showed signs of distress, which further strained the atmosphere. Zaratina remained comparatively strong, and I felt he would outlast us all. He spoke in an almost inaudible whisper before dawn, expressing the growing fear that we could now perish easily in these inhospitable ranges. He tried to remember places of water from when he lived here as a boy, but to no avail. We had no option but to continue on like doomed madmen.

At sunup, as the fierce sun gave the hills shape, it dawned on me that our only hope of survival was to try to locate the spoor of some animal and follow it in the hope it would lead us to water or at least provide the liquid of its guts or blood. But was there any game to be found?

It seemed a remote hope; the only signs of life we had seen were baboons on the first day at the base of the escarpment. The sun had risen, and one could feel the steady increase of hot air developing in the gullies and reflecting off the slopes. My mind wandered, and I had visions of us lying helpless and dying, unknown and unfound in this inhospitable country. I thought of friends, my childhood, parents, and the interesting people I had met and decided that it was better to die here than in a bed succumbing to an incurable disease as some of them had done. The hunting life had moulded my mental makeup, and having lived with savage fate more closely than others, I had a different philosophy. In the end there was always the rifle to terminate life if it became unbearable.

The comfort of being able to control my destiny to the last drove me on, and late dawn saw us moving through the gullies again. Once or twice I thought I heard the distant barking of baboons, but I dismissed it because the tracker, who had sharper ears than I, would surely have heard them as well.

Perhaps these were the first signs of "bush tap." In our hopeless state I became sick at heart. At midday we were desperate for water, and Jacoba could do no more than stagger a hundred yards or so before having to rest again. He had a hazy apathy about him and did not seem to want to participate at all any more. The vegetation had changed—there was at last some shade from the burning sun. I noticed this and despite my dulled mind scanned the area, finding an olive-green belt on a hillside. It seemed the obvious place to head for. So in slow stages we moved toward it. Just prior to entering this patch of vegetation—and to my great delight—we came across the fresh spoor of rhino. It seemed incredible to suddenly see signs of life after all the interminable days in the hills. Jacoba could hardly move, so Zaratina and I decided to leave him temporarily and track the rhino.

The spoor led into the same green belt on the sloping gully, and the freshly chewed thorn scrub indicated the animal was feeding. The beast was close now, and we were overwrought with anxiety and apprehension. Determined not to lose the element of surprise, we used all the skill we had. Then we heard it feeding close by. There is a moment when the hunter either overcomes his prey or loses it. We could not afford to lose it. When the rhino chewed, we stealthily moved in; when it hesitated, we too instantly stopped.

Suddenly baboons began barking from an adjoining hill. We heard the rhino rush off through the bush, and after a while it remained still. Were the baboons just barking or warning the rhino? In desperation the tracker took the spoor again, but the rhino sensed us coming and moved off once more. It was no longer feeding—a bad sign. We could tell from the spoor that it was in a trot, and my last hopes faded. If only I'd had the strength, I could have attempted to overtake it.

Suddenly the tracker paused, and as I followed his gaze I saw what looked like a bushbuck darting off into some cover—"*Umvura ere pano*!" Zaratina said (There is water here). We searched in vain until the tracker located more rhino spoor, which led us into a cleft close by in the hills, and to our profound joy we found water—a small seepage at the base of the hill. It was in deep shade hidden from the sun. Gratefully we drank our fill of the precious life-giving fluid.

Having recovered a little, Zaratina began to make hysterical bursts of semi-suppressed laughter in recognition that we had been spared. In the blessed coolness of the shade I checked my rifle, laid it next to me, and instructed the tracker to take water to Jacoba. I gazed at the small pool of water and resisted the temptation to gorge on it, knowing what would happen. I placed my hands in the pool, then carefully extracted my fingers and licked them dry. Exhausted, I fell asleep and awoke in darkness to see my two companions cooking our biltong and rice in the small pot on a cheerful fire. We were for the time being saved, and the water had rejuvenated our spirits.

Here in the cleft of the hills we tried to recover our lost strength. It was obvious that we could not travel too far from our present source of water until we could locate the Ruwee Pools, or until the first rains fell. The next few days were spent in the shade, and Jacoba started to recover, assisted by the well-salted food ration. On the second day we followed bushbuck spoor, then lost it over the stony ground. But later we picked up a fresh rhino spoor, and as we closed in it rushed us and I shot it. It seemed uncanny that the beast had escaped us so easily before when we needed it so badly. We cut off sufficient meat to eat fresh and would dry the rest for future use.

For days we stayed at the spring, living on our new rations. In the meantime Zaratina, with his instinctive sense of direction, had been exploring the surrounding country. To us at this stage the Ruwee Pools was just the name of a place somewhere in the mountain complex. Zaratina moved away daily, always returning at sunset. On the fifth night he arrived back at the camp just after dark to report that he had found the Ruwee Pools a day's walk from here. He described them briefly, explaining that there was evidence of numerous elephant, but he had not seen spoor of any large bulls.

This, however, did not dampen my expectations—bulls were likely to be there. In the morning Jacoba and I followed Zaratina to the Ruwee Pools and arrived toward sunset. The country here was different: The hills were widespread and interspersed with open valleys of tall grass and thickets. The pools were clear and good-tasting, but we purposely camped about four hundred yards from them so as not to disturb the game. Toward sunset I heard the roars of lion and later the noises of elephant in large numbers, drinking and bathing in the pools.

There was much animal disturbance around the pools during the night, including rhino snorting. Once I was tempted to approach the activity in the cover of darkness, but then I recognized the sounds of lion pulling down their prey close by and knew from the cries that the victims were zebra. After this we thought it wiser to shift our camp a little farther from the water.

Dawn seemed to announce itself with much promise that morning as we eagerly examined the many spoors at the water's edge. We moved away from the pool in large circles and discovered the spoors of a large herd of elephant. Tracking the herd was relatively easy. They entered thick patches of mixed scrub and began to wander apart to feed; this is what we had hoped for, as it made individual spoor noticeable.

We eventually found the tracks of three bulls, but they were not large tuskers. From experience we knew that they would probably leave the herd to join other bulls, and this is what happened. At times I was alarmed in our follow-up because these elephant did not stop to have the customary rest during the heat of the day.

When the sun had passed its zenith, they veered off into a particularly thick forest of *jess*. Here tracking was slow and dangerous, the wind seeming to move in continuous large swirls. By afternoon we were exhausted, having had miles of these trying conditions. From past hunts I knew that time was no problem. If we did not find them today, we would find them eventually. But it troubled me that the elephant had not stopped to sleep during the heat of the day—could it be that they sensed danger? Then the tracker showed us where they had rested for a short while before moving off again.

We followed on their tracks, and after a few hundred yards Zaratina halted, looked at me, and quietly said, “I think there are two large bulls here now along with the others. They must have all joined where they rested.”

I questioned this idea, so he returned to the ground that had betrayed the animals and said, “I am sure they are very large bulls.”

Now I had no doubts at all, and if the wind kept true we might be able to close in on them. The bush was thick enough to be unnerving, and it was mostly leafless and gray, the same colour as the elephant’s hides. The atmosphere seemed imbued with the presence of unseen bulls. I knew my tracker so well that by the way he moved I could tell the animals were close by. We came across another resting place where fresh dung droppings indicated that they had just moved off. Now the hunted seemed disturbed, perhaps aware of our presence. Our past thirst was having an adverse affect on my nerves, and I felt apprehensive of things to come.

I asked Zaratina if he thought the elephant knew of us, and he dismissed my question with, “Wait a bit longer, and we shall soon find out.”

Hunters experience certain feelings at the penultimate moment. Adrenaline courses through the body, making you superalert but at the same time anxious and fearful as to what the next moments may bring. Well-worn elephant paths ran through the thick, dry bush, and close to one of these we heard our first elephant sounds, the rumbling and cracking and breaking of branches. This put us on the defensive, especially as the wind started its antics again. We decided on our course of action. The spoor led to their noises, so we ran in quietly toward them. But we moved in too fast: in a flash they were directly in front of us, a bull fanning his outstretched ears, head raised in alarm a few paces away. Instinctively I shot him. He lay still, and after reloading I killed two more bulls with brain shots.

I was breaking a hunting rule by firing the second barrel at close quarters. If surprised, I could find myself caught off guard with an empty rifle. Reloading and glancing over the kills, I saw that these were not the big bulls the tracker had described. We knew other elephant were about. The hot, silent, gray bush became our enemy, screening the animals. I thought of climbing onto a slain elephant, but that might have made a noise.

During these tense minutes I glanced occasionally at my tracker’s eyes and felt hope. What strange senses this man had! Gazing in that position, he could tell something was near and alert. Suddenly elephant plowed in our direction with a rapid snapping of dead vegetation. There was no doubt they had us pinpointed now, and in order to survive the onrush we had no option but to wait for their heads to appear through the parting *jess*. I was troubled by not knowing how many animals would come at us. Normally Zaratina would have been armed with a second rifle. In our present circumstances he must have felt quite helpless. We were so deep into the hills that an accident could well be the end of any one of us.

“Concentrate!” I repeatedly drummed into my mind when apprehension seemed about to overwhelm me. Then the nerve-tormenting noise of snapping thickets increased and the bush parted to reveal the head of a large enraged bull rushing us. I killed him with a snapshot, but he almost crushed me as he collapsed into a giant mound. He was closely followed by a second bull. I fired a hasty second shot into this one's head. There had been no time to reload or aim properly, and so I had missed killing him outright. He slumped, temporarily stunned for a second, which saved us—then he swerved to one side, exposing large ivory, and lumbered away. There was no time to reload before he disappeared from sight in the dense vegetation. Then he stood still, listening for our movements.

A wounded bull is at his most dangerous, but now my blood was up and my nerve had returned, and the thought of his fine ivory made me reckless. "I'll hunt you in hell now!" I shouted.

At this shout we heard him turn and make straight for us, accompanied by crashing bush and the roaring, trumpeting sounds that enraged elephant usually make. I felt reassured by my efficient, dependable rifle and knew that surviving the moment only required coordination, steady nerve, and accurate shooting. He was coming at top speed, and when his large head rose in front of me I saw him for barely a split second in the sights of my rifle. Then he fell from view, dead a few paces from us.

We were all visibly relieved and for a while stood in silence. Then the tracker, as if mocking me, ran up the elephant's back leg and began to dance. After a short period he stopped, placed some snuff in his mouth, and softly said, "You must have shot him well this time."

He was lost in thought, then added, "We truly understand the value of living after moments like these. Still, although this time there was no mishap, there will be other times of danger." With that he resumed his slow, triumphant dance on the elephant.

We took refuge from the glaring sun in shade provided by the back of the largest bull, fell asleep, and awoke to find evening was approaching. We made our way back to the Ruwee Pools and near them shot two more bulls without incident.

The herds had now become restless, and it began to rain heavily. We knew that despite our sodden discomfort we could now proceed safely back through the mountains with no threat of thirst. It would be ten days before I could send tribesmen back to collect the ivory and return with it.

As we walked back through the mountains, where before we had almost perished of heat and thirst, now the gullies and rivulets ran with rain water. We were sodden and at times chilled. But when we reached the Zambezi Valley floor, we were back in the heat, baked earth, and dead-looking forest vegetation. We found ourselves depending again on water bags.

The waters from the rain up on the escarpments were winding their way down to the valley floor, where they petered out in the sun-scorched dry watercourses. Much later in the main rainy season, the large rivers would penetrate across the valley floor to empty themselves into the mighty Zambezi. Rains would come to the Zambezi Valley itself. The Zambezi's banks were our destination.

Even the insects were getting ready for the rains; the mopane flies plagued our eyes for liquid, and we had to swish them away with small branches. When the rains fall in this valley it becomes an entomologist's dream. The great variety of insects includes the Christmas beetle of the mopane forests, which makes a maddening sound. The tsetse flies were there in great numbers and very active, attaching to any living creature to get their blood.

After walking a long full day in these trying conditions, we reached the Chipandahoure dry river where it passes through a mixed *jess* forest. Here there was shade of sorts. Then we moved down the dry watercourse above the Chipandahoure Swamps and off at an angle through the riverine forests to reach the Zambezi River. As we came out exhausted on the high banks, some large crocodiles slipped into the water and were gone from view in seconds.

Zaratina said to them, "I have many years left in me to get you yet."

We slid down the high bank to get much-needed water for our parched throats. Tired that night, we pounded and ate dried meat and slept under a large Natal mahogany tree. In the morning we moved along the bank upstream to Mudzeemo's riverside village. Most of the people were at the inland village awaiting the rains, but the chief was still here. The time was near for me to leave the Zambezi Valley, so I had Jacoba and Zaratina use the tribesmen to collect our dispersed ivory and bring it to one central point. I lounged for some time here.

My mind had plagued me for a long time about avenging myself with the snake in the grass, the half-caste who resided across the river farther down. I wondered if I should confront him and then thought, *No, I would get at him through his possessions or take him on physically.*

Mudzeemo informed me that Faanie had returned from Tanganyika and was at Kam Cha Cha's. I got word to him, and he came across the river and then overland to me. They had made good money from the crocodile skins, and I was surprised to hear they had used dynamite in the Nemana Pools to force the crocodiles from their sanctuaries.

As the explosives went off, the crocs would apparently rush from one pool to another. In between these pools, on the land, the hunters would take the crocs with shoulder shots, spiking them later with choppers to the brain. The hunters came close to suffering fatalities themselves as a few crocs managed to put some skinners down with their tails. And on one occasion when Faanie was alone, a croc not properly immobilized grabbed his arm as he bent down to chop it. But Faanie had managed to hack at its head and the chopper fortunately got to the brain. He said he had learned that even a medium-size croc, even if shot through the shoulders, could throw a man with ease by merely flexing its neck. I laughed as he showed me his arm scars.

"Serves you right, you son of a bitch. I said you are prone to underestimating danger. Pity it did not grab you between the legs." And so we laughed about it.

I then told him I might become a game ranger. He was stunned, and accused me of lying.

"You're trying to frighten us out of the valley," he said. "You want it all to yourself. There is not enough oxygen on the plateau—they have no brains there. Why the hell would they want a man like you? You're incurable—a hungry ivory lunatic."

He said the shock of this was so great he no longer wanted ever to laugh again. It worried him. Then he said, "What ----head was stupid enough to offer you a game ranger's job?"

"Archie Fraser, the game officer who issued the tsetse-fly permits for us to hunt here," I said.

He stared at me for a while. "What's wrong with you? I have only left you for a few months and now you are talking of game ranging. You have more faith than brains. Don't you know Archie Fraser must be an only child, a spoiled brat? You with your experience will be walking behind him carrying his rifle or doing his shooting for him or making sure he does not get killed. Wait until Jeffrey hears about this. He will put you on his 'wanted list.' You had better not come back to this valley as a game ranger, not even to greet us."

He was so disturbed and annoyed that I thought I might lose his cooperation for my coming venture. I then told him of my conversation with Jeffrey when he had been drunk, and of the caste giving information about us to the authorities.

"You had better make sure of your facts before acting," he said.

"I am sure now," I told him. "This information makes the troubles of the past fit into place. He and the customs officer were at the root of our troubles."

Faanie reminded me of the time I got Zaratina to shoot the white bobbins that held the communication wires every two miles, to break down communications. "Within hours," he said, "Kam Cha Cha saw the caste motoring across the valley to the plateau. Within a day the forces were searching for you."

There was no way I could tolerate the treacherous activities of the caste. He had to be made to realize that if he continued his efforts of informing on us, running with the hares while hunting with the hounds, it could cause imprisonment for us all. I had to reach him now because during the rains I would be on the plateau.

By arrangement with Zaratina and Jacoba, Faanie and I made sure we were seen leaving Mudzeemo's village for the plateau. We took my truck and hid it in some vegetation, and both of us walked to a place close along the swamps. Here Chief Mudzeemo had left a dugout, which on his instruction had been stolen from the west bank. I had a snake outfit, water bag, rifle, bandolier, boots, and an extra pair of tribesman's sandals. I slipped off in the dugout in the dark.

Faanie had wanted to come with me, but it would have spoiled the plan. He went back to the truck, motored farther, and left the truck at an agreed-upon place while I felt my way down the Zambezi River. I had to use care as it was very dark, so I stuck to the eastern bank in Southern Rhodesia. Canoe speed going downriver was a little faster than walking, and I had to allow time for Faanie to reach Kam Cha Cha's. I took my time and gently made my way, making sure to avoid hippo.

When I thought I had passed Kam Cha Cha's, on the opposite bank about a quarter-mile away, I felt my way through a section of sluggish, meandering current. The intense darkness seemed to distort perspective, but with my sharp instincts and hearing I could feel the current strengthening and knew that somewhere across the river the Kafue River junction was having its influence, so I crossed the wide waters. Here in the velvet darkness I was more conscious of the sounds of the mighty Zambezi. It made me feel puny and at its mercy for a short while. Then I felt the current speeding up and knew I had passed the Kafue River junction. Eventually, close by, I could barely make out the deeper darkness of the west bank of the Zambezi. Everything was hidden from view except branches silhouetted against a dark sky. From here on the current would speed me downriver. At this time Faanie would be close to arriving at Kam Cha Cha's.

Caught in the fast current. I had to make sure that I did not overshoot the caste's place. From time to time I had to land and climb on the high banks to try to recognize places and determine my exact whereabouts. Finally I found a place with a small gully and knew the caste was about a quarter-mile below me.

Gently now I felt my way and stuck to the calmer waters near the shoreline. Then I saw the small reedbed above his place. I was here. I drove the dugout into the reeds, jamming it in as well as could be. I would be in danger of reprisal if I lost the boat. I listened for a long time and detected only the sounds of the night. Then I heard a stick explode some distance away. This happens at campfires when one patch of a branch is more flammable than others. I heard no human voices. I removed my boots, put on the native sandals, then waded through the shallows and climbed the bank to peer across the opening that I knew would be the caste's yard.

I saw glowing embers, the remains of two fires where they had no doubt sat talking and having their meals. In the darkness I made my way to the side of the caste's large house to listen. Behind it were huts and to my left the storerooms. I had to get at the main house first, the storerooms second, and then disappear inland for a short while before circling back to the dugout. I moved slowly to the surrounding forest and checked the fires again at a distance—there were more than enough glowing branches for my purpose.

Everything was set, but I checked myself for another half-hour to make sure of any human activities. I heard hyena howling in the distance and wondered what they could find to eat on this side of the river. Then from across the river came the roars of lion. Roaring lion have an effect on sleeping men, and I wondered why the lion should choose these moments of all times. They continued roaring for some time, then settled. It was likely that they would start up again after a time. The sounds of the night were my directives.

Thinking of the caste's facade of false friendship and treachery provoked in me a passion of murderous revenge. I thought of the time his treachery had sent me to prison, while he, a poacher, had remained undetected. We could have done the same to him, but it was not in our natures. Who, I wondered, would be next among us? He was obviously confident that his double dealings had been undetected.

Silently, gun in my left hand, I went to the fires and flung two brands, one to the thatched roof of the house and the other onto the large storeroom. I then moved off across the yard to the adjoining forest. The darkness lit up behind me, and I knew the fires had taken. In the forest I watched as the flames on the main house moved to the apex of the roof. The yards were aglow now, and I realized that if the occupants remained inactive they would burn to death.

I now thought of the caste's wives and children. I thought of firing a shot that would bring them all out when I suddenly heard shouting above the noise of the flames. The doors burst open and people came running out from the main house and the huts behind. I watched them running in confusion, silhouetted by the firelight, and saw the caste shouting and issuing orders. I had the almost irresistible urge to shoot him in the firelight glow. If I did this, I would be a murderer for the rest of my life. It was not such a bad thought, though, and I had to fight it. In addition to being a compulsive and sometimes violent young man, I had the calculating mind of a veteran hunter. Were it not for that, I think I would have shot him.

I could see from the flames that they would be lucky to get anything out of the building except themselves. The firelight was extending itself to the fringes of the forest. Time was of the essence now, so I circled and moved quickly to the dugout and began paddling across the Zambezi. On the open waters I no longer thought of hippo or other dangers for the moment as I watched the leaping flames and heard the shouts of people. It all slowly receded in sight and sound as I crossed the river. When I reached the opposite bank, all I could see was a glow in the distance.

I removed my possessions from the dugout and pushed it out into the fast waters. In the darkness it disappeared in seconds. By morning, unless beached, it would be twenty miles downriver in wild country. I walked most of the night, wanting to reach my truck and be on the plateau before dawn. The lion had started up again, and I had to move off course to get around them. But I knew the human and elephant paths and felt confident with the .450 rifle in my hands.

I had to be cautious but made good time, and before morning I crossed the Zambezi Valley floor and motored up the escarpment. This was to be my last action as an ivory hunter. Within weeks I was appointed the first game ranger in Southern Rhodesia with the newly formed game department. And so it was that I left my friends and our dying breed of men.

Game Department:

civilization's impact on the wilds—1954-1958

Life has many contrasts, especially my life in an office of the Game Department in Salisbury. I had became a game ranger.

As a prerequisite to this appointment I had a medical examination and to my surprise passed it. When I first started hunting, I'd had a faulty heart valve that had caused me pain and fatigue, so I cannot explain my physical improvement except to attribute it to having lived so close to nature. The wild ways had made me strong like other men.

Archie Fraser, the game officer, left me to absorb the details and records of events in the Game Department. I had to study the Game and Fish Preservation Act, the guiding game laws of Southern Rhodesia. At times I felt like laughing as I had committed so many of the misdeeds covered by these laws. The Act was basically legislation to ensure government control of the wild creatures as a natural resource to protect or destroy, depending on need.

Complaints came in through the various district native commissioners. Some of these commissioners, being magistrates, knew of my past and had their reservations about my being employed as a game ranger. But they eventually accepted me as a changed man.

It was toward the end of the rainy season when the first complaint about game came through, from European farmers past the village of Sinoia, close to the tribal trust and crown lands. An inspection showed little damage other than broken fences where elephant had passed through two farms. It was only a matter of repairing those few fences.

But I followed these elephant to the adjoining crown land, where they took refuge. Eventually I found them in a forest close to a bush-type house with gaps in the walls for windows. About thirty domestic cats were lounging around. As I walked up, an elderly European woman emerged. She was a Mrs. Cook and had the look of a recluse about her. I explained why I was here, and she became upset at the idea of shooting elephant to appease farmers. I tested her by pointing at her vegetable garden with the elephant in the background, but she said the bull elephant could have their share. Considering their large capacity for food, one feed would be enough to flatten the garden.

"Oh, I don't care," she said. "Just leave them alone; I will shoo them away later."

The more I met the English in Africa the madder they seemed to become. I thought at the time that she may have been too long away from her own kind and wondered why she was so isolated. I left her to her elephant garden party.

My first case certainly gave me a wrong impression about wild-animal complaints. Because I did nothing about the situation, the people here probably thought I did not have the ability to get rid of elephant. Later, complaints came in of genuine raiding elephant and other wild-animal damage to man and his property. It seemed a novelty to the complainants to have somebody to sort out their problems, and since I had to cover the whole of Southern Rhodesia by myself, I had to be on my toes. In between cases I would be in Salisbury writing reports. There were some dangerous moments requiring my skills and past experience—but nothing remotely to compare with the life of an ivory hunter.

It was strange to have been involved in so much ivory poaching and now to be the guardian of the elephant—or destroying them in my control work. Considering the chance Archie Fraser was taking by employing me as a game ranger, I had to make sure I stayed clean. Eventually it became common practice for me to deal in large quantities of ivory.

But hunting had lost much of its appeal now that I no longer had to evade searching men and attacking beasts to get at it. The wild adventure, risks, and intrigue of it were fading. In their place were my duties of assisting others and controlling wild animals. There was still, however, the excitement of hunting dangerous animals to make a man feel he was alive.

I had a natural resistance to apprehending poachers as they were mainly of the petty type, buck and bird hunters and fishermen. At times they made my life difficult and embarrassing. Sometimes they challenged me. Then I would physically go for them. I never bothered to report such incidents, which saved a lot of bother and had better effects. However, I was always on the side of men ranging in freedom, and I could not accept the thought of being responsible for their imprisonment.

Tribal poaching in Africa was traditional; using wire snares, on the other hand, was not. Because of the development of mines and business, poachers now had access to cable wires for use as snares. Snaring is probably the most devastating and cruel way to kill wild animals. Snared animals thrash around, panicking and cutting their necks or legs, sometimes to the bone. If the animal is lucky, the snarers come back to spear or club it to death—otherwise, it suffers loss of blood, pain, shock, and a slow death.

In my wanderings I came across a snared buffalo near the M'kwasini River in the Sabi Valley. Because of its struggles, the snare had penetrated parts of its neck. As I approached it turned to challenge me and then in desperation tried to charge me, but the cable snare was attached to a tree and it mercilessly jerked itself. In seconds I shot it. This was a classic example of how incredibly brave and tenacious a buffalo is.

In the vicinity of towns and cities, game animals were also at risk from night hunters using torch lights to blind them. It seemed to be an accepted practice—to the extent that people often planned it as their weekend's entertainment. Farmers, on a license that cost £1 per year, constantly shot game for labour rations and biltong, diminishing the numbers of game on private land. I had now lived on both sides of the game laws and consequently could see the problems from a broad perspective. Most people little realized what a financial benefit African game would become, especially on the large private properties, given the breeding potential and instinct of wild animals to survive. Ranging from thirty thousand to millions of acres, places such as Liebegs and the great Nuanetsi ranches were all well stocked with wild animals.

Another menace to the game was the Veterinary Department. Whenever it could not overcome diseases that were killing domestic stock, especially cattle, it called for the destruction of wildlife as the cure. I was called out to destroy buffalo in the Sabi Valley because of the disease known as tyleriosis. I did so, but then a new outbreak developed about thirty miles from Marandellas, a town in a region where there were no buffalo. It was frustrating and demoralizing to have to carry out the decisions and wishes of a more influential department.

It struck me how little government officials knew or valued wildlife. Those in authority liked to apply game laws to the well-known offenders, the celebrities, because these cases would be well publicized, but nothing was done about the thousands of other poachers operating on the fringes of the tribal trust lands as it would have involved too much work and bother. In the meantime the country was developing rapidly, many new farms were encroaching wherever land and rainfall were suitable. These farms required steady increases in their labour forces, some of the workers imported from Nyasaland (Malawi). Possibly one-quarter million people were involved. As the land was developed, game environments were destroyed. In addition the Tsetse Fly Department continued its campaign against the wild animals, shooting them by the thousands.

The official decimation of game made me feel like an angel by comparison, and I wondered how government could ever have considered people like me and my past life a menace. Government attitude only began to change slowly after official policy had utilized all the prize land, leaving marginal and low-lying rainfall areas. Even these were taken up later by man's needs. A few years previously D. C. Lilford, Fergus du Toit, and one other—it may have been D. K. Smith—had approached government to form a Hunters' Association to control hunters and to regulate hunting as a private enterprise. Government instead stepped in and formed the Game Department, deciding it had better keep the game's potential for itself. Archie Fraser was appointed the Game Officer with the authority to issue permits to the public for the destruction of wildlife on tsetse-fly operations. He became the head of the new department, and I came in to take over the fieldwork.

There were many complaints about game, some without foundation, and the most serious ones were given preference. In the crop seasons elephant would raid wherever they had access to farming and tribal trust lands, especially if those lands had previously been their ranges. In the center of the country was a large tract of land known as Rhodesdale Estates. It was now to be subdivided into many ranches, which meant it would be paddocked, and consequently the elephant had to be driven off. I had to concentrate on this area, which was particularly time-wasting as the vegetational cover was poor, meaning that the elephant had to move continuously during the day to protect themselves. Eventually they were driven down the Umniati River, but from time to time they came back in smaller numbers.

I remember on one occasion following them to their refuge on a small, flat hill. I was feeling tired and nervous, not so much from animals but from humans, and on reaching the summit I saw the elephant standing close to a stonewalled ruin. The remains of these walls were three to six feet high, and I took cover behind them and opened fire on the herd. This time there was no runaway panic. Well led, they came at me, wall or no wall. Leading were two cows that had pinpointed me. In urgency I shot the lead cow, but the second cow, screaming in rage, came on. I fired the second barrel and got her brain, and she fell onto the first one. Then I shot some others to turn the herd, and they raced off down the slope in squeals of fear and rage.

As the dust was clearing, I climbed the nearest high wall to try to visually follow them, but they were out of sight. Afterward, as I raised my eyes above the sparse forest, I saw the town of Que Que in the distance, about forty miles away. On my return to Salisbury I phoned Reay Smithers, the curator of the Bulawayo Museum, to advise him of the discovery of the ruins.

The more the Game Department did to sort out complaints, the more genuine the complaints became. In the Sabi Valley I followed elephant where they had broken down irrigation canals and pulled over telephone posts. The irrigated lands were given preference, and the manager here, a Mr. Cameron of the Sabi Tanganda Estates, welcomed me, saying he was losing his experimental wheat and other crops. I told him that if I contacted the elephant in the morning I would settle their hash, jokingly saying it would cost him a crate of champagne.

In the early morning I got these bulls where they had just finished raiding and flattening the wheat and other crops. I put the lot down, and that afternoon Mr. Cameron arrived at my camp with a crate of champagne. He had motored to the town of Chipinga to get it.

I said, "I don't drink the stuff."

He said, "You do now," and departed, saying I was invited to dine with him the next day. I tasted some of it and it was very dry, so I gave the lot to my staff and two trackers.

These two trackers were at times enemies, having different backgrounds, beliefs, and mentalities. One, Manwere, was much more mentally balanced than the other. The other one, Pafure, was at times dense and at other times unresponsive and silly. But both trackers worked well and were courageous and physically well matched.

I remember my wife, Joan, one time trying to chase Pafure from her kitchen with a broom after he had infuriated her. He calmly took the broom from her and snapped it. Amused and watching from a distance, I called him. As he came up, still annoyed as if it were his kitchen, he said "All women are mad, but some are madder than others and yours is the worst." I was later tempted to tell my wife of this but refrained as she did not have our type of humour.

The second cow, screaming in rage, came on. I fired the second barrel and got her brain.

Anyhow, on the Sabi River my staff got drunk on the champagne, and the two trackers squared up to each other, all fear gone and full of malice. I knew that in the long run Manwere would kill Pafure, so we pushed them into the Sabi River, where they tried to fight it out in the water, which half-drowned them. Exhausted, they eventually clambered out to regain their breathing, and as they did so the mad Pafure said he was enjoying himself and accused me of hiding the champagne. It was not so—they had drunk the lot.

A few days after this I left Manwere with the staff to remove the ivory while I crossed the Sabi River with Pafure and a water carrier to pursue a lone bull elephant that had been walking through the fenced paddocks. It was on Devuli Ranch, reputed to have herds of wild horses. We followed this lone bull the whole day in dry heat, and Pafure, uncomplaining, stayed on the spoor. The bull kept going through the fence lines and never stopped. At last, close to sundown, we heard him at a distance in front of us. In urgency we hastened as fast as we dared in the fading light.

Then Pafure suddenly froze, raised his hand, and pointed. The elephant was staring down at us, only the top of its head barely visible above a short tree. He was on the point of pushing the tree onto us.

Pafure then ducked down to get behind me, shouting, "*Chia ena*!" (Kill him). Not knowing whether I should kill the elephant or the elephant should kill me, I instantly fired into the gloom, and the bull lurched forward and crashed over on its side. I suspected that it might only be stunned, so I put a second shot into it at the breast, the slug traveling up to the heart—a common body shot I used when not sure. Darkness had set in, and we now had the long march back to camp and would have to cross the Sabi River. Hour after hour we walked through the bush scrub country in darkness.

Not thinking of much except the comfort of our distant camp, my eyes were mostly on Pafure's feet in front of me when he suddenly leaped into the air. He had walked into a large snake, an Egyptian cobra. It had raised itself to strike him, but he had leaped aside, and I now found myself facing a hooded cobra. In the darkness I could see its hood and part of its head, no doubt glaring at me. It was about four feet distant. With my rifle pointing at it from the hip, I realized that even if I missed it at this distance, the flame from the muzzle would make its attack ineffective. I figured its strike would be about the same speed as my gun reaction. We froze; then it lowered itself and slithered away.

Tired as we were, this incident woke us up. Pafure started complaining about how first the elephant and then the snake had wanted to kill him. He said it was the work of witchcraft by his enemies, and they would not dare do it to him in his own country. He lived about two hundred miles away in the very dry country of the southern lowveld, near the Bechuanaland border.

Ahead and to the sides we heard rustling leaves and bushes—no doubt minor game—and then a crash of larger animals. It was the wild horses of Devuli. We later heard buffalo. By this time Pafure, unnerved by superstition and by the snake and elephant, had stopped on a slight rise, knowing that the Sabi River and our camp were close by. Here he beat his chest with his clenched fists, shouting down the slope, "*Pafure m'kunzi manama!*" (I am Pafure, the male animal.) It was a warning to his unseen enemies. He felt his courage was being restored and wanted his enemies to know it. We moved downstream and located our camp on the opposite side. There was a makeshift boat, and the camp attendants came across and took us back across the Sabi.

Because of persecution, elephant had started to take refuge on an adjoining large ranch. So we had to pursue them and try to drive them away from this developing area along the Sabi River. The ranch in question, named Humani, was owned by Jimmy Whittall. He was the cooperative type, and he sent his staff to locate elephant movements. The Sabi is a long river, and these animals could water almost anywhere along its length. Eventually we traced the elephant to the reed islands and riverbanks and to inland scrub. I thought it best, where possible, to destroy them near the river as the smell of carcasses would help to discourage the remainder.

I did not consider this to be dangerous country, judging by my previous experiences in the Zambezi Valley, so we casually followed some fresh spoor—the tracker in front, a gunbearer, myself, and then the water carrier. We occasionally passed through thick bush, but it was not really frightening enough for me to carry the rifle. It was obvious that the elephant were looking for bush cover to relax in during the heat of the day.

As we passed through a small thick patch, the tracker suddenly jumped aside and ran off, and at the same time the gunbearer jumped back violently, hitting me square on the nose between my eyes with the butt of my rifle stock. The blow put me on the ground half-stunned, and then I heard the word "*magu*," meaning wasps. From previous experience I knew these *magu* as terrible stingers, aggressive if their clusters or nest systems are disturbed. Unlike bees, these wasps can sting many times, producing an effect much like shock. On hearing *magu*, semi-stunned or not I came to life again and dashed off, seeking scrub to fight my way through to be rid of them. I got a few stings, and you cannot imagine what they are like until you have actually been stung.

Afterward we called to each other from various points and regathered. We had all been stung. Although I was annoyed with the gunbearer for jumping back and clouting me, it was not really his fault. I asked him why he did not jump sideways instead. He did not reply, but then Pafure started again, saying his enemies in this new place were powerful enough to get at the white hunter. I let him ramble on as it seemed to appease him. The top of my nose and forehead were swollen, and Pafure said, "See, the spirits of the witch doctors even change your face."

We continued tracking, a little demoralized by the stings. The elephant knew we were hunting them as the wind at times had changed in their favour. It meant a long march, but at least we had reasonable vision in the bushy scrub. Finally, in late afternoon I could see the gap closing and then, for a change, fresh dung droppings. I kicked one open and placed the back of my hand on it—it was still warm, so if our luck held we would be able to come up to them. They were a small troop of about five bulls. The tracker's instincts took over and we moved cautiously, pausing sometimes in the hope of hearing the elephant ahead of us. It was painstakingly slow work, and it must have taken us an hour to do a quarter-mile through the bush. The pauses to listen were numerous and longer, and we eventually came to a standstill. Somewhere close in front of us were the elephant.

There were no sounds, not even bird or insect life, and no rustle of leaves as there was no air movement. The bush here was thick but not dangerous and was of a height to allow vision of elephant heads and backs. My instincts told me to rush the elephant, catching them unaware.

The tracker Pafure, known for his reckless courage, now told me that the spirits of his enemies were telling me to rush the elephant and also telling the elephant to be ready for me. We were in tense moments here with the elephant close by, and I had to guard against being influenced by the tracker's thoughts. The primitive beliefs of Africa can obsess people and make them unreasonable. A man like Pafure could not be influenced under these circumstances. Not even a rifle butt thrust to his neck would change the fearful power of his beliefs. This otherwise plucky tracker was now reluctant to move forward, and as his heart was not in it, it was up to me to go in alone.

I took the ash bag, tested the wind, and tucked it under my gunbelt. Then I slowly moved forward. At sixty yards I saw the dull white of ivory, and then elephant came partially into view, most of their bodies hidden by the bush. I was no longer an ivory hunter, so tusk selection did not make any difference.

Up close now, as a precaution, I very slowly went down on one knee to establish the angle at which the elephant were standing. The lower bush was leafless, giving me vision of their giant feet. It was well I had done so—a large bull was facing me close by, covered by bush. The others I could partly see. If the tracker had been here now, I would have been able to concentrate on the elephant while he tried to give me a better position. The tracker and water carrier were way behind me, unarmed, or had moved off. They were in more danger than I was right up against the elephant. If I fired from here, the hidden bull would overrun me. It was a point of no return, so I stepped forward into their midst. Their ears came out in alarm and their stances altered, raised heads intently looking at me. I knew in seconds there would be action, and for safety I must shoot to kill the closest elephant facing me. I got three of them, and as the bull hidden in the scrub moved off, I saw his large hindquarters and thought of taking a shot at its hip joint. If I missed, however, it would certainly kill the tracker and water carrier if they were still in its path of flight. Before I could take the shot, another bull came from farther back to join its companion.

This bull had taken me by surprise, and it was unlikely to have happened if the tracker had been here. I barely had time to fire, shooting from my hip as it passed. The moment I fired I knew I had wounded him instead of giving a fatal shot. It crashed off, and then the total silence of the bush enveloped me again. I ran up onto one of the dead elephant and called for Pafure.

He did not answer, but sometime later he silently came up to me. He told me they had heard the one bull coming and had silently slipped off. No doubt they had joined together in their escape. There was no real need to tell them I had wounded a bull, because by hearing the sounds they would have known this, but I confirmed it anyhow.

It was afternoon now, and I had no time or patience for superstitions or spirits. I told the tracker to follow the elephant. He said we would never catch them now. This I knew, but we had to have a direction and locality at sunset so we could try again on the morrow. These elephant slowed down from their run and settled into a shuffling pace that is about twice the speed of a fast-walking man. We abandoned them in fading light, but they brought us close to our camp on the Sabi, which seemed a good omen.

The next day I took Manwere, the other tracker. He was always clear-minded and steadfast; I had put him to many tests and found him reliable. We found the spoor of the two bulls where they had entered the Sabi River, and unless they had emerged on the other side it was likely that they would be on one of the reed islands.

This is the country of the Mandau, a short, stocky, athletic people related to the Shangani tribe. They are tremendous dancers, impressive to watch, making other tribes by comparison look anemic in their dancing ability.

They sometimes have a peculiar disregard for danger, and I have seen them, after running for their lives, collect in groups again to laugh at the adventure. Although, I was not completely familiar with them at the time, I certainly liked them as a people. One of these tribesmen told us he had seen an elephant in a reedbed downriver. He volunteered to take us there. The Sabi is at most times not a deep river, but there are deep channels where you have to cross in dugouts. We reached the spot and could hear elephant on a reed island.

I thought of crossing there, but on wading into the water it soon came up to my thighs and there were deep currents ahead. We retreated because of our fear of crocodiles. There was nothing to convey us across the water, so I asked the Mandau what was on the other side.

"Nothing," he said, "only low-lying scrub, not well shaded and with bushes like here."

It was quite a predicament. The elephant were in the reedbed islands, and we could not reach them. I sent the water carrier overland upstream about three miles to our camp to have the other tracker, Pafure, come down on the opposite bank and make noise, hoping to disturb the elephant so that they might cross the water to our side.

Toward late afternoon we heard Pafure and others shouting and banging drums and tins on the opposite bank. As a result, the noises from the reeds increased and the elephant came to our side of the reed island but did not come to the water's edge, and I could see only parts of them now and then. Both were big bulls, but I suspected my wounded one was the smaller.

Elephant in reedbed islands.

I was hoping the noise would drive them across the river, but they were reluctant to leave the reeds. In desperation I aimed the heavy rifle at a massive shoulder through the reeds, over 150 yards away. The elephant received the shot and turned to go deeper into the reeds, and I let fly the second barrel at its hip joint. I had little faith in these shots, but it was better than doing nothing since this elephant had already been wounded. It now turned and came back, leaving the reedbed and rushing across the water as if to reach us. I knew it was unlikely that it was aware of our position, so as it came dashing on I reloaded and waded into the river to meet it in case it should turn back.

It was spectacular to see it coming fast, the water parting under its great feet. It crossed a shallow place about four feet deep, and here I felt I could have a go, so I fired. The bull dropped in a splashing mass. I waited in case it should rise again, then fired at the water level where the current was flowing past its upper chest. I knew from its size that it was my wounded elephant. The other bull rushed off to the opposite bank somewhere. I had often seen elephant lolling and splashing in African rivers, at times completely hidden by the currents with their trunks above the surface to get air, and also crossing rivers like the mighty Zambezi.

Elephant partially hidden in water, with trunk above surface for air.

Here on the Sabi I watched the current passing the fallen elephant and felt the need to get the ivory before its flesh attracted crocodiles. But we were still in the same position, separated because of the deep channel. It was government ivory and so I was not overly concerned, but it had to be brought into camp eventually. We had to abandon the situation for this day. The next morning I left Manwere and another tracker, Kadigedige ("the small drum"), to use the locals to extract the ivory. I armed them in case of crocodiles. It would be useless to expect Pafure to do this job as he was sure to use the excuses of spirits and crocs. I took Pafure and a water carrier upriver to check on elephant presence. We found old spoor only.

I was trying to determine whether elephant were giving way to hunting pressure. About seven miles on we came to a village on the opposite bank. Here one could wade across the Sabi in places as it was wide and ran over flat, slippery rock formations. We called out across the river, asking the inhabitants if they had seen or heard of any elephant. They had not. It was hot and the river was comparatively safe here, so I casually strolled about seeking a suitable bathing place and found one just below a reed island with some large trees and short grass. The area was like an oasis by comparison to the dry bushland forests away from the river.

Pafure had gone farther upstream, and later, as I left the water, he came back to say I had missed a crazy scene—a bull elephant on an island fighting with a *picanin*, as we called black children. I thought the fearful spirits had reached Pafure's brain as I could not understand his ravings. I dressed, took the rifle, and with Pafure reached the upper part of this island close by.

I could see nothing unusual. But then I heard vegetation bending and breaking as a *picanin* of about eleven years came running out of the reeds and grass,

I had often seen elephant lolling and splashing in African rivers, at times completely hidden by the currents with their trunks above the surface to get air, and also crossing rivers like the mighty Zambezi.

followed by a small herd of about twenty cattle. Then I heard the low roar of a bull elephant behind them and saw him standing dimly visible in the reeds.

The elephant walked back deeper into the reeds, and this encouraged the *picanin,* who vigorously drove the cattle toward the elephant, shouting his defiance all the while. The *picanin* was oblivious of us. The entire chase now disappeared back into the reeds, but not long after that the cattle came streaming out again with the *picanin* in among them, still wielding his stick and shouting defiantly at the elephant, which again chased them out.

The cattle stopped at the water's edge. I finally understood what was going on as the boy shouted at the almost unseen elephant, "This is my father's grazing for our cattle, so you, bull elephant, must get out." What a loyal, brave little fellow he was to defy a towering bull elephant!

The boy was getting ready for a third drive when we called out to him, and Pafure walked halfway across the water to bring him to me. If he continued to pester the bull this way, it would kill either him or some of his cattle. He was plucky but ignorant of the dangers involved, and when we explained the situation to him he was doubtful of our opinion. It was a drought year and all animals, including cattle, had to depend on greenery that was available only on the banks of the river and on the islands. It was probably one of the reasons the elephant had raided the irrigated lands.

This was a semi-tame bull: Had it wanted to it could have easily chased and killed the *picanin* and his cattle. There was an incongruity here between this single small child and the bull elephant—similar to the clash between the needs of civilized man and the ever-diminishing wild Africa.

There was only one immediate answer here. As I did not want to shoot this particular bull, I had to drive it from the island and in so doing would be taking man's side against animals. We instructed the *picanin* to stay where he was, but he later followed us as we crossed to the island. Here, as we passed the cattle, we could hear the bull feeding. Allowing for enough vision in case it should turn on me, I fired a shot into the air. The bull paused in silence. Then I fired another shot, and the bull crashed off away from the sound of the gunfire. It knew what we were, and we heard it splashing as it crossed the water. The boy now had possession of the island for his cattle, so we left him to go back to camp and watched him driving his father's cattle back into the reedbeds again.

Mandau men now came to visit the camp, and I met the father of the boy who had challenged the bull elephant. Others called the father Shasha, meaning "someone knowing;" it was probably a nickname as they sometimes referred to it laughingly. They were quick to realize I was interested in their culture. I mentioned having seen their long bark-covered beehives placed in tree branches, and they brought some yellow cones of honey for us. They had previously heard of the champagne party and asked me if I would again be rewarded with similar presents of liquor for shooting elephant. I laughed at them and said, "No." They were disappointed, saying that this was why they had gathered here, and they did not mind waiting a few days for it. I assured them there would be no liquor. The Mandau men are a bit mad while sober, so one can only imagine what they would be like drunk.

Shasha then said, "We don't care; we will share with you as you have shot elephant." He said they would send me some cane-rat meat.

These cane rats are about the size of a fox terrier but thickset and good swimmers, frequenting the reedbeds close to the rivers. Their meat was considered a delicacy. I told them I did not have their hyena stomachs, capable of digesting old meat.

"No," they said, "we can get it fresh. We will hunt them together whenever you are ready."

"When I am ready?" I scoffed. "I am a hunter of elephant—why would I hunt cane rats? Hunt them yourself."

"No," Shasha said, "we do not hunt them like elephant but with bows and arrows."

Having aroused my curiosity, they explained that they hunted the hippo tunnel paths through the reedbeds, and as the cane rats dashed across these paths to get to the river the men would snap-shoot at them with bows and arrows. It sounded interesting, and as a change I accepted their invitation.

The next morning found us moving along the hippo paths, bent over to avoid the top layers of vegetation, alert to shoot arrows at cane rats. They had given me preferential position behind the first man, who led us down the hippo tunnels. Occasionally I heard the cane rats running as we approached. Some ran across the hippo tunnels, but I was too slow to get any. After missing a few, I told the leading man to use his own arrows to show me how they managed to get them.

We came around a bend in a tunnel, and there close in front of us stood a hippo listening to our approach. What followed was totally unexpected. The leading Mandau let fly an arrow at the hippo, and then they all, as one man, turned and ran. I was left alone facing an angry hippo with a puny bow in my hands. For seconds I was stunned stupid, wondering how I could have gotten myself in this position.

The hippo grunted and I took off, bending to run in an awkward position. I could hear the Mandaus running and laughing ahead and the hippo rushing from behind in threat to my life. I wondered what the hell I was doing with these lunatic people and with this ineffective bow in my hands instead of my .450 rifle, which was in camp. Fear helped me to run faster, even in a crouched position.

As I cleared the tunnel and emerged into the waters of the Sabi River, the Mandaus were already splashing their way across, laughing and shouting. Once I hit the water I could run upright, and I had longer legs than these short people, who in the hippo tunnels had had the advantage of not having to bend as low as I had to. I passed them in the water and clambered up the bank.

Some of them shouted in laughter, "See how this white man runs away from the cane rats!"

Once safe on the bank, I could not help laughing with them. After this they named me "he who runs staring at his own feet," meaning bent over in the reed tunnels. I could see Pafure liked these people—they were a little crazy like himself—but he had reservations, saying some of them were his enemies. He still had witchcraft on his mind.

On the east side of the Sabi Valley there is a plateau known as Chipinga, and a town there of the same name. About fifteen miles from this town was a farm called Redwood, owned by a Mr. Sletcher, who farmed dairy cows and crops. The farm overlooked part of the Sabi Valley and was on the brink of the escarpment, and from it a watercourse known as the Espungai wound its way steeply down the escarpment to the valley floor. For some time now the farm owner, referred to as "Sletch," had been plagued by wild dogs.

Most of the game of the Sabi Valley had been destroyed, which had caused unnatural conditions. As a result the wild dogs would range the valley floor and, if they found no game, move up the Espungai to Sletcher's farm, where they would attack his dairy cattle. In an effort to see if these wild dogs were resident, I arranged with Sletcher to camp at the bottom of the Espungai so that I could cross it daily to check for dog spoor while he checked the top part of it near his farm.

If wild dogs have burrows with young, they are easy to exterminate, but without this advantage they are almost impossible to locate because they range great distances, certainly too far for a man on foot. Sletch had a mixed pack of mongrel dogs that he used to keep baboons off his crops. He was having a hard time from both the wild dogs and the baboons.

On the second day I saw where wild dogs had passed after having killed some cows that night, and a few hours later Sletch arrived with two horses and his pack of dogs. He was of the opinion that we could track and overtake the wild dogs with the advantage of the horses. I was always a keen horseman and would have liked to fall in with his plans but told him to forget it as I had known wild dogs to far outlast horses. He did not think so, so I told him to use both horses as he would need them. I used my Land Rover and every ten miles or so cut across sections of the Sabi Valley, which is not nearly as massive as the Zambezi Valley.

At a twenty-mile range I found the wild dog spoor and then found it again after another twenty-odd miles, all from the comfort of the Land Rover. It was about midday, which meant the wild dogs would probably cover about sixty miles in that single day, excluding any night travel. I knew I was licked—unless I happened upon these wild dogs, there was no chance of finding them. They would lie low for some time and strike again later. Poor Sletch had to take the brunt of all their raiding because to his farm was the first on the plateau up the Espungai.

It was rumoured that some rhino had escaped the slaughter in the valley and had taken up refuge here. I was able to confirm this as I saw their spoor. What an impact civilization has had! Of the many rhino that had once roamed the valley, there were probably now only three survivors in the broken country of the Espungai. Unlike the wild dogs, they were easy to follow and were later exterminated by a government employee. Another price to pay for progress.

I returned to my camp on the lower Espungai and found that Sletcher had just arrived before me. We spent the night there as Sletcher did not want to go up the gorge cliff at night with his pack of exhausted dogs. In the meantime I had had staff searching for wild dog spoor in the hope of finding their burrows or lairs. It was a hopeless task, as all evidence showed that these relentless predators were not resident.

In early morning a troop of baboons barked close to the camp. Pack dogs of all shapes and sizes seemed to be everywhere, and the baboon barks acted as a signal, sending all the dogs off in pursuit, some running over me as I lay on my stretcher. Sletch went into action, pulling on his boots and saying he must back up his dogs or the baboons would lacerate them. The dogs were too fast and acted in haste, and when I came up behind Sletch I saw that some of the dogs were already in a bad way, having been ripped by the long fangs of the baboons. Some baboons had been treed by the dogs, and Sletch shot them as they showed up against the skyline.

Any dogs with terrier blood are known for their nippiness and daring tactics. Dogs and baboons taunted each other as the baboon pack stood at bay. If it came to a bet, I would put my money on the baboons, regardless of what an owner says his dogs can do. In Africa domestic dogs are not suitable for hunting dangerous game unless they have been bred for that purpose. There are, of course, exceptions, such as a Fingo dog owned by Pafure that actually attacked the back legs of elephant, but more of that later. The exceptions in this dog pack were those with bull-terrier blood. One little half-breed bull-terrier bitch named Lady was the boldest and consequently the most damaged. She had deep, gaping wounds, but her blood congealed quickly, giving her a chance of survival. Nine dogs were lacerated out of a pack of about twenty.

Sletch asked me if I would help him by taking the wounded dogs to his farm in my vehicle. I was only too willing for I knew these dogs would die otherwise. Sletch had his helpers take the horses and the unharmed dogs up the Espungai to his farm. We placed the damaged dogs in the back of the vehicle and took off. It would take some time, but at least the dogs would get there. In the proximity of the vehicle the lacerated dogs gave off a nauseating canine smell.

We motored up the escarpment and onto the plateau, then through the small town of Chipinga and on to Sletcher's farm. I pulled up at the back of the house. Sletcher issued orders for helpers to remove the dogs. As we walked into the dining room, where his wife and children were eating, he shouted a few words and everybody grabbed their plates and ate elsewhere. Evidently they were used to these affairs. The table, which was concrete or stone, was his emergency operating theater.

I watched him nimbly stitch and patch his dogs. He did the most valued first, the bitch called Lady, then the others. The Alsatian types had to be muzzled, for he had no anesthetics and their pain tolerance was very low, unlike that of the bull-terrier types. I left him to it, secretly hoping the crossbred bull-terrier bitch would survive—but what for I was not sure, since she would only go hell-bent at the baboons again.

The attempt to curb the wild dogs was a failure. Sletcher's only chance would be to suddenly come upon them. This happened later, and he told me his biggest disappointment involved his own pack of domestic dogs. On contact with the wild dogs they wagged their tails while he was shooting the wild species. He had thought his dogs would assist him, but they did not.

There were more problems on the massive Liebegs ranch, where elephant from Bechuanaland had taken up residence over the years, because of the better vegetation and water supplies. They had been increasing and had now reached problem proportions.

Archie Fraser with Ernest Glover and Ore van Bart, two resident hunters contracted to exterminate wildebeest and zebra to make more grazing available to cattle, and I covered the area in Land Rovers. In the winter this is dry country and it is easy to determine elephant numbers, mostly by the availability of water. The elephant were there in the hundreds. Archie Fraser eventually left, and I started to hunt these elephant in the hope of driving them back to Bechuanaland. It would be an ongoing practice involving a few seasons.

I started by trying to drive elephant from the most northern areas and was successful most times, keeping them southwest of the main road between Beit Bridge and Bulawayo. At times I had to return to Salisbury to handle other complaints.

At this stage the great Kariba Dam was being built across the Zambezi River Gorge. These waters were to flood some of my old hunting grounds and were later to drown thousands of wild animals.

There were additional complaints of lion killing cattle near the M'kwasini River, a small watercourse that runs into the Sabi. The area was open parklands, something like parts of Tanganyika. Lion in this piece of wilderness were living off the game but were at times raiding cattle on adjoining farms and ranches.

I moved through these places, but the lion had stopped their stock killing. Besides, I felt these farmers, who were always resident, were quite capable of dealing with lion with their poisons, traps, and dogs. I saw little danger for them under such conditions. On one occasion I set a trap borrowed from Ian de la Rue, a farmer who had lost stock to lion. He also used an empty four-gallon tin, cut and designed as a call to allow the human voice to imitate of the roaring of a lion. Such a call was used in Mozambique also, for clients who wanted to shoot lion the easy way. It was effective up to a few hundred yards. Anyhow, I set the trap on a rise, between large, high boulders. Using a zebra as bait, we covered the trap with leaves, leaving one entrance.

During the night I heard the angry roar of a lion and knew one had caught itself. It had been a halfhearted attempt on my part, done more to please the farmers, but it had worked. I had no torch and tried unsuccessfully to get the Land Rover into position so its lights would illuminate the lion. The lion's roars reverberated across the M'kwasini dry riverbed.

In the dawn a Mandau tribesman armed with bow, arrows, and spear came up to our firelight. He said lion had killed his cattle from time to time, causing hardships and poverty for him and his family. He had heard the lion roar and was pleased to know it was caught in the trap. He seemed obsessed about killing the lion himself, ill-armed as he was. I sensed he had a deep emotional hatred of them. As soon as there was proper daylight, we walked up the slope to where the lion was. It no longer roared, but we knew it was there. As we came close, the lion spotted me and faced us in rage. Had it not been caught by the front paw, it would have charged us. We were very close yet safe, but as I was thinking of how lousy it was to trap a lion to shoot it, the Mandau suddenly let fly with an arrow from his bow. It was an amazingly lucky shot as the arrow pierced the lion's eye and penetrated its brain. It slumped over as effectively as if shot by a heavy rifle. I left the Mandau the skin and carcass to help relieve him of his hatred of lions.

Various complaints called me from one side of the country to the other. I remember having to destroy crop-raiding elephant in the Chikore tribal reserve. There is an attractive running river there called the Ruenya, and not far from it I came across two elephant raiders. They could not be allowed to reside in this human settlement. Game control was the name commonly used for what I did, and though it sounded benign, wherever it was applied animals died, sometimes in disturbingly large numbers, to make way for man's needs.

Previously I had ranged thousands of miles over wild parts of Africa that were populated by few people but impressive numbers of wild animals. Now as a game ranger in Southern Rhodesia, I was finding that the game would have to be destroyed as humanity surged. The pace would vary, but it was a certainty. I wondered if the powers that be would be able to save some animals by adding more national parks and game reserves. I saw some hope that game's inherent value would eventually be recognized on large, private land holdings. But time had not yet changed man's mental makeup, and so I continued to hunt animals to make way for humanity.

As I approached these two crop-raiding elephant on the Ruenya River, I took cover behind some scant bush. There was a good distance between us, so I thought of a right and a left barrel to reach their brains on the first shots. On firing I heard a "twang" sound, which was worse on the second shot. The bulls were dead, but on examining my double rifle I discovered that the barrels were coming apart from each other. This gun had had thousands of rounds fired from it and had served me well.

I suspected, though, that it had lost some of its penetration power through barrel wear. It was my own rifle, the one for which I eventually paid D. C. Lilford the unprincely sum of £80. I am sure that Lilford accepted this amount mostly to help me to have a more suitable weapon for my dangerous hunting. Without it, I would never have survived. The gun was sent back to the original makers, Rigby of London, where it was re-regulated, tested, and reblued at no cost—wonderfully fine service.

While this gun was being repaired, I had to use double-barreled .500-caliber rifles that had been ordered by the Game Department. These were postwar makes, nice to look at but rubbish. I had misfires, the ammunition manufacturers blaming the gun manufacturers and vice-versa. Also, expended cartridge cases would jam in the chambers when the guns were heated, which often happened while shooting large herds of elephant. I remember one occasion when elephant faced me in tall grass. I fired and to my dismay heard only a fizzing sound—a hang-fire. Then, as I kept my aim, the cartridge went off. Such risks were necessary until my own rifle was sent back from London—and pleased I was to feel it in my hands again.

This young country, Rhodesia, was attracting overseas investors. One was the Bata Shoe Company, which set up in Gwelo, a town in the Midlands. Plans were made to take the owner hunting. Archie Fraser said they would want an unspoiled area, and so I was sent to select a place. I chose the vast Sebungwe, the so-called last wild stronghold of the country, the land of the wild Matonga people, previously described.

In this district, a large portion of which had been used for game destruction by the Tsetse Fly Department, the last station was a place called Lusulu. Here was stationed a tsetse-fly officer with many black hunters working under him. He would issue them .303 rifles and ammunition with which they destroyed game over their large range. It was the same type of campaign as described in the chapter on the Kariba/Chirundu areas of the Zambezi Valley. In addition there was another massive game-extermination area, the Mtoko, Mudzi, and Rushinga region to the northeast near and adjoining the Mozambique border.

My destination in the Sebungwe district was the area known as Kariangwe and the Lubu and M'belele Rivers and along their lengths for some miles to where they converged. At the last outpost, Lusulu, arrangements had been made for me to collect a large drum of petrol.

I was to use a four-wheel-drive vehicle to penetrate the bush and forest country as far as possible. I arrived at Lusulu camp with my staff and found that the officer, a Mr. Bond, was gone to the Gwaai River Hotel and stores some sixty-odd miles away on the Bulawayo-Victoria Falls road. I knew the lonely bush roads in this area, having used them. Bond's wife was in the camp, and she advised me to wait for him as he was due at sundown.

They had just recently got married, and his wife was new to this strange environment, having come from England. So I thought he would surely be back at nightfall. But he did not arrive, and so I was stuck without petrol, which was in a locked store, and Bond had the keys with him. Mrs. Bond offered me the hospitality of her house and above all a bath, which was welcome after all the sandy travel through the country. The dust seemed to cling to my clothing, acting as an abrasive on the skin. Next day I waited until midday, but no Mr. Bond, so I rode off in the general direction of Kariangwe, having made up my mind that when I could proceed no farther with the vehicle I would take water and provisions and attempt to walk to this new safari place. In the meantime I had acquired a young tribesman to help with directions as he said he knew some of the country.

I saw there were hills of a minor escarpment ahead, but the diminishing track petered out in some thick bush and forest. As I stopped to investigate further passage, I heard the drone of a vehicle and waited. Finally it arrived and out jumped this fellow Bond, short of stature, cocky as a bantam rooster—and drunk.

He was alone; apparently his staff had at some point vacated his truck, probably in fear. He told me this was his territory and demanded to know what I was doing here. He had a peculiar habit of rolling up his sleeves every now and then as if bracing himself for a brawl. Amused, I pointed at my government license plate and said I had come to his house for the prearranged petrol and was looking for a hunting place for Bata, the millionaire investor.

"I don't care about him!" he shouted.

"Neither do I," I said, "but I have to go through your tsetse-fly-control area to reach an unspoiled place."

I then told him I had been waiting a day and a half and had slept at his house last night. On hearing this he leaped into the air like a Masai warrior. What does one man say to another under these ridiculous circumstances?

"Call me a bastard if it makes you feel better," I said, "but give me the petrol."

He took advantage of this encouragement and enjoyed going into my pedigree. I found it amusing but less so when I saw a rifle in his vehicle. I had come across other men stationed in isolated places, and many of them were not really suited to it. The loneliness and great silences that fed an ivory hunter's soul had the opposite effect on such men, for they did not have the stimulus of continuous hunting to keep them sane. I had witnessed these types go native or find relief and sanctuary in liquor. Bond had the advantage now of a female companion of his own kind and choosing. I felt it would alter his life for the good, which it did. After this mishap I met him again much later in Salisbury, where his wife had given birth.

Now having got the poison from his system, Bond cooled down and said I was all right but must come home with him to have a few drinks. He at first had wanted to kill me and now wanted me as a drinking companion. Liquor for me was either a feast or a famine. On the rare occasions that I drank, I enjoyed only its effect, finding the taste unpleasant. I returned with Bond, saying I would only have a few drinks to satisfy him, collect the petrol, and be off. We sat on his veranda, and I listened to and questioned him in reasonable conversation on the area of his control. I then rose to collect the petrol and be off. But he said he had not had enough liquor yet.

My patience was running out, and I could see myself shooting the lock off the storeroom door to get at the petrol. Luckily for me Bond had been drinking all day, and as he became ineffective and more under its influence his wife took the keys from him and I managed to get the petrol and leave. I drove on past where I had met Bond, my helpers finding ways to get through the bush forest until darkness overtook us and we camped.

In the morning we continued for a full day, slowly negotiating places where no vehicle had ever been before. I crossed a slope between two large hills—like a small escarpment—to find myself in a series of smaller hills and rugged country. I camped a few miles farther on. At sundown I climbed a rise to see a decline in front of me. There was not much daylight left, but the view suggested a fall-away of topography, indicating less rugged country to negotiate.

That night we heard lion roaring and then a distinct rumble of earth behind us. The latter sound diminished, but the lions' roars continued. In the morning we found a way down the slope and crossed some flat bush and forest country to come up to a minor riverine forest verging on an open, dry, sandy riverbed. The place was bristling with impala and other minor game.

Reluctantly I shot an impala to provide the makings for a food commonly known as *sadza ne nyama*, which is a mealie-meal and meat stew, sometimes with vegetables or the leaves of certain bushes added. The gravy of this mixture is called *chisewa*, and the maize-meal is dipped into it before being eaten. It is the customary diet wherever maize is grown or obtainable. In fact, the food provides a reasonably balanced diet of carbohydrates, protein, and vegetable matter and is the staple diet for millions of people in Africa.

The lion gave us hell that night, coming close to the camp where the carcass of the impala sat on the bonnet of the Land Rover near the fire. We rustled up the fire to give a greater sphere of light. I could hear the heavy sighs of hungry lion in the darkness. While wondering how much safe sleep we would have, I saw the face and then the body of a lioness come into the firelight. I doubted if these lion were familiar with human beings, but she knew exactly where the dead impala was.

Lazy bitch, I thought, *why don't you hunt for yourself, there is so much wildlife here?* I could have shot at her but was intrigued by her boldness. She warned us with her snarls and came forward stealthily, the muscles rippling under her furry coat giving an indication of the power of her physique. As she reached the vehicle, she slightly turned her head to me and snarled a final warning; then she raised herself, pulled the impala carcass from the Land Rover, and, with deep-throated snarls of rage and then satisfaction, she dragged the impala off effortlessly, disappearing into the darkness.

We heard other lion fighting, no doubt wanting a share of the meat, and then they all moved off farther where we could hear them occasionally growling and feeding. I hoped there was enough for them all, so that we could feel secure enough to sleep undisturbed.

Other lion roared far off, and this lot of ours answered them. Later we heard the weird wails of hyena and the rasping grunts of leopard, the invisible masters of the night. It was awe-inspiring. I was listening to the grand sounds of my slowly diminishing wild, savage Africa, and the realization of it brought a loneliness to my soul.

I felt at home here. It was much like being in the wilds of Mozambique—less hot, but the night sounds, even the occasional snort of antelope reacting in alarm in the darkness, were similar. I knew such places could not survive the advance of civilization intact, and so it came to pass. This paradise was later totally obliterated while occupied by the Matonga people, who were removed from the middle Zambezi Valley to make way for the rising waters of the massive lake that was to be known as Lake Kariba.

In early morning we walked along the banks of the river in the forest flats. Animals in great variety were sighted all along. I saw some hills rising and another sandy river course holding large pools with crocodiles, a sign that these pools held out in the very dry seasons. Close to the river I came across two mounds of rocks indicating graves, no doubt placed there by men. I later traced these graves to two white men who had come here in the year 1903 and perished, probably from malaria or sleeping sickness. No doubt this place had not changed since then.

We entered the hills, climbing into a steep gorge until the sides became dangerous to maintain a foothold. Above us baboons barked as if to goad us on to our deaths. I accepted their judgment, and we eventually climbed higher onto safer ground.

Below us lay large crystal-clear pools in rock, some with subterranean caves. Occasional crocodiles lay in the pools, and I wondered how they had gotten there. To slip from our precarious positions here, even if not physically smashed, meant death, for no human could escape these pools with their almost perpendicular sides. In this rugged, dangerous country I now felt the need to gain safe ground.

The rifle was an encumbrance here as we clung to the hillsides and tested footholds, but men without weapons were doomed in this wild country. On reaching higher, more level ground, we gazed down to see beautifully coloured, streamlined birds of the duck family dive into the pools with their wings thrown back to disappear under the surface. At first I thought they were fishing, but as they did not reappear I realized they must have some sanctuary under the cliffs, probably nesting places on shelves safe from the crocodiles. My exploring instincts were strong—how I would have liked to investigate, but without the power of flight it was impossible.

We gave it a day's rest, and then I and the two others carried water and supplies across the dry river to explore the country farther on. Within two days we were well into a rugged, then smooth plateau where there was evidence of bull elephant and some large herds. Nowhere had we come across the Matonga people, but I did see paths that I judged might have been made by human use. It was hard to tell with all the movement of game. Finally the land below me leveled, and I got a strong impression that the vastness in front of and below me could only be the higher portion of the great Zambezi Valley. I realized I had overshot my mark, and so we made our way back to our camp, a full two days' walk. I had found what I had been sent for.

We spent a few more days walking the area but never saw anything as alluring and dangerous as the gorges we had climbed. We did, however, come across a recent landslide. That had been the rumbling noise we had heard when the lion were roaring. A massive part of the hill had subsided, blocking our exit. Luckily we were carrying extra water, and within a few days I found another way out of this country. I was later informed that the would-be hunter Bata had changed his mind. It made no difference—I had enjoyed exploring this unique country, and it was a break from game control.

On this trip we had not seen the Matonga tribe, so on the return journey I motored to Sewale, along a flood course where there was a large pan of water. It was in another one of the tsetse-fly hunting cam-

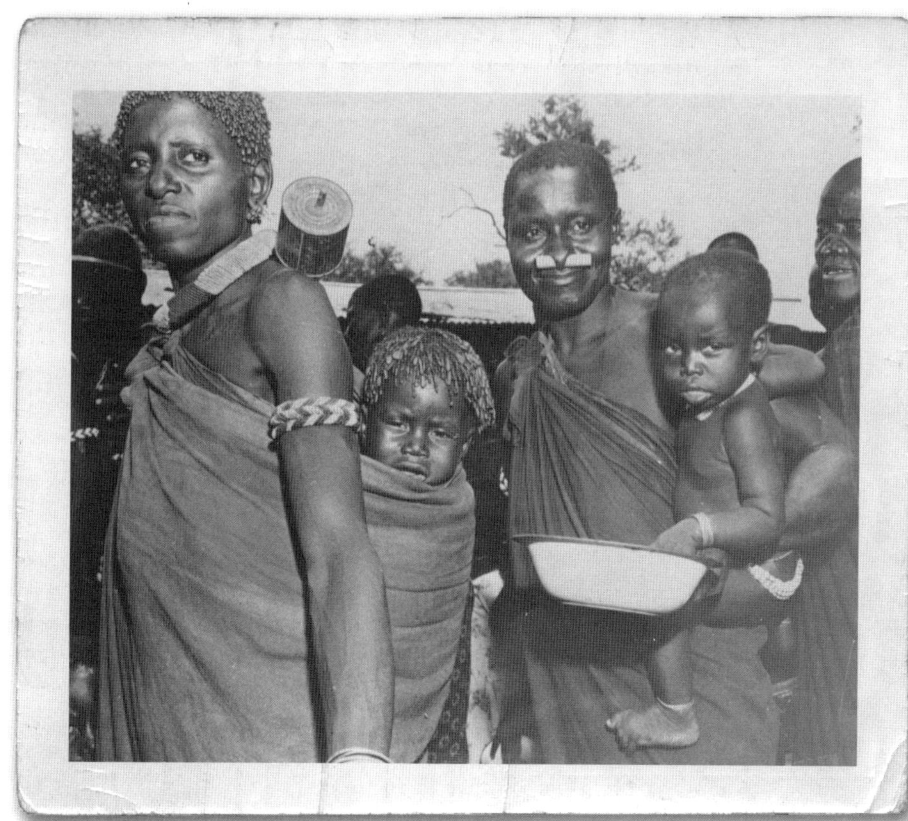

The Matonga people, who were removed from the middle Zambezi Valley to make way for the rising waters of the massive lake that was to be known as Lake Kariba.

paign areas. The resident tsetse-fly control officer was not there, so we camped at the edge of an opening behind his bush house.

We met Matonga people on the road and at some small villages. We gave some of them lifts between villages and got to know them. I heard of the "dance of the sable horns." Always intrigued by primitive people's ways of life, I asked them if they could perform this dance. They agreed and we made arrangements for the dancers, drums, and fluted sable horns to be brought to us at our camp.

I had barter materials and some money and with it procured quantities of beer. A large group gathered, and as the sun sank orange-red, the flames of the fires took over in the darkness, and many black bodies became intoxicated by liquor in the glare of the flames. When they were in the right spirit, one of them started to blow a pleasant high-pitched note through a sable horn.

The introduction was much like a European band tuning up before the main play. There were eight of these fluted sable horns, and as the men blew them in individual sequence they leaped into the air like the Masai of East Africa but not so high. The fluted horns had different tones, and the effect was appealing, almost soothing—that was, until the drummers brought their instruments into play. The scene then changed, with rhythmic, pulsating beats accompanying the piping sounds of the sable horns. Then the drums began to dominate, driving the movements of fast hands and dancing feet. It pleased me to see the tribesmen's feet pounding the earth in quick rhythm and at the same time enabling them to flow across the ground. The more they drank, the better they danced, and the scene reached a stage of ecstasy. One could feel the very soul of Africa in the sounds and dancing as the dust rose in the firelight.

At this stage the tsetse-fly ranger arrived, the beams of his vehicle passing over us and then stopping at his house. Just about that time my trackers told me the Matongas were going to act out the "smelling-out process." So for a while I took no notice of the newly arrived vehicle, thinking the ranger would come to investigate the dancing, but he did not and must have gone into his house.

The tribespeople lined up shoulder to shoulder in a subdued attitude. Then one, supposedly the witch, came forward to the drums with three attendants behind her. Actually it was a man acting as a woman and holding an animal-tail fly-swish in his hand.

They now danced all along the line of men, pausing now and then to gaze at this or that victim, then moving up and down the line in rhythmical, savage dancing. So impressive and real was this scene that the players seemed fearful of the witch in her state of evil dominance. The drummers watched the scene closely and altered their drumbeats accordingly. Then the witch became decisive and gazed at the first selected victim, dancing to and fro in front of him and coming right up to stare into the face. Dancing back a little, the witch struck the man across his face with the fly-swish. Instantly the victim was seized by the attendants and brought forward with head forced down, and then the act of spearing him in the back was depicted. It was so well done that I could see how it must have occurred in the days gone by.

This herdsman was later killed by a buffalo.

It was past midnight, and as I had seen what I wanted, I slept close by, confident in the sounds of the pounding drums and the large fires. Sometime before dawn the drums stopped, and I woke to see some Matongas moving off. I rose with the sun and saw others lying around the fires, having had too much to drink and incapable of going back to their villages. I told the trackers to pack and then went across the opening to visit the fly ranger.

His name was Mayhew, an Englishman out here in the bush. It must have been only a job to him since, when questioned, he expressed no interest in the primitive environment. He was well stocked with books of all descriptions and gave me one. Mayhew was hospitable and intelligent, but it surprised me how he could live here and yet divorce himself from almost everything around him.

After a small break in Salisbury, I had to try to discourage more elephant from Liebegs Ranch. It was easier said than done, but at least the country did not have the dangerous cover of the Zambezi Valley. It was thick enough in places but mostly low-growing scrub foliage, giving a view of elephant backs and heads. Consequently these elephant, upon being persecuted, would travel long distances in the dry heat of day and the cold nights of the southern lowveld. Obviously I had to cover the same distances. The bulls here acted as the forerunners to the herds, and so I had to go for them first. After a while they receded toward Bechuanaland and left the cows to take the brunt of the human pressure.

These elephant were reluctant to leave the good bush of Liebegs Ranch to return to the dry harshness of Bechuanaland. At the time, three ranches of previous crown land were made available, lots of 70,000 acres each, and some of the elephant took refuge from me there. These efforts to get the elephant back to Bechuanaland took years of hunting during seasonal dry winter when water was at its scarcest.

On one occasion, prior to going to Liebegs Ranch, I had to visit a man named John Posselt because of elephant complaints. He was stationed in the Gwanda tribal trust lands and had a menagerie of uncaged wild animals around his place. I spent half of a day viewing his setup and was particularly impressed by

John Posselt's eland being herded. He had a way with wild animals, usually a sign that a person is less fearful of them.

his domesticated herd of eland living with the cattle. He had a way with wild animals, usually a sign that such a person is less fearful of them.

That night we spoke of the elephant, a cow herd, that had to be hunted out of the area. John showed serious interest in hunting elephant, and so I suggested that we hunt them together, which was what he wanted. I went to the trouble of roughly drawing an elephant and explaining the shots vital to the hunter's survival, with particular emphasis on the frontal brain shot. As we always used to say, elephant don't charge sideways—you have to face them head on.

It was just as well I did this for the next day I nearly lost my life. After a good half-day, John Posselt and I finally caught up with the cow herd. I had left the good trackers at the Umzingwani River on Liebegs about sixty miles away to locate elephant movements. The bush here was of the dry, thick, short type, giving reasonable vision of elephant heads.

The Game Department had recently bought .425 Westley Richards magazine rifles, and I was now trying one out. We got to the side of the herd, and I put a large cow down, hoping to give John a shot at them, for I knew at least one of them would turn. This happened, but the new magazine rifle jammed, putting me at the mercy of the herd. Another cow came forward and charged me. Quick and silently she closed the gap, her ears flat, and would have had me but for John, who fired at the right moment. He hit her straight to the brain, and grateful I was when she crashed to earth. It was the greatest reward I ever received from a lecture.

The warlike Matabele tribe.

There were other interests at John's place, such as a tame warthog and a mongoose that played with his children. In addition there was a large brick- wall enclosure in which were many snakes, mostly puff-adders. In this pit were many pieces of sheeting and tin for these snakes to lie under, and as John removed these from outside the walls with the help of a long stick, the snakes became exposed and would slither around. He used them to extract their venom, which was sold to laboratories in South Africa. Each snake to be "milked" was noosed with a long stick, then held by hand behind the head, facing a glass covered with a fine material like chamois. The glass was used to antagonize the snake. Its mouth covered the fine material, and its fangs penetrated it as it released its venom into the glass. Seeing this deadly venom being released made me think of how lucky I had been to avoid contact with snakes—and made me determined to do so even more in future.

I had no sooner gotten back to my base camp on the Umzingwani River on Liebegs Ranch when John arrived, saying a small plane had been chartered to fly us over the country where large herds of elephant were reported to be migrating. We returned to Gwanda, where there was a landing field, and took off in a small four-seater aircraft. Eventually, about twenty miles west of Jopempe, a small mountain standing out in this otherwise flat country, we located the elephant. There were a lot of them. The pilot, who had flown over many elephant herds, estimated them at one thousand, but I thought them to be more like eight hundred and certainly not less than five hundred. We flew around the outer circle of the herd and then across them a few times, coming in low. They were disturbed by our presence and some panicked a little, but one bull in particular challenged us as we flew low over him.

He was a magnificent sight, standing his ground with raised head and trunk and outstanding ears and no doubt emitting trumpets and roars. He must have thought we were a great attacking eagle. Now that I no longer needed ivory, I had serious reservations about having to shoot such elephant.

As I looked down on this massive herd spread across the land, all visibly moving through the scrub forest, the realization that I was expected to drive these giants back toward the Bechuanaland border became staggering. Here

John also kept snakes, which he milked for their venom. In a large brick-wall enclosure were many snakes, mostly puff addlers.

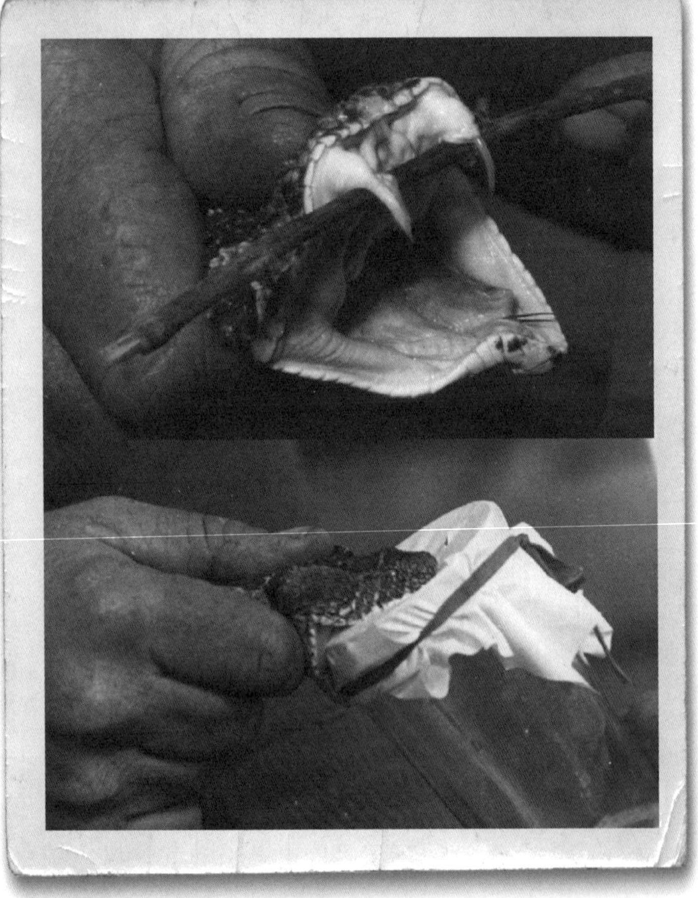

He extracted their poison, which was sold to laboratories down in South Africa.

in the aircraft my mind tried to leap across the curvature of the earth to reach the Angwa and Zambezi Rivers, the two places where Faanie and Jeffrey, my hunting companions of many past dangerous ventures, would be. I wondered if they could feel my desperate need of them and my fear of things to come. With these two men heavily armed and with good trackers to assist, I knew we could not only check these elephant on the first encounter but could drive them back to their original overgrazed range. Therein lay the reality of the problem that was causing their migration and could cause their deaths.

These elephant were simply moving across the earth by instinct to seek food, as they had done for countless ages, but the land now belonged to man. His title deeds proved it. It was 1956 and Southern Rhodesia had been occupied only for sixty years. Prior to this the warlike Matabele had been the nearest tribe and lived in Bulawayo, some 150 miles away. (These people, speaking Sindebele, are an offshoot of the mighty Zulus of south-east Africa, who referred to themselves as "Amazulu" or people of heaven. What a misnomer! They were the fiercest and most ruthless nation in savage Africa.) The Shona people were spread to the north, and the wild animals had vast ranges in which to survive. Then in 1896 the great mafioso of Africa, Cecil Rhodes, sent his civilization ahead of him. No doubt among them were men of real character, but it did not alter the fact that because of man's hunger for land, the wildlife was doomed.

My mind returned to the sight below me. John Posselt asked me how

In 1896 the great mafioso of Africa, Cecil Rhodes, sent his civilization ahead of him.

I would tackle these elephant. I said I really would not know until I was on the earth facing them.

Then the pilot said, "Rather you than me."

We stared at each other for seconds, and I said, "I would rather have my feet on the ground than my arse in the air."

"You don't like flying?" he inquired.

"No, I don't," I said, "I am a man of the earth. Let us get out of here to land on it."

As we banked and shot low over the herd for the last time, I jokingly said, "You are putting these elephant in a bad mood, hoping they will stay that way for me."

This pilot had flown over many wild places. "Progress," I joked. "It's all a matter of progress—me and the elephants, John and his snakes, and you with your arse up in the air hoping never to crash."

We laughed as only men of adventure can laugh and later landed at the Gwanda air strip. On parting, the pilot shook my hand and said, "I have got the feel of you now just in case I don't see you in one piece again." We both understood each other, and I could tell by this man's attitude that he had been in danger before.

I motored back to the camp of Ernest Glover, an old bush type, and his nephew, Ore van Bard, zebra and wildebeest hunters at Mazunga Pools close to the Bulawayo/Beit Bridge road on Liebegs Ranch. I did not go into detail but said that I had seen large elephant herds coming this way, probably heading for the Mazunga Pools, and requested using their camp as a base. Always helpful and hospitable, they agreed. It was essential that I contact this massive movement of elephant before they got to the pools because finding water and good leaf and grass cover there, they could split into smaller herds and family pockets, spreading my targets over a vast area. I motored down to the Umzingwani River about twelve miles south and collected my gear, trackers, and staff to take up temporary residence at Mazunga Pools. The elephant would first stop on the Umzingwani River, where they would have to dig in the sand to get water.

Here at Mazunga Pools we had the shelter of brick rondavels. It was well organized but a slaughterhouse for wildebeest and zebra, which were being killed at a rate of twenty-five per day by Glover and van Bart, the two resident game exterminators on contract to this massive ranch. The purpose was to make way for cattle feeding grounds.

The dried biltong meat was sold to the mines for labour rations at a price of six pence a pound and zebra skins were sold for £1 to £3 each. Obviously wild animals were vastly undervalued.

The mere fact that game was plentiful and available for killing meant it could not be ignored, even at these miserable prices. As long as the income from game animals paid the costs of transport, hunters, and butchery with a profit, the slaughter would continue until there was no more serious competition for grazing. In other areas there was the trade in furs of the magnificent leopard and other animals such as dassies (hyrax) to make coats and such. There were no roars of lion here; they had been eliminated with the other predators. We heard only the sounds of antelope, giraffe, zebra, wildebeest, domestic cattle—and the guns of men.

In the predawn I awoke, restless in anticipation of the day to come. I could hear the distant calls of zebra, which would move far off from this place in the daylight hours in fear of the commercial hunters. Outside the buildings I warmed myself at the fires, then instructed the trackers to prepare food, water, guns, and ammunition. They placed the guns in front of me for my approval. I checked the weapons carefully, satisfied with the reassuring feel of them, as this was to be a test day. "*Handeyi!*" I called (Let us go), and we moved off in the Land Rover. As I left I saw Old Man Glover, well into his seventies, surrounded by helpers. I slowed down to greet him.

"There is something going on here," he said. "You have not told us all of it. Do you need us with you?"

He was of the old stamp of hunters, the dying breed of days gone by. I said, "No, it will be all right, I hope." We parted and I thought to myself there are not many men like that any more. We got onto the bush tracks, and miles inland I began to work my way through the area, hoping to come up in front of the large herd or find its spoor. Only now did I tell the trackers of the many elephant I had seen from the air. As I turned I saw a *picanin* of about twelve years of age sitting with the water carrier behind me in the open truck bed.

"What the hell is this boy doing here?" I inquired. "Where does he come from?"

They answered, "He is the son of Hunyan, the wildebeest and zebra tracker at Mazunga. He got into the Land Rover when you were talking to the old white hunter."

They called Old Man Glover "the man of the marabou stork birds," scavengers that hung around Mazunga for the offal. As if I did not have enough to think about, now we had this boy in our midst. Black people can do the most peculiar things at the oddest times. I was annoyed with the trackers for letting this happen and at the same time realized I could not spare anybody to get the boy back to Mazunga. I questioned the *picanin*, and he said he wanted to see the elephant crash to the guns and that he would carry an additional waterbag for us. He stunned me by saying he had not even seen an elephant before. I felt anxiety, fear, and now annoyance and frustration. If I had been following a single herd, I would have chased the boy off to find his own way home, but at this time I did not know whether the elephant were still massed or spread out over miles in smaller herds. We had no option but to take the *picanin* with us.

We motored on, and soon some of the scrub became so thick that we had to abandon the Land Rover. We cut across the game paths, hoping to make contact, but after some miles I realized we were no longer on the elephant's line of march from the Umzingwani water area to the Mazunga Pools. We came back, and in an anemic-looking forest of sparse trees the *picanin*, of all people, drew our attention to a pall of dust hanging over some trees in the distance. Such a massive dust cloud could only be caused by elephant.

We stood and watched this for some time and determined that the elephant were moving toward us and were no more than a half-mile off. The dust continued to rise and drift behind them as they moved forward en masse. I had four people with me: the two trackers, both of whom could shoot reasonably well at close quarters but lacked the refinement of very accurate shooting; a water carrier; and the *picanin*, also carrying water.

Among us we had three rifles, two doubles and a bolt-action, but to avoid wounding or making mistakes at critical moments I preferred to do the firing myself. I also had the advantage of quick firepower, the trackers having been trained to remove a fired gun from my hands, reload, and pass it back to me. In this way I would almost constantly have a loaded rifle in my hands without having to take my eyes off the elephant.

Now that we had located the elephant, my anxieties diminished somewhat, but uncertainty and fear were still at the fore. I had never had to stand in front of so many oncoming elephant. I wondered how many of them had been persecuted before. We heard the occasional trumpet as they communicated across the herd. We were directly in their line of progress, and my instincts and testing of the wind made me move to one side to allow for a panicked rush of elephant into the wind.

I could not position our party until the elephant fully emerged into view to give me an idea of their collective width. When they did emerge from the trees about three hundred yards away, we all saw them, big cows slightly ahead, moving ponderously forward, unaware of us.

They came forward in great numbers, ears flapping against their sides and calling to each other in constant rumblings, sometimes in low and high-pitched squeals, trumpets, and low roars. From the middle and back of this large herd the dust rose well above the trees. I wondered how those at the back could breathe properly in it. Time seemed to stand still.

One hundred yards. I looked at the trackers Manwere and Kadigedige, positioned on both sides of me, where they would remove empty guns from my hands, reload, and pass them back to me again. They were well trained for times of danger, but this mass of elephant had fearful effects on us all. Then the *picanin* fell to his knees next to the water carrier and wailed in pitiful sounds of sorrow and hopelessness. In my mind I cursed the little bastard because he was diverting my attention from the oncoming mass.

If I did not do something, his wails would warn the elephant, which can pick up foreign sounds even amongst their own noises. I was thinking of giving him a crack on the head with the butt of the rifle when suddenly the forerunners pulled up and in less than a minute the whole herd became silent. It was uncanny how quickly it happened. Incredibly, they had detected the human wails and had sent their signals throughout the other hundreds of elephant behind and to the sides of them.

In the great silence we were in view of the foremost elephant, but they were not sure of our identity because of our immobility. Most were facing slightly away from us; two large cows were a little ahead, facing us. I had the set of double rifles loaded, one in my hand half-raised. I took in the view of this mighty herd in front of us. They were an overwhelming presence. Under these circumstances it did not seem possible that these two puny pieces of manufactured metal and wood could become the deciding factor in the coming confrontation.

The dust hung in a large pall over the massive herd and steadily rose in the heat. The *picanin* was on his knees with his forehead on the sand, in a hopeless state of sobbing and despair. In the uneasy silence I again had an urge to hit him on the head with the rifle butt. His noise had changed everything. Two large cows and then many others, alarmed at the noise, stared at all of us. If we moved, especially sideways, they would identify us as humans. The low, sparse scrub hiding our legs and feet caused the elephant to stay undecided. Wild animals, especially elephant, positively identify people quicker if arms or legs move or heads tilt and turn. To be sharply identified in their sight is as effective as being scented.

This menacing situation could not last much longer. Either men or beasts would have to react in some way. I had fleeting visions of the Zambezi River and Faanie and Jeffrey with all their combined hunting abilities. They were distant now, and I might never see them again. I realized they were the best I had ever hunted with and now in my desperate moments wished they were here.

I heard one of the trackers whisper, "*Navamware vadzi baba—midzimu yeru vimba inesu*?" (By the gods of our fathers, will the hunting gods be with us?.

When men reach a low ebb of spirit, they tend to fall back on their gods, something greater than themselves to renew a failing spirit. These massed elephant were demoralizing even to experienced men. In my indecision I was trying to maintain my own morale and confidence, but I feared this mighty herd was beyond my control. I had doubts that we would survive this day. If the trackers lost their nerve, we would be all finished, and I felt the sobbing *picanin* was getting to them.

The elephant had come up to about forty yards—still a doubtful distance for safe shooting, but the magnitude of the herd and atmosphere were too much for me to let them get right up to us. This herd was simply too large to apply the customary tactics. Now that the mass had come up to us, there were only two decisions: Either we try to step away unseen, in which case the elephant were sure to see human movements and charge, or we attack here and now, at the hollow heads of big cows, facing us, to get the herd moving away from us. It took more than just willpower to fire the first shot.

I fired a left and a right barrel quickly. The two nearest cows dropped dead in their indecision. Many of the elephant close enough had our position now. It was vital that I drop them before they could react. I fired furiously. The guns passed into and out of my hands without my having to take my eyes off the herd. I had a few thoughts of my children, wondering if I was going to get out of this alive. Then my blood rose, and it did not matter any more. I hardly remember seeing rifle sights but was conscious of the recoil from the heavy rifles pounding my shoulder.

Just as I was anticipating rushing up to take cover behind the dead animals, the elephant started to turn. Those that did not turn I aimed for. The shooting had its effects, and I knew, from the high-pitched trumpets and roars, they were about to stampede.

We all rushed forward to the fallen elephant. The movement was on, and the sounds of elephant in fear and fury penetrated everywhere. We were dwarfed into insignificance by the noises, which dulled even the rifle blasts. As the elephant raced off, the sounds became less and the dust more, rising above the trees and slowly drifting toward us. Eventually we could see the great pall of dust in the distance getting bigger where the elephant were changing their course, going back in the direction of the Umzingwani River.

I followed for a short while, looking for wounded stragglers, but there were none. The earth had been churned up by the elephant's great, wide, heavy feet. The elephant had flattened what trees there were, knocking them down as they stampeded away. They were out of sight now, but the noise of stampede remained in my head for some time. I wondered at the incredible ability of calves to survive such a massive rush since they would have run next to their mothers' forefeet. How well coordinated they must have been.

We came back to the water carrier and the *picanin*, who was still on his knees with his forehead on the sand. He had an appealing, disturbed look about him. With shivering frame and outstretched hands he offered me a waterbag. His otherwise black-brown skin was a louse gray. Kadigedige and Manwere said he had the "sickness of the shivers," meaning shock. They collected wood for two fires and placed the *picanin* close to keep him warm. I drank some water, and we sat down near the fires. Afterward I leaned back and slept to restore my mental health. When I woke, calm enough to think of other things, my mind turned to the *picanin*. He looked better but had a weak look in his eyes. We gave him food and water, and then he started to sweat, so we let him leave the fires but still kept him in the sun. He had much improved. I watched and thought about him.

There was no doubt his wails and sobs had halted and alerted the elephant coming up to us. But it is probable that without him we may have been stampeded or attacked by too many elephant at once. Strange it was that this *picanin*, who had wanted to see the elephant crash to the guns, had seen nothing but only heard the elephant, as he had remained with his forehead on the ground during the shooting. I felt strongly enough about it to accept that fate had played a part in our survival.

We returned to the Land Rover and motored to the Mazunga camp, where I explained briefly what had happened. I knew I would have to follow these elephant south, but rested the night here and in predawn motored down to the Umzingwani River. Close to its banks, as the sun rose, we could see fresh spoor everywhere and signs of feeding. I worried that they could become resident here. It meant I would have to get stuck in the middle of them again. I was not sure I could drive them from this riverine forest and adjoining bush, but even if I kept them south of the Bulawayo/Beit Bridge tar road I would be doing well.

They were now spread for miles up and down the river, making the hunting harder, but at least safer. If I was going to drive them farther, I must find as large a herd as possible. At midday I spotted a herd of about 150—probably more—in the riverine area and closed in on them. The situation was much less hazardous than the previous day, and as I started putting them down, they signaled to each other and rushed across the wide sand of the Umzingwani River, their great bulks plunging up the opposite bank to disappear into the vegetation.

Later a dust cloud appeared at a distance, indicating their presence farther inland in dry scrub country. For days I pursued the elephant in the riverine forest and adjoining bush country. Some doubled up behind me to reach the Mazunga Pools, but on contact with me they moved on. Others I traced for long distances up and below the Umzingwani River, but most of them stayed south of the river. I was pleased that none of them had so far crossed north of the main tar road. They were at least being contained, and seasonal hunting would eventually drive them off. In the urgency of it all I was fatiguing myself and the trackers, but I needed to keep up the hunting pressure for a while.

On Section Four of the ranch, there was a manager by the name of Freddy Odendaal, a character of sorts who lived an isolated existence to raise cattle for the land barons. He had two bush-type horses and kindly loaned them to me. I corn-fed them and used them to carry me on the elephant trails, changing trackers and water carriers on alternate days so that they were not physically overtaxed. It was a change to come up to the elephant unfatigued, dismount, and then close in on them on foot. Some elephant doubled back north across the main Bulawayo road, but I drove them back, the use of the horses giving me greater mobility.

I thought of these and other elephant drives and the general persecution of these animals. All they were really doing was seeking food, and to do that they had to range across what was now man's land. As I used to say in my ivory poaching days, when I had twinges of developing conscience: *What the hell, people and governments will kill them all anyway, replacing them with domestic stock so that they can regulate their commercial slaughter and then put up pictures on their walls depicting wild animals as the real thing that once was.* I had seen much evidence of this in South Africa, where all the land had been taken up—though President Kruger of the Boer Republic had seen fit to instigate the establishment of Kruger National Park.

As fate would have it, a game ranger from the Transvaal—which called rangers "fauna and flora" inspectors—was invited by the Southern Rhodesian Game Department to see the problems on our adjoining borders. I was amazed to realize that their department had such inexperienced men hunting dangerous game, especially elephant. It was explained to me that, when dangerous game had to be shot, a few inspectors fired all at once at a single animal. I marveled that they had lost contact with their forefathers, whom I knew had been able to do better even with the muzzleloading firearms of their time. I demonstrated to this inspector the frontal brain shot on elephant and on other occasions had him demonstrate to others for his future safety.

In a reciprocal response I was invited to hunt a troop of bull elephant that had vacated Kruger National Park in the Transvaal. They were in the area of Klein Chipise, not far from Sebaza. I had my own arms and trackers with me. As we searched from the inspector's truck, he told me that my trackers could not use rifles for the purpose of shooting elephant in the Transvaal. We had been invited here, far from our own hunting grounds, and been told that despite our vast experience we would have to hunt under their restricted conditions. I loaded the rifles and handed one and a full gunbelt to Kadigedige, who was a better shot than Manwere. If there was to be a flash point it must be now.

"Stuff you and your setup," I said to the inspector. "These men of mine have more ability and experience than any of your lot who are supposed to be the cream. They are naturals, not overcivilized men trying to become hunters."

By way of an apology he said that he was tied by the laws of the country and that my trackers must not use rifles in the Transvaal.

"Take me back to the border," I said, "I am not interested in your elephant. We have tens of thousands of them. I am only here under sufferance."

"No," he said, "we have come this far. Let us drive the elephant back to Kruger Park, and I will take my chances with the administration."

We searched around and spoke to some locals who had seen elephant spoor, and then we found it. The inspector had a black-skinned tracker of his own, but his tracking was so unprofessional that I lost patience and put Manwere on the spoor. It became apparent to me, through this single contact, that Transvaal's Fauna and Flora Department largely emphasized the administration of game laws and had lost contact with old Africa. It was obvious from staff I later met that these men did not have the background we had.

Life in the northern Transvaal was less enticing and more civilized than in Rhodesia. The Limpopo River was unimpressive, and the dry, stony country with low bush scrub was uninviting. By our hunting and living standards these people were overfed and soft; far too many were overweight. It suggested that there were many cases of heart disease in this country.

It was a picnic to hunt in the limited scrub, which gave much vision. Manwere followed about ten bull elephant to the slope of some rugged, stony hills covered in low bush, and as we came closer I got a picture of how it must have been in the time of the Boers. The elephant were spread a little, finding partial shade under the almost leafless, scrubby trees. The wind was right, so I halted the party to view them. They were large old bulls with a slightly different look about them—gnarled, rough-looking skins and massive bodies and heads, sporting good ivory—certainly better than ours in Rhodesia. I felt they must be select old bulls, the more impressive of their species, and wondered why they had risked leaving the Kruger Park, one of the biggest in Africa. It could only be their instincts to wander, seeking food in new country, or perhaps a lack of suitable feed in Kruger. I doubted the latter, for Kruger's scientific employees would certainly have done their studies of feed relative to environment. They had been organized for so long and had all the aids of scientific study.

The hunting of these elephant was not my responsibility. I had advised the inspector always to go for the frontal brain shot wherever possible—a habit of survival. I had told him, "Don't forget, you are not immortal—concentrate on nothing else but the elephant and the rifle in your hands."

I thought it necessary to stay with him for the final short period so he could become as efficient as possible. He was no youngster, a man of about fifty years, but tough as they come. My tracker Manwere gave him his line of approach, and as they were closing in on the animals the inspector seemed to falter. I had taught him to get up close to the elephant so that they would have short rushes at him rather than speedy runs from a distance in which the chances were good that other elephant would follow.

The principles of hunting in thick cover, which can be used by both man and beast, are simple: If you are very close to elephant bulls when you fire, they will either rush you individually or run off to collect themselves. Even with individual charges, the animals tend to mushroom around the area of the shot, giving the hunter scope for further firing, defensive or offensive. Firing at a distance can either bring them collectively at you or send them rushing away from you, but if they come in your direction you risk being trampled or flushed into the open because of their speed and the impetus of their large bodies crashing through the vegetation.

It is a hide-and-seek game at top speed, and if you lose nerve or ability to fire fast and effectively, your career ends right there. Elephant are afraid of the overall happening, but once they see or smell you the fear usually turns to rage, followed by determined attacks. If you fire amidst a herd, as often happens, they usually run off, especially if they have not got your position.

If you are surrounded by a herd, don't think of extracting yourself by retreating; continue forward and fire—that way they will move either left or right of you, depending on the wind angles. As you move forward, it is likely that others will move close behind your original position—and herein lies another danger: The matriarch cows may catch your scent and come at you from behind. It is important, once you emerge from the herd, to immediately change direction in accordance with the wind, to throw them off your scent.

Time is of the essence. It is now a matter of either attacking them again unseen from your new position or slipping away quietly. If determined, they will come seeking you. By your maneuvering, you will have actually drawn them to you in a position advantageous to yourself, and thus can reenact the scene. But often the hunter not conditioned to being a few paces from live elephant is afraid to see the pattern through. Having come halfway, he ends up in greater danger than is necessary.

Being in proximity to enraged wild beasts has a demoralizing effect on most men, but in ivory hunting it is a matter of forcing yourself to handle these conditions until it becomes a rewarding and less fearful practice. This ability and great stamina are the ivory hunter's advantages. I had taught men successfully to hunt dangerous game, but I failed to get most of them to condition themselves to accept being a few paces from large, dangerous animals—especially elephant, where you had to look up at them.

I have described these hunting patterns to bring about an understanding of some of the experiences now to come. Here in the Transvaal, with easy conditions and elephant that were probably unpersecuted, I had to watch one of my unarmed trackers confidently closing in on elephant bulls with the inspector, unknown to him, standing stationary. I could not shout to warn my tracker that he was alone.

As the gap between these two men got longer and the gap between the tracker and the elephant got shorter, I thought of running up behind the unarmed tracker to back him up, even though it would alarm the elephant and destroy the element of surprise. As I got into my stride, the inspector, ahead and to one side of me, fired his .470 double-barreled rifle. He hit the brain and a bull crashed, but most of the others came forward in a rush at me and the other armed tracker, Kadigedige.

I knew we would have to put some of them down quickly to allow the others to pass to our sides. We both had .425 magazine rifles in our hands. I fired in haste, but it was a misfire. With only seconds left I reloaded, and as I raised my rifle Kadigedige fired his, bringing down a bull coming at me. I felt it was only stunned by the way it had crashed in front of me. I fired and another bull dropped, then Kadigedige fired at an oncoming bull. Another turned toward me, and the inspector shot it from where he stood at a distance away from us. I fired at the last oncoming elephant, which dropped.

In this action we had reached the foremost tracker, Manwere—it was miraculous how he had survived the rush unarmed. The other bulls raced past on our sides. Because they had got up their speed, we had barely managed it.

These were huge bulls, and as I was admiring their ivory Kadigedige's original bull suddenly rose up within reach of me, and then a shot went off as Kadigedige shot it again from somewhere behind me. I had been saved by the actions of Kadigedige and the inspector, but the situation had been totally unnecessary to begin with.

The inspector was apologetic—a useless gesture. He said he had been afraid to move up close to the elephant alone without a second gun behind him. It is so common of modern hunting for the sportsman to shoot with another armed man backing him up instead of developing the ability to depend only on the rifle in his hands. I am talking about reliable rifles. It is far better to be dependent on yourself, unless you need fast, multiple firepower in stampedes or other emergencies.

Some days afterward we all crossed the border from South Africa back into Rhodesia to rehunt the Liebegs elephant again. On motoring down from Mazunga Pools to the Umzingwani River, we came across the spoor of hundreds of elephant where they had crossed the sand road in a wide mass. We alighted from the vehicles to examine the spoor. It was recent, meaning the animals were still resident in the region.

I wondered how many of these would have to be killed before they moved away and how many miles I would have to walk. The inspector was amazed that so many elephant could be in a herd. I explained that they were not really a herd as such; they moved in a mass when it suited them and sometimes stayed that way feeding. When relaxed, they usually split into many smaller groups, and in their home territory they would further split into family units. I said that with the four of us firing—meaning the inspector, my two trackers, and myself— there would be a miniature war here within a few days.

I should never have said that. When I was deep in thought about the elephant movements, I heard the inspector saying, "I have a lot of work in the Transvaal." Then he jumped into his truck and rode off in a cloud of dust. The silence developed again, and I must have looked very serious because Manwere said, "What are the *murungos* (white men) fighting about?"

I said, "Nothing. He has a lot of work to do and has just remembered it."

Then Kadigedige said, laughing, "*Ena saba ko heenya.*" (He is afraid to ---- himself.)

We camped farther on at the Umzingwani River in the shade of the sparse riverine forest. For weeks I stayed on these elephant, but most of them were reluctant to leave the feed of this place, moving great distances during the day and escaping persecution by occupying three adjoining ranches during the afternoon, through the night, and past dawn. It meant that the distances I would be traveling on their spoor were not justified in terms of results, so I abandoned them temporarily to work elsewhere.

Because of my past I knew every poacher of any consequence in the Zambezi Valley. Now that I was a game ranger they conveniently vanished, unless I sent for them when I visited their areas. I was about to meet one I knew very well.

I was preparing a camp for a VIP, a political minister who had been invited to hunt in the Zambezi Valley. He was to arrive shortly. It was close above the Nyakasanga Swamps on the Zambezi River, and I had temporarily managed to get the services of my old tracker Zaratina and some of his associates. That night the lion roared almost continuously in a deep gully about thirty yards from the campsite and kept us awake most of the night. In the morning, while standing in the river having a wash, I saw upriver near the west bank a dugout heading across the current toward me. I picked up the forms of three tribesmen, two of them rowing. Their crossing took some time, and when they arrived they remained stationary about two-hundred yards away, paddling against the current. I had already climbed the riverbank.

The usual calls of greeting came across the water, and on questioning them I learned they had come from Chief Chiawa across the river. They appeared relieved to see that I was still alive after hearing the lion roaring all night. I wondered why these tribesmen should be so concerned, but suddenly it dawned on me that the third man, sitting in the middle of the dugout with a loincloth on his head, could only be my friend of days gone by—Jeffrey!

I took a chance and called out, "Jeffrey, I know it's you. I can smell you." The others in the boat remained silent and did not laugh, and because of this I knew it was Jeffrey.

"You are a game ranger now," he called out. "Do you think you can catch Jeffrey?"

"You're the easiest of all," I said.

He moved his body to face us. "I am armed," he said, "and I am coming across."

I shouted back, "I have never seen you unarmed," and as he landed on shore on his bad leg, the paddlers faltered and he verbally abused them, swearing at their mothers and fathers as can only be expressed in an African language. It was the same Jeffrey—time had changed nothing.

I watched him struggle up the bank, and on higher ground we faced each other.

"Do you know, little boy," he said, "I can shoot faster and better than you. You must remember that when you are tempted to catch me." He was cautious and kept me at gun's-length for a while, then relaxed.

I laughed at him, and he said, "Have you any baby food and liquor?" By baby food he meant the drink mix called Milo.

"Yes," I said, "we will make some to drink."

"You do not need to be afraid of Jeffrey, little boy," he said. We laughed and sat around the fire.

"Before I go you must find me some liquor."

"I have none," I said. He did not believe me, so he questioned Zaratina and two trackers as to where I was hiding the liquor. Disappointed, he cursed them, saying we had already drunk the liquor the previous night to hold back the fear of the roaring lion. The trackers knew him, and we all laughed at him.

Then came the news. He said he had married one of the Vlahakis girls. I thought to myself: *How unfortunate can a girl get?*

"There is a problem," he said. "I was only with her two days when I got homesick for the river again, and I have been downstream more than a month."

"But your men said you came from Chiawa's," I said.

"You know how these people lie," he replied. "Why do you listen to them? I am Jeffrey, and I know where I have been and for how long."

I asked him what he had been doing, and he said if I was not a game ranger he would tell me, but since I was indeed a ranger I must mind my own business, and I knew he meant it.

"I need you to come back with me to the Kafue River junction," he said. "I have built a house, and my wife may be stupid enough to still be there."

"Why me?" I asked.

"Because she will be normal when she sees you."

"And you, Jeffrey, are you normal?"

"What sort of question is that, little boy—you know I am normal."

This man, so serious of nature, had no idea of how hilarious he sometimes was. As a game ranger I was not supposed to cross the river, but I had a governor's permit, and because he was an old friend and I wanted to see his house, I agreed. He left, crossing the river.

In the morning at sunrise I heard him calling from the shoreline. We traveled upstream in the slower waters, then crossed to the other side, where we were joined by two of Jeffrey's dugouts carrying goods and paddlers. I suspected that he had ivory but thought little of it. A day's hard journey brought us to the Kafue junction in the afternoon. We climbed the bank, and I saw the small house he had built.

His wife came forward with some servants and said, "Where have you been?" He said I had arrested him and only today had decided to let him go. *What a convenient liar,* I thought. She looked me up and down, then started to complain to him about lion. Apparently they had tried to get through the outer door of the house and, failing, pulled out and killed a woman from one of the surrounding huts. As we walked toward the house, she kept on at him about leaving her alone in such a dangerous place. Although born and raised in this country, she continued to make an issue of it all the way to the house. Knowing Jeffrey as I did, I was sure this relationship would not last. We saw the lions' claw marks on the door where they had tried to force an entry. Jeffrey boasted about his good carpentry. He had, I guessed, made these doors.

"Pity," he said, feeling the claw marks on the wood.

"Yes, pity," she said, thinking that he may now be repentant.

"Pity," he said, staring at her. "Pity they did not eat you!"

Highly amused, I had to turn away. The romance ended there and then.

The next morning Jeffrey's paddlers took me downstream to my camp on the opposite bank. Other than avoiding the hippo and shooting an Egyptian goose for myself, there were no incidents. It was a pleasant time, and the miles passed quickly. We stayed with the strong current; it was evident that Jeffrey's paddlers knew the character of the river. They stayed that night, and because we were short of meat for camp rations I took the spoor of a lone old buffalo in the morning.

After a few hours we entered a miniature forested plateau with soft, sandy ground. This buffalo did not have much more time to live as it was very old. Even unwounded and probably tired of life, it eventually stood at bay. We stood and watched him from about thirty paces. Perhaps his eyesight was failing for he stared ahead, threatening with his large bullish body and wide horns, cool and brave as only buffalo can be. This admirable species is much more courageous when wounded than other animals.

In admiration I was reluctant to shoot. I stood there, hoping he would turn away to give me a side shot to his neck to make it as painless as possible, and then hit the back of the brain. But he stood his ground.

Zaratina, perhaps knowing my thoughts, whispered, "The lion will pull him down anyhow."

It was one of those occasions when I did not want to become involved in what I considered a noble and courageous animal's death. I thought of the times he must have faced lion to protect the herd. Now he was ostracized or had voluntarily left the herd, a loner in the forest facing us. Is it possible to admire and love animals and at the same time kill them?

Feeling cornered, he bravely came forward in a rush. I fired, hitting him just below the horn boss. The heavy bullet, even if it failed to find the brain, would paralyze him by traversing the length of the neck. As he dropped, I put a shot into the heart. Death was instantaneous—he did not have the customary chance to bawl. There he lay, a massive buffalo bull at the very end of his life.

There he lay, a massive buffalo bull at the very end of his life.

I had often, when shooting dangerous game in the brain, hoped that my own death would be so merciful and quick. One can even do it oneself. I live by the gun and certainly would want the privilege of dying quickly rather than be taken by some incurable illness or a frightening and humiliating situation. *Well,* I thought, *to each his own.*

I had camp followers, and I left them here to cut and carry the meat to camp. It would be part of their rations for the next week. Jeffrey's paddlers, who were still with me, were given a share of the meat to take back up the river. I told them to tell Jeffrey that since he had crocodile teeth, the old meat would be suitable. It was easy to cross swords with him when he was far away. They left that afternoon, covering their meat in the dugout with small branches and leaves to shade it.

I think it appropriate here to enlarge on some aspects of buffalo behavior, especially for the benefit of people who these days are allowed to go on walking safaris, unarmed, in certain game areas.

On the plains of Marromeu in Mozambique, we often came across buffalo by the thousands. Several times individuals rushed at us from the herds. Although unexpected, it was something I could cope with as there was always a reasonable distance between us to allow for defensive action. We examined a few of them. All except two had been previously wounded. It is those two that I will now discuss.

In Southern Rhodesia I once stopped at a shallow water pan near the Rukometje River in the Zambezi Valley to collect water for the radiator of my truck. I sent Frau, a tracker, to collect the water. On the opposite side of the pan, two middle-aged buffalo gazed at him as he approached. One became alarmed and moved off into the surrounding open forest, but the other one rushed across the shallow water at Frau. He dropped the tin and ran for his life toward the truck, but the buffalo was too close for him to jump into the truck. Consequently he ran around the vehicle with the buffalo chasing him. It was a small, enclosed, one-ton truck. The tracker was shouting for assistance—the buffalo was wearing him down. I had no option but to get out of the truck to use the rifle, a .375 loaded with softnose ammunition. As the buffalo passed my door in pursuit, I jumped clear, and as Frau came around again I placed a shot past him and hit below the boss of the buffalo's horns.

It died instantly. Then Frau came back almost breathless, accusing me of enjoying the scene and wanting to know why I had waited so long to take action. The problem was the unexpected situation and the fact that it took just the right timing to get into a position to stop the buffalo. We later examined the buffalo, but there was no indication of wounding or anything to suggest why it had deliberately come across the pan of water to attack.

These days I remember such incidents while walking unarmed in game reserves. Many people do this in the dry seasons, especially animal lovers—some inexperienced, others ignorant—and sometimes trusting fools like myself. Wherever possible, however, I always had a reasonably climbable tree in view just in case of emergency. But there are not always convenient trees around. Should a buffalo turn aggressive in such a situation, it would be fatal.

Faanie and I once amused ourselves with an aggressive buffalo. He was between two good trees spaced about seventy yards apart with termite nests sloping up the lower parts of the trees. Faanie apparently wanted to become a matador. We were both armed, and as we passed the buffalo Faanie turned back, dancing and shouting at it. It was typical of his humour to make us sprint. We were in a game reserve illegally, with officials only a few miles away, and Faanie knew I would not fire unless I had to. The buffalo, in reaction, came at us in a straight line. It so happened that I ran for one tree and Faanie the other. These were easily climbable. The buffalo pulled up at my tree, but I was safe above his horns. It pawed the ground, circled the tree, and gazed up at me with a fearless, hateful stare. It is hard to believe disturbed buffalo belong to the bovine species.

From my vantage place I cursed Faanie's parentage and also the buffalo for being so stupid as to pick on me when it had been Faanie who started this contest. Meanwhile, Faanie was watching from the foot of his own tree, in full view of the buffalo. Up until then Faanie had remained silent, amused at my predicament. Then he shouted, "Since you look like a sick English fowl in the branches, I will call my dog off." He shouted at the buffalo, which slowly turned as if it did not want to break its concentration on me. Faanie did his matador

Whenever possible, however, I had a reasonably climbable tree in view just in case of emergency.

dance again, and it lumbered into a rush and charged him. Faanie was always athletic and agile, and now he allowed the buffalo to come close before pulling himself into the branches of the tree. The buffalo, apparently surprised to realize that men can climb trees, ran up the slope of the anthill and butted the tree base. From where I was perched I could see it getting into a rage as Faanie kept antagonizing it.

Sitting in the branches of a tree cradling a rifle for a long time is not a natural position, and I was uncomfortable. And I realized that we had to move from here before sunset. While Faanie was still antagonizing the buffalo, I slipped down the tree, but the buffalo saw me and came lumbering up. I had to climb into the tree again. Then Faanie tried to vacate his tree, but the buffalo turned back on him also. Now we were in an unusual and dangerous predicament whereby we could not leave our trees. It was late afternoon, and I did not fancy staying in the tree at night with the July cold developing and an enraged buffalo somewhere in the dark. I shouted at Faanie, "How in the hell are we going to get out of here without shooting the buffalo?" He shouted back, "I can see you came from the apes, so stop complaining, stupid. All you have to do is get out of the tree so that the buffalo can gore you and allow me to escape." I shouted back that when the sun set it would get chilly.

He shouted back, "When you evolved, you should have retained your fur." That was one hell of an Afrikaner, fearless and unconcerned, but he knew I was becoming agitated, so he shouted, "I will save you as a remnant of the British empire. Get the buffalo's attention, and I will sprint for a farther tree until I can lengthen the distances."

Using his knife, he pulled strip bark from the tree, and tied his rifle on his back. "Call him now, and if he looks as if he's turning back on me, for Christ's sake shoot straight! You don't have to get the shivers, since you are not facing a Boer commando, only a buffalo living under the protection of the Union Jack." Humourous he was to the last. Now that he had strapped his rifle to allow him to climb easier, his main chance was his sprinting ability. Faanie remained silent in his tree, and I climbed down mine to attract the buffalo. It was not interested at first, still preferring Faanie, until I gesticulated and shouted at it. Then it came rushing over again, and I climbed back into my tree.

I kept the buffalo occupied while Faanie descended the back of his tree to sprint to another not-so-climbable tree; there he paused to look back and sprinted farther while I was shouting at the buffalo below me. He was at a considerable distance now and I faintly heard him calling something like, "Enjoy the buffalo's company. You both have dull brains like an ox, and the very best of British luck to you." But Faanie kept calling his abuse, and as I remained silent the buffalo wandered off in his direction, obviously confused. By now I was determined to get away at all costs, even if I had to shoot the damn thing. I climbed down the tree and ran off silently, using some bush for cover. Sometime after this, as I had not heard a shot, I assumed Faanie had also escaped. I waited, and Faanie came up spooring me.

Buffalo often come forward in a menacing way but eventually halt, perhaps simply curious. But who knows what goes on inside a buffalo's head? In later years my son Clive and I had to walk around three buffalo on a small scrubby riverine area adjoining the Chipandahoure, by then developed from swampland into a bare plain. One buffalo came on menacingly, and I jokingly told Clive to give him a good blow with his fist between the eyes. But these were anxious moments as we were armed only with a 9mm pistol, just enough to get him into a bad mood. He stopped as we slowly gave way, but who is to say that they will always stop?

But back to my work as game warden. I was waiting for Archie Fraser, who was to bring the Minister of Labor of South Africa, B. J. Schoeman, and his friend Lategan, also from South Africa, down to the Zambezi Valley to hunt. These two men had left Cape Town on the southern tip of Africa, and were not due for a few days, and what with exploring and enjoying the river again I lost sense of time.

I had, on occasion, taken tourists hunting in East Africa to assist safari hunters and it was not an occupation I enjoyed—depending, of course, on the character, control, and outlook of these clients. It could be either an exciting and pleasant effort or a bush hell with spoiled and abusive people who expected wild animals and men to bow to the power of their money and authority. The best people I ever accompanied were Europeans, and the worst were those with newly acquired wealth. The latter tried to bring the influences of their environment with them, and, like wine, their money had gone to their heads, making them unreasonable.

I once had to take a governor hunting, and he had the audacity to plant a pole with his large flag on the banks of the river. The trackers asked me what it was about. Because I did not know how to explain to them the intricacies and pomp of Europeans, I told them the flag was planted so that the elephant would realize how important the governor was and so would cooperate by standing sideways in the open to give the governor his shot at them. We were being watched by the party concerned, and the trackers laughed at my ridiculous version of the power of the governor's flag.

That night the governor's wife asked me what the joke was. I told her outright and at the same time asked the governor how he thought anyone could be impressed by his flag here. This conversation did not set the tone for an amiable safari—they just could not forget their own background, even for that short while. With such memories in mind, I was not looking forward to the coming safari.

I was walking up a track that had been cleared here and there to allow vehicles to pass to the established camp when Zaratina heard the drone of motors. It was the vehicles of the new safari. Eventually the sound came close, and we stepped out of the bush to greet them. Fraser was leading in a Land Rover. In a second Land Rover were Schoeman and Lategan, and behind that was a big truck loaded with gear. I pointed to the back bumper of the truck, saying it would catch on some storm-water gullies ahead. The two visitors were of the opinion that it was not necessary to remove it, saying that they had used this vehicle in other parts of Africa. When you are responsible for others and they are uncooperative, life can be tough.

I left them to it and returned to the camp. In the distance we could hear the truck was stuck, the back bumper no doubt having been caught on the deep gully. Eventually they arrived and established themselves around the fires.

Schoeman's reputation as a hunter was well known in South Africa, and he was known as the "hunting minister." In a conversation between these two visitors I heard Lategan describe me as being too young to have enough experience and said I would be more trouble than I was worth. They spoke in Afrikaans, which I understood. I said nothing in response but took the initiative and suggested that since Schoeman was experienced, he might wish to hunt alone. I told him I had excellent trackers, and if he followed them he would have a safe and pleasant hunt. He said he would think about it.

Fraser called me aside and asked me why I was trying to ditch them. Fraser was not the type of man to lie to, so I asked him if he understood the Afrikaans language. He said "No," so I left it at that.

I woke in predawn to the sounds of the camp and by habit went to the trackers' fire. Here Schoeman asked us where we thought we might find elephant spoor. I pointed at Zaratina, Frau, and Jaubek, the three trackers, saying that I had already instructed them. Zaratina was always reluctant and most times refused to hunt with white men, saying they were excellent until conditions got very dangerous—and then they became useless and could cause his death. I had given him a rifle for the occasion, and he seemed satisfied.

I thought I had escaped the hunting scene and had already planned to wander the islands naked to get some sun in this midwinter, and to shoot wild fowl for the camp. But Schoeman suddenly interjected, saying I should hunt with them on the first day to teach them something of the place. I told him the trackers knew the score, but he insisted, so I joined them.

We moved inland parallel to the Zambezi River in the direction of the Nyakasanga River swamps, where I knew that elephant stragglers sometimes remained behind the herd to feed. This is the swamp where Jeffrey, Faanie, and I had shot for our lives when the cow elephant herd came down on us through the reeds. It was where Faanie and I had had the parting of the ways. Schoeman had brought along his trackers, light-skinned natives from South Africa. They walked ahead of Schoeman, then paused on bull elephant spoor. Zaratina, I, and the water carrier came up and watched them studying its direction. I did not want to condemn them, but even from a distant Zaratina said the spoor was old, probably six hours.

I had hunted with some of the best trackers in Africa, and I could see that these light-skinned men sorting out the spoor were inferior. I could feel the resentment rising in me. We men, far superior in our skills, were being subjected to much lesser men in our own environment. I considered myself of reasonable temperament at most times, but certain incidents tended to set me ablaze. Then it occurred to me, why should I fight people about their own good? Let them fight Africa. So we ambled along with them on the old spoor.

In estimating time lapse, wind action has an effect on the imprint of spoor. In the Zambezi Valley in August and September, the gentle warm winds most times sweep through from the east, though at times they swirl in all directions. The wind action often occurs during the hours of darkness, and consequently in the mornings the spoor's finer surfaces appear disturbed, making it look old. The opposite occurs when there is no wind. Trying to read spoor can be misleading and confusing, except to those who are knowledgable about such conditions.

Schoeman's trackers in their ignorance had misinformed him and deceived themselves into thinking they were following recent spoor. They spoored well enough until they reached forested areas where fallen, decayed leaves confused them. They lost the spoor several times and Zaratina pointed it out to them, but still they did not concede to us. We were almost halfway across the valley floor when they began to tire and became sensible enough to realize they were not going to overtake these bull elephant. I always found in the African wilds that when the body grows fatigued, the brain becomes reasonable.

The trackers had actually made the mistake of following an even older spoor that had crossed their original track. They may have been good elsewhere but were useless at spooring on forested ground. Schoeman became doubtful of us ever overtaking the elephant, and then I told him that the spoor was old from the start.

He did not want to believe me, so I said, "Well, carry on then!"

They had marched a half-mile more when Schoeman called a halt. "What has really been going on here?" he demanded to know.

I knew, of course, but called Zaratina and had him tell the complete story. I translated for Schoeman, emphasizing that the opinion of this excellent tracker was indisputable.

"How long have you known this?" he added.

I said, "From early this morning when your trackers first took the spoor."

Schoeman was aghast, and I was short with him: "Since you know so much about our country, carry on—we are fit and will follow you. You will eventually learn the first lesson, which is that Africa will tame you or make you realistic."

He was angry and said, "What sort of man are you?"

I replied, "I was wondering the same about you! Even if we use my tracker we will be lucky to get back to the camp by sundown, and there is no way your trackers will bring us back to the banks of the Zambezi River at night, so we had better let Zaratina guide us back now."

They were all tired. Schoeman said he had been sitting at a desk almost continuously for eleven months and could feel the stiffness developing in his body. I told Zaratina to head back for the river as straight as possible. Schoeman and party were definitely flagging.

As the sun set, Schoeman became anxious about our direction, and I assured him that even in the dark it was almost impossible for Zaratina to become lost, especially here in the Zambezi Valley.

We walked for hours into the night. We had used our water and now felt the need for it. At last Zaratina told me he could smell the river, and a little later I scented it myself about a half-mile off. Then we emerged under some trees close to the camp to drink the water of the Zambezi River.

Schoeman relaxed in camp for some time but then was ready to have a go at the elephant again. In the meantime Lategan, with Fraser and a tracker, had shot antelope for the camp. We were well supplied with other foodstuffs, and they noticed how little meat I ate, preferring carbohydrates, the flesh of birds, and fish.

After eating it was usual for me to join the trackers and other staff at their campfire. It was interesting and amusing to hear their stories from far and wide. Schoeman thought he was missing something, and I told him he was, as the best company is around the campfire with the people of the wilds. He sat with us, and I translated. He found it amusing, but his presence caused them to tone things down until they lost interest and eventually wandered off to sleep.

Schoeman was chairman of the Transvaal Hunter's Association, and was against "professional" hunters—including and perhaps especially those who followed the ivory trail as I had. I have trouble viewing hunting as a "sport." Relations in camp were cool at best.

Schoeman and Lategan got their various game animals, but I accompanied them only for the dangerous ones. One night around the fire we heard the movement of bush as a kudu came past and plunged off the bank into the Zambezi River. It was in a state of terror, being followed by wild dogs. The incident ended quickly as the dogs veered away from our camp. We heard the kudu splash from the water farther down, no doubt taking a new direction into the bush. *A lucky kudu*, I thought. Without our presence the dogs would have waited on the riverbank for the kudu's exit from the water. Few antelope escape from the chase of wild dogs.

I had endeavoured to impress on Schoeman the vital necessity of the frontal brain shot on elephant—an imaginary line across the eyes and about three inches up the forehead, depending to a small degree on the angle of the head—whether raised in alarm or lowered in a charge. I always urged hunters to attempt this shot in preference to all others because they might have to use it for their survival.

One day we found a herd of elephant, and because there was no ivory worth having I got Zaratina to demonstrate his ability to follow them and to penetrate the herd unseen, unheard, and unscented. Schoeman, I could feel, was tense as we moved among the elephant in thick, high bush, able to see only their thick lower legs, sometimes at just a few paces. That night around the campfire I made the statement that in all walks of life there are the so-called experts and the real experts. Zaratina was a man of great skill and much experience, which added to his courage. After this Schoeman said he understood our resentment to his inferior trackers. We began to understand each other.

A few days later we came across a large troop of bull elephant making their way in the thickets and bush of the Nyakasanga dry watercourse. During the rainy season this river spilled into the Zambezi, where it formed a large swamp of dense reeds. I pressed the trackers to close the distance, hoping to get the elephant before they entered the swamp, but we failed and emerged from the bush to see a few of their backs and tops of heads moving through the reeds. Then the animals disappeared in the dense mass of reeds.

Once we reached the higher ground at the edge of the swamp, Zaratina paused slightly to see my reaction to the situation, and we then both plunged down the bank to enter the reeds. The others—Schoeman, Lategan, and the two remaining trackers, Frau and Jaubek—paused on the bank. Realizing that they were no longer behind us, I looked back and signaled for them to follow, but there was no response. The thought of penetrating the tall reeds after these elephant was frightening to them. I came back up the bank to Schoeman. He said he felt we had no chance and did not want to enter the swamps. It was getting late, and the bulls were close at hand. It struck me that this was an opportunity to express the mentality of an ivory hunter. I reminded Schoeman that he and Lategan had traveled two thousand miles from Cape Town to hunt elephant, and now that the animals were here in front of us in the swamps they were trying to abandon the hunt.

"Imagine," I said, "that you are an ivory hunter and in order to survive you must have that ivory. You cannot come back tomorrow or next week like a "trophy hunter" or seek safe hunting elsewhere. The elephant are here now in the swamps below us."

Then I asked him if he had ever been so hungry that he had to hunt to live. He still refused to enter the swamps. "I will shoot them for you," I said and started walking down the bank.

"No, you won't," Schoeman said and walked up behind me. Then he added, "Whatever happens, this was not my idea."

I signaled for the others to follow, telling Lategan that when the shooting started some elephant might stampede up the bank. It had the desired effect.

As he joined us, he asked Schoeman in Afrikaans if he was sure about what he was doing. I told them that the first time I had entered a dense swamp after elephant I had to repeat to myself the words of a prayer my mother taught me from the Psalms: "Yea, though I walk through the valley of the shadow of death. . . . " I told them that confidence must come from your nerve and the rifle in your hands.

They were now partly conditioned to enter the reedbed swamps, but to my dismay the tracker Frau started blabbering, saying that we would all perish under the feet of the elephant. Except for Zaratina, I felt increased responsibility for these people and took action before the fear spread. I switched the rifle from my right to my left hand and drove a hard blow into Frau's neck with my fist. He fell, stunned, and when he rose I drove him in front of me to take a position behind Zaratina.

We were on the move, and as the denseness of the reeds increased, we all had to adjust to the conditions. Frau got a grip on himself. I recalled that this was the same swamp where Faanie, Jeffrey, and I had managed to shoot open the large, stampeding cow herd. I doubted if anything as dangerous and close as that could happen here again, and besides, these were bulls, not cows.

We had the familiar fearful feeling as we approached the noisily feeding bulls. Now came the task of trying to locate those bulls with reasonable ivory by the sounds of their feeding. We skirted the rear of the herd, occasionally pushing the reeds aside to get a view of parts of their bodies. I warned Schoeman to be prepared to defend at close quarters once he had fired his initial shots, as the elephant would group with some stragglers to the side and rear of the troop. Eventually Zaratina found a small opening where a bull was standing broadside away from the others. As the tracker's hand parted the reeds, Schoeman's rifle came up to his shoulder.

I quietly said, "All hell will break loose after this shot." He fired. The bull fell but was only stunned, and as it rose he fired again. It crashed down in the reeds, still alive, so I had to break through to get at it since it was almost out of sight. I had no sooner finished it off than I heard the rustling and snapping of reeds. The sounds increase in intensity as I made my way back to the party. Then came trumpets and angry roars. Would the bulls come at us, forcing us to take the initiative, or would they rush away?

We were in the right position from the standpoint of the wind, testing it as it blew through the reeds. The elephant communicated with each other. Then came a single, high, penetrating trumpet blast receding into a deepening roar, and I knew they would move now. The snapping of reeds grew louder—they were coming at us.

Zaratina was armed and looked calm, the only indication of excitement being the visible pulsing of blood in his neck artery. I took a position to wait. Schoeman was between Zaratina and myself; the others were behind us, some of them wide-eyed.

I said to Schoeman, "These elephant have our whereabouts. I need your firepower now."

He had a double-barreled .470 rifle in his hands. "Just remember," I advised, "to dismiss from your mind the frightening sounds and concentrate on elephant foreheads, and never stop firing until they have all passed by."

I turned slightly to the others behind us and said, "Move away or run and you will die. Stay behind the guns."

My mind flashed back to the past when Faanie, Jeffrey, and I had stood waiting in front of the stampeding cows. There was danger here but nothing like that occasion, and I felt confident that we would turn the oncoming elephant or shoot an open path through their midst. The hail-like sounds came closer, huge feet and bodies snapping the reeds. Then they broke cover close up. I saw one drop to Schoeman's rifle—he had accomplished the frontal brain shot. Zaratina and I opened fire.

Time seemed to stand still during the continuous firing. The surviving bulls passed by on our sides—we had shot them open. I called for Zaratina to get us out of the reed swamps quickly: *"Buda u teesa!"* We moved fast with Zaratina leading. The fear now was that if the elephant regrouped, the wind would be in their favour, allowing them to make an accurate attack. There was absolute urgency to change our position and keep moving.

Schoeman and especially Lategan were much older than I, but age did not come into it as we all scampered through the reeds. Then Zaratina pulled up, so I made my way forward to him. We could still hear the elephant in the distance.

"What is it?" I asked.

He said, "We are close to the Nyakasanga River mouth, but there is an elephant moving in front of us."

I told him, "Get us out of here. If it shows, put it down."

He indicated that he wanted me with him and not guarding the rear. Time was of the essence, so I stayed close to him as we jogged along a path, watching in anticipation all the time. I felt relieved when we ran up the slope to the Nyakasanga riverbed, but there was a bull in front of us, standing alarmed with ears and trunk testing sound and scent. We were in five feet of grass; the bull was exposed.

"Your frontal head shot," I said to Schoeman.

Together we moved through the grass toward it. Halfway, I started running toward the bull, knowing that as it heard me coming it would face me, giving Schoeman the desired position to fire at it. On hearing me surge through the grass, the bull turned to face the oncoming noise. His fearsome, massive bulk, with outstretched ears and raised head, was impressive. He came forward a few steps at a time toward where I had stopped, crouched on one knee, waiting for the shot from Schoeman, who was somewhere behind me. The bull kept coming, hoping to flush me. It seemed to take ages. It was too close now for me to look back.

I wondered where the hell Schoeman was—there is a limit to how close you can allow an elephant to get. I was toying with the thought that Schoeman might not be there at all, and I might have to kill the bull myself at the last moment. Then a shot rang out and the bull collapsed. I watched its back legs stretch out and then relax, an indication of a brain shot.

The party had witnessed it all, and as they came forward I declined to allow them to stop and got them going again. The remaining elephant were cutting up rough farther back in the swamp, and I wanted us all out of here in case something unforeseen should happen. Not long after this we reached the mopane forests, and I let the group relax. There were flushed faces and the heavy breathing of excited men. Frau said in the Cha Lapa Lapa language, "*Teena duse ena heenya*!" meaning we had come close to sh--ting in fear. I regretted having had to hit him, because on other occasions we had successfully hunted together, so I took the opportunity to explain my action to him. Having escaped the elephant in the swamp, he was humourous again and bore no grudge.

The following day was set aside to take photographs of elephant in the swamp. Schoeman was keen to get these pictures so that other people could see the dangerous hunting that had occurred here. I had no interest in this and felt I had earned a clear day for myself. I suggested that they go with the trackers to do their photographing, but Fraser would not have it, hinting that I had nearly got the minister killed the previous day and must return with them to the swamps. There went my dreams of relaxation, and so we all eventually arrived in the swamps again.

There Fraser said to me, "How could you bring people into this place to hunt elephant?"

I was astounded at his ignorance of that situation, but needed my wits about me and was not going to let him get me angry. Schoeman took the liberty of reproaching Fraser and asked him why he had not been with us the day before.

Zaratina suddenly detected the top of a bull's head standing next to the dead ones. It probably wanted to be near a dead companion, further proof of how the live ones feel about their fallen comrades.

These people had come all this way to photograph the hunting scene so that others would believe it, so I moved forward to put the bull down. Fraser was against it, obviously afraid. He said, "Leave it—let's get out of here. There are already enough dead elephant."

As if one more would make any difference now, I thought to myself. They were being shot in hundreds for the tsetse-fly campaign. All I had to do was shoot one more elephant to get the photos. If not, what were we doing here? Fraser had not even been here during the shooting, but he was the "boss man," so Schoeman lost his photo opportunity.

Years later I had a friend, Pat Bromfield, photograph these swamps near the Nyakasanga River, and I sent the photos to Schoeman in South Africa. But the photos were not the same, for the hunting opportunity had gone forever. In his short period in the swamps, Schoeman had learned much of the professional side of hunting and had stood up for it. Considering his position as chairman of the Transvaal Hunters' Association, it was a valuable learning experience. He had experienced the full realization of danger, and after this occasion he became interested in the other side of the law, namely the life of the ivory hunter. He often questioned me on my previous way of life, finally saying that his attitude had changed, and he would be more selective in what he said at future Hunters' Association functions in the Transvaal.

Schoeman had a particular liking for the tracker Zaratina and toyed with the idea of enticing him to accompany him on other trips. He said he would install him on his farm in the Transvaal so that he could use him as a tracker once a year.

Knowing how impossible this was, I called Zaratina into the conversation. He said he had heard the country to the south was cold and had no wild places, and he did not want to develop a light skin like Schoeman's Africans. He said he would go with me any time to the north, where people got blacker and the climate warmer. We laughed at his descriptions. Schoeman was only trying to say he would miss the skill and knowledge of the tracker. It is interesting to note that the good trackers know the value of their skills but do not see themselves as admirable.

Fraser had left, and the safari was getting ready to break up and depart back to South Africa. As a change, I crossed the dry bed of the Nyakasanga flood river. Chief Dandawa lived farther on down the valley on the Rukometje flood river. His people were spread along the Rukometje from the Zambezi to the base of the escarpment, in small villages with large tracts of land between. The country was well stocked, especially with elephant, which gave the tribesmen a hard time in the crop-raiding season. We were now well into the dry winter, when the Zambezi Valley climate is ideal.

With Zaratina and Jacoba walking in front of me on a path, we entered a forest where the mottled shade always reminded me of the spotted leopard that also frequent these parts. We had short branches to swish off the tsetse flies, which were particularly bad in shaded gullies. Suddenly Zaratina stopped, saying that there were two feet ahead of us, meaning a man. We stood on this winding path with limited vision, and then I heard someone approach and waited in a clear place. It was Chief Dandawa, alone and with spear in hand, no doubt on his way to one of the villages of his people. I wondered about this as the old man was going blind. So as not to startle him, I called out his name. He came on and then stopped. "*Indiane*?" (Who is it?)

Jacoba said, "*Kaporamujese*."

I expected the usual warm greeting of a chief I knew well, but, standing close in front of me, he suddenly raised his spear as if to plunge it. My trust of him was so great that had he thrust he would have impaled me.

Then he raised his voice, impassioned with hatred: "My father was right—we should have put you white dogs to the spear before you became too many."

Had it been another man I would have put a heavy bullet into his chest to avoid the flash of his spear, but my instincts cautioned me and I had a liking for this man.

I said by way of appeasement, "Why kill the hunter of elephant? Kill some other whites instead."

Slowly he lowered the spear. He was in the grip of a terrible racial hatred. Because of the presence of Zaratina and Jacoba, he started to calm down, but his hatred for all white men remained. I now got the story.

The native commissioner at Miami on the plateau had been instructed by the government in Salisbury to advise the tribes that they were to be removed from the Zambezi Valley because of the building of the new Kariba Dam upriver. There was such a good balance here between man and beast that the thought of it disturbed me. It was the first I had heard of it. I wondered why they would remove people who were downstream and would be unaffected by the dam. It would turn their way of life upside-down for a while.

"Where will they settle you?" I asked.

"*Magunge*, on the plateau," he replied.

I knew of this place—it was a good area with fertile ground in a cool, high-rainfall climate with no elephant to raid lands and no tsetse flies.

"All white men think the same," he said. "But this is the land of our forefathers. We can live here well—it is warm and the Zambezi River is close by in case other water fails. We had the tsetse and malaria before you came, and if the elephant raid our lands and we are quick, we have dried meat."

My heart went out to the chief. Later he rose to go, his muscular old frame shining in the sun.

"You, *Kaporamujese*, you are now a government man—you must speak to the native commissioner. Tell him it is our country and we have a right to decide." I knew it would be useless but said I would try.

This was also the first that Zaratina and Jacoba had heard about this situation. It would affect them as members of the KoreKore tribe, which was spread from Kariba to the Mupata Gorge on the east side of the Zambezi River. It occurred to me that once the KoreKore tribe was removed from the Zambezi Valley, there would be absolutely no information from this vast, game-rich land.

The opposite bank of the Zambezi River was mentioned in David Livingstone's journals as the place where he had seen the greatest concentration of big game in Africa. Almost no wildlife was there now except animals that crossed the river from our side, the east bank. Those that went there were likely to die as the west bank had hundreds of tribesmen with firearms, mostly muzzleloaders but some heavy enough to bring down the big game. Wounded game would seldom make it back across the Zambezi River to their previous sanctuaries.

As I had other obligations from various parts of the country, I left Zaratina and Jacoba to the sadness of having to leave the Zambezi Valley. They were concerned that I would no longer be able to find them where they were destined to be settled in the Urungwe area, a vast tract of tribal land on the plateau above the Zambezi Valley. I assured them I would find them through their chiefs or the native commissioners.

I had to see to many complaints, mostly about elephant, and found it tough and demanding to be an effective one-man band. These excursions took me all around the country, and it was difficult, if not impossible, to get effective help from people. But my travels from Mpoengs, Sansuke, Mabali, and down the Ramagua Bane and Shashe Rivers, past the Tuli circle and on to Maramani in the west and south, gave me an idea of the movements of Liebegs Ranch elephant to Bechuanaland and back again.

At one stage I was close to that mad tracker Pafure but was too caught up in affairs to visit him. I did, however, come across the legendary poacher van Heerden. This was a man who challenged all authority when it came to what he considered his heritage to hunt wildlife. I had heard that he was no ordinary man and had shot at and wounded people who had tried to stop him from poaching in the Transvaal into Rhodesia and Bechuanaland.

Rumour had it that he used mares in milk with nursing foals. These young horses he corralled at his base in the Transvaal. He would cross the Limpopo River into Rhodesia with the mares to shoot antelope. He would strap the antelope to the mares, which he then released. They would unhesitatingly head back to the kraaled foals, carrying the carcasses of the antelope, and he would follow later on horseback. Just listening to the stories told me a great deal about this man. He and others like him believed so emphatically in their way of life that they would attack and die to protect it. He must have been a marauder by nature and was reputed to be very fast and accurate with a rifle.

As fate would have it, I came close to his horses tethered in some shade and saw part of him—armed and facing me behind a tree. I deliberately put my rifle up against another tree, walked up to him, and engaged him in his own language, Afrikaans. I told him I was a game ranger on elephant control and not looking for anybody—especially him.

He had a Kalahari bushman half-caste assistant who looked as if he could murder a man in his sleep, and I jokingly said so. Van Heerden replied that the looks of all men were deceiving. He then asked me why I had deliberately come up to him unarmed. I could not help laughing as I said he had a bad reputation, and I did not fancy a shootout with him over wild animals and civilized men. We understood each other. He was not very communicative, but I could feel the dangerous physical nature and ruthless expertise of this man. I asked him how long he hoped to continue his way of life in the face of developing civilization. As long as there were game rangers like me, he replied with humour. He had three horses with thoroughbred blood in them, and after we had spent some pleasant time together van Heerden and his assistant mounted to follow the mares, which had left prior to my arrival. Our paths met just this once; I never saw him again.

It was not the hunting that really tired me but rather the traveling. After dealing with elephant trespassing in the Malapati area, I drove back along the main Bulawayo/Beit Bridge road to the West Nicholson area, where elephant had broken out on a ranch. On arrival at the ranch, I was greeted from a large veranda by the owner, who cautioned me not to alight from my vehicle until his pack of some twenty fox terriers became used to me. He came up, and we conversed as the pack of piranha, as he put it, growled and smelled around. Eventually I alighted from the vehicle and the dogs accepted me. They were a vicious bunch, ready to go at anything they thought needed sorting out.

The elephant here had crossed the main Bulawayo/Beit Bridge road, probably from a large ranch to the south belonging to the Henderson brothers, who, thank God, did their own game conservation and control work. I had arrived at midday, and while having lunch at the rancher's house—I no longer remember his name—his cook came in to tell us that a leopard had just killed a newborn calf. The rancher sprang up, calling me to come along and see his dogs in action. Reluctantly I left the good food on the table. He handed me a shotgun and took one for himself.

Outside the house the dogs became excited on seeing the guns, sometimes fighting with each other. We jumped into an open vehicle and arrived at a cattle kraal. The dogs moved all around the kraal and then ran off away from it. This leopard, the rancher said, had made his last mistake, killing for the first time in daylight, and the dogs would get him now. Apparently the leopard had taken many calves, but always at night, and afterward moving into broken, hilly country where the dogs could not follow. In following the dog spoor, I could see where the leopard had dragged the calf. Then we heard the dogs barking at a distance. "They have got him treed," the rancher said as we moved off in that direction.

It was only a matter of locating the sound, and as we came to a clearing I saw a large leopard in a tree, his ears flattened as if to warn the dogs below. Some were trying to run up the tree trunk. As they reached their maximum height, they came over backward and spun to land on their feet again. But the leopard's claws made him the master of the situation, and at any rate the dogs could not reach him. On seeing us approach, the leopard flattened himself out on a stout branch and the dogs went berserk—a moving mass of activity all around the base of the tree.

The next morning I followed elephant spoor.

I had my regrets at being here and decided to hang back. The rancher had taken only a few steps when the leopard sprang out of the tree toward us. He knew he was cornered, and he knew who the real enemy was. After landing squarely on the ground, he came straight at us, the dogs racing behind to get at him. The racing cat was spectacular to watch. The rancher shouted "Shoot!" and did so himself. The heavy, spreading shot hit the leopard in the face and chest. It crouched over, still alive, and I drove a second shot at it to make sure it was dead before the dogs got there. Then the dogs closed in. These small domestic fox terriers were a bloodthirsty, effective, aggressive pack and tore the leopard apart.

The next morning I followed elephant spoor and found where they had recrossed to go south of the Bulawayo/Beit Bridge road. I left them, hoping they would stay there. I had come all this way for nothing.

I had a friend, Tom Williams, a medical doctor who was interested in the ways of wildlife. Elephant were raiding cultivated lands at Biriwiri, about eighty miles west of the town of Sinoia, so I took him along with me. Adjacent to the tribal trust lands was a sea of dense, thick grass about sixteen miles long and almost as wide. It was an ideal refuge for elephant as the grass gave them good cover in the semi-silence of the whispering air currents. The place had a distinct atmosphere of danger. Amid the miles of grass were occasional stunted trees, indicating a struggle between grasslands and what might at one time have been savanna. In this sea of grass the raiding elephant took refuge, reappearing at night to raid the maize lands.

In the villages there was a menace in the form of a witch doctor (*muroi*) known as Mhondoro, meaning the lion. He was an evil bastard who held sway over the people and was firmly established as someone to be feared and obeyed. The power of witch doctors often enraged me, especially those who were evil and took advantage of the ignorance of others. Mhondoro was fully aware of the grassland conditions, knowing that other hunters had penetrated but failed to stop the elephant depredations and had wounded some of them. His objective was to intimidate people into a state of obedience whereby he could enrich himself.

On entering the first village, I was informed by the inhabitants that without Mhondoro's authority it would be impossible to hunt here. I brushed these beliefs aside but in so doing made life difficult for myself as the villagers became obstructive, even lying to me. It was now up to the trackers, Manwere and Kadigedige, to trace elephant activities. Finally, on the second day, we found elephant spoor and knew that if we did not overtake them they would probably raid other lands miles away during the coming night hours.

The animals entered the sea of grass and kept ahead of us all day. Eventually we had to abandon the spoor at sunset. In these frustrating conditions Mhondoro, who was no doubt well informed, had the audacity to send for me. I arrived the following day at sunset after another futile hunt. He was sitting at a fire with some elders of the tribe. He was old and emaciated, wearing a piece of lion skin draped from the top of his head down over his shoulders. In the firelight he had an aura of mysterious evil as he looked out at me from under the lion skin. He did not know that I had had experience with his kind, particularly in Mozambique, where we gave them the usual rifle butt thrust to the neck if they interfered with us. At that time it was our mode of survival. But I had been cautioned by the native commissioner not to use such tactics as they were trying to build up a law case against Mhondoro.

I asked Mhondoro why he had sent for me, and he threateningly stated that if I did not pay homage to him I would be unable to locate elephant in his area, and if I did find some I would be killed by them.

Homage would entail a ceremony in which, for a payment, he would give my weapons, myself, and the trackers success against the elephant. Thus brought into the open was a clash of two sides: I having to hunt crop-raiding elephant and he demanding profit and further prestige. He was so confident of his demands that I wondered what he knew of the sea of grass that I did not. I did not succumb to Mhondoro's pressure.

I felt that we would need to be prepared to track for days, but that meant we needed porters to carry food, water, and bedding. Here we were partly curtailed because the tribesmen would not help, thanks to Mhondoro's influence. And so it was that we took the barest essentials and started tracking in the grasslands. I wondered what would happen in the cold of night as there were almost no trees for firewood.

On the first day we failed to contact the elephant and consequently spent a miserable night in the cold. Grateful I was when the rising sun warmed the earth. We tracked the same elephant, about ten of them, but then they split, so we continued to follow the smaller group of three bulls. At midday, having gone from one extreme to another, we were exposed to a brilliant, hot sun in shadeless country. The elephant arrived at a depression of trampled grasses, and I hoped to get them there, but they had just moved off, so we continued in their wake. My hopes rose as the signs indicated that the elephant were about to leave the grass cover and enter adjoining forest. There, with visibility, I felt we could track them at speed.

In the grasslands on the fringe of the forest was a dead forked tree about twelve feet high. I was unsure of the proximity of the forest, so I climbed the dead tree, leaving my rifle lying on its exposed root system. The trackers helped me scramble up the smooth surface and reach the exposed fork. From there I saw a large elephant at the base of an anthill about thirty yards off, with two others partly obscured behind it. I felt confident that we would get them, but suddenly the nearest bull gazed in my direction, then unexpectedly and silently charged through the tall grass. My companions were defenseless and unaware at the base of the tree. I jumped down to retrieve my rifle and barely had it in my hands when the bull's head broke cover. Luckily his trunk was curled to his chest: I shot him within trunk reach.

That was too close for all of us, though the situation had been beyond my control. If it had gotten me, no doubt it would have flushed my companions out in the grass cover as there was nowhere to hide.

A second elephant came at us, but I heard the whispering sounds of the grass as he came and was ready for him. The third ran off into the forest and then, farther on, back into the grasslands. The first elephant, we later discovered, had a sinus infection—its head-bone formation was filled with thick mucus. No doubt its discomfort had caused it to attack at the sight of my movements in the tree fork. It was an unusual hunt, but it had broken the authority of Mhondoro. The news spread fast, and thereafter we had the cooperation of the people. As a matter of interest, Mhondoro was eventually prosecuted and died of old age in confinement.

We managed to shoot more crop-raiding elephant. And one afternoon, on arrival at a village, I passed a man with emaciated legs sitting on the ground. Immediately I knew what his problem was. I waited for my doctor friend and some water carriers to come up to us, thinking this would be interesting to a medical man. I said, "Tom, what do you think is wrong with this man's legs? Why are they so withered?"

"Some form of paralysis," he casually remarked.

"No," I said, "It is the curse of the witch doctor."

"Bull," he replied. I then had the trackers partly raise the man from the ground, and he wailed pitifully, saying that if he stood on his feet he would die. He was so terrified that we lowered him again, but not before I got the doctor to examine his legs. He must have been off his feet for years as there was almost no response to tapping his legs below the knees.

"I don't want to believe what I am seeing," the doctor said, and a little while later he accepted the truth of the matter. This tribesman was destined to crawl on hands and knees for the rest of his life. The doctor asked me how it was possible, but I could not explain it other than belief, fear, and dominance. There are happenings in Africa that are beyond the comprehension of the European mind.

On returning to Salisbury, I was told by Archie Fraser to proceed to the Gwaai corridor, to inspect it for purpose of tribal occupation. It struck me as strange. Why use a game ranger to define agricultural land usage?

The Gwaai corridor was used as an access to the Wankie Game Reserve. It was used mostly by elephant seeking the waters of the Gwaai River, especially in the dry season. Without that access, masses of elephant would have to break out of the game park to find water on adjoining properties. That would lead to outcries against the park and its personnel.

We were politically considered a federation, meaning the British had decided to amalgamate the three territories of Northern Rhodesia, Nyasaland, and Southern Rhodesia. They called it the Federation of Rhodesia and Nyasaland. It turned out to be another one of those British experiments that failed. Having created it, the British then scrambled and disbanded it in ten years' time. Some high-up theorists had drawn lines across the map of Africa again, without paying attention to the tribes that lived in the areas. At the time it was an appealing idea, since it registered a strong block in opposition to South Africa, which controlled most of the trade. The federation could have worked, but the British destroyed it at the first sign of African nationalism.

Anyhow, I moved over the length and breadth of the Gwaai River corridor, coming down to the Gwaai River and following elephant that had crossed into the Sebungwe district outside the park. There was little harm in this at the time, but it was an indication that the elephant preferred the better feeding outside the park. The next day I walked through mostly broken country from the Gwaai River to the Wankie Game Reserve. The corridor was unsuitable for agricultural settlement—that anybody could see. The idea of human occupation of the corridor struck me as a setup that would cause enough trouble so that the Game Department, which was territorial, could get control of the Wankie Game Reserve, which was federal at the time. In my mind it was obvious that I was to be instrumental in this ploy.

I came clean and spoke to Ted Davison, the chief warden, who was suspicious of my having been sent here in the first place. He was reluctant to give me free range in the Wankie Game Reserve, but I took it anyhow. Casually I told Bruce Austen, his assistant, what I thought the setup was and that I was going to stick out my neck. There was little response, so I thought they either did not believe me or were disturbed by what I had disclosed. Both were game men of an excellent stamp and would know what it would all mean.

I completed a tour of the Wankie Game Reserve and got a good idea of game populations relative to feed and available water. Wankie was not a natural reserve; a lot of its water came from boreholes drilled into pans, and any rivers that held their water in the dry season were a bonus. I had followed elephant for thousands of miles in their migrations and wanderings for food, and I realized that parks and game reserves, although sanctuaries, forced elephant to adopt a way of life foreign to them. Elephant in parks do not lose their instinct to wander for food, and that is why they would occasionally break out of parks and only gunfire could keep them confined.

The whole setup put me in a predicament. I had been instructed on what the political minister, Ben Fletcher, wanted. I was already becoming slowly disillusioned by the Game Department. I thought to myself that I was a game man, so game must come first. In Salisbury I reported that the Gwaai Corridor was absolutely essential for the welfare of the Wankie elephant. The next day I was told that the minister wanted to see me. In early morning I walked to the minister's office and reported my presence to his secretary. I was told to wait, so I sat on a bench. Toward midday I spoke to the secretary again, asking him if the minister knew I was here. He went into the minister's office and returned to say I must wait until the minister was ready to see me. Toward lunchtime the minister came out and passed me, leaving the building.

I thought to myself, "Stuff you," and strolled downtown, had something to eat, and found a cinema, where I spent the afternoon.

The next morning I appeared at the Game Department. Fraser was concerned about my disappearance, saying that the minister had sent his secretary for me, only to find I was missing. Fraser asked me where I had been, and I told him. The phone rang; it was the secretary saying the minister wanted to see me with Fraser. We walked down to his office. I told the minister's secretary that I would wait but half an hour. Fraser at this stage was dismissed. To my surprise I was soon admitted to the minister's office, but after I greeted him he kept his head in some papers. It reminded me of the attitude of some wild tribal chiefs when you first come up to them. Having nothing to do, I moved around the large room to study the pictures of previous politicians and administrators on the walls. Just as I completed my tour the minister asked me to explain my report, which he had in front of him. I told him exactly what it meant.

"I am a game man, and game must come first," I said. "The corridor is unsuitable for tribal occupation."

He asked me how qualified I was to reach a decision regarding agricultural and pastoral needs. I countered by saying he had sent the wrong man to do his task. He was obviously trying to intimidate me, but since I was past caring, it did not work.

I told him it would be much more interesting to see a picture of Selous the hunter on the walls here instead of those others. He became angry and again tried to intimidate me, so I goaded him and his kind. He showed me the door, saying he would break me.

I said, "You can't, for the simple fact that I don't care much about my position here."

Much later, officials assembled at Binga, a place on the Zambezi River in the Matonga country of the Sebungwe. The gathering consisted of representatives of the Game Department, led by Fraser; the National Parks and Game Reserves, led by Ted Davison and Bruce Austen; the Native Department; the Tsetse Fly Department; and the Veterinary Department. We were assembled to sort out the problems of these various departments. Ben Fletcher, the minister, flew in on a light plane, and the palaver started. On the first day I became bored listening to them talking around problems, imaginary and otherwise. But inevitably they came to the wildlife situation.

I never heard so many experts who knew so little about game and its movements. Their knowledge was mostly theory and misinformation from the locals. The minister was being misinformed, especially by the Native Department. I became impatient and asked permission to speak, but the minister told me to wait my turn. I had had previous experience with this, so I lost interest and went to find my trackers. With one to guard me, I bathed in the river.

Here on the bank I thought of this and other similar events. Illogical as it is, man can be intelligent but ignorant at the same time. Often the ignorance arises from the conceit of one who thinks he knows, but in actual fact does not. It becomes an act of self-importance done for prestige. These idiots wish to be admired at all costs. Listening to them brought about in me feelings of loneliness and despair, and to protect my mental makeup I had to withdraw from the discussions. They were too unrealistic for me. I preferred the practical intelligence of tribesmen sitting around campfires.

In the meantime the minister called for me, but some thoughtful person made an excuse for me. That night, amid the campfires, I walked up to where the minister was standing with his wife and took the liberty of telling him the facts as I saw them. He was in an amiable mood and listened, and I made sure that the information he received was precise and factual. But he told me that my perceptions were contrary to what the others had said.

"Suit yourself," I told him. "I am not here to influence you but only to give you the facts as I see and know them, of the game's position relative to man." It was the end of the conversation, and I moved on.

The next day I listened to the officials talking through interpreters to the various chiefs and headmen of the Matonga tribe. Some were given choices of places to settle their people because of the rising waters of Lake Kariba. Sadly disturbed, I heard one chief say he wanted to settle his people at Kariangwe, the place where I was sent to find a hunting camp for the Bata industrialist. I knew that the abundant Kariangwe wildlife was doomed to destruction from that moment onward, and so it was.

To me it did not make sense to move tribes into previously unoccupied but game-filled areas—semi-gameless places were available—and then to unrealistically expect the tribesmen not to hunt wild animals for food. But I later learned that it was a political concession made in the shadow of African nationalism. I drew the minister's attention to the coming destruction of the Kariangwe game area. He said everything would have to give way to the building of the new Kariba Dam for electric power.

Besides, the government wanted the resources of the minor rivers and watercourses for tribal occupants. It did not take much imagination to realize what would happen and who would get the water—at the expense of the wildlife. The minister then made the remark that the game laws would just have to be applied. It was laughable and unreal, especially here in the Sebungwe district, the last so-called stronghold of the wilderness. Tribesmen do not hunt for sport—they do not even know what it is. They hunt out of the necessity to provide food, so they see nothing wrong in their activities. Civilization, of course, condemns them as poachers.

The minister was knighted Sir Patrick Fletcher for his removal of the Matonga people to other places in the threat of the rising waters of the Kariba Dam.

The minister was knighted Sir Patrick Fletcher for his removal of the Matonga people to other places in the threat of the rising waters of the Kariba Dam.

Zambezi Valley:

The Coming of Kariba—1958

I now had to start the campaign of procuring elephant meat for the labour employed in the building of the Kariba Dam. As a base, I selected a small, dry watercourse called the Kasese about eight miles from the dam site. The local tribesmen were reluctant to work for the white men on the project. Consequently hundreds of labourers were brought in from Nyasaland and others were sent to me from Salisbury to cut meat and make racks on which to dry and smoke elephant meat for transportation to the dam site. Where possible fresh meat would be collected, which was better as I did not want to become involved in the butchery process.

I sent for Zaratina and Jacoba. These men, besides being hunting companions, were invaluable in dense thickets and could be relied upon under the worst circumstances. I felt complete with the right men around me. Then, to my surprise and joy, Juda, the bent-legged medicine man, arrived and brought some other tribesmen with him. One in particular, old Chakadama, was an excellent tracker with his heart in the right place. He was humourous and often kept us going when we were tired and thirsty. How his body produced such energy I don't know, but I remember that on one occasion he danced into a village where there was a woman he fancied—this after a thirty-mile walk under trying conditions.

As we hunted elephant for meat in a dense forest, we veered off to one side of a path to avoid a puff adder. In so doing I disturbed some buffalo-bean plants above me. The fine, fiberlike hairs came gently down and covered my arms, legs, neck, and face. I dusted off what I could, using a leafed branch, but I had gotten a shower of it and so had Jacoba, some of it getting into his hunting sandals. Within hours irritations developed.

In late afternoon we found some damp mud in the Naodza River, stripped, and plastered ourselves with it. According to my tracker, the mud, allowed to dry, could then be removed and would bring the fine hairs of the buffalo bean away from the skin. It worked well and we got relief, but during the night I felt irritation in my eyes, and by morning they were inflamed. One does not realize the value of powerful eyesight until it becomes faulty. I had to take the problem seriously, so Jacoba and I left in the Land Rover, heading for the high plateau and the town of Sinoia, where I sought medical attention. About ten miles from the main road junction, Jacoba pointed out a sizable camp. My eyes were inflamed and giving me hell, so I motored in for a break. It was a camp of surveyors from South Africa. Two survey groups were working toward each other to complete the road to Kariba.

There was a white woman in the camp, and when she saw me she thought a snake had spat venom into my eyes. I explained to her what buffalo bean was and its effects. She rummaged through lots of paraphernalia and produced a tube of penicillin or something like that—whatever, it was the latest from South Africa. She applied it to my eyes, and in hours I began to get relief.

I slept there that night and by morning could feel much improvement. She gave me the tube, and because of this I returned to the Kariba area, but it took a week before I could see spoor properly again. I had apparently allowed this irritation to remain untreated for too long, and it must have scarred my eyes.

It so happened that Rex Bean, a labour recruiter at the Sanyati River, visited one day. I gave him the remains of the ointment tube to take back to the surveyors' camp in case they needed it. The survey route got into rough country, so rough and steep that expensive bridges would have to be built along the last miles of the new road.

The story I got was that some old KoreKore tribesman had told them to route the road along some elephant migration paths. They, of course, paid no attention, but when the going got tough they sent for the tribesman. He showed them the route, they altered it to suit themselves, and it worked. This was hearsay, but I sometimes wonder if that is why this section of the road is called "elephant walk."

From my camp on the Kasese watercourse, I ranged the area to hunt elephant for the Kariba construction workers. Large quantities of meat were always drying in smoke racks, but most of the carcasses were collected by Kariba personnel. One afternoon a tribesman said he had seen a black mamba come from under my stretcher and crawl off into the forest surrounding our clearing. Not wanting contact with such a snake, we removed the stretcher and sure enough, he was right: There was a hole in the ground right where I had been sleeping for days. The locals said jokingly, "He is a friend of yours, but don't step on him at night or it will make him angry."

The lion here had become lazy and scavenging, not wanting to hunt anymore. They boldly came into our camp at night and helped themselves to the meat on the racks. At first their visits were a novelty, and I thought little of it, but soon they increased in numbers, making us fearful and uncertain.

I had no torch, so I had the fires kept large to illuminate our sleeping places and the low-lying racks. Eventually the lion became so bold that they came into the firelight in full view and took the meat, sometimes silently and at other times with low, warning growls.

I was tempted to shoot at them, but realized that if I wounded any in the uncertain light, they could land among the many sleeping meat cutters, creating a disaster of mauled or dead men. The lion had become so fearless that I felt they might turn on us if there was no meat on the racks. I no longer admired them in the firelight but wanted to be rid of them. They were about sixteen in number. I felt poison would be the answer to our problem and certainly was the safest method. I knew Rex Bean had poison, so I borrowed some and dosed chunks of elephant meat.

The lion arrived as soon as it was dark, and we fed them by throwing the dosed meat away from the fires into the darkness. In no time we heard the grunting roars of lion in pain, and then the whole area became quiet. We kept the fires up in case some of the predators were unscathed. In the middle of the night I woke to the maniacal laughs of hyena and calls of other animals in the distance. I knew by the sounds that there were large packs in the darkness. Then the wails became concentrated, indicating that they were all coming together nearer to our camp.

We heard their powerful jaws feeding on what we assumed were the dead lion. It had taken them some time to become bold enough to do this. Then there were shrieks from the hyena and noises that I had never heard before as the scavengers felt the effects of the poison. After that we had silence for a long time. Toward dawn I woke to the roars of lion miles off, but there were no answering calls.

At first light Zaratina checked the activities of the night. He came back and told me there were many dead lion and they had been eaten by hyena, which in turn had died. Some of the poisoned meat was still lying around intact, so I did not know whether the hyena had poisoned themselves from the meat or the lion carcasses. The next day some of the men found dead vultures, which they prized, using the heads dried and ground for medicine, which they believed gave the power of identification in dreams. I ordered the vultures burned in the fire because I did not want any more chain-reaction deaths. We now had respite from the predators, and our lives became safe again around the campfires at night.

During the predawn a herd of elephant trumpeted a mile or so from our camp. It meant that at sunup we would have to follow them. These elephant went through thick bush and showed signs of restlessness, and from the spoor we could see where a large cow had taken up a position facing to the rear of the herd, alert to any follow-up. Zaratina said we must try to anticipate her as she could be one of the Chirundu cow elephant—the Zambezi Ladies. We eventually came up behind them in forest country with reasonable visibility. I jumped up onto a fallen tree trunk to get a better view. Our group included Zaratina with a .416 rifle, myself, Jacoba, and the medicine man Juda, who was very brave considering his bad leg. Although he had the great stamina of wild people, because of his leg he had little maneuverability.

From my elevated position I fired at a cow at the back of the herd, hoping it would turn some of the others and give us additional chances. The cow dropped, followed by total silence. Then without any sound a large cow came from the back through the herd straight at us, her ears flat to her head and trunk curled and tucked back to her chest in true charging fashion. Because she was only a single animal, I decided to let her get up close to make sure of killing her. But she suddenly let out a roar and a trumpet, causing all the other elephant to swing in behind her. In seconds we had a lot of cows streaking toward us. Zaratina was right as always—she must have been a Zambezi Lady, charging at the sound of the rifle. I put her down, but the others came on. On this particular day I was not wearing the customary left-hand glove that protected that hand from the heat of the barrels (my double rifle had a limited wood forestock). As I had to fire rapidly, the heat from the barrels burned my left hand badly.

Zaratina was right as always—She must have been a Zambezi lady. Zararina in the background.

The cows came faster than I could shoot. They had got into their top speed and were guided by a wind that had changed against us. I had become casual and overconfident, taking them initially at a distance of about forty yards instead of getting up close to them. Zaratina, who was a poor shot at distance but efficient at close range, now went into action as some of the cows closed in on him. My fingers were burning from the hot barrels, but I dared not stop firing, death being more fearful than pain.

A cow that saw me but was blocked by three dead elephant caught hold of the top part of the tree trunk I was standing on and jerked it so vigorously that I fell off. In midair I shouted to Zaratina to kill her. I hit the ground and then heard his rifle go off. I pulled my feet under me and shot another cow as she turned to close in, and then the remainder stampeded off. These cows had come much too close and too fast for safety.

Despite all the times I had hunted elephant, I was learning a new lesson about the intelligence and determination of a charging cow. I just could not get over how she had shaken me from the fallen tree. How could she have known how to get at me unless at some time previously she had learned to shake baboons from a tree—which was highly unlikely.

The pain of my burned hand was penetrating, and I could hardly stand still. In minutes there were large blisters where the fingers had gripped the barrels of the .450 rifle. It put me out of action for a while.

Prior to this, in Salisbury, a vacancy had been created for a game ranger. I emphasized to Archie Fraser that the job be given to a man of practical ability so he could shoulder some of the field work. There were many applicants, and Fraser had me make a short list. On paper six men seemed suitable or trainable for the job of dangerous game control and other duties.

I did not know any of these men personally but knew one by reputation because of a hunting incident in which his brother was killed by elephant in Mozambique. The brothers and their father lived as a family near the Mozambique border in Rhodesia, and from early manhood these two brothers and the father were often after elephant. They must have had considerable experience in Mozambique, which at that time was a stronghold of crop-raiding elephant. When I was sent off to hunt elephant at Kariba, I thought that one of these six men would be employed. I was looking forward to it as I sure as hell had my hands full of game problems.

There are certain elements involved in driving off elephant. The first and most important is that the herds must be vigorously harassed and their numbers reduced quickly and efficiently, regardless of how dangerous the conditions are. It is essential that they find no sanctuary in the area you are clearing for human settlement. Treated that way, elephant vacate the area and you save about three-quarters of the herd. On the other hand, if you shoot them halfheartedly here and there over long periods, they remain resident, especially if the hunter is afraid to tackle them in their sanctuaries of thick bush. The elephant accept slow, continuous persecution over long periods and become conditioned to it. In that case you probably shoot three-quarters of the herd in the long run and sometimes all of them, saving nothing. The same rationale applies to most wild animals.

These concepts assume that there are sanctuaries *to which* the unwelcome elephant can be driven—which in Rhodesia at the time there usually were. Even the Rhodesdale elephant were driven from this massive estate in the center of the country down the Umniati River to the vastness of the great Sebungwe district, an area probably the size of England.

Word came through that Fraser was bringing a new game ranger to Kariba to relieve me. I was pleased, knowing that I would have a small break in Salisbury and then could continue the elephant persecution on Liebegs Ranch at the opposite end of the country. To my disappointment, the new game ranger was not one of the six men on the short list, but rather a man named Rupert Fothergill. On speaking to him I had my doubts but thought I might be overstressed and consequently overcritical, so I reserved my judgment and hoped for the best.

Fraser emphasized that Fothergill had considerable experience in buffalo hunting, having shot a few hundred of them, but I wondered how an occasional hunter had managed to shoot hundreds of buffalo. I casually questioned him on this and decided it was not so, but I still hoped for the best.

He remained at Kariba to continue what I had established, and within a short period I was back again at Liebegs Ranch to continue driving its elephant southwest to the Bechuanaland border. In the meantime others had since taken sanctuary on three Limpopo ranches—an area of about 90,000 acres—and also had access to tribal trust lands of sparse human occupation. These places would have to be hunted in addition to Liebegs. The total area embraced probably a million acres, a vastness I had to penetrate to follow elephant herds that usually walked long distances.

Left to right: Rupert Fothergill; Sir Robert Tredgold, acting chief justice; Garfield Todd, prime minister of Rhodesia; Archie Fraser, game officer; and the author . . . amusing company for the ex-jailbird.

I started the campaign again on the Umzingwani River, where there were plenty of elephant to be driven off, and got as many as possible at each contact. It was sparse, dry, low-lying scrub country with thousands of zebra and wildebeest, hundreds of impala, and some kudu and the odd giraffe.

About fifty miles east was another ranch known as the great Nuanetsi. It was much larger, with similar conditions and game, but was known for its epidemics of foot-and-mouth disease. This disease causes the death of domestic stock, especially cattle, which were ranched there. Except for the Umzingwani riverine areas, Nuanetsi was a featureless place of flat, low-lying, dry country in the winter with low rainfall in the summer. Consequently maize was seldom grown. The main crops were *munga*, watermelons, native vegetables, and pumpkins. Liebegs Ranch, except for the Mateke Hills, was similar but larger and even more featureless. This whole area was the complete opposite of the Zambezi Valley, which was so full of atmosphere and charm. "Another planet," as we used to say.

In the afternoon, having harassed elephant, I came back to camp on the Umzingwani River. A *picanin* came through the sparse trees and said he had been sent ahead of an important man who was coming to see me. He said he had been instructed to tell us to wait and be polite and respectful. Most of the language spoken here is N'debele of the Matabele people. I did not think I was hearing right, so I called an N'debele man to question the child. He added more to the story, saying we would shiver in fear when this man arrived, like we did with the elephant. I knew there was insincerity here.

While trying to find out who the *picanin* was, I saw a full-grown, well-built man approaching. It was that mad bastard Pafure, who lived about forty miles from here in the tribal trust lands. He approached slowly, taking his time, looking down his nose at us all, tilting his head back in a supercilious attitude of arrogance. I was pleased to see him and burst out laughing. The *picanin* was his son. Pafure never for a moment indicated that he knew us. He said he had come to complain of crop-raiding elephant, and his complaint seemed to give him a sense of importance. I was amused watching my old hunting companion.

One of our N'debele people said, "What crops? They were reaped three months ago."

"Wait, dog," Pafure said. "When you come out of your dreams, you will know what I am saying." He tried to intimidate us, saying that if we did not assist him and give him preference, he was going to see the native commissioner at Beit Bridge. We were all laughing at his strange antics and attitude, and I told him to "pi-- off."

Unconcerned, he said he did not speak like that even to his cattle. Then he beat his chest with clenched fists and shouted, "I am Pafure *M'koenzi manama*" (the male animal). Everybody burst out laughing. He then sat at the fire and accused me of staying away during the rains of the crop season because I was afraid of the dense leaf cover here, but now that he was here I need not be afraid of the elephant anymore. He wanted to know if I had brought any champagne and was disappointed when there was none.

The last words of his act were, "You are afraid—you cannot walk far anymore, and now you have grown stingy."

After much bantering he eventually settled down and told us that elephant had boldly come into his village to raid the grain bins. He had so far managed to keep them off with dogs and a large whip, making a cracking sound in imitation of a rifle.

One of the N'debele men said jokingly, "Why did you not mount the elephant and ride them out of your village?" In reply he said some things about this man's forefathers that are unprintable. It was good to be back among friends again, even if this one was mad and had to be watched because his crazy antics could get you into trouble with the elephant. By our standards, he was definitely a bit touched but was considered brilliant by his own. He was a good and courageous tracker.

Listening to his anxieties, I thought it would be a break for us all to attend to his needs, so we packed hastily and crossed the bush road into the tribal trust lands, arriving at Pafure's village after sunset. It consisted of huts spaced about ten yards apart. That night, as we settled in around the fires, Pafure stood up, looked worriedly into the darkness, and said, "Can you hear that?" It was the elephant browsing around in his old *munga* lands. Pafure had an impressive well-fed dog built like a greyhound but more powerful and taller. The dog would rise in the firelight each time Pafure became agitated about the elephant.

Then Pafure said, "Come, let us get them before they reach my grain bins in the village." It was a semi-dark night, but I could not see myself moving across the noisy *munga* lands to approach the elephant, for whatever antics we used, the elephant would know we were coming. I said we would spoor them in the morning, but Pafure was agitated and said something about my being gone too long in the land of hyena and jackals.

Some of the Matabele people are inclined to be boastful, but others are truly courageous and reckless. Pafure, in disgust at my refusal, disappeared with his dog into the darkness. About an hour later we heard the cracking of his long whip and the excited barking and yapping of dogs. The elephant in the disused *munga* lands became angry, trumpeting and roaring in the dark. The dogs started to yelp more and bark less and came running toward us into the village. Close behind them I heard the elephant's ears flapping against their sides and knew they were chasing the dogs. We all realized it would be only a matter of moments before these elephant came streaming through the village in the darkness.

There were women, children, and some men in these huts, and I wondered at the irresponsibility of Pafure—what other lunatic would be bold enough to approach elephant in the dark, cracking a whip and backed by a pack of half-starved mongrel dogs! To stand illuminated next to a fire would be an invitation to being seized by an elephant on the run, so it was every man for himself. We took what refuge there was behind the huts, hearing the elephant coming at speed and angry as well. I knew that if an elephant decided to run through a hut instead of around it, there would be human fatalities.

Then the elephant were among us, the dogs yapping and panicking as they passed out of the village. We mostly heard but also got glimpses of huge shapes as the animals passed near the fires. Here I was without a suitable weapon, having to take refuge behind a flimsy hut of all things, hoping to God that the elephant would run around and not through it. I silently cursed that madman in those few tense moments. It was a great relief to us all when the last elephant passed. Immediately behind them came Pafure cracking his whip. On seeing us returning to the fires as a bunch of dejected, frightened men, he joined us.

In the firelight, excited and flushed, he shouted, "You can see my complaints are genuine. If they get at my grain bins, my family will starve this year." Everybody stared at him. At the moment he seemed like an alien from another planet, his shiny black body sweating in the fire glow. What does one say to such an irresponsible, courageous, untamable wild man? Nothing would penetrate his mind, given his obsession to rid himself of these elephant. Then most of the dogs came back, having escaped the elephant somewhere in the surrounding scrub forest, but we could still hear Pafure's dog in the distance barking at the elephant.

Pafure got angry with the dogs, chastising and chasing them away by throwing lighted brands at them. He shouted across the fires, "Go to your masters—you are as useless as the elephant hunters." Most of our fears and tensions had subsided, and I started laughing. How does one reach the unreachable?

One of our Shona people said, smiling at Pafure, "*Uno penga*," meaning "You are mad." This fact needed no confirming, but it made everybody laugh. There was not so much as a smile from Pafure, so great was his concern for his grain bins, and he was agitated because we did not share his concern, as if we were all shareholders in his grain.

Eventually people dispersed to their huts and we fell asleep around the fires. I had come across two other men in Mozambique similar to Pafure, including one who got us into unnecessary dangers through his recklessness. At the time I beat him severely in frustration and anger, but it was a waste of effort as such wild men seem almost immune to pain. They are as tenacious as a bull terrier and can be reached only by mentally appealing to them.

Every few hours Pafure would rise, alarmed, from his sleep, his magnificently built dog jumping to its four feet as well. He would then call out loudly, "Can you hear them?" meaning the elephant—even if there were no elephant noises. Half-sleeping men muttered about madness. Eventually we felt the coming of dawn. In the slight chill I moved close to one of the fires. I saw Pafure and his dog at the farthest fire listening to imaginary sounds. They came over to my fire, and the dog growled at me. It is interesting to note that in cities most dogs growl and bark at black men; in the wilds they do the same to whites. The reason is probably something simple like scent, or a presence felt by the dogs. This dog was not relaxed in white company, and I could see it was the type that would rush at a white man and fight him. It kept threatening me. I did not fancy having my fingers chewed while trying to defend myself, so I told Pafure to tone the dog down. He said it had never bitten a white man yet.

"How many white men has it seen?" I asked.

"You are the first," he said.

To avoid an incident, I took my rifle and went to sit at another fire.

All our people were waking now. Pafure came over to us, and the dog started threatening me again, but this time Pafure shouted at it and it immediately dropped down and gave no more trouble. It must be understood that such dogs are used to chase and attack game and are extremely fit and strong, as some of the game they tackle are decidedly dangerous.

Although I was a game ranger, I always spoke openly to tribesmen. Because Pafure had much dried meat, I asked him if he had a hidden rifle. This was forbidden by law. He said he did not need one—with the help of his dog they always had meat but had to go far for it, away from the tribal trust lands. I always considered tribesmen, armed or not, to be subsistence hunters, and I closed my eyes to their illegal hunting as long as it was satisfying their hunger needs only.

Pafure disappeared for a while in the developing light of dawn as I gathered our gear, rifles, gunbelts, water, and some hard rations. He came back later, and by the look of him I knew he had found fresh spoor. We came to a place where the elephant had lounged around feeding most of the night, and then the spoor moved off in a straight line—too straight, I thought. I did not like it as I suspected they had a definite destination and were in that shuffle movement whereby they can go all day, easily twice the speed of a fit walking man.

Pafure was right: These elephant had hung around in the dark, no doubt having smelled the grain bins, and if it were not for the fracas of dogs, they would certainly have advanced into the dark village to raid. Bins are common in this country, built off the ground because of the activities of white ants. They are circular in shape, and all an elephant needs to do is push them over to spill out the grain.

After a mile or so, to my dismay, Pafure's dog appeared, passing me with a growl and joining his master at the front. I called a halt.

"What about this dog of yours?" I said. "We had enough of dogs last night."

"I will use him," he answered me.

In my experience dogs and elephant do not mix. Though the agile dogs were in little danger unless they got too close, their harassment would cause the elephant to get fed up, alarmed, and frustrated, and then they would move for miles to get peace again. Under such conditions a man on foot cannot come up to them since they usually move over great distances. I said, "All right, these are your elephant, and if we do not get them it is up to you to save your grain bins!" We continued for a few miles, and at no time did these elephant waver from a straight course.

Eventually I called a halt and asked Pafure, "What does the ground tell you?"

This man knew the wilds and said, "The elephant are not afraid of dogs, but they resent the harassment and our presence in the village and are yearning to come back as soon as you are gone," meaning me. "They have smelled you from last night."

Interesting-—this coming from him—but I had already proved to myself that elephant know the difference between the scents of white and black men. If conditions are right, they will certainly attack both types or flee from them, but in an attack elephant prefer to charge a white man—no doubt being less familiar with him than with black men and associating the white hunter with danger.

I told Pafure we would not catch these elephant on foot. He agreed.

"Let us use the Land Rover," I said, "and try to cut the spoor, hoping they will keep a straight course." We returned to the village and prepared everything to leave. At the last moment Pafure asked permission to take his dog, saying it could hunt anything. The heat was taking over, and because I doubted that we would see the elephant on this first day, I had the time and patience to question and listen to him.

I told Pafure that we had always hunted elephant without dogs, and asked why his insistence of having this dog? "You know, your dog thinks I am white game," I said. They all laughed. I gave way and Pafure thong-tied the dog at the back of the Land Rover. We cut the elephant spoor after about twelve miles and then again ten miles farther, where they crossed an unimpressive dry gully called the Hunga.

Here we followed the spoor on foot for a few miles. The herd was less than two hours ahead of us, which meant the elephant had done a good thirty-two miles. It was late afternoon, and they had passed through tracts of sparse open country—no wonder they were in a hurry. They were heading in the direction of Liebegs Ranch, which was not far from here. There were sledge breaks (cattle pull wooden sledges to transport goods) cut along its border, and if the elephants crossed these it would be easy to find their spoor, but once these bulls got in among other elephant they would be unidentifiable. They would probably feed in cover of darkness tonight and then penetrate the adjoining thicker cover of Liebegs Ranch the next day.

We returned and camped at the Hunga not long after sunset, and next morning we found where the bulls had gone over the sledge breaks. They had crossed before dawn and were moving at a slow pace, so we walked the spoor, the bush being too thick for Land Rover progress. They zigzagged and fed a lot, and their spoors indicated five bulls, well spread out, which caused us to halt from time to time. It was new for me to see a tracker (Pafure) spooring with a keen dog in front of him held by ox thongs. In fact, the dog did most of the tracking.

I noticed that once the dog was on a fresh spoor it no longer resented me; perhaps it thought it was the undisputed leader of the pack. At times when Pafure and I came together, the dog stood at my side with no aggression. It is definitely less physically taxing to use a dog on spoor because the dog does not look for tracks but rather detects the freshest scent, thereby allowing a follow-up in a straight line.

I could see by the dog's keenness that we were nearing the elephant, and then we found fresh droppings. Pafure kicked one open to feel for heat—it was still warm. I told him to keep the dog at the back in case it made a noise or whined with excitement, but he assured me it would be silent until the quarry ran; then it would call out as it always did after game.

We were in the heat of the day and the elephant were seeking a shaded spot. Pafure became tense, and the dog started shivering in anticipation. I wondered how it could be so keen with these giants ahead of it. Then Pafure suddenly stopped to listen, pulling the dog close to him and indicating that the elephant were behind some bush in front of us.

What to do—I had not anticipated a screen of scrub between us and the elephant, and I did not want to use Pafure and the dog to approach. If we left the dog with some of the others and advanced, the dog could become anxious and whine, knowing it was being held back. Elephant hunting is strictly for the human species, except in semi-open country, where well-trained dogs can be used. I signaled Pafure to stay behind and advanced alone—not a good practice as the others were no longer protected by the man with the gun. As I moved through the scrub undetected, I could easily see two elephant and parts of the three others.

I shot the first two, and another one turned slightly to face in my direction and I shot him as well. Two others crashed off through the bush forest. Pafure heard this and released the dog. It came tearing past me, running on the scent with a howling call. After a while we heard it barking furiously and bush crashing in the distance.

Pafure came past me, and I called to him: "Don't run after the dog. This is not minor game, and you are unarmed."

We followed the noises, changing direction a few times but eventually coming up to the scene. I was intrigued to see the elephant stopping; they normally run on, regardless of dogs. They were trying to corner and trap the dog in the thick bush. Buffalo are brave, but elephant have more intelligence than most large animals. The dog, sure of its speed and mobility, always managed to outmaneuver them, and though they wanted to run off again, its furious actions kept attracting their attention. "*Chia ena*!" (Kill them), Pafure said. But I did not wish to do so under these conditions.

After some time spent watching the infuriated elephant and the fierce, antagonistic dog boldly going for their back legs, I signaled and we moved off. Pafure scowled as I told him to entice the dog back. He did so halfheartedly and it did not respond, so we moved on. Eventually it came back to us. I now realized why Pafure was never short of meat; from what I had seen of this dog's performance, no zebra or wildebeest could survive it.

We spent the next day removing the ivory from the three bulls. The day after, at dawn, we loaded up and I took Pafure close to his village. I watched him walking off with his elephant meat, cut in strips tied to a pole draped across his shoulders, the dog walking in front of him. I thought we would hunt together again, but that was the last time.

I motored in the opposite direction and arrived at my Umzingwani camp, where I had left Manwere and Kadigedige to monitor the elephant. They informed me that a troop of bulls had crossed the main Beit Bridge/Bulawayo road, and they had followed them to see if there were unknown watering places. The bulls had walked continuously and drunk during darkness at a borehole, where water was pumped to the surface into a long trough for the cattle. I had been informed prior to this by a Mr. Vavaseur, the ranch manager, that thirsty elephant had passed through the cattle, tusking and crushing them to get at the water.

I had to give priority to eliminating the elephant north of the main road, so I arrived at the watering trough. What little spoor I could see among all the cattle tracks indicated these elephant were regular visitors, which meant waiting for their arrival at night.

There was a long cattle kraal close to the water, built of hard wooden railway sleepers with their ends embedded into the ground. This was thirsty country, and I was hoping the elephant would arrive during the late daylight hours. I felt quite safe about shooting as I planned to be in the kraal, where my scent would be dissipated amongst the many cattle. From this position I could fire through the gaps between the vertical sleepers.

No sooner had the sun gone down than the elephant arrived, closely passing the cattle kraal. My eyes had accustomed themselves to the dark, but there was little visual detail. As the last two elephant were passing, I fired a left and a right barrel in the direction of their massive shoulders. These two ran off into the darkness, and the cattle behind me panicked, stampeding around the enclosure. I had created a dangerous situation.

As the bunched cattle rushed my way, I also panicked. A five-foot wall of sleepers was no barrier to a frightened man, and in seconds I was atop it, standing with rifle in hand and trying to see the elephant. I thought they loomed out there in the darkness, which surprised me because the firing should have caused them all to run off. If I had to fire from here, the recoil might put me back into the kraal, where the stupid, panicking cattle were rushing up against the barriers. They had already stampeded past me once, and the thought later occurred to me that if the sleepers I was standing on had not been properly planted in the ground, I could have fallen in amongst the milling cattle. There I was with panicking cattle on one side and elephant on the other.

I realized I could not stay on the sleepers, so I took my chances on the elephant and jumped down outside the kraal. Now safe from the cattle, I was at first reluctant to move forward to the water trough, which was built of brick and about three feet tall. I knew it was unlikely that the elephant had scented me and wondered how well they could see in the dark—certainly better than humans. I realized that it would be hard for them to identify me against the sleeper wall behind me, so I stealthily moved forward, silently opening the rifle to make doubly sure I had reloaded in the panic among the cattle. There were two large, obscure forms in front of me, and as I slowly approached, they moved. It looked like two elephant, and I thought their heads were raised in alarm.

There was definite danger here. I believed that the elephant could see me. I was conscious of their great bulks, silent in the night, but could see no details. Both were facing me, on the opposite side of the trough, thank God. I could make out the top of their raised heads against the lighter skyline. They had seen me long before I had seen them and were determining what course of action to take. If they split and came on either side of the trough, one might get me. For a second I wondered what I was doing.

It is one thing to walk up to a dangerous situation you have created but quite another to try to walk away from it with your back exposed in the dark, especially considering the attack instinct of dangerous game. I could see the movement as one elephant turned away. It was unlikely that he would swing back, so I fired into what I thought was the chest of the other. In the flash of the rifle I knew I had hit it right. It was either starting to attack or turning to run off as the other had done. This elephant lurched forward, smashing the trough and coming in my direction. I knew I could stop it with a shot from the second barrel, provided I could see to hit the head-bone formation.

It was about twenty-five yards off, but with the disadvantage of darkness I had to allow the elephant to rush up closer to me. Suddenly it let out a piercing trumpet so paralyzing that it made me inactive for moments. Luckily the bull crashed onto its knees and rolled over. I knew from past experience that the bullet had penetrated the top part of its heart. It works that way: The lower the heart is penetrated, the farther an elephant will run before collapsing. Their speed also determines how quickly they fall.

I sat down, staring into the darkness at the outline of the fallen giant. This area held mostly the Kalahari-sand-veld strain of elephant, which usually had short, thick ivory. It was too dark to see the ivory. Having managed to come through another harrowing experience, I wondered what was driving me and why I was risking my life to kill these great creatures to make way for man. Most of the elephant I shot had not known what hit them; if I did not do this job, others would and perhaps not so mercifully.

Even so, it seemed a waste of life, mine perhaps and certainly theirs. I was becoming bewildered, disillusioned, and resentful of the killings and the reason for them—I no longer had to have ivory for survival. Perhaps my hunting instincts weren't as powerful as they had been. Whatever it was, for my own survival I had to tone myself down. Here in the dark, amid the sounds of milling cattle, I realized that the responsibility of driving away these massive elephant herds was too much for a single hunter, whatever his background.

Laughter came easily—probably a release from the tension—as I thought of myself being a civil servant. These people are known for being steady plodders—why couldn't I become the same? The idea amused me as I realized it was impossible for a man of my makeup. I resented the fact that the more I came in contact with people and their needs, the more I had to bend to their ways and destroy wildlife. I thought too of the powers that be. There will always be governments. But can governments effectively control and lead the masses, with their civil servants plodding the way for them?

My mind came back to where I was. It was unlikely that the remaining bulls would stay here; their temporary safety lay across the main road past the Umzingwani River to the southwest and into Bechuanaland.

The next day, complaints came through the bush telegraph that elephant were causing damage to three newly developing Limpopo ranches. Unexpectedly, Archie Fraser arrived with the new game ranger, Rupert Fothergill. I learned that Fothergill had been at Kariba for a month, supposedly to hunt elephant meat for the workers at the dam wall, but had failed to kill a single animal.

"What do you expect of him here?" I asked.

Fraser said, "Here it is easier country, and with you he will learn."

So I said, "You employ the wrong personnel for your own private reasons, and you expect me to work miracles. What do you think I am—a magician?" Here I was living on my nerves, driving hundreds of elephant—admittedly with two good men, Manwere and Kadigedige—but Fraser saw fit to anchor me.

I asked him what had happened to the six suitable men on the application short-list. He avoided my questions. I advised Fraser to have the new man posted elsewhere—a game reserve, national parks, or anywhere the killing of dangerous animals was rarely required. To my disappointment, Fraser tried to lecture me on tolerance, but it was like a drizzle on a duck's back. Then a messenger brought a letter from Hans van der Merwe, the owner of Limpopo Ranch Number One. It had been named River Ranch, probably because it was located along the lower Umzingwani River. Elephant herds were breaking newly erected fences and had become aggressive. Attempts had been made to hunt them, but some had being wounded. Fraser returned to Salisbury and left Fothergill behind.

At this stage I developed a fever with headaches—partly the reason I had become short-fused. I knew it was not malaria. Any unknown sickness is worrisome, and so I left Manwere and Kadigedige, in addition to Fothergill's own staff from Liebegs ranch, to help him hunt elephant, while I went off to Beit Bridge to see a doctor.

At Beit Bridge, a customs post on the South Africa-Rhodesia border, I met Hans van der Merwe, who took me to see his doctor across the border at Messina, a small town about eight miles inside South Africa. Dr. Bachman took one look at me among other patients in a waiting room and said, "You first." I told him my symptoms. He said, "Tick-bite fever," and looked at my palms and at the membranes of my eyes.

"These are the indications," he said, "but it must be confirmed by finding the little swains."

He then took a blood sample, placed it under a microscope, and called me to see for myself.

"There," he said, "have a look at the squiggly-wigglies that are making you sick."

He injected me and said I must return for other injections. Hans van der Merwe, besides having the ranch in Rhodesia, had a house in Messina and kindly suggested that I stay there until the worst had passed. There was good food—including salads and vegetables that we did not have in the bush—but it did not interest me as I felt nauseous and had continuous headaches. After the second injection I started to recover, but I had lost my strength and speed of movement. I poked around the town, and Hans van der Merwe found me lying in the sun at a swimming pool. He suggested I come with him for a few days to the city of Johannesburg, about 350 miles away. It is concrete jungle, and decidedly un-African in its atmosphere.

"The change will help you pass the time and give you strength," he said. We were both amused at the idea that instead of hunting elephant in Rhodesia I would walking the streets of Johannesburg.

It was an easy ride on good roads. En route, in Pretoria, I asked van der Merwe to stop at the Union Building, the center of government. I wanted to see the fish ponds where as a small child I had caught and stolen goldfish—my earliest poaching experience. It pleased me to see the old haunts.

"Somewhere in this building," I said, "is a man I once hunted with in the Nyakasanga Swamps. I doubt if he will have forgotten it."

"Who is it?" he queried.

"B. J. Schoeman," I said.

"Hell," van der Merwe said, "he is a powerful man in these parts. Why don't you phone his secretary to see him?"

I shook my head and said, "What for? Anyhow, he wasn't so powerful when he was in the swamps."

Van der Merwe said in his slow drawl, "You're a bit crazy, you know—nothing brushes off on you."

"That's not true," I said. "It does, but I don't show it. And anyhow, this is where the crazy people are. There are millions of them who will never know any other world. Wherever there are extremes in riches, as there are here, there must be millions of underprivileged."

"I still say you are a bit touched," van der Merwe said, and we motored on.

On Koch Street I found the large jacaranda trees I used to climb, running on the branches like a monkey. On our way to Johannesburg we came to the Swartkop airfield, where I had spent many days on horseback crossing the rolling grasslands. I would gallop a horse across the well-kept flat plain, and when the military personnel gave chase in their vehicles, I would race through the trees in the gullies to escape them. I was a weakling in those days, and fast horses gave me the power I did not have.

We motored into Johannesburg, and I said to van der Merwe, "Can you see the gold on the pavements?"

"*Lekker mal*," he said, meaning "Nicely mad," referring to me, of course. Van der Merwe looked after me well, and we stayed with his various friends. He delighted in telling people I was wild, and it made good conversation in their social circles. One old woman who, with her large family, had invited us and other guests to a lunch party held outside in parklike grounds, came up to me. She was the old-stamp Afrikaner type.

"My," she said, "it must be hot and dangerous in your world!"

"Not as much as here," I said. "Look at all these nice, shapely women."

She laughed, saying with regret that she was better than them once. Then a striking woman came along. I searched my mind, knowing that I had seen her before. As she slowly passed, I reached for her. She frowned, and the old woman introduced us.

"Nyschens," she said. "I remember an Aubrey Nyschens."

"That is my brother," I said. But she said there were only two brothers, one of them was a weak, sickly boy. "That's me," I said. There was a look of disbelief on her face.

"How did this transformation come about?" she asked—but before I could answer, a strong-looking chap came over, took her by the arm, and glared at me. Hans van der Merwe had also come up and said he was my bodyguard. He looked the type, something like the portraits of Hindenburg, with a powerful-looking square head. The strong husband took his wife away, and I never saw her again.

The old woman said, "What was that about?"

"The hot, dangerous conditions you spoke of," I said.

We all laughed and looked for more liquor.

On another occasion, at a wedding party on my last day in Johannesburg, somebody vacated a chair next to me just as a pretty woman came along. She dropped into the chair as if she had won the Grand National, throwing her arms above her head, leaning back and then forward to reach for a glass. She engaged me in conversation, and because her social grace was so exaggerated, I asked her where her hair was. She had a glorious mop of black hair and indicated it.

"No," I said, "the hair under your arms."

She paused for a while. "They said you are wild, but I don't believe that—strange, maybe."

Van der Merwe, who was sitting on my left side, got up and leaned toward her, saying, "Lady, if this man gets you into a bed, you will think you are in the company of a leopard." She rose, looked at us both, and was glad to be gone.

I asked van der Merwe what he was doing, and he said, "Saving you, of course."

"From what?" I asked."

He said he knew this woman by reputation; she had been married four times, and each time she got richer.

"You are not rich," he said. "I could not stand to see you drooling over her raven hair. Such a woman could cut you up and throw you away." I later spoke to her, but she had lost interest, wanting instead someone she could control and certainly not a leopard man.

Van der Merwe was right—the change had done me good, and as we motored back through the northern Transvaal, where he had another farm, he said, "I wonder what is left of my paddock fencing, thanks to your Game Department elephant."

We crossed the Limpopo River, unimpressive at Beit Bridge, and I camped on the lower Umzingwani River, leaving van der Merwe to go on to his ranch house. It had been a worthwhile change that I had needed. The next morning two locals arrived, saying one could track and the other knew the area. This was not dangerously thick country to hunt in, but the tick-bite fever had sapped some of my fitness, so I sent these men off without me to scout for elephant. I lay in the camp, letting the sun bake the cold Johannesburg climate from my body.

That afternoon, Fothergill, and my two trackers arrived. They had been hunting for three weeks on Liebegs Ranch and had accounted for one elephant, which Fothergill had wounded and abandoned. The two trackers had followed up the next day, and one of them shot it. The trackers were embarrassed and sensitive about it, and I had to draw the information from them. The whole business upset me. In Africa it was important to set examples, especially in the wilds; once you proved something to the locals, they would willingly assist and follow you almost anywhere. But it worked the other way as well.

During the morning I had heard gunfire at a considerable distance. I thought it was someone hunting zebra and wildebeest for biltong as there were hundreds of these animals about. It so happened that van der Merwe was off after the elephant. That afternoon the two searchers came back to camp to say they had found where elephant had been smashing fences while going from paddock to paddock to seek food and water. Then van der Merwe arrived, saying he had shot an elephant and wounded others.

He said I must not be angry. In reply I said, "Since you have started it, finish it—it is better for me to do my hunting on the Liebegs Ranch."

Hans van der Merwe was an Afrikaner, and they generally have a tenacious stubbornness about them, particularly those who can express their freedoms away from the restrictions of large cities. Now I had on my hands a man incapable of successfully hunting elephant and another capable of wounding them.

That left the two trackers, Manwere and Kadigedige, to do the hard work. It was such a bugger-up that I could not see how it could get any worse.

The next morning they found fresh elephant spoor. I strolled behind this army, making sure my two trackers were armed and able to defend themselves, principally because of the human factor.

The damage to fencing was everywhere between the large paddocks, and van der Merwe complained of the costs involved. I reminded him that the government had sold him this vast tract of land with its large variety of game at the cost of a bottle of whiskey per acre. He jokingly said how many bottles of whiskey he could have drunk if he had not bought it. At that moment the party ahead stopped, and I came up from the back. Manwere indicated the presence of two cow elephant, stragglers from the main herd, browsing in easy country with no thick bush. Any of my trackers could have stalked up in the low scrub and shot them, so ideal were the conditions. I told Fothergill, who had previously had much instruction and encouragement from me, to take these elephant and try to get a frontal brain shot should any of them turn to face him. He hesitated, so I sent the best shot, Kadigedige, with him. They advanced a few paces, and then Fothergill stopped. When the tracker realized the ranger was no longer there, he stood waiting.

That truly annoyed me, so I came up to Fothergill and said, "It is all in your mind—if you slip, the tracker will shoot for you." You would think I was trying to extract money from a beggar.

"Watch!" I told him. "I will demonstrate." I moved on with the tracker. Under these conditions, it was simply a matter of approaching until the elephant saw or heard us and became alarmed. There would be plenty of time to shoot them. The first cow crashed at my shot without knowing we were there, but the second one turned to face us and had our position. I thought she might turn to run off, in which case I would have time to make sure of her. But this cow had other ideas—she silently charged us. I still had a shell in the left barrel, and it was just a matter of waiting for a sure shot, which I did.

The other people came up, and van der Merwe said in his own language, "God, today I have seen elephant hunting—it is a matter of not losing your head."

"Exactly," I said. "Tell Fothergill in English—he never seems to learn." Van der Merwe told him.

Van der Merwe then paced the shot off. The elephant lay about five steps away, and he asked me why I had allowed it to come so close. I said it was all a matter of conditioning. Any experienced hunter of dangerous game prefers close shots to make sure. I was tempted to explain about *jess*-bush hunting, but if five yards disturbed them, how could I?

I was not myself yet physically, so after watching the others go after the elephant herd ahead, I made a straight course with a water carrier back to my camp, where I saw an elderly man waiting. He said his name was Sussens and that he had a son commercially shooting wildebeest and zebra for skins and meat on van der Merwe's ranch. He had come to capture pythons resident in low-lying hills with small caves, where his son had previously observed them. He sounded like a city-type bull-tosser to me. He stayed a while and then moved off to find his son somewhere up the riverine area.

That afternoon the main party came back, having had no success. The next morning van der Merwe appeared with one of his locals, who had heard the elephant at predawn far off. It seemed an uninviting hunt was about to take place. In the first place, there were too many of us, which usually leads to chaos and uncertainty—like men under enemy fire for the first time.

We found the spoor, and as our party ambled off it reminded me of Hollywood scenes I had seen of the Mexican army. The herd of some thirty-odd elephant led us into broken country with small kopjes (hills), large boulders strewn around, and scrub growing between them. The place was higher than its surroundings and suggested a dry scrub sanctuary with openings leading to it. As we approached one of these openings, with large boulders around, the party with my two trackers, Manwere and Kadigedige, stopped while I came up from the back. They had heard the elephant, and I could see a few half hidden about a hundred yards away. Experience told me that their only line of escape would be along one of the openings. The trackers also realized this, but the others knew only that they had come upon a herd of elephant.

At this stage of assessment van der Merwe raised his large-bore .505 Gibbs magazine rifle and said, "I can see a head," and started firing.

I did not know if he hit his target, but the whole herd came streaming out of the opening toward us. I was disturbed and annoyed by this amateurish attempt at elephant hunting. You don't fire simply because you can see the head of an elephant, regardless of others, both man and beast. As the elephant stampeded onto us, I saw van der Merwe duck behind a large rock, taking refuge even with a powerful .505 rifle in his hands. Kadigedige and Manwere, thank God, were armed.

Fothergill stepped back as if to run, and I cautioned him, "Stand!" Give us a hand—we will cut them up." But the sight of the stampeding elephant was too much for him and he wanted to escape at all costs. I should not have tried to stop him, as it turned out. The trackers were conditioned to such events and knew that as soon as the elephant were close enough we would open fire to create dead elephant bodies as barriers to the other oncoming animals. We seemed to know when to use our combined firepower.

As these final moments were about to take place, Fothergill fired from behind, next to my right ear. He was armed with a double-barreled .500 rifle and was so close that the flash drove me to my knees. I half-turned and saw his feet running off to escape or take refuge. On my left side I saw great elephant feet come looming up in long strides and heard distant trumpets of fear and rage. The sounds seemed faint, but the elephant were close to me. My brain was not clear. I felt I was finished and had fleeting thoughts of my children. These powerful feet would bash me, and in seconds I would be dead. Then I heard distant firing and elephant began falling in front of me forming a barrier, and my dull brain realized that the trackers were at work and the stampede was passing on both sides of us.

I thought the elephant's speed and numbers might be too great, so with effort I turned on my knees to help. I could not see over the dead elephant up against me, so I struggled to raise myself, leaning on the head of a dead cow. I still could not see properly, but the rifle fire suddenly ceased. Now I could see that my two trackers had protected me more than themselves—the main body of dead elephant was in front of me. My ears were ringing, and I must have been groggy because the trackers poured water over my head. I cupped my hands to drink some, and my brain partly cleared, but the ringing continued.

Then I saw van der Merwe and Fothergill coming forward, and a murderous rage rose in me. Take them now, I said to myself—don't think about it, take them! A shot in the chest each from the .450 rifle. It would have been a greatly satisfying. Then Manwere stepped in front of me, and thank God he did. He must have known how I felt. I had been forced to kill men before, but never had I felt this yearning urge to do so. Then sanity came back and the urge passed, but my contempt for them remained. The thought of being sacrificed because of my tolerance of these cowardly amateurs in the first place brought about an anger that did not subside.

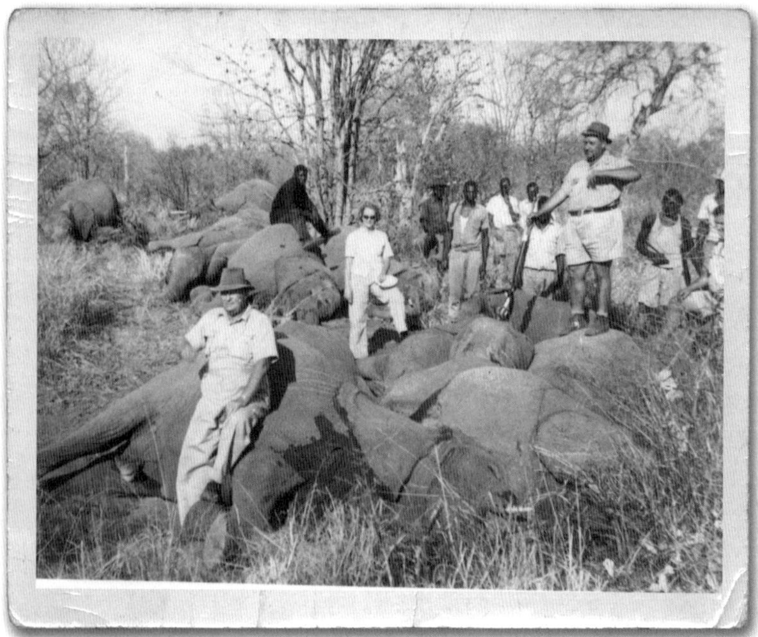

My two trackers had protected me more than themselves—the main body of dead elephant was in front of me.

The time had come for me to completely take over, but first I had to be rid of the human jackals. I told van der Merwe that, regardless of this being his property, I did not want him anywhere near these elephant, and I told Fothergill to go back to his own staff on Liebegs Ranch. With the two trackers I took the spoor of the stampede and found blood on the leaves, indicating wounded animals. I made an attempt to follow, but what with my recent fever and the latest escape, warning bells told me to abandon this hunt, and so the two trackers, the water carrier, and I returned to camp. Fothergill had already left.

That night at the campfire the trackers suggested that I let them hunt these elephant. It was a good idea, and I told them that if I felt inadequate in the morning they should do so together. I had a bad night, sometimes waking to the discomfort in my right ear, and was thankful for the dawn. A runner came into the camp saying he had heard the elephant performing and that they sounded disturbed and angry. He took us close to where he had heard them, and we let him go on his way to van der Merwe's ranch house. We closed in on the place he had indicated and found a dead elephant. No doubt the noises the runner had heard were elephant "rites." The rest of the herd had abandoned this place so we followed them through sparse dry bush, then into lightly shaded, anemic-looking forest.

I was hoping to get them here, but they moved on, crossed rocky ground, and entered low scrub. We saw them ambling along, and Manwere skirted to get to their downwind side. We had almost completed this move when the elephant became alarmed and many cows faced us. I went into action and put down about five of them before the herd could properly react, and as they did, the tracker rushed toward them. Those that tried to break off to the sides I put down. I was hoping the remainder would stampede off and leave this part of the country, but some old cow leaders, instead of stampeding—which they usually do at this late stage and sometimes long before it—came forward, leading the herd to attack. I had the advantages of time and openness to see the charge developing. I had a left-hand glove, so other than the impact on my shoulder, the firing did not distract me.

By the time I had put the last ones down, there was a mass of bodies—the herd no longer existed. Having annihilated an elephant herd, I was perhaps unfeeling to be concerned about my own condition, but I had the shivers and felt cold even in the heat, with a painful ear and developing headaches. I tried to figure it out, but my brain was dull. There was only one solution: I had to get medical attention.

Walking back to camp was an enormous exertion. I sometimes became giddy and felt so faint that I had to sit down for long periods. To get my wits and to relieve the fatigue, I lay on a camp stretcher for some time. Then the trackers packed and we motored to the Beit Bridge post a few hours distant.

After dumping the staff close by the Limpopo River, I crossed the bridge to Messina and was examined by Dr. Bachman. I complained of my ringing ears, but he was more interested in my general condition and said that I was in a state of nervous disorder. He then examined my ears and said the right eardrum was perforated to the extent that he doubted I would have the same sharp hearing as before. But he gave me hope, saying time would tell. He cautioned me to rest and stay away from excitement.

I had respect for this man's ability. He gave me the necessary drugs and medicines to last a few weeks. I returned to Rhodesia and camped on the Limpopo, which is far less impressive than the Zambezi, but at least the climate was warm. I spent a week or so there, having small walks and a few times illegally wading across the river into South Africa and back, just for the hell of it. The drugs were having an effect, and I was beginning to feel myself. I understood that there were occasional crocodiles in the Limpopo River, so I did my swimming in a small pool belonging to the native department at Beit Bridge.

While I was there, some prison bandits came to weed the lawns, followed by an armed guard who was a bit fat, probably from having to watch others working. Then to my surprise I saw among the prisoners the well-built proportions and walk of a man I knew, and I called out to him. He turned, and it was Pafure. We were both surprised and pleased to see each other. The guard was amazed to see the friendship and came up to warn me that this was a dangerous man, strong and a terrible fighter. I took no notice of him and asked Pafure what had happened since our last visit, and he said someone had stolen some of his cattle and he later beat up the wrong man and another who came to his assistance.

I could not help laughing when he said his dog had also gotten into the fray.

"When they arrested me," he said, "I shouted at the dog and, as it was well-trained, it took refuge in the bush."

No doubt the dog was back at Pafure's home and his wives would see to it. It was strange for me to be lounging in the sun while Pafure was made to weed the lawns. He did not seem disturbed by it, saying that the food was good and, as he put it, "Cooked by these women who wear men's clothing," meaning the prison guards and staff. I conversed with him and said I would get the facts of his case from the native commissioner, a Mr. Hagerthorn, whom I knew because of inter-departmental business with the Game Department. Pafure seemed unconcerned and said he would outlast all these dogs, meaning the guards and prisoners, referring to them as *masweenas* (the dirty gut of an ox).

The guard, probably because of my presence, relaxed and later dozed against a tree. On seeing this, the mad Pafure rose from the lawn, silently walked up to the guard, took his single-barreled shotgun, and removed the shell. Then he retreated, hid the shell in some bush, and sat down to weed the lawn again. I knew I was the impetus for this laughable demonstration but decided to leave anyway as I wanted to see the commissioner about Pafure.

I got the facts from Hagerthorn. It appeared that Pafure and his dog had badly damaged two men and had been sentenced to a year's imprisonment. I explained to Hagerthorn about Pafure and his amazing ability in the wilds, his individuality, and his mad ways. He promised to reduce the sentence, but also said Pafure must be punished to discourage him from beating up people, especially the wrong people. More than that I could not do.

We then discussed the game situation, most of which he was aware, so I brought him up on the rest, adding that civilization here was destroying the game, men, dogs, residents, and visitors. He said it was a sign of the times. Because of the general non-response I received to such opinions, I had reached the stage where I hardly bothered to make written reports of incidents, especially now that civilization's impact was so great.

As I came out of the building, Fothergill pulled up in a Land Rover with his staff and gear. He had a message from headquarters saying we were to proceed to the Sabi Tanganda estates in the Sabi Valley, where buffalo had become resident again. I had driven these buffalo off previously during the tyleriosis scare. The next day I packed my gear and followed him. It was a drive of about 260 miles on good roads. As I neared Birchenough Bridge across the Sabi River, I pulled up where I saw Fothergill's vehicle parked in some shade. He informed me that he had failed to shoot any elephant on Liebegs Ranch. There were plenty of them, but he just could not get himself to approach them. Then he broke down, saying it was the elephant's terrible size that had demoralized him.

We motored on to the Sabi Tanganda estates and saw the manager, Mr. Cameron, who had previously presented me with the champagne. In the morning we arrived at a place where I knew the buffalo should be, and sure enough they were, but of course in the reedbeds. As we penetrated the reeds, Fothergill came up behind me and said one of his trackers had found blood stains on reed leaves. It meant some of these buffalo were wounded.

By this time I had had enough, so I said to Fothergill, "You are supposed to be the buffalo expert, so follow them."

I abandoned the buffalo spoor and returned to the manager, Mr. Cameron, presented him with the bloodstained leaves, and left for Salisbury, saying, "Between your staff wounding these animals and the "buffalo expert," conditions here should balance themselves out." A few days later, Fothergill also arrived in Salisbury. No buffalo had been hunted or shot.

At this stage the Game Department had acquired the services of two additional game rangers, Tommy Orford and Barrie Ball. Archie Fraser's position as head of the Game Department gave him the power and influence that he would never have had otherwise. Especially in Mozambique, which had a poor reputation amongst the colonial powers, I had experienced the intelligence and manliness of some of the administrators by the way they implemented their authority. Some others wielded their power mainly to remind others of who they were. The intelligent ones used their authority to implement only what rulings were necessary.

Fraser's activities put me in a sensitive position. It was important to show that the Game Department could curb the activities of dangerous game to the benefit of private land owners, trust lands, crown lands, and any developments where assistance was needed. Barrie Ball, who had been a policeman, was seconded to the Game Department to become a game ranger. It was part of my duties to take him with me occasionally to teach him the hunting of elephant for control purposes. Considering my past, it was of some amusement to me that as a policeman he had been stationed at Miami, the control center for the Zambezi Valley.

I had first met Ball when Fraser sent me down to the tribal trust lands where baboons were raiding maize lands. The tribesmen had complained through the native commissioner, and help was sent in the form of three game rangers, Barrie Ball, Tommy Orford, and Rupert Fothergill. The last two were useless anywhere near dangerous game, although Fothergill did later become famous for his daring feats with darted, doped rhinos. He was a naturalist by heart, not having the mental makeup for killing, and from the first should have been posted to a game reserve or national park to make the most of his abilities. I stayed a day or so with these rangers and witnessed their amateurish attempts to capture baboons—of all the clever species—in stone-age traps built of wooden poles! It was a pathetic effort, and I think they caught one in one month (apparently even among baboons there are stupid ones). I felt more than saw the difference between Barrie Ball and the two other rangers and his natural resentment at carrying out this backward approach to the baboon problem.

Now I had Ball on my team. I took him with me because I could see this man had the makeup to deal with dangerous wild animals. He also had an intelligent caution to danger, but I had faith that he would not give way to charges.

Elephant were raiding lands on a farm called Journey's End, which joined on the crown lands. About eight bulls were raiding at night, and in daylight they took refuge in the *msasa* forest country, which abounded here. It was appealing to walk for miles in the semi-shaded forests, with green-gray lichen in patchwork all over the bark of the trees. Eventually I sensed the bulls moving slowly ahead of us unseen. My instincts must have been sharp that day for I suddenly felt uneasy, expecting something unforeseen. Suddenly the elephant turned and came rushing at us where we had taken an elevated position on the slopes of a large antheap. We opened fire and put them down. What a pleasure it was to at last hunt with a fellow government worker who would stand up to elephant.

Many years earlier, Barrie had had a close encounter with an elephant cow. It was during my ivory hunting days in 1954, when bush was being cleared along the Zambezi River at Chirundu for future sugarcane fields. Barrie at the time was a policeman. He arrived at Chirundu on a motorcycle with a servant as a sidecar passenger and camped in what was a particularly beautiful mopane forest before the bush clearing occurred. It was above the Chipara Swamps near Ka-Koma-Marara (the small hills of the palms).

During the night a herd of elephant passed by a hundred yards away. Lying on his bedding, he listened to them disappear into the darkness. Unexpectedly a cow trumpeted in rage, and by the sounds he knew it was coming at him, apparently having picked up the scent of his camp. Coming over a distance of about

A cow trumpted in rage and attacked the motorcycle. While this was going on, Barrie opened fire from only five paces away.

three hundred yards, it continued to trumpet in rage and speedily appeared in the semi-dark. It attacked the motorcycle, bending the handle bars, jamming the hooter, and tearing off various pieces. While this was going on, Barrie opened fire from only five paces away, using a ten-shot .303 magazine rifle, aiming mostly at its forehead in the dark. In the fury of it all he managed to place seven shots before the elephant collapsed. Those moments so close to an enraged elephant must have been fearful, especially with a light .303 rifle in hand and considering that prior to this occasion Barrie had hardly gone near a wild animal.

Having survived the ordeal, his next concern was his servant, who had disappeared. Barrie called and searched to no avail. He feared that his servant must have been under the dead elephant, but then he looked up into a tree and saw his servant, who was totally speechless. This elephant could only have been a Zambezi Lady, and to make matters worse she was tuskless—those are the ones with the most formidable reputation for unprovoked attacks. Barrie spent the remainder of the night in dread, armed only with the rifle and three remaining rounds of .303 ammunition.

When I got back to Salisbury, I told Fraser I wanted to instruct Ball on elephant and other dangerous field work as I felt he would stagnate where he was. Elephant were raiding lands at Chief Dandawa's in the Zambezi Valley, one of my favorite places, and I decided to take Barrie Ball with me. At the last moment Archie Fraser decided to come with us. At Dandawa's it turned out that Fraser wanted to shoot first.

The elephant crop raiders at Dandawa's were generally easy to hunt, especially if previously undisturbed. We spotted a lone bull in grass short enough for us to look it over and approached it. The grassland was fringed with a thick patch of forest. I had trouble getting Fraser close enough to the elephant so as not to make any mistakes. He did not want to close in to my preferred safe ranges, so I had to give way to his distance of about forty yards. As we closed in, the hair on his forehead started dancing, indicating the stress he was under.

Fraser missed the vital brain shot, and as the bull, partly stunned, lurched forward to take sanctuary in the adjoining forest, Barrie Ball fired a shot into its side. I hoped the bull would turn toward us, but it rushed off and disappeared in the forest in seconds. Fraser, fearful and agitated, now turned on Barrie Ball, shouting and using his authority, wanting to know why Barrie had fired.

I followed the bull to where it had entered the forest. The rest of the party—two trackers, Fraser, and Barrie—eventually arrived. Fraser declined to follow the bull and forbade us to enter the forest, using his authority again to force us to circle the whole forest area in the hope that the bull had run off through it. I told him the bull would stay in the sanctuary of the forest patch, especially since it was wounded. He was adamant, so I circled the area again and found no spoor. The bull was still in the forest.

We came back to our original place. With all this unnecessary indecision, my patience ran out. To get the job done, I instructed the tracker, Manwere, who I knew was courageous, to take the spoor. As he and I disappeared into the forest, I heard Fraser in a raised voice saying something about me being irresponsible and having a wife and children at home. But I had to put him from my mind to concentrate on what lay ahead.

It was toward the end of the rainy season, and the forest was thick and lush, with mottled shade where the sun streaked through the leaf cover. Moving cautiously, we came across the bull lying dead on its side, frothed blood evidencing a lung shot—the shot Barrie Ball had fired. Fraser's shot, because he'd had the shakes, had gone high above the brain into the head-bone formation.

We sat for some time in the deep shade on separate legs of the fallen giant, and Manwere asked me why we had had to follow another man's wounded elephant while the man stayed behind. I knew Manwere well and liked him.

"We do this," I said, "because the elephant may kill some of the tribesmen."

I fired a shot to see what would happen. Some time after that we heard the rest of the party approaching: the other tracker, Kadigedige, in the lead and then Ball and Fraser.

For the next few days we walked from village to village along the banks of the Rukometje sand river. At one place a crop-raiding bull was foraging on the land of an old woman. She was perturbed, as the bull had already flattened half her crop lands. I knew her son, who worked on a farm on the plateau, and it was he who had planted these lands. My intention was to shoot this bull to get rid of him once and for all. Fraser used the word "posterity" in saying we must not shoot this bull.

"Posterity," I said. "That word is the price of a rich man's hunting license."

I put the bull elephant down. The old woman was elated, raising her arms in thanks. But I was trying to do my job in disagreeable company and was grateful when we left the Zambezi Valley.

On another occasion, Fraser and I were down in the Sabi Valley at the river bridge, where there was a hotel. The owner, Mr. Stock, was a nice stamp of an Englishman who had survived a lion mauling. There were many lion skulls on display at the back wall of the bar, and having had more than my share of whiskey, I asked him which lion had mauled him, saying that I wanted to buy it a drink.

"You can't fool me," he said. "I know who you are," and placed a bottle of whiskey in front of me.

He was alarmed because we were about to shoot elephant that were raiding the cultivated lands of the newly established Mutema and Devuli irrigation projects. It was a pity to have to do so: Tourists from the hotel could see the elephant from the bridge bathing in the river in late afternoons.

The elephant had to be killed for the expansion of man's activities. Fraser had come with me to see the setup to report back to the political minister of the day, and to make sure that I did not shoot too many at once since they wanted to do the killing in stages to avoid any bad publicity.

Sitting in some shade, we heard the elephant herd feeding toward us. I entered the riverine forest with Jaubek, a trained tracker from the private farm of Fergus du Toit. Fraser followed, saying he wanted the first shot. As we waited in their path of feeding, Fraser hesitated. By the time he woke up to the reality of a dangerous situation, the elephant had fed up to us and to our sides. He muttered his usual words about what he considered dangerous situations and then said, "What do I do now?"

Because these were semi-tame, unpersecuted elephant, I found it amusing. "Shoot!" I said. "What the hell else?"

Moving cautiously, we came across the bull lying dead on its side, frothed blood evidencing a lung shot. At left is Archie Fraser. Barrie Ball is on the right.

Despite the shakes, he fired and wounded a cow elephant. The herd panicked a little but not much. I knew the shot would be heard at the hotel, so I shot another cow as they came past to disguise the fact that an elephant had been wounded. The herd rushed off but then pulled up—the bush and forest stopped rustling. The tracker was ready to take after the elephant again, but Fraser would not have it, saying he would pursue them later but now wanted to go to the river, which was close by. He removed his shoes and put his feet in the shallow flowing water. It looked inviting, so I did the same.

He had stopped shivering, but as he lit up a cigarette his hands quivered, making the cigarette do the same. It was one of my humorous days, so as I watched him inhaling the smoke I asked if he was enjoying it. He said very much so, under the circumstances.

He endured my continuing gaze for a while and then said, "What is it?"

I replied, "I hope you are enjoying it, really I do, as I have the feeling it is going to be your last cigarette on earth." I was joking and should not have said it, for the effect was electrifying. He point-blank refused to follow the elephant.

"Ian," he said, "you are conditioned to this and seem to enjoy it! You have learned to adjust to danger."

"Not always," I said. "I sometimes have more than my share and need a break."

After a while I showed Fraser a slight rise where there were some family huts. We accompanied him to the huts, and I said that I would come back later.

The tracker, Jaubek, and I moved off through the riverine forest to get in front of the elephant. We heard them coming toward us, and I climbed a large tree pulling the tracker and gun up after me, thinking I might be able to see Fraser's wounded elephant before tackling others. They fed directly below us, and it was grand to see them from above undetected. Their movements were majestic and deliberate. We were standing on a heavy branch when I realized the tracker had taken a bad turn. He looked queer. I wondered how the elephant could affect him this high up. I thought he might collapse, so I put my non-gun hand in front of him and pressed him with my body to the trunk of the tree. I refrained from speaking as the remainder of the herd passed by underneath us. The man had vertigo, and I was lucky not to have lost both him and my rifle.

I got him down, but it took some time before he recovered. He was still not capable of spooring, so I took his position, using him to do the sighting ahead, though I also kept an eye out, no longer trusting his diminished ability. We came up to the elephant again, and I shot one at the tail end of the herd so I could say to those who might enquire that it was the wounded elephant.

Although senior in the Game Department, I usually had no assistance from anyone other than Barrie Ball. I am not writing this in complaint, because I was infinitely better off and safer on my own with good trackers.

In later years, after I moved on from the Game Department, it was amalgamated with the Department of National Parks and Wild Life Management, which definitely had better personnel—the Cetsee brothers, for instance, and Bruce Austen, whom I knew personally.

Bruce had a preference for the .375 rifle, having had much success with it. Once he was sent by Ted Davidson, warden of the Wankie Game Reserve, to destroy a bull elephant that had been wounded by a native commissioner and then abandoned.

The bull had entered a *sinanga (jess)* section of the Gwampa Forest and, the locals told him, had not come out of it. Bruce verified this by circling the area in search of spoor, but it puzzled him because he knew there were no water pans in the area. With a black tracker and a white companion he entered the *sinanga* and found the bull's spoor. Eventually they found water stains on the ground at the base of a large tree. The bull had reached high up into the tree and located water from past rains in a hollow. They continued on the spoor and eventually heard the bull moving ahead. But it also became aware of them, spun around, and rushed them in a true charge, ears back and trunk curled to the chest. With the elephant coming down on him, Bruce placed the first shot at the brain, but it had no effect except that the impact caused the elephant's ears to flop forward and then backward again as it continued its charge.

Bruce's second shot was, as he described it, "two finger widths" below the first one, causing the bull to collapse at close quarters. The first shot had barely missed the top of the brain, and the second, lifesaving shot had barely hit the top section of the brain. This episode is another example of how inadequate medium-caliber rifles are when it comes to shock transmission in heavy bone formation, especially under adverse conditions. A fondness for such calibers can, under bad conditions, be the eventual end of you. In Mozambique, because of their cheapness and availability, there was a preference for 9.3 and 9.5mm rifles, and friends and I jokingly referred to the class of hunters who used them as being lured to the mythical happy hunting grounds.

Bruce Austen was at most times a loner like myself, having no doubt learned about his fellow man the hard way. He was a stout, aggressive hunter who stood his ground, a parks officer who later became the warden of the Wankie National Park. Ted Davison, the previous warden, had built up the park from almost nothing. I knew him as a grand old man and a dedicated conservationist, a man who deserved to be head of the National Parks and Wild Life Management Department.

My case was different: Fraser needed someone to curb the activities of dangerous game, and this is what I was—no longer an ivory hunter but an official killer with authority. All these were simply facts of the times.

A complaint came from the southern lowveld at a place called the Bubye Ranch, which adjoined the great Nuanetsi Ranch. Mr. Nel, a rancher battling to establish himself, had elephant smashing his fences. I was puzzled because two rangers, Rupert Fothergill and Tommy Orford, had just come back from this complaint without success. Knowing these two, I had not bothered to ask why. In the meantime Mr. Nel had complained again.

"Take Barrie Ball with you," Archie Fraser said. "You can check the complaint at Malapati as well." Elephant were raiding croplands there. "Go easy on the native commissioner," he said. "He does not like elephant being shot."

"If I don't shoot a lot of them," I said, "he will keep complaining about them, so why bother—just leave the elephant."

It was unreal—I was assigned to shoot elephant that were breaking fences and raiding crops because two rangers for some reason had failed to do the job—but was limited in the number to be destroyed because of the native commissioner's sentiments!

"Well, anyhow," Archie Fraser said, "see what you can do, but take it easy."

Dealing with the destructive power of dangerous game is a hard undertaking. As I think back on those days, flying to places of complaint would have saved a lot of time and I could have done so much more, but all travel was by Land Rover and it took a day for this journey. We arrived and camped at a dry watercourse in some shade near the homestead. Mr. Nel, the ranch owner, came down to see us. The sun had just gone down as we sat around the fire.

He said, "Which one of you is going to get malaria first?"

He was an Afrikaner and his English was poor, and I did not fully understand him. I asked him to repeat it and then to explain. He said that after his first complaint he had been visited by rangers Tommy Orford and Rupert Fothergill. As they came close to the elephant, Orford kept showing signs of malaria, complaining that he was in no condition to hunt. Fothergill, covering for him, said he needed extra assistance, and so none of them, even after following these elephant, accomplished anything.

They had then returned to Salisbury and Mr. Nel had complained again, and that is why Barrie Ball and I were here now. The story of the two rangers sounded farfetched, and I felt sensitive about it. Life had taught me that Afrikaners have a powerful, stubborn resistance to anything that threatens them or their way of life. The sad part was that these elephant were the last of the Nuanetsi herds, the few survivors that were now to be eliminated to accommodate progress. Man required the meat of cattle for his consumption, and so the elephant had to be destroyed to protect cattle range. This was a common happening as man advanced and robbed the game of its original ranges. It was time to establish more parks and reserves before it was too late, and even then man would eventually want the park and reserve land unless it was totally useless for cattle or man's other needs.

I thought of Mr. Nel's statement about the two rangers and knew there must have been something in it, but the malaria sham seemed ridiculous. Anyhow, we would try to help this landowner.

So it was that the three of us, Ball, Nel, and myself, followed two bull elephant the next day. They moved up a miniature riverine bush forest in a dry watercourse, and finally we heard them ahead.

Nel, watching us closely as we paused, said, "This is the time to get malaria!" I was anxious about closing in on the elephant, so I took no notice of Nel's remarks.

I had previously instructed Barrie Ball not to fire a second barrel at close quarters from a double rifle and always to reload singly in case of a sudden attack at close range. Here, unknown to me, he was about to do the wrong thing. I left him on his own to close in while I stood a short distance behind. I could see an elephant's head, and as Ball approached and tested the wind, he stopped and opened his hand as if to say, "What now?"

On other occasions he had had ample instruction, so I just bowed slightly to show that it was his problem—giving him the stage, so to speak. He paused, then fired, and the bull dropped. In its place another rose from an antheap. Barrie fired the second shot at its shoulder, and the elephant, being close, spun and attacked him. This man had guts, all right, but now he was caught with an empty rifle. He turned slightly to avoid the sight of the bull as it came down on him, and I shot it from where I was standing. Nel was pleased as he had got rid of his elephant menace and had elephant meat at the same time.

Bruce Austen with a cheetah and a female tourist.

We left at midday to reach the village of Malapati. As the sun was setting, we passed into an area where small palm trees had been cut and bowls placed on the trunks to tap the sap. This produced *malala* palm wine, delicious to the taste but intoxicating. I was busy filling water bags with this wine when the owner arrived, and so I paid him for it. I asked him to call us out if the crop-raiding elephant showed up on his lands. Elephant at night would move through the *malala* palm forest gently sucking up the wine from the bowls attached to the trees. In the morning the owners would wake to see they had been robbed.

We camped in a small riverine a few miles farther on. Now that we had shot the "malarial" elephant, we were expected to chase others from the area without seriously disturbing them. In the morning we were informed that cow elephant had raided certain lands so we took the spoor. In addition to water I took a bag of *malala* wine with me. Being frustrated with my impractical instructions, I drank the wine in the course of the morning, and when we located the elephant I was intoxicated. I was supposed to be showing Barrie Ball how to hunt elephant, but because of my condition I did things I was not supposed to do, like shouting at the elephant and enticing them to charge so that I could report that I'd had to shoot to ward off an attack. It was one hell of a way to teach a game ranger.

The next day on our way back, as we slowed to cross a wide, dry watercourse, I heard a European swearing outrageously in the riverbed. His truck had become stuck, and he was in the process of winching it out. The locals assisting him were half-amused and half-afraid, expecting him to explode at any moment. Though he was a missionary, he aggressively asked me what I wanted here, as if it was all his domain. I let him blow steam and then asked him if he belonged to the new generation of swearing, ill-tempered missionaries. He said it was not my business and since I was standing here I should give him a hand.

Barrie and I did so, using our four-wheel-drive rig and the man's winch to pull his vehicle across the soft sand. He invited us to his house close by, where his wife was delighted to try out the new unbreakable crockery they had acquired in the States. She said that locals were always breaking her crockery and now she could frustrate them, possibly enough to break their hearts. She must have had a bad time with them before she bought this new crockery.

This missionary was quite a character. He told me he had a good racket here, living in the bush surrounded by ignorance and teaching the locals the good Lord's works, which he himself did not really believe. When verbally cornered, he would always say, "Mind your own business," and he said just that when I asked him how he had become a missionary. He was quite keen to go hunting, and I knew we would have a good time with him, but as there were no complaints in the area, we moved on back to Salisbury.

In our absence Fraser himself had seen to a complaint of a lone lion having killed cattle on the Elephant Hill ranch owned by a Mr. Culverhouse, an Australian. It was one of the many ranches that had been subdivided from the previously mentioned Rhodesdale Estate. Selous, the hunter, in his book *The Wanderings of an Elephant Hunter* mentions hunting on horseback on Elephant Hill ranch.

I never knew the full circumstances of this event, but Fraser wounded the lion. It then crossed a small river, probably the upper Umniati where one can wade across. Fraser, although he had good trackers, did not follow it up, leaving the wounded beast and returning to Salisbury.

He was later sent cheap miniature statues of lion with red ink marks indicating the wounds he had inflicted. These presents kept arriving for some time until he eventually suspected me of sending them. I had never met the ranch owner, Culverhouse, but these presents most probably came from him or some associates involved. Always outspoken, I eventually questioned Fraser about the incident and asked him how he was qualified to hunt lion. The mere fact that he had failed to follow up the wounded animal, especially as he had the capable and armed tracker Kadigedige with him, called his abilities into question.

In case the reader should get the impression that such events were mere clashes of personalities, they were not; rather they were events leading to disillusionment and disappointment. In its initial stages, the Game Department had failed to take advantage of the excellent men available in Rhodesia to be trained as game rangers. With these characters the Game Department could have emerged as the best in Africa. This opportunity had not been allowed to get off the ground. There were many other game-control incidents, but my pen power is running out.

On the horizon loomed the spectacular events leading up to the building of the great Kariba Dam on the Zambezi River. For one, the Matonga tribe was to be moved onto higher ground beyond the reaches of the rising waters, to be resettled in other wilderness areas such as the beautiful, unspoiled valleys of Kariangwe, Lubu, and Umbelele. The Matongas, resident on both sides of the Zambezi River, had been instructed not to grow food because the government of the day would be moving them. One result was human suffering caused by stupidity and ignorance. Some of the Matongas were starving, and children in particular were suffering from dysentery. It was reported that they were grinding grass seeds for food. In view of this, it was suggested that I, the trackers Kadigedige and Manwere, and a Dr. Parker should be parachuted into the area. The doctor would attend to the sick, and I would hunt elephant for the starving people. This was the information we had at the time.

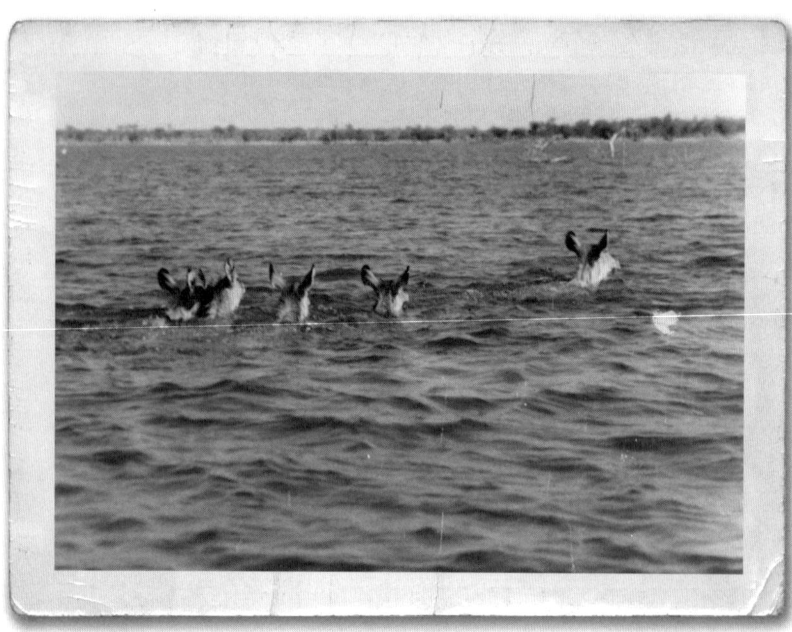

We saw animals swimming in the rising river, some of them exhausted and sinking.

The Sengwa and Umi Rivers were in flood, making it impossible to go overland. I was afraid to parachute down through the trees, not wanting a broken leg or other injury and fearful of jumping from an aircraft into nothingness. The only solution lay in tackling the rising floodwaters of the Zambezi River, and I looked forward to it with pleasure. At the Kariba Gorge great floods were racing over the cofferdam, the first step in building the huge Kariba Dam, causing the Zambezi above it to spread out to a width of about eight miles. We took to the waters above the cofferdam in a boat powered by an outboard motor, and it brought nostalgic feelings. Some of my old hunting grounds were flooded, and we were now traveling over them on the water. I thought of Rice, the plucky headman; the tracker, Chakadama; Juda, the medicine man; and others I had hunted with, all forced to take up residence elsewhere. The swollen river above Kariba had already covered some hill land while other hills still protruded, their tops visible and wild animals stranded on some.

Unless the game animals were chased from the Zambezi Valley, they would be drowned by the thousands. Only the cofferdam had been built thus far, and there was plenty of time to drive the game to safety before the main dam wall, which was under construction, would eventually raise the water levels enormously and create the great Lake Kariba. We boated over what had been the village of Sambakaruma, about eight miles upstream of the Zambezi's confluence with the Sanyati River. Here, traveling the wide waters, one could see and feel the deadly disaster that would occur if these animals were not hunted and driven away from the areas to be flooded. Why shouldn't that happen? That was what the tsetse-fly campaigns had always been about, and it could easily be accomplished at the cost of issuing permits to the public. Unlike the tsetse-fly campaigns, this hunting could be justified, and even if one-quarter of the animals were shot, the remaining three-quarters would be driven from the flooding valley and thus be saved. I wondered why this solution had not been thought of as yet. After this expedition I brought these facts to the attention of the authorities.

We occasionally saw animals swimming to escape the rising waters, some of them exhausted and sinking, never to breathe again. A lot of plankton or algae was developing from the rotting vegetation, causing the water to become slightly murky. Once we came across a herd of sable antelope clustered together on a small rise surrounded by water. Occasionally one seemed to jump back into the center of the herd. On coming close we witnessed water disturbance, indicating that tigerfish were attracted to their rotting feet. They were in bad condition, and I told the trackers to shoot them all as they were doomed anyway.

Our destination was a small river, the Sibilo Bilo, where it ran into the Zambezi about fifty miles upstream from Kariba. Within about ten miles of this place our outboard motor seized. It was late evening, and, now powerless, we floated with the moving waters. Though the cofferdam was about forty miles downriver, I panicked at the thought of going over it, for the boat and all our equipment would be smashed and we would be killed. No one could survive the leaping waters as they passed over the cofferdam to continue into the Kariba Gorge. In the semi-gloom we managed to land on a hillock with scrubby trees. It was at least a temporary shelter from the dark waters.

During the night we distinctly heard the grunts of a leopard, and knowing that this might be an island of starvation, we kept the fires going and took turns in keeping watch.

At dawn we saw a large barge floating downriver toward us and thought our problem would be solved. The tracker fired a few shots to draw attention to our plight, and even at that distance we could see everybody suddenly paddling with hands and planks toward us. As the barge was passing us, someone managed to catch a rope on some partly submerged trees, and we assisted by pulling the barge to shore. On board was Rex Bean, the labor recruiter from Kariba, who was delivering a large load of maize to the starving Matongas. He was not the humourous type and was in a bad mood. Leaks had developed where the inboard motor was mounted on a frame at the bottom of his large wooden boat. He could not use the motor, because the vibrations caused the leaks to worsen.

I offered him something to drink as we sat around the early morning fire, and between anxiety and the mosquitoes he reached for a bottle of whiskey. He had a drink, and then the barge shifted in the darkness. In trying to maintain his balance he dropped the bottle, which fell between the duck-boards. He reached hastily to retrieve it in the darkness, but the bottle had broken and he cut his fingers. I had a medical kit and patched him up.

The Zambezi River above Kariba was turning into a lake.

So here we were, stranded with one small boat and a large barge on top of a little hill island, a miserable place of scrubby trees and stony ground. I told Rex there was a leopard here, probably hiding and waiting for him to fall asleep. He said leopard didn't scare him, and he would sleep on his barge anyway. I told him the leopard was so hungry that it would tightrope-walk to prod him. I was trying to get him out of his gloom.

"I have a gun," he said, "and if you don't shoot it, I will."

We sent the trackers off, and they shot the leopard and hauled it into our camp. It was in such a starved and miserable condition that I told them to throw it into the water. We spent a few days here hoping for the sight of a boat, but nothing happened. We would now have to drift downriver, but we all were afraid of the waters roaring over the cofferdam, where the whole river converged. I had previously seen it from the heights of hills overlooking the gorge, and the turbulence was frightening.

We cut adrift in the early morning, our two boats connected by a length of rope. Lounging on the barge, I was surprised to learn that Rex could not swim, not even dog paddle, which most tribesmen could do. Drifting in sheer freedom, our morale was high, but we knew it would be replaced by fear as we neared the Kariba Gorge. As we basked in the sun, I discussed our plight with the trackers. They all preferred dangerous game to the rising waters, but unfortunately there was no option.

We sat well above the waters on maize sacks, and all seemed well as we moved with the current. The crew had a flat piece of iron and made a small fire for cooking. For the moment we had all the luxuries of a water expedition.

I was for fighting the current, paddling to reach the west bank. If we could get out of the main currents, we could reach Siavonga. I had walked this country in my poaching days and remembered that the Sanyati River, at its confluence with the Zambezi, tended to influence the larger river, causing calmer waters along the west bank. Rex would not have it, saying we must stay to the east side of the flowing mass. This was risky: If the Sanyati River was also in flood, we could be caught in its flow as well.

The Zambezi River, surging over the cofferdam.

I later realized that I should have used my own small boat and crossed the currents to reach the west bank. We had time, for it would take a day or more of drifting to reach the gorge ahead of us. However, we were failing in the battle to get the barge to the east side of the currents, and I advised Rex to dump the maize. The resistance, I said, to the heavily loaded barge was too great and the craft was too deep in the water.

There was opposition to this suggestion, so I put it to him squarely: "If you want us to stick together, dump at least most of the maize and get some rowing strength from your staff or everything else will be in vain. If not, I will try to save myself and my own men by cutting my boat adrift."

Finally things began to happen. Most of the maize was dumped, and it floated along with us for some time. Some of the men looked longingly at it, for it represented years of food to them. These men did not seem to grasp the danger we were drifting into. In such cases one must "rule by force and fear," and so I drove them on the paddles.

The miles passed and eventually we could see that we were crossing the currents. The east bank came closer, and we could see the Matussadona Mountains in the far distance beyond a large, flat land mass. We could not go too close to the shoreline because without power and steering we might crash into the partly submerged forest there. We stayed close enough so that if necessary we could catch onto one of the many half-submerged trees—provided we came onto them at the right angle. Otherwise the strong current would crash us into them. Slowly the mountains of Kariba came closer, and then we heard the distant roar—it was the whole of the Zambezi River surging over the cofferdam. Now the full realization of our peril took over, and a mixture of fear and hope showed on the faces of the men.

Some said they had rowed as hard as they could and there was nothing else they could do—it was not their fault if we went over the cofferdam. At this stage I was past caring about anybody except myself and the two trackers, Manwere and Kadigedige. Other than danger from crocodiles, I was not unduly worried about myself—I was a strong swimmer, and even with the .450 rifle tied to my back I knew I would make it. But the thought of losing these courageous, faithful trackers worried me.

Then I thought of the outboard motor; even if it had seized, we should surely be able to start it again and get at least a short burst of speed at a critical time. We pulled the small boat in and the trackers and I occupied it, tying the rope from its storm to the front of the barge. I tested the motor, and it started; then I cut it. The roar of the water at the cofferdam was close now as we came under the swelling influence of the Sanyati River where it poured into the Zambezi. One could feel the change in the flow, and I realized the Zambezi's influence caused a slowing where the two river currents joined. About four hundred yards downstream, across the Sanyati's current, the banks were spread in forest trees, mostly submerged but some partly above water. I shouted at Rex, who knew what it meant. Then I started the motor, took up the rope slack, and opened the throttle. We had a burst of power that took us about two hundred yards across the Sanyati before the motor seized. Momentum carried us to the half-submerged trees, which caught the rope and brought us to a halt. As we swung around in the current, we knew we were saved. People were watching from the bank, and in less than an hour a boat came out to pull our boats to the shoreline.

The trackers and I were still intact as a hunting unit except for the motor, which we loaded into my Land Rover (I had left it at Kariba). A new road had just been surveyed and supplies of frozen meat were arriving for the Kariba project, so the hunting of elephant to feed the construction workers had ceased.

The only place to get the motor repaired was Salisbury, 250 miles away. I drove there and returned within days with a motor, and we tackled the waters of the Zambezi again. This time all went well, and on reaching the Sibilo Bilo River we camped a little upstream to get away from the mosquitoes that had steadily increased in numbers with the rising waters. Fish and bird life had become abundant.

In the morning I sent the two trackers to see Chief Mola, about eight miles off, requesting his presence, mostly to determine the situation of the starving people. They came back in late afternoon without the chief and told me he had said, "If the white man wants me, he must come to my village." I had been warned by the authorities in Salisbury that there was political agitation in the Matonga tribe, and I was not to revert to violence. So the next day I put my pride in my pocket and took supplies to Chief Mola's village. It was toward the end of the rains, and all the leaves and grasses were now brilliantly green.

As we entered the village, we came across a group of men with Chief Mola, who sat on a low, carved wooden stool. I walked up and greeted him, and he spat on the ground at my feet. Under normal circumstances one good kick would have removed his teeth for life and put him out of action, but knowing the circumstances, I took his abuse. I attempted to question him on conditions, but he became more and more abusive, saying the whites had caused his people to reach a point of starvation and so on. He even refused to tell us the whereabouts of the elephant so that we could help feed his people. I took the initiative and told Manwere to examine the grain bins that stood above the ground on supports. From the very tops he pulled out handfuls of maize to show me. If the people were starving, this bastard certainly was not. When questioned on this, he spat on the ground again. I was sorely tempted to fly into him but struggled to restrain myself because of my superiors back in Salisbury.

This discontent had been instigated from the west bank, across the Zambezi River. It was the first indication here of the rise of African nationalism that was eventually to follow. To me, most politicians, black or white, were subtle liars and schemers, exploiting the aspirations and fears of people. I personally did not give a damn who was in power as long as they ruled intelligently, justly, and efficiently.

I said to Chief Mola, "Your people are starving—hunt with us, or are you a hyena?"

More spitting. I then went into his pedigree, and he rose in anger and said, "White dog, you will not hunt here." So that's what it was about: He had food and was willing to let others suffer for political reasons.

I felt I had the pulse of the place now, so we walked off up the Sibilo Bilo River. We saw tribesmen here and there in settlements, but no one knew the whereabouts of elephant. It was obvious they had been instructed not to help. We came across cultivated lands, some with good stands of maize hardening on the cob. I was beginning to doubt the reports of starvation. The owners of these fields were unresponsive as to the whereabouts of elephant.

At sunset we came to a few huts on a rise with a well-swept yard and chickens here and there. This was the home of Nilos, a young Batonga tribesman of good physical build and manner.

I asked him outright if there were any starving people among the Matongas, and he said, "Yes, many stupid and lazy ones who did not grow crops." He said the elephant were farther up the Sibilo Bilo watercourse. He was not unfriendly. I asked him for details, and he explained that instructions had come across the Zambezi River for the people not to grow crops, and the innocent fools who had followed these directions were starving.

We camped that night in this pleasant spot. Around the fire I told him of how I'd had to condescend to Chief Mola's attitude and about our need to find elephant. Nilos was an individualist by nature and cared little for Chief Mola. He said he would show us where the elephant sometimes stayed.

In the morning, guided by Nilos, we took our gear and moved farther upriver and then away from all settlements. Eventually we found the spoor of a large mixed herd, including some large bulls. We followed through forest, scrub, and small *dambos* of high grasses. Here the animals crossed to watering places in low-lying areas. There was other game but nothing impressive in numbers, and some were shy and timid. The elephant eventually entered what Nilos called the "*sekete jess* bush," referred to in the local language as the *sinanga* thickets. The elephant took refuge on the fringes of the *sinanga*; thank goodness they did not penetrate far into these dense thickets or we would have been involved in another close-quarters wars. They eventually moved off to hills we could see in the distance and were about an hour ahead of us.

Then we came upon an unusual happening. A leopard had caught and killed an impala ram and had started feeding on it under some overhanging branches. It was completely in our view, and I thought it would drag off the carcass, but it stood in defiance of us. We paused, and I indicated that we should move around to avoid any confrontation. At that moment Nilos, the Batonga guide, placed his spear under his right arm, thrust it forward with the left hand, and moved ahead to approach the leopard.

For a moment I thought it a mad and stupid act. He slowed as the leopard snarled, warning him. But he kept moving ahead, poised for action. He got so near that I saw little chance of assisting him were the cat to make a rush. The closer he got, the fiercer the leopard became, its ears flattened and fangs exposed, emitting rasping growls. I marvelled at how a man could make such a foolish move on so fast an animal for the prize of impala meat.

Man or beast had to give way, and on viewing Nilos's slow, tense advance it did not seem as if it was going to be the man. If the leopard charged, it would rush into the spear—if the spear was properly poised in the last critical moments. Then, suddenly, the cat turned and slunk off. These had been tense moments for us all, but Nilos did not consider it much of a feat. I learned that he had done this before with isolated lion as well. I believe it, for the leopard is the more dangerous of the two predators. I watched Nilos use bush *tambo* to tie the dead impala to a branch, and he and Manwere carried it on the elephant spoor that Kadigedige was following.

Within the hour the spoor became fresh, so they placed the impala high in the fork of a shaded tree. We were now free of it and moved forward cautiously. The elephant went between two close hills into what looked like a small valley completely enclosed by hills. Here there was dense scrub and good feeding. We followed, then moved up the slope of the nearest hill, where we could see their backs and heads as they spread out to feed. We were safer here than below.

Out of danger for the moment, we sat watching in low, sparse grass, stunted because of the poor topsoils of the hillside. It was pleasant to see the animals and hear their low roars communicate their delight at being surrounded by so much good feed. The wind conditions were right, and occasionally, in openings of vegetation, we could see young calves at their mother's front feet feeding on leaves, their quick little trunks whipping here and there as if it was a game of sorts. The domestic scene caused my mind to wander.

I thought my ivory-hunting days with Faanie, Katasoro, Jeffrey, and the many other rare, admirable trackers of the wilds. I pictured them all with their individual characteristics. Were their lifestyles still the same? Were any dead? Since joining the Game Department I had lost touch with my old companions, and amidst the encroaching influences of civilization I missed the company and steadfastness of my associates of the past and the wild country we had traveled.

Mozambique, I felt, would have changed little, but here in Southern Rhodesia the changes were staggering and their effects on the game disastrous. Civilization was penetrating everywhere, even here in the great Sebungwe, the last isolated stronghold of the wilderness.

Politics had penetrated the wilds, causing me to hunt and kill elephant because of ideology. I was in reality a pawn of the Game Department. Did this realization mean that my attitudes were maturing, or were these elephant calves getting to me? Perhaps it was both. It was hard to picture these same calves, grown one day, coming down through the thick stuff to try to eliminate me, as had happened so often in the past. They seemed so innocent, feeding and playing, but if man allowed them to mature, they would be hemmed into ever decreasing land, competing for food. The proximity of man would mean they would inevitably break fences and raid crops, and then the government could destroy them, for their ivory would represent revenue. In the future elephant will likely be allowed to grow up only in parks and reserves for man to view at his pleasure—and there they will be annually culled to suit their restricted areas and vegetation.

The big bwanas don't care for the Matongas, but they don't want any other country's influence here, and so I rose and moved into the thick scrub in full leaf and started killing the elephant. These elephant, trapped in the little hill-surrounded valley, could only rush out the way they had come, having to pass me where I stood on the higher ground and running the gauntlet of my rifle power. They paid a heavy toll.

In all this excitement, Nilos was moving around oblivious of the masses of elephant, which at times were only yards from us. Fascinated, he was picking up the expended cartridge cases as they were ejected from my rifles. These were valued by the locals as snuff containers. Nilos had shown great courage in the presence of leopard, lion, and now elephant—it seemed to make no difference to him. He was obviously born to this type of life. Later I tried to incorporate him into the Game Department. He refused but said he would always be available in the Sebungwe district should I come back. He so reminded me of Zaratina in his ways, and I later concluded that he would never work for any organization unless absolutely necessary.

I was becoming more disillusioned with the Game Department. As long as I had the ability to destroy dangerous game, I was going to be utilized for this purpose continuously. This last shoot was particularly devastating. I sat on the rise viewing the destruction. There were more than enough dead elephant for the starving people. When I was an ivory hunter, I thought that game numbers were inexhaustible. The advance of civilization was proving me wrong.

Already some hill land had been covered by the rising waters while other hills still protruded, their tops visible and wild animals stranded on some.

It made me think the best tracker in Rhodesia, that little man Zaratina. He was without any education but had vision, wisdom, and unbiased common sense. He had refused to join the Game Department, saying it was a refuge for privileged jackals from what he had seen of it. And he had challenged me by asking what it was that had influenced me to join the department. In the wilds he cared not a whit for any man's influences, opinions, or authority.

"Stay wild," I said to him at the time. "That way, disturbing thoughts won't reach you."

A few days after this latest hunt there was hardly any evidence of elephant having been shot, for the Matongas came from far and wide to remove the meat, bones, and skin. On the last day, to my amusement, Chief Mola came past with his attendants, wanting to know why I had not reserved a dead elephant for him. I told them the hyena always follow in the wake of the lion and that he should look and see what he could scavenge. He then instructed me to shoot a buffalo for him. I agreed but said, "Only on the condition that it is just you and me, and you do the tracking." He refused, muttering something about hunting being beneath him, and moved off in a state of discontent.

Our trip back down the Zambezi River was pleasant, and in many places we moved over the flooded forests, cruising amongst the trees for many miles. It reminded me of film scenes I had seen of the Okefenokee Swamp and the Everglades in America. Halfway down the river we met the new native commissioner, Mr. Pitou, from Kariba, also cruising amongst the trees in a boat. We tied up to a tree, and I told him of the Matonga people's plight upriver. We discussed other matters as well, and then we left him to move on down the river to Kariba.

En route we tried to spend a night on the top of an island hill with starving impala and other antelope but were driven off by the creeping insects, scorpions, centipedes, and snakes. We had to push off in the boat again and in the dark landed on the east bank near the Matussadona Mountains. In the morning we clearly saw this range and walked inland to view the game, then took to the waters again.

On this second day, our last on the river, we saw many stranded animals. I had previously pointed this problem out to higher authority and on my return would do so again, hoping that it would eventually have some effect. It was afternoon when we landed at Kariba. We were now unconcerned about going over the roaring waters of the cofferdam below us as we had the power of the outboard motor.

On landing we packed quickly to get away from the bustling activity and motored out of town, passing a makeshift hut where a queue of men waited. It was the place of one of the Kariba whores—another indication that civilization was here to stay.

About four miles from Kariba, on our way back to Salisbury, I sighted some men on a hillside. As we got closer I saw the bulk of an animal lying in the short scrub, so I pulled up to investigate and walked up to them. An entomologist had shot a rhino. I was puzzled since he wasn't the big-game hunting type and no one seemed interested in the carcass other than the horns, which had been hacked out. I asked him why he had killed it. I was taken aback when he told me he required the ticks from its anus. They had collected these insects using tweezers and placed them in a bottle of preservative.

"You shot the rhino for its ticks? " I asked.

"Yes," he said. "We will send them to England, as they have requested them."

In Africa I had heard of and seen all types of hunting and hunters, but to shoot a rhino for ticks was something new and beyond my understanding. I asked him about the rhino horns, and he said he had removed them with the sanction of the Game Department. I knew it was true but did not like it. It was a great leap from starving primitives who had to hunt for food to this "civilized" act of securing ticks! It was unfathomable! What kind of world was developing around me? I feared that I might succumb and find myself conforming to it.

Back in Salisbury there was news of two people having been killed by elephant. A black man had been cycling on the Victoria Falls road across the Gwaai corridor. He apparently saw an elephant, fell from his bicycle, and ran off down an elephant path. The elephant ran on a parallel path, and where the two paths met, the elephant picked him up in its trunk and smashed him. The other case involved a white prospector, Victor Stroebel, and occurred in the Mtoko area where there was a large tsetse-fly game-extermination program. Stroebel, armed with a .375 magazine rifle, had tracked a family herd of elephant in semi-open forest country. He fired, they turned on him, and they threw him into a deep rock cleft, killing him. I visited the site and concluded that his rifle may have been loaded with softnose ammunition because he failed to stop the cows. These elephant were so angry that they snapped off some of their tusks trying to get at him where he lay dead on the rocks.

To add to all this, a tsetse-fly officer who was mentally depressed over a romantic association shot himself near the border post of Nama Panda in the same area. I had met him a few times but did not know him well.

At this stage I started to do a game survey on crown land along the Lundi River. I came across a man sitting in a large American-type station wagon and blazing away at a herd of impala antelope. I pulled up next to him and asked what he was doing.

"Shooting game for labour rations," he said, "on an owner's game license."

I asked him how he could use an owner's game license when he was shooting on crown land. Annoyed because I believed he was lying, I demanded his name and address. He said it was Stockhill, M.P. I thought at first that M.P. were his initials, but they meant he was a member of the Rhodesian Parliament. Anyhow, he told me to come along and see for myself that this was no longer crown land. A mile away, near the Lundi River, bulldozers were clearing bush and trees to make way for irrigation projects. When I had left Salisbury the day before, this was crown land, but here in front of me at least fifty acres had already been cleared, meaning it was no longer crown land. I did the game survey for what it was worth, knowing that the wild animals would eventually be eliminated as the land was taken away from them, even if they found temporary sanctuary in adjoining areas. It turned out that this area became highly developed, affording employment for many people, but it was the end of a prolific wildlife population.

Numerous other events angered and saddened me. All the evidence pointed to the elimination of game in the steady advance of man's needs. It was like a great wave in the distance, looming over the land. The lucky animals would be those that were allowed to survive on privately owned land, national parks, and game reserves. But in the future even the national parks could go.

This wonderful world I knew was dying, so it made no difference whether I was in or out of the Game Department. I had made up my mind to resign as I no longer wanted to be part of it.

My resignation meant that I would become divorced from the game world, and that thought deeply disturbed me. The great pity in life is that what you have learned mostly dies with you—there is no finer teacher than experience. But I also had to accept that endings are a natural part of the cycle of life, for without them there would be no evolution.

In the beginning was the hunt. It helped man evolve into a state of intelligence. Fishing was man's first hunt and will probably be his last. We have evolved from hunting to herding, fishing to farming, providing humans with ever more food, and now the human population seemed uncontrollable. I knew the time would come when the wild Zambezi River, like the American Colorado River, would be no more, and the adventurous life associated with it would fade beyond all memories. Man is concerned that he may perish from the face of this earth, but I concluded that everything would perish before man. In the hunting life I had managed to stay alive, but I knew that eventually time would become my enemy, and I had visions of a gray-bearded, weather-beaten old man approaching with his scythe to cut the grass from under my feet.

What worried me most was the fate of the Zambezi Valley, particularly the area between the Kariba and Mupata Gorges. Having lived there, I realized that the annual flooding of the Zambezi River would be restricted, its floodwaters held in check by the massive Kariba Dam wall. Even if the floods were too great to contain, the floodgates could be opened to allow some water to escape. Never again would the Zambezi River below the dam wall have its impressive strength to flood the banks and nourish the swamps as it had done for millions of years.

Many of the wild animals of the valley depended on this annual flooding for their food and water in the dry winters. Without the floodwaters, the life-giving green vegetation would not last through the Months of the Sun.

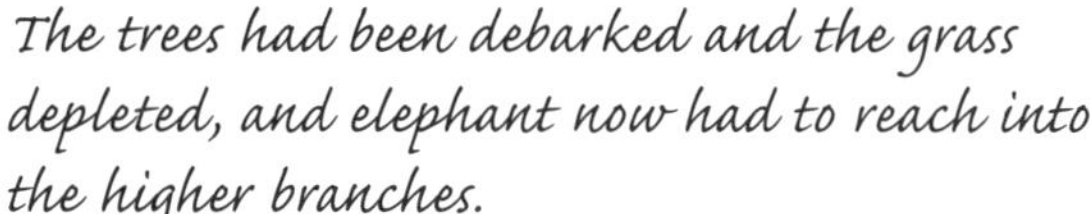

The trees had been debarked and the grass depleted, and elephant now had to reach into the higher branches.

The dark spot shows where there was a water pan. Eighteen years of elephant overabundance destroyed this former forest.

Because of my wild background I could visualize the great floodplains, such as Nemana and particularly the swamps, slowly drying up until nothing edible was left. The game would be forced to destroy its own environment and move on to cull another area. And what if man needed to irrigate? I could not imagine the massive waters of the Zambezi River remaining untapped.

If the great Zambezi Valley with its wild atmosphere, abundant game, and warm climate could be utilized for tourists and provide a financial return, it could survive. Otherwise I pictured it like the west bank in Northern Rhodesia, where all the animals had already been eliminated, almost as if they had never existed. Even the trees there had quickly disappeared, making the land look foreign.

I had to live in hope that the great Zambezi Valley would be preserved for future generations. But in the long run, as populations and poverty grew, and pressures for land intensified, wildlife would pay the price until finally it became scarce and eventually exterminated.

These were my thoughts in 1958, the year of my resignation from the Game Department. The building of the Kariba Dam created a lake approximately 120 miles long by 20 wide, causing the deaths of thousands of wild animals from drowning and starvation. Some attempts were made to rescue animals, but the effect was insignificant. The publicity about the Kariba Dam put Southern Rhodesia on the map of Africa and the world. But the game animals paid the price with their lives.

So much has happened since then. A long drawn-out bush war resulted in Rhodesia becoming Zimbabwe. And, of course, most of the casualties were civilians. Wild animals were blown up by land mines, some lying helpless for long periods to die of shock, pain, and loss of blood. Elephant in particular had legs and shoulders blown off. Military personnel were at times reluctant to shoot them because the sound would have given their positions away to the enemy. Mines must be the cheapest soldiers in the world.

Game in the eastern districts seem to be holding their own, but in most places neither the game nor the vegetation is as impressive as before. The great swamps no longer exist. They now look like desolate places with almost no vegetation. The country no longer has the same game-carrying capacity, so the animals must be culled to protect the depleted environment. But it is still a place of interest and has amenities for modern tourists. Foreigners in particular think it is wonderful, so different from their own world.

I often, these days, canoe down the gorges and open waters of the Zambezi River. Ever conscious of its charm, I stop at places that evoke nostalgic memories. Usually armed with a spear, I go inland illegally to view the game and places of old human contacts. The valley is now run under strict control by the Department of National Parks and Wild Life Management.

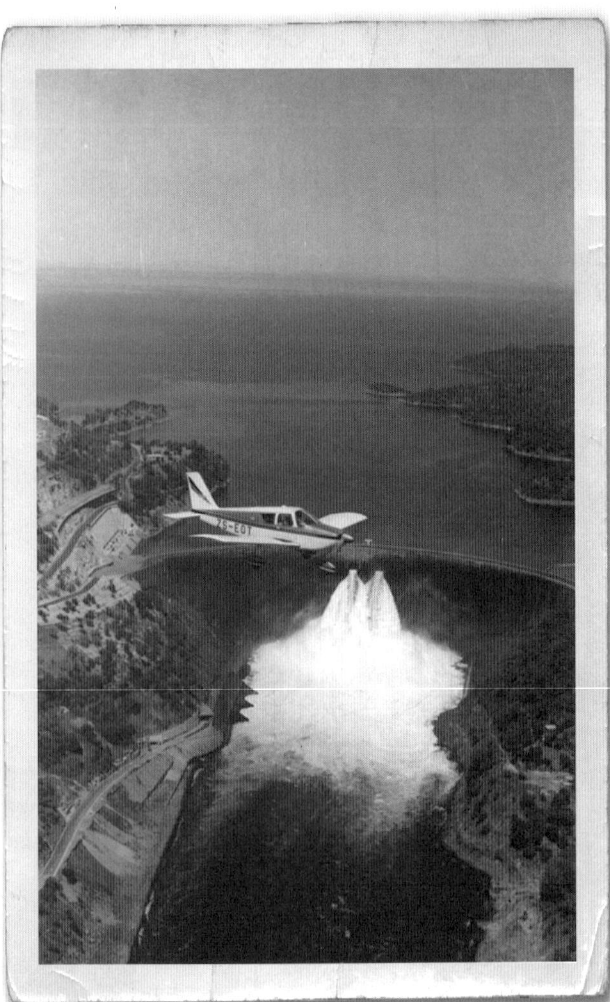
The swamp conditions had deteriorated because of the building of the Kariba Dam upstream.

Walking the banks and inland, in the influence of the riverine forests, I notice that the vegetation in places is seriously depleted, but the land has much the same atmosphere and comforting warmth of climate that it used to have, and the now-protected game is sometimes plentiful. My visits bring back memories of places, people, and events when I roamed freely as an ivory hunter. And so I come to the end of a great era of freedom, excitement, and the privilege of having lived wild.

In 1987 I accompanied my daughter Cheryl, her husband Michael, and their son Gary from Chirundu to Mudzeemo's old village site. The Chirundu Hills has been developed into a township, and throughout the Zambezi-Kariba tourist area the tsetse fly has greatly declined, a result of research and a scientific approach to the problem. We reached Chief Mudzeemo's old village site but found no traces of it except for a flat, red, sandstone maize grinder that my daughter found partly buried. We retrieved it.

Armed with a spear, we walked through the area of previous occupation, viewing the wild animals. Because we were ill-armed and this had always been a favorite place for lion, I was cautious.

The infamous Zambezi Ladies had disappeared, and this place was now a controlled hunting area. We came across a herd of buffalo and some lion in their wake. The lion were no doubt trying to get the buffalo to run off so that they could flank them for killing, but the buffalo remained together and stationary. The lion grunted, but the herd remained compact.

Indeed the Mana Pools area is so overgrazed that elephant debark the musango trees and sometimes even eat out the insides the massive baobab trees until they collapse.

Michael reacted to these snorts by grabbing the spear from me. I found it amusing that this relative of mine was suddenly overtaken by the primitive instinct to survive. Young Gary did not like the setup and said, "Do we have to be here at all?" We circumvented the buffalo herd and returned to Chirundu, crossing what had once been the Chipandahoure Swamps, now a level plain with occasional scant, struggling vegetation.

One of the factors contributing to the possible survival of the Zambezi Valley is that Zimbabwe is isolated in terms of hard currency, and foreign tourists supply this badly needed revenue. All manner of tourists and a lot of our own residents enjoy these wilds—from the Zambezi Valley to the shores of the giant Kariba Lake right up to Victoria Falls, where they ride the rough "white waters" of the gorges. Indeed much of this land is a paradise.

It pleases me now, as I push the years, to see much of the wilds still intact. Considering how small the world is becoming in terms of man's ever-increasing numbers, I feel it is unfortunate that so many people do not know of or will never have the opportunity to enjoy this wild wonderland of the great Zambezi Valley.

The Kariba Dam greatly disrupted the land. Today it would help if minor dams were built at the base of the escarpment to hold back and collect flood waters from rains on the plateau before they cascade to the Zambezi Valley floor. It would be a relatively inexpensive and practical undertaking to dam such narrow rivers as the Sharu, Chikomba, Reefa, Dekete, Chimba, Nyakasanga, Chimutsi, Musekera, Kamchara, Rukometje, Chewuyu, Chitake, and Chewori. There are ideal dam sites on all these rivers, which flood during the rainy season on the adjacent higher plateau country and wend their way down to the Zambezi Valley floor, where most of them peter out and eventually disappear under the sandy riverbeds in the heat of the valley. Capturing their waters would certainly draw large numbers of wild animals away from overgrazed places and back toward the escarpment base and its lush vegetation.

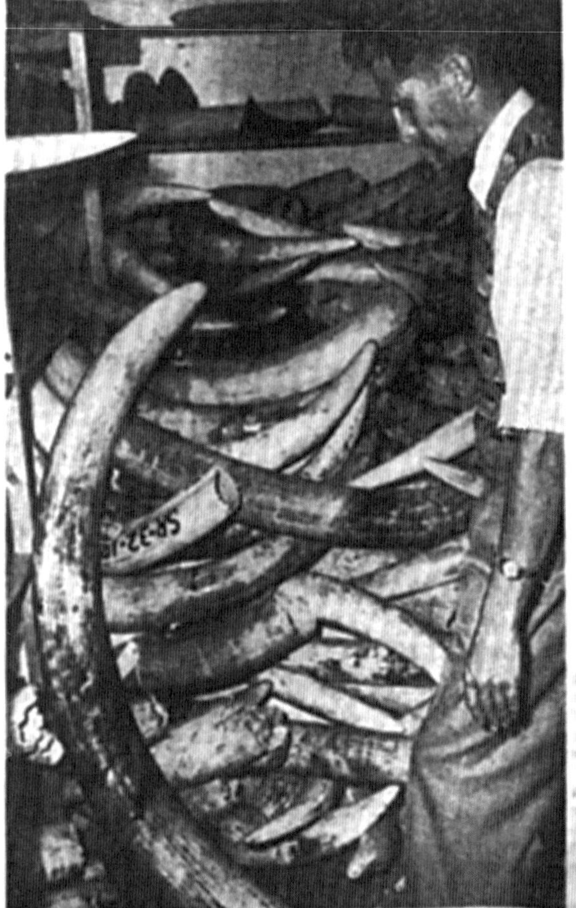
Ivory For Sale

A TWO-YEAR stockpile of ivory and rhino horn resulting largely from tsetse fly control and game control, is to be sold by the Southern Rhodesia Government. This picture shows Mr. Ian Nations, game ranger, examining part of the pile.

The proximity of man would mean elephant would inevitably break fences and raid crops, and then the government could destroy them for their ivory.

About eight years ago I was asked to write an article on Mana Pools. I described it as a dying area, now fed only by rainfall and having a restricted game-carrying capacity. Indeed, the Mana Pools area is so overgrazed that the elephant debark the *musango* trees and sometimes even eat out the insides of the massive baobab trees until they collapse. Prior to the building of the dam, when the great floodwaters of the mighty Zambezi River annually renewed the land, this was unheard of.

There are plans to build another dam in the Mupata Gorge, which would flood the Mana Pools area. Because of the area's unique beauty, this has become an emotional issue. But in my mind the whole complex will continue to deteriorate without the great Zambezi River floods.

Maybe they will not build this dam, for there are alternative sites in the Batoka Gorge below Victoria Falls. If the new dam is ever built at Mupata Gorge, it will back-flood the area, probably causing much overfeeding on the shoreline grass, as has developed at the Kariba Dam. Unfortunately the new dam would also inundate the opposite bank in Zambia in what was the country of Chief M'Baruma, an alluring place of wild beauty with mountains rising in the background.

Sometimes, in the company of starry-eyed, oversensitive, unrealistic people, I am asked if I have regrets. Yes, like most humans I have regrets, but not always the kind they think I should have. Even today I come alive at the thought of tracking dangerous beasts through thick bush or swamps, and I often long for the great silences of the dense *jess*.

Today I am deeply disturbed to witness the ruthless destruction of elephant herds by helicopters in radio contact with marksmen on the ground. While the elephant are in a state of frightened confusion, the marksmen open fire, annihilating the herds from the sides in a terrific barrage. The bullets strike the elephant at all angles, and the animals, from the largest to the smallest, are totally unable to defend themselves. An occasional cow with some fight left may attempt to charge, but only to defend her young.

In the confusion of gunfire coordinated by modern science, the elephant succumb in a pitiful state of total confusion. It is man gone to war against elephant. They call it culling. How inoffensive that sounds. But it clearly reflects civilized man in his greed for land. In the long run he will want even the limited ranges that wild animals at present frequent.

Because of my background I see further than the niceties of social occasions. I wonder how many people will believe that elephant in national parks are "culled" in large numbers away from the tourist areas. There is, of course, no publicity about the culls because man wants to hide his crimes against nature.

Now there emerges a new scientific man called a Conservationist. I don't envy him his task. His information and assessments are given over to those who decide how many elephant herds are to be culled, where, and when. The elephant continue to breed despite their restricted environment, so it is an ongoing process. Man the predator wants the land. Even the peasant farmer cares not whether wildlife survives; indeed, he prefers to slaughter it for food. To him wild animals, especially elephant, do not belong. His needs are to get food and to procreate, and so he has no sentiment for the intriguing beauty of nature. We might do the same in his position.

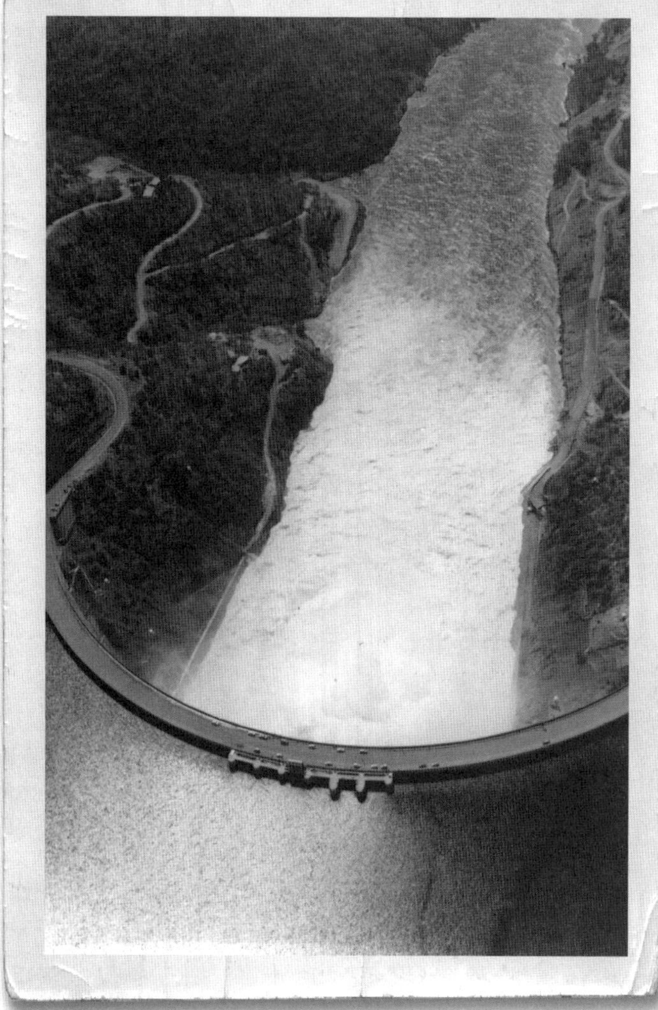

The annual flooding of the Zambezi River would be restricted, its floodwaters held in check by the massive Kariba Dam wall.

When you consider the mentality of our modern African thinking—our hunger for Western-style development, the corruption, and the overbearing autocracy—the problems seem insurmountable. In addition the excessive human population explosion forecasts for failure regarding wildlife preservation.

In this respect Africa will constantly be the beggar, depending on foreign currency to bolster our ever-failing economies. Wild animals may be permitted to survive as long as outside tourists pay for the pleasures of enjoying game reserves and national parks. Some African countries, even with foreign aid, have gone back to the Stone Age, and the finance houses of the world have learned a lesson the hard way. It is evident that the African continent is in for hard times. To some of us in Africa it is no surprise.

Prior to the coming of Arabs, Asians, and, later, Europeans, Africa had uncountable numbers of elephant, sparse populations of people, and huge land areas unoccupied by man. Elephant were hunted; we have historical records of ivory coming from Africa in Egyptian and Roman times. With the advent of colonization, however, need and greed took over and the use of modern firearms became common. Elephant and other animals are protected in national parks and reserves, which average about 8 percent of the land mass of most African countries. With shifting political winds and new governments, however, designated wildlife areas and similar enterprises declined. Today some parks suffer from poor control, minimal staff, and lack of facilities.

My son Clive riding shotgun on a ration run during the bush wars in 1974.

Any game park in a state of decline is open to abuses such as organized poaching for ivory, rhino horn, skins, and meat. People living near parks will also wreak havoc by penetrating them to destroy the wild animals for their own consumption. People have no sentiment in the face of hunger. Parks staff, as they lose the fight, can and do become demoralized enough to turn blind eyes to the problems or even indulge themselves in the poaching of ivory and rhino horns for profits. They apparently feel they are fighting for a lost cause and might as will reap some benefits while they can.

Kenya and parts of Zaire, as two examples, lost over half of their elephant and large percentages of other species to the encroachment of humans in their need for land. For this to happen, there had to have been corruption and inefficiency. Kenya was a showpiece in my time, and I once considered Tanganyika the greatest stronghold of wildlife in Africa.

Angola and Mozambique are other classic examples. In the course of internal wars there, game animals were slaughtered indiscriminately by many people using military firearms, and the more valuable commodities such as ivory and rhino horn were sold as a boost to help maintain their armies. A curse of Africa is the availability of firearms to the wrong people.

As soon as political parties no longer agree, the lead starts flying. To make matters worse, most killings are not of army personnel but of innocent civilians. These events are often followed by starvation. This is man out of control, and still our numbers continue to increase alarmingly. The balance of nature's forces in Africa took millions of years to develop to its state of perfection earlier in this century. Today the imbalance caused by the struggle of man against beast will help determine the face of Africa's future.

In my heyday I witnessed the natural balance between primitive men and wild beasts. A certain percentage of animals was killed by the primitives to protect crops and stock and to provide protein. Diseases, plagues, and droughts took their toll on both man and beast.

Animals were hunted in primitive ways; consequently, though these men must have been the greatest hunters of all time, only small numbers of animals were killed, helping to maintain the natural balance. This balance was also partly determined by available vegetation and water, and the inroads of predators on lesser game. There were, of course, fluctuations in this balance, but most species survived in profusion.

That was old Africa, probably the most magnificent wildlife center on earth. But modern man—with his medicines, industrial and agriculture organizations, modern facilities and firearms—has closed the gap between himself and the animals. Today he controls wild animal populations in a way primitive man never dreamed of. Inevitably this wild, magnificent continent will be completely commercialized at the expense of its wildlife, causing an irreversible change on the surface of Africa. Eventually man will kill man in order to survive. Indeed we are already doing just that as our numbers demand more land and resources.

Hunting taught me what one species can do to a continent. The elephant was a major factor in determining the balance of vegetation in Africa. In their great wanderings across the face of Africa, these animals opened up the overgrown forests and dense bush. When they moved on, new vegetation

I often these days canoe down the gorges and open waters of the Zambezi River.

established itself. In my hunting days there were few places where no elephant paths meandered, even across the great open plains of Marromeu. Thus the elephant populations caused bush country to become plains, which in turn allowed the antelope, equines, and buffalo to thrive.

Animals are self-centered but honest in their needs. Man, supposedly a higher form of life, is arrogant, conceited, entirely self-satisfying, and thoughtlessly unconcerned and indifferent. Unless something substantially reduces man's destructive power and numbers, you must eventually reach the same conclusions as I have.

I remember the noted paleontologist Louis Leakey saying that when we were few our weapons were mostly ineffective, but with our increasing numbers came great destructive power. He jokingly said that we could never decimate world populations with spears and pangas. One would have to seek far and wide to find a more realistic man.

So we come to the end of the *Months of the Sun.* I hope I have managed to take the reader into the world of the matchless African wilds and into the wilderness of the human mind.

Afterthoughts

I have come to realize that man in advanced civilizations is compelled to dominate ruthlessly, which he does with cunning and organization. With all his niceties, charm, and manners, man prefers to think of himself as civilized, not as ruthless and cunning. When he deems it necessary, or when it suits him, he ignores the devastation and misery that he causes. He has many characteristics of the lion pride. Indeed, by comparison lions are amateurs. As our history continues to prove, man does not kill only for food, he kills for hatred, sport, pleasure, gain, and in madness. He is a natural marauder. We are basically predators by the very nature of our evolution.

Man is a masterful hypocrite. Most of us deceive ourselves into believing what suits us rather than what really is. Our outlooks are determined by what we believe or care to believe in. I escaped from the rat race, and that enabled me to walk this wild earth as a primitive man. I am heartily grateful for the lifestyle I chose. I would like to remain wild but have to accept that I am a product of civilization, and civilization is a product of evolution. It is not what I want to be true, but I believe it because it is inescapably so. In my final words on an adventurous life, I hope you have seen Africa, as it was, through my eyes as an ivory hunter and a primitive man.

Appendix A:

In 1963 the Game Department was incorporated into Zimbabwe's Department of National Parks and named the Department of National Parks and Wildlife Management. As appreciation for wildlife has increased, this organization has gone from strength to strength. Today there are still wonderful facilities for tourist attractions, not only in the Zambezi Valley but in other parts of Zimbabwe as well.

These wildlife areas are comparable to any in Africa, except perhaps the great Serengeti Plains, the Ngorongoro Crater, and the buffalo stronghold of Marromeu, but it must be taken into account that those three places are risk areas, whereas Zimbabwe is comparatively safe. In terms of humans, Zimbabwe certainly has the edge, as it has always been known for its relaxed, friendly people. In addition there is the attraction of its climate—from its high mountain ranges to the low-lying warm areas.

The following tables list the tourist attractions of Zimbabwe. Without the presence of the Department of National Parks and Wild Life Management, these wild areas would not exist.

NATIONAL PARKS	AREA IN SQUARE HECTARES
Chimanimani	17,110 ha
Chizarira	191,000 ha
Gona re zhou	505,000 ha
Hwange	1,465,100 ha
Kazuma Pan	31,300 ha
Mana Pools	219,600 ha
Matopos	42,400 ha
Matsusadona	140,700 ha
Nyanga	33,000 ha
Victoria Falls	2,340 ha
Zambezi	56,010 ha
TOTAL	**2,703,860 ha**

BOTANICAL RESERVES	AREA IN SQUARE HECTARES
Bunga Forest	495 ha
Chisekera Hot Springs	95 ha
Haroni Forest	20 ha
Mawari Raphia Palm	34 ha
Mazowe	46 ha
Pioneer	38 ha
Rusitu Forest	50 ha
Sebakwe Acacia Karoo	60 ha
Sebakwe Great Dyke	165 ha
Sebakwe Mountain Acacia	53 ha
South Camp	26 ha
Tingwa Raphia Palm	290 ha
Tolo River	44 ha
Vumba	42 ha
TOTAL	**1,558 ha**

BOTANICAL GARDENS	AREA IN SQUARE HECTARES
Ewanrigg	286 ha
National Botanic	67 ha
Vumba	200 ha
TOTAL	**553ha**

SANCTUARIES	AREA IN SQUARE HECTARES
Chimanimani Eland	1,800 ha
M'Baze Pan	40 ha
Manjinji Pan	300 ha
Mushandike	12,900 ha
Nyamanyetsi	2,480 ha
Tshabalala	1,002 ha
TOTAL	**8,620 ha**

SAFARI AREAS	AREA IN SQUARE HECTARES
Charara	169,200 ha
Chete	108,100 ha
Chewori	339,000 ha
Chipinge	26,100 ha
Chireza	171,300 ha
Dande	52,300 ha
Deka	51,000 ha
Doma	94,500 ha
Hartley 'A'	44,500 ha
Hurungwe	289,400 ha
Island 52	4 ha
Malapati	15,400 ha
Matetsi	295,500 ha
Sapi	118,000 ha
Sibilobilo	4,400 ha (vii)
Tuli	41,600 ha
Umfurudzi	76,000 ha
TOTAL	**1,896,304 ha**

RECREATIONAL PARKS	AREA IN SQUARE HECTARES
Bangala	2,700 ha
Chibwatata	10 ha
Chinhoyi Caves	120 ha
Lake Cunningham	4,172 ha
Lake Kariba	287,200 ha
Kavira	50 ha
Kyle	16,900 ha
Manjirenji	3,400 ha
Lake Matopos	2,900 ha
Robert McIlwaine	6,180 ha
Ngezi	5,800 ha
Lake Robertson	11,200 ha
Sebakwe	2,600 ha
Umfuli	12,700 ha
Umzingwani	1,233 ha
TOTAL	**357,165 ha**

Parks and wildlife estates cover 12.7 percent of Zimbabwe and include national parks, recreational parks, safari areas, sanctuaries, botanical gardens, and reserves.

Address of the National Parks and Wildlife Management:

P.O. BOX 8365, CAUSEWAY
HARARE, ZIMBABWE, AFRICA

Appendix B:

NAMES OF PEOPLE	PRESENT WHEREABOUTS
Antonio Alves—*The very young Portuguese hunter attacked by leopard possibly the nephew of the* chefe do poste	Unknown
Archie Fraser—*Head of the game department*	Resident, Zimbabwe
Arnold and his tracker	Killed by buffalo
Athena Vlahakis	Resident, Zambia
Barrie Ball—*Game ranger*	Resident, Zimbabwe
B. J. Schoeman—*Minister of labour, Republic of South Africa*	Deceased
Boss D.C. Lilford	Lured from his house and murdered
Bruce Austin—*Later warden, Wankie Game Reserve*	Resident, Zimbabwe
Chakadama—*The tracker*	Unknown
Chakama—*Mozambique tribesmen (who actually attacked elephant with a spear)*	Unknown
Chief Chiawa	Deceased
Chief Chundu	Deceased
Chief Dandawa	Deceased
Chief Mola	Deceased
Chief Mudzeemo	Deceased
Chief Nyamunga	Deceased
Chikati—*The Great Mozambique tracker*	Unknown
Chirenge—*The Great Mozambique tracker*	Unknown
Culverhouse—*The Australian*	Unknown
Dakati—*The thief and deserter*	Unknown
Demetri Vlahakis	Succumbed to a lion mauling
Dinka tribesmen	Unknown
Doctor Bachman	Unknown
Doctor Parker	Unknown
Doctor Riley	Deceased

NAMES OF PEOPLE	PRESENT WHEREABOUTS
Doctor Tom Williams	Unknown
Faanie Jooste *(Machenahooche)*	Committed suicide on the Angwa River in Zimbabwe—the place of his gold dreams.
Fergus Du Toit	Deceased
Fore the tracker	Unknown
Frau the tracker	Unknown
Freddy Odendaal—*the Liebegs Ranch section manager*	Unknown
Furese—*the camp attendant*	Unknown
George Jeffrey	Suicide or probably murdered
Galanakis	Unknown
Glover and Van Bard	Deceased
Guy Patterson	Killed by elephant
Hans Van De Merwe	Deceased
Hunyan the zebra & wildebeest hunter *(the* picanin's *father)*	Unknown
Ian De La Rue	Unknown
Ian R. Nyschens (kaporamujese)	Resident, Harare, Zimbabwe
Jackie Waddell (Farmer)	Resident, Zimbabwe
Jacoba—*the plucky water-carrier*	Deceased
Jainaki	Unknown
Jaubek–*the tracker*	Deceased
Joan Nyschens–*my ex-wife*	Resident, Namibia
John Connor *(Lord Muck)*	Resident, Zimbabwe
John Posselt	Deceased
John Taylor *(Pondoro)—The expert on rifle ballistics*	Deceased
Joram—*the cowardly tracker*	Unknown
Juda–*the medicine man*	Unknown
Kadige Dige—*courageous tracker of the game department*	Resident, Zimbabwe
Kam Cha Cha—*(the dancer)*	Deceased
Kampari and his wife and child—*the Machikunda tribesmen of the Mupata Gorge*	Unknown
Kapessa	Deceased
Karl Larsen—*the boat captain*	Unknown

NAMES OF PEOPLE	PRESENT WHEREABOUTS
Kasoko	Killed by a man-eating lion
Katasoro	Deceased
Katasoro's two excellent trackers	Unknown
Keto-Keto—*the honey hunter*	Unknown
Klem Coetsee	Resident, Zimbabwe
Lategen B. J. Schoeman's hunting companion	Deceased
The Chinaman	Resident, America
Lofty Stokes—*tsetse fly officer*	Deceased
Louis Leaky	Deceased
Manwere—*courageous tracker of the game department*	Resident, Zimbabwe
Marcel Mitton	Deceased
Martin Jooste	Resident, Republic of South Africa
Mayhew—*tsetse fly officer*	Unknown
Meyer—*the Roman road-builder*	Deceased
Mr. & Mrs. Bond	Unknown
Mr. Cameron—*manager Sabi Tanganda estate*	Unknown
Mr. Nel—*the rancher*	Unknown
The Entomologist	Resident, Zimbabwe
Mr. Pitout—*native commissioner*	Unknown
Mr. Stock—*of the Sabi River Hotel*	Deceased
Mr. Vavaseur—*manager, Liebegs Ranch*	Unknown
Mrs. Cook—*the recluse*	Unknown
Native Commissioner Hagelthorn	Unknown
Nicholas Vlahakis	Deceased
Nilos the brave Batonga leopard man	Unknown
Norman Payne and his nephew Sunny	Deceased
Old-man Hinze	Deceased
Pafure—the mad tracker and his fingo dog	Unknown
Pat Bromfield	Immigrated to Australia
Paul Coetsee–*ex warden*	Resident, Republic of South Africa
Peter Grobelaar	Deceased
Pop Du Toit–*Fergus Du Toit's father*	Deceased
Rankine *(seized by crocodile)*	Unknown
Reay Smithers—*curator, Bulawayo Museum*	Deceased

NAMES OF PEOPLE	PRESENT WHEREABOUTS
Rex Bean	Unknown
Rice–*the brave headman and his friend Kamptepere*	Unknown
Rupert Fothergill—*game ranger*	Deceased
Shasha	Unknown
Sinoia—*John Conner's servant and tracker*	Unknown
Sir Patrick Fletcher—*Minister of Lands*	Deceased
Sletcher—*(Sletch) of the wild dogs*	Unknown
Stockhill—*Member of Parliament*	Deceased
Sussens	Unknown
Ted Davison—*warden, Wankie Game Reserve*	Deceased
The aircraft pilot	Unknown
The angry disturbed armed tribesmen	Unknown
The Bata industrialist	Unknown
The beautiful Ceylonese woman and her doctor husband of Zanzibar	Driven into the ocean waves and murdered
The caste resident on the Zambezi River whose house and Storerooms were burnt down	Resident, Zambia
The *chefe do poste*	Unknown
The customs officer	Unknown
The fat magistrate	Unknown
The governor	Unknown
The Henderson brothers	Unknown
The Kraut	Unknown
The lost Portuguese child and parents	Unknown
The Magotcha lion hunter	Killed by buffalo
The Mandau tribesmen *(obsessed lion killer)*	Unknown
The Northern Rhodesian police officer	Unknown
The old Makorekore tribesman of the road survey	Unknown
The *picanin* *(child of the island in the Sabi River)*	Unknown
The *picanin* on his knees facing the massive elephant herd	Unknown
The Northern Rhodesia African constable	Unknown
The porter killed by snake	Unknown
The remittance man Northern Rhodesia	Unknown
The road surveyors	Unknown

NAMES OF PEOPLE	PRESENT WHEREABOUTS
The Swedish hunter who spoke Portuguese on my behalf in court	Unknown
The Survey white woman	Unknown
The swearing missionary	Unknown
The tracker (Kari) who ran off on the elephant path	Killed by elephant
The Transvaal fauna and flora inspector	Unknown
The tribesman who rescued us in the dugout	Unknown
The tsetse fly officer Mtoko	Committed suicide
The West Nicholson rancher and his pack of Fox Terrier dogs	Unknown
Tien Dieney—*the faulty-eyed tribesman*	Unknown
Tommy Ferreira—*Boss Lilford's farm manager*	Deceased
Tommy Mitton	Murdered in the Zambezi River
Tommy Orford—*game ranger*	Resident, Zimbabwe
Van Heerden—*the legendary poacher*	Unknown
Venturas	Deceased
Zaratina—*the great Zambezi Valley tracker*	Resident, Zimbabwe
Zekoni—*the well-built tribesman going blind*	Unknown

Appendix C:

TRIBAL NAMES	ENGLISH MEANINGS
Ani	He/Who
Batonga (singular)	Batonga tribesman
Behrey	Hyena
Bwana	European financier or person of power
Bwana	Also means "the boss"
Buda uteesa	Get away quickly
Changa mira	Someone greater Than yourself
Chia ena (lingua franca)	Kill it
Chief Mudzeemo	Chief of the ancestral spirits
Chigeedi	Muzzleloading rifle
Chikwari	Red-necked francolin
Chipara	Name of swamp
Chipandahoure	Name of swamp
Chifua	Influenza
Damuka	Waterbuck
Dongoosa	Roan antelope
Duruwe (*dingingwe*)	Cheetah
Ena saba koheenya	He is afraid to sh-- himself
Enda	Go
Gondonga	Hartebeest
Gotcha (singular)	Hunter/He who "gotchas" cooks game meat
Handeyi/tiendeyi	Let's go
Hungwe	Fish eagle
Humba rumi	A man who hunts to live
H'wato	Dugout boat
Imba	A hut
Kamwendo	He who drags a leg
Kamchacha	The dancer
Kaporamujese	The penetrator of the dense thickets
Ka-tondora	Small emerald-spotted wood dove
Kakomamarara	The small hills of the palms
Ko heenya	To sh-- in fear
Machende pamusoro	Raised testicles
Machena hoochie	Tigerfish fearless
Magora	Vultures
Magotcha (plural) - ***Magosha***	Hunters
Magu	Wasps/hornets

TRIBAL NAMES	ENGLISH MEANINGS
MakoreKore	Tribe
Makuee (Mozambique)	Cobra
Mambo *(nduna)*	Chief
Mandaus	Tribe
Manyanedzi	Pools of the reflecting stars
Mara *(mhara)*	Impala antelope
Marire	A tuskless bull elephant
Masawo *(musuwa)*	Paddle pole
Masweena *(maswinwa)*	Mutation of a word, gut of an ox or something dirty squeezed out
Matabele (plural)	People of Zulu descent (Bulawayo area)
Matonga (plural)	Matonga tribe (Tonga people)
M'bada *(n'alugwe)*	Leopard
M'gwarati	Sable antelope
M'komana *(picanin)*	Young black child
Mondoro or pondoro	Lion
Moomi *(mhumhi)*	Wild dog
Mopani	Mopane trees
M'kondi *(mukondi)*	Poisonous bulbs used to stun fish in pools
Muchene *(mucheni)*	Tigerfish
Mujese *(muchesa)*	*Jess*-bush thickets
Mudzeemo Mhondoro	A hunter who has tribal spirits' *Mondoro* or lion (someone to be feared)
Muntomanama *(muntu omnyama)*	A black skinned person
Murowiyi - Muroi	Witch/wizard (travels in spirit at night)
Murungu	White man
Murungu una penga	White people are mad
M'sanga	Papyrus reeds
Muto - chisewa	Gravy/vegetable mixture
M'vou	Hippopotamus
M'wari	God
Mudzeemo ndzou	Ancestral elephants' spirit
M'zweete (mudzviti)	Native commissioner
Nanga	Medicine man (also a thrower of the bones)
Nanja (language)	People of Chinanga (Nyasaland) now Malawi
Nasi teena heenya	Today we will sh-- ourselves in fear
Naukaranga	*Jess*-bush forest in which your feet enter but do not return
Nemah *(chipembere)*	Rhinoceros
Ndebele (singular)	People of Zulu descent (Bulawayo area)
Ndiani uyo	Who is it?

TRIBAL NAMES	ENGLISH MEANINGS
N'dzou	Elephant
N'gwena or garwe	Crocodile
N'koo-koto	Loincloth
Noroh	Kudu antelope
Nyati	Buffalo
P'fumo-dati-m'seve	Bow and Arrow
Rodzi *(tambo)*	Rope
Rota *(dota)*	Ash Bag (to test wind direction)
Sadza ne nyama	Millie-meal and meat
Shasha	Expert (the knowing one)
Sinanga *(chinanga)*	Thickets
Tambo	Bush Rope
Teena duze ena heenya	We came close to sh---ing in fear
Tsoro	Honey-guide bird
Umvura eere pano	There is water here
Una penga	You are mad
Uria ndzou	Kill the elephant
Wamama	To tremble in fear
Wa-wa	Native beer
Waafa zehzeh *(vafa vose)*	All dead
Wadomas *(vadomas)*	A clan of isolated tribespeople
Zimba *(dzimba)*	Many huts

ANIMAL NAMES	LATIN NAMES
Black-backed jackal	*Canis mesomelas*
Blue duiker	*Cephalophus monticola*
Buffalo	*Syncerus caffer*
Bush-baby	*Galoga grassicaudatus*
Bushbuck	*Tragelaphus scriptus*
Chacma baboon	*Papio ursinus*
Cheetah	*Acinonyx jubatis*
Crocodile	*Crocodilus nilioticus*
Egyptian cobra	*Naja haje*
Eland	*Taurotragus oryx*
Elephant	*Loxodonta africana*
Hartebeest	*Acelaphus lichtensteini*
Hippopotamus	*Hippopamus amphibius*
Honey bird guide	*Indicator-indicator*
Honey badger	*Mellivora capensis*
Impala	*Aepyceros melampus*
Kudu	*Tragelaphus stripsiceros*
Leguan	*Varanus niloticus*
Leopard	*Panthera pardus*
Lion	*Panthera leo*
Nyala	*Tragelaphus angasi*
Oribi	*Aurebia ourebi*
Reedbuck	*Redunca arundinum*
Rhinoceros	*Diceros bicornis*
Roan	*Hippotragus equinus*
Sable	*Hippotragus niger*
Side-striped jackal	*Canis adustus*
Spotted hyena	*Crocuta crocuta*
Tigerfish	*Hydrocynus vittatus*
Tsessebe	*Damaliscus lunatus*
Warthog	*Phacochoerus aethiopicus*
Waterbuck	*Kobus ellipsiprymnus*
Wild dog	*Lycaon pictus*
Wildebeest	*Connochaetes taurinus*
Zebra	*Equus burchelli*

VEGETATION	LATIN NAMES
Baobab tree	*Adansania diagatata*
***Jess* bush**	*Combretum caffrum*
Mopane	*Colopospemrmum mopane*
Masango (apple-ring thorn trees)	*Acacia albida*
Natal mahogony	*Trichilia ametica muchichire*
Pampas grass	*Cortaderia selloana*
Papyrus reeds	*Cyperus papyrus*
Red-flame lianas (burning bush)	*Combritum panialatum*
Sausage tree	*Kigelia pinnata mubvee*
Yellow-tailed acacia (tamarind tree)	*Tamarundus indica*

INSECTS	LATIN NAMES
Christmas beetle	*Cycada*
Tsetse fly	*Morsitani palidipes*
Malaria mosquitos	*Anophelees*
Mopane bees (mopane flies)	*Xylocodo rufa*
Scarab (dung beetle)	*Scarabeidae*

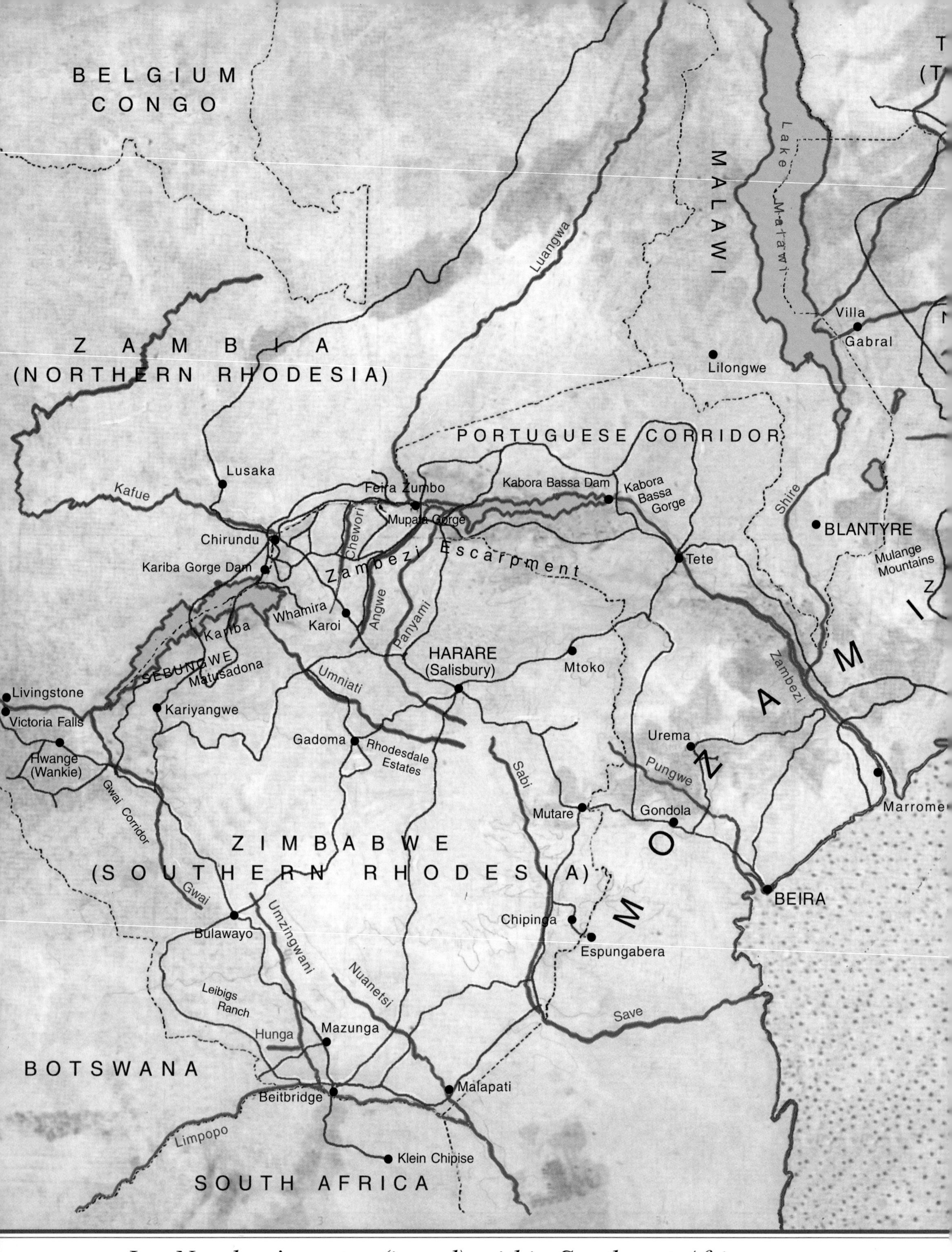

Ian Nyschen's routes (in red) within Southeast Africa
1947-1958